# Human Resource Management | 4e

## Managing Employees for Competitive Advantage

**Mary Gowan**

*James Madison University*

**David Lepak**

*University of Massachusetts Amherst*

CHICAGO
BUSINESS PRESS

CHICAGO
BUSINESS PRESS

HUMAN RESOURCE MANAGEMENT:
MANAGING EMPLOYEES FOR COMPETITIVE ADVANTAGE, FOURTH EDITION

For product information or assistance, visit www.chicagobusinesspress.com

ISBN-13: 978-1-948426-08-4

## Dedication

*This book is dedicated to my husband, Ed Moore, whose patience as I worked through this challenging revision was nothing short of exemplary.*

# In Memoriam . . .

*Many years ago, I had the privilege of being a colleague of David Lepak's at the University of Maryland while serving as a visiting professor there. We quickly recognized that we had a shared vision for how human resources management should be taught. That shared vision led us to write the first edition of this textbook, and to keep it going over the years.*

*Those who had the honor of knowing Dave understand what a unique and special person he was as a husband to Ellen, father to his four children, Reilly, Addy, Henry, and Rowan, colleague, scholar, mentor, coach, and friend. I never understood how Dave managed to do all that he did with his family, his doctoral students, and as a soccer coach (many children were fortunate to have him as a role model as their coach). His scholarship was highly regarded and published in the top academic journals. Numerous doctoral students, other students in his classes, and students who have used this textbook, have benefited from his knowledge, wisdom, and guidance. Through it all, Dave was unflappable. His quick wit and patience saved the day many times.*

*Few who pass at such a young age leave the legacy left by David Lepak. I am honored to have known him as a colleague, co-author, and, most of all, friend. He is deeply and sincerely missed.*

*This book is possible because of Dave and is dedicated to his memory. The publisher and I are committed to ensuring that proceeds from the sale of the book will continue to go to his family for many years to come. For all he contributed to so many, in so many ways, they deserve no less.*

*With much gratitude . . . here's to you Dave.*

*Mary Gowan*

# Brief Table of Contents

# Table of Contents

PART 1

# HR Challenges  31

## PART 2
# Work Design and Workforce Planning  109

## 4  Job Design and Job Analysis  111

PART 4

# Managing Employee Attitudes and Behaviors  335

## 12    Employee Benefits and Safety Programs   457

## PART 5
## Special Topics 505

# Preface

## A Different Perspective on Human Resource Management

Talent acquisition, development, motivation, and retention affect the success of every type of organization—for profit, nonprofit, governmental, and nongovernmental organizations. Making sure that these efforts are managed well is one of the greatest challenges all managers face, regardless of their role in the organization. Baby boomers are retiring in record numbers, while organizations are growing. Available workers often do not have the right mix of skills and abilities for jobs that are available, leading to labor shortages and requiring more expenditures for training and development. New technologies require larger investments in hiring and training at the same time that technology offers exciting possibilities for how to identify, secure, and manage top talent. Employing a multicultural workforce is critical to organizational success but calls on managers to develop and use new skill sets domestically and abroad. At the end of the day, in order to navigate the complexities of the 21st century workplace, every manager has to understand the importance of designing jobs that affect the organizational mission and goals, planning for the types and numbers of workers needed to do those jobs, managing employee competencies through selection and learning and development opportunities, and managing employee attitudes and behaviors through the reward structure and policies of the organization.

This book is written for anyone interested in understanding how to manage employees well in a dynamic and rapidly changing business environment. The paragraphs that follow describe some of the ways that the approach to human resource management (HRM) in this book differs from many other HRM textbooks available.

## Major Themes of the Book

Faculty and organizational consultants have noted that the framework in this book is right on target with what students need to learn, regardless of major, and what clients need, regardless of organization. Based on feedback from students, the goal of providing a readable and engaging textbook has been met. This edition continues the focus of earlier editions on providing a strategic framework for managers that is applicable across large and small organizations, regardless of industry or for profit or nonprofit status. The overarching goal is to provide the information and context that any manager needs to know to effectively identify and empower the right talent to move the organization forward. To do so, the focus of the book is built from the following three points:

- **Managing Employees Rather than Managing the HR Function.** Students often have difficulty separating the concept of employees as human resources from a discussion of the human resources (HR) department of an organization. Our unique framework, woven throughout the book, places equal emphasis on the principles of employee management practices and the application of those practices in different organizational and environmental contexts. These are contexts in which all managers must make daily decisions that affect firm performance, how work is structured, and the terms and conditions of employment. The goal is for those using this book to understand both the theory behind effective employee management practices and the reality that managing employees under different scenarios presents unique challenges and requires different responses. Our managerial perspective, as opposed to an HR perspective, makes the book accessible to all students interested in learning about managing employees, while still being applicable for future HR professionals.

- **Managing Employees in Context.** A second point of differentiation for this book is how we place management of employees directly in the broader context of organizations and their external environments. We devote a significant amount of coverage to the role of employee management in supporting business strategy, company characteristics, organizational culture, and employee concerns. We also address the external pressures that come from globalization, technology, labor force trends, ethics, regulatory issues, and related topics. The importance of context is highlighted in the overarching framework for the book and incorporated into every chapter. Each chapter discusses contextual pressures on the use of various tools for managing employees and focuses on how contextual pressures influence the effectiveness of these practices. Most current textbooks present this information primarily in the early chapters.

- **Integrative Framework.** A third point of differentiation is the book's overarching framework. Students learn better when they have a clear framework for understanding how different practices are used independently and interdependently. In this case, they will learn about issues related to individual employee management and the larger work group, as well as how to address this independence and interdependence relative to different internal and external contingencies. We highlight three primary activities for managing employees and show their interrelationships: work design and workforce planning, management of employee competencies, and management of employee attitudes and behaviors. We approach these themes from the context of understanding how employee management affects the ability of an organization to achieve its objectives and attain a competitive advantage. We have developed a matrix that outlines the topics covered for each employee management role relative to the organizational demands and environmental influencers to aid students in understanding the many interrelationships that exist in managing employees.

## Approach

This book will help current and future managers understand what practices and tools are available for managing employees, how to use them, and when to use them in different situations. Knowing that a picture is worth a thousand words, the work on this book began by developing an integrative framework for the strategic management of employees. This framework, which is woven throughout the chapters, shows the relationships among organizational demands, environmental influences, regulatory issues, and the three primary HR activities noted previously: work design and workforce planning, management of employee competencies, and management of employee attitudes and behaviors. These HR activities, when managed in concert and within the context of the HR challenges, lead to the desired employee contributions and create a competitive advantage for the organization.

## Three Primary HR Activities

In essence, the strategic management of employees requires managers to attend to three primary HR activities. First, managers must design and manage the flow of work and the design of specific jobs that employees perform to ensure that employees are in a position to add value to the company. Second, managers must identify, acquire, build, and retain the critical competencies that employees need in order to effectively perform their jobs. Third, managers must guide and motivate employees to use their abilities to contribute to company goals. By describing the activities in this manner, students understand the interrelationships that exist among them.

All managers need a solid understanding of the practices available for managing employees. Managers can use a wide array of practices for job design, workforce planning, recruitment, selection, learning and development, performance evaluation and appraisal, and compensation and other rewards. To effectively manage employees, a manager has to know how and why the various practices work, as well as when to use them.

## HR Challenges: The Importance of Context

Employee management activities do not happen in a vacuum. Rather, managers must keep in mind the context of the organization in terms of the company's strategy, characteristics, and culture. In addition, managers must consider the concerns of their workforce. Beyond organizational demands, the strategic management of HR requires managers to anticipate and take steps to meet the environmental influences associated with labor force trends, advances in technology, ethics, and globalization, as well as to ensure that companies comply with legal requirements. Having a good understanding of the various options for recruiting new employees is not very useful if managers do not also have a good understanding of when the options are likely to be effective. Knowing when to use the different practices requires that you know the context of managing employees.

## Chapter Design

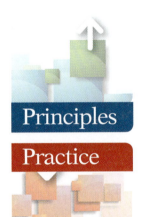

Each chapter in this book focuses on more HR activities than other HRM textbooks and builds on the idea that context matters. Thus, each chapter has two parts.

The first part describes the principles of the HR activity. The goal is to help students acquire the tools appropriate for each activity. For example, when performance management is discussed, aspects of measuring employee performance, trade-offs with different performance evaluation approaches, and considerations of the process for evaluating employee performance are emphasized.

The second part of each chapter is where the difference between the approach of this text and other textbooks becomes clear. Emphasis is placed on the importance of context and how the context—the organizational demands and environmental factors—affects the choices made when applying the technical knowledge. Also emphasized is how HR challenges—the various organizational demands and numerous environmental influences—affect decisions about which performance management approach to apply and how to use it.

The fundamental principles for each HR activity are explored first, followed by a perspective on how these practices can be used to meet contextual challenges. This approach is used to help students put together the pieces better, rather than simply discussing context at the beginning of the semester and then focusing on each of the major functional activities, with only minor discussion of context. In many ways, a decision-making approach is taken, asking, "What if A? What if B?" Included are examples and Company Spotlights to highlight this information, followed by discussion questions, exercises, and short cases that give students a chance to apply chapter concepts.

This book also provides an edge for students interested in a career in HRM. These students will complete the course well grounded in the bigger organizational picture and be better able to make decisions about the HR tools to apply in different contexts. They will better understand the possible consequences of designing and implementing practices that support or conflict with organizational goals.

## New to this Edition

This edition incorporates the latest research and practice thinking on managing HR to achieve a competitive advantage. Topics such as the impact, value, and challenges of technology are woven throughout the chapters. Legal, political, and economic information and data were current at the time the book went to press. This extensive revision includes many new Company Spotlights and examples, as well as a number of new key terms. Here is a chapter-by-chapter overview of many of the key revisions. Additionally, the instructor will find numerous new or updated end-of-the-chapter questions, exercises, and cases.

## Chapter 1: Managing Employees for Competitive Advantage

Workforce planning, labor force trends, globalization, and regulatory issues are among the updated discussions with new examples and data. New Company Spotlights feature Costco Wholesale, Wegmans, Facebook, and Impahla Clothing.

## Chapter 2: Organizational Demands and Environmental Influences

Updated coverage includes work/life balance, the aging workforce, demographic diversity, technology, globalization, and ethics and social responsibility with new examples and current data. New Company Spotlights feature Amazon, Michelin North America, and Apple Inc.

## Chapter 3: Regulatory Issues

New company examples for discrimination and disparate impact are given; equal pay, racial, religious, and discrimination coverage is enhanced, and new Company Spotlights feature Texas Roadhouse, Stemilt Growers, Mission Hospital, and Wells Fargo.

## Chapter 4: Job Design and Job Analysis

This chapter introduces new topics, such as job crafting, and updates the discussion of job analysis, job descriptions, job specification, current research on job design, formalization of jobs, breadth and depth of tasks, job design decisions for the aging labor force, telecommuting, virtual teams, ethics and job design, and physical conditions of job design. New Company Spotlights feature Lockheed Martin, Uber, and Unilever.

## Chapter 5: Workforce Planning

A new exhibit covers contingent and alternative work arrangement percentages and numbers of workers, and the exhibit on employee versus independent contractor has been revised. Updated topics in this chapter include importance of workforce planning, internal factors, turnover, succession planning, transition matrix, employee productivity, external factors, economic conditions, outsourcing and contingent labor, employee retention, layoffs, early retirement, where the workers are, and which workforce planning tactics to use. A new Company Spotlight features REI.

## Chapter 6: Recruitment

Among the topics updated for this chapter are advertising, career fairs, recruitment process outsourcing (RPO), gig workers, employer branding, labor force and recruitment, technology and recruitment. New Company Spotlights feature Staples, LinkedIn, and Cisco.

## Chapter 7: Selection

Updated topics include applications and résumés, new key terms, reference checks, background checks, credit reports and honesty checks, methods of selection, labor market at home, and the labor market abroad. New Company Spotlights feature the National Science Foundation (NSF) and Automattic.

## Chapter 8: Learning and Development

This chapter includes updated and new discussions of the following: onboarding, designing an effective training process, on-the-job training (OJT), training methods, tips to increase e-learning rates, compliance training, benchmarks for effective diversity training, behavioral training, the future of career development (a new section), work/life balance. New Company Spotlights feature L'Oréal, UPS, Pal's Sudden Service, and Marriott International.

## Chapter 9: Performance Management

Topics covered and updated include why performance management is so important, the purposes of performance management, performance measurement standards, specificity, individual comparisons, behaviorally anchored rating scales (BARS), sources of performance data, trends in performance management, the performance evaluation method used, technology and performance management, and globalization. New Company Spotlights feature Deloitte, Patagonia, and MRA Systems.

## Chapter 10: Compensating Employees

Topics updated in this chapter include total compensation, salary surveys, broadbanding, market pricing, internal value of jobs, employee concerns and compensation, the level of a firm's compensation, pay rates, a living wage, minimum wage issues, and exempt versus nonexempt employees. There is also a new exhibit on aging salary survey data. New Company Spotlights feature Fairfield City Employees, Siemans AG, and Costco.

## Chapter 11: Incentives and Rewards

Theories of motivation, individualized incentive plans, merit pay and bonus eligibility by band, group/organizational incentives, executive compensation, technology and incentives, globalization, and incentive plans are among the topics revised and made current. New Company Spotlights feature Nike and WinCo Foods.

## Chapter 12: Employee Benefits and Safety Programs

Improved coverage in this chapter includes health and wellness programs, health care plans, managed care, availability of benefits and safety programs, and globalization. New Company Spotlights feature Hasbro and Milliken & Company.

## Chapter 13: Labor Unions and Employee Management

Union membership, right-to-work states, union-organizing process, decertification, new forms of worker organizations, global trends are among the updated discussions. New Company Spotlights feature Amazon and Communities Organized for Public Service (COPS) of San Antonio.

## Chapter 14: Creating High-Performance HR Systems

Among the topics updated are strategic value, strategic performance drivers, HR practices, and HR deliverables. There is also a new table on contingent and alternative employment arrangements.

## Audience

The approach of this book has worked well with students, especially those who are taking an introductory HRM course because it is required for their business or another degree, and has worked equally well for undergraduate and graduate students. Often, these students are focused on careers in marketing, accounting, finance, psychology, or information systems and would rather be taking courses in those areas. They do not plan to work in HR and quickly are turned off by an HR textbook because of its emphasis early on in describing HR careers and focusing on what HR departments do. Many of the current texts acknowledge the general manager's role in HR management. However, those textbooks often focus more on the functional or technical aspects of HR management, with little integration within and among chapters of organizational and environmental demands.

Also, we have found that even our students planning a career in HR welcome a focus on the contingencies that have to be addressed in HR activities. They know that a broader organizational perspective—understanding some of the critical decision factors—will give them an edge in their future careers. This approach is supported by professional organizations, such as the Society for Human Resource Management (SHRM), that recognize the need for HR leaders to take a more strategic approach to their areas of responsibility.

## Prerequisites

Each university makes its own choice about how to sequence courses. This book has been written so that a course using it would not have to have prerequisite courses at either the graduate or undergraduate level. Many students may have little or no knowledge of the subject matter before taking a course that uses this text. We have written it to provide full coverage of the major principles associated with HR.

## How to Use this Book: Tips for Success

This textbook has been designed to be learning-centered. The chapters have been specifically designed to help students bridge the gap between theory and practice. Each chapter contains a set of learning tools—learning objectives, chapter summaries, key terms, discussion questions, learning exercises, and case studies. All of these are intended to help students master the material covered in the chapters.

**Learning Objectives.** Each chapter begins with a set of learning objectives. Read these before you read the chapter, then revisit them after you read the chapter. Can you discuss or explain all of the concepts covered in the learning objectives? If not, make sure that you review that part of the chapter and ask your professor after class to clarify anything about which you are still uncertain.

**Chapter Summary.** The chapter summary provides a broad overview of what was covered in the chapter. There will be many concepts and much more detail that you will need to know to be successful in your class, but the summary provides a way to bring together the concepts covered in the text.

**Key Terms.** Because the field of HRM includes many terms and concepts that are new to most students, key terms are defined in the margins of each chapter and listed at the end of each chapter. Students are advised to read the chapters before they are discussed in class and then review the key terms and concepts after class to ensure understanding.

**Review Questions.** The review questions are designed for you to explore how well you have learned the major points and themes covered in each chapter. Completing the review questions requires students to reflect on the material in the chapters and demonstrate a clear understanding of the major theories, issues, and challenges associated with HRM.

**Learning Exercises and Case Studies.** In addition to the key terms and review questions, each chapter contains several learning exercises and case studies. The learning exercises are designed to encourage students to think about how the principles of HRM might inform the use of HR practices in different situations. The case studies provide specific situations and ask you to reflect on HRM-related problems and devise solutions to those problems. Responding to the learning exercises and case studies will give you a greater understanding of the application of the concepts you have studied in the class.

**Company Spotlights.** Each chapter contains several Company Spotlights that demonstrate the importance of the topics in the chapter, provide examples of how actual companies have been involved with HR issues, and bridges the gap between principles and practice of HRM.

## Instructor Supplements

The comprehensive Instructor's Manual includes chapter outlines, answers to the in-text questions, guidance for each case, and a sample syllabus.

The Test Bank provides a wide range of questions for each chapter and includes a mix of descriptive and application questions.

A PowerPoint deck is available for easy downloading and provides a recap of the highlights in each chapter.

Visit www.chicagobusinesspress.com to request access to the instructor supplements.

## CourseBank

This book is available with CourseBank, a system that allows instructors to easily assign and automatically grade activities. CourseBank provides a comprehensive and flexible bank of media, assignments, and quizzes. Use it to assign homework that results in students coming to class better prepared, or use it as a turnkey solution for your online section, sparing the time and effort of creating an online course from scratch.

CourseBank works with Blackboard, Canvas, D2L, or any other popular learning management system for single sign-on and gradebook integration.

## Acknowledgments

A special thanks goes to Paul Ducham of Chicago Business Press for his continued belief that this book is important, and an especially big thank you goes to Jane Ducham, coach, copy editor, and composition coordinator extraordinaire, who spent an incredible amount of time making sure that edits and more were accurately incorporated throughout the text.

Janet Marler provided invaluable contributions to Chapters 1, 2, and 4, getting us off to a strong start with this edition.

We also owe deep gratitude to several instructors for their input on this revision:

Suzanne Crampton, *Grand Valley State University*

Kim Hester, *Arkansas State University*

Kathleen Jones, *University of North Dakota*

Kurt Loess, *East Tennessee State University*

Kimberly Lukaszewski, *Wright State University*

Erin Makarius, *University of Akron*

Maura Mills, *University of Alabama*

Kelly Mollica, *University of Memphis*

Tracey Porter, *Cleveland State University*

Susan Stewart, *Western Illinois*

Sheng Wang University of Nevada Las Vegas

Brian Webster, *Ball State University*

## Special Thanks to . . .

Brian Chupp of Purdue University for his contributions to the online course content. Susan Jackson of Old Dominion University for her careful, line-by-line review.

## A Note from the Publisher

We at Chicago Business Press share with the academic community a great sense of loss and sadness at the passing of our good friend David Lepak. Dave was an exceptional academic, professional, and author. We are honored to have worked with him on the previous two editions of this textbook. He is greatly missed and will always be remembered.

Dave would be extremely proud of his coauthor, Mary Gowan, who has worked tirelessly to bring about this revision. Mary has honored her colleague and friend and his family by working diligently on every line of every page of every chapter.

Dave will be remembered in so many ways. Together with Mary, we honor him in the best way we know, by publishing the very best fourth edition of this textbook.

# About the Authors

**MARY GOWAN** is a professor in the School of Strategic Leadership Studies at James Madison University and the former dean for the College of Business at James Madison University. She received her Ph.D. in business administration from the University of Georgia. Her teaching, research, and consulting experience focuses on human resource management and organizational behavior and includes international teaching and research. She is currently on the board of the Southern Business Association of Administrators and has been a board member of the Society for Human Resource Management Foundation, the Human Resource Division of the Academy of Management, and Southern Management Association, along with a number of other nonprofit organizations. She has served on a number of journal editorial boards, including serving as an associate editor for the *International Journal of Human Resource Management*. Her research has focused on career transitions and related HR topics and has been published in the *Academy of Management Journal, Journal of Applied Psychology*, and numerous other HR related journals.

**DAVID LEPAK** was the Berthiaume Endowed Chair of Business Leadership in the Isenberg School of Management at the University of Massachusetts at Amherst. He received his Ph.D. in business from the Pennsylvania State University. His research, teaching, and executive education outreach focused on strategic HRM with interests in mediators of the HR-performance relationship, international HRM, and managing contingent labor for competitive advantage. His research has appeared in outlets such as *Academy of Management Review, Academy of Management Journal, Journal of Applied Psychology, Journal of Management, Personnel Psychology, Human Resource Management Review*, and *Human Resource Management*. He was editor-in-chief of the *International Journal of Human Resource Management* and was a former associate editor of *Academy of Management Review* and *British Journal of Management*. David also served as chair of the HR division of the Academy of Management. Sadly, Dave passed away in December 2017.

# Chapter 1

# Managing Employees for Competitive Advantage

## Learning Objectives

**AFTER READING THIS CHAPTER, YOU SHOULD BE ABLE TO:**

1 Discuss the potential costs and benefits associated with managing employees.

2 Explain what it means to manage employees strategically.

3 Identify and explain the three primary human resource (HR) activities.

4 Discuss the management practices associated with each primary HR activity.

5 Explain the importance of HR activity alignment.

6 Discuss how organizational demands influence the management of employees.

7 Describe how the external environment influences the management of employees.

8 Understand the importance of regulatory issues in establishing HR practices.

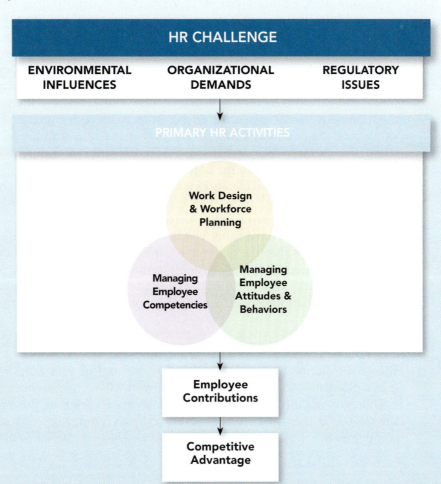

**HR CHALLENGE**

| ENVIRONMENTAL INFLUENCES | ORGANIZATIONAL DEMANDS | REGULATORY ISSUES |

**PRIMARY HR ACTIVITIES**

Work Design & Workforce Planning

Managing Employee Competencies

Managing Employee Attitudes & Behaviors

Employee Contributions

Competitive Advantage

Each year, *Fortune* magazine publishes its list of "The World's Most Admired Companies." *Fortune* identifies the highest-revenue companies in every industry, invites executives, directors, and managers to rate the selected companies in their industry, and then choose the 10 they most admire across all industries. Panelists use the following nine equally weighted criteria in their rankings:

- Quality of management
- Quality of products and services
- Innovativeness
- Long-term investment value
- Financial soundness
- Talent management
- Community responsibility
- Global business effectiveness
- Use of corporate assets[1]

These criteria reflect various aspects of company operations that ultimately relate to company success. Including *talent management*—defined as a company's ability to attract, develop, and keep talented employees—in this list of criteria acknowledges the role that employees play in the success of an organization. When a company has the right employees in place and properly develops and motivates them, the likelihood of sustaining a competitive advantage increases dramatically.

## Managing Employees

This book is about managing employees—the people who make organizations successful. The talent that employees bring with them when they start work or acquire after getting hired plays a key role in determining what the company does and how well it does it. Consider the company GlaxoSmithKline. Its website indicates that the company's mission is to help people "do more, feel better, live longer." The business is focused on the delivery of three strategic priorities that aim to increase growth, reduce risk, and improve its long-term financial performance. The priorities are: (a) grow a balanced global business, (2) deliver more products of value, and (3) simplify the operating model.[2] Now, consider the type of employees this company must have to even begin to achieve its goals. Without the right employees, the company simply could not succeed. In addition to having the right talent, the company must make sure that it motivates its employees to work as hard as possible to contribute to the company's success.

Our goal for this book is to provide you with an understanding of how to attract, develop, motivate, and retain employees, and to equip you with the knowledge and skills that managers need to perform these activities. We also consider how organizations can leverage the talents of their employees in facing the challenges and opportunities that the external environment presents. We focus on both what organizations need to do now to achieve their goals through employees, and what organizations will need to do in the future to maintain and enhance a competitive advantage through the practices that they use to manage their employees.

### WHAT'S IN A NAME?

Before we discuss how to maximize the potential of your employees, we want to take a moment to clarify a few terms that you will see throughout the text.

Different organizations use different terms to refer to the members of their workforce. Disney has its *cast*, and Walmart employees are *associates*. Other companies use the terms *human resources* and *human capital*. While the terms used by companies may vary, we use the term **employees** to refer to the individuals who work for a company.

Throughout this book, we use the term **human resources practices**, often shortened to **HR practices**. When we refer to HR practices, we are not talking about the responsibilities of the HR department of a company unless we specifically say so; rather, we are talking about the practices that a company has put in place to manage employees. We have chosen this term because it is the one that most companies use to represent these activities. Also, most schools refer to the course you are taking as "Human Resource Management," and most of the tools that you will have at your disposal as a manager to attract, develop, motivate, and retain employees are related to human resource concepts and principles.

We use the term **line manager** (or **manager**) to refer to an individual who is responsible for supervising and directing the efforts of a group of employees to perform tasks that are directly related to the creation and delivery of a company's products or services. For many years, line managers had the responsibility for most, if not all, aspects of managing employees. As more employment-related laws were passed, however, many companies began to assign much of the responsibility for employee management to the **human resources department** (also called simply the **HR department**), a support function within companies that serves a vital role in designing and implementing company policies for managing employees. Over time, the role of HR departments expanded to include a wide variety of tasks, including record keeping and payroll, compensation and benefits, recruitment, selection, training, performance management, and regulatory issues. Now, however, companies are increasingly recognizing that managing employees is a key organizationwide responsibility, not solely the responsibility of the HR department—and line managers are being held accountable for how effectively they attract, develop, and motivate the employees they oversee.[3] After all, managers are successful only if they are able to get the highest-quality work from their employees.

Of course, many companies still maintain HR departments, and the employees within HR departments serve an important role in company success. But, increasingly, managers must work with the HR department to design and implement HR practices that maximize the contributions of their employees. Smart managers understand that people matter, and without people, a company cannot begin to achieve its goals. As we look at some of the potential costs and benefits, you will begin to understand why managing employees is the job of every manager, not just the job of the HR department.

## THE COSTS AND BENEFITS OF MANAGING HR

A company's **competitive advantage** is its ability to create more economic value than its competitors. A company achieves this outcome by providing greater value to a customer relative to the costs of making a product or providing a service.[4] Historically, companies focused on achieving a competitive advantage by holding protected assets, having extensive financial resources, competing based on price, or benefiting from economies of scale.[5] Companies often considered employees as a cost to minimize rather than as a competitive advantage. After all, maintaining a workforce is one of the largest fixed costs for most organizations. In addition to compensation costs, employers incur costs as a result of the time and effort needed for activities such as recruiting, hiring, training, evaluating, mentoring, coaching, and disciplining employees.

Increasingly, companies are recognizing that employees and how they are managed may prove to be as important to competitive success as other organizational attributes. When employees are mismanaged, they may not be able or willing to work

**employees**

individuals who work for a company

**human resources practices (HR practices)**

the practices that a company has put in place to manage employees

**line manager (manager)**

an individual who is responsible for supervising and directing the efforts of a group of employees to perform tasks that are directly related to the creation and delivery of a company's products or services

**human resources department (HR department)**

a support function within companies that serves a vital role in designing and implementing company policies for managing employees

**competitive advantage**

a company's ability to create more economic value than its competitors

toward organizational goals. If employees do not have the necessary skills for their jobs and are not provided the training to succeed, they may not know how to work effectively or efficiently which leads to lower performance and greater costs to the company. How employees are managed also influences their attitudes and behaviors.[6] Employees who feel undervalued or underappreciated will not expend as much effort in performing their jobs.[7] Unhappy or unmotivated employees may be less likely to be responsive to customer needs, which can cost the company customers.[8] Mismanaging employees may lead to higher levels of employee turnover and absenteeism[9] or even sabotage,[10] all of which can have both direct and indirect costs for the organization. An employee who is not properly trained to do a hazardous job may make mistakes that lead to injury for the worker and a lawsuit for the company.

In contrast, effectively managing employees can lead to improved firm performance.[11] Studies have shown this link in industries as diverse as banking, apparel, and manufacturing.[12] When employees have the skills they need, they are able to contribute to meeting company goals. And when employees feel valued by their company, they are likely to display greater levels of commitment, loyalty, and morale.[13] Armed with the skills they need and greater motivation, employees may be more productive. Greater productivity may more than offset the costs associated with managing employees.

Given what we know about the outcomes of effective management, many companies increasingly view employees as an asset rather than just a cost to control. These companies know that employees are a potential source of competitive advantage and that their talents must be nurtured.[14] In fact, many companies now emphasize the value of employees to the company directly on their websites. Cigna, a company that provides employee benefits, state on its Careers website: "Cigna is a global health service company, dedicated to helping the people we serve improve their health, well-being, and sense of security. Cigna serves its customers with nearly 35,000 dedicated employees worldwide. When you work at Cigna, you can count on a different kind of career. Work with us, and you'll make a difference, deliver results, and share in the reinvention of health care. Cigna understands and nurtures your individual strengths to help you achieve what matters most to you in your life."[15] This company recognizes that when employees are managed effectively, they can be an important source of competitive advantage.

Keep in mind that there is no single best way to manage employees. Rather, each company is different and must manage employees in a way that is most appropriate, given its unique situation. The internal organizational demands and the external environment determine the context for setting HR practices. The framework we present next and reference throughout the book shows the relationship among three sets of HR challenges in an organization's internal and external environment, three primary HR activities, and the path to competitive advantage. Understanding this framework will better equip you with the skills to strategically and effectively manage employees while minimizing the costs of mismanaging them.

## Framework for the Strategic Management of Employees

Have you ever tried to assemble a jigsaw puzzle without the picture on the box? You have all these odd-shaped little pieces of colored cardboard, but no clear idea of how to start putting them together. For many managers, knowing how to hire employees, give them performance feedback, and decide on pay raises feels much like trying to complete that puzzle without the picture. Just as soon as the manager begins to feel as if she has a handle on some of these aspects of employee management, changes occur in the business environment. Maybe new technology or new laws emerge, and the manager begins to feel like the shapes of the pieces have changed.

## COMPANY SPOTLIGHT  1.1

### Costco Wholesale

Costco Wholesale, a low-priced retail company regularly on *Fortune's* "America's Most Admired Companies" list, serves as an exemplar for how the strategic management of human resources can lead to competitive advantage in a highly competitive industry. Most low-priced retailers have a business strategy that is cost-focused. They believe that if they pay more for employees, customers will have to pay more, leading to less competitiveness and profits. Rather than following industry practice of managing profits by cutting employment costs, however, Costco invests in training its employees, providing generous pay and benefits even to part-timers, giving employees greater discretion to make on-the-spot decisions to help customers, and promoting from within. In this highly cost-focused industry, Costco's approach to managing employees strategically results in a key competitive advantage: employee productivity that is almost double that of the company's main competitors. Employee reviews on Indeed.com speak to the positive culture that produces one of the lowest turnover rates in the industry. As one Costco sales advisor noted in a posted review, "Excellent environment to work in. Good salary. Opportunities to grow professionally. Excellent benefits and good work area. Flexible work schedules." Sounds simple, but not so easy to execute well, which is why Costco has a competitive advantage.

*Sources:* Zeynep Ton., "Some Companies Are Investing in Their Workers and Reaping Healthy Profits," *Harvard Business Review*, January–February (2012): 3–9. Michael Stallard, "Why Culture Makes Costco America's Best Employer," October 2017, www.td.org/insights/why-culture-makes-costco-americas-best-employer; Abhijeet Pratap, "An Analysis of Costco's Organizational Culture and Human Resource Management," August 25, 2017, https://www.cheshnotes.com/2017/08/an-analysis-of-costcos-organizational-culture-and-human-resource-management/; "Costco Wholesale Employee Reviews," indeed.com, https://www.indeed.com/cmp/Costco-Wholesale/reviews.

The framework that we introduce in this chapter and use throughout the book (Exhibit 1.1) is like the guiding picture on the puzzle box. It shows the relationship between the organization's context, both external and internal, and the HR activities that the organization needs to use to manage employees to achieve its ultimate goal: competitive advantage. By understanding the relationships among these components and how the HR activities build on each other, managers can equip and position employees to maximize their contribution to company performance, which in turn creates competitive advantage. The picture of the puzzle does exist, and it helps managers put together the pieces. Company Spotlight 1.1 describes a company, Costco Wholesale, that understands the importance of strategic human resource management.

Exhibit 1.1 shows that the strategic management of employees centers around three categories of HR activities. These activities occur within the context of three main HR challenges. The **primary HR activities** are:

1. *Work design and workforce planning*—Designing jobs and planning for the workforce needed to achieve organizational goals
2. *Managing employee competencies*—Identifying, acquiring, and developing employee talent and skills
3. *Managing employee attitudes and behaviors*—Encouraging and motivating employees to perform in appropriate ways to contribute to company goals

**primary HR activities**

encompass work design and workforce planning, managing employee competencies, and managing employee attitudes and behaviors

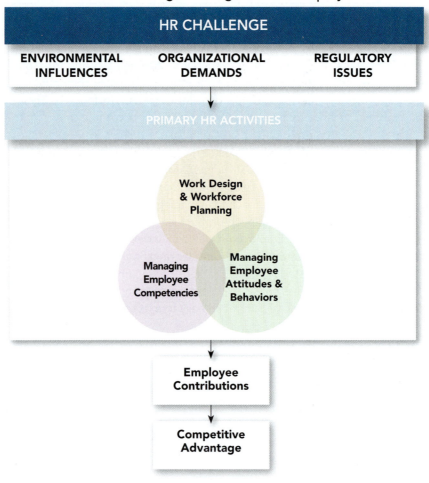

**EXHIBIT 1.1**

Framework for the Strategic Management of Employees

Managers carry out these three primary HR activities in the context of three main **HR challenges**:

1. *Organizational demands*—internal factors, including strategy, company characteristics, organizational culture, and employee concerns
2. *Environmental influences*—external factors, including labor force trends, globalization, technology, and ethics and social responsibility
3. *Regulatory issues*—a special subgroup of environmental influences that includes federal, state, and local legislation that protects the rights of individuals and the company with regard to the employment process

We discuss these primary HR activities and HR challenges in more detail in the following section. Regulatory issues are so critical to employee management that we devote a full chapter to discussing them (Chapter 3).

**HR challenges**

challenges that managers must consider in the management of employees that relate to organizational demands, environmental influences, and regulatory issues.

## Primary HR Activities

Exhibit 1.2 highlights the three primary HR activities. First, companies must decide how to design jobs and ensure that employees are where they need to be to meet organizational goals. Second, companies must ensure that employees have the competencies that they need to perform those jobs. Third, employees must be motivated to use their competencies productively.

**EXHIBIT 1.2**

Primary HR Activities

# Work Design and Workforce Planning

Work design and workforce planning are two critical components of managing employees. Managers must design jobs in a way that ensures that employees perform tasks and responsibilities that have the most potential to add value to the company. Managers also must engage in workforce planning to make sure that the right people are in the right place in the company, at the right time, to meet company goals.

## JOB DESIGN

Job design involves deciding what employees will do on a day-to-day basis, as well as how jobs are interconnected. In part, job design is a function of the tasks that employees are expected to perform. However, job design also represents the choices that managers make regarding how those tasks are to be carried out. There are many different ways to design jobs.

Some employees work on an assembly line, others work in self-managed teams, and still other employees work in relative isolation. Managers may design similar jobs in different ways in different companies—no single design fits all situations. Think about how the job of an accountant in an accounting firm might differ from the job of an accountant in a retail store chain, or how the job of a marketing manager might differ in a professional services firm from the job of marketing manager in a manufacturing firm. In both examples, many of the tasks will be the same, but the importance of those tasks for company success and how the jobs are performed will differ. Some questions that managers need to consider for job design are:

- What tasks should you emphasize when designing a job?
- How simple or complex are these tasks?
- How many tasks can your employees perform?
- How much flexibility do you provide to your employees in terms of how and where they carry out their tasks?

The choices managers make about the tasks that employees perform and how they are expected to perform those tasks have several important implications. From a company perspective, when jobs are designed to align tasks with company objectives, employees in those jobs are in a position to add value and increase company success. If managers do not consider company objectives in job design, employees may unknowingly focus on tasks and activities that are not necessarily the most important. From an employee perspective, job design influences employee satisfaction, as well as intentions to remain with the company.[16]

## WORKFORCE PLANNING

The number of employees in different parts of an organization is always changing. Factors such as employee turnover and company growth challenge managers to make workforce planning decisions to maintain the necessary number of employees.

Companies also must decide how to allocate employees—through promotions, demotions, and transfers—to areas where they can contribute most significantly. Changes in strategic emphasis, a reorganization of operations, or the introduction of new products or services also influence the demand for different jobs in different parts of a company. At any point in time, some parts of a company may be facing a shortage of employee talent, while others may have a surplus.

Some companies hire full-time employees or promote current employees to address a growing demand for products or services; other companies turn to outsourcing and send work to other companies, often in other countries, or use other forms of labor such as contingent workers, temporary employees, and independent contractors.[17] In 2017, there were 5.9 million contingent workers (defined as workers who do not expect their jobs to last or who report that they have temporary jobs) and another 15.5 million workers in alternative work arrangements (independent contractors, on-call workers, temporary help employees, and workers provided by contract firms).[18] This number is expected to continue to increase with the emergence of the technology-enabled gig economy. Companies such as Uber, Lyft, TaskRabbit, and Freelancer, with technology platforms that match people willing to supply labor or work on a short-term engagement with those looking for someone to perform a short-term task or service, are creating a new source of work for independent contractors, or "gig workers", as they are now called.

When faced with a labor surplus, managers often must consider tactics such as downsizing, early retirement programs, and demotions or transfers to reduce the number of employees in certain parts of the company and balance supply and demand. Some of the important questions concerning workforce planning are:

- How should you address a labor shortage? A labor surplus?
- When should you require current employees to work overtime, as opposed to hiring additional full-time staff?
- When should you outsource work rather than hire new employees?
- What can you do to minimize the negative effects of downsizing?

While there are many options available to address labor shortages and surpluses, the challenge is to understand when different options are likely to be most effective to meet each company's unique situation.

## Managing Employee Competencies

As shown in Exhibit 1.2, the second primary HR activity for managers is ensuring that employees have the necessary competencies to perform their tasks effectively. **Competencies** are the knowledge, skills, abilities, and other talents that employees possess. These competencies directly influence the types of jobs that employees are able to perform. Managing competencies means recruiting and selecting the right people and training them to succeed in their jobs.

**competencies**

the knowledge, skills, abilities, and other talents that employees possess

## RECRUITMENT

*Recruitment* refers to the process of generating a qualified pool of potential employees interested in working for your company or encouraging individuals within your company to pursue other positions within your company. The challenge with recruitment is having a clear understanding of the competencies needed to succeed in a job and designing a strategy for identifying individuals in the labor market who possess those competencies and who would be a good match for the organization's culture and goals. Identifying a potential chief executive officer (CEO) or an individual with rare scientific skills, for example, requires a different recruitment approach than identifying people who could fill a clerical or assembly-line job vacancy. Placing an advertisement for a job opening in the local newspaper is not likely to maximize a company's opportunity to identify a good CEO. Similarly, placing an advertisement in the *Wall Street Journal* is not likely to be an efficient way to identify individuals for a janitorial position. Where and how companies recruit influences the type and quality of candidates who respond to a job opening. Management has to create an employee value proposition that will attract the right individuals to apply for the open positions. A *recruitment value proposition* addresses the question: "Why would someone want to work for this company?"[19] Some key issues to address in creating a recruitment strategy are:

- For what competencies do you recruit?
- What groups do you target with your recruitment message?
- Do you recruit internally, externally, or both?
- How do you ensure that you offer an employee value proposition that will attract the right applicants?

## SELECTION

Whereas recruitment focuses on generating a qualified pool of candidates for job openings, *selection* focuses on choosing the best person from that pool. As with recruitment, there are a number of important questions to consider when deciding among candidates. Each job candidate brings a unique blend of knowledge, skills, talents, and abilities. Perhaps the most critical issue to address is whether the candidate possesses the competencies that you have identified as the most important for a particular job. Some companies may emphasize past experiences while others may emphasize personality when making a selection decision. Certainly, the emphasis is influenced by the nature of the job. Consider making a selection decision for a firefighter. How important is personality? How important is physical strength? How important is experience? Your answers to these questions directly influence who is hired from the pool of job candidates identified in the recruitment process.

Once a company has made a selection decision, it has made a commitment to an individual. Considering the time, money, and energy spent recruiting and selecting new employees, managers need to ensure that selection decisions are based on sound reasoning and do not violate employment laws. Some of the key issues in making selection decisions are:

- How do you generate the information that you need to make an effective, and legal, hiring decision?
- Which tests are most effective for identifying employees with high potential?
- What questions should you ask candidates during an interview?
- Who makes the ultimate hiring decision?

There is no "one best way" to recruit and select employees. Each company is unique and has different needs. Yet the choices that managers make influence the effectiveness of the staffing process and, ultimately, who is employed. The goal of recruitment and staffing is to ensure that employees have the competencies they need to contribute to the company's success, or have the potential to develop those competencies.

## LEARNING AND DEVELOPMENT

Recruitment and selection focus on finding and choosing the right person for the job. *Learning and development* ensure that new and current employees know the ins and outs of the organization and have the skills that they need to succeed, both now and in the future. Training is part of learning and development. Even when a company successfully hires employees who have a great deal of potential, the employees are still likely to need training, depending on the company's needs. Employees also need to learn about the company itself, its culture, and the general way that it operates.

Beyond new hires, many other situations warrant training for both new and current employees. All employees may need to learn how to use new technology effectively and safely, and the decision to merge with another company may require employees to learn new procedures. Beyond training for the needs of a particular job, companies engage in training activities to develop individuals for future positions. Doing so requires the foresight to identify employees who may potentially fill positions throughout the organization and then engaging in activities to provide them with the skills that they will need to be able to move into those positions when the vacancies emerge.

Given the time, cost, and effort required to build employee competencies, it should come as no surprise that companies place great emphasis on these processes. If companies are going to work hard to select the right people, it is important that they focus on providing employees with the specific know-how that they need to be successful in their current position, as well as potential positions that they might assume. Some of the important decisions in training are:

- How do you know which employees need to be trained?
- How do you design an effective training program?
- Which training methods are most effective to meet your needs?
- How do you know if your training efforts have been successful?

## Managing Employee Attitudes and Behaviors

Building competencies is critical, but keep in mind that it is only part of the equation. How well employees perform is a function of the effort they expend, as well as their competencies. Encouraging the right employee attitudes and behaviors requires motivating workers to continually improve their performance. This need forms our third group of primary HR activities. Some of the major tools that managers use to guide employee efforts on the job are compensation, incentives, performance management programs, and employee benefits, health, and wellness programs.

### PERFORMANCE MANAGEMENT

Many managers may think that performance management is simply sitting down with an employee once a year to discuss her or his performance during that time. The manager may review an evaluation form with the employee to rate her or his performance on certain items and then use those ratings to discuss appropriate merit raises and possible promotions. But good performance management is more complex than that. Much like with incentive systems, which we discuss next, the criteria that managers use to evaluate their employees need to represent the attitudes and behaviors managers expect of their employees. When managers clearly communicate performance criteria, employees are more likely to have a good understanding of the steps that they need to take to achieve successful job performance. When these performance criteria are aligned with organizational goals, managers and employees become more confident that they are focusing their efforts on important activities.

Effective performance management involves more than just evaluating employees, however. It also focuses on providing employees with feedback (positive and negative), on an ongoing basis, and on using employee learning and development activities to improve current and future performance. The continuous improvement part of this process entails giving clear feedback regarding performance, praising good performers, and disciplining poor performers. Perhaps most important, effective performance management means helping employees understand how to continually improve.

There is no single best performance management system. The most appropriate system depends on the unique context of each company. Some critical issues in performance management are:

- What is the best way for you to measure employee performance?
- How should you communicate that information to employees?
- In addition to performance evaluation, how can managers give employees developmental feedback to improve their performance?
- How should you manage poorly performing employees?

## COMPENSATION AND INCENTIVES

A company's compensation system exerts a strong influence on the attitudes and behaviors of employees because it sends a message regarding the employees' value to the company. If employees feel that their company does not value them, they may not work as hard as possible. Instead, they may search for other employment opportunities. In contrast, if employees feel that their company compensates them at a fair level for the job that they perform, they are more likely to work harder to help the organization meet its goals.[20]

In addition to compensation in the form of base pay, a rewards and incentives system shows employees how managers expect them to focus their time and energy. Some companies are more likely to reward seniority, while others may emphasize performance-based pay. Even among companies that reward their employees based on performance, the criteria may differ. Companies may value efficiency, creativity, knowledge sharing, and teamwork. Lincoln Electric's incentive system, for instance, is geared toward rewarding productivity, whereas 3M's incentive system places greater emphasis on creativity and new product design.[21] The incentive systems of these two companies differ because their employees add value in different ways. The size of an incentive is also an important indicator of how a firm values a particular activity or level of performance.

Some of the key questions when designing incentive systems are:

- What factors should you consider when determining the salary range for a job?
- What is the best way to determine how much employees should be paid?
- How much of that pay should be guaranteed, and how much should be based on incentives?
- What types of incentives should you use to encourage the employee attitudes and behaviors the firm wants?

## EMPLOYEE BENEFITS, HEALTH, AND WELLNESS

The last piece of managing employee attitudes and behaviors is managing benefits, health, and wellness. Some companies offer benefits in an attempt to help recruit, select, and retain employees. Think about that for a second. Would you be more willing to work for a company that had an attractive benefits program that included coverage for dental care, vacation time, tuition assistance, and the like, or a company that did not offer these practices? In addition to serving as a recruitment or a retention tool, benefits may help ensure the health and well-being of a company's workforce. Considering the value-creating potential of employees, it is only logical that companies help ensure that employees are able to work effectively over time.

Some benefits, including some health and wellness programs, are required by law. For example, Social Security, workers' compensation, and family and medical leave are governed by regulations with which most employers must comply. Similarly, employee safety is a key concern for companies, and is governed by the Occupational Safety and Health Administration (OSHA). As a manager, it is important that you understand your responsibilities to ensure that your employees work in a safe and healthy environment.

There are also a wide array of voluntary benefits programs that companies typically offer. These include paid time off, health care, and retirement programs. Some critical issues when considering employee benefits, health, and wellness are:

- Which benefit programs are most appropriate for your workforce?
- What are the legal requirements regarding benefit programs?
- How can you ensure the safety of your employees?

As you can see, managing attitudes and behaviors requires careful attention to a host of issues. The challenge lies in the fact that each manager's situation is unique. This uniqueness is the result of differences in organizational strategies and in characteristics of the employees supervised. We'll discuss some of these challenges shortly, but keep in mind that instead of trying to identify a single way to manage employee attitudes and behaviors, it's important to identify the different tools that managers have at their disposal to guide and motivate their employees within the unique context of their organization.

## HR Activity Alignment

 Each of the three HR activities described is critical, but none is effective in isolation. Work design and workforce planning, managing employee competencies, and encouraging the right employee attitudes and behaviors must align with each other to be effective.[22] When we discuss **alignment**, we are describing the extent to which HR activities are designed to achieve the goals of an organization. Company Spotlight 1.2 discusses the importance of HR activity alignment with company goals at Wegmans, a large, family-owned supermarket chain.

**alignment**

the extent to which HR activities are designed to achieve the goals of an organization

## COMPANY SPOTLIGHT  1.2

### Wegmans

A private, family-owned supermarket chain with over 42,000 employees, Wegmans exemplifies the value of investing in employees, particularly, training. Included in Fortune's "100 Best Companies to Work For" for more than two decades, Wegmans describes itself as a mission-driven, values-based, family company. Its mission is to help people live healthier, better lives through food and by providing incredible service in a warm, welcoming atmosphere from its caring, knowledgeable employees. To execute its mission, Wegmans invests more than $50 million each year to provide its employees with learning and development opportunities. For example, new cashiers receive over 40 hours of training before they can serve customers. Wegman's butchers go to Colorado, Uruguay, and Argentina to learn about beef, and its deli managers are sent to Wisconsin, Italy, Germany, and France to learn about cheese. For employees who want to attend college, Wegmans provides flexibility and financial assistance. Since 1984, Wegmans has given $110 million in scholarships to 35,000 employees. The Wegmans model is simple: A happy, knowledgeable, and superbly trained employee creates a better experience for customers. Profits and accolades follow.

*Sources:* Freile, Victoria E. (2015), "Wegmans Again Named Top Workplace by Fortune Magazine," February 15, 2018, https://www.democratandchronicle.com/story/money/2018/02/15/wegmans-again-named-top-workplace-fortune-magazine/340352002/; Great Place to Work, "Wegmans" (http://reviews.greatplacetowork.com/); Wegmans Website: Learn & Grow https://jobs.wegmans.com/learn-grow; Rohde, David, "The Anti-Walmart: The Secret Sauce of Wegmans Is People," *The Atlantic Daily,* published March 23, 2012, https://www.theatlantic.com/business/archive/2012/03/the-anti-walmart-the-secret-sauce-of-wegmans-is-people/254994/.

## EXHIBIT 1.3
Internal Alignment

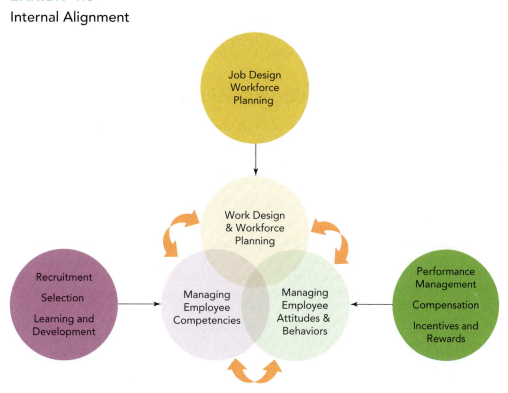

Alignment can be broken down into two parts—internal and external alignment. As shown in Exhibit 1.3, to achieve **internal alignment**, you must first make sure that the specific practices used *within* each HR activity are consistent with one another, as well as aligned *across* the primary HR activities.[23] If you have ever been on a sports team, you know how important it is for all participants to have a common understanding of how to play the game, the skills required to play, and the desire to win. That is the same thing that we are talking about here:

- If employees know the goals of the organization and are motivated to work toward those goals, but do not possess all the competencies to do so, the results will be diminished employee performance and reduced organizational productivity.
- If employees possess the competencies that they need and know the goals, but lack sufficient motivation, their contributions to the company's success will be limited.
- If employees are capable and motivated, but are limited in what they can do or if the company is short staffed due to inappropriate or poor job design and workforce planning, their ability to contribute to the organization will be limited.

In addition to internal alignment, you must achieve **external alignment** by ensuring that the design of the three primary HR activities takes into account the HR challenges that companies face. We discuss these challenges next.

**internal alignment**

the outcome of ensuring that specific practices within each HR activity are consistent with one another and aligned across the primary HR activities

**external alignment**

the outcome of ensuring that the design of the three primary HR activities takes into account the HR challenges that companies face

# HR Challenges

We have already discussed how managing employees in different contexts presents unique challenges. Let's take a look at these challenges in more detail. Internal factors, including company characteristics, strategic objectives, organizational culture, and employee concerns of the workforce, vary across organizations. Also, environmental factors outside the company, including competitive and regulatory forces, are constantly changing. The variety of internal and external forces affecting a company, and the challenges they pose, are briefly introduced next. In Chapter 2, we discuss internal organizational demands and environmental influences in more depth; and in Chapter 3, we focus on regulatory issues.

# Challenge 1: Meeting Organizational Demands

**organizational demands**

factors within a firm that affect decisions regarding how to manage employees

**Organizational demands** are factors within a firm that affect decisions regarding how to manage employees. We focus specifically on the demands highlighted in Exhibit 1.4: strategy, company characteristics, organizational culture, and employee concerns.

## STRATEGY

**strategy**

a company's plan for achieving a competitive advantage over its rivals

A company's **strategy** is its plan for achieving a competitive advantage over its rivals. Strategy drives the activities that a company performs to attract and retain customers relative to its competitors.[24] Companies realize a competitive advantage when they implement a strategy that has value for customers and that rival firms are unable to duplicate.[25]

Companies have a wide range of strategies from which to choose.[26] A company may strive to become the low-cost leader in an industry, or it may strive to sell some unique product or service that differentiates the firm from its competitors and commands a higher price. A look at the retail industry provides a good example of these differences. Walmart is the low-cost leader in the retail industry and outperforms its competition by having the lowest costs in the industry. On the other hand, Nordstrom's strategy focuses on providing a high level of customer service under the theory that people will pay more for goods if the service is exceptional. While both companies operate successfully in the retail industry, they pursue distinctly different strategies for how they compete with their rivals.

The strategy that a company chooses influences the types of jobs that must be performed to meet its objectives and, consequently, influences its primary HR activities.[27] A company with a low-cost strategy is likely to have different expectations and objectives for its employees than a company with a strategy emphasizing customer service or creativity.[28] By shaping how employees work and add value, a company's strategy also affects the competencies that employees in those jobs must possess, as well as the specific attitudes and behaviors they need to display. Consider the food service industry. The tasks that employees perform in a four-star restaurant, in which service, ambience, and excellent quality are likely the focus, are very different from the tasks that employees perform in a local diner or a fast-food establishment in which speed and price are the focus. The strategies of these types of companies vary, resulting in differences in the required competencies, attitudes, and behaviors of employees. Strategy is a key influential factor for managers as they carry out the primary HR activities. As with all the other HR challenges, we will cover strategy in each chapter throughout this book.

## COMPANY CHARACTERISTICS

Companies differ in size and stage of development. Whether a company has a handful of employees or millions, it must manage its employees. However, the challenges associated with managing employees correspond (at least in part) to the size of the organization. Smaller businesses often do not have the same amount and type of resources as larger companies, and they may not be in a position to provide the same level of pay, benefits, and training opportunities. Size also influences the degree of

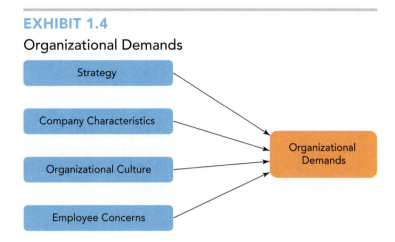

**EXHIBIT 1.4**

Organizational Demands

autonomy and discretion that managers may expect employees to display in their jobs. As a result, the competencies that employees need in small companies versus large ones may differ. Companies also vary in terms of their stage of development. As you might imagine, the pressures of managing employees in a young start-up company are likely to differ from those in mature organizations striving to protect their market share.[29]

As we discussed earlier, the way a job is designed depends on the industry. Differences in job tasks also vary based on company size. An accountant in a small firm probably will handle all aspects of the firm's accounting, including accounts payable and accounts receivable. In a large firm, she will likely handle only one aspect of the job (perhaps accounts payable), and then the accounts of only a few vendors. Employee attitudes and behaviors also can have different consequences for companies of differing sizes. A high- or low-performing employee in a small company is likely to have a much more direct influence on the company's success than one in a company that has thousands of employees.

## ORGANIZATIONAL CULTURE

**Organizational culture** is the set of underlying values and beliefs that employees of a company share.[30] What is particularly interesting about organizational culture is that it is unwritten, yet understood and often taken for granted. Each organization has a distinct culture that represents the beliefs of the company's founders, decisions of its top managers, types of people who work in the company, and environment in which the company operates.

Culture influences how employees do their jobs, how managers and employees interact, and the acceptable practices for executing primary HR activities. A positive culture can be a tremendous asset to an organization.[31] When a culture is positive and consistent with the organization's objectives, employees are likely to have a clear understanding of what they need to do in their jobs to contribute to the company's goals and to have a willingness to engage in those activities. Such a culture can also be a strategic asset in attracting and retaining employees. Facebook, described in Company Spotlight 1.3, provides an example of a company in which organizational culture matters.

**organizational culture**
the set of underlying values and beliefs that employees of a company share

## EMPLOYEE CONCERNS

Timely address of employee issues and concerns is a critical component in a company's success. Employees may experience the stress of single parenting, caring for aging parents, or juggling schedules with an employed spouse. Successful companies are helping employees find a balance between the demands of work

## COMPANY SPOTLIGHT 1.3

### Facebook

Facebook, founded in 2004, is a social-networking technology company whose mission is to give people the power to build community and bring the world closer together. Regularly ranked by Glassdoor and *Fortune* as the best employer to work for (number 1 and number 2, respectively, in 2018), Facebook demonstrates the power of HR activities that are aligned with meeting employee needs. With an average employee age of 28, one of the lowest among large technology companies, Facebook seeks to "build a set of policies that support being good workers, family members, and friends in every life stage," according to Lori Goler, Vice President of People. To back this up, new parents have benefits that include parental leave that is equal for men and women, $4,000 in baby cash for parents of newborns, and reserved parking spaces for pregnant mothers. Working long hours is made easier with a come-to-work culture that includes free train passes, van pools, a full-service bike shop, on-site laundry services, and no meetings on Wednesdays. Facebook also offers gourmet and healthy meals for free all day long which contributes to employee energy and enjoyment, encourages coming to the office, and sustains a pleasant work environment. Refueling employee energy is also supported with 21 days of paid vacation, unlimited sick days, and a $700 subsidy for gym memberships. Workspaces are open, with no private offices, to encourage collaboration and equality. To promote boldness and risk-taking, Facebook offices are decorated throughout with inspirational slogans painted on the walls, such as "All glory comes from daring to begin" and "Nothing at Facebook is somebody else's problem." All these things support their young, hard-driving employees' needs, and add up to make the work experience at Facebook very positive.

*Sources:* "Facebook's HR Head Reveals Why Staff (Really) Love Working for It," http://www.humanresourcesonline .net/fuels-facebooks-talent-asia/; Crum, Rex, "Facebook Employee's Favorite Perks—Here's 8 of the Best," November 22, 2015, https://www.thestreet.com/story/13371353/1/facebook-employees-favorite-perks-here-s-8-of-the-best.html; Pratap, Abhijeet, "HR Management at Facebook: Amazing Benefits for Amazing Talents," January 9, 2018, https://www .cheshnotes.com/2018/01/hr-management-facebook-amazing-benefits-amazing-talents/; Mejia, Zameena, "Facebook's HR Chief Discusses 5 Key Tenets of Its Winning Culture," July 17, 2017, https://www.cnbc.com/2017/07/17/facebooks-hr-chief-reveals-no-1-reason-for-the-social-media-giants-succeess.html; Allen, Robert, "Average Age of Tech Company's Employees," May 31, 2016, https://www.smartinsights.com/manage-digital-transformation/average-age-tech-companys-employees-chartoftheday, Glassdoor, "Facebook Overview," https://www.glassdoor.com/facebook, https:// newsroom.fb.com/company-info/; Heath, Alex, "Facebook Has a New Mission Statement: 'To Bring the World Closer Together'," June 22, 2017, http://www.businessinsider.com/new-facebook-mission-statement-2017-6; Sullivan, John, "A Case Study of Facebook's Simply Amazing Talent Management Practices, Part 1 of 2," September 9, 2013, https:// www.ere.net/a-case-study-of-facebooks-simply-amazing-talent-management-practices-part-1-of-2/

and their personal lives. Many companies now offer more flexibility, including flexible work schedules, family-friendly benefits, and telecommuting, to address this growing need. For example, Unilever permits its 100,000 employees, with the exception of factory production workers, to work anytime, anywhere, as long as they meet business needs.[32]

## Challenge 2: Environmental Influences

**environmental influences**

pressures that exist outside of companies that managers must consider to strategically manage their employees

**Environmental influences** are pressures that exist outside companies that managers must consider to strategically manage their employees. Exhibit 1.5 highlights the point that managing these influences requires tracking labor force trends, taking advantage of technological advances, addressing the globalization of industries, and meeting social and ethical obligations.

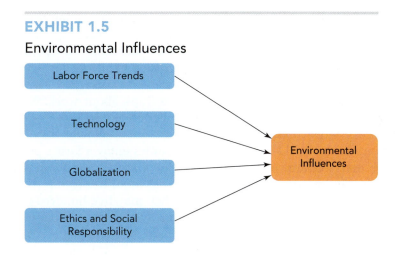

**EXHIBIT 1.5**

Environmental Influences

## LABOR FORCE TRENDS

According to the Bureau of Labor Statistics (BLS), the labor force is increasingly diverse, especially in terms of the number of women and minorities and the age of the labor force. The number of women in the labor force is expected to grow by 5.8% between the years 2014 and 2024.[33] Similarly, while white, non-Hispanics are projected to remain the largest group in the labor force, the two fastest-growing groups are Hispanics and Asians.[34] The size of the labor force in the 55-and-older age group is increasing faster than the rest of the workforce.[35] In 2024, those aged 55 and older will make up nearly 25% of the U.S. labor force, up from 22% in 2016.[36] For some companies, these older workers represent a potential source of highly qualified applicants often overlooked by other employers.

The changing composition of the labor force influences the primary HR activities in several ways. A diverse workforce requires that managers reevaluate how they recruit and select individuals to make sure that any potential for direct or indirect discrimination is eliminated. Further, employers need to educate employees about the value that different backgrounds and perspectives can bring to organizational performance and create an inclusive climate in the workplace. By directly addressing diversity issues, companies are more likely to capitalize on the many benefits associated with a diverse workforce.[37] Google, in an effort to increase gender diversity in its technology and leadership ranks and to build a more inclusive culture, has voluntarily released demographic data about its workforce each year since 2014.[38] Most companies have kept this information confidential for fear of being targeted for a discrimination lawsuit. Google's former senior vice president of people, Lazlo Bock, however, thought that bringing greater transparency to the lack of diversity in the technology industry might help spur change.[39] But change has been slow. Their 2017 report shows that although women make up 31% of their workforce, only 20% are in technology jobs, up from 17% three years ago. Unfortunately, progress has been slow for increasing the number of Black, Hispanic and Latino employees.[40] In a surprising twist, however, Google's diversity efforts have come under fire from an unanticipated source: white male former employees alleging discrimination at Google, whose workforce is 80% male, 53% white, and 39% Asian.[41] Google's experience illustrates how aligning HR activities with labor-force trends is an HR environmental challenge not to be underestimated.

## TECHNOLOGY

Technology continues to shape the nature of competition. The increasing prominence of the Internet and information technologies (IT) has considerable implications for how employees function within companies. Many employees today must possess a basic level of computer proficiency to perform their jobs. IT has created new avenues for how employees interact, share information, and learn from one another.[42] In addition, technology has created challenges in terms of privacy issues and has increased the potential for employee misuse.

Advances in IT also have changed how we think about work. Not long ago, it was important to live within a reasonable distance of one's job. Today, high-speed Internet access, videoconferencing, Skype, and email allow a firm's employees to live anywhere in the world. As a result, companies enjoy a larger pool of potential employees, and workers experience a wider variety of potential employers.[43] JetBlue allows its reservation agents, many of whom are trying to balance work and family demands, to work from home. They may live hundreds of miles from JetBlue's headquarters, but they work and contribute to the company as if they were physically located in the headquarters.[44] Of course, managing a virtual workforce introduces new challenges regarding staffing decisions, performance evaluations, and learning and development, as we will explore in later chapters.[45]

## GLOBALIZATION

**globalization**

the blurring of country boundaries in business activities

An increasingly significant factor companies face in today's environment is the increased **globalization** of industries—the blurring of country boundaries in business activities. Many companies are actively competing on an international level, setting up production or service facilities in other countries, or establishing international joint ventures and partnerships. Companies that still operate primarily in domestic markets often find themselves competing with international companies. To some extent, all companies operate in a global arena, which creates challenges and opportunities in terms of managing employees.

Capitalizing on the global labor market requires understanding how differences in cultural values and beliefs influence working relationships among employees. When companies expand across borders, helping expatriates—employees sent to work in company facilities in another country—to work with the local labor force and thrive in a different culture is paramount.

**offshoring**

sending work to companies in other countries, or opening facilities in other countries to do the work

Another challenge in globalization today is **offshoring**—sending work that was once performed domestically to companies in other countries, or opening facilities in other countries to do the work, often at a substantially lower cost.[46] Many companies have offshored some work to India, China, and the Philippines to take advantage of excess labor and low labor costs, and a recent report indicates that 23% of surveyed organizations outsource work internationally.[47] Making the decision to offshore jobs has become more complicated lately, however, with rising wages in emerging economies, particularly in India and China, coinciding with the rapidly decreasing costs of robots and automated factories in the United States.[48] In fact, in 2016, there were more jobs returning from overseas than leaving, for a net gain of 25,000 jobs. Indeed, a newer trend is for foreign companies to acquire and expand manufacturing plants in the United States. For example, Lenovo decided to keep a manufacturing plant in North Carolina's Research Triangle Park that it had acquired from IBM because the location boasts competitive costs, highly skilled workers, and a business-friendly environment.[49]

## ETHICS AND SOCIAL RESPONSIBILITY

Every company operates in a social environment based on implicit and explicit standards of ethical behavior and social responsibility. The importance of ethical

# COMPANY SPOTLIGHT  1.4

## Social Responsibility at Impahla Clothing

Since its founding in 2004 in Cape Town, South Africa, and starting with 60 employees, Impahla Clothing has demonstrated the power of investing in the well-being of its employees and community. The company's Code of Conduct states that it is committed to the goals of reducing waste, using resources responsibly, supporting workers' rights, and advancing the welfare of workers and communities. "When we bought the business, the South African clothing industry was at a very low point, with people losing their jobs in droves," says William Hughes, Impahla Clothing owner and managing director. "We realized very quickly that we had to find a niche for ourselves and do something different to everybody else." Thus, while Imphala struggled to establish itself as a small clothing manufacturer in a very challenging economic environment, it never lost sight of the importance of its employees. The company paid above market wages and provided performance bonuses, sick leave bonuses, and health benefits. The company also encouraged employees to join the union to have their interests represented to management. Moreover, Impahla maintained a strong commitment to an impressive sustainable manufacturing record, being the first carbon-neutral garment manufacturer in South Africa, planting more than 3,000 trees in needy communities and making a commitment to reduce electricity usage by 25% through installing solar panels. Today, the company employs more than 400 people, and in 2013, it was awarded first place in the Job Creation category and first place for Sustainability at the 2013 Business Awards. Impahla's success is an inspiring example of how even a small company can prosper financially by being socially responsible.

*Sources:* "Impahla Clothing: You Have to Learn to Walk Before You Can Run," http://www.sportstrader.co.za/pages/issue%20articles/2015January/impahlaclothingyouhavetolearntowalkbeforeyoucanrun.php; Cohen, E., Taylor, S., Muller-Camen, M. *HRM's Role in Corporate Social and Environmental Sustainability* Alexandria, VA: SHRM Foundation, 2012; "The Story of Impahla Clothing," March 20, 2013, https://www.westerncape.gov.za/110green/news/story-impahla-clothing www.impahla.co.za 2015; *Impahla Integrated Annual Report,* http://www.impahla.co.za/wp-content/uploads/2015/09/Integrated-Annual-Report_2015.pdf; *Impahla Clothing Sustainability Report 2010,* http://www.corporateregister.com/a10723/40898-11Su-10674378J6343770576V-So.pdf.

behavior has gained renewed prominence in recent years as a result of the widely publicized unethical behavior of companies such as Equifax, Uber, United Airlines, Wells Fargo, and Volkswagen. Financial performance may be critical, but, increasingly, companies and their managers are being held accountable for ethical behavior.[50] The problem is that ethical standards are not always clear. To address these ambiguities, many companies, such as Lockheed Martin, Texas Instruments, Raytheon, and GlaxoSmithKline, have implemented formal policies and procedures to help their employees act ethically. For example, Lockheed employs a large group of ethics officers and requires that all its employees attend ethics training each year.[51]

Beyond ethics programs, many companies are also taking steps to demonstrate enhanced levels of social responsibility. For example, Starbucks has garnered considerable attention by going above and beyond its legally required responsibilities to provide a work setting that places a strong priority on taking care of its employees. Also, as shown in Company Spotlight 1.4, even small companies in an emerging economy can flourish economically by being socially responsible.

## Challenge 3: Regulatory Issues

Regulatory issues present the challenge that has probably had the most direct influence on the management of employees. During the past 50 years, many U.S. presidential executive orders, as well as much federal, state, and local legislation, have been specifically concerned with the employment process. At a basic level, legislation describes what is legally acceptable in the employment process and focuses on protecting the rights of individuals to have an equal opportunity to enjoy the benefits and privileges of employment.

The challenge with regulatory issues is that the influence of legislation on employment is very broad, and the interpretation of these laws continues to evolve. Moreover, legislation is continually introduced that broadens existing statutes and creates new ones. The Americans with Disabilities Act of 1990 (ADA), for example, provides specific guidelines and provisions regarding the treatment of individuals with disabilities in employment situations.[52] This law covers management-related activities such as interviewing, selection, promotion, job design, access to training opportunities, compensation and benefits, and even layoffs. The ADA is only one of the many laws and executive orders that influence the management of employees in direct and indirect ways. Other laws, such as Title VII of the Civil Rights Act of 1964, the Occupational Safety and Health Act, and the Civil Rights Act of 1992, have important implications for how companies manage their workforce.

When a company fails to comply with legal requirements, it is at risk of considerable costs. For example, in a very high profile case that led to the resignation of its longtime news chief, Roger Ailes, Twenty-First Century Fox Inc. reached a $90 million settlement of shareholder claims arising from the sexual harassment of female employees at its Fox News Channel.[53] In another high profile case, the Weinstein Company, once seen as "a crown jewel of moviemaking," said it would file for bankruptcy in the aftermath of sweeping allegations of sexual harassment and unlawful sexual misconduct perpetrated by its founder and CEO, Harvey Weinstein.[54] Both examples illustrate the significant financial penalties, debilitating damage to a company's reputation, and the diminished morale and productivity associated with the failure to address regulatory requirements. Consequently, given the breadth of influence that the legal environment has on the management of employees, this is a critical area for managers to understand. In Chapter 3, we focus on the major employment-related laws and executive orders that affect the management of employees.

## The Plan for This Book

Before moving on to the remaining chapters, it is important to have a clear road map of where we are heading and why we are heading there, much like having the picture to help put the jigsaw puzzle together. The plan for this book is to explore the primary HR activities in detail. First, though, we will focus on the three sets of HR challenges to help you recognize the dynamic context of organizations so that you will understand how to strategically manage employees. We will reference the overarching framework for this book, first introduced in Exhibit 1.1, throughout each chapter as we explore the interrelationships among the HR activities, HR challenges, and organizational goals. Exhibit 1.6 shows how the chapters fit within the framework.

The following is a brief overview of the chapters to come.

**EXHIBIT 1.6**
Chapter Overview

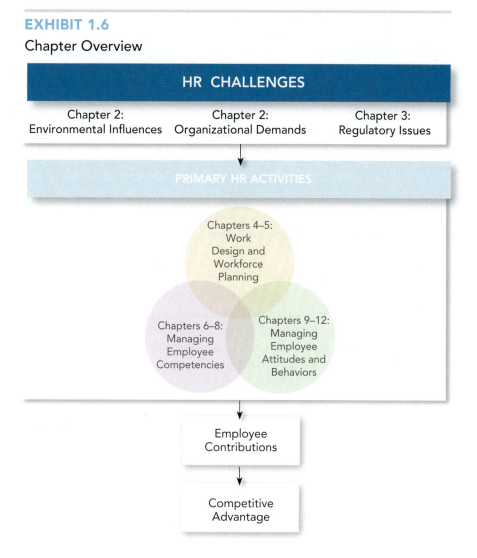

## CHAPTERS 1–3: HR CHALLENGES

As noted previously, effectively managing employees requires that managers have a firm understanding of how the organizational, environmental, and regulatory issues influence companies. In Chapters 1–3, we focus on these three sets of HR challenges.

## CHAPTERS 4–5: WORK DESIGN AND WORKFORCE PLANNING

In Chapters 4–5, we focus on the nature of work and allocating people throughout a company to maximize the contributions of employees to company success. In doing so, we explore the viability of alternative types of job designs to meet different organizational goals, how to use job analysis to help ensure that employees' jobs focus directly on achieving important organizational objectives, and how to balance the supply and demand for employees throughout organizations.

## CHAPTERS 6–8: MANAGING EMPLOYEE COMPETENCIES

In Chapters 6–8, we explore various options for building and maintaining needed competencies for different jobs. We focus on how to use recruitment and selection to identify and choose the right people for the unique needs of the organization. We also focus on how to use learning and development to translate employee potential into functional competencies.

## CHAPTERS 9–12: MANAGING EMPLOYEE ATTITUDES AND BEHAVIORS

In Chapters 9–12, we focus on how to encourage and motivate employees to focus their efforts on contributing to important organizational objectives. We focus on performance management systems and emphasize how to evaluate, appraise, and develop employees to increase their contributions; how compensation systems are established and which are most appropriate in different circumstances; how to establish incentive and reward systems to encourage continued employee effort toward important objectives; and how to design benefits, health, and wellness programs to meet employees' needs.

## CHAPTERS 13–14: SPECIAL TOPICS

In Chapters 13–14, we focus on two additional topics associated with the strategic management of employees. Beyond the HR challenges, managing employees who are covered under collective bargaining agreements introduces important issues about how unions work, the unionization process, legal aspects of labor relations, negotiating collective bargaining agreements, and managing the labor agreement. We take a closer look at these issues in Chapter 13. In Chapter 14, we explore the specific issues associated with reaching alignment among the primary HR activities, as well as between the primary HR activities and the HR challenges to create high-performing organizations. We also focus on how to measure the impact of alternative decisions regarding the primary HR activities to continually improve the strategic management of employees.

## SUMMARY

There are many benefits associated with effectively managing employees. When employees have the necessary competencies, they can contribute to meeting company goals. When employees are motivated, they are likely to display increased levels of commitment, loyalty, and morale. And when the work environment is designed appropriately, employees are in a position to turn their abilities and motivation into greater productivity. In contrast, when employees are mismanaged, they may not be able or willing to work toward organizational goals. If employees do not have the needed skills, they may not know how to work most effectively, resulting in decreased performance and morale and greater turnover and absenteeism. Employees who feel undervalued or underappreciated are not likely to expend much effort in performing their jobs.

The strategic management of employees requires managers to pay attention to three primary HR activities. First, managers must design work and engage in workforce planning to ensure that employees are in a position to add value to the company. The specific HR practices that are used to manage the flow of work are job design and workforce planning. Second, managers must identify, acquire, build, and retain the critical competencies that employees need to effectively perform their jobs. This is done through recruitment, selection, and learning and development activities. Third, managers must provide employees with guidance and motivation to use their abilities to contribute to the company's goals. Performance management, compensation, incentives, benefits, and health and wellness programs are the primary tools to influence employee attitudes and behaviors.

When companies are able to leverage the talents of their workforce, they are more likely to achieve competitive advantage. However, this is not an easy task.

Managers must make sure that the tactics they use within the three primary HR activities are in alignment. The context of a company's strategy, characteristics, and organizational culture also must be kept in mind. In addition, managers must consider the concerns of their workforce. Beyond organizational demands, the strategic management of human resources requires managers to anticipate and take steps to meet the environmental influences associated with labor-force trends and advances in technology. Finally, the design and implementation of the primary HR activities must be done in a manner that is in compliance with legal requirements.

## KEY TERMS

| | |
|---|---|
| alignment | human resource (HR) practices |
| competencies | internal alignment |
| competitive advantage | line manager (manager) |
| employees | offshoring |
| environmental influences | organizational culture |
| external alignment | organizational demands |
| globalization | primary human resource (HR) activities |
| human resource (HR) challenges | strategy |
| human resource (HR) department | |

## DISCUSSION QUESTIONS

1. How does managing employees contribute to a company achieving a competitive advantage?
2. Given the importance of employees for a company to sustain a competitive advantage, why do you think so many companies have engaged in layoffs, outsourcing, and offshoring of work to other countries?
3. What does it mean to strategically manage employees?
4. Identify and explain the three primary HR activities.
5. Which of the three primary HR activities is most challenging? Why?
6. Discuss the management practices associated with each primary HR activity.
7. Some people think that there are certain practices for managing employees that are always beneficial for companies, while others maintain that the best practices depend on the circumstances of each company. Which approach do you think is right? Why?
8. Which of the environmental influences identified in this chapter is most important for managing employees in a company pursuing innovation? What about a company with a strategy emphasizing low costs or customer service? How does a company's strategy influence the importance of different environmental influences?
9. Discuss how regulatory issues influence the management of employees.

## LEARNING EXERCISE 1

Now that you have read about how companies differ, and how those differences can affect employee management practices, here's a chance for you to begin applying those concepts. Lockheed Martin and Panera Bread are two very different, and very successful, companies. Lockheed Martin is an advanced technology company and a major defense contractor, while Panera Bread is a fast-expanding bakery-café chain.

Lockheed Martin was formed in 1995, when two major defense contractors, Lockheed Corporation and Martin Marietta Corporation, merged. The corporation

reported net sales of $51 billion in 2017. Net income from continuing operations (excluding the impact of the Tax Cut and Jobs Act) were $3.9 billion, and cash from operations amounted to $6.5 billion.[55] Clearly, the corporation is doing well. Lockheed's vision statement is, "Be the global leader in supporting our customers' missions, strengthening security, and advancing scientific discovery."[56]

Panera was founded in 1981 as Au Bon Pain, Inc. In 1993, the company bought St. Louis Bread Co., and in time it changed its name from St. Louis Bread to Panera Bread. Because of the success of Panera, in May 1991, the company sold all the Au Bon Pain, Inc., business units except Panera Bread and then changed the name of the company itself to Panera Bread. The rest, as they say, is history. Annual sales now exceed $5 billion. Panera Bread's mission statement is simple: "A loaf of bread in every arm."

Visit the websites of Lockheed Martin Corporation (www.lockheedmartin.com) and Panera Bread (www.panerabread.com). Use the information provided in the "About Us" section and other parts of each company's website to answer the following questions.

1. Prepare a chart comparing the two companies based on the organizational demand characteristics discussed in this chapter.
2. Discuss two or three of the key environmental influences that each company would likely face. Why would there be different key environmental influences for each company?
3. Describe how the organizational demands and environmental influences identified for each company would differentially affect work flow, employee competencies, and employee attitudes and behaviors for each company.

*Sources:* Lockheed Martin website, http://www.lockheedmartin.com/us/news/press-releases/2017/january/0123hq-earnings.html, http://www.lockheedmartin.com/us/who-we-are.html; Panera Bread website, www.panerabread.com, https://www.panerabread.com/en-us/company/about-panera/our-history.html.

## LEARNING EXERCISE 2

What exactly does it mean to be a manager? This may seem like an innocent question. But do you really know? Throughout this chapter, we have discussed many of the tools that managers have at their disposal for managing their employees. For this exercise, interview three managers and ask them how they spend their time. Then answer the following questions.

1. What does it mean to manage employees?
2. What aspects of each manager's job create the most challenges?
3. Compare the responses that you get from the three managers with the primary HR activities discussed in this chapter. What role do these managers play in work design and workforce planning? Managing employee competencies? Managing employees' attitudes and behaviors?

## CASE STUDY 1: THE NEW JOB

After graduating from school, you are fortunate to receive an offer as an assistant manager of a marketing department in a company located in New York City, working for a fast-growing company that provides marketing support for companies. Your department specializes in marketing strategies for the Internet and currently has 10 employees—you, your direct supervisor (the manager of the department), and 8 marketing associates. Your job is to help the manager lead the unit to develop long-term strategies for your unit, to maintain excellent customer service with your clients, and to strive to build future business opportunities. The marketing

associates in your department work a very flexible schedule and are often off site, working with the clients at their locations to help develop marketing campaigns to improve their business presence and performance via the Internet.

After being on the job a short while, you realize that you need to create another position to help make sure that all the necessary work gets completed on time. Essentially, while you and your manager are focusing on the long-term interests of the department and the associates are working very hard to help the clients, many of the administrative aspects of the work are falling by the wayside. For example, no one is currently tracking accounts payable from clients or handling accounts payable to your service providers. As a result, you are spending time on these tasks that are beyond your job expectations. In addition, you are spending an increasing amount of time making travel arrangements, such as booking hotels and arranging transportation for your staff. After you talk with the manager of your unit, she agrees that something needs to change to allow you to devote your time to more of the strategic issues in the unit, and she permits you to create a new position to help out in your department. Your challenge now is to determine what this position will be.

### Discussion Questions

1. What job would you create? Why?
2. What are the key tasks and responsibilities that this new employee would be expected to perform?
3. What are the employee competencies this position needs to be successful? Why?
4. What are your ideas for how you might design performance management, compensation, and incentives for this new position? Why?
5. Are there any particular challenges you would expect to encounter that would make successfully filling this position difficult? How would you overcome these challenges?

## CASE STUDY 2: EMPLOYEES LOVE WEGMANS

In 2018, *Fortune* magazine ranked Wegmans Food Market number 2 in its list of 100 Best Companies to Work For. This should not come as a surprise because it has been a mainstay on this list for 21 years. As noted in Company Spotlight 1.2, Wegmans, a regional supermarket chain, exemplifies the value of strategically managing employees. While the average turnover rate for supermarkets is 26.8%, at Wegmans, turnover is much lower—it is 5%. In an industry that has not historically been known for generating intense employee satisfaction and loyalty, Wegmans stands out. But what is it about this supermarket that generates employee loyalty, productivity, and commitment from its workforce?

Wegmans' outstanding reputation allows it to be very selective in its hiring processes. Once employees are hired, Wegmans also does a good deal to enable employees to be successful both personally and professionally. Wegmans invests more than $50 million per year in providing its over 42,000 employees with many amazing training and development opportunities. (See Spotlight 1.2). On average, customer service representatives earn just over $31,500 in base pay and $3,000 in extra compensation per year. In addition to above-average compensation and training, Wegmans provides its employees with a generous work/life balance program that includes job sharing, compressed workweeks, and telecommuting. Both part- and full-time employees can participate in medical insurance and prescription plans, 401(k) retirement savings plans, dependent-care reimbursement plans, adoption assistance, and an employee assistance program. In addition, full-time employees enjoy access to dental coverage, life insurance, and personal days.

### Discussion Questions

1. Why do you think other regional supermarket chains haven't been able to achieve the same awards as Wegmans?

2. Thinking about the three primary HR activities, how do they affect employee loyalty and financial success?

3. Would the Wegmans approach to managing employees work in other companies? What types of companies are most likely to benefit from a similar approach to managing their workforce?

4. If you were going to compete against Wegmans, what would you do differently?

*Sources:* Wegmans website, "Great Place to Work and Fortune Magazine Name Wegmans One of the 2018 Fortune 100 Best Companies to Work For, Ranking #2," 2018, https://www.wegmans.com/news-media/press-releases/2018/great-place-to-work--and-fortune-magazine-name-wegmans-one-of-th.html; Harrison, S., and Gordon, P. A., "Replacing Misconceptions of Turnover with Evidence-based Information for the Retail Grocery Industry," The Clute Institute International Academic Conference, Orlando, FL, 2014, http://cluteinstitute.com/conference-proceedings/2014DWPapers/Article%20212.pdf.

## NOTES

[1] "World's Most Admired Companies, 2018," *Fortune*, http://fortune.com/2015/02/19/wmac-ranked-by-key-attribute/.

[2] "Shared Value Initiative," GlaxoSmithKline (GSK), sharedvalue.org, https://www.shared-value.org/partners/funding-partners/glaxosmithkline-gsk.

[3] Jeffrey Pfeffer, *The Human Equation: Building Profits by Putting People First* (Boston: Harvard Business School Press, 1998).

[4] Jay B. Barney and William S. Hesterly, *Strategic Management and Competitive Advantage* (Upper Saddle River, NJ: Prentice Hall, 2006).

[5] Jeffrey Pfeffer, *Competitive Advantage Through People: Unleashing the Power of the Work Force* (Boston: Harvard Business School Press, 1994).

[6] Mark A. Huselid, "The Impact of Human Resource Management Practices on Turnover, Productivity, and Corporate Financial Performance," *Academy of Management Journal* 38 (1995): 635–672; James P. Guthrie, "High-Involvement Work Practices, Turnover, and Productivity: Evidence from New Zealand," *Academy of Management Journal* 44 (2001): 180–192; John E. Delery and Dorothea Roumpi, "Strategic Human Resource Management, Human Capital and Competitive Advantage: Is the Field Going in Circles?" *Human Resource Management Journal* 27(1) (2017): 1–21. https://doi.org/10.1111/1748-8583.12137; David E. Guest, "Human Resource Management and Employee Well-Being: Towards a New Analytic Framework: HRM and Employee Well-Being: New Analytic Framework." *Human Resource Management Journal* 27 (1) (2017): 22–38. https://doi.org/10.1111/1748-8583.12139; Kaifeng Jiang and Jake Messersmith. "On the Shoulders of Giants: A Meta-Review of Strategic Human Resource Management." *International Journal of Human Resource Management* 29 (1) (2018): 6–33.

[7] Eisenberger, Armeli, Rexwinkel, Lynch, and Rhoades, "Reciprocation of Perceived Organizational Support"; Robert Eisenberger, Robin Huntington, Steven Hutchison, and Debora Sowa, "Perceived Organizational Support," *Journal of Applied Psychology* 71 (1986): 500–507; and Shari Caudron, "The Myth of Job Happiness," *Workforce,* April 2001, 32–36.

[8] Benjamin Schneider, Susan S. White, and Michelle Paul, "Linking Service Climate and Customer Perceptions of Service Quality: Test of a Causal Model," *Journal of Applied Psychology* 83 (1998): 150–163.

[9] For research findings regarding HR practices and turnover, see Timothy M. Gardner, Patrick M. Wright, and Lisa M. Moynihan, "The Impact of Motivation, Empowerment, and Skill-Enhancing Practices on Aggregate Voluntary Turnover: The Mediating Effect of Collective Affective Commitment," *Personnel Psychology* 64 (2011): 315–350; Jason D. Shaw, Tae-Youn Park, and Eugene Kim. 2013. "A Resource-Based Perspective on Human Capital Losses, HRM Investments, and Organizational Performance." *Strategic Management Journal* 34(5) (2013): 572–589.

[10] Abdul Karim Khan, Samina Quratulain, and Jonathan R. Crawshaw, "The Mediating Role of Discrete Emotions in the Relationship Between Injustice and Counterproductive Work

Behaviors: A Study in Pakistan," *Journal of Business and Psychology* 28 (2013): 49–61; and Jennifer Laabs, "Employee Sabotage: Don't Be a Target!" *Workforce,* July 1999, 33–42.

[11] David Guest and Neil Conway, "The Impact of HR Practices, HR Effectiveness, and a 'Strong HR System' on Organisational Outcomes: A Stakeholder Perspective," *International Journal of Human Resource Management* 22 (2011): 1686–1702; Huselid, "The Impact of Human Resource Management Practices on Turnover, Productivity, and Corporate Financial Performance"; Guthrie, "High-Involvement Work Practices, Turnover, and Productivity"; and Kaifeng Jiang, David P. Lepak, Jia Hu, and Judith C. Baer, "How Does Human Resource Management Influence Organizational Outcomes? A Meta-Analytic Investigation of Mediating Mechanisms," *Academy of Management Journal* 55(6) (2012): 1264–1294, https://doi.org/10.5465/amj.2011.0088.

[12] John E. Delery and D. Harold Doty, "Modes of Theorizing in Strategic Human Resource Management: Tests of Universalistic, Contingency, and Configurational Performance Predictions," *Academy of Management Journal* 39 (1996): 802–835; Thomas Bailey, Peter Berg, and Carola Sandy, "The Effect of High-Performance Work Practices on Employee Earnings in the Steel, Apparel, and Medical Electronics and Imaging Industries," *Industrial and Labor Relations* 54 (2001): 525–543; and Mark A. Youndt, Scott A. Snell, James W. Dean, Jr., and David P. Lepak, "Human Resource Management, Manufacturing Strategy, and Firm Performance," *Academy of Management Journal* 39 (1996): 836–866.

[13] Laurie J. Bassi, Ed Frauenheim, and Daniel P. McMurrer. Good Company: Business Success in *the Worthiness Era* (San Francisco: Berrett-Koehler, 2011); Ellen M. Whitener, "Do 'High Commitment' Human Resource Practices Affect Employee Commitment? A Cross-Level Analysis Using Hierarchical Linear Modeling," *Journal of Management* 27 (2001): 515–535.

[14] Pfeffer, *The Human Equation.*

[15] CIGNA website, "You Have the Talent to Help Us Make a Difference," http://www.cigna.com/careers/.

[16] J. Richard Hackman and Greg R. Oldham, "Motivation Through the Design of Work: Test of a Theory," *Organizational Behavior and Human Performance* 16 (1976): 250–279; and Frederick Herzberg, "One More Time: How Do You Motivate Employees?" *Harvard Business Review* 65 (1987): 109–120.

[17] Susan N. Houseman, "Why Employers Use Flexible Staffing Arrangements: Evidence from an Establishment Survey," *Industrial and Labor Relations Review* 55 (2001): 149–170.

[18] Bureau of Labor Statistics, "Contingent and Alternative Employment Arrangements—May 2017," June 7, 2018, http://www.bls.gov/news.release/conemp.pdf.

[19] Elizabeth G. Chambers, Mark Fouldon, Helen Handfield-Jones, Steven M. Hankin, and Edward G. Michaels, III, "The War for Talent," *The McKinsey Quarterly* 1 (1998): 44–57.

[20] For discussion of the influence of perceive equity and inequity, see J. Stacy Adams, "Toward an Understanding of Inequity," *Journal of Abnormal and Social Psychology* 67 (1963): 422–436. For discussion of social exchange, see also Anne S. Tsui, Jones L. Pearce, Lyman W. Porter, and Angela M. Tripoli, "Alternative Approaches to the Employee–Organization Relationship: Does Investment in Employees Pay Off?" *Academy of Management Journal* 40 (1997): 1089–1121; and Lynn M. Shore and Kevin Barksdale, "Examining Degree of Balance and Level of Obligation in the Employment Relationship: A Social Exchange Approach," *Journal of Organizational Behavior* 19 (1998): 731–744.

[21] Lincoln Electric website, "Why Lincoln Electric," August 7, 2014, http://www.lincolnelectric.com/en-us/company/careers/Pages/lincoln-tradition.aspx; http://solutions.3m.com/wps/portal/3M/en_US/3M-Careers-NA/Home/Innovation/.

[22] R. Miles and C. C. Snow, "Designing Strategic Human Resource Systems," *Organizational Dynamics* 13 (1984): 36–52; Randall S. Schuler and Susan E. Jackson, "Linking Competitive Strategies with Human Resource Management Practices," *Academy of Management Executive* 1 (1987): 207–219; Brain E. Becker and Mark A. Huselid, "High Performance Work Systems and Firm Performance: A Synthesis of Research and Managerial Implications," in *Research in Personnel and Human Resources Management*, ed. G. R. Ferris (Greenwich, CT: JAI Press, 1998), 53–101; and John Paul MacDuffie, "Human Resource Bundles and Manufacturing Performance: Organizational Logic and Flexible Production Systems in the World Auto Industry," *Industrial and Labor Relations Review* 48 (1995): 197–221.

23 Ibid.

24 Michael E. Porter, "What Is Strategy?" *Harvard Business Review*, November 1, 1996, 61–78.

25 Michael A. Hitt, R. Duane Ireland, and Robert E. Hoskisson, *Strategic Management: Competitiveness and Globalization* (Cincinnati: South-Western College Publishing, 2001).

26 Michael E. Porter, *Competitive Strategy* (New York: The Free Press, 1980); and Michael E. Porter, *Competitive Advantage* (New York: The Free Press, 1980).

27 Jeffrey B. Arthur, "The Link Between Business Strategy and Industrial Relations Systems in American Steel Minimills," *Industrial and Labor Relations Review,* 45 (1992): 488–506; Susan E. Jackson, Randall S. Schuler, and J. Carlos Rivero, "Organizational Characteristics as Predictors of Personnel Practices," *Personnel Psychology* 42 (1989): 727–786; and Schuler and Jackson, "Linking Competitive Strategies with Human Resource Management Practices."

28 Jackson, Schuler, and Rivero, "Organizational Characteristics as Predictors of Personnel Practices"; Miles and Snow, "Designing Strategic Human Resource Systems"; and Delery and Doty, "Modes of Theorizing in Strategic Human Resource Management."

29 Lloyd Baird and Ilan Meshoulam, "Managing Two Fits of Strategic Human Resource Management," *Academy of Management Review* 13 (1988): 116–128.

30 Edgar H. Schein, *Organizational Culture and Leadership* (San Francisco: Jossey-Bass, 1985).

31 Cheri Ostroff and David E. Bowen, "Moving HR to a Higher Level: HR Practices and Organizational Effectiveness," in *Multilevel Theory, Research, and Methods in Organizations: Foundations, Extensions, and New Directions*, ed. K. J. Klein and S. W. Kozlowski (San Francisco: Jossey-Bass, 2000), 211–266.

32 SHRM, "Managing Flexible Work Arrangements," SHRM Toolkits, shrm.org, June 14, 2016, http://www.shrm.org/resourcesandtools/tools-and-samples/toolkits/pages/managing-flexibleworkarrangements.aspx.

33 U.S. Bureau of Labor Statistics, December 2015. "Table 1. Civilian Labor Force, by age, gender, race, and ethnicity, 1994, 2004, 2014, and projected 2024 (numbers in thousands). Monthly Labor Review, http://www.bls.gov/opub/mlr/2015/article/labor-force-projections-to-2024.htm."

34 U.S. Bureau of Labor Statistics, "Employment Projections: 2016–26 Summary," https://www.bls.gov/news.release/ecopro.nr0.htm.

35 U.S. Bureau of Labor Statistics, December 2015. Table 1. Civilian labor force, by age gender, race, and ethnicity, 1994, 2004, 2014, and projected 2024 (numbers in thou- sands). Monthly Labor Review, http://www.bls.gov/opub/mlr/2015/article/labor-force- projections-to-2024.htm.

36 U.S. Bureau of Labor Statistics, Employment Projections: 2016-26 Summary, https://www.bls.gov/news.release/ecopro.nr0.htm.

37 David A. Kravitz, "More Women in the Workplace: Is There a Payoff in Firm Performance?" *Academy of Management Executive* 17 (2003): 148–149; and Orlando Richard, Amy MacMillan, Ken Chadwick, and Sean Dwyer, "Employing an Innovation Strategy in Racially Diverse Workforces: Effects on Firm Performance," *Group and Organization Management*, March 2003, 107–127.

38 Grace Donnelly, "Google's Diversity Report Shows Progress Hiring Women, Little Change for Minority Workers," June 29, 2017,http://fortune.com/2017/06/29/google-2017-diversity-report/.

39 "Google Finally Discloses Its Diversity Record, and It's Not Good," May 24, 2014, https://www.pbs.org/newshour/nation/google-discloses-workforce-diversity-data-good.

40 "Google's Diversity Report Shows Progress Hiring Women, Little Change for Minority Workers," June 29, 2017, http://fortune.com/2017/06/29/google-2017-diversity-report/.

41 Nitasha Tiky, "New Lawsuit Exposes Google's Desperation to Improve Diversity," March 2, 2018, https://www.wired.com/story/new-lawsuit-exposes-googles-desperation-to-improve-diversity/.

42 Janet H. Marler and Xiaoya Liang, "Information Technology Change, Work Complexity and Service Jobs: A Contingent Perspective." *New Technology, Work & Employment* 27(2) (2012): 133–46; Janet H. Marler and Emma Parry, "Human Resource Management, Strategic Involvement and E-HRM Technology." *International Journal of Human Resource Management* 27(19) (2016): 2233–53.

43 "The Push Forward," *Workforce*, January 2000, 29.

44 JetBlue website, "Work Here," August 7, 2014, http://www.jetblue.com/work-here/job-descriptions.aspx; Amy Rottier, "The Skies Are JetBlue," *Workforce*, September 2001, 22; and Chuck Salter, "Calling JetBlue," *Fast Company*, May 2004, http://www.fastcompany.com/magazine/82/jetblue_agents.html?page=0%2C1.

45 Charlene Marmer Solomon, "Don't Forget Your Telecommuters," *Workforce*, May 2000, 56–63.

46 Charlene Marmer Solomon, "Moving Jobs to Offshore: Why It's Done and How It Works," *Workforce*, July 1999, 51–55.

47 Kathleen Maclay, "Report: Offshoring and Outsourcing a Mixed Bag for American Jobs, Wages," UC Berkeley News Center, February 18, 2014, http://newscenter.berkeley.edu/2014/02/18/report-offshoring-and-outsourcing-a-mixed-bag-for-american-jobs-wages/.

48 April Glaser, "Why Manufacturing Jobs Are Coming Back to the U.S. Even as Companies Buy More Robots: But for how long?" May 26, 2017, https://www.recode.net/2017/5/26/15656120/manufacturing-jobs-automation-ai-us-increase-robot-sales-reshoring-offshoring.

49 "What to Do Now: Shape Up," January 19, 2013, https://www.economist.com/special-report/2013/01/19/shape-up.

50 Dayton Fandray, "The Ethical Company," *Workforce*, December 2000, 75–77.

51 Lockheed Martin website, "Ethics," Lockheed Martin's Vision, August 7, 2014, http://www.lockheedmartin.com/us/who-we-are/ethics.html; and Andy Meisler, "Lockheed Is Doing Right and Doing Well," *Workforce Management*, March 2004, http://www.work-force.com/archive/feature/23/65/12/index.php.

52 "Information and Technical Assistance on the Americans with Disabilities Act," http://www.ada.gov/.

53 Jonathan Stempel, "21st Century Fox in $90 million Settlement Tied to Sexual Harrassment Scandal," Reuters, November 20, 2017, https://www.reuters.com/article/us-fox-settlement/21st-century-fox-in-90-million-settlement-tied-to-sexual-harassment-scandal-idUSKBN1DK2NI.

54 Amy Chozick, "Where's Harvey," *The New York Times*, March 9, 2018, https://www.nytimes.com/2018/03/09/style/harvey-weinstein-in-arizona.html.

55 "Lockheed Martin Reports Fourth Quarter and Full Year 2017 Results," https://news.lockheedmartin.com/2018-01-29-Lockheed-Martin-Reports-Fourth-Quarter-and-Full-Year-2017-Results.

56 Lockheed Martin website, https://www.lockheedmartin.com/en-us/who-we-are.html.

# Part 1

# HR Challenges

# Chapter 2

# Organizational Demands and Environmental Influences

## Learning Objectives

**AFTER STUDYING THIS CHAPTER, YOU SHOULD BE ABLE TO:**

**1** Describe how differences in company strategies shape the primary human resources (HR) activities.

**2** Explain how company characteristics influence the way that employees are managed.

**3** Discuss the role of organizational culture in effective employee management.

**4** Explain how employee concerns influence employees' interpretation and response to different HR activities.

**5** Discuss the impact of labor force trends on how companies manage employees.

**6** Identify how advances in technology affect employee management.

**7** Explain the challenges of managing employees in a global context.

**8** Understand how ethics and social responsibility influence managerial decisions.

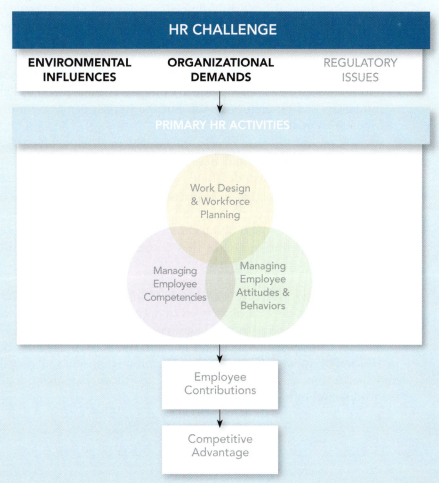

**HR CHALLENGE**

| ENVIRONMENTAL INFLUENCES | ORGANIZATIONAL DEMANDS | REGULATORY ISSUES |
|---|---|---|

**PRIMARY HR ACTIVITIES**

Work Design & Workforce Planning

Managing Employee Competencies

Managing Employee Attitudes & Behaviors

Employee Contributions

Competitive Advantage

# The Importance of Context

Have you ever heard the phrase *the right tool for the job*? It is a simple but meaningful phrase. After all, would you ever consider mowing a lawn with a pair of scissors? Would you ever dig a hole with a screwdriver? Would you ever try to saw a piece of wood with a hammer? Sure, the hammer might work—it could break the wood in half, but you would end up with two damaged pieces of wood, neither of which would be likely to serve their intended purpose as well as wood cut with a saw.

Managing employees strategically is a lot like looking for the right tool needed for the task to be completed. When we think about tools, we usually think about things in a garage—a hammer, a saw, or a screwdriver. But a tool is anything that gets a particular job done. The practices used to carry out the primary human resources (HR) activities are managers' tools. These practices could involve a particular recruitment strategy or offering specific benefits, but they are nonetheless tools that you use to accomplish organizational goals through employee management.

In Chapter 1, we defined *HR activity alignment* as the design of the primary HR activities to reinforce one another to build the needed competencies, motivate the right attitudes and behaviors, and manage the allocation of work to make sure that the right people are doing the right things that need to be done. In addition to *internal alignment* among HR practices, companies must achieve *external alignment*—making sure the HR activities are set up to help companies confront the HR challenges of meeting organizational demands, navigating environmental influences, and complying with regulatory issues. To be an effective manager, you have to understand which HR tools, or practices, are available, how to use them, and which ones are the most appropriate in different circumstances. In short, you have to know which HR tool is right for the job. This knowledge requires an understanding of how different HR challenges affect organizations and your management options. We provide you with three axioms as a foundation for this understanding:

1. *No two companies are the same.* Each company's strategy, characteristics, culture, and employee needs are unique. Companies may face similar environmental influences and regulatory issues, but the impact of these influences is different for each company.
2. *There is no one best way to manage employees.* What is effective in one company may not be effective—and may even be damaging—in another company. As a manager, you need to understand how and when to use the different HR practices.
3. *Using the wrong practice, or using the right practice poorly, can cause more harm than good.* Sometimes people may pick the wrong practice for the job because they don't know enough about the different tools at their disposal. Other times, managers may use a practice that is appropriate for a particular scenario, but they may implement it poorly.

In this chapter, we have two objectives, as highlighted in Exhibit 2.1. First, we will provide an in-depth look at types of organizational demands within companies. Second, we will examine the environmental influences that exist outside companies that affect employee management. Later in the book, as you build your knowledge of HR activities, we will tie specific HR practices—such as recruitment, training, and performance management—back to these organizational demands and environmental influences.

**EXHIBIT 2.1**

Framework for the Strategic Management of Employees

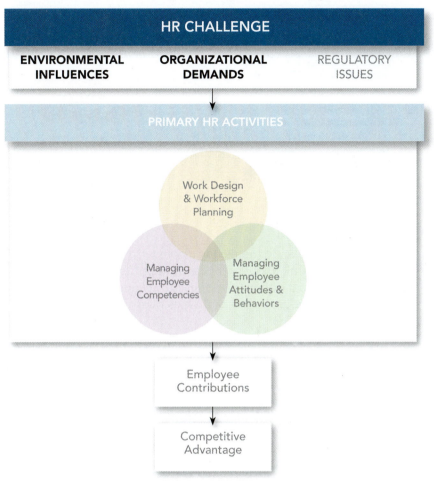

## Meeting Organizational Demands

Organizational demands are factors inherent within a company that influence how employees are managed. There are four key challenges associated with organizational demands:

1. *Strategy.* Employees contribute to the achievement of strategic goals and, ultimately, company success. Differences in company strategies influence the specific competencies and behaviors that managers require of employees.

2. *Company characteristics.* Each company has unique characteristics that affect what it asks of employees and its options for how it manages employees.

3. *Organizational culture.* Companies have distinct cultures that influence what work is done, as well as how it is done, within companies.

4. *Employee concerns.* Managers are most likely to be effective if they take into account the concerns of their employees.

Exhibit 2.2 depicts these challenges.

**EXHIBIT 2.2**

Organizational Demands

## Strategy

A company's strategy is its plan for achieving a competitive advantage over its rivals. At a basic level, you can think about business strategy as positioning, meaning the decisions that companies make about how they attract and retain customers relative to their competitors.[1] There are two broad types of strategies that companies can choose.

**cost leadership strategy**

focuses on outperforming competing firms within an industry by maintaining the ability to offer the lowest costs for products or services

A **cost leadership strategy** focuses on outperforming competing firms within an industry by maintaining the ability to offer the lowest costs for products or services.[2] For companies that concentrate on cost leadership, issues related to efficiencies and cost reductions dominate management decisions. Because costs are the underlying focus, facilities need to run smoothly and at maximum capacity, and the company must minimize overhead and extraneous costs associated with administration, service, advertising, and research. Companies with a cost leadership strategy may serve one or many different industry segments, but they typically focus on products that are capable of reaping the benefits of high volume or economies of scale. To be successful, however, a company must be *the* cost leader in its market because the benefits of this strategy result from consistently achieving higher profits, relative to costs, than competitors. In other words, there can be only one cost leader in an industry. While more than one company may focus on providing low costs to consumers as a potential source of competitive advantage, only one company is able to be the lowest-cost leader. For example, Walmart retains its cost leadership position by maintaining the most efficient operations in the retail industry. As a result, Walmart is able to offer lower prices for its products than competing firms while remaining profitable. Indeed, many smaller and midsized stores have faced financial difficulties trying to compete directly with Walmart stores in their area because of the significantly lower prices at Walmart.[3] However, we should also note that Amazon has increasingly become a strong competitor for Walmart in terms of being the leader in the low-cost retail industry.

**differentiation strategy**

emphasizes achieving competitive advantage over competing firms by providing something unique for which customers are willing to pay

A **differentiation strategy** emphasizes achieving competitive advantage over competing firms by providing something unique for which customers are willing to pay.[4] Unlike with a cost leadership strategy, many companies within an industry may succeed with differentiation strategies, particularly when they each provide something unique to their customers. In fact, there are an unlimited number of potential sources of differentiation from rivals. For example, companies may focus on unique product features, location, innovation, reputation, status, customer service, or quality as a source of competitive advantage. Consider the automobile industry. There are a large number of different types of cars that claim to offer something

## EXHIBIT 2.3

### Strategy and HR Activities

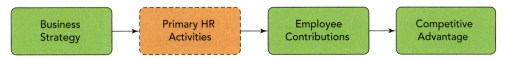

unique. Different cars are known for being rugged, sporty, safe, or luxurious (and a few can claim all of those categories which gives them another level of uniqueness). Tesla Motors is an automobile maker, but its mission is not to build a better or even different car. Tesla differentiates itself with a mission "to accelerate the world's transition to sustainable energy."[5] By focusing on attributes that different customer groups value, multiple companies can succeed within the same industry. For example, companies competing in the minivan segment target different customer groups from companies competing in the sports car automobile segment. Within each segment, car companies offer different attributes in an attempt to reach consumers. The key success factor for a differentiation strategy is providing something that competing firms do not provide, but that customers value. By doing so, companies are able to either reduce the importance of price in the customer's decision-making process or command a price premium for their products that exceeds the cost of providing the differentiation.

As shown in Exhibit 2.3, while strategy sets the overall objectives for a company, it also sets the parameters for the needed employee contributions or how people add value within a company. Different strategies require different employee contributions to create a competitive advantage. A company focused on low cost, for example, requires employees to be highly productive and efficient. A company with a differentiation strategy focused on innovation likely requires employees to be creative and generate many new potential products or services. Just as strategy influences how employees add value toward competitive advantage, it affects the types of jobs that employees perform, the specific competencies employees need, and the attitudes and behaviors employees must display on the job to help reach company goals. In short, strategy affects all three of the primary HR activities.[6] Let's now look more closely at some of the basic differences in the primary HR activities for different strategies.

### Low-Cost Strategy and Managing Employees

Given their focus on efficiencies and cost reduction, companies with a cost leadership strategy tend to design jobs in a way that maximizes predictable employee outcomes. Consider an assembly line. The jobs on an assembly line are designed to maximize employee productivity while minimizing errors and deviations from the expected output. In this type of work environment, employees are expected to perform jobs that are narrow in focus, with an emphasis on standardized and repetitive actions. When jobs are narrowly structured and well defined, the competencies that employees need to perform these tasks are generally relatively simple, and the required behaviors are likely to be fairly well understood. As a result, managing employees in a cost leadership strategy often focuses on ensuring acceptable job performance by hiring individuals with the basic skills needed for these jobs, training employees to efficiently carry out their responsibilities, making sure employees clearly understand the specific expectations of their jobs, paying employees based on the jobs they perform and how efficiently they perform them, and evaluating employees based on adherence to established job expectations.

### Differentiation Strategy and Managing Employees

A differentiation strategy requires employees to perform jobs geared toward a particular objective, such as creativity or customer service. Employees need to possess specific skills related to the source of differentiation and need to engage in behaviors that help set the company apart from its competition. For example, a company with a differentiation strategy focused on innovation would not likely succeed if employees were required to perform narrow tasks and rigidly defined jobs. Instead, in companies such as Tesla, Under Armour, Monster Beverage, and Incyte, innovation often requires cooperation, creativity, and knowledge-sharing among employees, all of which call for broad job responsibilities. To foster creativity, managers may recruit employees who bring new skills or new perspectives to the company. Rather than focus on efficient job performance, managers may adopt a long-term HR orientation for employee growth to help employees develop new skills that might prove valuable in the future. Similarly, pay decisions are more likely to focus on individual potential, unique experiences, team accomplishments, and long-term results than on volume and efficiency.

As you can see, by influencing the types of jobs that employees perform, strategy shapes the competencies, attitudes, and behaviors required of employees. While the specific HR practices that are most appropriate vary across different strategies, effectively managing employees requires managers to align the primary HR activities with strategic objectives to maximize employee contributions. Early studies found improved organizational performance in companies with better alignment than their peers.[7]

## Company Characteristics

No two companies are the same. Companies differ in the size and stage of their development, and these differences directly affect how firms manage employees. Company characteristics represent the second organizational demand in our framework.

### Company Size

When we talk about jobs, most of us think about working for a large company with an established reputation and clientele and a long history. Yet, did you know that

- Small businesses represent 99.7% of all firms with paid employees.
- From 2010 to 2016, small businesses accounted for 63% of net new jobs in our economy.
- Small employer firms represent 98.5% of all employer firms in high-tech industries.
- Small businesses employ 47.8% of all private sector employees.
- Approximately 20% of small businesses have paid employees.[8]

The reality is that small businesses comprise a major portion of the U.S. economy. Whether a company has only a handful of employees, such as a local diner or landscape firm, or is a giant such as Amazon or General Motors (GM), employees have to be managed. However, the challenges of effectively managing employees differ with the size of the company.

Larger companies typically have more resources to hire staff dedicated to supporting the management of employees than do smaller companies, which often lack formal HR departments to provide similar support.[9] Of course, this does not eliminate the need to attend to personnel issues in smaller companies;

rather, line managers or company owners must perform HR practices as well as their other activities.[10] Also, smaller businesses often do not have the resources to provide the same level of pay, benefits, and training opportunities to employees as larger companies. For example, less than 25% of all employees in companies with fewer than 10 employees have employer-paid health insurance, compared to 95% of companies with over 1,000 employees.[11] One recent study found that some of the most pressing issues for small business owners were the availability of quality workers and the ability to provide competitive wages, benefits, and training.[12]

Although small companies often do not have the same type or level of resources enjoyed by larger companies, the importance of effectively managing employees may be magnified in smaller companies. With a smaller staff, managers may expect employees to display greater autonomy and discretion.[13] As a result, the types of knowledge, skills, and abilities that employees may need in small versus large companies, even for the same job, differ. Moreover, in contrast to large operations, in a small company, the performance of each employee is likely to have a larger, more direct impact on company success. After all, a single employee in a company of 100 employees has a greater influence on the bottom line than a single employee in a company with more than 10,000 employees. For these reasons, effective employee management is of heightened importance in smaller companies.

## Stage of Development

As shown in Exhibit 2.4, companies differ in terms of their stage of development. As you might imagine, the pressures of managing employees in a young, start-up company are different from those in a mature organization striving to protect its established market share and competitive position.[14] The objectives and needs of companies at different stages of development introduce new and distinct challenges for effectively managing employees.[15] While young companies tend to focus on growth and survival, mature companies may be more concerned with customer retention and perhaps extending their operations into new markets for future opportunities.[16] In addition, mature companies often have more resources and support staff, as well as established policies and procedures, for handling employee-related issues. Young companies face pressures to identify and hire people who can help the company grow. Given the limited resources that small companies typically have for pay and other benefits, it is sometimes very difficult for small firms to attract top-notch employees.

As companies mature, the pressures regarding the management of employees evolve as well. Companies such as Apple and Microsoft, regarded as highly informal and entrepreneurial in their early years, have had to adopt more formalized approaches to managing their employees as they have become more established. Increased size and success often bring more bureaucracy to govern how things are done. Managers in more mature companies must pay particular attention to how employees do their jobs to ensure that they comply with established procedures and routines. As you can

## EXHIBIT 2.4

Organizational Life Cycle

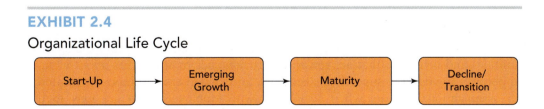

see, a company's stage of development affects company goals, the role of employees in meeting those goals, and the most appropriate way to manage employees.

## Organizational Culture

Have you ever noticed how different companies seem to have unique personalities? If you have worked for several different companies, you probably noticed that each one had its own way of doing things. Differences in how companies operate and how employees act signal what is called *organizational culture*.

**organizational culture**

the set of basic assumptions, values, and beliefs of a company's members

As defined in Chapter 1, **organizational culture** is the set of the basic assumptions, values, and beliefs of a company's members.[17] In some ways, it is useful to think about a culture as the informal or unwritten side of organizations; these values and beliefs are not necessarily spelled out but are of great importance. In fact, the observable elements of a company's culture—how employees talk to one another, how employees interact with customers, and the practices used to manage employees—represent the values that organizational members share.

There is no predetermined list of types of cultures from which a company chooses its culture. Each company has its own distinct culture. Some cultures may be more bureaucratic in nature, valuing rules, formalization, and hierarchy as the appropriate ways of doing business. Other cultures may be more entrepreneurial, emphasizing creativity, knowledge exchange, and innovation. Similarly, some companies may have a culture that values competition among employees, while others may be more team oriented, valuing cooperation and support for one another. While there is no right or wrong culture, nor is there a limited set of cultures, the nature of a company's culture exerts a significant influence on how employees behave on the job.

Compare most banking and financial institutions and their traditionally white-collar bureaucratic cultures, which value formality, with high-technology companies, such as Google or Facebook, which value employee flexibility, autonomy, and employee growth. Company Spotlight 2.1 provides a window into the organizational culture at Amazon. How do you think its culture would fit in a company that values formality, procedures, and tradition?

While employees might not be able to clearly articulate the exact culture of their company, most employees understand that within their company there are certain ways of doing things, making decisions, and interacting with each other and with customers. Some employees may describe their company as fun, others might describe their company as being like a family, and still others might refer to their company as a tightly run ship. All are describing some aspect of their company's culture.

It is important to acknowledge that culture is shaped by a number of factors. For example, the values and beliefs of a company's founder, as well as important decisions that the founder makes in the early stages of a company, shape subsequent values and beliefs of organizational members. The history of a company also has a strong influence. Consider Southwest Airlines. In its early years, it faced a long, drawn-out legal battle with existing airlines simply for the right to enter the industry and fly its planes. This early event significantly affected the future actions of the company and helped define an "us" versus "them" feeling that solidified the culture among Southwest's employees.[18]

Similarly, the actions of top managers and the HR practices used to manage employees send messages to employees that signal the values and behaviors that are most appropriate. What companies look for in new employees and the specific attitudes and behaviors that are rewarded provide cues to employees about what is important. In addition, supervisors, mentors, and coworkers continuously reinforce an organizational culture when socializing with employees who are new to the company. Because of the evolution of cultures and the continued reinforcement of the underlying values through history, stories, and socialization, cultures tend to be fairly rigid once established. In fact, even as people come and go, the company's culture tends to persist which makes trying to change an organization's culture difficult.[19]

Organizational culture influences employee management in several ways. First, the culture of a company affects managerial decisions about which specific practices to use with regard to job design and workforce planning, building of competencies, and management of attitudes and behaviors. In many ways, employee management practices are mechanisms to transfer cultural values into expectations of how employees should carry out their everyday tasks and activities.[20] For example, a company with a competitive culture might be more likely to reward people for individual sales rather than for being good team members.

## COMPANY SPOTLIGHT  2.1

### Amazon: A Most Admired Company

In 2018, Amazon was ranked number 2 on *Fortune's* list of "The World's Most Admired Companies" and ranked number 1 by LinkedIn as the "Top Company to Work For." Amazon has been described as "ceaselessly inventive, unafraid to try something and fail." The company's ambitious goal is to "sell to everyone everywhere." To accomplish its goals, Amazon focuses on how to extract the most from its employees, recognizing that employee dedication and obsession constitute the real engine behind the company's success.

Not all descriptions of the company culture have been glowing, however. For example, a *New York Times* feature story on the company, entitled "Inside Amazon: Wrestling Big Ideas in a Bruising Workplace," described the company's hard-driving, strong culture. The article noted that Amazon's CEO, Jeff Bezos, encourages his employees to stave off mediocrity, bureaucracy, and big spending—ideas that he has encoded into a set of leadership principles that describe the way that Amazon employees should act.

The first principle in this set of leadership principles is "Customer obsession, an unwavering commitment to the customer." The remaining principles talk about how to achieve the first principle and include thinking long-term, inventing and simplifying, being right a lot, always seeking improvement, hiring and developing the best people, insisting on the highest standards, thinking big, a bias for action, frugality, earning trust, operating at all levels, disagreeing and committing, and delivering results. In practice, employees are encouraged to tear apart one another's ideas in meetings; work smart, hard, and long; and do big, innovative groundbreaking things. Employees are also expected to embrace frugality, from bare-bones desks to the cell phones and travel expenses that they often pay for themselves. There are no daily free food buffets or regular snack supplies either. The focus is on relentless striving to please customers. Such a demanding culture is not for everyone, but Amazon doesn't mind its high turnover because it only wants to retain those who can handle a driven, customer-obsessed culture. Perhaps this reason is part of how Amazon recently surpassed Walmart as the most valuable retailer in the country.

*Sources:* "World's Most Admired Companies," fortune.com, http://fortune.com/worlds-most-admired-companies/amazon.com; Paul Schrodt, "The 50 Best Places to Work, According to LinkedIn," time.com, March 21, 2018, http://time.com/money/5208407/best-places-to-work-linkedin; Jodi Kantor and David Streitfeld, "Inside Amazon: Wrestling Big Ideas in a Bruising Workplace," *The New York Times*, August 16, 2015, Section A1; Jodi Kantor and David Streitfeld, "Bezos Says Amazon Has No Room for 'Callous' Acts," *The New York Times*, August 19, 2015, Section B:1; https://medium.com/@NYTimesComm/dean-baquet-responds-to-jay-carney-s-medium-post-6af794c7a7c6 "Leadership Principles," amazon.jobs, https://www.amazon.jobs/principles.

Second, the culture of a company also influences the effectiveness of different HR practices. The same HR practices may be acceptable or unacceptable to either employees or managers across different companies, depending on the cultural values of the organization. Even if a practice itself is a good idea, it might not necessarily fit with the underlying cultural values of a company. For example, employee participation and empowerment might be more accepted by employees, managers, or both in a company with an informal culture than in a company with a formal culture that values hierarchy and status. When HR practices are consistent with organizational culture, they are likely to be more effective.

Third, the strength of the culture further influences the effectiveness of employee management practices.[21] Strong cultures provide clear, consistent signals to employees regarding how they should behave and what is or is not acceptable. In contrast, weak cultures are ambiguous and lack a clear, coherent message.[22] When a culture is strong and consistent with organizational objectives, employees are likely to have a clear understanding of what they need to do in their jobs to contribute to company goals and a willingness to undertake the efforts to meet those goals. It is possible, however, that a strong culture might conflict with company goals. This situation is most likely to happen when companies make strategic changes without considering the cultural values of the company. Culture conflict may also occur in the case of mergers and acquisitions. In fact, one of the reasons mergers and acquisitions fail is lack of attention to blending cultures from different companies.[23]

## Employee Concerns

Up to this point, we have focused on aspects of companies—their strategies, characteristics, and cultures. There is one additional component of organizational demands that is critical to consider for effectively managing employees—the employees themselves. After all, this book is about managing people, and without consideration of their needs and concerns, companies are unlikely to be successful in getting employees to work toward company goals.

To understand how employees view and react to different HR practices, think about how employees view their relationship with their company. In many ways, this is an exchange: Companies use pay, benefits, and training as incentives for employees to perform their jobs in exchange for the employees' commitment to the organization. There are two ways employees evaluate this exchange. First, there is a rational component: Do employees perform the work they are expected to perform, and do they receive what they are promised? Second, there is a perceptual component of this exchange. The term **psychological contract** means the *perceived* obligations that employees believe they owe their company and that their company owes them.[24]

**psychological contract**

the perceived obligations that employees believe they owe their company and that their company owes them

The perceptions of these obligations are certainly influenced by the rational side of employment. But they are also based on interpretations that might not be explicitly stated. For instance, did employees receive the raise that they believe they earned? Choices that managers make regarding job design,[25] pay systems,[26] job security,[27] and performance appraisal systems[28] send strong messages to employees about their company's intentions toward them. Employees' perceptions of these signals influence the extent to which they feel a need to reciprocate through certain attitudes and behaviors. When employees perceive that their company values them, they often feel obligated to provide the organization with something of equal or greater value in return.[29] This favorable perception leads to greater loyalty, commitment, and effort among employees toward the company.

The importance of a psychological contract is that it governs how employees evaluate company decisions regarding how they are managed, and, as a result, it governs how they act on the job. When we view the management of employees from the employees' perspective, two concerns emerge. First, employees expect that their company will help them balance work and life obligations. Second, employees constantly evaluate the extent to which their company holds up its end of the bargain and fulfills what they believe the company owes them for their hard work and dedication. A leading aspect of this assessment is whether an employee thinks the company behaves in a fair and just manner.

## Work/Life Balance

As noted in Chapter 1, an issue that is gaining increased attention from many companies is a need to help employees with **work/life balance**—the balance between the demands of work and the demands of employees' personal lives. Consider that roughly 70% of mothers in the U.S. workforce today have children under the age of 18, and mothers are primary or sole earners for 40% of households with children under 18 today, compared with 11% in 1960.[30] Moreover, approximately 60.5% of households today are dual-career households.[31] Work/life balance isn't about only caring for children. The U.S. population is getting older and, as a result, many employees today need to care for their elders. Many employees are caring for both older family members and children. Some are working as single parents; others as part of dual-career couples. One estimate is that 47% of adults in their 40s and 50s have a parent aged 65 or older and also are raising a young child or supporting a grown child.[32] Yet another work/life issue for some employees is dealing with traffic or long commutes to get to and from their jobs.

> **work/life balance**
>
> the balance between the demands of work and the demands of employees' personal lives

In response to these issues, many progressive companies are taking steps to help employees achieve work/life balance by providing them with more flexibility to attend to their personal or family needs. One increasingly common approach is to provide employees with flexible schedules. According to a 2016 national study of employers, 81% of companies are allowing some employees to change their starting and quitting times, 66% of employers allow for employees to work some of their regular hours at home, and 81% of the companies allow some employees to take time off during the workday to attend to important family or personal needs.[33] As noted by Steve Lyle, former director of diversity and workforce development at Texas Instruments, Inc., "At the end of the day, it's not about where you do your work or when you do your work, but that you do your work."[34]

Many companies are also committed to helping parents meet their childcare demands; however, doing so is primarily in the form of providing information or providing dependent-care-assistance plans to pay for childcare with pretax dollars.[35] Only 7% of employers offer childcare at or near the worksite.[36] Abbott Laboratories is part of the 7%. The company built a $10 million state-of-the-art childcare center for its employees.[37]

Other companies use family-friendly benefits and telecommuting to increase the ability of their employees to balance their work and personal lives. In 2016, 40% of employers allowed some employees to work some of their regular hours at home on a regular basis. In 2017, the International Foundation of Employee Benefit Plans reported that 74% of companies were allowing employees to telecommute.

While establishing work/life balance programs clearly involves considerable costs and effort, companies are finding that family-friendly practices help current employees remain effective contributors toward company goals and also provide an additional point of attraction for many potential job applicants. A Society for Human Resource Management (SHRM) survey of HR professionals reported that 75% of survey respondents stated that offering various flexible work benefits had a positive effect on retention, 61% indicated that the benefits helped attract employees, and 71% indicated that they led to improved productivity.[38]

## Justice

Whereas work/life balance programs strive to meet the personal needs of employees, issues of justice focus primarily on the expectations of employees about how they should be treated while at work. Understandably, employees expect to be treated fairly. The challenge is that, unlike with legal issues that also govern how companies manage employees, there are no clear-cut standards regarding fairness. Fairness is in the eye of the beholder—what is fair for one person may not be perceived as fair by another. Managers and employees may disagree regarding the extent to which the company has met its obligations to the employee.[39] But even while individuals differ in how they view fairness, there are three primary aspects of their relationship with their companies that employees tend to monitor: distributive, procedural, and interactional justice.

**distributive justice**

perceptions of the fairness of what individuals receive from companies in return for their efforts

**procedural justice**

perceptions of whether the processes that are used to make decisions, allocate rewards, or resolve disputes, or that otherwise affect employees, are viewed as fair

**interactional justice**

how employees feel they are treated by their managers and supervisors in everyday interactions

**Distributive justice** is the fairness of what individuals receive from companies in return for their efforts.[40] Ideally, this is a balanced exchange, with employees receiving compensation or other benefits that they view as being of equal value for the time and effort that they put into their jobs. **Procedural justice** focuses on whether the processes that are used to make decisions, allocate rewards, or resolve disputes, or that otherwise affect employees, are viewed as fair.[41] As shown in Exhibit 2.5, a number of factors influence employee perceptions about procedural fairness. For example, employees are more likely to accept evaluations or decisions regarding their pay raises when they believe that the methods used to make those decisions are consistently applied to all employees and are based on valid, accurate data.

**Interactional justice** represents how employees feel they are treated by their managers and supervisors in everyday interactions. Do managers treat employees politely and respectfully? The underlying principle of interactional justice is that *how* managers treat their employees is something that is as important to employees as the actual decisions regarding their treatment.

Perceptions of justice are particularly noteworthy because they influence the extent to which an employee believes that the company has met its obligations within the psychological contract.[42] When employees perceive that their company has not met its obligations, they are likely to display less trust of and commitment toward the company and are more likely to leave it.[43] According to Denise Rousseau,

---

## EXHIBIT 2.5

### Understanding Procedural Justice

Procedural fairness has been shown to be related to six criteria:

1. **Consistency:** Managers should ensure that allocative procedures are consistent across people and over time.

2. **Bias suppression:** Managers need to prevent personal self-interest and blind allegiance to narrow preconceptions.

3. **Accuracy:** Decisions must be based on good information and informed opinion.

4. **Correctability:** Managers must be open to opportunities to modify or reverse decisions based on inaccurate information.

5. **Representativeness:** The allocation process must represent the concerns of all important subgroups and individuals.

6. **Ethicality:** The allocation process must be compatible with prevailing moral and ethical standards.

*Source:* D. M. Rousseau, *Psychological Contracts in Organizations: Understanding Written and Unwritten Agreements* (Thousand Oaks, CA: SAGE Publications, 1995), 128.

a leading expert on psychological contracts, employees may engage in several actions in response to perceived violations of psychological contracts:

- *Voice*—Actions an employee might take to correct a situation that he or she views as unfair
- *Silence*—A form of nonresponse and a willingness to live with the circumstances, even if they are viewed as unfair
- *Neglect*—Failure to completely fulfill one's duties
- *Exit*—Departure from the company
- *Destruction*—Counterproductive behaviors that damage the company, such as vandalism, theft, and aggression[44]

A number of factors influence the specific course of action that an employee chooses. For example, the history of the relationship between the employee and the company, as well as the degree of trust that an employee has toward the company, may encourage the employee to exercise his or her voice before exiting or acting destructively. The presence of other job alternatives for an employee may encourage the person to leave sooner rather than later in response to unfair treatment. The presence of a formal grievance procedure may encourage an employee to try to remedy the situation before choosing another action.

It is important for managers to maintain open lines of communication with employees to monitor their attitudes about justice in their jobs. In larger companies, this is often difficult to do on an informal level. Many companies now conduct attitude surveys of their employees on a regular basis to monitor their overall perceptions. This provides useful information to management, and it also reassures employees that the company cares about their views and opinions. In addition, some companies perform exit interviews with employees who have voluntarily terminated their employment in order to better understand why they are leaving and what changes might improve the environment for current employees.[45]

# Environmental Influences

Whereas organizational demands are factors that exist within the boundaries of a company, environmental influences are pressures that exist outside a company. And while there are certainly many different influences, our framework focuses on four, as shown in Exhibit 2.6: labor force trends, technology, globalization, and ethical and social responsibility.

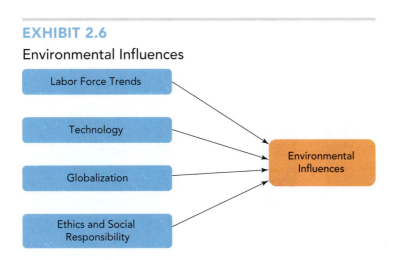

**EXHIBIT 2.6**

Environmental Influences

## Labor Force Trends

The labor force means the individuals who are available for work. According to the U.S. Bureau of Labor Statistics, the future labor force will be markedly different from the labor force of the past. Companies will have to consider several notable trends in the labor force in the coming years. Specifically, the composition of the workforce is becoming older and more diverse.[46]

### The Aging Workforce

The years immediately following World War II (1946–1964) witnessed a boom in births in the United States compared to other years. In the year 2020, the youngest "baby boomers" will be 56 years old. The 65-and-older population in the United States is expected to grow from 48 million to 88 million in 2050.[47] Companies are now realizing the need to start planning for the graying of the workforce. As shown in Exhibit 2.7, the percentage of individuals in the 55-and-older age group will continue to grow compared to the rest of the workforce.[48] In contrast, the percentage of the workforce of people 16–24 is expected to be 11.7% in 2026, down from 14.8% in 2006.[49] In 2017, the United States ranked 36th on a list of countries with high proportions of people age 65 and older, at 15.41%.[50] Japan was the oldest population in the world, with 27% of the population 65 or older, followed in the top 5 oldest by Italy, Portugal, Germany, and Finland.[51]

**EXHIBIT 2.7**

### Percent Distribution of Civilian Labor Force, by Age

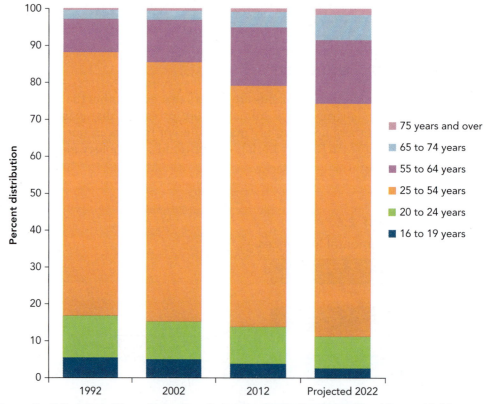

*Source:* The Editor's Desk, "Share of Labor Force Projected to Rise for People Age 55 and Over and Fall for Younger Age Groups," Bureau of Labor Statistics, January 24, 2014, http://www.bls.gov/opub/ted/2014/ted_20140124.htm.

An aging workforce brings with it a number of challenges for companies, as well as opportunities. For example, there are likely to be increased challenges with workforce planning. As the baby boomers approach retirement, companies are facing a situation in which a considerable number of their employees may leave the workforce. With the smaller number of younger workers to replace them, many companies are increasingly competing for a limited supply of workers to replace individuals who retire. Some companies have already started capitalizing on the aging workforce by explicitly recruiting and retaining older individuals beyond their retirement years. As highlighted on the next page in Company Spotlight 2.2, Michelin North America has taken a number of innovative steps to help older employees remain in the workforce. Another innovative initiative is the idea of paid internships for older workers, developed by Carole Fishman Cohen, CEO of iRelaunch. Credit Suisse, Goldman Sachs, J. P. Morgan, MetLife, Morgan Stanley, and the Onramp Fellowship for Lawyers are some of the companies that have implemented paid internships for mature workers. Between 50–90% of these internships were subsequently converted to full-time positions.[52]

### Demographic Diversity

In addition to the population aging, certain demographic groups are expected to grow more rapidly than others. For example, the number of women in the labor force is expected to grow by 8% between the years 2016 and 2026.[53] Women are expected to make up 47.4% of the U.S. labor force in 2026. This stands in contrast to the 1950s when the share of the workforce for women was less than 40%.

Similarly, while white non-Hispanics are projected to remain the largest demographic group, the fastest-growing groups in the labor force are Hispanics and Asians.[54] In 1990, the population of Hispanics was 22.6 million. That number increased to 35.7 million in 2000 and 57.5 million in 2016. An earlier forecast had predicted that the Hispanic population in the U.S. would reach 48 million by 2030 but that number clearly has already been surpassed. The Bureau of Labor Statistics projects that by 2050, Hispanics will make up 24% of the U.S. labor force, blacks 14%, and Asians 11%.[55] In 2017, the foreign-born labor force in the United States comprised 17% of the total U.S. labor force, with 48% of these workers being Hispanic and 25% Asian.[56] Foreign-born workers lived in every state in 2010, and half of all foreign-born workers lived in California, New York, Texas, and Florida.[57]

Trends in migration, coupled with differences in birth rates across demographic groups, will continue to shape the racial composition of the workforce. These changing labor force demographics have implications for managing employees. For example, how companies manage diversity and inclusion in their workforce affects their ability to attract future employees, as well as their overall reputation. Companies must take steps to manage diversity and inclusion to help employees learn the value that different backgrounds and perspectives offer in terms of organizational performance. By directly addressing diversity issues, companies are more likely to be in a position to capitalize on the benefits associated with a diverse workforce.[58]

The growing presence of a diverse workforce also requires that managers continue to pay attention to issues of discrimination and eliminate any potential biases that might harm one or several demographic groups. As we will discuss in Chapter 3, an array of federal, state, and local regulations, as well as presidential executive orders, govern the decisions that companies make regarding the management of employees, especially to ensure that practices are not discriminatory.

## COMPANY SPOTLIGHT  2.2

### Michelin North America

The Urban Institute predicts that 35% of the U.S. workforce will be age 50 or older by 2019. This aging of the population is not just a U.S. issue. Older workers are staying in the labor force longer in countries throughout the world. For some, this prediction might raise concern. However, studies show that contrary to stereotypical beliefs that older employees are more expensive, older workers have lower absenteeism, fewer accidents, and are more loyal to an organization than younger workers. Older workers tend to stay with an organization longer, and therefore, organizations incur lower costs for recruitment and training. A study conducted for AARP showed that replacing an experienced worker of any age can cost 50% or more of the individual's salary in turnover-related costs, and the cost is even higher in jobs requiring the specialized skills and extensive experience often possessed by employees over 50. Moreover, as the economy continues to do well and unemployment continues to drop, companies that know how to attract and retain older workers have an advantage.

Michelin North America is one company that understands the value of attracting and keeping older workers. In fact, Michelin's staffing management strategy centers around the premise that employees will remain with the organization for the bulk of their careers. Older workers have an average tenure of 23.6 years with the company, and about 36% of Michelin's U.S. workforce is age 50 or older. These data mean Michelin has a significant number of people with a large base of knowledge and long tenure.

To handle its future staffing needs, Michelin introduced a return-to-work retiree program. Every employee who leaves is asked as part of the company's off-boarding interview if the person is interested in returning to work in some capacity after retirement. One recent retiree, a vice president of sales for North and South America for Michelin's Aircraft Tires, had retired at age 64 after 37 years of service. He went back to work as part of the company's returning retiree program. Fifteen months after retirement, he was rehired on a part-time contract to help the government relations team prepare aircraft tire contract bids for the U.S. Navy and Air Force.

Among the employment perks at Michelin are continuing education for midcareer development and a variety of wellness and financial services benefits that are geared toward preparing workers for retirement and keeping them healthy as they get older. For instance, discounts on Weight Watchers programs and fitness center memberships are among the benefits offered. Workers also have an option to buy into the company's health-care plan after they retire. Michelin's strong business performance in its competitive industry demonstrates the value of challenging myths about an aging workforce. Michelin, the only major manufacturer to receive an AARP 2013 Best Employers for Workers Over 50 award, has one of the highest net profit margins in the tire industry.

*Sources:* "Preparing for an Aging Workforce," Society for Human Resources Management, December 2015.; Appannah, A., and Biggs, S. (2015). Age-Friendly Organisations: The Role of Organisational Culture and the Participation of Older Workers, *Journal of Social Work Practice*, 29: 37–51; "Michelin, NIH See Value in Recruiting Older Workers." *Employee Benefit News*, September 30, 2015; Shelley Emling, "Employers Are Going After Older Workers with New Programs," AARP, April 14, 2018, https://www.aarp.org/work/working-at-50-plus/info-2018/older-workers-programs.html; Robert J. Grossman, "Invest in Older Workers," *HR Magazine*, shrm.org ( August 1, 2013), http://www.shrm.org/hr-today/news/hr-magazine/pages/0813-older-workers.aspx.

# Technology

Technology continues to shape the nature of competition and how companies conduct business. There was a time when customers actually had to go to a store and talk with a salesperson to purchase a product. Today, many people do much of their shopping online. Companies such as eBay, Etsy, and Amazon are convenient, online sources for virtually any product imaginable. Most companies now have their own sophisticated websites that allow a customer to shop from the convenience of his or her home or office.

The prominence of the Internet and information technology (IT) has considerably changed how employees function within companies. An increased reliance on the Internet as a medium for meeting customer needs influences the types of competencies that employees must possess. In today's environment, most employees need a certain level of computer proficiency as most people work with a computer at some point during the workday. Even manufacturing jobs, traditionally viewed as manual labor, are becoming more high-tech with advances in computer-aided procedures, robotics, analytics, and artificial intelligence.

In many companies, technology has also created new avenues for how employees interact, share information, and learn from one another.[59] For example, it is possible to have group meetings online or through videoconferences that do not require employees to meet physically in a central location. Indeed, advances in technology have expanded how we think about work.

Not long ago, employees typically lived within a reasonable distance of a company. Now many employees **telecommute,** which involves working away from the traditional office setting. With high-speed Internet access, videoconferencing, email, and mobile technologies, it is conceivable that employees can live anywhere in the world and perform their work remotely. Of course, the downside to telecommuting is that work can be done, and expected, 24/7.[60]

**telecommute**

working away from the traditional office setting

And because employees can work from home or from a satellite location, they do not have to waste time commuting to and from a particular location. By providing employees with more flexibility in terms of when and where they work, telecommuting helps employees manage their work/life balance.

Of course, there are downsides to telecommuting. One recent study found that with an increase in telecommuting, nontelecommuting workers had fewer emotional ties to their coworkers, felt less obligated to the organization, and found the workplace less enjoyable. One explanation for this reaction is that nontelecommuters are faced with a greater workload and less flexibility because they have fewer coworkers available to share work.[61] Another study indicated that up to 75 percent of nontelecommuting employees have concerns about their telecommuting colleagues.[62] Some workers are reluctant to telecommute out of fear that doing so might reflect poorly on their dedication and commitment to their organization.[63]

Nevertheless, advances in technology have thrust telecommuting into the daily lives of companies, and employers and employees alike are exploring whether it is a good option for their circumstances. In one of the boldest moves to reconsider telecommuting, IBM announced in May 2017 that thousands of their remote workers in the United States had to relocate to a regional office or leave the company. The reason given was a desire to accelerate the pace of work and to improve collaboration. This last reason is interesting because many U.S. workers at IBM work on projects with colleagues around the globe, and those projects run 24/7.[64]

As technology enables employees to work anywhere and anytime, it also expands the pool of potential employees for companies. Individuals who require flexibility to stay at home and care for children or aging parents might not be able to commit to a traditional 9-to-5 workday, especially with a long commute. With the option to work off site and with flexible hours, this portion of the labor force becomes more accessible to companies. In addition, companies may expand their workforces to include people around the globe, thus creating a larger pool of applicants and facilitating work around the clock, without having to establish formal offices. Digital technologies are also leading to the creation of a lot of atypical jobs—jobs that have grown the so-called gig economy, a work environment in which companies hire independent contractors to do temporary work. These employees can be working anywhere around the world.[65]

## Globalization

Many companies are actively competing on an international level through exporting products and services, sending work to foreign companies, setting up production or service facilities in other countries, or establishing international joint ventures and partnerships with foreign firms. Even when companies focus primarily on their domestic market, they are increasingly finding themselves competing with international companies for a share of that market.

The push toward globalization is influenced by various trade agreements among countries around the world. The North American Free Trade Agreement (NAFTA) is a pact among Canada, the United States, and Mexico that called for the gradual removal of tariffs and other trade barriers on most goods produced and sold in North America. Since its implementation on January 1, 1994, NAFTA has had a considerable impact on business in North America. For example, the total trade among NAFTA partners increased from $652 billion in 2003, to $944.6 billion in 2010, to over $1.2 trillion in 2017.[66]

Similarly, the European Union (EU), a union of 28 independent countries, was founded to enhance political, economic, and social cooperation. The goal of the European Union is to establish a single market unifying the EU members through a common commercial policy, reducing economic differences among its richer and poorer members, and stabilizing the currencies of its members.[67] In 2019, the United Kingdom (UK) will leave the European Union as the result of a 2016 referendum against staying in the EU approved by citizens of the UK. However, the date for exit may be delayed by negotiations between the UK and the EU. Another trade agreement is the Asia-Pacific Economic Cooperation (APEC) which has a membership of 21 Pacific Rim countries. APEC has worked to reduce tariffs and other barriers to free trade throughout the Asia-Pacific region.[68]

These agreements are serving as catalysts for globalization; however, starting in 2016, there have been growing concerns in the United States and the United Kingdom among citizens and politicians over the effects of globalization on domestic jobs. These concerns have led to attempts to renegotiate trade agreements, such as NAFTA, by the United States, and the already noted withdrawal from the European Union by the United Kingdom. The growth in globalization has implications for how companies compete, where they establish operations, and the location of their labor force. It also brings new challenges for managing employees.

### International Strategies

While globalization exerts a considerable impact on just about every industry, companies differ in the extent to which they compete on a global level. Christopher Bartlett and Sumantra Ghoshal, two leading experts on international strategy, provide a useful framework that views international strategies in terms of their focus on local responsiveness and global efficiency.[69]

A **domestic strategy** focuses primarily on serving the market within a particular country. In contrast, when firms follow an **international strategy**, they expand the markets in which they compete to include multiple countries. An international

**domestic strategy**
a strategy that focuses primarily on serving the market within a particular country

**international strategy**
a strategy used by companies to expand the markets in which they compete to include multiple countries

strategy is an extension of a domestic strategy that focuses on penetrating markets in other countries through exports or moving some operations into other countries. When following a **multinational strategy**, companies take an international strategy a step further and establish autonomous or independent business units in multiple countries. One of the major objectives of a multinational strategy is that it provides business units in other countries with the authority to meet the unique local needs of their country (local responsiveness).[70]

While a multinational strategy strives to be responsive to local preferences, a **global strategy** strives to achieve global efficiency. When following a global strategy, companies are not aligned with a particular country, nor do they target the unique tastes and preferences of individual countries. Rather, a global strategy focuses on aligning business units across countries to realize gains in efficiency and scope. It does this by focusing on standardizing products that are valued across multiple markets. Finally, companies that follow a **transnational strategy** strive to achieve the benefits of both a global strategy and a multinational strategy. This is done through a combination of extensive efforts to foster a shared vision and coordination across business units, while maintaining a commitment to provide each unit with the ability to tailor products to meet the needs of the local country. For example, automobile manufacturers such as Ford try to increase efficiencies in the production process through plants across the globe, while enabling variations in the specific attributes of the vehicles that are sold in different markets. Additionally, Ford decided to limit the types of cars made in the U.S. and focus on truck and SUV manufacturing in response to consumer demand for those types of vehicles in the U.S.

The importance of international strategies has gained increased attention recently with the greater reliance on offshoring by U.S. companies. **Offshoring** is the practice of sending work that was once performed domestically to companies in other countries or opening facilities in other countries to do the work, often at a substantially lower cost.[71] Companies such as GE, Dell, and General Motors have turned to other countries such as China and India as sources of labor to supplement their full-time employees in the United States. The prevalence of offshoring and the supporting benefits associated with access to skilled labor for lower costs influence how investors view a company. Some venture capitalists now expect a company to have an offshoring strategy before they will fund new business ventures for the company. Of course, offshoring has limitations, which we will discuss throughout this book. For instance, to address quality issues, some companies are bringing work back to the U.S. that was once offshored.

### Global Factors

The success of different international strategies depends in large part on the management of employees. As companies become more global in focus, they have to make important decisions regarding the locations of their international operations. These decisions are certainly affected by factors such as proximity to the target market and access to resources, but it is also critical to consider how differences across countries influence the management of human resources and the effectiveness of different HR practices. There are two major factors that are particularly important in an international context: economic considerations and cultural differences.

**Economic Considerations**   We noted earlier that labor costs are a vital factor when companies consider alternative locations for international facilities. As you might imagine, average wages for employees, even for performing the same types of jobs, vary dramatically across countries.

For example, Exhibit 2.8 shows a comparison of hourly manufacturing labor costs for the United States and many other countries around the world for 1997, 2015, and 2016. Switzerland has consistently had the highest hourly labor costs. Other

**multinational strategy**

a strategy where companies establish autonomous or independent business units in multiple countries

**global strategy**

a strategy whereby a company strives to achieve global efficiency

**transnational strategy**

a strategy that strives to achieve the benefits of both a global strategy and a multinational strategy

**offshoring**

the practice of sending work that was once performed domestically to companies in other countries or opening facilities in other countries to do the work, often at a substantially lower cost

**EXHIBIT 2.8**

Hourly compensation costs in manufacturing, in US dollars and as a percent of costs in the United States (US =100)

| | Hourly Compensation Costs(1) | | | | | |
| Country | in US dollars | | | US = 100 | | |
| | 1997 (2) | 2015 | 2016 (3) | 1997 (2) | 2015 | 2016 |
|---|---|---|---|---|---|---|
| Switzerland | 30.43 | 61.01 | 60.36 | 132 | 161 | 155 |
| Norway | 25.88 | 50.96 | 48.62 | 112 | 135 | 125 |
| Belgium | 28.95 | 47.96 | 47.26 | 126 | 127 | 121 |
| Denmark | 23.72 | 44.57 | 45.32 | 103 | 118 | 116 |
| Germany | 28.86 | 42.27 | 43.18 | 125 | 112 | 111 |
| Sweden | 25.05 | 41.64 | 41.68 | 109 | 110 | 107 |
| Austria (5) | 24.88 | 38.99 | 39.54 | 108 | 103 | 101 |
| United States | 23.04 | 37.81 | 39.03 | 100 | 100 | 100 |
| Finland | 22.36 | 38.44 | 38.72 | 97 | 102 | 99 |
| Australia | 19.29 | 38.59 | 38.19 | 84 | 102 | 98 |
| France | 24.87 | 37.31 | 37.72 | 108 | 99 | 97 |
| Ireland | 17.42 | 35.84 | 36.23 | 76 | 95 | 93 |
| Netherlands | 22.71 | 35.02 | 34.60 | 99 | 93 | 89 |
| Italy | 19.77 | 32.40 | 32.49 | 86 | 86 | 83 |
| Canada | 18.49 | 30.74 | 30.08 | 80 | 81 | 77 |
| United Kingdom | 19.30 | 33.01 | 28.41 | 84 | 82 | 73 |
| Singapore | 12.16 | 25.87 | 26.75 | 53 | 68 | 69 |
| Japan (4) | 22.00 | 23.60 | 26.46 | 96 | 62 | 68 |
| New Zealand | 12.04 | 23.23 | 23.67 | 52 | 61 | 61 |
| Spain | 13.96 | 23.40 | 23.44 | 61 | 62 | 60 |
| South Korea | 9.24 | 22.54 | 22.98 | 40 | 60 | 59 |
| Israel | 11.62 | 21.85 | 22.63 | 50 | 58 | 58 |
| Argentina (4) | 7.55 | 20.20 | 16.77 | 33 | 53 | 43 |
| Greece | 11.61 | 16.01 | 15.70 | 50 | 42 | 40 |
| Estonia | NA | 11.00 | 11.60 | NA | 29 | 30 |
| Slovakia | 2.84 | 11.08 | 11.57 | 12 | 29 | 30 |
| Portugal | 6.44 | 10.99 | 10.96 | 28 | 29 | 28 |
| Czech Republic | 3.25 | 10.39 | 10.71 | 14 | 27 | 27 |
| Taiwan (4) | 7.07 | 9.49 | 9.82 | 31 | 25 | 25 |
| Hungary | 3.05 | 8.21 | 8.60 | 13 | 22 | 22 |
| Poland | 3.29 | 8.52 | 8.53 | 14 | 23 | 22 |
| Brazil | 7.03 | 7.73 | 7.98 | 31 | 20 | 20 |
| Turkey | NA | 5.68 | 6.09 | NA | 15 | 16 |
| Mexico | 2.62 | 4.38 | 3.91 | 11 | 12 | 10 |
| Philippines | 1.24 | 2.15 | 2.06 | 5 | 6 | 5 |

NA means data not available.

For complete definitions and country information, see Technical Notes and Country Notes.

(1) Compensation costs include direct pay, social insurance expenditures, and labor-related taxes.

(2) With the exception of Estonia and Turkey, 1997 is the first year data for all countries are available.

(3) Data are ranked on the 2016 value of Hourly Compensation, US Dollars.

(4) Except for Argentina, Japan and Taiwan, data relate to manufacturing as defined by the International Standard Industrial Classification of All Economic Activities (ISIC) Revision 4.

(5) For Austria, ISIC C Manufacturing excludes ISIC 12 Manufacture of tobacco products.

*Source:* The Conference Board, International Labor Comparisons program, February 2018

countries reporting high hourly compensation costs for 2016 are Norway, Belgium, Denmark, Germany, Sweden, Austria, and then the U.S. Note the considerable difference between the hourly costs of the top 10 countries versus the bottom 10 countries.

In addition to labor costs, an important consideration is the availability of qualified labor. Countries differ in the types of skills that their workforces have, as well as the level or supply of workers with those skills. For example, companies face a labor shortage in the United States for people with the appropriate technology skills. As a result, some companies look to the global labor market to fill positions with individuals from other countries as a solution.

A country's unemployment level influences the availability of skills and workers. Higher levels of unemployment create a larger supply of workers with certain skills. In contrast, lower levels of unemployment force companies to work much harder to identify and hire qualified employees. Relatively high unemployment in countries such as Eastern Europe, Brazil, and Spain make those countries attractive locations for companies looking to expand internationally because they provide a relatively high number of skilled, available workers.

When considering establishing operations in foreign countries, countries with low levels of skills or facing a shortage of workers with certain skills are less attractive locations for international operations, while countries with high levels of skilled workers are more attractive. For example, countries such as Mexico, Brazil, and Taiwan have a large supply of workers with desired skills who command relatively low wages compared to U.S. companies. This fact is one reason many companies have established *maquiladoras* (U.S.-owned manufacturing plants located in Mexico). Maquiladoras provide labor for much lower costs than in the United States. Other countries are more attractive for companies that need higher-skilled workers. One reason that companies increasingly offshore facets of their operations to India is the availability of highly skilled workers who command lower labor costs.

**Cultural Differences**   In addition to differences in skill levels and economic conditions, companies must also consider cultural differences when managing employees internationally. Geert Hofstede, a leading scholar on cross-cultural differences, identified five major cultural dimensions on which cultures tend to differ:[72]

*Individualism–collectivism*—The degree to which people in a country prefer to act as individuals rather than as members of groups

*Power distance*—The degree of inequality among people that a population of a country considers normal

*Uncertainty avoidance*—The degree to which people in a country prefer structured situations with clear rules about how one should behave over unstructured situations that are more ambiguous

*Masculinity–femininity*—The degree to which a society stresses values that have traditionally been viewed as masculine (assertiveness, performance, success, and competition) over values that have traditionally been viewed as feminine (quality of life, personal relationships, service, care for the weak, and solidarity)

*Long-term versus short-term orientation*—The degree to which the population of a country focuses on future-oriented values such as saving and persistence versus more short-term values such as respect for the past, tradition, and fulfilling social obligations

Hofstede's dimensions represent only one of many frameworks for understanding cultural differences.

**Implications of Global Factors on Managing Employees**   In addition to assessments of locations for international operations, globalization also creates unique challenges for managing employees on international assignments.

First, cultural differences affect what HR practices and management decisions employees deem acceptable. For example, employees in a *collectivistic* culture may be less receptive to placing a strong emphasis on individual performance in reward systems and performance-management systems than those in a more *individualistic* culture. Similarly, individuals from a *high power distance* culture may accept a work environment that emphasizes multiple layers of hierarchy and strong status distinctions between managers and employees more easily than those from a *low power distance* culture.

Second, cultural differences also influence which HR activities managers and supervisors view as appropriate for how they manage employees. Asking managers in a *high power distance* culture to encourage employee participation and decision-making might be viewed as contrary to their strong values for maintaining status differences. Similarly, companies might encounter resistance when asking managers to reward individual achievement in *collectivistic* cultures that value the community more than the individual.

The importance of effectively managing international assignments cannot be emphasized enough. Companies that fail to develop international work experience among their managers may not be able to achieve their long-term strategic goals in a global context. Lack of international management experience may be a factor in less-favorable productivity of operations located in foreign countries and in lost opportunities for creating or penetrating markets. Lack of experience also may cause difficulties with building and maintaining relationships with stakeholders in the country in which the operations are located.[73] Not surprisingly, international work experience is now one of the major requirements for promotion to higher-level managerial positions.[74] CEOs with more international experience are often more highly recruited than those who lack that experience.[75]

## Ethics and Social Responsibility

Organizations are increasingly expected to cope with HR challenges in an ethical way, which leads to the fourth environmental challenge in our framework: ethics and social responsibility. Ethics and social responsibility have always been important to companies. Questions of child-labor abuse in sweatshops have received considerable attention for years in the retail industry. Public awareness regarding financially unethical behavior in companies gained prominence as a result of the widely publicized problems at Lehman Brothers and Madoff Investment Securities. Toyota and GM came under scrutiny for questionable handling of defective parts when their automobiles were involved in accidents with some of those accidents including fatalities.[76] GM hired attorney Kenneth Feinberg to compensate victims killed in crashes caused by defective ignition switches in a number of the company's models.[77] Toyota paid out $1.2 billion to avoid prosecution for covering up safety problems with unintended acceleration. More recently, several companies have been scandalized by allegations of sexual harassment and misconduct.[78]

But what exactly is ethical behavior? How much responsibility do companies have toward the environment? Toward other countries? Toward minority groups? According to *Business Ethics* magazine, it is useful for companies and managers to think about ethical behavior with regard to eight stakeholder groups:[79]

- Shareholders
- Community
- Governance
- Diversity
- Employees

- Environment
- Human rights
- Product

Each of these stakeholder groups is affected by the actions of companies, and each has a vested interest in evaluating how companies are performing to meet their needs. How ethically companies behave toward these groups has several implications for their success. Would you shop at a company that offered a great product for a low price? What if that company was able to achieve exceptionally low costs by using child labor in another country? What if that company achieved its low costs by dumping chemical waste in a local stream?

Ethical actions and socially responsible behavior can help foster a positive reputation that spurs additional consumer support. Bristol-Myers Squibb, Johnson & Johnson, Gap, Inc., and Microsoft are a few companies that have had the honor of being identified as some of the 100 best corporate citizens by *Corporate Responsibility Magazine*.[80] In 2018, Microsoft was named as the number 1 Best Corporate Citizen by the magazine. Microsoft was one of the first companies to offer flextime and job sharing, family benefits, and bereavement leave. Microsoft has a strong record on human rights and on the environment, making sure that its server rooms are as energy efficient as possible. They also have a large corporate giving program.[81] Research shows that companies rated among the 100 best corporate citizens financially outperform their business counterparts.[82]

Given the importance of ethics, how can you encourage your company to act ethically? Perhaps the best place to start is by recognizing that ethical decisions are made by people. Employee behavior, from the entry-level new hire up to the CEO of a corporation, defines the ethical nature of companies. In a survey of accountants sponsored by the European Federation of Accountants and Auditors for SMEs and the Accountants Association in Poland and reported in 2017, 64% of the 662 respondents representing 23 countries indicated they had been pressured during their professional career to act in an unethical manner. Around 37% of the respondents indicated that such pressure had occurred on five or more occasions.[83] Exhibit 2.9 highlights the top five causes of unethical behavior according identified in a SHRM survey. When asked what types of unethical behavior were most prevalent,

---

**EXHIBIT 2.9**

**Pressure Points for Unethical Behavior**

As noted by the Society for Human Resource Management 2003 business ethics survey, the top five causes of pressure to compromise ethical standards were:

Following the boss's directives (49%)

Meeting overly aggressive business/financial objectives (48%)

Helping the organization to survive (40%)

Meeting scheduling pressures (35%)

Wanting to be a team player (27%)

*Sources:* "How to Help Reinvigorate Your Organization's Ethics Program," *HR Focus* 80 (June 2003); and J. Schramm, "A Return to Ethics?" *HR Magazine* 48 (July 2003): 144.

the respondents reported misrepresenting hours of work; lying to supervisors; management lying to employees, customers, vendors, or the public; misusing the organization's assets; and lying on reports or falsifying records.[84]

Considering that a company's ethical behavior rests on employee decisions and actions, it is important that employees understand how to act ethically. There are several steps that companies can take to encourage ethical behavior in employees:

- Appoint an "ethics officer"
- Constantly monitor the aspects of the company's culture that concern its value system, including ethics
- Provide ethics training
- Perform background checks on incoming employees
- Devote time at regular staff meetings to talking about responsibilities[85]

## COMPANY SPOTLIGHT   2.3

### Apple, Inc.'s Ethical Decisions

Apple, Inc., recognized as one of the most admired companies in the world, is continually challenged to meet ethical and corporate social responsibility (CSR) standards, particularly with respect to its parts suppliers in China. Just recently, Apple suspended the use of one Chinese mining supplier when it learned the supplier used child labor as young as age 4. In response to the situation, an Apple spokesperson stated, "Apple is deeply committed to the responsible sourcing of materials for our products, and we've led the industry in establishing the strictest standards for our suppliers." Apple developed these tough standards after it was scandalized in 2010 by its supplier relationship with Foxconn, a major assembly manufacturer with locations throughout China. A series of suicides took place among Foxconn employees as a result of the company's harsh working conditions.

In its 2018 Supplier Responsibility Progress Report, Apple underscores its commitment to human rights, environmental protections, and sound business practices. Every year, Apple conducts assessments to ensure that suppliers meet their Supplier Code of Conduct. The company also sponsors an 18-month training program that aims to improve employee health and safety throughout the globe. A total of 240 suppliers participate in this program.

Despite making great progress, however, Apple saw its CSR reputation slip from 7th place in 2016 to 49th in 2017 in the annual ranking of social responsibility reputations conducted by the Reputation Institute, a reputation-management consulting firm. Foxconn, still a key Apple iPhone supplier, was accused of using illegal intern labor and breaching Chinese labor law. In addition, in 2017, Apple was unwilling to unlock its iPhone to assist the Federal Bureau of Investigation (FBI) in its investigation of a domestic terrorist attack. Pursuing social responsibility and ethical standards is not easy for a competitive, global business.

*Sources:* Karsten Strauss, "The 10 Companies with the Best CSR Reputations in 2017," September 3, 2017, Forbes. com, https://www.forbes.com/sites/karstenstrauss/2017/09/13/the-10-companies-with-the-best-csr-reputations-in-2017/#76345f75546b; Mallen Baker's Respectful Business Blog, "How Tim Cook Brought Corporate Social Responsibility to Apple," March 10, 2016, http://mallenbaker.net/article/clear-reflection/how-tim-cook-brought-corporate-social-responsibility-to-apple; John Dudovskiy, "Apple Corporate Social Responsibility," Research Methods, January 23, 2018, https://research-methodology.net/apple-corporate-social-responsibility-csr; Tom Cheshire, "Child Miners: Firm Refuses to Apologize Over Cobalt Sourcing," https://sky.com/story/child-miners-firm-refuses-to-apologise-over-cobalt-sourcing-10785313; "Apple Supplier Responsibility 2018 Progress Report," https://www.apple.com/supplier-responsibility/pdf/Apple_SR_2018_Progress_Report.pdf.

Once accused of abusing child labor around the globe, Nike has a large team of corporate responsibility and compliance managers working in locations around the world focusing on ensuring that their vendors and suppliers comply with the Nike Code of Conduct.[86] In fiscal year 2015, Nike conducted 654 audits of its factories and had fewer factories with noncompliance issues than in 2014 when it had 685 audits. Sixteen percent of the factories recorded violations in 2015 with wages and hours worked as two of the top issues of concern.[87] Similarly, as described in Company Spotlight 2.3, Apple conducts audits of suppliers' factories to ensure that the company's foreign labor has satisfactory working conditions. Beyond asking employees to behave ethically, some companies take steps to show employees how to behave ethically. For instance, Lockheed Martin requires all employees to attend ethics training each year.[88]

Financial performance has long been a measurement tool for company success. However, the ethics and social responsibility that companies display are increasingly playing a role in how people evaluate organizations. Companies need to not only set ethical standards for employees, but also take steps to show employees how to carry out ethical actions in their jobs. After all, if employees don't adhere to ethical standards, social responsibility and ethics may become simply an exercise in public relations.[89]

## SUMMARY

To be an effective manager, you have to understand which HR practices are available. Just as important, managers need to understand which HR practices are most appropriate for different circumstances. In short, you have to understand how employees add value and how HR challenges affect your options for managing employees. In this chapter, we have explored the organizational demands that exist within companies, as well as the environmental influences that exist outside companies that affect how to manage employees.

Organizational demands are factors within the boundaries of a company that affect what you need to do to manage employees. One of the key challenges facing managers is to understand how employees contribute to realizing strategic priorities and, ultimately, company success. Different strategies require employees to perform in different ways, and employees in different companies add value in unique ways. Moreover, each company is unique in how it is set up to carry out its operations. Companies vary in terms of size, stage of development, and transformation process. These differences affect what resources are available to manage employees, as well as the types of tasks and responsibilities that employees are expected to perform. Beyond strategy and company characteristics, each company has a unique culture that influences how employees interact with each other and with customers based on differences in values and beliefs. Finally, managers are not likely to be very effective if they do not take into account the concerns of the individuals that they are managing—their employees.

While organizational demands focus on factors that exist within the boundaries of a company, environmental influences are pressures that exist outside companies. Changes in the labor force are occurring, and the workforce is becoming older and more demographically diverse. Technological advances have provided companies with new options for when and where employees work, as well as how employees are managed and controlled. Globalization continues to introduce new challenges regarding where companies establish facilities, as well as how to manage cultural differences. In addition, companies are increasingly being expected to cope with these challenges and opportunities in an ethical way.

Successful companies are able to navigate these HR challenges by understanding how to use the primary HR activities to cope with the challenges and take advantage of the opportunities that the changing competitive landscape presents.

## KEY TERMS

cost leadership strategy
differentiation strategy
distributive justice
domestic strategy
global strategy
interactional justice
international strategy
multinational strategy

offshoring
organizational culture
procedural justice
psychological contract
telecommute
transnational strategy
work/life balance

## DISCUSSION QUESTIONS

1. Create a list of differentiation strategies. What implications do these strategies have for employee management?
2. What are some of the unique HR challenges associated with managing employees in start-up companies versus long-established, larger companies?
3. As a manager, what can you do to help instill new values and beliefs among your employees?
4. How much responsibility do companies have to help employees balance their work and personal lives? What options are available to help achieve work/life balance? Which of these options are best?
5. Research the benefits and challenges of having a diverse workforce. How can you help employees embrace diversity and create an inclusive environment?
6. What types of managerial challenges would you expect to encounter if your employees telecommute to work? How would you address those issues?
7. Companies are increasing their global operations. What are some of the challenges that a company would face when going global? What could you do, as a manager, to help people working internationally deal with these challenges?
8. How have advances in technology affected the way that companies manage their employees?
9. As a manager, what can you do to encourage your employees to act in an ethical and socially responsible manner?

## LEARNING EXERCISE 1—ENCOURAGING ETHICAL BEHAVIOR

Given the well-documented scandals in corporate America involving unethical behavior, many companies are increasingly encouraging their employees to act ethically. For this exercise, choose four different companies. Research their approaches to ethics and their codes of ethical conduct by visiting their company websites and reading about them in the popular business press. Then answer the following questions.

1. Which company's approach to ethics impresses you the most? Why? Which is least impressive? Why?

2. If you were to write a code of ethical conduct for your employees, what would it say? In your opinion, what are the key components of a good code of ethical conduct?

3. What are some ways that you would make sure employees comply with your code of ethical conduct?

# LEARNING EXERCISE 2—MANAGING IN A SMALL FIRM

In light of the trends highlighted in this chapter, there is a good chance that you will work in a small company—or even create one! It is important, therefore, to think about some of the issues that you might encounter in managing employees in a small or entrepreneurial firm.

1. What challenges would you expect to encounter as a manager in a small company that are different from those you might encounter in a larger, more established company?

2. How would these challenges influence how you manage your employees?

3. If you were to create a new company, or at least be part of the founding team, how you manage employees would set the tone for the culture of the company as it grows. Would this influence your decisions about how to manage your employees? How?

# CASE STUDY 1: SUSTAINING SUCCESS AT ST. STEVENS COMMUNITY COLLEGE

Emma Barnes is a senior administrator at St. Stevens Community College (SSCC), and recently, she has been asked to assess the sustainability of SSCC's strategic mission and to develop a long-term plan for SSCC to overcome any pending challenges and capitalize on any potential opportunities. Established in 1965, SSCC is a midsized community college serving the local population that partners with students to maximize their college experience. SSCC's competitive advantage is to be a high-quality educational option for diverse students at an affordable price and to serve a valuable role in the community. It provides small classes, cutting-edge classrooms, and great resources to enable students to get the most out of their educational experience. Based on all assessments, SSCC has been successful. In its 50-plus years, the college has grown to more than 12,000 students and enjoys financial profits, with enough funds to reinvest in maintaining the administrative infrastructure of the college, enhancing the technology in the classrooms, and bolstering the quality of the athletic facilities.

Despite the college's success, Emma is worried that it may be experiencing the calm before the storm. There are several reasons for her concerns. First, many members of the faculty are approaching retirement age, and hiring faculty replacements is difficult because newly minted PhDs have many options for employment. Moreover, new hires are demanding salaries that are above what SSCC is typically able to afford. The quality of the faculty is a key attraction for students, and Emma worries that SSCC may not be able to maintain the level of education that it offers without planning now for the future. In addition, there has been a growing increase in the number of students who have decided to pursue distance education rather than attend community college, with the goal of attending a four-year university after the completion of an associate's degree online. Finally, the composition of the student population continues to become increasingly diverse in terms of gender, race, national origin, and age. While everyone at SSCC agrees that it is a great asset, Emma wonders what implications the increased diversity of the student body might have for how SSCC moves forward.

While everything seems to be fine, Emma is determined to develop a plan to ensure that SSCC is able to take advantage of its opportunities and minimize its constraints. The problem is that she doesn't have a clear answer for how do so.

### Discussion Questions

1. What is your assessment of the organizational and environmental challenges facing SSCC?

2. Which of these HR challenges would you view as most important and least important for Emma to consider as she develops a plan for the future?

3. Given your assessments of these challenges, what recommendations would you make to move forward in a way that ensures that SSCC is able to sustain its strategy of high-quality education at affordable prices? Explain the logic behind how you ranked the HR challenges.

## CASE STUDY 2: GLOBALIZATION AT LEVI STRAUSS

Blue jeans are a legendary component of American culture. They were created in the United States in 1873, when Levi Strauss patented the riveted denim jeans that proved so successful among customers that they launched an entire industry. Yet, the one company that has perhaps been most synonymous with blue jeans—Levi Strauss—doesn't actually make its blue jeans in the United States.

In the late 1990s and early part of the 2000s, Levi Strauss undertook a substantial shift in the location of its manufacturing operations. In 1997, the company closed 11 plants and laid off 7,400 employees to cut excess production. In 1999, Levi's announced a large-scale layoff of almost 6,000 jobs and the closing of more factories in Georgia, North Carolina, Virginia, Texas, Tennessee, and Arkansas in an effort to move production to foreign facilities. Over time, the layoffs and the closings continued. Once a mainstay of U.S. manufacturing, plants in areas such as San Antonio, San Francisco, El Paso, and Brownsville were closed, and by 2004, Levi Strauss had shut its domestic operations and moved production facilities to foreign countries such as Mexico and China. Costs were a major factor for this decision. What might cost $6.67 to make in the United States costs about $3.00 in Mexico and $1.50 in China. While Levi Strauss was reluctant to move these jobs, it faced a competitive market operating with lower costs and lower prices.

### Discussion Questions

1. How did the four environmental factors discussed in this chapter influence Levi's decision to move its manufacturing outside the United States? Which environmental factor do you think had the strongest impact on Levi's?

2. How would you evaluate this decision from a business perspective? What about from an ethical perspective?

3. Assume that you are an employee working for Levi Strauss and are assigned to the management team in one of the manufacturing facilities in Mexico. What differences would you anticipate in terms of how you manage your Mexican employees versus how you manage employees located in the United States?

4. Why do you think those differences exist?

*Sources:* L. Kaufman, "Levi Is Closing 11 Factories; 7,600 Jobs Cut," *The New York Times*, February 23, 1999, http://query.nytimes.com/gst/fullpage.html?res=9405E6DC103DF930A15751C0A96F958260; L. Kaufman, "Levi Strauss to Close 6 U.S. Plants and Lay off 3,300," *The New York Times*, April 9, 2002, http://query.nytimes.com/gst/fullpage.html?res=9F06E6DB133DF93AA35757C0A9649C8B63; and M. Thiruvengadam, "Apparel Industry No Longer a Good Fit in El Paso," *San Antonio Express-News*, October 15, 2005, http://www.citizenstrade.org/pdf/sanantonioexpress_apparelindustryoutofelpaso_10152005.pdf.

# NOTES

[1] M. E. Porter, "What Is Strategy?" *Harvard Business Review*, November 1, 1996, pp. 61–78; and M. A. Hitt, R. D. Ireland, and R. E. Hoskisson, *Strategic Management: Competitiveness and Globalization* (Cincinnati: South-Western College Publishing, 2001).

[2] M. E. Porter, *Competitive Advantage: Creating and Sustaining Superior Performance* (New York: The Free Press, 1985).

[3] Montana State University, Center for Applied Economic Research, "The Impact of Big Box Retail Chains on Small Businesses," January 2000, http://www.msubillings.edu/caer/bix%20box%20report.htm; and K. E. Stone, "Impact on the Wal-Mart Phenomena on Rural Communities," *Proceedings of Increasing Understanding of Public Problems and Policies 1997* (Chicago: Farm Foundation, 1997).

[4] Porter, *Competitive Advantage*.

[5] "About Tesla," tesla.com, https://www.tesla.com/about.

[6] L. C. Christiansen and M. Higgs, "How the Alignment of Business Strategy and HR Strategy Can Impact Performance: A Practical Insight for Managers." *Journal of General Management* 33, no. 4 (2008): 13–33; S. E. Jackson, R. S. Schuler, and J. C. Rivero, "Organizational Characteristics as Predictors of Personnel Practices," *Personnel Psychology* 42 (1989): 727–786; and R. S. Schuler and S. E. Jackson, "Linking Competitive Strategies with Human Resource Management Practices," *Academy of Management Executive* 1 (1987): 207–219.

[7] S. E. Jackson, R. S. Schuler, and K. Jiang, "An Aspirational Framework for Human Resource Management," *Academy of Management Annals* 8 (2014): 1–56; David P. Lepak and Jason D. Shaw (2008), "Strategic HRM in North America: Looking to the Future." *International Journal of Human Resource Management* 19 (8): 1486–1499.

[8] Small Business Bulletin, June 2015, "Small Business Market Update, A Snapshot of the Small Business Economy," https://www.sba.gov/sites/default/files/Small_business_bulletin_June_2015.pdf; Small Business Bulletin, June 2015, "Small Business Market Update," https://www.sba.gov/sites/default/files/Small_business_bulletin_June_2015.pdf. Small Business Bulletin, August 2017, "What's New with Small Business?" https://www.sba.gov/sites/default/files/Whats-New-w-Small-Business-20175.pdf.

[9] D. Finegold and S. Frenkel, "Managing People Where People Really Matter: The Management of Human Resources in Biotech Companies," *International Journal of Human Resource Management* 17 (2006): 1–24; and J. G. Heneman and R. A. Berkley, "Applicant Attraction Practices and Outcomes Among Small Businesses," *Journal of Small Business Management* 37 (1999): 53–74.

[10] M. R. Allen, J. Ericksen, and C. J. Collins, "Human Resource Management, Employee Exchange Relationships, and Performance in Small Businesses," *Human Resource Management* 52, no. 2 (March–April 2013): 153–172; and J. S. Hornsby and D. F. Kuratko, "Human Resource Management in U.S. Small Businesses: A Replication and Extension," *Journal of Developmental Entrepreneurship* 8 (April 2003): 73–92.

[11] P. Fronstin, P., "Fewer Small Employers Offering Health Coverage; Large Employers Holding Steady," *EBRI Notes,* 37 (2017): 1–6.

[12] S. Mayson and R. Barrell, "The 'Science' and 'Practice' of HRM in Small Firms," *Human Resource Management Review* 16, no. 4 (December 2006): 447–455; and Hornsby and Kuratko, "Human Resource Management in U.S. Small Businesses."

[13] J. D. Kok and L. M. Uhlaner, "Organization Context and Human Resource Management in the Small Firm," *Small Business Economics* 17 (December 2001): 273–291.

[14] O. C. Richard, D. Ford, and K. Ismail, "Exploring the Performance Effects of Visible Attribute Diversity: The Moderating Role of Span of Control and Organizational Life Cycle," *International Journal of Human Resource Management* 17 (2006): 2091–2109.

[15] L. Baird and I. Meshoulam, "Managing Two Fits of Strategic Human Resource Management," *Academy of Management Review* 13 (1988): 116–128.

[16] Ibid.

[17] E. H. Schein, *Organizational Culture and Leadership* (San Francisco: Jossey-Bass, 1985).

[18] Southwest Airlines website, "About Southwest," July 29, 2014, https://www.southwest.com/html/about-southwest/.

[19] A. Canato, D. Ravasi, and P. Nielson, "Coerced Practice Implementation in Cases of Low Cultural Fit: Cultural Change and Practice Adaptation During the Implementation of Six Sigma at 3M," *Academy of Management Journal* 56 (2013): 1724–1753; and J. R. Harrison

and G. R. Carroll, "Keeping the Faith: A Model of Cultural Transmission in Formal Organizations," *Administrative Science Quarterly* 36 (1991): 552–582.

[20] R. A. Guzzo and K. A. Noonan, "Human Resource Practices as Communications and the Psychological Contract," *Human Resource Management* 33 (1994): 447–462; see also D. M. Rousseau, *Psychological Contracts in Organizations: Understanding Written and Unwritten Agreements* (Thousand Oaks, CA: SAGE, 1995).

[21] C. Ostroff and D. E. Bowen, "Moving HR to a Higher Level: HR Practices and Organizational Effectiveness," in *Multilevel Theory, Research, and Methods in Organizations: Foundations, Extensions, and New Directions*, ed. K. J. Klein and S. W. Kozlowski (San Francisco: Jossey-Bass, 2000), 211–266.

[22] D. E. Bowen and C. Ostroff, "Understanding HRM-Firm Performance Linkages: The Role of the 'Strength' of the HRM System," *Academy of Management Review* 29 (2004): 203–221.

[23] I. Drori, A. Wrzesniewski, and S. Ellis, "Cultural Clashes in a 'Merger of Equals': The Case of High-Tech Start Ups," *Human Resource Management* 50 (2011): 625–649; R. A. Weber and C. F. Camerer, "Cultural Conflict and Merger Failure: An Experimental Approach," *Management Science* 49 (2003): 400–415; and S. Fister Gale, "Memo to AOL Time Warner: Why Mergers Fail," *Workforce*, February 2003, p. 60.

[24] Rousseau, *Psychological Contracts in Organizations*.

[25] J. R. Hackman and G. R. Oldham, *Work Redesign* (Reading, MA: Addison-Wesley, 1980).

[26] B. Murray and B. Gerhart, "An Empirical Analysis of a Skill-Based Pay Program and Plant Performance Outcomes," *Academy of Management Journal* 41 (1998): 68–78.

[27] S. L. Robinson, M. S. Kraatz, and D. M. Rousseau, "Changing Obligations and the Psychological Contract: A Longitudinal Study," *Academy of Management Journal* 37 (1994): 137–152.

[28] M. S. Taylor et al., "Due Process in Performance Appraisals: A Quasi-experiment in Procedural Justice," *Administrative Science Quarterly* 40 (1995): 495–523; Peter Cappelli and Martin J. Conyon (2018), "What Do Performance Appraisals Do?" *ILR Review* 71 (1): 88–116.

[29] R. Eisenberger, R. Huntington, S. Hutchison, and D. Sowa, "Perceived Organizational Support," *Journal of Applied Psychology* 71 (1986): 500–507; K. Alfes, A. D. Shantz, C. Truss, and E. C. Soane (2013), "The Link Between Perceived Human Resource Management Practices, Engagement, and Employee Behaviour: A Moderated Mediation Model." *International Journal of Human Resource Management* 24 (2): 330–351; Peter Cappelli (1999), *The New Deal at Work: Managing the Market-Driven Workforce* (Cambridge, MA: Harvard Business Press).

[30] Bureau of Labor Statistics, "Table 6: Employment Status of Mothers with Own Children Under 3 Years Old by Single Year of Age of Youngest Child and Marital Status, 2014–2015 Annual Averages," http://www.bls.gov/news.release/famee.t06.htm.

[31] Bureau of Labor Statistics, April 22, 2016, "Employment Characteristics of Families Summary," http://www.bls.gov/news.release/famee.nr0.htm.

[32] Kim Parker and Eileen Patten, "The Sandwich Generation: Rising Financial Burdens for Middle-aged Americans," Pew Research Center, pewsocialtrends.org (January 30 2013), http://www.pewsocialtrends.org/2013/01/30/the-sandwich-generation/.

[33] K. Matos and E. Galinsky, "National Study of Employers. Co-sponsored by the Families and Work Institute and the Society for Human Resource Management and the Alfred P. Sloan Foundation," 2016, http://whenworkworks.org/downloads/2016-National-Study-of-Employers.pdf .

[34] Ibid.

[35] Ibid.

[36] Ibid; Bureau of Labor Statistics, June 24, 2016. News Release, "American Time Use Survey—2015 Results," http://www.bls.gov/news.release/pdf/atus.pdf.

[37] "Abbott's On-site Child Care Center Recognized Amongst the Country's Best," National Association for the Education of Young Children, July 28, 2104, http://www.prnewswire.com/news-releases/abbotts-on-site-child-care-center-recognized-amongst-the-countrysbest-72238327.html; A. Tugend, "It's Unclearly Defined, But Telecommuting Is Fast on the Rise," *The New York Times*, March 7, 2014, http://www.nytimes.com/2014/03/08/your-money/when-working-in-your-pajamas-is-more-productive.html?_r=0; Mauerle Backman, "Telecommuting Has Pros and Cons," The Motley Fool, usatoday.com, December 28, 2017, https://www.usatoday.com/story/money/careers/2017/12/24/74-of-employers-offer-this-crucial-benefit/108121966/?utm_source=feedblitz&utm_medium=FeedBlitzRss&utm_campaign=usatodaycommoney-topstories.

[38] F. Hansen, "Truth and Myths of Work/Life Balance," *Workforce*, December 2002, pp. 34–39.

39 S. W. Lester, W. H. Turnley, J. M. Bloodgood, and M. C. Bolino, "Not Seeing Eye to Eye: Differences in Supervisor and Subordinate Perceptions of and Attributions for Psychological Contract Breach," *Journal of Organizational Behavior* 23 (February 2002): 29–56.

40 Rousseau, *Psychological Contracts in Organizations*, p. 128.

41 Ibid., p. 53.

42 "Why Loyalty Is Not Enough,' *HR Focus* 77 (November 2000): 1–3.

43 J. M. L. Poon, "Distributive Justice, Procedural Justice, Affective Commitment, and Turnover Intention: A Mediation-moderation Framework," *Journal of Applied Social Psychology* 42 (June 2012): 1505–1532; J. Coyle-Shapiro and I. Kessler, "Consequences of the Psychological Contract for the Employment Relationship: A Large-Scale Survey," *Journal of Management Studies* 37 (2002): 39–52; S. L. Robinson, "Trust and Breach of the Psychological Contract," *Administrative Science Quarterly* 41 (1996): 574–599; and W. H. Turnley and D. C. Feldman, "The Impact of Psychological Contract Violations on Exit, Loyalty, and Neglect," *Human Relations* 51 (1999): 895–922.

44 Rousseau, *Psychological Contracts in Organizations*, p. 90.

45 B. N. Carvin, "New Strategies for Making Exit Interviews Count," *Employment Relations Today* 38, no. 2 (Summer 2011): 1–6; and F. Hansen, "Weighing the Truth of Exit Interviews," *Workforce*, December 2002, p. 37; E. Spain and B. Groysberg, "Making Exit Interviews Count," *Harvard Business Review* (April 2016): 89-95.

46 Bureau of Labor Statistics, "Employment Projections: 2016–26 Summary," https://www.bls.gov/news.release/ecopro.nr0.htm.

47 B. Cire (March 28, 2016), "World's Older Population Grows Dramatically," National Institutes of Health, https://www.nih.gov/news-events/news-releases/worlds-older-population-grows-dramatically.

48 The Editors Desk, "Share of Labor Force Projected to Rise for People Age 55 and Over and Fall for Younger Age Groups," January 24, 2014, http://www.bls.gov/opub/ted/2014/ted_20140124.htm; and M. Toossi, "Labor Force Projections to 2022: The Labor Force Participation Rate Continues to Fall," *Monthly Labor Review*, December 2013.

49 Bureau of Labor Statistics, "Employment Projections: 2016–26 Civilian Labor Force, by Age, Sex, Race and Ethnicity," https://www.bls.gov/emp/tables/civilian-labor-force-summary.htm.

50 W. He, D. Goodkind, & P. Kowal (March 2016_, "An Aging World: 2015," U.S. Census Bureau, https://www.census.gov/content/dam/Census/library/publications/2016/demo/p95-16-1.pdf.

51 R. Martin (August 21, 2016), "New England Public Radio Weekend Edition Sunday," http://www.npr.org/2016/08/21/490820273/how-japan-is-dealing-with-impacts-of-supporting-the-oldest-population-in-the-wor; S. Yoon (September 9, 2015), Bloomberg news online, "These Will Be the Older Populations by 2050," http://www.bloomberg.com/news/articles/2015-09-09/these-will-be-the-oldest-populations-by-2050; "Populations Ages 65 and Above (% of Total)," 2017 Revision, World Bank Group (US), https://data.worldbank.org/indicator/SP.POP.65UP.TO.ZS.

52 Sheryl Smolkin "Michelin, NIH See Value in Recruiting Older Workers." *Employee Benefit News*, benefitnews.com, September 30, 2015; https://www.benefitnews.com/news/michelin-nih-see-value-in-recruiting-older-workers; Randy Lilleston, "It's Never Too Late For an Internship," Work & Jobs: Job Search, AARP, aarp.com, February 28, 2018, https://www.aarp.org/work/job-search/info-2018/internship-employment-gap-fd.html.

53 U.S. Bureau of Labor Statistics, "Table 3.1 Civilian Labor Force by Age, Sex, Race, and Ethnicity, 1996, 2006, 2016, and Projected 2026 (Numbers in thousands)," https://www.bls.gov/emp/tables/civilian-labor-force-summary.htm.

54 M. Toossi, "Projections of the Labor Force to 2050: A Visual Essay," *Monthly Labor Review*, 2012, p. 14.

55 M. Toossi, "A Century of Change: The U.S. Labor Force 1950–2050," *Monthly Labor Review*, 2002, pp. 15–28; "How the U.S. Hispanic Population Is Changing," Fact Tank, Pew Research Center, September 18, 2017, http://www.pewresearch.org/fact-tank/2017/09/18/how-the-u-s-hispanic-population-is-changing/.

56 Bureau of Labor Statistics Economic News Release, "Labor Force Characteristics of Foreign-Born Workers Summary," May 17, 2017, https://www.bls.gov/news.release/forbrn.nr0.htm/Labor-Force-Characteristics-of-Foreign-Born-Workers-Summary.

57 E. M. Grieco, Y. D. Acosta, G. P. de la Cruz, C. Gambino, T. Gryn, L. J. Larsen, et al., "The Foreign-Born Population in the United States: 2010," American Community Survey Reports, U.S. Census Bureau, May 2012, http://www.census.gov/prod/2012pubs/acs-19.pdf.

58 O. C. Richard, S. L. Kirby, and K. Chadwick, "The Impact of Racial and Gender Diversity in Management on Financial Performance: How Participative Strategy Making Features

Can Unleash a Diversity Advantage," *International Journal of Human Resource Management* 24 (2013): 2571–2582; D. A. Kravitz, "More Women in the Workplace: Is There a Payoff in Firm Performance?" *Academy of Management Executive*, 2003, p. 148; A. Konrad, "Leveraging Workplace Diversity in Organizations," *Organization Management Journal*, 3 (2006): 164–182.

[59] S. Greengard, "Surviving Internet Speed," *Workforce*, April 2001, pp. 38–43.

[60] M. C. Noon and J. L. Glass, "The Hard Truth About Telecommuting," *Monthly Labor Review* 38 (June 2012); and M. Mariani, "Telecommuters," *Occupational Outlook Quarterly*, Fall 2000, pp. 10–17.

[61] T. Golden, "Co-workers Who Telecommute and the Impact on Those in the Office: Understanding the Implications of Virtual Work for Co-worker Satisfaction and Turnover Intentions," *Human Relations* 60 (2007): 1641–1667.

[62] C. Cooper and N. B. Kurland, "Telecommuting, Professional Isolation, and Employee Development in Public and Private Organizations," *Journal of Organizational Behavior* 23 (2002): 511–532.

[63] B. Moore, M. Rhodes, and R. Stanley, "Telework 2011: A World at Work Special Report," http://www.worldatwork.org/waw/adimLink?id=53034.

[64] John Simons, "IBM, A Pioneer of Remote Work, Calls Workers Back to the Office, wsj .com, May 18, 2017, https://www.wsj.com/articles/ibm-a-pioneer-of-remote-work-calls-workers-back-to-the-office-1495108802.

[65] "Managing Flexible Work Arrangements" June 14, 2016, Society for Human Resource Management, https://www.shrm.org/resourcesandtools/tools-and-samples/toolkits/pages/managingflexibleworkarrangements.aspx; "How Can We Make Labor Shifts Work for People?" May 2018, McKinsey Global Institute, https://www.mckinsey.com/featured-insights/future-of-organizations-and-work/how-can-we-make-labor-shifts-work-for-people.

[66] "The North American Free Trade Agreement (NAFTA)," *Export.Gov*, July 28, 2014, http://export.gov/FTA/nafta/index.asp. "NAFTA: A 10-Year Perspective and Implications for the Future: Hearing Before the Subcommittee on International Economic Policy, Export, and Trade Promotion of the Committee on Foreign Relations," United States Senate, April 20, 2004, http://www.gpo.gov/fdsys/pkg/CHRG-108shrg95375/html/CHRG-108shrg95375.htm; Global Affairs Canada (July 27, 2016), North America Free Trade Agreement (NAFTA). http://www.international.gc.ca/trade-commerce/trade-agreements-accords-commerciaux/agr-acc/nafta-alena/fta-ale/archived-archivees.aspx?lang=en; Holly K. Sonneland, "Chart: NAFTA By the Numbers in 2017," Americas Society/Council of the Americas, March 1, 2018, https://www.as-coa.org/articles/chart-nafta-numbers-2017

[67] Delegation of the European Union to the United States website, July 28, 2014, http://www.euintheus.org/.

[68] Asia-Pacific Economic Cooperation (APEC) website, July 28, 2014, http://www.apec.org/About-Us/About-APEC/Member-Economies.aspx.

[69] C. A. Bartlett and S. Ghoshal, *Managing Across Borders: The Transnational Solution* (Boston: Harvard Business School Press, 1998).

[70] S. Ghoshal, "Global Strategy: An Organizing Framework," *Strategic Management Journal* 8 (1987): 425–440; and Hitt, Ireland, and Hoskisson, *Strategic Management*.

[71] A. R. Owens, "Exploring the Benefits of Contact Centre Offshoring: A Study of Trends and Practices for the Australian Business Sector," *International Journal of Human Resource Management* 25 (2014): 571–587; and C. M. Solomon, "Moving Jobs to Offshore Markets: Why It's Done and How It Works," *Workforce*, July 1999, pp. 51–55.

[72] G. Hofstede, "Cultural Constraints in Management Theories," *Academy of Management Executive*, February 1993, pp. 81–90.

[73] P. J. Dowling, M. Festing, and A. D. Engle, *International Human Resource Management: Managing People in a Multinational Context*, 5th ed. (Cincinnati: South-Western College Publishing, 2013).

[74] N. Doherty and M. Dickmann, "Exposing the Symbolic Capital of International Assignments," *International Journal of Human Resource Management* 20 (2009): 301–320; M. A. Carpenter, W. G. Sanders, and H. B. Gregersen, "Bundling Human Capital with Organizational Context: The Impact of International Experience on Multinational Firm Performance and CEO Pay," *Academy of Management Journal* 44 (2001): 493–511; and C. M. Daily, S. T. Certo, and D. R. Dalton, "International Experience in the Executive Suite: The Path to Prosperity?" *Strategic Management Journal* 21 (2000): 515–523.

[75] Daily, Certo, and Dalton, "International Experience in the Executive Suite."

[76] A. France-Presse, "General Motors VP Knew of Ignition Switch Defect, Documents Show," *Industry Week*, June 27, 2014, http://www.industryweek.com/corporate-responsibility/general-motors-vp-knew-ignition-switch-defect-documents-show.

[77] Jessica Bennet (November 30, 2017), "The #MeToo Moment: When the Blinders Come Off," *The New York Times*, https://www.nytimes.com/2017/11/30/us/the-metoo-moment.html?rref=collection%2Fseriescollection%2Fmetoo-moment&action=click&contentCollection=us&region=stream&module=stream_unit&version=latest&contentPlacement=8&pgtype=collection.

[78] S. P. Graves, S. Waddock, and M. Kelly, "The Methodology Behind the Corporate Citizen Rankings," *Business Ethics: Corporate Social Responsibility Report*, March/April 2002.

[79] Anonymous, "Corporate Responsibility Magazine Announces 2018 100 Best Corporate Citizens," May 7, 2018, CSR Newswire, http://www.csrwire.com/press_releases/41014-Corporate-Responsibility-Magazine-Announces-2018-100-Best-Corporate-Citizens.

[80] S. Adams (April 22, 2015), Forbes Online, "America's 100 Best Corporate Citizens in 2015," http://www.forbes.com/sites/susanadams/2015/04/22/americas-100-best-corporate-citizens-in-2015/#34707e9a61df.

[81] Z. Tang, C. E. Hull, and S. Rothenberg, "How Corporate Social Responsibility Engagement Strategy Moderates the CSR-Financial Performance Relationship," *Journal of Management Studies* 49 (2012): 1274–1303; J. S. Chun, Y. Shin, J. N. Choi, and M. S. Kim, "How Does Corporate Ethics Contribute to Firm Financial Performance? The Mediating Role of Collective Organizational Commitment and Organizational Citizenship Behavior," *Journal of Management* 39 (2013): 853–877.

[82] D. Brown, "HR Feeling Pressure to Act Unethically," *Canadian HR Reporter* 16 (May 19, 2003): 1.

[83] Sarah Perrin, "Resisting the Pressure to Act Unethically," accaglobal.com, February 1, 2017, http://www.accaglobal.com/us/en/member/member/accounting-business/2017/02/corporate/ethics-pressure.html# (accessed June 7, 2018).

[84] "How to Help Reinvigorate Your Organization's Ethics Program," *HR Focus* 80 (June 2003): 7.

[85] Nike website, www.nikebiz.com; "Survey: Sweating for Fashion," *The Economist*, March 6, 2004, p. 14; and R. Locke, T. Kochan, M. Romis, and F. Qin, "Beyond Corporate Codes of Conduct: Work Organization and Labour Standards at Nike's Suppliers," *International Labour Review* 146 (2007): 21–40.

[86] Nike website, "Quick Facts: As of the End of FY13," July 29, 2014, http://www.nikeresponsibility.com/report/content/chapter/labor.

[87] "Ethics Awareness Training," Lockheed Martin, https://www.lockheedmartin.com/en-us/who-we-are/ethics/ethics-awareness-training.html (accessed May 30, 2018) A. Meisler, "Lockheed Is Doing Right and Doing Well," *Workforce*, March 2004, http://www.workforce.com/articles/lockheed-is-doing-right-and-doing-well.

[88] A. Mees and J. Bonham, "Corporate Social Responsibility Belongs with HR," *Canadian HR Reporter* 17 (April 5, 2004): 11–12.

[89] Sarah Perrin, "Resisting the Pressure to Act Unethically," accaglobal.com, February 1, 2017, http://www.accaglobal.com/us/en/member/member/accounting-business/2017/02/corporate/ethics-pressure.html# (accessed June 7, 2018).

# Chapter 3

# Regulatory Issues

## Learning Objectives

**AFTER READING THIS CHAPTER, YOU SHOULD BE ABLE TO:**

**1** Discuss why we have equal employment laws.

**2** Describe basic equal employment opportunity (EEO) concepts.

**3** Identify the categories of discriminatory activity and how to prevent their occurrence.

**4** Explain the background and basic principles of the main EEO laws.

**5** Describe the EEO responsibilities of multinational employers.

**6** Explain the filing process for discrimination charges.

**7** Identify the components of an affirmative action plan.

**8** Discuss the main points of legislation related to employment.

HR CHALLENGE

ENVIRONMENTAL INFLUENCES | ORGANIZATIONAL DEMANDS | **REGULATORY ISSUES**

PRIMARY HR ACTIVITIES

Work Design & Workforce Planning

Managing Employee Competencies

Managing Employee Attitudes & Behaviors

Employee Contributions

Competitive Advantage

# Equal Employment Opportunity and Other Workplace Laws

Regardless of your main motivation for working, we expect that you would like to be treated fairly and with respect in the workplace. You want an equal chance to get interesting and challenging jobs, promotions, and, ultimately, the bigger paychecks that come with all those opportunities. The employees that you will manage or currently manage want the same things.

In Chapter 2, we described how two sets of HR challenges, organizational demands and environmental influences, affect employee management. This chapter is about the third HR challenge, regulatory issues (highlighted in Exhibit 3.1). We devote a full chapter to this topic because of its extensive impact on employee management practices. Compliance with employment regulatory requirements strengthens the ability of a company to attract and retain top talent. Noncompliance can negatively impact the reputation of a company and lead to monetary fines.

Employment regulations derive from laws passed by Congress, state legislatures, and local governing bodies. They also originate from executive orders enacted by the president of the United States for the purpose of managing the operations of the federal government and the operations of federal contractors. Employment regulations focus on the fair treatment of individuals in the workplace. They require

**EXHIBIT 3.1**

Framework for the Strategic Management of Human Resources

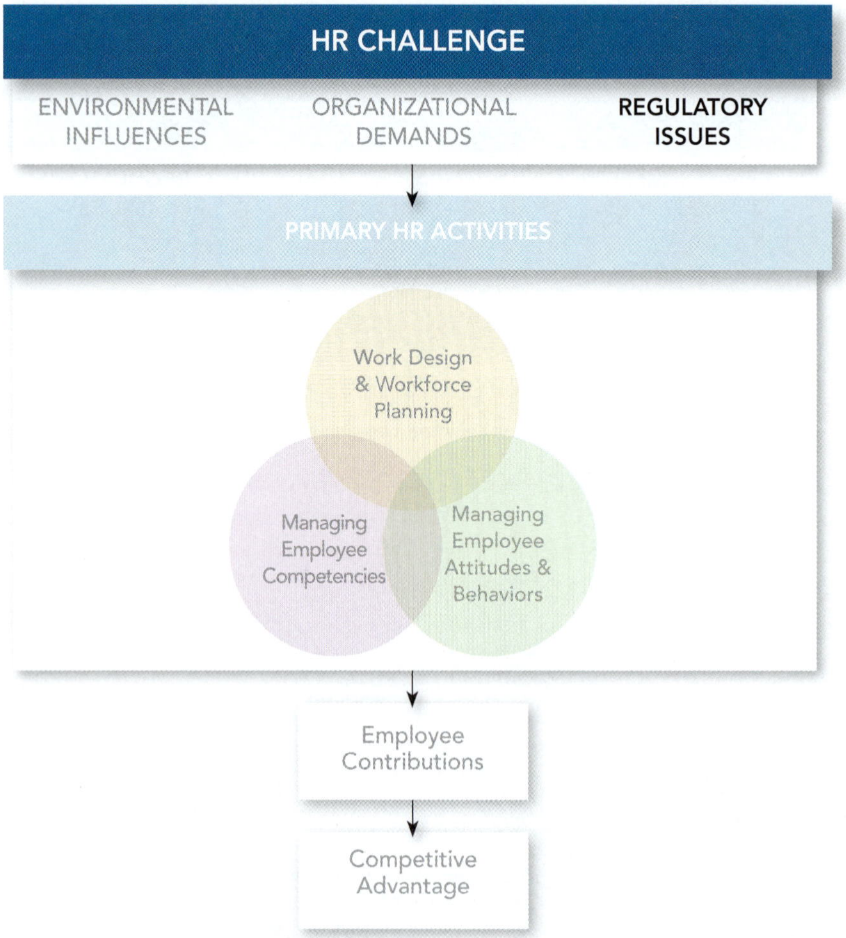

employers to concentrate on the qualifications of the individuals that they employ rather than gender, nationality, or other characteristics not related to an applicant's or employee's ability to perform the job. These regulations influence employee contributions to organizational performance by guiding managers in the design of work and in the management of employee competencies, attitudes, and behaviors. A vital factor in whether the organization can gain and maintain a competitive advantage is how an organization manages its workforce.

In this chapter, we focus primarily on regulations in the form of **equal employment opportunity (EEO)** laws and other regulations related to fair treatment of employees. We will cover additional regulations in the chapters for which they are most relevant. For instance, Chapter 10 focuses on compensation. In that chapter, we will talk about the Fair Labor Standards Act (FLSA), which emphasizes what employers can and cannot do with regard to paying employees for work done. We introduce issues related to diversity management in this chapter and then expand on them throughout the text.

**equal employment opportunity (EEO)**

the term used to describe laws, regulations, and processes related to fair treatment of employees

## Introduction to Equal Employment Opportunity (EEO)

EEO laws and executive orders are intended to eliminate discrimination in the workplace. **Discrimination** means treating people differently. We choose to treat people differently every day. How we treat our supervisor is different from how we treat our peers at work. Discrimination becomes problematic, however, when people are not treated fairly because of characteristics they possess that have nothing to do with their ability to perform a particular job.

EEO laws exist on the federal, state, and local levels and are created following the same basic model as other laws. Exhibit 3.2 illustrates a simple overview of the process that leads to the passage of an EEO law and what happens following passage of such a law.

**discrimination**

treating people differently in employment situations because of characteristics, such as race, color, and gender, that have nothing to do with their ability to perform a particular job

### EXHIBIT 3.2
#### Development and Implementation of EEO Laws

Congress lobbied to address societal or economic problem

Law passed to address problem

Enforcement agency designated to oversee compliance with law

Agency develops and communicates guidelines and regulations

Employers comply

Courts hear cases of violations of law or issues of interpretation

**Equal Employment Opportunity Commission (EEOC)**

the federal agency responsible for enforcing compliance with antidiscrimination laws such as the Civil Rights Act of 1964 (CRA 64), the Age Discrimination in Employment Act (ADEA), and the Americans with Disabilities Act (ADA)

**Office of Federal Contract Compliance Programs (OFCCP)**

the federal agency responsible for developing guidelines and overseeing compliance with antidiscrimination laws relative to executive orders

Two regulatory agencies oversee compliance with the equal employment regulations: the **Equal Employment Opportunity Commission (EEOC)** and the **Office of Federal Contract Compliance Programs (OFCCP)**. The EEOC is responsible for developing guidelines and overseeing compliance with most antidiscrimination laws. The OFCCP is responsible for the same activities relative to executive orders.

Noncompliance with antidiscrimination laws and executive orders can lead to negative consequences, including fines to the company and charges of discrimination that result in costly, time-consuming legal battles. Here is an example. In July 2017, Bass Pro Outdoor World settled a lawsuit brought by the EEOC in September 2011. In that lawsuit, the EEOC charged Bass Pro with engaging in a practice of discrimination for years by passing over African-American and Hispanic job applicants because of their race or national origin. Further, the charges claimed that Bass Pro unlawfully retaliated against employees who raised concerns about this widespread pattern of discrimination and noted that the company failed to keep appropriate hiring records. In the settlement of the lawsuit, while not admitting liability, Bass Pro agreed to pay $10.5 million and to hire a director of diversity and inclusion. A portion of the $10.5 million was designated to provide monetary relief to applicants who claimed they were discriminated against. Funds from the settlement were also designated to strengthen the company's efforts to recruit minorities. Also, some of the funds may be used for programs for engaging inner city youth in outdoor activities. As a result of the EEOC case, the company lost much productive work time and had to pay extensive legal fees. More importantly, competent applicants believed they were the victims of discrimination solely because of their race or ethnicity.[1]

Before we discuss the EEO laws, we introduce some of the concepts that you need to know in order to understand the laws. These concepts include protected classifications, bona fide occupational qualifications (BFOQ), business necessity, and discriminatory practices such as disparate treatment, disparate impact, harassment, and retaliation. A good understanding of these concepts will be important throughout this book.

## Protected Classifications

**protected classifications**

the demographic characteristics that cannot be used for employment decisions, also called *protected classes*

The primary objective of antidiscrimination legislation and executive orders is to ensure that individuals are given equal opportunity in the workplace. Each law or executive order identifies one or more demographic characteristics that a company generally cannot use to make employment decisions. An employer cannot refuse to hire Asians or Muslims simply because they are Asian or Muslim. Doing so violates EEO laws, which specifically forbid using the characteristics of race (Asian) or religion (Islam) as the basis for employment decisions. The demographic characteristics that cannot be used for employment decisions are known as **protected classifications**, or protected classes. The main protected classifications are:

- Race
- Sex (including gender identity and sexual orientation)
- Religion
- Color
- National origin
- Age (being 40 or older)
- Disability
- Veteran status
- Pregnancy
- Genetic information

As you read through this chapter, you will see that some laws specify which group within a protected classification is protected, while others do not. When you read about the Age Discrimination in Employment Act (ADEA), you will see that it specifies that individuals age 40 and older are the protected class. In contrast, when you read about Title VII of the Civil Rights Act of 1964 (CRA 64), you will see that the Act specifies that sex is one of five protected classes. It does not state that being female is the only sex protected from discrimination. People sometimes believe that is the case because traditionally females are more likely to be the victims of discrimination in the workplace than males.

## Bona Fide Occupational Qualification (BFOQ) and Business Necessity

Are there times when sex or nationality or another protected classification *can* be used to make an employment decision? That's a good question. Let's take a look at when that can happen, by way of an example.

A modeling agency has a client that designs clothes exclusively for women. Perhaps not surprisingly, the agency decides to hire only women to model the clothes. The employer in this example would claim that *gender* (the term that we will use interchangeably with *sex* in this book, and the more common term used now) is a **bona fide occupational qualification (BFOQ)**. A BFOQ exists when a protected classification can legally be used to make an employment decision. The modeling agency could argue that it can give preference in hiring to one gender, female, over the other gender, male, because of **business necessity**. Claiming that a protected classification is a business necessity means that the employment practice has some relationship to legitimate business goals and that it is essential to the company's survival. In our example, the clothing designer focuses exclusively on women's clothing and needs to sell the clothes to buyers looking for women's clothing to stay in business. Gender, therefore, would be an acceptable BFOQ in this case.

The general guideline accepted by the EEOC and the courts to determine the appropriateness of a protected class as a BFOQ came from a landmark 1971 case, *Diaz v. Pan American World Airways*.[2] Celio Diaz wanted to be a domestic flight cabin attendant for Pan American World Airways (Pan Am). He did not get the job because he was the wrong gender. He subsequently filed a charge of gender discrimination. Pan Am argued that females are more nurturing, give more courteous personal service, and generally make flights more pleasurable for passengers than can males. In the late 1960s and early 1970s, most air travelers would have been business*men*.

In response, the 5th Circuit Court of Appeals noted that gender can be a selection criterion only if it affects business operations. Business convenience is not a reason for using gender as a BFOQ. Consequently, an employer who uses gender as a BFOQ needs to show that all or substantially all members of that sex cannot reasonably perform some aspect of that job, and that the aspect is a business necessity. By the way, Pan Am already had 283 male stewards (what we now call flight attendants) on its foreign flights at the time of the case, providing further evidence that gender was not an appropriate BFOQ.[3]

In summary, sometimes an employer *can* make a case that gender, religion, national origin, or age is a BFOQ. The likelihood of successfully doing so, however, is usually very low. Employers can never use race or skin color as a BFOQ, for any reason.

## Discriminatory Practices

Discriminatory practices can typically be grouped under one of four categories: disparate treatment, disparate impact, harassment, and retaliation. Let's take a look at what each of these involves.

**bona fide occupational qualification (BFOQ)**

a BFOQ exists when a protected classification can legally be used to make an employment decision

**business necessity**

an employment practice that has some relationship to legitimate business goals and is essential to the company's survival

### Disparate Treatment

Most people think of discrimination as being obvious and intentional in nature, occurring when a protected classification is used as the basis for an employment decision. Not hiring a qualified woman simply because she is female would be obvious and intentional discrimination. Under this definition, if someone is turned down for an employment opportunity and can show that it was because of a particular attribute that is protected by law—religion, sex, race, or whatever protected class is at issue—that individual has the right to file charges against the employer. This type of discrimination is known as **disparate treatment**. In disparate treatment cases, an individual is treated differently *because of* the characteristic that defines the protected class. This term also means that the company *intentionally* discriminated against a person or persons because of the characteristic and a BFOQ for that characteristic does not exist. Company Spotlight 3.1 describes a case of disparate treatment discrimination in which age discrimination occurred.

An employee who believes that he or she has been the victim of disparate treatment must make a ***prima facie* case**, or preliminary case, using the **McDonnell Douglas test**, named after the *McDonnell Douglas Corp. v. Greene*[4] 1973 U.S. Supreme Court case, which identified a four-step test. To make a case for disparate treatment, the plaintiff must show all of the following:

1. That he or she is a member of a protected class
2. That he or she applied for the job (or other employment opportunity, such as being eligible for a raise or promotion) and was qualified
3. That he or she was rejected
4. That someone else got the job, or the employer continued to seek applications from individuals with the plaintiff's qualifications

If the plaintiff successfully makes a *prima facie* case, the burden of proof shifts to the employer to provide a legitimate, job-related reason for the decision.[5] For instance, an employer might show that the person selected had more relevant experience or performed better on selection measures.

**disparate treatment**

treating individuals differently in employment situations because of their membership in a protected class

***prima facie* case**

establishing the basis for a case of discrimination

**McDonnell Douglas test**

a four-step test used to make a case of disparate treatment

## COMPANY SPOTLIGHT  **3.1**

### Disparate Treatment at Texas Roadhouse

In March 2017, Texas Roadhouse agreed to settle an age discrimination suit brought by the EEOC. The company was charged with engaging in a nationwide pattern of disparate treatment against individuals age 40 or older. Such discrimination is in direct violation of the Age Discrimination in Employment Act (ADEA). The EEOC had filed the suit on behalf of a class of applicants alleging that they had been denied front-of-the-house jobs as servers, bartenders, hosts, and server assistants at the restaurants in the chain because of their age.

Texas Roadhouse entered into a consent decree that included a $12 million settlement for payment to individuals who were discriminated against on the basis of age between January 1, 2007 and December 31, 2014. The company also agreed to change its hiring and recruiting practices, add a diversity director, and fund a position for a compliance monitor who is tasked with ensuring that the company abides by the terms of the consent decree. The decree is in force for three and a half years.

*Source:* Adapted from Equal Employment Opportunity Commission, Texas Roadhouse to Pay $12 million to Settle EEOC Age Discrimination Lawsuit March 31, 2017, http://www.eeoc.gov/eeoc/newsroom/release/3-31-17.cfm.

The courts have been clear that even though an employer may have had a job-related reason for a decision, discrimination has occurred if protected class membership played any part in the outcome. In other words, a **mixed motive** has affected the outcome. A legitimate reason for an employment decision exists, but the decision also was motivated by an illegitimate reason (such as membership in a protected class).

**mixed motive**

a legitimate reason for an employment decision exists, but the decision also was motivated by an illegitimate reason.

## Disparate Impact

*Disparate treatment* refers to intentionally unfair and illegal treatment of a particular individual. But discrimination also may take a more subtle and usually unintentional form, known as **disparate impact**, or adverse impact. Disparate impact occurs when a company uses an employment practice that unintentionally discriminates against members of a protected class. For example, a job requirement at a home improvement store might state that all employees must be six feet tall to perform a job that requires regularly reaching up to obtain items from high shelves. This job requirement might not be intended to discriminate against anyone. It may, however, lead to discrimination against several protected classifications, including females and members of some minority groups. The average height for women in the United States is 5′4″; the average height for men is 5′9″.[6] Although it would not be intentional discrimination, the height requirement would yield an unequal outcome for women because, on average, fewer women than men would be tall enough to be hired.

**disparate impact**

discrimination that occurs when an employment practice results in members of a protected class being treated less favorably than members of a nonprotected class, even though the discrimination was not intentional

A useful way to think about the difference between disparate treatment and disparate impact is that disparate treatment focuses on the *treatment* of a particular person or group of persons within a protected class, and explicitly considers the *motivation* for the company's actions. Disparate impact, on the other hand, focuses on the *consequences* of the employment practices.

The court case that identified disparate impact as discrimination was *Griggs v. Duke Power Company*,[7] decided in 1971. At a Duke Power generating plant, black employees challenged the employer's selection requirements. Specifically, to be hired for or to be transferred to other jobs at the plant, applicants had to possess a high school diploma and pass two professionally prepared aptitude tests—selection requirements not designed to measure an applicant's ability to learn a particular job. Also, prior to the passage of major civil rights legislation in 1964, the company had a history of discriminating on the basis of race, even to the extent of restricting black employees to the lowest-level jobs within one department and paying them less than the lowest-paying job in the other four operating departments.

In reviewing the case, the U.S. Supreme Court held that the company had not intended to discriminate; however, the selection criteria resulted in discrimination. The relevance of the criteria was suspect because there were employees doing just fine in the jobs in question who did not have high school diplomas and who had not taken the tests. Also, blacks in the area were less likely than whites to have a high school diploma and would be less likely to pass the tests because of their lack of education. The employer could not show that having a high school diploma and passing the tests were necessary to be able to perform the jobs. Thus, discrimination occurred, even though that was not the company's intent.[8]

The issue in disparate impact is whether the employer can show that there is a valid, job-related reason for using the selection criterion that discriminates. In establishing selection criteria or deciding who gets raises or promotions or training, managers need to think through the possible outcomes of their choices. Lack of intent is not an acceptable defense in a disparate impact case. Most important, using nonjob-related criteria for making such decisions ultimately affects the success of the organization as it rewards the wrong behaviors and attitudes. We will discuss these issues in more detail later, after we elaborate on how a plaintiff can make a case that disparate impact has occurred.

To make a case for disparate impact, the plaintiff must first demonstrate that the outcome of the employment practice was less favorable for his or her protected class than for the majority. The **four-fifths rule** is a guideline generally accepted by the courts and the EEOC for making such a *prima facie* case of disparate impact. To see how it works, let's consider an example.

Assume that your company is expanding and needs to hire multiple people for the same job. You place an advertisement in the local newspaper and 475 people apply for the 38 openings. Some applicants are white, and some are Asian. A selection criterion used in the hiring process requires passing a test written in English, even though English was not listed in the advertisement as a job requirement. After your company completes its hiring process and fills the 38 openings, several Asian applicants express concern that they were not selected for the job even though they were qualified. To determine whether there is disparate impact, as these individuals believe, you will need to know the number of job applicants from each group and the number hired from each group. The breakdown looks like this:

| Applicants | Number Hired | Selection Ratio |
| --- | --- | --- |
| Asian = 120 | 7 | 7/120 = 5.8% |
| White = 355 | 31 | 31/355 = 8.7% |

Once you have this information, you need to determine whether 5.8%, the selection rate for the Asian applicants, is equal to at least four-fifths, or 80%, of the 8.7% selection rate for the majority group. In this case, when you divide the selection rate for the Asian applicants by the selection rate for the white applicants, you find the following:

5.8% (selection rate for Asian) / 8.7% (selection rate for whites) = 67%

67% is less than 80% (or the desired four-fifths rate)

Because 67% is below the four-fifths threshold, evidence of disparate impact exists.

A cautionary note is in order here. As a manager, you should not try to "hire by the numbers." A manager should not simply calculate how many minority group members need to be hired and hire that many to be in "compliance" based on the four-fifths rule. Doing so defeats the purpose of hiring based on job-related qualifications. Remember, your goal as a manager is to ensure that you have the best-qualified employees so that your company can achieve its goals. Hiring by the numbers is not the way to accomplish that goal. In later chapters, you will learn how to develop job-related selection criteria so that you will know how to hire the best talent.

Once the plaintiffs (in our example the Asian applicants) make a *prima facie* case of disparate impact for the particular practice that is discriminatory, the employer can use one of several defenses to support use of the practice, as shown in Exhibit 3.3. First, companies may provide evidence that the practice in question is *job related*. Companies can do this by demonstrating that the employment practice is connected to a measure of job performance or that it is directly related in some other way to the ability to perform the job. Requiring a pilot's license for a job as a first officer for a commercial airline would be job related, even if it meant that certain protected classes would be less likely to be hired for the job.

---

**four-fifths rule**

a guideline generally accepted by the courts and the EEOC for making a *prima facie* case of disparate impact by showing that an employment practice results in members of a protected class being treated less favorably by an employment practice than members of a nonprotected class

---

**EXHIBIT 3.3**

Acceptable Defenses in Disparate Impact Cases

| |
|---|
| Provide evidence that the practice is *job related*. |
| Demonstrate the practice is a *business necessity*. |
| Show the decision results from a *bona fide seniority system*. |

A second possible defense in a disparate impact case is that the practice is a *business necessity*. A strenuous physical-ability test as a job requirement for a firefighter might have disparate impact for women, but it is a business necessity for fire departments. Firefighters must be physically fit and capable of lifting heavy loads, such as fire hoses and people. A fire department can readily show that passing the test is a strong predictor of firefighter safety on the job. On the other hand, CSX Transportation ended up paying $3.2 million to settle a class action lawsuit filed by the EEOC over the use of physical strength tests. CSX had used physical strength tests for current and potential employees in several job categories, which resulted in disparate impact for women. The tests were a requirement for workers to be hired or promoted or transferred into various jobs, including conductors and material handler/clerks.[9]

The existence of a *bona fide seniority system* is a third defense that companies can offer. Seniority systems give employees rights based on their length of time with the company. Rights can include opportunities for better working hours, for instance. A bona fide seniority system is one that is officially sanctioned by the organization. To successfully use this defense, the employer must show that the seniority system has been in effect for some time and was not created to keep certain protected classifications from being eligible for the job in question. Most union contracts include seniority systems.

## Harassment

The type of harassment that you are probably most familiar with in the workplace is sexual harassment. However, **harassment** occurs when employees are subjected to unwanted and unwelcome treatment because of their race, color, religion, sex, national origin, age, disability, or genetic information.[10] Harassment can include, but is not limited to, offensive jokes, unwelcome comments related to a person's protected class, graffiti targeting the protected class, and physical threats. Because of the harassment, employees experience a hostile work environment. A **hostile work environment** exists whenever an employee is the subject of unwelcome harassment because of his or her membership in a protected class, and that harassment is severe and abusive.

Such was the case for three former employees of Olympia Construction in Alabama. The three were subjected to racial slurs and intimidations and then were fired because they complained about their treatment to the EEOC. In settling the suit, the EEOC required the company to pay $100,000 to the former employees and put in place policies and practices to ensure that future harassment and retaliation do not occur.[11]

Later in this chapter, we provide more details about the types of harassment that can occur in the workplace. Exhibit 3.4 outlines what a company and its managers should do to reduce the likelihood of harassment. There is a lot of overlap among the lists. Managers are agents of the company and have the responsibility for implementing the company guidelines, hence the overlap.

**harassment**

occurs when employees are subjected to unwanted and unwelcome treatment because of their race, color, religion, sex, national origin, age, disability, or genetic information

**hostile work environment**

exists whenever an employee is the subject of unwelcome harassment because of his or her membership in a protected class and that harassment is severe and abusive

## EXHIBIT 3.4

### Guidelines for Reducing Harassment in the Workplace

| Steps Company Should Take | Steps Managers Should Follow |
|---|---|
| 1. Develop and regularly communicate antiharassment policy to all employees, providing examples of the behaviors that are considered harassment. | 1. Recognize that you are responsible for creating a harassment-free environment for your employees. |
| 2. Provide training to managers, making sure that they understand the policy and know that they are responsible for its enforcement. | 2. Make sure you understand what constitutes harassment and what your role is when a problem occurs. |
| 3. Establish a process for reporting incidents to someone other than the employee's supervisor.[a] | 3. Ensure that employees receive training on and understand the antiharassment policy and know their role in following the policy. |
| 4. Investigate all reports of harassment immediately. | 4. Report any incidents of harassment immediately. |
| 5. Treat individuals reporting harassment with respect. | 5. Make sure that incidents are investigated and individuals making the reports are not further harassed. |
| 6. Take prompt action against harassers, ensuring that disciplinary action is appropriate to the nature of the offense. | 6. Participate in any follow-up actions requested. |
| 7. Follow-up with the victim of harassment to ensure that the behaviors have stopped and no retaliation is occurring. | 7. Always maintain confidentiality about situations that occur. |

[a]This step is especially important in case the harasser is the supervisor or in case the supervisor knows about but has ignored the harassment. A member of the HR department or the affirmative action officer can serve in this role. In a smaller firm without an HR department or affirmative action officer, employees may be directed to speak with a designated manager as long as that person is not the direct supervisor of the employee. In the event the designated manager is the supervisor of the employee with the concern, the policy should direct the employee to an alternate manager.

## Retaliation

**retaliation**

occurs when an employer takes an adverse action against an employee who has filed a discrimination complaint

Many of the laws that prohibit discrimination have nonretaliation requirements. **Retaliation** occurs when an employer takes an adverse action against an employee who has filed a discrimination complaint.[12] Retaliation is often a punishment, or a threat of punishment, because an employee exercises the rights provided under the antidiscrimination laws. Retaliation can take many forms, including but not limited to,

- denying a promotion to the employee who is otherwise qualified,
- demoting the employee,
- suspending the employee for a period of time,
- writing a negative evaluation of the employee, and/or
- threatening the employee if the complaint is not withdrawn.

When a manager takes any of these actions, he or she is discriminating against the employee. Company Spotlight 3.2 describes the case of a company in Washington State charged by the EEOC in a sexual harassment and retaliation case.

Now that we have defined many of the terms associated with EEO and regulatory issues, let's explore the laws themselves.

## COMPANY SPOTLIGHT  3.2

### Sexual Harassment and Retaliation at Stemilt Growers: The Case of the Female Tractor Driver

Stemilt Growers and its wholly owned subsidiary, Stemilt Ag Services, is the largest grower of organic tree fruit in the United States. Stemilt has over 150 acres of orchards in eastern Washington State. In April 2018, the company was ordered to pay $95,000 to a female tractor driver who was sexually harassed by her direct supervisor. On the second day on her job at a new location at the orchard where she worked, her supervisor drove her to a remote area and propositioned and tried to kiss her. She asked him to stop and told him she was only there to do her job. Following her rebuff of the supervisor, she was assigned to pick up trash and was excluded from meetings with other tractor drivers. After she reported the harassment to upper management, she was told that she could continue working under this supervisor or take a transfer to a lower-paying job sorting fruit at a warehouse.

The EEOC brought the lawsuit on behalf of the plaintiff and charged the company with sexual harassment and retaliation. Such conduct is a violation of Title VII of the Civil Rights Act of 1964. The EEOC first tried to reach a prelitigation settlement with the company through the agency's reconciliation process, but that effort failed.

In addition to the $95,000 that the company has to pay the tractor driver, it has to provide antidiscrimination policy and annual training for management and staff, develop a complaint handling process, and hold supervisors accountable for how they respond to allegations.

*Sources:* Adapted from "Stemilt Growers and AG Services to Pay $95,000 to Settle EEOC Harassment, Retaliation Suit," Equal Employment Opportunity Commission, https://www.eeoc.gov/eeoc/newsroom /release/4-3-18b.cfm; D. Wheat, "EEOC Alleges Sexual Harassment of Stemilt Employee," Capital Press, June 13, 2017, http://www .capitalpress.com/orchards/20170613/eeoc-alleges-sexual-harassment-of-stemilt-employee.

## Equal Employment Legislation

By now, you should have a good understanding of the basic concepts underlying EEO laws and the types of problems that can occur in the workplace. These problems have led to the creation of laws and executive orders to protect employees from discrimination. As you study them, remember that even though you may be thinking about them from the perspective of a manager, they provide protection for you as an employee as well. Exhibit 3.5 outlines the main EEO laws that we discuss in this chapter.

### Equal Pay Act of 1963 (EPA)

Most people today agree that marital status, gender, and other nonjob-related factors should not influence how much a person gets paid. However, prior to 1963, employers frequently considered gender and marital status when making such decisions. It was not uncommon for employers to pay males more than females, particularly if the males were married. Newspaper advertisements often had separate listings for male and female jobs, and companies routinely reserved their higher-paying jobs for males. The assumption was that males were the primary breadwinners for their families and needed to make the most money. Even when males and females performed the same jobs, males generally received higher pay.

## EXHIBIT 3.5

### Equal Employment Opportunity Laws and Executive Orders

| Regulation | Provisions | Covered Employees and Enforcement Agency |
| --- | --- | --- |
| The Equal Pay Act of 1963 (EPA) | Prohibits discrimination in pay on the basis of gender for individuals performing jobs with the same skill, effort, responsibility, and working conditions unless a factor other than gender is being used to determine the pay difference. | All employers with one or more employees, including the federal government. *Enforced by EEOC* |
| Title VII of the Civil Rights Act of 1964 (CRA 64) | Prohibits discrimination on the basis of race, color, religion, sex (includes gender identity and sexual orientation), or national origin; established the EEOC as an enforcement agency. | Employers with 15 or more employees, including all private employers; federal, state, and local governments; educational institutions; private and public employment agencies; labor organizations; and joint labor management committees that control apprenticeship and training programs. *Enforced by EEOC* |
| Executive Order 11246 (EO 11246) | Similar to Title VII; prohibits employment discrimination on the basis of race, color, religion, sex, national origin, sexual orientation, and gender identity by federal contractors; requires affirmative action plans for federal contractors. | Federal contractors with contracts greater than $10,000 must not discriminate; federal contractors with 50 or more employees and contracts over $50,000 must have affirmative action plans. *Enforced by OFCCP* |
| The Age Discrimination in Employment Act of 1967 (ADEA) | Prohibits employment discrimination of individuals aged 40 or older. | All employers with 20 or more employees, including employment agencies and labor organizations; federal, state, and local governments; and school districts. *Enforced by EEOC* |
| The Pregnancy Discrimination Act of 1978 (PDA) | Specifies that women who are pregnant or who are affected by pregnancy-related conditions are to be treated the same as other applicants or employees with similar limitations or disabilities. | Same as Title VII of the Civil Rights Act of 1964. *Enforced by EEOC* |
| Title I of the Americans with Disabilities Act of 1990 (ADA) and ADA Amendments Act of 2008 (ADAA) | Prohibits discrimination in employment practices against qualified individuals with disabilities who can perform the job with or without reasonable accommodation. | Same as Title VII of the Civil Rights Act of 1964. *Enforced by EEOC* |
| Sections 102 and 103 of the Civil Rights Act of 1991 (CRA 91) | Clarifies the defense in disparate impact cases, provides for monetary damages in cases of intentional discrimination, and eliminates race norming. | Same as Title VII of the Civil Rights Act of 1964. *Enforced by EEOC* |
| Title II of the Genetic Information Nondiscrimination Act of 2008 (GINA) | Prohibits discrimination against employees or applicants because of genetic information and restricts requesting, requiring, or purchasing genetic information, as well as disclosing such information. | Same as Title VII of the Civil Rights Act of 1964. *Enforced by Department of Labor's Employee Benefits Security Administration* |

In 1963, Congress made it clear to employers that such pay differences were no longer acceptable when it passed the Equal Pay Act (EPA) as an amendment to the Fair Labor Standards Act (FLSA). The FLSA of 1938 had established general guidelines for employee pay, but the EPA specified that gender could not be a factor in paying employees. We will cover the FLSA in detail in Chapter 10; we include the EPA in this discussion because it is an antidiscrimination law.

Today, if a male and a female in the same company are performing jobs that require *substantially* equal skill, effort, and responsibility and that have similar working conditions, the law requires the employer to pay them equally. Pay differences for employees in the same job are allowed if they are based on merit, seniority, quality or quantity of production, or another nongender-related factor, such as night shifts versus day shifts. It is up to the employer to prove that the stated reason for the pay difference is an allowable **affirmative defense**.[13]

**affirmative defense**
factual information presented by the defendent that leads to a claim by a plaintiff being defeated even if her or his claim is true

The EPA was passed more than 50 years ago, and yet a gender pay gap still exists. In 2016, females working full-time in the United States typically were earning only 80 percent of what males were earning according to research by the American Association of University Women (AAUW). In 2017, females with a bachelor's degree were earning only 74 percent of what males were earning.[14] Several arguments have been offered to explain this continuing gap including women's later entry into the workplace compared to men's, women taking time out to have and raise children, gender differences in negotiation skills at time of hire, percentage of women in traditionally female jobs, and ongoing gender discrimination.

The state of Massachusetts took a novel approach to attempt to close the gender pay gap by passing a pay equity law. Effective in 2018, employers in Massachusetts are prohibited from asking job applicants about their previous salaries. This prohibition applies to both application forms and the interview. The law also broadens the definition of "equal work" and prohibits employees from discussing salary among themselves. Applicants can still volunteer previous salary information, and employers can still negotiate their salary with potential hires. Other cities and states, such as New York City and Oregon, have begun to pass laws that prohibit asking applicants about previous salaries as well.[15]

## Title VII of the Civil Rights Act of 1964 (CRA 64)

Imagine this scenario: You get on the bus to go to work and are told that you have to move to the back even though there are plenty of seats up front. You get to work and are thirsty. When you go to the water fountain, you find that there are two fountains, and one has a sign above it that says "Whites Only." Later, you try to talk to your boss about a promotion. He tells you that "your kind" are not eligible for promotions. Blacks in the United States, and to an extent Hispanics, had just these experiences before the passage of the Civil Rights Act of 1964. Across the nation, but particularly in the South, Blacks were considered second-class citizens. They were not allowed to vote, were denied entry to many public places, and were restricted to separate seating areas in public places. These events were commonplace even though the Civil Rights Acts of 1866 and 1871, plus the 13th and 14th Amendments to the U.S. Constitution, had attempted to provide equal rights to all persons.

Not surprisingly, Blacks were extremely disadvantaged economically. Education was segregated, with Black schools traditionally lower in quality than white schools. Think about what it would be like not to have an education, and to have a job in a segregated workplace that offers only low-level, low-paying jobs. These conditions help you begin to understand why Blacks had little money and few opportunities to improve their quality of life during that time in history. Many U.S. citizens at the time believed that these conditions affected the entire nation negatively. Low income led to reduced buying power, which led to reduced production, which led to fewer jobs. A segregated society led to the need for duplicate facilities, such as schools and other public services, as well as duplicate spaces in the workplace, such as cafeterias and restrooms. Money that could have been used for increased wages and in other productive ways was used to keep Blacks segregated.[16]

The civil rights movement of the 1960s brought to light the need for reform. The world watched as peaceful demonstrations led by Martin Luther King, Jr. and others to call attention to discrimination and its outcomes turned violent. Police beat up and abused demonstrators in other ways. Seeing this abuse galvanized the nation, forcing it to confront the issue of discrimination.[17] Finally, Congress passed the Civil Rights Act of 1964 to address the societal and economic need for change. The passage of the Act sent the message that the time had come to abolish discrimination in employment and in other areas of society.

Title VII is the part of the Civil Rights Act that specifically addresses employment discrimination. Title VII prohibits employers from discriminating against any individual on the basis of that individual's race, color, religion, sex, or national origin. Employers with 15 or more employees, including federal, state, and local governments, employment agencies, and labor unions, have to abide by this law. Also, the law covers U.S. citizens and legal residents of the United States who are working for U.S. companies in other countries.

Title VII further states that it is against the law for an employer to discriminate with regard to selection, termination, compensation, terms and privileges of employment, promotion or transfer of employees, work assignments, and any other activity related to employment.

As a manager, you need to make sure that you are aware of antidiscrimination laws and that you treat all employees fairly. Note that the law applies to employment agencies and labor unions, as well as to private employers. Remember that the law does permit the use of religion, sex, and national origin as BFOQs, but only when necessary for the normal operation of the business.[18]

As part of the Civil Rights Act, Congress created the EEOC to provide oversight of Title VII for all covered entities except the federal government. The Office of Special Counsel and the Merit Systems Protection Board oversee discrimination issues related to federal employees. The OFCCP oversees compliance by federal government contractors.

The EEOC has developed and continues to develop regulations and guidelines to help employers and employees interpret Congress's intent in the Civil Rights Act. It provides a very informative website (https://www.eeoc.gov), and numerous other resources to answer questions that managers have about equal employment opportunity. A section of the website provides answers to many questions about compliance requirements for small businesses (https://www.eeoc.gov/field/phoenix/smallbusiness.cfm).

The EEOC is involved in interpreting the meaning of the term *discrimination*, determining how individuals can prove that discrimination has occurred, identifying what remedies are available in the law, and addressing how to reconcile seniority rights of current employees with the rights of victims of discrimination.[19] Title VII's influence on the management of employees and HR activities is best understood by closely examining each of the protected classifications covered in the Act. Exhibit 3.6 provides an example of each type of discrimination covered under Title VII that this book addresses.

Congress amended the Civil Rights Act in 1972 by passing the Equal Employment Opportunity Act. The amendment broadened coverage of the Civil Rights Act to state and local governments, as well as to public and private educational institutions. The Act also gave the EEOC the right to sue employers to enforce the provisions of Title VII.

**EXHIBIT 3.6**

Examples of Discriminatory Practices Under the Civil Rights Act of 1964

| Type of Discrimination | Common Example |
|---|---|
| Race and color | Not hiring dark-skinned applicants because they don't fit the company image |
| Religious | Requiring a Seventh-Day Adventist to work on Saturday |
| Gender | Providing males with different benefits than females receive |
| National origin | Giving preferential treatment in employee decisions to individuals born in the United States |

## Race and Color Discrimination

Much progress has been made in reducing racial discrimination in the workplace since the passage of Title VII. However, in 2017, the EEOC reported that the number of race-based harassment charge filings had increased from 5,783 in 1997 to 9,009 in 2017.[20] Also, in 2017, the EEOC received 28,528 charges of race-based discrimination and resolved 34,229 cases (cases carry over from one year to the next), with monetary benefits of $75.9 million for plaintiffs. This last figure does not include monetary benefits obtained through litigation.[21] Under certain conditions, plaintiffs can file charges in court and may receive additional monetary benefits.

Employers violate Title VII when they use race itself or race-related characteristics and conditions to make employment decisions, tolerate the harassment of employees because of their race or color, segregate or classify employees based on race or color, or collect preemployment information about race in such a way that it is available to those making the hiring decisions.

The following are examples of race and color discrimination by employers in violation of Title VII:[22]

- *Using race or race-related characteristics and conditions to make employment decisions.* A "no-beard" policy may discriminate against African-American men because they are predisposed to a medical condition that makes shaving difficult. Selecting only light-skinned employees because they best fit the preferred company image is discrimination on the basis of skin color.
- *Tolerating the harassment of employees because of their race or color.* Permitting racial slurs and racist graffiti creates a hostile working environment. Making derogatory remarks about an employee's skin color and then firing the employee for complaining to management is a violation of Title VII.
- *Segregating or classifying employees based on race or color.* Assigning racial groups to work only in areas where the customer base is predominantly of the same racial group is discriminatory. Assigning employees of a certain racial group exclusively to work in certain jobs in the company is also discriminatory.
- *Collecting preemployment information about race in such a way that it is available to those making the hiring decisions.* Asking for information that would identify race as part of the preemployment process is not permissible. Coding applications or résumés so that the interviewer knows the race of applicants is another example of illegally classifying employees.
- *Dismissing an employee because of his or her association with someone of a different race.* Learning that an employee has a biracial child and using that information to discriminate against him in the terms and privileges of employment is discrimination. Finding out an employee is part of an organization that supports minority rights and using that information against her in the employment decision process is also a violation of the law.

### Religious Discrimination

Religious discrimination is either occurring more often or is being reported more often than in the past. In 1997, 1,709 religious discrimination complaints were filed with the EEOC, with 2,137 resolutions (some cases carried over from the previous year) and reasonable cause found in 4.4 percent, or 95, of those cases. *Reasonable cause* exists when the EEOC believes that there is enough evidence that discrimination has occurred to make a case. In 2017, the number of charges was slightly more than double that of 1997, at 3,436, with 3,997 resolutions and reasonable cause found in 3.0 percent, or 119, of the cases.[23] This rise is undoubtedly related to the increase in the proportion of people of various religions represented in the workplace in recent years, as well as the prejudices against certain religious groups exacerbated by the wars in the Middle East.

Religious discrimination occurs in a variety of forms. An employer might refuse to hire an applicant because of her particular religion, in which case disparate treatment occurs. Or an employer might have a policy that requires Saturday work. Such a policy could have disparate impact on an employee whose religion does not permit working on Saturdays, such as the Seventh-Day Adventists. In the former case, the employer is blatantly violating Title VII. In the latter case, the employer is not intentionally discriminating, but that is the result of the policy. The employer would either have to accommodate an employee by permitting him or her to work on a day other than Saturday or prove that adjusting the schedule would impose an undue hardship on the company. **Undue hardship** can take the form of diminished job efficiency, higher-than-usual administrative costs, impaired safety in the workplace, need for coworkers to perform hazardous or burdensome portions of the employee's work, or violation of a law or regulation.[24]

Employees also may experience *religious harassment*, which occurs when employees are subjected to a hostile work environment because of their religious affiliation. Since the terrorist attacks on the United States on September 11, 2001, members of some religious groups, such as Muslims, have experienced direct discrimination and harassment in the workplace.

Another important issue for companies is the extent to which employees can express religious beliefs at work. Employers are obligated to make reasonable accommodation for employee's religious beliefs unless doing so would result in undue hardship for the employer.[25] If an employer allows employees to keep personal books on their desks to read during breaks, the employer would have to allow an employee to keep a Bible or a copy of the Koran on his desk to read during breaks. Company Spotlight 3.3 describes another situation in which the EEOC showed that an organization should have provided a reasonable accommodation for a sincerely held religious belief.

Religious organizations are permitted to use religion as a BFOQ for certain positions. If a professor at a church-affiliated university is teaching a course based on the religious principles of the denomination with which it is affiliated, the university may specify that the person hired must be a member of the university's religion. But it would be hard to make a case that the custodial staff or clerical staff at the same university had to be members of that particular religion.

### Gender Discrimination

The Equal Pay Act, which you read about earlier, specifically prohibits employers from discriminating on the basis of gender in terms of pay. Title VII makes it unlawful for an employer to discriminate on the basis of gender in *any* employment situation or opportunity. For example, an employer cannot refuse to hire a woman for fear that she will get married, have children, and decide to quit her job. Additionally, the EEOC interprets Title VII as forbidding discrimination on the basis of gender identity or sexual orientation. Denying a promotion to someone who is gay, firing

**undue hardship**

a situation that exists when accommodating an employee would put the employer at a disadvantage financially or otherwise would make it difficult for the employer to remain in business and competitive

# COMPANY SPOTLIGHT 3.3

## Religious Discrimination Lawsuit Costs Mission Hospital $89,000

A requirement that all hospital employees receive a flu vaccination seems logical. Approximately 50,000 people die from the flu annually. Vaccinating hospital employees is about patient care. Mission Hospital, Inc., based in Asheville, North Carolina, has a flu vaccination requirement. The hospital does allow employees to request an exemption from getting the vaccination, so long as they do it by a specified date and have a legitimate reason. Sincerely held religious beliefs against being vaccinated can qualify an employee for the exemption. Also, Title VII of the Civil Rights Act of 1964 requires reasonable accommodation when employees have strong religious beliefs, so long as the accommodation does not cause undue hardship for the employer.

Three employees of Mission Hospital requested an exemption from obtaining a flu vaccination, but they did so after the stated deadline for making such a request. In making this request, the three noted that being vaccinated was against their religious beliefs. Mission Hospital refused to accommodate them because they had missed the deadline, which coincided with the start of flu season. All three were ultimately fired.

The EEOC brought a case against the hospital on behalf of the three workers, citing that a violation of religious discrimination had occurred under Title VII. Ultimately, Mission Hospital agreed to a settlement in this case, which included monetary relief for the terminated employees and issuance of a consent decree. The consent decree is in place for two years. The terms of the consent decree require the hospital to revise its immunization policy to allow employee exemptions during the time period in which flu vaccinations are given, provide annual training for supervisors and managers about Title VII and religious accommodations, and make periodic reports to the EEOC about requests for religious exemption from the flu vaccination requirement.

*Sources:* "Mission Hospital Agrees to Pay $89,000 to Settle EEOC Religious Discrimination Lawsuit," Equal Employment Opportunity Commission, http://www.eeoc.gov/eeoc/newsroom/release/1-12-18.cfm; K. Killen (2016) "Mission Hospital Under Fire for Possible Religious Discrimination," WLOS.com, http://wlos.com/news/local/mission-hospital-under-fire-for-possible-religious-discrimination.

an employee who plans a gender transition, or denying an employee access to a common restroom for his gender identity are all examples of unlawful gender discrimination in employment.

We now review some of the ways in which employers have engaged in gender-based discrimination. These ways include gender as the basis for an employment decision, gender-plus discrimination, and sexual harassment.

First, employers engage in gender discrimination when they use the person's gender as the basis for an employment decision. This form is the most straightforward and obvious way that gender discrimination occurs. Let's say that you have an opening for a sales associate at your car dealership. You may think that men are the best employees in this job because you believe that they know more about cars than women (which may or may not be true, but is a stereotype). As a result of your stereotype, you will not even consider a woman for that job. You have just discriminated on the basis of gender.

The second form of gender discrimination occurs when an employee would have been treated differently had it not been for that employee's gender. This form is known as *gender-plus discrimination*. An employer who refuses to hire women with preschool-age children but hires males with preschool-age children is guilty of gender-plus discrimination. In this instance, the women would have been hired "but for" their gender. Personality, as the next case shows, and appearance also can be factors in gender-plus discrimination.

In the 1982 *Price Waterhouse v. Hopkins*[26] case, Hopkins, an associate, brought a lawsuit against Price Waterhouse when she was denied a partnership. Apparently, some of the firm's partners didn't like her use of profanity and thought she was too macho and too aggressive, even though she had an exemplary record. This attitude existed even though she had played a critical role in securing a multimillion-dollar contract for the company with the U.S. Department of State. She also had been lauded as "an outstanding professional," and clients found her to be capable. Her aggressive manner did upset some coworkers and partners, however. After the firm refused to make Hopkins a partner despite her qualifications, she filed a sex discrimination lawsuit against the firm. She charged that she would have been treated differently had she been a male. In the end, the court found that gender-based discrimination had occurred: A male behaving as she had likely would have been made a partner. The firm, however, considered the behaviors unfeminine. In other words, Hopkins would have been promoted to partner, "but for" her gender.[27] This case is an example of mixed-motive discrimination.

The third form of gender discrimination is sexual harassment. You already know that under Title VII any form of gender discrimination is illegal. In 1986, the Supreme Court ruled on a gender discrimination case, *Meritor Savings Bank v. Vinson*. This case made it clear that creating a hostile environment for someone because of her gender was also prohibited under Title VII and constituted sexual harassment. Sexual harassment is a form of gender-based discrimination because the harassment is directed at members of one gender, but not the other. Females are directing the behavior at males but not at other females; males are harassing females, but not harassing other males.

Keep in mind that sexual harassment can involve two members of the same gender. This type of sexual harassment occurs, for instance, when a gay male makes sexual overtures or otherwise sexually harasses another male. The gay male would not be treating a female the same way.

The EEOC guidelines define what sexual harassment includes, but does not limit the definition to the statement below.

Unwelcome sexual advances, requests for sexual favors, and other verbal and physical conduct of a sexual nature when:

1. submission to such conduct is made either explicitly or implicitly a term or condition of an individual's employment;
2. submission to or rejection of such conduct by an individual is used as the basis for employment decisions affecting such individual; or
3. such conduct has the purpose or effect of unreasonably interfering with an individual's work performance or creating an intimidating, hostile, or offensive working environment.[28]

The EEOC has identified two types of sexual harassment. The most straightforward type is called **quid pro quo harassment**. *Quid pro quo* means "something for something." When this type of harassment occurs, submission to sexual conduct is made a condition of employment, whether explicitly or implicitly. A manager might agree to give an employee a raise or a promotion in exchange for her going on a date with him—no date, no raise. The manager's request constitutes *quid pro quo* harassment.

The other form of sexual harassment is referred to as *hostile work environment sexual harassment*. We defined the concept of a *hostile work environment* in an earlier discussion of harassment. Hostile work environment sexual harassment is quite controversial in some instances and more straightforward in others. The

*quid pro quo* **harassment**

occurs when submission to sexual conduct is made explicitly or implicitly a condition of employment

challenge arises because what may not appear to be a hostile work environment to one person may appear to be so to another person. Some people are offended by jokes with sexual overtones, while others are not. Whether or not employees might be offended, though, these jokes do not belong in the workplace.

Managers have an obligation to take corrective action once they are informed of a potential sexual harassment situation. According to the EEOC, a company may be guilty of harassment if the company knew, or should have known, about the harassment. A manager who ignores a complaint is allowing a climate to exist that is offensive to an employee in the work unit.

If the employee pursues action through the EEOC or through the courts, the question becomes whether there is a pattern of such behavior in the firm's workplace, and whether a *reasonable person* would find the behaviors offensive. In sexual harassment cases in which the victim of the harassment complains to management and nothing is done, or management should have known about the problem even if the victim did not speak up, the victim will have a better chance of winning the case. Therefore, it is important for managers to act quickly and decisively when any suggestion of sexual harassment occurs. Managers are agents of the company and put the company at risk if they are the harassers, or if they fail to take complaints seriously when their employees tell them about possible sexual harassment incidents.[29] Organizations spend a lot of time and money fighting sexual harassment charges when those charges frequently could have been avoided with proper training of managers and an established process for dealing with sexual harassment in the workplace. The #MeToo movement is in large part a response to the failure of organizations to address sexual harassment in the workplace.

In sexual harassment cases, the EEOC and courts generally respond more favorably to employers who have clearly communicated to employees that behavior of a sexual nature is not welcome in the workplace, and those who have taken immediate and decisive action to investigate and resolve any reports of sexual harassment. Also, a company can improve its chances of defending a case brought against it by showing that the plaintiff did not take advantage of corrective and preventive opportunities that it offered.[30] If the company can prove that the incident was never reported even though it had a clearly defined complaint process and the employee should have been aware of the process, the company will have a better chance of defending its lack of responsiveness.

Company Spotlight 3.4 provides an example of a situation in which the damages awarded the plaintiffs were large, in part because the company did not respond to their concerns. The EEOC has clearly articulated basic guidelines for employers to follow to reduce the incidence of sexual harassment in the workplace. These guidelines are the same as those outlined in Exhibit 3.4 for reducing the likelihood of any type of harassment.

## National Origin Discrimination

Discrimination on the basis of national origin can take the form of harassment, disparate treatment, or disparate impact, and results from

- treating an individual differently from others in employment situations because of his or her ancestry, ethnicity, or accent;
- treating an individual differently because he or she is married to or associates with someone of a particular nationality; and/or
- assuming that a person is of a particular national origin because of physical, linguistic, or cultural traits associated with an ethnic group.[31]

After the terrorist attacks on the United States on September 11, 2001, often referred to as 9/11, many individuals of Arab ancestry experienced discrimination

## COMPANY SPOTLIGHT  3.4

### Same-Sex Sexual Harassment at Wells Fargo

Does sexual harassment exist when the plaintiffs and the accused are the same sex? The U.S. District Court for the District of Nevada ruled that it did. The court required Wells Fargo to pay $290,000 to four female bank tellers who were the subjects of sexual harassment by a female manager and another bank teller at the bank branch in Reno, Nevada.

The manager and bank teller had subjected the plaintiffs to graphic sexual comments, gestures, and images and engaged in inappropriate touching. They also had suggested that the bank tellers dress provocatively if they wanted to advance in the workplace. Management had failed to address the issues even though there had been multiple complaints. One employee quit her job because of the harassment.

In addition to the monetary fine, a consent decree was put in place for two years for all the branch locations in the Sierra Mountains District. The decree required a number of steps designed to prevent future harassment and to ensure that any other victims had their concerns properly addressed.

*Source:* Adapted from "Wells Fargo Settles EEOC Same-Sex Sexual Harassment Lawsuit for $290,000," Equal Employment Opportunity Commission, https://www.eeoc.gov/eeoc/newsroom/release/9-15-14b.cfm; Scott Sonner, (2014),"Wells Fargo Pays $290,000 in Sex Harassment Case," washingtonexaminer.com, September 17, 2014, https://www.washingtonexaminer.com/wells-fargo-pays-290-000-in-sex-harassment-case.

in the workplace. One such case involved the Plaza Hotel and Fairmont Hotel and Resorts, Inc. The EEOC lawsuit in this case alleged that after 9/11, Muslim, South Asian, and Arab employees were called "terrorist," "Taliban," and "dumb Muslim." Such names were written down instead of the employees' actual names when they were given their room keys for the day's work. In addition, they were cursed at and accused of being responsible for the events of 9/11. According to the EEOC, the employer knew about, or should have known about, the harassment.[32] The EEOC reached a $525,000 settlement agreement with the company on behalf of the 12 affected employees, and the company agreed to train managers and employees about diversity to prevent future hostile environment situations.[33]

The EEOC has identified a number of ways in which language requirements used by employers can lead to national origin discrimination. Exhibit 3.7 provides examples of some of the ways that this discrimination occurs.

### EXHIBIT 3.7

#### National Origin Discrimination Resulting from Language Requirements

*Accent discrimination*
Making an employment decision based on an applicant's or employee's accent when the accent does not interfere with job performance

*Fluency*
Requiring fluency in English or a foreign language when such is not required for effective job performance

*English-only rules*
Having a rule that employees must speak English when it is not essential for the safe or efficient operation of the business

*Source:* Adapted from "National Origin Discrimination," Equal Employment Opportunity Commission, https://www.eeoc.gov/eeoc/publications/fs-nator.cfm.

## Pregnancy Discrimination Act of 1978 (PDA)

In 1978, Congress passed the Pregnancy Discrimination Act (PDA) as an amendment to Title VII. The purpose of this Act is to prohibit employers from discriminating against women because of pregnancy, childbirth, or a related medical condition. That means that an employer cannot refuse to hire a woman because she is pregnant, nor can an employer fire a woman because of her pregnancy. Also, an employer must treat pregnancy the same way that it would handle any other medically related condition or temporary disability of an employee. If an employer modified work tasks for an employee with a broken leg (a temporary disability), the employer would have to make similar temporary modifications for a pregnant employee, if needed. In addition, the PDA spells out employer requirements regarding benefits. Company health insurance plans cannot exclude pregnancy. Employers are required to provide the same health coverage to spouses of male employees as they do to spouses of female employees. Companies have to provide the same benefits and privileges to pregnant employees, regardless of marital status, that they would provide to other employees who are temporarily disabled.[34]

## Civil Rights Act of 1991 (CRA 91)

The outcome of a number of Supreme Court cases in the late 1980s led Congress to revisit the issue of civil rights in the workplace and amend CRA 64. The Civil Rights Act of 1991 (CRA 91) was needed to "strengthen and improve federal civil rights laws, to provide for damages in cases of intentional employment discrimination, to clarify provisions regarding disparate impact actions, and for other purposes."[35]

The provisions of CRA 91 strengthened employee rights in several ways. The following is a summary:[36]

- *It clarifies the burden of proof in disparate impact cases.* After the plaintiff shows that a particular employment practice has disparate impact, the burden of proof is on the employer to show that the practice is job related and is consistent with business necessity.
- *It addresses rights of U.S. employees working abroad.* CRA 91 specifies that U.S. citizens working outside the country for U.S. employers are to receive the same equal employment protections as employees working within the United States under Title VII of CRA 64.
- *It prohibits race norming.* Companies cannot use lower cutoff scores or otherwise adjust the outcome of employment-related tests based on race, religion, gender, or national origin to give minority groups an advantage.
- *It eliminates the use of the mixed-motive defense in disparate treatment cases.* CRA 91 makes explicit that employers cannot defend their discriminatory actions in disparate treatment cases by arguing that the outcome would have been the same because of some additional reason, even if the protected class had not been a consideration.
- *It allows jury trials and damage awards.* CRA 91 provides plaintiffs with the option for a jury to decide discrimination cases and permits punitive and compensatory damage awards in disparate treatment cases. (Punitive awards are paid to address the harm caused by discrimination done with malice and reckless indifference to legal rights. Compensatory damages under CRA 91 are not to compensate for back pay and related costs, but rather to compensate for emotional damage and other anguish caused by the discrimination. Punitive and compensatory damages under CRA 91 are not to exceed $300,000.)

## Age Discrimination in Employment Act of 1967 (ADEA)

Many of you reading this book might think that 40 is a really old age. Others of you know that is definitely not true! (Maybe 90 is old, but some of us are not so sure about that anymore.) You may remember that when we first defined the term *protected classification* at the start of the chapter, we mentioned the Age Discrimination in Employment Act of 1967 (ADEA) as one of the few EEO laws that specifies which group the law protects. The ADEA makes it illegal for an employer to discriminate against any individual age 40 or older because of that individual's age when making employment decisions. These decisions include activities such as promotions, layoffs, and pay raises.

The ADEA resulted from employment practices in which employers preferred younger workers over older workers, and even terminated older workers to avoid having to pay retirement benefits to them. The Act applies to employers with 20 or more employees, and includes state and local governments, employment agencies, labor organizations, and the federal government. The ADEA applies to apprenticeship programs, job notices and advertisements, preemployment inquiries, and benefits, as well as most other employment practices. Years of service cannot be used by employers as a proxy for age when making employment decisions.

Age discrimination can occur even if both individuals are in the protected class.[37] Here is how that might happen. An employee who is age 50 is denied a promotion, and the promotion goes to someone who is 42. Both individuals are over 40, but discrimination may have occurred. The older employee would use the four-step McDonnell Douglas test to make a *prima facie* case of disparate treatment. If he could do so, the company would then need to defend its actions by establishing a nondiscriminatory reason for the decision.

Courts have tended to uphold early retirement incentives and waivers offered by employers so long as the employees were not coerced into signing the agreements, the agreements were presented in a way that the employees could understand, and the employees were given enough time to make a decision. The courts also have supported the use of BFOQs based on age when a company can demonstrate that age affects performance in a job and could create a risk to public safety or adversely affect company efficiency. Further, the law includes a provision for compulsory retirement of high-ranking executives who are guaranteed by their employer a certain level of retirement income.

The ADEA was amended in 1990 by the Older Workers Benefit Protection Act (OWBPA). This Act specifically prohibits employers from denying benefits to older workers. The OWBPA does allow employers in limited circumstances to use age as the basis for reducing benefits, so long as the cost of those benefits is still equal to the cost of providing the benefits for younger workers.[38]

The National Council on Aging predicts that by 2019, the workforce will include over 40 percent of Americans aged 55+. This group will make up over 25 percent of the workforce. Older Americans have returned to or stayed in the workforce because they simply are not ready to retire, and because businesses are realizing that their knowledge and skills are important.[39] A downside to the increase in older Americans in the workplace is an increase in age discrimination charges. The number of complaints received by the EEOC increased from 15,785 in 1997 to 18,376 in 2017. Meanwhile, monetary benefits awarded in EEOC settlements related to age discrimination more than doubled, climbing from $44.3 to $90.1 million, not counting awards made as a result of litigation.[40]

Organizations are finding that older workers make excellent employees and are actively recruiting them for the skills and knowledge that they can bring to the job. One such organization is the home-improvement retailer Home Depot. In 2004,

Home Depot partnered with AARP to recruit older applicants to fill some of the 35,000 new positions the company anticipated having that year. This alliance between AARP and Home Depot was successful and led to the creation of the AARP National Employer Team, a group of employers who are friendly to older workers. Today, AARP invites employers to become part of the AARP Employer Pledge Program. This program includes over 500 employers who have signed a pledge recognizing the value of workers of all ages and especially noting that workers 50+ should have a level playing field in competing for jobs. Employers signing the pledge cover a range of sizes and industries.[41] The older workers typically have a strong work ethic and like the challenges that work provides for them. Additionally, often they can pass along important knowledge to younger workers.[42]

## Americans with Disabilities Act of 1990 (ADA) and ADA Amendments Act of 2008 (ADAA)

Legislation to provide equal employment opportunity for individuals with disabilities dates back to the Vocational Rehabilitation Act of 1973. The Vocational Rehabilitation Act applies to companies with federal contracts over $10,000 and is administered by the OFCCP. As noted earlier, the OFCCP is part of the Department of Labor's Employment Standards Administration and is specifically tasked with administering regulations for federal contractors. Companies covered by this Act are required to affirmatively seek and hire qualified individuals with disabilities. The OFCCP revised the regulations for Section 503 of the Vocational Rehabilitation Act in 2014 to strengthen the affirmative action and nondiscrimination responsibilities of federal contractors.[43] Court cases that occurred as a result of this Act have provided guidance for implementation and interpretation of the Americans with Disabilities Act (ADA), which applies to all employers with 15 or more employees.[44]

In 1990, Congress passed the ADA to provide greater opportunities for access in general and employment in particular for individuals with disabilities. A study by the U.S. Census in 2010, which coincided with the twentieth anniversary of the ADA, revealed that nearly one in five people in the United States has a disability.[45] The ADA specifically prohibits employers from using a disability as the basis for discriminating against qualified individuals in making employment decisions. *Qualified* is a key word in interpreting the ADA—and in other employment laws as well. Keep in mind that none of the laws that we have discussed, including the ADA, requires an employer to hire someone who is not qualified—that is, someone who does not have the knowledge, skills, and abilities or other characteristics required to perform a job. The ADA further defines *qualified* in terms of individuals with disabilities: a qualified employee or applicant with a *disability* is an individual who, with or without *reasonable accommodation*, can perform the *essential functions* of the job.[46]

The Act was amended in 2008 following several Supreme Court rulings that many perceived as diminishing the intent of the original ADA.[47] In passing the original law, Congress tried to be clear regarding the terms and conditions of compliance with the Act. As often happens, a number of issues were left open to interpretation. For example, were individuals covered if they had medical or corrective devices that compensated for their disability? And does a disability automatically mean that you are covered by the Act if you cannot do a particular job but can do other jobs? In an attempt to remove some of the confusion, President George W. Bush signed into law the Americans with Disabilities Act Amendments Act of 2008 (ADAA). The ADAA made it easier for individuals to establish the existence of a disability. Exhibit 3.8 provides a summary of the main provisions of the ADAA.

## EXHIBIT 3.8

### The ADA Amendments Act (ADAA) of 2008

- Clarified that "substantially limits" is to be interpreted broadly, thus allowing for more expansive coverage

- Requires an individualized assessment of whether an impairment substantially limits a major life activity

- Specified that mitigating measures, except eyeglasses and contact lenses, should not be considered when assessing if an individual has a disability

- Clarified that episodic impairments or those in remission were a disability if they substantially limited a major life activity when active

- Changed the definition of "regarded as" to mean person is disabled if subject to an action prohibited by ADA based on nonminor, nontransitory impairment

- Noted that individuals covered under "regarded as" are not entitled to reasonable accommodation

*Source:* Adapted from "Fact Sheet on the EEOC's Final Regulations Implementing the ADAA," Equal Employment Opportunity Commission, https://www.eeoc.gov/laws/regulations/adaaa_fact_sheet.cfm.

**disability**

a physical or mental impairment that substantially limits one or more major life activities

**essential functions**

the job tasks, duties, and responsibilities that must be done by a person in a job

**reasonable accommodation**

making modifications in how the work is done or in the work environment so that someone who is qualified for the job and who has a disability can perform the job

According to the ADA, as amended in 2008 with the ADAA, a **disability** is a physical or mental impairment that substantially limits one or more major life activities. Individuals who have a record of such impairment or who are regarded as having such impairment are also covered.[48] Major life activities include caring for oneself, performing manual tasks, breathing, walking, eating, and similar activities, as well as the operation of major bodily functions such as the immune system.

**Essential functions** are the job tasks, duties, and responsibilities that must be done by a person in a job. *Must* is another important word in the context of the ADA. If there is someone else who can perform the function instead of the person in the particular position, or if someone else can assist in performing the function, then it probably is not an essential function for that specific position. If the job exists to perform that function, or if there is no one to assist with doing it, then the function is considered essential. The question then becomes whether the person with the disability can perform the function with or without *reasonable accommodation*.

The EEOC defines **reasonable accommodation** as making modifications in how the work is done or in the work environment so that someone who is qualified for the job, and who has a disability, can perform the job. A reasonable accommodation might include restructuring a job, modifying a work schedule, acquiring or modifying equipment, or making existing facilities easily accessible and usable for someone with a disability.[49] Over 50 percent of accommodations cost $500 or less, the median cost is $240, and one-fifth do not cost anything. Tax incentives often offset the cost to the employer.[50]

Some people may wonder if employing individuals with disabilities raises the costs of benefits or creates workplace safety issues for a company. Research has shown that the levels of benefits offered by employers and the incidence rates of occupational illnesses and injuries in the workplace have been unaffected since the ADA went into effect.[51] Exhibit 3.9 provides examples of reasonable accommodations that employers can make.

Reasonable accommodation is not required if providing it will create an undue hardship for the employer. In other words, an employer with limited financial resources would not be required to spend a large sum of money to make a reasonable accommodation. The EEOC notes that undue hardship is determined by the difficulty and expense of the accommodation relative to the size, financial resources, structure, and nature of a company's operations. For instance, a hotel that requires all housekeepers to clean a certain number of rooms per day is not required to lower the requirement for an employee with a disability.[52]

**EXHIBIT 3.9**

## Examples of Reasonable Accommodation

- Providing a sign language interpreter for an interview with someone who is deaf

- Changing the design of store displays so that a sales associate in a wheelchair can have access to do his job

- Reallocating a nonessential task, such as occasionally taking boxes to a storage room, for an employee with a back problem to another employee and replacing it with a different task

- Allowing an employee to work from home if doing so will not create an undue hardship on the employer

*Source:* Adapted from "The Americans with Disabilities Act: A Primer for Small Business," Equal Employment Opportunity Commission, https://www.eeoc.gov/eeoc/publications/adahandbook.cfm.

We cover employment selection issues in greater detail in Chapter 7, but we need to highlight a few issues related to employee selection and the ADA here. Specifically, the ADA prohibits employers from asking job applicants whether they have a disability or asking about details of a disability. As a manager, you may ask a candidate if he or she can perform the essential functions of the job. In fact, that should be a question you ask of *all* applicants. If there is a job-related reason to require the applicant to take a medical examination, you may do so, but only after you have made the job offer, and only if you require all entering employees in similar jobs to have the same medical exams. Tests for illegal drug use are not considered medical examinations under the ADA and can be administered per the employer's policy. Applicants and employees who use illegal drugs or are alcoholics are not protected under the ADA.[53] Recovering drug addicts and recovering alcoholics, or drug addicts and alcoholics currently in a treatment program, are covered by the ADA.

Companies need to keep all medical information separate from other personnel records to ensure that the information remains confidential and is seen only by individuals who have an absolute need to see it. For instance, a supervisor working to make a reasonable accommodation or an emergency medical technician who is called in to treat an individual for a workplace injury would need to see the information.

## Title II of the Genetic Information Nondiscrimination Act of 2008 (GINA)

How would you feel if the following experience happened to you? You applied for a job and did not get it. The reason given was that the family medical information you provided suggested that you were likely to become "disabled." Do you think such a decision is fair if you are qualified to do the job? Founders Pavilion, a nursing and rehabilitation center in Corning, New York, learned the hard way that acquiring and using such information is illegal. The company had to pay $110,400 to 138 individuals to settle a discrimination suit that included a charge of requesting employees to provide family medical history as part of the post-offer, preemployment medical exam.[54]

Title II of the Genetic Information Nondiscrimination Act of 2008 (GINA) is designed to prevent such discrimination from happening. GINA prohibits employers from using **genetic information** for making employment decisions. The Act also prohibits employers and other covered organizations from requesting or otherwise acquiring genetic information about applicants or employees. There are times when an employer may have access to genetic information, such as family medical history, but GINA strictly limits the employer's use and disclosure of such information.

**genetic information**
information about an individual's genetic tests and genetic tests of family members and/or about an individual's or family member's diseases or disorders

# Use of Social Media and Employment Discrimination

 Before moving away from the topic of employment discrimination, it is worth noting the possible discriminatory implications of the use of social media in employment situations. In March 2014, the EEOC convened a meeting to discuss the increased use of social media and the implications of that on the laws enforced by the agency.[55] We will discuss the use of social media for human resource decision making in several chapters in this book. For instance, social media sites such as LinkedIn are frequently used for recruiting employees. The ability to learn the race, age, gender, and other information related to protected classifications of potential applicants through such sites, unfortunately, creates the opportunity for bias to enter into the decision-making process.

The use of social media also can affect other employee decisions where bias can affect outcomes. Here is an example: An employee announces on her Facebook page that she has just found out she is pregnant. She could potentially lose a promotion opportunity if the employer has a bias against giving management roles to women with young children (remember the "but-for-her-gender" description of gender discrimination discussed earlier). Exhibit 3.10 provides a list of ways that social media can potentially result in discrimination in the workplace.

# EEO Responsibilities of Multinational Employers

Managers need to consider several questions regarding multinational corporations and employee law:

1. Do the U.S. EEO laws apply to employees of U.S. companies in other countries?
2. What are the responsibilities of U.S. companies operating abroad relative to the laws of those countries?
3. Do non-U.S. companies operating in the United States have to follow U.S. equal employment laws?

Employees of U.S. companies who are working for U.S. companies in other countries are covered by Title VII, the ADA, and the ADEA. You may remember that we noted this coverage as one of the provisions of CRA 91. U.S. employers are not

## EXHIBIT 3.10

Examples of How Social Media Use Can Result in Possible Employment Discrimination

| Activity | Possible Outcome |
|---|---|
| A supervisor views pictures and other information posted online about applicants during employee recruitment. | Available information such as race, gender, and disability can lead to discrimination against members of protected classes. |
| An employee posts information about other employees on a social media site. | If information is harassing or derogatory, the employee may be creating a hostile work environment. |
| A supervisor "friends" an employee on Facebook and has access to information about that employee's "likes" or other personal information. | The supervisor may use that information against the employee in making employment decisions (e.g., learning an employee is gay). |

*Sources:* "Social Media Is Part of Today's Workplace But Its Use May Raise Employment Discrimination Concerns," Equal Employment Opportunity Commission, March 3, 2014, http://www.eeoc.gov/eeoc/newsroom /release/3-12-14.cfm; Lisa Rein, "Gay Man Sues Library of Congress, Alleging Discrimination" *Washington Post*, August 22, 2012, https://www.washingtonpost.com/politics/gay-man-sues-library-of-congress-alleging-discrimination/2012/08/22/ad23e0a0-ebca-11e1-9ddc-340d5efb1e9c_story.html?utm_term=.d15502f02c2e.

required to abide by these laws, however, if doing so would result in the company violating a law of the country in which the workforce is located. This situation provides employers with a *foreign law defense*. For example, if a country has a mandatory retirement age law, the U.S. employer has to honor that law. The EEOC does caution that a U.S. employer is not permitted to transfer an employee to another country to keep the company from having to treat the employee in accordance with the U.S. EEO laws. In other words, an employer cannot purposefully send an employee to a country that has a mandatory retirement age law to force the employee to retire.[56]

Companies headquartered in other countries but doing business in the United States are generally bound by U.S. EEO laws. The exception to this requirement occurs when there is a binding international agreement or treaty in effect that states otherwise. If such an agreement or treaty exists, the international company is not bound by U.S. EEO laws and can give hiring preference to citizens of their own country. Likewise, U.S. employers operating abroad have a responsibility to know the employment laws of the countries in which they are working and to ensure that they do not violate those laws when managing the local country's employees.

Let's turn now to the steps that an employee would take if she believes that her employer is in violation of an employment law.

## Filing Process for Discrimination Charges

An individual who believes she has been discriminated against in violation of an EEO law can file a charge of discrimination by contacting the nearest EEOC office. The EEOC website (https://www.eeoc.gov) provides contact information for all the district, field, area, and local offices. Individuals also can contact their state's Fair Employment Practices Agency. These offices work closely with the EEOC and vice versa. The charge should be filed within 180 days from the occurrence of the alleged violation. The time to file can be extended to 300 days under limited circumstances.

Once a charge is filed, the EEOC will review it and decide if it warrants investigation. If deemed appropriate, the agency will begin an investigation, seeking to collect as much factual information as possible about the allegation. At any point in the process, the EEOC can seek to settle with the employer.

If settlement efforts are not successful, and if the investigation indicates that discrimination occurred, the EEOC will try to work with the employer for conciliation. As opposed to litigation, *conciliation* is a voluntary, less formal, and less costly process used to resolve a discrimination charge. The EEOC may also select the case for its more formal Mediation Program, which is a voluntary program that uses a neutral third party as a mediator and is available at no cost to the employer or employee. Like conciliation, mediation is a good way to avoid a costly, lengthy litigation process.[57] In fact, the EEOC is increasingly encouraging employers to use these techniques, known as **alternative dispute resolution (ADR)**, to resolve discrimination complaints. ADR provides a process for resolving disputes among employees and employers using a mediator or an arbitrator, and it generally leads to a more productive outcome than taking a case to court.[58] If settlement, conciliation, or mediation efforts are not successful, the agency will decide whether to take the case to court. In the event that the EEOC decides not to sue the employer on the individual's behalf, the individual has 90 days to file a lawsuit on his or her own.[59]

**alternative dispute resolution (ADR)**
a process for resolving disputes among employees and employers using a mediator or an arbitrator

## Executive Orders and Affirmative Action

Recall from earlier in the chapter that executive orders are enacted by the president of the United States for the purpose of managing the operations of the federal government, including the operations of federal contractors. The executive orders discussed here are those that directly influence how an employer manages human resources. They require employers to do more than just not discriminate. They require employers to make concerted efforts to bring underrepresented groups into the workplace and to help them advance once hired. Compliance with antidiscrimination executive orders is under the jurisdiction of the OFCCP.

## Executive Order 11246 (EO 11246)

Executive Order 11246 (EO 11246) was signed into law in 1965 to prohibit discrimination based on race, color, religion, sex, or national origin. In 2014, sexual orientation and gender identity were added as protected classifications. You may be wondering how this EO differs from Title VII. Good question. In many ways, it doesn't, except that it applies specifically to federal contractors and subcontractors, most of which also have to abide by Title VII regulations. The big difference is that EO 11246 specifically requires federal contractors and subcontractors to put into place *affirmative action* programs, which we will describe shortly. Under EO 11246, federal contractors are required to do all of the following:

- Ensure that the job application process and subsequent employment experience are not based on race, color, religion, sex, or national origin
- Conspicuously post notices from the OFCCP describing the provisions of the nondiscrimination clause in EO 11246
- Provide notices to labor unions or other groups with whom the employer has a collective bargaining agreement
- State on all job advertisements that the company is an EEO, affirmative action employer

The federal government can withhold payment to contractors that fail to comply with this executive order.

The affirmative action requirement of EO 11246 is very important. The following sections describe what is meant by *affirmative action* and what employers do as affirmative action employers, whether because they are required to or out of goodwill.

## Affirmative Action

**affirmative action**

the process of actively seeking to identify, hire, and promote qualified members of underrepresented groups

**Affirmative action** employers actively seek to identify, hire, and promote qualified members of underrepresented groups—that is, they do more than simply not discriminate. Affirmative action programs exist for one of three reasons. You already have learned about the first reason, which is to comply with EO 11246. Second, any employer can decide to engage in affirmative action, even if not required to do so by law. Many managers understand the contributions that a diverse workforce can make to company success, and they actively seek to recruit, hire, and promote individuals from many racial and ethnic groups. This type of affirmative action program exists out of the goodwill of the employer, the belief that affirmative action is the right thing to do, and the belief that it can help the company prosper in the long run. After all, if your customer base is diverse, doesn't it make sense for your workforce to be diverse too?

Third, companies may have affirmative action programs resulting from a court-ordered consent decree. This type of decree results from a court finding that an employer is guilty of discriminating against a protected group in its employee management practices. In such cases, the court will identify what the employer needs to correct and for how long the decree is in effect.

Affirmative action plans under EO 11246 are periodically reviewed by the OFCCP and require the company to engage in three activities:[59]

1. *Conduct a utilization and availability analysis.* This analysis is a profile of a company's current workforce relative to the pool of qualified workers in the relevant labor market. Companies must first identify the demographic profile of current employees in certain job groupings (e.g., managerial, secretarial, technical). Second, companies must identify the percentage of individuals in the *relevant labor market*—the appropriate comparison group of skilled employees—who are in each job grouping. Third, companies must compare these two demographic profiles. For example, the company will have to determine what percentage of professional sales personnel already in the company are female, and what percentage of individuals in the workforce that may work in professional sales are female. If a company's percentage for a demographic category is considerably lower than the percentage of that demographic category available in the labor market, that protected group is said to be *underutilized* for that job.

2. *Identify goals and timetables.* The next step is to establish goals and timetables to address underutilization. It is important to understand that goals are not the same as quotas. *Quotas* stipulate hiring a certain number of employees from a protected classification and are often met by hiring unqualified applicants or applicants who are less qualified than others, just to make the numbers. The OFCCP explicitly bans quotas.

3. *Develop and implement an action plan.* The last step in an affirmative action program is to develop and implement an action plan to accomplish the goals established in step 2 to eliminate underutilization in the company's workforce. Companies may use a number of tactics to provide greater opportunities to underutilized groups. Companies can modify where they advertise open positions to target certain demographic groups. Also, they can train current employees to increase the potential for promotions into job categories that are underutilized.

The OFCCP and research studies report many successes as a result of affirmative action programs required of federal contractors, including more females moving into management positions in *Fortune* 1000 companies, employment of people with disabilities, and minority groups entering positions in companies that might not otherwise have been as accessible to them.[60] There is a downside to affirmative action, however. Employees hired under affirmative action plans may be perceived as less qualified than other workers. As a result of this perception, they may end up not receiving equal treatment in the workplace.

By now, you know that affirmative action leads to greater diversity in the workplace. Throughout this book, we will talk about the importance of diversity. As you read this information, keep in mind that researchers and managers are not always convinced of the benefits of diversity. Some argue that it improves the quality of group performance and creativity and can lead to a greater variety of perspectives. Others point out the negative outcomes, such as less group integration and lower organizational attachment.[61] Another problem associated with affirmative action is **reverse discrimination,** a type of discrimination in which members of a protected group are given preference in employment decisions, resulting in discrimination against nonprotected groups. However, if two parties—one minority and one not—are equally qualified and the company is an affirmative action employer, hiring the minority applicant may be appropriate.

**reverse discrimination**
a type of discrimination in which members of a protected group are given preference in employment decisions, resulting in discrimination against nonprotected groups

## Related Employment Legislation

We will discuss other laws and executive orders in later chapters, where we can show their direct effects on HR activities in more depth. There are, however, a few more laws that we need to discuss in this chapter because of their focus on fair treatment of employees. These laws include the Immigration Reform and Control Act (IRCA), the Family and Medical Leave Act (FMLA), the Vietnam Era Veteran's Readjustment Assistance Act (VEVRAA), the Uniformed Services Employment and Reemployment Act (USERRA), state and local government fair employment practice laws, and the doctrine of employment-at-will.

## Immigration Reform and Control Act of 1986 (IRCA)

Immigration has long been part of the fabric of the United States. In recent years, it has become an important topic for many people, including the president of the United States and members of Congress as they struggle to decide how open the U.S. borders should be. Immigrants who have a legal right to work in the United States are protected under the national origin provisions of CRA 64. In 1986, Congress passed the Immigration Reform and Control Act (IRCA) in an attempt to control unauthorized immigration to the United States. The law also has antidiscrimination provisions. Specifically, employers with 4 or more employees are prohibited from using national origin or citizenship as a basis for their employment decisions. This portion of the law provides protection against national origin discrimination to a group not covered by Title VII—employees in firms with 4–14 employees.

Employers are responsible for verifying that all employees that they hire have the legal right to work in the United States. Companies confirm this by having their employees complete INS Form I-9, "Employment Eligibility Verification," and by collecting the specified documentation that verifies their identities.[62] To prevent discrimination on the basis of citizenship, employers are encouraged to wait until after a job offer has been made to request that Form I-9 be completed.

The Immigration and Naturalization Service (INS) enforces the IRCA. Employers who hire workers who are not eligible to work in the United States can be fined, debarred from government contracts, receive criminal penalties, and be ordered by the courts to hire the individual who was discriminated against, give back pay to that individual, or both. U.S. Immigration and Customs Enforcement (ICE) agents or auditors inspect Forms I-9 for compliance. Employers found to have technical or procedural violations are given 10 days to make corrections and may be fined. Employers who knowingly hire or continue to hire unauthorized workers must cease the activity, may be fined, and can even be criminally prosecuted. Monetary fines and penalties range from $110 to $16,000 per violation and are determined on the basis of the size of the business, good faith efforts to comply with the Act, history and seriousness of violations, and whether unauthorized workers were involved.[64]

In recent years, the enforcement of this law has garnered greater attention as more focus has been placed on national security issues and as efforts have been made to more closely guard U.S. borders since 9/11. Form I-9 has undergone several revisions since it was first put into effect, including changes to the list of documents that someone could use to verify employment eligibility and clearer instructions for employers and employees. Employers also may use E-Verify to determine if employees are eligible to work in the United States. E-Verify is an Internet-based system that allows employers to compare information from the employee's Form I-9 to data from U.S. Department of Homeland Security and Social Security Administration records, thus verifying eligibility to work. This service is fast and free to employers through the official Homeland Security website (www.uscis.gov), and is currently used by more than 600,000 employers.[65] Exhibit 3.11 provides steps for companies to follow to reduce their risk of violating the IRCA.

## EXHIBIT 3.11

### Steps to Reduce the Risk of Violating the IRCA

1. Make sure that staff are designated and trained to handle the I-9 process.

2. Provide clear and complete information to all managers about the importance of compliance and penalties to them of noncompliance.

3. Ensure that the I-9 form being used is the most current one required.

4. Review files periodically to make sure that I-9s are completed and up to date.

5. If in doubt, seek legal assistance to ensure that your policy and practices are in compliance.

## Family and Medical Leave Act of 1993, 2008 (FMLA)

What would you do if you had to choose between taking care of a sick child and going to work? In 1993, Congress passed the Family and Medical Leave Act (FMLA) to provide job protection for employees in just such situations. The FMLA requires employers with 50 or more employees in a 75-mile radius to grant up to 12 weeks of unpaid leave to an employee who needs to take time away from work because of his or her own illness; to care for a sick member of his or her immediate family (such as a child, spouse, father, or mother), but not including his spouse's immediate family; and for the birth, adoption, or foster care of his or her child. Employees must have worked for the employer for at least 12 months and for 1,250 hours during the 12 months preceding the beginning of the leave.

In 2008, the FMLA was amended to allow leave for family members of soldiers who are on or about to go on active duty for any qualifying exigency. Also added was the provision for caregiver leave for wounded service members. This provision extends leave eligibility to a spouse, son, daughter, or next of kin for up to 26 weeks of unpaid leave. In 2015, the definition of *spouse* was amended to ensure that eligible employees in legal same-sex marriages would be covered under the FMLA.[66]

The Act requires prior approval for leave to count as FMLA leave. Under the FMLA, the employer can permit or even require its employees to designate vacation or sick leave time as FMLA leave so that they receive pay during at least a portion of the 12 weeks. In addition, the leave may be taken intermittently throughout a 12-month period. Except in the case of key employees, the law requires that the employer provide the same or an equivalent job for the employee when he or she returns from FMLA leave. *Equivalent* refers to both pay and duties. Key employees are those whose absence could lead to substantial and grievous economic loss to the company.[67]

## Vietnam Era Veteran's Readjustment Assistance Act of 1974 (VEVRAA)

The Vietnam Era Veteran's Readjustment Act of 1974 (VEVRAA) provides employment protection for Vietnam-era veterans, special disabled veterans, and other veterans who served on active duty during a war or recognized military campaign. Employers with federal contracts or subcontracts of $25,000 or more are required to give equal opportunity and affirmative action to this group of protected-class individuals. Affirmative action under this Act includes listing all job openings with the local state employment service, with the exception of top management and executive positions, positions of less than three days' duration, and positions to be filled internally.[68]

## Uniformed Services Employment and Reemployment Rights Act of 1994 (USERRA)

The Uniformed Services Employment and Reemployment Act of 1994 (USERRA) was passed after the Gulf War of 1990–1991. The purpose of this Act is to ensure that noncareer military personnel can keep their civilian employment and benefits when volunteering for duty or being involuntarily called to duty. Noncareer military include individuals in the reserve units of any branch of the uniformed services (e.g., the Army or Air Force), as well as members of the National Guard. In addition, the USERRA is designed to ensure that these individuals can seek employment without being discriminated against, and to encourage others to join the uniformed services noncareer programs.[69] With some exceptions, the total length of time that a covered individual can be absent from work and retain his or her employment rights is five years.[70]

The U.S. wars in Iraq, Afghanistan, and other parts of the world have led to greater use of the provisions of this Act, as large numbers of reservists have been called away from their regular employment. Most employers are required to abide by the USERRA even if they have only one employee. Any individual who has served in the uniformed services has rights if that individual seeks employment after serving or was employed and took a leave of absence to perform the service. These rights affect initial employment, reemployment after serving, employment retention, promotion, and other benefits.[71]

When employers choose not to comply with USERRA, the Department of Labor can and has intervened. Law enforcement officer Brian Benvie was an Army reservist who had been called up for service in Kosovo, Iraq, and Kuwait. Because of his military service, he missed taking the promotional exams for sergeant and lieutenant. He did eventually take one of the exams. Other officers who took the exam were promoted ahead of him, even though he had higher scores. Eventually, because of USERRA and the intervention of the U.S. Department of Justice, a settlement was reached, resulting in $32,000 in back pay awarded to Benvie, promotion, and retroactive seniority.[72]

## Fair Employment Practices

**fair employment practice laws**

state and local governments' employee management regulations

Many state and local governments or municipalities have employee management regulations known as **fair employment practice laws**. These laws are often more stringent than the federal government's regulations. When these regulations exist, the more stringent regulations are to be followed. If the state laws are less stringent, then the federal regulations must be followed. Differences between state and local laws and federal laws can exist in all aspects of the employer–employee relationship, from minimum wage to protected classifications. For instance, prior to a landmark U.S. Supreme Court case in June 2015, only 37 states allowed same-sex marriage. These state laws had implications for employers, including the requirement to provide employee benefits for same-sex couples that are equal to those provided to other married individuals.[73] Managers need to be sure that they are familiar with and abide by the laws of the states in which they work. Information about the regulations for each state is readily available online from each state's labor department.

## Employment-at-Will and Wrongful Discharge

What happens when an employee receives consistently negative evaluations because of poor work performance and her company wants to terminate her?

**Employment-at-will** provisions give employers the right to terminate (or hire or transfer) employees at any time unless it is illegal to do so. Firing someone because of his or her membership in a protected class would be illegal. Firing someone because he or she is not performing the job or has violated company policy would be allowable.

Essentially, under the employment-at-will practice, there is no contractual obligation to which either an employee or the employer must adhere. Either party can terminate the relationship at any time, for any legal reason. Wrongful discharge and terminating an employee for illegal reasons or for reasons that the courts have found to be inappropriate for discharge are known as exceptions to the employment-at-will doctrine, or *common law claims*. Not every state recognizes all three exceptions to the employment-at-will doctrine. Florida, Georgia, and Rhode Island do not recognize any of the exceptions. A list of the exceptions and the number of states recognizing each follows:[74]

- *Public policy exception.* An employee can sue if he was fired for a reason that violates public policy—that is, if his company acted in bad faith, malice, or retaliation. Serving on jury duty, refusing to violate one's code of professional ethics, and refusing to commit a white-collar crime at the company's urging are examples. The public policy exception is recognized by 43 states.
- *Implied employment contract.* An implied contract is one that is inferred (orally, written, or otherwise) by the conduct of the parties involved. Telling employees that they will not be fired so long as they do their jobs is an example. Policies printed in corporate employment manuals can constitute implied contracts, too. The implied contract exception is recognized by 42 states.
- *Implied covenant of good faith and fair dealing.* Employers have an implied contractual obligation to act in good faith toward their employees, and vice versa. If an employee has been promised a bonus and then is fired so that the company does not have to pay that bonus, the company will not have acted in good faith and fair dealing. The covenant of good faith and fair dealing exception is recognized by only 20 states.

## Regulatory Issues and Competitive Advantage

We have spent a lot of time discussing employment legislation, especially equal employment legislation. As we close this chapter, it is important to make one additional point. A company must not get so caught up in regulatory issues that it loses sight of its purpose as a business. Some companies make hiring decisions to meet quotas and fail to terminate employees who are not contributing to organizational goals out of fear of getting sued. These decisions yield dysfunctional employees and resentment from other employees who have to work with them. The result is lost productive time and often more, rather than fewer, charges of discrimination. Managers face a delicate balance. Imposing controls to reduce harassment and discrimination can overly restrict employee behavior and lead to low morale and lower productivity.[75]

Successful organizations know the value of finding the most qualified applicants, treating them fairly once hired, and treating them fairly and with respect if they have to be terminated. These companies make hiring and other employment decisions with a focus on finding and keeping the most qualified employees rather than on the basis of one of the protected classifications or solely to be legally compliant. As we will show throughout each of the following chapters, this focus, combined with efforts to treat all employees fairly, helps organizations stay legally compliant and advances their ability to have a competitive advantage.

**employment-at-will**

hiring provisions based on state laws that allow employers to terminate (or hire or transfer) employees at any time and that allow employees to quit at any time

## SUMMARY

Equal employment opportunity laws exist to prevent employers from discriminating in employment practices. Specifically, EEO laws prohibit discrimination on the basis of race, color, religion, gender, national origin, age, disability, and genetic information. The laws seek to ensure that individuals are treated fairly in the workplace.

Disparate treatment occurs when employers use a protected classification to make employment decisions. Employers can defend a charge of disparate treatment by providing evidence that the employment decision was based on a reason not related to the protected classification. Disparate impact occurs when a neutral employment practice leads to an unfavorable outcome for a protected classification. Disparate impact charges can be defended by showing the job relatedness of the practice, business necessity, or the presence of a seniority system or BFOQ.

The main EEO laws include the Equal Pay Act, Title VII of the Civil Rights Act of 1964, the Age Discrimination in Employment Act, the Americans with Disabilities Act as amended, and the Pregnancy Discrimination Act. Each of these laws identifies protected classifications, and the EEOC oversees employer compliance with the practices. In addition, the Civil Rights Act of 1991 provides guidance on discrimination issues.

EEO laws prohibit harassment in the workplace on the basis of race, color, religion, national origin, and gender. While national origin and religious harassment is becoming more of a problem in the workplace, sexual harassment continues to be of particular concern. The EEOC has issued guidance on what an employer should do to discourage sexual harassment in the workplace.

The ADA requires that employers look at whether an individual with a disability is qualified to perform the essential functions of the job, with or without reasonable accommodation. Most reasonable accommodations cost less than $1,000. The ADAA clarified a number of issues about enforcement of the ADA.

The EEOC has developed guidelines for multinational companies to assist them in knowing to what extent they are bound by EEO laws. These guidelines cover U.S. employers with U.S. employees in other countries, employers from other countries operating in the United States, and responsibilities of U.S. companies with regard to the laws of the countries in which they are operating.

In addition to EEO laws, a number of executive orders prohibit discrimination by federal contractors and subcontractors and require that these employers engage in affirmative action activities. Affirmative action means the employer goes beyond not discriminating by actively seeking to increase the representation of minority groups in the organization.

Other related employment laws that affect employee rights include the Immigration Reform and Control Act, Family and Medical Leave Act, Rehabilitation Act, Vietnam Era Veteran's Readjustment Assistance Act, Uniformed Services Employment and Reemployment Rights Act, state fair employment practice laws, and the employment-at-will doctrine.

## KEY TERMS

| | |
|---|---|
| affirmative action | disparate impact |
| affirmative defense | disparate treatment |
| alternative dispute resolution (ADR) | employment-at-will |
| bona fide occupational qualification (BFOQ) | equal employment opportunity (EEO) |
| business necessity | Equal Employment Opportunity Commission (EEOC) |
| disability | essential functions |
| discrimination | fair employment practice laws |

four-fifths rule

genetic information

harassment

hostile work environment

McDonnell Douglas test

mixed motive

Office of Federal Contract Compliance Programs (OFCCP)

*prima facie* case

protected classification

*quid pro quo* harassment

reasonable accommodation

retaliation

reverse discrimination

undue hardship

## DISCUSSION QUESTIONS

1. Discuss why EEO legislation is still needed today.

2. Research and report on why Congress included both race and color and ethnic origin as specified protected classifications. Why can race and color never be used as BFOQs?

3. What is required for someone to make a case that discrimination has occurred? Discuss both disparate treatment and disparate impact.

4. Write an executive summary for employers to help them understand that sexual orientation is considered sex discrimination under Title VII of the Civil Rights Act of 1964. Include a few examples of relevant cases that have been settled or are being reviewed by the EEOC that relate to this topic.

5. Your employer is a Japanese company doing business in the United States. Research employment law practices in that country, especially related to the role of females. Explain to your Japanese boss why he cannot refuse to hire women for managerial jobs in his company in the United States even though he can do so legally in his own country.

6. A friend is concerned that he has been discriminated against at work because of national origin. Write an email to him explaining the process for filing a discrimination charge.

7. Discuss the difference between affirmative action and quota systems. Why do you think employers often confuse these concepts?

8. Your best friend, Katelyn, is six months pregnant. She just interviewed for a job for which she is highly qualified and was turned down. A friend of hers, Elsie, who works at the hiring company, told her that a man with lesser qualifications was hired. Elsie also told Katelyn that she did not get the job because the hiring manager did not want to have to "deal with maternity leave and all of that stuff that goes with new mothers." What options are available to your friend? What do you recommend she do, and why?

9. Choose a state different from your home state. Identify the EEO protected classifications in that state. Discuss your findings with your classmates. What are the implications for employers doing business in a state that has a protected class that is not protected by federal law (e.g., political affiliation or belief, questions allowed on applications)?

## LEARNING EXERCISE 1

You have just learned that one of your employees has told another employee that she was sexually assaulted by a coworker at the company holiday party. The party was held off site and was not a mandatory event.

1. Describe how you would handle this situation.

2. What information would you need from the employee?

3. If your company does not have a policy prohibiting sexual harassment, how would you handle the situation? Would the absence of a policy affect how you deal with the situation?

4. What should be included in an antiharassment policy?

5. Discuss with your classmates the implications of the #MeToo movement in the workplace and how employers should deal with this issue.

## LEARNING EXERCISE 2

Jose Martinez is the new plant manager for a small manufacturing firm that assembles products for other companies. The assembly tasks are not difficult. A number of very good employees have intellectual disabilities. Unfortunately, you have a new supervisor who has been overheard making derogatory remarks about some of these employees. He has even commented on their disabilities on his Facebook page, calling them derogatory names.

1. How should you handle this situation?

2. What law, if any, has been violated?

3. If a law has been violated, is there evidence of disparate treatment, disparate impact, both, or neither? Make a case for your answer.

4. Discuss with your classmates what a manager can do to reduce the likelihood of this type of problem occurring.

## CASE STUDY 1: NATIONAL ORIGIN DISCRIMINATION IN PAY—LEGAL OR NOT?

According to the Equal Pay Act, employers are permitted to pay males and females different wages under a limited set of circumstances. What about differences in national origin, however? Are there legitimate reasons that a company can use to pay individuals differently based on their national origin?

Winner Ford of Cherry Hill and Winner Ford evidently thought so. They employed Chinese and non-Chinese emergency and accessory installation (EAI) technicians. The company paid the Chinese EAI technicians as much as $3 per hour less than it paid the non-Chinese technicians. The dealerships are part of Chas. S. Winner Inc. The company is a large automotive dealership based in Cherry Hill, New Jersey. The dealership offers direct sales and leasing of cars and trucks, fleet management services, police responder vehicles, delivery vehicles, and more.

The technicians performed the same work, regardless of national origin. Some of the non-Chinese workers had less experience than the Chinese technicians, and others had no experience. Because of the pay disparity, one of the Chinese EAIs complained. The company responded by reprimanding him for complaining and suggested that he could lose his job if he sought legal advice.

The EEOC brought charges against the company in U.S. District Court for the District of New Jersey when attempts at conciliation were not successful. The court ordered the company to pay $150,000 in lost wages and damages to the members of the class action lawsuit. The courts also required a consent decree for three years.

### Discussion Questions

1. Visit the EEOC website and read about national origin Discrimination, especially noting the "Facts About National Origin Discrimination" under the "More Information" section. Prepare a memo to explain to the owners of Winner Ford why what they did was a problem.

2. What type of discrimination occurred? What would Winner Ford need to do to defend their actions successfully?

3. Why do courts require consent decrees? What were the specifics of the consent decree in this case? (Information is available on the EEOC website in their "News" section and in other places online.)

4. Under what circumstances could Winner Ford justify paying Chinese employees less than non-Chinese employees and not be breaking the law? Would you recommend that they do so? Why or why not?

*Source:* Based on Ryan Felton, "Ford Dealership to Pay $150,000 Back to Chinese Technicians It Allegedly Underpaid," jalopnik.com, November 27, 2017, https://jalopnik.com/ford-dealership-to-pay-150-000-back-to-chinese-technic-1820774142: "Winner Ford to Pay $150,000 to Settle EEOC National Origin Discrimination Suit," Equal Employment Opportunity Commission, https://www1.eeoc.gov/eeoc/newsroom/release/11-22-17.cfm; "Company Overview of Chas. S. Winner Inc.," Bloomberg LP, https://www.bloomberg.com/research/stocks/private/snapshot.asp?privcapId=6487648.

## CASE STUDY 2: CHANGING THE CULTURE AT STARBUCKS: RACIAL-BIAS TRAINING

On April 12, 2018, a manager at a Starbucks in Philadelphia called police to arrest two black men in the store. The two men were waiting for a friend to arrive for a business meeting when one of them, before he ordered any food or drink, asked to use the restroom. The white store manager responded by calling 911. Witnesses say that the black men had not done anything to warrant this response. The video of the arrest went viral quickly.

Both the chief executive officer (CEO) of Starbucks and the chairman met with the two men to publicly apologize for the incident. They also announced that the company would close all 8,000 of its stores on May 29 for racial-bias training designed to prevent discrimination at its locations in the United States. Topics to be included in the training were "implicit bias" and "conscious inclusion." The company reached out to groups such as the Equal Justice Initiative and the NAACP for assistance in designing the antibias training. Starbucks already had policies that prohibit discrimination, but it now plans to add antidiscrimination and antiharassment training to the employee onboarding process in the future.

Employee reactions to the planned training were mixed. Some employees thought that it was a good move. Some saw it as a public relations stunt. Some questioned how much could be achieved in a few hours. Other employees shared their own experiences of ethnic and racial harassment from customers. Nonwhite employees make up 40 percent of the workforce at Starbucks.

This latest move by Starbucks to address issues of race follows a 2015 campaign in which the company had invited baristas to write "#RaceTogether" on cups and have dialogues with customers who asked about it. Many workers were uncomfortable with being assigned this responsibility.

### Discussion Questions

1. Discuss why Starbucks reacted to this incident as an employee training issue. How does the situation relate to the content of this chapter regarding discrimination?

2. Is a company responsible for the discriminatory behavior of its customers toward its employees? Could an employee charge the company with discrimination if subjected to harassment by a customer and, if so, under what law?

3. Research antibias discrimination programs. Use the information that you discover to develop an outline of the content and activities that are considered effective in such training.

4. Why do you think the 2015 #RaceTogether campaign did not succeed? Can a company require employees to participate in such an activity? Why or why not?

5. What other options should Starbucks consider to ensure that future incidents such as the April 12 event do not occur?

*Sources:* Based on Kate Taylor and Leanna Garfield, "Starbucks Is Closing All Stores Nationwide for Racial-Bias Training—Yet Baristas Say the Problem Runs Deeper than Many Customers Realize," businessinsider.com, April 23, 2018, http://www.businessinsider.com/starbucks-racial-bias-training-what-baristas-think-2018-4; Julianne Slovak, "Starbucks Pledges to Learn From Its Mistakes In Racial Bias Case, Reports Record Revenues," forbes.com, April 26, 2018, https://www.forbes.com/sites/julianneslovak/2018/04/26/starbucks-pledges-to-learn-from-its-mistakes-in-racial-bias-case-reports-record-revenues/#7c87a7204a96; Ziati Meyer, "Starbucks CEO Vows to Learn from 'Mistake' in Racial Incident," usatoday.com, April 26, 2018, https://www.usatoday.com/story/money/2018/04/26/starbucks-ceo-apologizes-mistake-racial-incident/554597002/.

# NOTES

[1] Lisa Nagele-Piazza, "Bass Pro to Pay $10.5 million to Settle Hiring Discrimination Claims," SHRM.org, https://www.shrm.org/resourcesandtools/legal-and-compliance/employment-law/pages/bass-pro-$10.6-million-hiring-discrimination-claims.aspx; "Bass Pro to Pay $10.5 million to Settle EEOC Hiring Discrimination and Retaliation Suit," Equal Employment Opportunity Commission, http://www.eeoc.gov/eeoc/newsroom/release/7-25-17b.cfm; Wes Johnson, "Bass Pro, EEOC Reach Agreement On Discrimination Claims; Company Will Pay $10.5 Million," *Springfield News-Leader*, news-leader.com, July 25, 2107, https://www.news-leader.com/story/news/2017/07/25/bass-pro-eeoc-reach-agreement-discrimination-claims -company-pay-10-5-million/508002001/.

[2] *Diaz v. Pan American World Airways, Inc.*, 442 F.2d 385 (5th Cir. 1971).

[3] Ibid.

[4] *McDonnell Douglas v. Green*, 411 U.S. 793 (1973).

[5] "Selected Supreme Court Decisions," Equal Employment Opportunity Commission, http://www.eeoc.gov/eeoc/history/35th/thelaw/supreme_court.html.

[6] Amanda Onion, "Why Have Americans Stopped Growing Taller?" ABC News, http://www.abcnews.go.com.

[7] *Griggs v. Duke Power*, 401 U.S. 424 (1971).

[8] Ibid.

[9] "CSX Transportation to Pay $3.2 million to Settle EEOC Disparate Impact Sex Discrimination Case," *National Law Review*, natlawreview.com, June 13, 2018, https://www.natlawreview.com/article/csx-transportation-to-pay-32-million-to-settle-eeoc-disparate-impact-sex.

[10] "Harassment," Equal Employment Opportunity Commission, http://www.eeoc.gov/laws/types/harassment.cfm.

[11] "Olympia Construction to Pay $100,000 to Resolve EEOC Racial Harassment and Retaliation Lawsuit," Equal Employment Opportunity Commission, March 12, 2014, http://www.eeoc.gov/eeoc/newsroom/release/3-12-14b.cfm.

[12] "Retaliation," Equal Employment Opportunity Commission, www.eeoc.gov/laws/types/retaliation.cfm.

[13] "Facts About Equal Pay and Compensation Discrimination," Equal Employment Opportunity Commission, http://www.eeoc.gov/eeoc/publications/fs-epa.cfm.

[14] American Association of University Women (AAUW), "The Simple Truth About the Gender Pay Gap: 2016 Edition," downloaded July 4, 2016, http://www.aauw.org/files/2016/02/SimpleTruth_Spring2016.pdf.

[15] Marguerite Ward, "4 Ways the Ban on the Interview Question 'What's Your Current Salary?' Could Affect You," CNBC.com, http://www.cnbc.com/2017/11/09/how-the-ban-on-asking-whats-your-current-salary-could-affect-you.html.

[16] Peter B. Levy, *The Civil Rights Movement* (Westport, CT: Greenwood Press, 1998).

[17] "Pre 1965: Events Leading to the Creation of EEOC," Equal Employment Opportunity Commission, http://www.eeoc.gov/eeoc/history/35th/pre1965/#content.

[18] "Title VII of the Civil Rights Act of 1964," Equal Employment Opportunity Commission, http://www.eeoc.gov/laws/statutes/titlevii.cfm.

[19] "Shaping Employment Discrimination Law," Equal Employment Opportunity Commission, http://www.eeoc.gov/eeoc/history/35th/1965-71/shaping.html.

[20] "Charges Alleging Race and Harassment (Charges filed with EEOC) FY 1997–FY2017," Equal Employment Opportunity Commission, http://www.eeoc.gov/eeoc/statistics/enforcement/race_harassment.cfm.

[21] "Race-Based Charges (Charges Filed with EEOC) FY1997–FY2017," Equal Employment Opportunity Commission, http://www.eeoc.gov/eeoc/statistics/enforcement/race.cfm.

[22] "Questions and Answers About Race and Color Discrimination in Employment," Equal Employment Opportunity Commission, http://www.eeoc.gov/policy/docs/qanda_race_color.html; EEOC Compliance Manual Directives Transmittal Number 915.003, "Section 15: Race and Color Discrimination," Equal Employment Opportunity Commission, April 16, 2006, http://www.eeoc.gov/policy/docs/race-color.pdf.

[23] "Religion-Based Charges (Charges Filed with EEOC) FY1997–FY2017," Equal Employment Opportunity Commission, www.eeoc.gov/eeoc/statistics/enforcement/religion.cfm.

[24] "Religious Discrimination," Equal Employment Opportunity Commission, http://www.eeoc.gov/laws/types/religion.cfm.

[25] Ibid.

[26] *Price Waterhouse v. Hopkins*, 490 U.S. 228 (1989).

[27] Ibid.

[28] "Facts About Sexual Harassment," Equal Employment Opportunity Commission, http://www.eeoc.gov/eeoc/publications/fs-sex.cfm.

[29] Anita Cava, "Sexual Harassment Claims: New Framework for Employers," *Business and Economic Review* 47 (2001): 13–16.

[30] Ibid.

[31] "National Origin Discrimination," Equal Employment Opportunity Commission, http://www.eeoc.gov/laws/types/nationalorigin.cfm.

[32] "EEOC Sues Plaza Hotel & Fairmont Hotels & Resorts for Post-9/11 Backlash Discrimination," Equal Employment Opportunity Commission, September 30, 2003, http://www.eeoc.gov/press/9-30-03b.html.

[33] "The Plaza Hotel to Pay $525,000 for Post 9/11 Backlash Discrimination Against Employees," Equal Employment Opportunity Commission, June 8, 2005, http://www.eeoc.gov/eeoc/newsroom/release/6-8-05.cfm.

[34] "Pregnancy Discrimination," Equal Employment Opportunity Commission, http://www.eeoc.gov/eeoc/publications/fs-preg.cfm.

[35] "The Civil Rights Act of 1991," Equal Employment Opportunity Commission, http://www.eeoc.gov/eeoc/history/35th/1990s/civilrights.html.

[36] "The Civil Rights Act of 1991" (Pub. L. 102-166).

[37] "Age Discrimination," Equal Employment Opportunity Commission, http://www.eeoc.gov/laws/types/age.cfm.

[38] Ibid.

[39] Dan Horn, "Older Workers Transform the Modern Workplace," *USA Today*, February 25, 2013, http://www.usatoday.com/story/money/business/2013/02/25/older-workers-transform-modern-workplace/1945711/.

[40] "Age Discrimination in Employment Act (Charges filed with EEOC) (includes concurrent charges with Title VII, ADA, EPA, and GINA) FY1997–FY2017," Equal Employment Opportunity Commission, http://www.eeoc.gov/eeoc/statistics/enforcement/adea.cfm.

[41] Kelly Greene, "AARP to Recruit for Home Depot," *Wall Street Journal*, February 6, 2004, p. B5; Employer Pledge Program, AARP.com, https://www.aarp.org/work/job-search/employer-pledge-companies/.

[42] Dan Horn, "Older Workers Transform the Modern Workplace," *USA Today*, February 25, 2013, http://www.usatoday.com/story/money/business/2013/02/25/older-workers-transform-modern-workplace/1945711/; Kerry Hannon, "Reaping the Benefits of an Aging Workforce," *Seattle Times,* March 15, 2018, https://www.seattletimes.com/explore/careers/reaping-the-benefits-of-an-aging-workforce/.

[43] "Frequently Asked Questions, New Section 503 Regulations," U.S. Department of Labor, Office of Federal Contract Compliance Programs (OFCCP), http://www.dol.gov/ofccp/regs/compliance/faqs/503_faq.htm#Q0.

[44] "Section 503 of the Rehabilitation Act of 1973, as amended," U.S. Department of Labor, Employment Standards Administration, Office of Federal Contract Compliance, http://www.dol.gov/ofccp/regs/compliance/sec503.htm.

[45] Matthew Brault, "Americans with Disabilities: 2010," *Household Economic Studies* (July 2012): 1–15, http://www.census.gov/prod/2012pubs/p70-131.pdf.

46 "Disability Discrimination," Equal Employment Opportunity Commission, http://www
.eeoc.gov/laws/types/disability.cfm.

47 "Notice Concerning the Americans with Disabilities Act (ADA) Amendments Act of 2008,"
Equal Employment Opportunity Commission. http://www.eeoc.gov/laws/statutes/adaaa_
notice.cfm.

48 Ibid.

49 Ibid.

50 "Employers and the ADA: Myths and Facts," U.S. Department of Labor, http://www.dol
.gov/odep/pubs/fact/ada.htm; "The Amercians with Disabilities Act: A Primer for Small
Business," Equal Employment Opportunity Commission, http://www.eeoc.gov/eeoc/
publications/adahandbook.cfm%20#reasonable.

51 B. A. Loy and T. G. Gebremedhin, "Disability Legislation: An Empirical Analysis of Employer Cost" (research paper 2001-3, West Virginia University Regional Research Institute,
Morgantown, WV, 2001).

52 "Disability Discrimination," Equal Employment Opportunity Commission, http://www
.eeoc.gov/laws/types/disability.cfm.

53 "Facts About the Americans with Disabilities Act," Equal Employment Opportunity Commission, http://www.eeoc.gov/eeoc/publications/fs-ada.cfm.

54 "Founders Pavilion Will Pay $370,000 to Settle EEOC Genetic Information Discrimination
Lawsuit," l January 13, 2014, http://www.eeoc.gov/eeoc/newsroom/release/1-13-14.cfm;
John Herzfeld, "Nursing Center Settle Charges by EEOC for Asking About Family Medical
History," Bloomberg BNA, January 15, 2014, http://www.bna.com/nursing-center-settles-
charges-by-eeoc-for-asking-about-family-medical-history/.

55 "Social Media Is Part of Today's Workplace But Its Use May Raise Employment Discrimination Concerns," Equal Employment Opportunity Commission, March 12, 2014, http://
www.eeoc.gov/eeoc/newsroom/release/3-12-14.cfm.

56 "The Equal Employment Opportunity Responsibilities of Multinational Employers,"
Equal Employment Opportunity Commission, http://www.eeoc.gov/facts/multi-employers
.html.

57 "Facts About Mediation," Equal Employment Opportunity Commission, http://www.eeoc
.gov/eeoc/mediation/facts.cfm.

58 "History of the EEOC Mediation Program," Equal Employment Opportunity Commission,
http://www.eeoc.gov/eeoc/mediation/history.cfm.

59 "Administrative Enforcement and Litigation," Equal Employment Opportunity Commission, http://www.eeoc.gov/eeoc/enforcement_litigation.cfm.

60 "Facts on Executive Order 11246—Affirmative Action," U.S. Department of Labor,
Employment Standards Administration, Office of Federal Contract Compliance Programs, http://www.dol.gov/ofccp/regs/compliance/aa.htm.

61 Ibid; Amano Noriko (2017). "What Are the Effects of Affirmative Action Regulation
on Workers' Careers?" Yale Institution for Social and Policy Studies, https://isps.yale.edu/
news/blog/2017/01/what-are-the-effects-of-affirmative-action-regulation-on-workers%
E2%80%99-careers.

62 Taylor Cox, *Creating the Multicultural Organization: A Strategy for Capturing the Power of
Diversity* (San Francisco: Jossey-Bass, 2001); Shelley Brickson, "The Impact of Identity
Orientation on Individual and Organizational Outcomes in Demographically Diverse Settings," *Academy of Management Review* 25 (2000): 82–101; and David Harrison, Kenneth
Price, and Myrtle Bell, "Beyond Relational Demography: Time and the Effects of Surface-
and Deep-level Diversity on Work Group Cohesion," *Academy of Management Journal* 41
(1998): 96–107.

63 "I-9, Employment Eligibility Verification," U.S. Citizenship and Immigration Services,
http://www.uscis.gov/i-9.

64 "Form I-9 Inspection Overview,' U. S. Immigration and Customs Enforcement, January 8,
2018, https://www.ice.gov/factsheets/i9-inspection#fineSchedule.

65 "USCIS Revises Employment Eligibility Verification Form I-9," U.S. Citizenship and Immigration Services, http://www.uscis.gov/news/public-releases-topic/employment-verification/
uscis-revises-employment-eligibility-verification-form-i-9; "What Is E-Verify?" U. S. Citizen
and Immigration Services, https://www.uscis.gov/e-verify.

66 "The Family and Medical Leave Act and National Defense Authorization Act for FY 2008,"
U.S. Department of Labor, Wage and Hour Division (WHD), http://www.dol.gov/whd/fmla/
NDAA_fmla.htm; "Final Rule to Revise the Definition of 'Spouse' Under the FMLA," U.S.
Department of Labor, https://www.dol.gov/whd/fmla/spouse/.

67 "The Family and Medical Leave Act," U.S. Department of Labor, Employment Standards Administration, Wage and Hour Division (WHD), http://www.dol.gov/whd/regs/compliance/1421.htm.

68 "The Vietnam Era Veterans' Readjustment Assistance Act (VEVRAA)," U.S. Department of Labor, http://www.dol.gov/compliance/laws/comp-vevraa.htm.

69 "The Uniformed Services Employment and Reemployment Rights Act (USERRA)," U.S. Department of Labor, http://www.dol.gov/compliance/laws/comp-userra.htm.

70 "Job Rights for Veterans and Reserve Component Members," U.S. Department of Labor, VETS USERRA Fact Sheet 3, http://www.dol.gov/vets/programs/userra/userra_fs.htm.

71 Ibid.

72 "VETS Assists Police Officer through USERRA," U.S. Department of Labor, Veterans' Employment and Training Service, Uniformed Services Employment and Reemployment Rights Act (USERRA) Information, http://www.dol.gov/vets/programs/userra/.

73 "Same-Sex Marriage in the United States," *CNN.com*, http://www.cnn.com/interactive/us/map-same-sex-marriage/.

74 Charles Muhl, "The Employment-at-Will Doctrine: Three Major Exceptions," *Monthly Labor Review* (January 2001): 1–11; "Employment At-Will Exceptions by State," National Comference of State Legislators, http://www.ncsl.org/research/labor-and-employment/at-will-employment-exceptions-by-state.aspx.

75 Mark Roehling and Patrick Wright, "Organizationally Sensible vs. Legal-Centric Responses to the Eroding Employment at-Will Doctrine: The Evolving Nature of the Employment Relationship: Protecting Workers from Unjust Dismissal Versus Safeguarding Employer Prerogatives," *Employee Responsibilities and Rights Journal* 16 (2004): 89–103.

# Part 2

# Work Design and Workforce Planning

# Chapter 4

# Job Design and Job Analysis

## Learning Objecties

**AFTER READING THIS CHAPTER, YOU SHOULD BE ABLE TO:**

**1** Explain the importance of job design.

**2** Describe how managers use efficiency and motivational approaches to design jobs.

**3** Explain the trade-offs between the efficiency and motivational job-design approaches.

**4** Understand the importance of job descriptions and job specifications.

**5** Discuss the advantages and disadvantages of different sources of data for job analysis.

**6** Understand how organizational demands influence job design.

**7** Discuss how environmental challenges affect job design.

**8** Explain the importance of job design and job analysis for legal compliance.

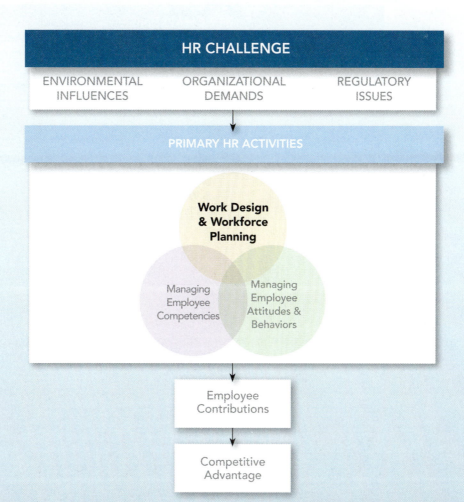

HR CHALLENGE

| ENVIRONMENTAL INFLUENCES | ORGANIZATIONAL DEMANDS | REGULATORY ISSUES |

PRIMARY HR ACTIVITIES

Work Design & Workforce Planning

Managing Employee Competencies

Managing Employee Attitudes & Behaviors

Employee Contributions

Competitive Advantage

# The Importance of Job Design and Job Analysis

Have you ever wondered why jobs are set up the way they are? Compare the job of a cook in a fast-food restaurant to that of a chef in a four-star restaurant. The cook typically follows a predetermined process to assemble the product that the customer has ordered in a timely manner. The chef has much more latitude in how to prepare the food, as well as what to include with the meal, and performs a wider array of tasks than the cook. Why are these jobs so different? Both jobs focus on preparing food to satisfy the customer. Both jobs use similar equipment to cook the food. Yet the duties that each job requires differ, as do the knowledge, skills, and abilities (KSAs) that each food preparer must possess to perform the job successfully.

Differences in the tasks and responsibilities for different jobs, or even for similar jobs in different companies, do not occur by chance. Managers consciously make decisions about how they design jobs to improve company performance. Looking at the framework for the strategic management of employees in Exhibit 4.1, you can see that a critical goal of managing *the primary human resources (HR) activities* is to maximize the employee contributions that yield competitive advantage. **Job design** involves determining the tasks and responsibilities that employees in a particular job are expected to perform, as well as how they need to interact with

**job design**

determining the tasks and responsibilities that employees in a particular job are expected to perform, as well as how they need to interact with their coworkers to realize those contributions

**EXHIBIT 4.1**

## Framework for the Strategic Management of Employees

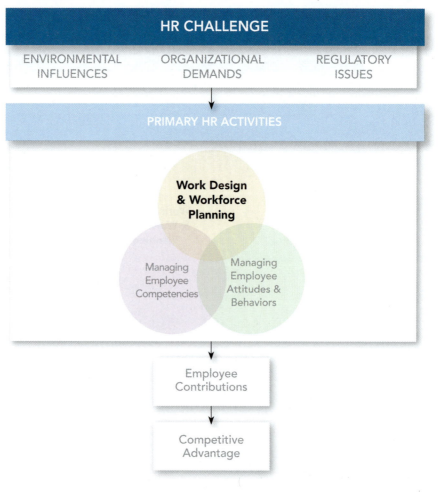

their coworkers to realize those contributions. Job design is a key component of effectively managing employees because it is one of the major ways to translate company goals into the specific actions that employees perform in their jobs. When done effectively, job design helps employees focus on the tasks and responsibilities that optimize their potential contributions for competitive advantage. Some of the key issues that managers must consider are:

- What tasks should you emphasize when designing a job?
- How simple or complex are these tasks?
- How many tasks can your employees perform?
- How much flexibility do you provide to your employees in terms of how and where they carry out their tasks?

In addition to deciding how to design jobs, managers must understand the competencies that an employee needs to possess to successfully perform a particular job. This secondary aspect of job design is called *job analysis*. **Job analysis** is the process of systematically identifying the tasks, duties, and responsibilities expected to be performed in a single job, as well as the competencies—the knowledge, skills, and abilities (KSAs)—that employees must possess to be successful in the job. Two important outcomes of job analysis are the creation of job descriptions and the identification of job specifications. *Job descriptions* are written summaries of the specific tasks, responsibilities, and working conditions of a job and include a list of the job specifications. *Job specifications* are the specific competencies a jobholder must possess to be able to perform a job successfully.

Job descriptions and job specifications serve as valuable tools for the other employee management activities that managers must perform. For example, by clearly articulating the abilities that employees must have to be successful in their jobs, job descriptions serve a critical role in managing competencies. After all, without a clear understanding of the necessary competencies to perform tasks successfully, how does a company know what to look for when recruiting employees, or which job candidate to hire? Similarly, as you may recall from our discussion of the legal environment in Chapter 3, hiring decisions must be based on job-related criteria. How do you know if the hiring standards you use are legally defensible? And how can companies make effective training decisions without knowing which competencies are actually needed to succeed in a current or future job? Later in this book, we explore how job descriptions and job specifications are valuable tools for *managing employee competencies*, especially when recruiting and hiring employees.

Job design and job analysis also serve a critical role in *managing employee attitudes and behaviors*. As we will discuss in Chapter 9, an effective performance management system is grounded in part on evaluating how well employees perform all aspects of their jobs and providing developmental feedback to improve their job performance. Similarly, compensation decisions are directly influenced by job design. If you have work experience, you'll quickly recognize that salary decisions are typically based on the relative worth of a job performed within a company. Establishing pay levels that are fair and equitable requires a good understanding of a job's tasks and responsibilities, as well as how the value of that job to company success compares with the value of other jobs within the company.

Exhibit 4.2 shows the relationships among job design, job analysis, and job descriptions and specifications. In this chapter, we examine the principles of job design and explore alternative approaches to designing jobs to increase employee efficiency and motivation. Our discussion focuses first on job design based on the logic that to perform a job analysis, there has to be a job, or at least the idea of a particular set of tasks and responsibilities to be performed. We then discuss the process of job analysis and wrap up with examination of how the HR challenges—organizational demands, environmental influences, and the legal environment—influence job design in practice

**job analysis**

the process of systematically identifying the tasks, duties, and responsibilities expected to be performed in a single job, as well as the competencies—the knowledge, skills, and abilities (KSAs)—that employees must possess to be successful in the job

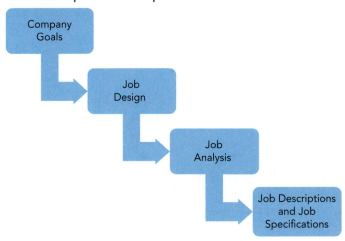

**EXHIBIT 4.2**

Relationships Among Job Design, Job Analysis, and Job Descriptions and Specifications

within companies. The appendix to this chapter provides more detailed information regarding the specific approaches to job analysis.

# Job Design

The ultimate goal of job design is to enhance company performance. There are two considerations in this perspective. First, managers have to understand the role that different jobs play in attaining competitive advantage for the organization. Each job is unique and adds value in different ways. What specific tasks and responsibilities, if performed as expected, will maximize the value added of each job? For example, within a single company, some jobs add value because their tasks contribute to efficient operations. Other jobs add value because their tasks create innovative products or services, maintain customer satisfaction, or contribute to another important aspect of organizational functioning. If customer service is a high priority for the company, what specific tasks, behaviors, and responsibilities lead to exceptional customer service? The challenge for managers is to understand *what* tasks and responsibilities need to be performed in each job to maximize the company's success.

Second, managers must make decisions about *how* employees will perform their jobs. These decisions shape the nature and extent of employees' contributions toward company objectives. Most jobs may be performed in many different ways. For example, in a manufacturing company, employees may work on an assembly line performing a limited set of tasks throughout the day without interacting with coworkers unless a problem is detected. In another manufacturing firm, employees may perform a broad set of tasks, work in self-managed teams, and have a high level of interaction with their coworkers. Similarly, for computer programmers, some companies may design jobs so that employees work in relative isolation in cubicles solving complicated problems. Alternatively, companies may design the job environment to encourage a high level of interaction among programmers, perhaps even requiring programmers to work with colleagues across the globe. The ultimate choice about which job design approach to implement should be based on how a job adds value within a company. Jobs can align with company goals and add value through a focus on efficiency or on motivation.

## Efficiency Approaches to Job Design

Not surprisingly, efficiency has been the dominant model for job design for much of the past 100 years. Fueled by developments of the Industrial Revolution in the late 1800s, companies began to employ large numbers of workers in a single location to take advantage of the technological breakthroughs in manufacturing. A growing workforce led to the need to coordinate and standardize the work performed, and increased the challenge of hiring and training employees. Scientific management, pioneered by Frederick Taylor in 1911, emerged during this time as the dominant perspective that examined how work should be structured to maximize worker efficiency.[1]

One of the primary contributions of scientific management was the standardization of production processes. This standardization focused on how employees performed their work, how employees' workdays were structured, when and how often employees took breaks from their work, and how much responsibility employees were allowed on the job. The use of scientific management principles guided the design of the first assembly lines. Company Spotlight 4.1 showcases Henry Ford and his production of the Model T. Ford's assembly line revolutionized the automobile production process. The same scientific management principles that guided the design of the first Ford assembly line are still in use in many automobile plants today.

The critical outcome of scientific management and other efficiency-oriented approaches to job design is a detailed analysis of the specific tasks and worker actions to identify the ideal method or procedure for carrying out each task.[2] One common method for this type of analysis is the use of a **time and motion study**—a systematic evaluation of the most basic elements of the tasks that comprise a job. Each job is divided into its most basic parts so that industrial engineers or managers can design jobs in a way that minimizes excessive movements or wasted time while maximizing the time that employees spend working on core job tasks.[3] Consider the traditional assembly line again. Rather than require employees to search for the necessary parts to assemble a product, the process is designed so that employees remain relatively stationary and a mechanized line brings the product to them.

**time and motion study**

systematic evaluation of the most basic elements of the tasks that comprise a job

## COMPANY SPOTLIGHT   **4.1**

### Henry Ford and the Model T

Just how important can job design be for a company's success? In the early days of the automobile industry, most cars were hand-built by craftspeople. Building cars was an art as much as a science. The components were not standardized, and the workers had to finesse them into place. Realizing the inefficiencies of this approach, Henry Ford implemented a mass-production assembly line in his automobile plant with each employee performing a single task throughout the day. As each task was completed, a mechanized assembly line moved the product along to the next worker. The result? Production soared because of the labor efficiencies of the process. The purchase price of the cars dropped as well. In 1912, Ford sold roughly 89,000 cars for $600 each. In 1916, Ford sold 585,388 cars for $350 each. Given this type of growth, it is evident that how jobs are designed can dramatically affect a company's bottom line.

*Sources*: M. Krebs, "The Starting Line," *Automotive News*, 77 (2003): 16, http://www.autonews.com/article/20030616/SUB/306160837/ford-at-100:-its-impact-on-a-community:-the-starting-line; "Putting America on Wheels," *Economist.com*, December 23, 1999, http://www.economist.com/business/displaystory.cfm?story_id=347288; and A. Harrington, "The Big Ideas," *Fortune* 140 (November 22, 1999): 98–103, http://archive.fortune.com/magazines/fortune/fortune_archive/1999/11/22/269065/index.htm.

As you can imagine, this substantially increases the efficiency of the process. Another effect of this type of design is that it alters the specific tasks and responsibilities of employees through job specialization and job simplification.

**Job specialization** is the process of identifying the core elements of a job. By focusing on these core elements, a company is able to limit the variety of tasks employees perform and increase the efficiency with which they perform them. When repetition is built into a job, employees are able to master a specific task and perform it with increasing efficiency, thus maximizing company productivity. Recall our earlier discussion of fast-food restaurants. When a company reduces the variety of tasks in each job, the individuals performing those jobs are able to carry out their tasks efficiently, quickly, and with minimal error. Speed is one of the key sources of competitive advantage for a fast-food restaurant so it is not surprising that an efficiency approach to job design enables employees to maximize their contribution toward that competitive advantage. In effect, a fast-food restaurant, such as McDonald's, operates much like a factory assembly line with its division of labor based on the tasks to be performed.

Another efficiency approach is **job simplification,** which involves removing decision-making authority from the employee and placing it with a supervisor. By removing the discretionary components of jobs, companies are able to lower the number and level of competencies required of new hires. One benefit of this approach, then, is that it opens up a wider pool of job candidates, and jobs often can be staffed more quickly because more workers are available in the labor market. Job simplification also reduces the amount of time that employees might spend thinking instead of doing their jobs. Employee training can be more focused and, as a result, more cost-effective.

The downside of job simplification and job specialization is that jobs are narrow in focus and without much (if any) discretion afforded employees. These jobs can be performed efficiently, but they often lack complexity and variety and can lead to boredom, fatigue, and diminished job satisfaction. An interesting note about Ford's production plants in the early 1900s is that productivity did increase with the implementation of scientific management principles but so did turnover.[4] However, because of job simplification, more people were able to perform the tasks and training requirements were reduced. These results allowed companies, such as Ford, to quickly fill their frequent vacancies. This pattern of high productivity but also high turnover still exists today in many industries, including the agricultural and service industries. The difference from Henry Ford's day is that the pool of low skilled workers has gotten smaller because of greater competition for the same workers.

## Motivational Approaches to Job Design

Motivational approaches to job design maximize an employee's drive to work as hard as possible. A useful way to think about the difference between efficiency and motivational approaches to job design is that an efficiency approach focuses on maximizing employee productivity by simplifying jobs so that employees make fewer mistakes and maintain a high level of performance according to preset job procedures,[5] whereas a motivational approach focuses on making jobs more interesting, challenging, and complex to encourage employees to want to work as effectively and efficiently as they can.

The most famous motivational approach to job design is the Job Characteristics Model, shown in Exhibit 4.3. The **Job Characteristics Model** identifies five job dimensions and three psychological states of employees that affect employees' internal motivation and satisfaction, as well as absenteeism, turnover, and productivity.[6] The three psychological states are (1) experienced meaningfulness of the work,

**job specialization**

the process of identifying the core elements of a job

**job simplification**

removing decision-making authority from the employee and placing it with a supervisor

**Job Characteristics Model**

a motivational model of job design based on five job dimensions and three psychological states of employees that affect employees' internal motivation and satisfaction, as well as absenteeism, turnover, and productivity

## EXHIBIT 4.3

### The Job Characteristics Model

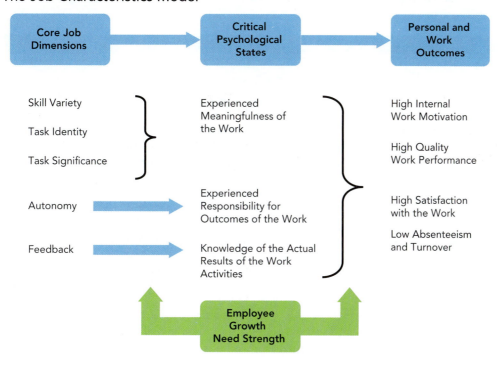

(2) experienced responsibility for outcomes of the work, and (3) knowledge of the actual results of work activities. The five core job dimensions are:

1. *Skill variety*—The degree to which a job includes different tasks and activities that challenge an employee's skills and abilities.
2. *Task identity*—The degree to which the job involves completing a whole, identifiable piece of work.
3. *Task significance*—The degree to which the job has a substantial and perceivable effect on the lives of others.
4. *Autonomy*—The degree to which the job permits substantial freedom and discretion to the individual in scheduling the work and in determining the procedures to perform the work.
5. *Feedback*—The degree to which performing the job requirements results in the individual receiving direct and clear information about the effectiveness of his performance.

Employees are more motivated in their jobs when these five dimensions are present. As shown in Exhibit 4.3, the first three job dimensions influence the psychological state of employees—whether they feel that the work they perform is meaningful and valued. The more skill variety, task identity, and task significance within a job, the more experienced meaningfulness an employee is likely to feel. The fourth job dimension shows that jobs that grant employees autonomy allow them to take ownership and responsibility for the outcome of their work. People with high levels of autonomy know that they are personally responsible for success and failure. The fifth job dimension emphasizes that when employees receive feedback, they understand how well they are performing and the direct results of their work.[7] Feedback allows employees to know whether their work performance is satisfactory.

**EXHIBIT 4.4**

Methods to Improve Employee Motivation and Satisfaction Through Job Design

| Approach | Method |
|---|---|
| Change job tasks | *Job enlargement*—Assign additional tasks of a similar level of difficulty and responsibility to employees. |
| | *Job rotation*—Move workers from one job to another within an organization. |
| Increase responsibility | *Job enrichment*—Increase the level of responsibility and control regarding tasks performed in a job. |
| | *Participation*—Permit employees to participate in decisions that may affect them in their jobs. |
| | *Voice*—Provide employees with access to formal channels within their company to express concerns about their work situation. |
| Create employee teams | Create small groupings of individuals who work collaboratively toward a common goal and who share responsibilities for their outcomes. |

Viewed together, when these job dimensions are low, employees tend to be less satisfied with their jobs and less motivated to work hard. They tend to have lower-quality performance and higher turnover and absenteeism.[8] In contrast, employees in jobs that are designed to support the three psychological states have higher internal motivation to perform well.[9]

How well this model works depends in part on individual differences and contextual conditions. For example, some employees have a higher need for growth in their jobs than others. **Growth need strength** is the extent to which individuals feel a need to learn and be challenged, a need to develop their skills beyond where they currently are, and a strong need for accomplishment. Employees with high growth need strength tend to respond more strongly to the presence of the three psychological states than employees with low growth need strength. One implication of this discussion of growth need strength is that it highlights the importance of considering the fit between individuals and job requirements when making staffing decisions (as we will discuss in Chapters 6 and 7).

Understanding how employees react to the absence or presence of the psychological states and core job dimensions helps managers decide which tactic to use to improve employee motivation and satisfaction. As shown in Exhibit 4.4, three primary methods for improving employee motivation and satisfaction through job design are to change the tasks that employees perform, provide employees with more responsibilities or authority regarding the performance of their jobs, and restructure the work environment to include teams.

### Changing Job Tasks

Managers may modify the variety of tasks that employees perform to make jobs less boring and more satisfying through job enlargement and job rotation. **Job enlargement** is the assignment of additional tasks to employees. This process involves increasing the volume or variety of tasks that are of a similar level of difficulty and responsibility. One of the primary benefits of job enlargement is that increasing the number of different tasks employees perform causes skill variety to increase as well. Greater task and skill variety are effective in countering boredom and fatigue.[10]

**growth need strength**

the extent to which individuals feel a need to learn and be challenged, a need to develop their skills beyond where they currently are, and a strong need for accomplishment

**job enlargement**

the assignment of additional tasks of a similar level of difficulty to employees

**Job rotation** involves moving workers from one job to another job within the organization to provide exposure to different aspects of a company's operations. Unlike job enlargement, job rotation does not change the tasks of a particular job. Rather, it changes the tasks that individual employees perform by moving them to different jobs in a systematic manner. One of the major benefits of job rotation is that it can break the monotony of performing relatively simple jobs while still ensuring efficiency in the performance of each specific task. Another benefit is that companies can use job rotation as a training tool to ensure that employees are able to perform a number of tasks and have a broader overview of the company.[11] A manager in training, for instance, may work for several weeks or months within the marketing department, rotate to a term within the production department, and then move into the design department. Company Spotlight 4.2 describes a leadership development program at Lockheed Martin that involves job rotations. Many other large companies have similar programs.

**job rotation**
moving workers from one job to another job within the organization to provide exposure to different aspects of a company's operations

## COMPANY SPOTLIGHT 4.2

### Job Rotation at Lockheed Martin: Human Resource LDP (HRLDP)

Companies have long known that a good way to build their leadership pipeline is through a job rotation program. Such programs provide an opportunity for participants to learn more about the company activities than they would learn by just working in one department. These programs also provide an opportunity for the company to assess where an employee might have the greatest potential for contribution as a leader down the road.

One such program is the Human Resource Leadership Development Program (HRLDP) at Lockheed Martin. This three-year rotational program is designed to provide participants with a well-rounded, integrated, and accelerated introduction to the HR activities at the company. Participants in the program form a cohort selected based on a demonstrated record of leadership potential and high performance. In addition to rotating throughout the HR functions at Lockheed Martin, participants take part in a well-designed curriculum program that includes technical and experiential development activities, two off-site Leadership Development Conferences (LDCs), and networking opportunities across the organization.

The HRLDP is just one of the many leadership development programs at Lockheed Martin. Others include the Communications LDP (CLDP), a two-year rotational program; the Engineering LDP (ELDP), a three-year program with three or four rotations during that time; the Finance LDP (FLDP), with three annual rotations; the Security LDP (SLDP), with two rotations; and the Operations LDP (OLDP), with three cross-functional rotations.

Rotational programs, such as these at Lockheed Martin, may be particularly attractive to new entrants to the workforce who want to continuously learn, work collaboratively with others, and work on a variety of types of projects, but do so in one organization. Companies are finding that job rotation programs often develop millennials into long-term employees who have greater depth in their contributions to the organization.

*Sources:* "Leadership Development at Lockheed Martin," lockheedmartinjobs.com, https://www.lockheedmartinjobs .com/leadership-development; Glenn Parker, "Designing and Implementing a Job Rotation Program," accenture.com, February 9, 2017, https://www.accenture.com/us-en/blogs/blogs-designing-implementing-job-rotation-program; Kaytie Zimmerman, "Are Rotational Programs the Key to Retaining Millennial Employees?" forbes.com, August 8, 2016, https://www.forbes.com/sites/kaytiezimmerman/2016/08/08/can-a-millenial-quarter-life-crisis-be-cured-by-their-employer/#4c57fe3d446f.

## Increasing Responsibility and Participation

**job enrichment**

increases the level of responsibility and/or control employees have in performing the tasks of a job

While job enlargement and job rotation focus on changing the breadth of tasks that employees perform, **job enrichment,** also called *empowerment* or *delegation,* increases the level of responsibility or control that employees have in performing the tasks of a job. In some ways, it is useful to think of job enrichment as an opposite approach to the job simplification that we discussed earlier in this chapter. While job simplification removes most of the cerebral or higher-level aspects of work and allocates them to managers and supervisors, job enrichment entrusts higher-level tasks and responsibility to employees. Company Spotlight 4.3 shows how Uber uses job enrichment to motivate its driver-partners (individuals who are officially not its employees) to maintain a competitive advantage in the on-demand digital platform business.

**empowerment**

providing employees with higher-level tasks, responsibility, and decision-making in the performance of their job

**Empowerment** builds on the dimension of autonomy in the Job Characteristics Model but takes it a step further by permitting employees to have input into how they carry out their tasks and also authority to modify the job itself.[12] When management delegates authority and responsibility to employees, the employees often realize heightened job satisfaction and enhanced task performance.[13] There are a number of ways to accomplish job enrichment, including the following:[14]

- Provide employees with discretion to set their schedules, decide work methods, check quality, and help less-experienced employees.
- Provide employees with more authority.
- Allow employees freedom to decide when to start and stop work, when to take breaks, and how to prioritize their work.
- Encourage employees to solve problems as they encounter them.
- Provide employees with knowledge about, and control over, budgets.

Of course, companies have to be careful when empowering employees through job enrichment. While it can be an effective means to increase employee motivation and to transfer authority to levels in an organization where decisions are implemented by employees,[15] job enrichment must be accompanied by ability and accountability. Both the employee and the company suffer when employees are asked to take responsibility for tasks that they do not have the competencies to perform effectively. And empowering employees without also holding them accountable for their decisions may result in haphazard decision-making.

**participation**

the extent to which employees are permitted to contribute to decisions that may affect them in their jobs

As an alternative to transferring decision-making authority to employees, managers also can improve employee satisfaction by increasing employee participation in decision-making processes. **Participation** is the extent to which employees are permitted to contribute to decisions that may affect them in their jobs. In contrast with job enrichment, participation does not necessarily transfer responsibility or discretion to employees. It does achieve a similar benefit, however, by allowing employees to take part in decisions that affect their jobs. A specific form of participation, called **voice,** gives employees access to channels within their company to complain or express concerns about their work situation. Whether the channels for employee participation are formal or informal, the more employees are able to have a say in aspects of their work that affect them, the more satisfied they are likely to be in their jobs.[16]

**voice**

a specific form of participation that gives employees access to channels within their company to complain or express concerns about their work situation

**job crafting**

ways in which employees redesign their jobs to increase job satisfaction

One way in which employees are gaining more say in their work is through **job craft** which empowers employees to redesign their own jobs. This process differs from the traditional top-down way in which jobs are designed. Employees engage in job crafting by taking on more or fewer tasks, altering the nature or extent of their interactions with others, or cognitively changing their jobs by changing their perceptions about the tasks that they perform. Through job crafting, employees increase their job satisfaction, engagement, and resilience. So long as the results of job crafting are in line with company goals, it is a net positive for the organization.[17]

# COMPANY SPOTLIGHT  4.3

## Motivating Uber's Drivers

Uber characterizes itself as a technology-based referral service that connects drivers to passengers through a proprietary rideshare app that uses the GPS on the user's phone. Drivers who partner with Uber (Uber refers to them as "driver-partners") provide the transportation services using their own cars and are officially independent business contractors rather than Uber employees.

This scheme means that Uber does not pay employment taxes or provide benefits, which saves labor costs. However, at the same time, Uber, wants to make sure that passengers can find a driver on demand, in five minutes or less. What is it about a job without a steady wage, security, and benefits that attracts enough Uber drivers to make this plan work? Established in 2009, Uber had an estimated 460,000 driver-partners actively driving for them by 2015 and an estimated 2 million in 2018.

Thinking about the Job Characteristics Model, four out of five job dimensions can be applied to explain the motivation for these drivers to agree to this work arrangement. First, there is *skill variety*, because driver-partners are running their own business , setting their schedule, and managing business assets and finances. There is *task identity*, because the job involves completing a whole, identifiable piece of work. Passengers are picked up and dropped off at their desired destination. *Task significance* is achieved because the drivers are providing a needed service for their customers and the income they earn meets their family's needs. Finally, the job provides *autonomy*. Uber driver-partners can choose to work whenever, wherever, and for however long they want. More than half of Uber drivers choose to drive for 15 or fewer hours per week, with no difference in hourly wage between those who work part time and those who choose to work full time. The most stated reasons for being an Uber driver, according to a recent survey, were "to earn more income to better support myself or my family" (91%); "to be my own boss and set my own schedule" (87%); and "to have more flexibility in my schedule and balance my work with my life and family" (85%).

Because driver-partners are independent contractors, Uber cannot compel drivers to show up at a specific place or time. So how does Uber manage to provide a service whose goal is to provide on-demand, seamless transportation to passengers who use it? Feedback. Uber provides their driver-partners with compelling (and some say coercive) feedback. To avoid shortages, Uber communicates with its drivers all day long with texts, emails, and pop-ups: "Hey, the morning rush has started. Get to [this or that area], that's where demand is biggest." Uber also sends messages to drivers when they log off, telling them how much they have earned and then asking if they wouldn't like to earn more. The feedback also is designed to encourage goal-oriented behavior. As reported recently in *The New York Times*, "At any moment, the app shows drivers how many trips they have taken in the current week, how much money they have made, how much time they have spent logged on, and what their overall rating from passengers is. All of these metrics can stimulate the competitive juices that drive compulsive game-playing." Despite criticisms of the sharing economy's contingent jobs, 81% of driver-partners overall said that they were very satisfied or somewhat satisfied with Uber in a recent survey.

*Sources*: R. Bales and C. P. Woo, "The Uber Million-Dollar Question: Are Uber Drivers Employees or Independent Contractors?" *Mercer Law Review*, 68(2017): 461–487; J. Hall and A. Krueger, "An Analysis of the Labor Market of Uber's Driver-Partners in the United States," *ILR Review*, 71(2018): 705–732; Seth Harris and Alan Krueger, "A Proposal for Modernizing Labor Laws for Twenty-First-Century Work: The 'Independent Worker'," The Hamilton Project, Discussion Paper 2015–10, Washington, DC: Brookings Institute; Noam Scheiber, "How Uber Uses Psychological Tricks to Push Its Drivers' Buttons," nytimes.com, April 2, 2017, https://www.nytimes.com/interactive/2017/04/02/technology/uber-drivers-psychological-tricks.html; J.C., "How Many Uber Drivers Are There?" https://www.ridester.com/how-many-uber-drivers-are-there/.

## Employee Teams

A third method of increasing employee satisfaction and motivation is the use of teams—small groups of individuals who work collaboratively toward a common goal and share responsibility for their outcomes. There are several basic types of teams: work teams, parallel teams, and project teams.[18] *Work teams* are typically well defined, stable, and have full-time members working under the direction of a supervisor to produce a good or service. *Parallel teams* pull people from different areas of a company to address a particular problem or issue. Parallel teams include quality circles and problem-solving teams. One distinction of a parallel team is that members retain their formal positions in their own departments while working on the team; the team exists in parallel to the existing organizational structure. *Project teams* are unique because they typically exist for a limited time, under the guidance of a project leader. Often, project team members disband once they accomplish a particular objective, such as the design of a new process or product.

Teams offer a number of benefits to managers. By integrating individuals with diverse experiences and talents, teams allow members to examine issues from multiple perspectives, which would not be possible with individual employees working in isolation. And when teams are composed of members with complementary abilities, they may be able to achieve performance levels that exceed the potential of individuals working alone.[19] Team-based job designs also have the potential to improve employee interaction and social support for team members. When team members are cross-trained, multiple people can perform team tasks, which increases task variety and reduces boredom and fatigue among employees.[20]

In addition to these benefits, research has shown that a higher level of self-management in any of these types of teams leads to greater motivation, job satisfaction, and effort among team members.[21] In a **self-managed team**, the team members, rather than a supervisor, work collaboratively to make decisions, including hiring, planning, and scheduling.[22] One of the major reasons that self-managed teams are effective is that they are based on the principle of empowerment described earlier. Decision-making rests with the team members, who in the end are responsible and accountable for carrying out the team's tasks. By giving authority to a team, a company may be able to cut down on bureaucracy in decision-making and improve the effectiveness of the team.[23] Of course, there are potential downsides to team-based structures. Teams require high levels of interaction among team members, and their success depends directly on the willingness of team members to share their knowledge and ideas. If there is a low degree of trust or either insufficient or too much face-to-face interaction, teams may not be able to meet their objectives.[24]

**self-managed team**

a type of team in which team members, rather than a supervisor, work collaboratively to make team decisions, including hiring, planning, and scheduling

## Current Research on Job Design

More recent research on job characteristics, for instance, has begun to identify characteristics that shape employee behavior beyond those originally included in the Job Characteristics Model. Some of these characteristics focus on the social aspect of work, such as *optional interaction* and *required interaction*, and are particularly relevant in the service industry. Research to understand how the social dimension affects work performance is ongoing. Additional streams of research related to job design include examining how job design influences organizational citizenship behavior, creativity, and even health and well-being, and how it enables workplace bullying and other negative behaviors. Also of interest is research on job design for temporary employees, job design across cultures, and job design and newer forms of work, for example working from home or working in an off-site location, such as a coworking space (also called a hub). Understanding more about these areas and the outcomes of various approaches to job design for each area will help enhance job design in the future.[25]

# Which Approach to Use? Balancing Efficiency and Motivational Approaches

Focusing on efficiency is certainly an important component of organizational effectiveness. After all, inefficient workers are less productive and contribute to higher company costs than efficient workers. However, when taken to the extreme, a focus on efficiency can lead to jobs that employees may view as boring and unfulfilling.[26] Similarly, focusing on employee motivation alone in job design neglects the potential benefits of efficiency that might be realized through task simplification and specialization.[27] Managers need to balance the tension between motivational and efficiency approaches cautiously. Each approach has fundamental trade-offs and distinct outcomes.[28] In addition, these two approaches are typically inversely related—that is, emphasizing one diminishes the odds of realizing the other.[29]

The job design choices that managers make should be driven by the strategic objectives of the company. Recall the framework in Exhibit 4.1. How jobs are designed dictates how employees add value to the company. When managers design jobs in a way that aligns the tasks and activities that employees perform with the primary objectives of the company, employees are in a position to contribute to their company's success. In contrast, when this alignment is weak or missing, employees may focus on tasks and activities that are not necessarily the most important for company success.

# Job Analysis

Before managers can effectively manage employee competencies, attitudes, and behaviors, they need to have a clear understanding of job tasks and job specifications and that information is acquired through job analysis, a term we defined earlier in this chapter. The primary goal of job analysis is to gain a clear understanding of what tasks, duties, and responsibilities are expected to be performed in each job for use in developing a **job description**. The job description describes the expected activities an employee will perform in doing a job and also lists the **job specifications**, the competencies that are necessary for successful performance of the job. We will discuss job descriptions and job specifications in more detail after we provide an overview of job analysis. Often, trained professionals from the HR department perform job analysis, but managers participate in the process in a variety of ways. Managers typically provide information during the process and, most importantly, verify the accuracy of the resulting job description.

**job description**

a written summary of the specific tasks, responsibilities, and working conditions of a job

**job specifications**

a description of the competencies—the knowledge, skills, and abilities (KSAs) or other talents—that a jobholder must have to perform a job successfully

## Job Information

To gather the necessary job information, *job analysts* (trained professionals who specialize in analyzing jobs) and managers typically rely on one of several methods: observations, diaries, interviews, questionnaires, and generic information available through the Occupational Information Network (O*NET). We will now describe each of the methods, as well as O*NET.

### Observations and Diaries

Observations are one source of information about the tasks performed in a job. Using this method of job analysis, a manager or a job analyst watches and documents all the activities performed by current jobholders while they work. One of the primary advantages of this method is that it is based on actual work behavior information rather than on someone's memory of what a job involves.

In addition, the neutral perspective of the job analyst helps reduce bias or inflation in identifying the tasks that jobholders may claim to perform. However, it is sometimes difficult to capture all aspects of a job through observation, or to see all the tasks for jobs that are not standardized or simplified. The job of a consultant or a supervisor, for example, may be difficult to analyze accurately using just observation because of its many diverse tasks. In addition, observation may miss tasks that are performed infrequently and may not fully capture tasks that require considerable judgment.

**diary**

a journal or log of the tasks and activities that an employee performs throughout the course of a day, week, or month

A variation of the observation approach is to ask employees to keep a **diary,** or log of the tasks and activities that they perform throughout the course of a day, week, or month. In this approach, employees, rather than a job analyst, observe their own actions on the job and document them. One advantage of this data-gathering method is that it relies on the source of information that knows the job the best—the employee. However, employees might log only the tasks that they tend to emphasize, and might not document other tasks that they also should be performing. In addition, employees may perceive keeping a diary as frustrating and time consuming. Managers and other employees can assist in validating the information collected from this method of job analysis.

### Interviews

Interviews provide another method for gathering data about a job. The method involves a job analyst conducting structured interviews with jobholders and supervisors using a series of job-related questions to identify the tasks and responsibilities of the job. The advantage of this approach is that it can uncover or clarify work tasks that are not directly observable. For example, gathering data on managerial positions through observation may not provide information on the cognitive components of the job that command a good part of the manager's time. The interview approach allows a job analyst to discuss such aspects of a job with the jobholder. Exhibit 4.5 provides a checklist for conducting a job analysis interview.

## EXHIBIT 4.5

### Checklist for Conducting a Job Analysis Interview

The process used to collect job information during a job analysis interview will influence the quality of the information obtained. Some pointers to enhance the outcome of a job analysis interview include the following:

_____ 1. Make an appointment in advance with the job incumbent or supervisor to be interviewed, and make the interviewee aware of the purpose of the appointment.

_____ 2. Engage in casual conversation when you arrive, including making introductions, to help put the interviewee at ease.

_____ 3. Answer any questions the interviewee may have about the job-analysis process and outcomes.

_____ 4. Use a predetermined set of interview questions to make sure the information obtained is the information needed for the purpose of the job analysis. This process also ensures that both the interviewer and interviewee stay focused on the task at hand.

_____ 5. Guide the interview assertively, if necessary, to stay on task and ensure that needed information is collected during the allotted time.

_____ 6. Allow the interviewee to return to a question if the answer is not immediately clear in his or her mind, but be sure to return to the question.

_____ 7. Before ending the interview, summarize the major points of the information you have gathered and allow the interviewee to make any corrections needed.

However, the interview approach can be time consuming for both the analysts and the interviewees. In addition, this approach depends on the ability of jobholders and managers to convey all the tasks and responsibilities for a position accurately. Employees and managers may believe there is a benefit to exaggerating or inflating the types of tasks performed on a job—a situation that is especially likely to occur if the results are linked with compensation decisions.[30]

### Questionnaires

Questionnaires provide yet another method of gathering information about job tasks and responsibilities. While the interview and observation methods are time-consuming, questionnaires can be used with a large number of individuals at the same time. In addition, using the same questionnaire for all positions provides standard types of data across jobs. As we will discuss in Chapter 10, one of the benefits of having similar data is to help establish equity or fairness in how much people are paid based on the relative value of their jobs. However, the questionnaire approach requires considerable up-front work to ensure that the questions capture all the dimensions of the jobs surveyed. Another limitation of questionnaires is that, unlike interviews, they don't offer an opportunity for immediate follow-up questions that may provide additional insights. Also, they assume that the individuals completing the questionnaire accurately understand all the questions and can clearly communicate the answers in writing.

### Occupational Information Network (O*NET)

A final method of collecting information about jobs is by using the **Occupational Information Network (O*NET)**, located online at www.onetonline.org. The O*NET database, created by the U.S. Department of Labor, is a comprehensive source of information for over 1,000 occupations.[31] For each job, O*NET provides a summary rating of the tasks and work-related behaviors performed in the jobs. In addition to task-oriented information, O*NET provides data on the job specifications of each job—the knowledge, skills, abilities (KSAs) and experience levels required to perform the job.

> **Occupational Information Network (O*NET)**
> an online database created by the U.S. Department of Labor that serves as a comprehensive source of information for many occupations

One of the primary advantages of O*NET is that it offers managers an online resource to help with the job-analysis process. It is especially helpful to managers who do not have a full HR department or job analysts to assist them as is the case in many small businesses. Rather than completing the entire job-analysis process themselves, managers can build on O*NET job descriptions that have been generated for similar positions across a large number of companies. This is especially an advantage for managers who may be creating a job description for a job that doesn't exist yet in their company. The job description on O*NET can be a starting point to understand the types of tasks that a person in a particular position might perform, as well as the specific KSAs to look for when hiring to fill the new position. Finally, accessing O*NET online does not require substantial capital investments—it is free. The appendix to this chapter contains more details about O*NET and a sample job entry from its database. Exhibit 4.6 provides a summary of each of the five data-collection methods covered here, along with recommendations for when each is most appropriate to use.

## Job-Analysis Techniques

Once the data about a job is collected, it must be organized in some way that supports the goals and objectives of the organization. Job analysis techniques provide that organizing mechanism. These techniques differ in terms of whether they focus on a standardized approach to categorizing jobs or a customized

**EXHIBIT 4.6**

Methods for Collecting Job Information

| Method | Source | Process | Applicable Jobs |
|---|---|---|---|
| Observation | Job analyst | Physical observation or videotaping of employees performing the job; notes are taken or videotape analyzed to determine the main tasks performed. | Jobs with repetitive tasks performed over a short cycle, such as an assembly-line position. |
| Diary/log | Employee | Records activities at specified intervals for a specific time period. Information analyzed to identify patterns suggestive of typical types of work performed. | Most jobs. May be disruptive to use in retail, manufacturing, and construction. |
| Interview | Job analyst/employee | Face-to-face question-and-answer session to identify tasks, duties, responsibilities, competencies, and working conditions. | Most jobs, especially at the managerial and professional level. Time-consuming and costly. |
| Questionnaire | Employee | Written survey instrument administered in a group setting or individually. Can be done electronically. Ensures that standardized information is collected. | All jobs. Literacy of participants can affect the quality of information collected. |
| O*NET | Occupational Information Network | Online database (www.online.onetcenter.org) of more than 1,000 occupations that includes information on tasks, work-related behaviors, and specifications needed to perform the job. | All jobs. Customization of jobs to specific company circumstances may be limited. |

approach to studying the unique dimensions of a particular job within a company. They also differ in terms of whether they focus on identifying the tasks performed in each job, the needed competencies (i.e., KSAs) required to successfully perform each job, or both. Exhibit 4.7 provides a summary of the primary job-analysis techniques.

Sometimes a company needs to perform job analyses on many different jobs.[32] For example, if a company creates a new unit with a variety of positions (secretarial, technical, professional) or if it wants to establish the relative worth of a variety of jobs for compensation purposes, it would benefit from using a standardized approach so that all jobs are analyzed based on similar standards or criteria. A standardized job-analysis approach uses a single instrument—typically a questionnaire or O*NET—to collect similar data that may be used to evaluate multiple jobs within a company or across many companies. This approach identifies underlying job dimensions that apply to a variety of different jobs and that allow comparisons of dissimilar jobs in meaningful ways.

The two most common standardized approaches used by companies for analyzing job data are Functional Job Analysis (FJA) and the Position Analysis Questionnaire (PAQ). The FJA is based on the notion that it is possible to systematically compare jobs

**EXHIBIT 4.7**

Approaches to Analyzing Job Information

| Standardized approaches | Functional Job Analysis (FJA) | Focuses on the level of three broad categories of work-related tasks in each job, related to *data, people,* and *things.* |
|---|---|---|
| | Position Analysis Questionnaire (PAQ) | Focuses on work-related behaviors that employees must display to successfully perform a job related to *information input, mental processes, work output, relationships with other persons, job context,* and *other characteristics.* |
| Customized approaches | Critical incidents | Focuses on obtaining specific, behaviorally focused descriptions of work behaviors that distinguish exceptionally good performance in a particular job from exceptionally poor performance. |
| | Task inventory | Focuses on identifying the specific tasks that are necessary to successfully perform a job. |
| | Job element | Focuses on identifying the employee competencies (i.e., KSAs) that are necessary to successfully perform a job. |

that are dissimilar in the tasks that they perform by focusing on job dimensions that apply to all jobs.[33] The *functional* part of its name represents functional categories, which are broad categories of work-related activities that are applicable to all jobs and focus on three distinct work domains related to data, people, and things. The PAQ is a standardized survey that measures a number of different employee work-related *behaviors* that are necessary to perform a wide variety of tasks in different jobs. The appendix to this chapter provides more explanation of these standardized approaches.

Sometimes managers need to conduct a more customized analysis of jobs within their company. Whether it is for a newly created position or a unique position that is simply not captured through standardized approaches, customized techniques allow managers to develop a job description and job specifications that represent the unique attributes of a job. The three primary approaches for customized job analyses are the critical-incidents approach, the task inventory approach, and the job elements approach. The *critical-incidents approach* focuses on obtaining specific, behaviorally focused descriptions of work activities that distinguish exceptionally good performance in a particular job from exceptionally poor performance. The *task inventory approach* focuses on collecting information to identify the tasks that are necessary to perform a job successfully. Finally, the *job element approach* focuses solely on analyzing the employee competencies that are necessary for successful job performance, rather than the tasks to be performed in a job. When adopting a customized approach, observations, diaries, and interviews may be preferred as data collection techniques to allow the collection of unique information about specific jobs and specifications. The appendix to this chapter provides more details about these customized approaches.

# Job Descriptions and Job Specifications

As already noted, a **job description** is a written summary of the specific tasks, responsibilities, and working conditions of a job. **Job specifications** are the competencies—the KSAs (knowledge, skills, abilities), or other talents—that a jobholder must have to perform a job successfully. Job descriptions and job

## EXHIBIT 4.8

Sample Job Description for an Accounting Associate

| | |
|---|---|
| **Job Title:** | Accounting Assistant |

**Job Identification Section:**

| | |
|---|---|
| Department: | Accounting |
| Reports to: | Director, Accounting |
| Position Number: | 05 0246 |
| Wage Category: | Non-Exempt |
| Salary Grade: | 04 |
| Analyst: | Ellen Kassman |
| Date Analyzed: | December 14, 2019 |

**Summary:**

The accounting assistant works under the direction of the accounting director and provides professional accounting, financial analysis, and budgeting support for assigned accounts.

**Essential Duties and Responsibilities:**

- Maintain financial planning and administration of the accounting office.
- Prepare a variety of financial documents, analyses, and reports, including year-end reports, for internal and external purposes within established deadlines.
- Reconcile administrative and overseas bank accounts, manage accounts payable and receivable, and perform financial planning.
- Analyze and reconcile financial data of internal records with the department's systems.
- Implement billing policies.
- Act as a liaison with other departmental units.
- Perform other duties as assigned by director of accounting.

**Job Specifications:**

- A bachelor's degree, preferably in accounting, finance, or related field, or an equivalent combination of education or related experience that demonstrates knowledge and understanding of general accounting principles and practices required.
- Two years of experience in a financial or accounting function required.
- Experience with computers and common word-processing, spreadsheet, and database applications required.
- Excellent communication and organizational skills required.
- A basic understanding of global finance and market forces on exchange rates desired.

specifications are technically separate, but most companies include job specifications as part of the job description as the example in Exhibit 4.8 illustrates. While there is no standard format, most job descriptions provide the following information:

- *Job title*—The first portion of a job description usually states the title of the job and the specific level, if any, of the job in a particular job grouping. For example, some job groupings have multiple levels, such as materials handler I, materials handler II, and materials handler III.
- *Job identification section*—The job identification section specifies important administrative aspects of the job, such as the department in which the job is located, who conducted the job analysis, when the job was last analyzed, the wage category of the job, and the job code, if the company uses a job classification system.
- *Essential duties and responsibilities section*—The essential duties and responsibilities section is a summary of the key tasks, worker behaviors, and responsibilities of the job. These statements, called *task statements*, typically appear in order of importance or in order of the time each task requires. Some companies distinguish essential duties from marginal duties and responsibilities in this section for legal purposes.
- *Job specifications section*—The final portion of the job description is the job specification. This section documents all the qualifications that a job candidate must possess to perform the job successfully, such as educational level, work experience,

## EXHIBIT 4.9

### Checklist for Writing a Job Description

_____ 1. Provide job-identifying information, such as title, assigned location, and classification.
_____ 2. Prepare a brief summary of the job.
_____ 3. Write task statements, making sure to include the following in each:
      a. What needs to be done (action verb)
      b. To whom or what (object)
      c. For what purpose
      d. Using what resources, tools, or equipment
_____ 4. Identify the job requirements, including the following:
      a. Knowledge
      b. Skills
      c. Abilities
      d. Minimum work experience and education
_____ 5. Describe the work context, including:
      a. Schedule
      b. Physical requirements
      c. Environmental conditions
_____ 6. Have job incumbents and supervisors review the accuracy of the description

or specific abilities, such as mathematical, language, or computer skills. A key point is that job specifications are _requirements_ for job success, not _desirable_ attributes that go beyond what is required. For example, a doctoral degree is not likely to be a true requirement for job success in many entry-level positions. Some companies identify desirable or preferred qualifications as well, as shown in Exhibit 4.8.

A clear job description with job specifications is critical for managing employee competencies and behaviors effectively. Managers often use the task statements in the job description as the performance standards that employees in a particular job are expected to meet. As we will discuss in Chapters 6 and 7, the job specifications section is particularly critical for recruiting and selecting employees to ensure that staffing decisions are relevant, effective, and nondiscriminatory. Exhibit 4.9 provides a checklist to keep in mind when writing a job description. And as discussed in Chapter 3, job relatedness is a key criterion for complying with regulatory issues. Given the importance of job descriptions and specifications, both for company success and legal compliance, it is critical that these documents accurately represent each job.

Principles

Practice

# Job Design in Practice: Organizational Demands

We have covered a lot of material regarding job design and job analysis within companies. With this background in place, we now turn to the decisions that managers must make in designing jobs to meet HR challenges, as outlined in Exhibit 4.10. We'll start with the first organizational demand—strategy.

## Strategy and Job Design

In Chapter 2, we discussed various types of business strategies. We noted that companies compete based on having the lowest costs in their industry or having some form of differentiation, such as customer service, high quality, or an image for which customers are willing to pay a premium. The type of strategy that a company pursues has two direct implications for job design: how jobs are structured and what tasks, duties, and responsibilities employees need to perform.

## Job Design in Practice

| Context | Practice Issues |
| --- | --- |
| **Organizational Demands** | |
| *Strategy* drives . . . | • Job design approach adopted<br>• Breadth of tasks, duties, and responsibilities performed |
| *Company characteristics* determine . . . | • Formalization of jobs<br>• Breadth and depth of tasks |
| *Culture* establishes . . . | • Managerial choices of job-design tactics<br>• Employee acceptance of job-design decisions |
| *Employee concerns* include . . . | • Perception of fairness of job duties<br>• Need for flexible work arrangements |
| **Environmental Demands** | |
| *Labor force* influences . . . | • Skill availability to perform tasks<br>• Job-design decisions for the aging labor force |
| *Technology* affects . . . | • Telecommuting<br>• Virtual teams |
| *Globalization* impacts . . . | • Need to address cross-cultural issues<br>• Relevant labor market |
| *Ethics/social responsibility* shapes . . . | • Concerns about types of tasks required<br>• Attitudes toward the physical conditions of the job design |
| **Regulations** | |
| *Regulations* guide . . . | • Importance of understanding essential and nonessential job duties<br>• Job design and employee safety |

## Job-Design Approach Adopted

Recall our earlier comparison of jobs in a fast-food restaurant to jobs in an upscale restaurant. While the types of jobs may be similar, how the jobs are designed differs considerably given the different strategies of these companies. Fast-food establishments, such as Chick-Fil-A and Arby's, compete based on costs and efficiency. One of the primary ways that their employees contribute to the company's strategy is to perform narrow jobs efficiently and quickly. This job design allows the company to serve its customers affordable meals without much wait time. In contrast, most upscale restaurants, such as the Inn at Little Washington in Little Washington, Virginia, in the U.S. or Le Cinq in Paris, France, are not focused on speed or cost. Instead, they focus on the quality of the food, the ambience, and the experience of being waited on for an evening. For these restaurants, a strategy of differentiation through customer service and high quality, rather than low cost, is the primary source of competitive advantage. Job design in these establishments gives employees, such as the wait staff and the chef, much greater latitude to modify how they perform their tasks to meet the unique needs of each customer.

Although the example about restaurant jobs is simplistic, the same logic applies for most positions in the workforce, including accountants, marketing analysts, and consultants. The focus of a company's strategy drives how managers structure the jobs to be performed. In companies in which employees contribute through creativity and innovation, managers might base their job designs on teamwork to facilitate knowledge sharing and knowledge creation. In companies that compete based on cost, managers are more likely to structure jobs to maximize efficiencies through the principles of scientific management discussed earlier (job simplification, job standardization, and repetition). A useful way to think about the relationship between strategy and job design is to think about what customers are paying for and how the job contributes to meeting customer expectations.

### Breadth of Tasks, Duties, and Responsibilities Performed

Jobs should be designed in a way that maximizes the potential contributions of employees toward implementing a company's competitive strategy. Given their focus on efficiencies and cost reduction, companies pursuing a cost strategy tend to design jobs in a way that maximizes predictable employee outcomes. In contrast, a differentiation strategy requires employees to perform jobs geared toward some particular objective, such as creativity or customer service.[34] Think about the job of designer at a creative services firm, the complexity of the job, and the significant role that it plays in organizational success. Of course, one direct implication of designing jobs in order to achieve strategic objectives is that how jobs are designed directly affects the scope or breadth of the tasks, duties, and responsibilities that employees need to perform to be successful in their jobs. When jobs are designed to maximize efficiency through job simplification and standardization, one outcome is that the range of tasks, duties, and responsibilities performed by an employee are often limited. Recall the discussion of the assembly line worker earlier in the chapter. By focusing on performing few tasks more frequently, this job-design approach strives to encourage maximum levels of productivity and efficiency among employees. In contrast, greater levels of autonomy and empowerment often involve a wider array of tasks for employees to perform on a regular basis.

## Company Characteristics and Job Design

Company characteristics, such as size and stage of development, influence job design in terms of the level of formalization or standardization of jobs, as well as the breadth and depth of tasks performed by the jobholder.

### Formalization of Jobs

Smaller organizations may be forced to adopt a more fluid, open-ended approach to the design of jobs simply because they have fewer people to perform the needed tasks. If you have ever worked at a small boutique or a coffee shop, you have likely been asked to take on multiple roles as needed to get the work done. Smaller companies also may be more able and willing to be more flexible in how and when employees perform their jobs. For example, smaller companies may be more likely to offer employees opportunities for workplace flexibility, and small business employees with access to formal workplace flexibility policies report greater job satisfaction and commitment to their employer.[35] Small employers are more likely to allow employees to change starting and quitting times within a stipulated range of hours, work some regular paid hours at home occasionally, have control over when to take breaks, return to work gradually after childbirth or adoption, and take time off during the workday to attend to important family or personal needs without loss of pay.[36] A similar study by the Small Enterprise Research Team at the Open University indicated that more than 75% of small businesses in the United Kingdom offer flexible working options.[37]

On the other hand, researchers have demonstrated that larger organizations are associated with greater formalization and bureaucratization.[38] As companies grow, they tend to develop more rules and regulations regarding how business is carried out on a day-to-day basis. Logically, this outcome makes sense. To ensure consistency and fairness in everything from hiring employees to conducting performance appraisals, rules and regulations are important. In addition, greater bureaucracy may be (and in fact often is) associated with greater levels of specialization in jobs that employees perform.

### Breadth and Depth of Tasks

A company's size and stage of development influence the breadth and depth of tasks that its employees are expected to perform. Given limited resources, smaller companies often need employees to perform multiple tasks that may or may not be within their job descriptions.[39] As a result, the types of knowledge, skills, and abilities (KSAs) that employees need for the same job in small companies as opposed to large ones can differ. An accountant in a small firm will have to do far more accounting tasks than an accountant in a large firm that has many other accountants who share the tasks that need to be done. For instance, in a large firm, an accountant may deal only with accounts payable. In the small firm, the accountant may do accounts payable and accounts receivable and many other accounting activities. Further, entrepreneurial companies or companies in an early stage of development may face growth opportunities that outpace their ability to staff all the necessary jobs fully. As a result, like smaller companies, younger companies may need employees to perform a wider array of tasks than an established company might require in the same job. Additionally, especially in start-up companies, hiring for leadership positions may focus on hiring for point of view (POV). This approach to hiring involves seeking new employees who can bring best practices from similar settings and apply those practices appropriately to the organization to enable it to continue to grow and become more competitive.

## Culture and Job Design

In Chapter 2, we described how organizational culture—the basic assumptions, values, and beliefs of organizational members—provides unwritten cues to employees about what attitudes and behaviors a company values. Because culture informs employees about the types of actions that are and are not appropriate, culture also influences managerial choices of job design tactics and employee acceptance of job designs.

### Managerial Choices of Job Design Tactics

Earlier in this chapter, we discussed a host of approaches that managers can use to increase employee efficiency (job specialization, job simplification, and repetition) and motivation (job enlargement, job enrichment, job rotation, and teams). Company culture is an important consideration when choosing a job design approach. In a company that has a very formal, hierarchical culture, managers may be reluctant to use empowerment and participation methods for lower-level employees. They may be more comfortable with a traditional, top-down approach for conducting business. In contrast, managers and employees in a company that has an egalitarian culture may have difficulty executing and accepting rigid or narrow job designs. Do you think officers in the military would adopt the same job design approach for soldiers as an IT company would for programmers or a pharmaceutical company would for its research and development scientists?

### Employee Acceptance of Job Design Decisions

Equally as important as whether managers are comfortable implementing various job design tactics is whether employees will accept these decisions. At its root, organizational culture is a shared perception of how things are, as well as how they should be within companies. Conflict between how jobs are designed and the cultural values shared by employees can result in unhappy and potentially unproductive employees. For example, employees who are content with and expect explicit instructions about how they are to spend their time at work may resist job design changes that increase their autonomy and decision-making because the changes are inconsistent with their cultural expectations. Similarly, employees who are used to and expect a very friendly and open culture might not easily accept an increase in rules and regulations that they must follow to perform their jobs. In other words, employees who enjoy the culture at Google or Facebook would most likely not do well in the work culture at General Motors (GM) which is more rigid and requires much less creativity from many of its employees. The key point is that while managers have many job design tactics at their disposal, they need to choose tactics based on the unique cultural values of their company.

## Employee Concerns and Job Design

Naturally, a critical organizational demand to consider when designing jobs is the effect of job design on employees. After all, employees are the ones who are directly affected by job design considerations. Two issues that are particularly important for employees are their perceptions of fairness in the job duties they perform and their needs for flexible work arrangements.

### Perception of Fairness of Job Duties

Beyond the tasks that employees of a company perform, each employee also has a role in the company. Roles are the expectations that companies and coworkers have regarding how employees are to allocate their time in the performance of their jobs. While the tasks may be straightforward in a job, employee roles may not be as clearly defined, resulting in employee stress. For example, some employees may experience **role overload**, which is having too many expectations or demands placed on employees in the course of performing their jobs. Many times, this occurs because employees perceive that their job demands exceed their abilities.[40] Alternatively, some employees may experience **role underload** from having too few expectations or demands placed on them. **Role ambiguity** is uncertainty that employees may experience about the daily tasks expected of them and how to perform them.[41] Finally, **role conflict** is tension caused by incompatible or contradictory demands on a person, which often stems from the simultaneous occurrence of two or more stressors (demands) such that focusing on one demand makes meeting another demand more difficult.[42] One particularly common form of role conflict that we discuss next is conflicting expectations between work and personal life.

**role overload**

too many expectations or demands placed on employees in the course of performing their jobs

**role underload**

having too few expectations or demands placed on employees in the course of performing their jobs

**role ambiguity**

the uncertainty that employees may experience about the daily tasks expected of them and how to perform them

**role conflict**

tension caused by incompatible or contradictory demands on a person

### Need for Flexible Work Arrangements

Balancing the conflicting demands of work and family or other personal obligations is difficult for many employees. Demands for travel or overtime, for example, may conflict with personal demands to spend time with family. To help employees achieve this balance, many companies offer flexibility through several alternative work arrangements: flextime, compressed workweeks, and job sharing.

**flextime**

a work arrangement in which employees may choose the starting and ending time of their workday, as long as they work the appropriate number of hours per day or week

**compressed workweek**

an arrangement that provides employees with the option to adjust the number of hours and days that they work within a week

**job sharing**

a work arrangement allowing two employees to work part time to complete the tasks of a single job

With a **flextime** work arrangement, employees may choose the starting and ending time of their workday, as long as they work the appropriate number of hours per day or week. Often, flextime requires employees to be at work during a predetermined set of core hours in which all employees must be at work. According to a National Study of Employers, about 42% of companies have flexible work schedules that allow employees to vary the time they begin or end their workday on a daily basis, and 81% can change their starting and quitting times periodically.[43] At Qualcomm, for example, 95% of employees have flexible work schedules.[44]

While flextime provides employees with choices regarding the hours that they work each day, a **compressed workweek** provides employees with the option to reduce the number of days that they work within a week. The National Study of Employers also reported that 43% of companies allow some employees to work longer hours over fewer days for at least part of the year.[45] The most typical form of a compressed workweek is the 4/10 or 4/40 approach, in which employees work 4 days in a week instead of 5 days, but work for 10 hours per day rather than the typical 8 hours per day. Another version of a compressed workweek is the 9/80 approach in which employees work 80 hours in a two-week period in 9 days instead of 10 days. Among the benefits of compressed workweeks are reductions in the number of shifts worked; in travel time and commuting costs; and in sick time, overtime, and personal leave.[46] For an employee, working a compressed schedule offers the benefit of more time for leisure activities and personal or family matters.[47] However, compressed workweeks can have potential negative consequences, such as fatigue, reduced work quality, and staffing challenges to ensure that the necessary numbers of people are at work each day.[48]

A third form of flexible work arrangement is **job sharing**,[49] which consists of having two employees work part time to complete the tasks of a single job. In this scheme, the two jobholders work out how to split the work and responsibilities and establish ways to coordinate with one another to complete the job tasks. Jobs may be split in any way, but a common arrangement is for both employees to work 2.5 days each week. The pay and benefits connected with the position are split between the two employees and the company does not incur any additional costs compared to the job being performed by just one person.[50] The prevalence of job sharing in organizations varies. One study noted that 19% of employers offered job sharing for some employees, while 2% allowed it for most of their employees.[51]

Establishing flexible work arrangements clearly requires costs and effort. Companies that implement these programs, however, often find that the programs help employees remain effective contributors toward company goals and provide an additional point of attraction for many potential job applicants. Indeed, practices such as job sharing may be particularly effective for attracting and retaining workers who otherwise might opt out of the labor force to raise families.[52] Research has even found a positive relationship between company initiatives that facilitate work/family balance and company performance.[53] Company Spotlight 4.4 illustrates how Unilever has successfully incorporated work/life balance solutions into its design of work arrangements.

## Job Design in Practice: Environmental Influences

Factors in the external environment influence job design within companies. Labor-force trends, technology, globalization, and ethical considerations each exert unique pressures on companies and must be considered when designing jobs.

## COMPANY SPOTLIGHT  4.4

### Agile Work Design at Unilever

Unilever, the Anglo-Dutch consumer goods company (which includes Hellmans, Lipton, Knorr, Axe, and Dove under its umbrella) has 171,000 workers and is at the forefront of offering work flexibility with its Agile Working Policy. This policy permits all employees worldwide to work anytime, anywhere, as long as they meet business needs. It covers everyone except some factory production workers, and they can use flextime.

To support this effort, Unilever provides employees with lightweight, high-performance laptops with Wi-Fi, virtual private networking (VPN) capabilities and the Microsoft Office 365 suite to access the company's mobile-optimized intranet, internal social media network, and email. All employees and contractors have Skype so that they can find each other in the global list, see their availability status, and chat (instant message), phone, or have video calls, share programs, edit documents, and collaborate virtually. In live and online training, managers learn virtual management techniques and technologies that support virtual work and learn to recognize that their teams must focus entirely on producing measurable results, such as making sales or production targets.

The Agile Working Policy was piloted in August 2008 at Unilever's Englewood Cliffs, New Jersey, location. After two years of using agile working, Unilever cut global travel costs by 50% and slashed office overhead by 40%. The company also started attracting a higher level of talent at the junior level. At the end of 2017, 47% of their managers were women, up from 38% in 2010. Named as the top company on the list of 100 Best Companies by *Working Mother* magazine in 2017 for its commitment to progressive workplace programs, and by *Fast Company* magazine as one of the most innovative companies, Unilever is capitalizing on a workforce that is more productive, happier, and less likely to leave than that of their office-bound, more traditional competition.

*Sources*: "Advancing Diversity & Inclusion," https://www.unilever.com/sustainable-living/enhancing-livelihoods/opportunities-for-women/advancing-diversity-and-inclusion/index.html; "Corporate Awards," https://www.unileverusa.com/news/corporate-awards/; Dana Poole, "How Unilever Makes Agile or Virtual Working a Remarkable Success," February 7, 2017, https://www.linkedin.com/pulse/how-unilever-makes-agile-virtual-working-remarkable-success-poole/; R. J. Grossman, "Phasing out Face Time: Flexibility Rules at Unilever as Long as Work Gets Done, "*HR Magazine*, April (2013): 33–38; Society of Human Resource Management, "SHRM Research: Flexible Work Arrangements," 2015, https://www.shrm.org/hr-today/trends-and-forecasting/special-reports-and-expert-views/Documents/Flexible%20Work%20Arrangements.pdf; Gary M. Stern, "Turning Cubicle Sitters into Telework Warriors, Unilever Moves Flexible Work Options to a New Level," *Investor's Business Daily*, August 26, 2012, A06.

## Labor-Force Trends and Job Design

Job design should be based on the strategic objectives of a company. But another part of making job design decisions is looking at the labor force. This means considering the competencies of the people in the labor force who may fill a job and the changing demographic composition of the labor force—particularly the aging labor force.

### Skill Availability to Perform Tasks

If a job is designed so that only a select few individuals are able to perform it, a company is likely to experience considerable difficulty filling the job. In this regard, the skills that are available in the labor market may influence what job designs are feasible. Think about industries such as health care that face labor shortages in the coming years. As the supply of qualified individuals decreases, companies may need to modify their design of jobs to reduce the necessary qualifications to perform them successfully. For example, a company may restructure a single job into two separate jobs, each with a narrow range of tasks to perform. By doing so, the company can increase the number of viable candidates to fill the positions. In contrast, when there is a labor surplus in a particular industry, occupation, or region, companies may be able to implement more of the job design dimensions that foster employee motivation and satisfaction. While these techniques often raise the necessary skills to perform a job, a labor surplus is likely to make it easier for companies to find qualified people to fill the jobs.

### Job Design Decisions for the Aging Labor Force

The aging of the workforce is a particularly important demographic trend that influences how companies design jobs. PKF O'Connor Davies, an independent accounting and advisory firm, has 800 employees, who range in age from 21 to 83. They go out of their way to hire older workers and offer them the options of shorter workweeks, flexible hours, relocation to offices nearer to home, or part-time work from home.[54] While some companies recruit older workers by choice, others do so out of necessity.[55] For example, faced with a shortage of qualified nurses, St. Mary's Medical Center, in Huntington, West Virginia, has drawn on its own retirees and older alumni of a local nursing school to fill vacancies. One approach that the medical center used to help these older employees readjust to working was to assign them to less physically demanding tasks.[56] To assist older nurses who can no longer lift and turn patients, Baptist Health South Florida has installed new hydraulic technology and allows older employees to change jobs internally to positions with less physical demands and less heavy lifting.[57] Another job-design modification that companies may use to help older employees succeed in their jobs is flexible scheduling and part-time shifts. For example, at Brethren Village, a continuing-care retirement community in Lancaster, Pennsylvania, employees receive generous time off benefits[58]—for instance, to spend time in Florida during the winter months.[59]

## Technology and Job Design

One of the most prominent environmental factors that has influenced job design in recent years is technology. Its presence has been felt in two ways—the emergence and rapid growth of telecommuting and the increased use of virtual teams.

### Telecommuting

**telecommuting**

employees working away from the traditional office setting, often with the use of technology

One major impact of technology on job design is the increased use of **telecommuting** in which employees work away from the traditional office setting. There are a wide range of statistics regarding telecommuting.[60] One recent report suggests that 22% of Americans work at least some hours at home each week.[61] A recent survey from SHRM suggests that the number of companies offering telecommuting increased from 20% to 62% between 1996 and 2017.[62] Full-time employees are four times more likely to have work-at-home options than part-time workers.[63] Technology also has contributed to the rise in home-based work, with an estimated 6.6% of all workers claiming to work exclusively from home.[64]

Telecommuting offers many benefits to companies and employees. Perhaps the most important benefit is that it provides flexibility in the hours and location of work. Because employees can work from home or from a satellite location, such as an urban hub where telecommuting workers from multiple companies work, they do not have to spend time commuting to and from a particular site. This arrangement also benefits individuals who might not be able to commit to a traditional 9-to-5 workday with a commute because of a life circumstance where, for example, they are caring for their children or aging parents or both. By providing flexibility in when and where work may be performed, telecommuting can help employees achieve better work/life balance.

Of course, there are potential drawbacks to telecommuting or working remotely. Establishing telecommuting policies requires technology. The costs of providing employees with computers, Internet access, scanners, smart phones, and the like may be costly for some companies. Smaller companies do not have the same resources that larger firms have, and they may struggle to provide these options to their employees. It is also possible that relying too much on telecommuting may erode the environment at work. If everyone is working offsite, who is at work? One possible outcome may be a disengaged work culture in which people no longer feel the need to attend to the social side of work, even though that is an important part of organizational functioning, communication, and knowledge exchange. Social networking technologies are ameliorating some of this concern. In addition, not all jobs are well suited for telecommuting. Working in retail sales often involves helping customers one-on-one to select merchandise to meet their needs—a task that is obviously difficult to do when telecommuting. However, most retail stores now have online shopping options and chat technologies that enable an interactive customer shopping experience online.

Despite the potential drawbacks of telecommuting, many companies realize that telecommuting can have a positive effect on employees and help them contribute to company success when done effectively. The Telework Enhancement Act of 2010, for example, has helped the federal government implement telecommuting to help ensure continuity of operations during emergencies, to promote management effectiveness to reduce costs, to affect the environment and transit costs, and to enhance work/life balance for employees.[65] Of course, managing a workforce that is not at work introduces new challenges, which we will revisit later in this book, regarding issues such as staffing decisions (Chapter 7), training and development (Chapter 8), and performance evaluations (Chapter 9).[66]

### Virtual Teams

Advances in information technology (IT) have provided companies with the ability to use virtual teams. The Internet, videoconferencing, and specialized software allow dispersed individuals to collaborate electronically as virtual teams that work together even when they cannot physically be in the same location.[67] General Electric (GE) and SAP are just a few of the companies that rely on virtual teams to work on important business objectives.[68]

The trend toward virtual teams is understandable, given the growth in telecommuting and the fact that virtual teams do not require face-to-face interaction. Virtual teams are able to respond quickly to pressing issues, problems, and opportunities. An additional organizational benefit of virtual teams is that their use dramatically expands who can be part of a team. Virtual team members may be located anywhere in the world—a benefit that is particularly helpful for companies operating on a global scale. Some of the practices that have been identified for effectively leading virtual teams are:[69]

1. Get the team together physically early on.
2. Clarify tasks and processes, not just goals and roles.
3. Leverage the best communication technologies.
4. Have regular meetings.
5. Create opportunities for informal interactions.

6. Clarify and track commitments.

7. Foster shared leadership.

## Globalization and Job Design

While technology has provided a medium for companies to pursue virtual teams, increasing globalization has provided a strong incentive for them to do so. As companies continue to expand into the global marketplace, they increasingly have employees located in multiple countries and continents who somehow have to work together to meet customer needs. Virtual teams help accomplish this coordination, and continual improvements in IT have enabled companies to be more prepared for long-distance working relationships that help meet the needs of globalization.

### Need to Address Cross-Cultural Issues

As companies continue to build their presence in other countries or employ people from other countries in a single location, they are likely to face challenges that stem from cultural differences. As noted in Chapter 2, different regions of the world have different norms, standards, and expectations that influence the way business is conducted. Diverse workplaces that have individuals from distinct cultural backgrounds may realize that assumptions about job design in the United States may not be consistent with the expectations of individuals from other countries. Individuals may differ in their comfort with formality, preference to work in teams or individually, perception of the importance of meeting deadlines and being on time, or view of how much work constitutes a workday. In short, different cultures have different job design styles, experiences, needs, and expectations. Employees in a collectivistic culture, for example, may be more willing to devote time and energy toward a work team's success than are employees from a more individualistic culture. Similarly, cultures vary in terms of their expectations of how much of their life revolves around work, and some of these values may be reflected by different laws. British employees, for example, have a statutory right to seek flexible work arrangements,[70] and this right might not be legally mandated in other countries.

### Relevant Labor Markets

Globalization also magnifies the importance of the labor-force trends that are unique to each country. The average education level of the workforce, the occupational background, and the supply of workers with different skill sets establish the parameters for the amount of autonomy, discretion, and variety that companies can feasibly build into different jobs. Companies must be attuned to the composition of the relevant labor-force trends when assessing which approaches to job design are most likely to succeed in different scenarios. For example, in developed countries with a ready supply of skilled labor, companies experience more success implementing more motivational tactics such as empowerment and job enlargement compared to countries in which the workforce tends to possess significantly lower skill levels.

## Ethics and Job Design

When we talk about how jobs are designed, we need to consider ethical issues. One issue that is of particular importance is the impact of job design decisions on the level of stress that employees experience. In general, a certain amount of stress is good; it helps employees stay excited and focused on the task at hand. Too much stress, however, may lead to employee dissatisfaction, illness, absenteeism, turnover, and reduced productivity.[71] Job-related stress can stem from many sources, but two of the most common ones are the types of tasks performed in a job and the physical demands of the job.

### Concerns About the Types of Tasks Required

Jobs vary in the extent to which the tasks that are expected to be performed inherently cause a high level of stress for employees. For example, it is easy to imagine that the job of a soldier during wartime is very stressful, but some of the other jobs that are considered high stress might surprise you. For the last 30 years, CareerCast has conducted an annual survey of 200 professions and rated them on 11 stress factors related to job tasks: travel, physical demands, competition, career growth potential, environmental conditions, hazards encountered, risk of death or grievous injury, meeting the public, immediate risk of another's life, working in the public eye, and deadlines. The top 10 most stressful jobs in 2018 were enlisted military, firefighter, airline pilot, police officer, event coordinator, newspaper reporter, broadcaster, public relation executive, senior corporate executive, and taxi driver. Information security analyst, diagnostic medical sonographer, hair stylist, audiologist, university professor, medical records technician, compliance officer, jeweler, pharmacy technician, operations research analyst, and medical laboratory technician had the least stressful jobs on the 2018 list.[72]

A study conducted by the American Psychological Association's Center for Excellence reported that over one-third of working Americans indicated they were experiencing chronic work stress. Only 36% felt their organizations were providing enough resources to help them manage that stress.[73] What are some of the causes of this stress? One survey reported that 81% of respondents said they checked email on the weekends, 55% said they logged in after 11 p.m., and 59% said they looked at email while on vacation.[74] Several of the key factors associated with stress on the job are directly related to job design, such as the expectation created by email of being available 24/7. Other factors include long work hours, over work, infrequent breaks, routine tasks with little meaning, little sense of control, uncertain expectations, too many responsibilities, too many tasks, lack of participation, and poor social support. As you can imagine, prolonged exposure to any of these types of job features would likely lead to increased stress for employees, which can have an associated impact on employee health, well-being, and safety. In an attempt to address these concerns, The National Institute of Occupational Safety and Health (NIOSH) has developed some basic tactics to help organizations prevent stress on the job. These are highlighted in Exhibit 4.11.

### EXHIBIT 4.11

#### How to Change an Organization to Prevent Job Stress

- Ensure that the workload is in line with workers' capabilities and resources.
- Design jobs to provide meaning, stimulation, and opportunities for workers to use their skills.
- Clearly define workers' roles and responsibilities.
- Give workers opportunities to participate in decisions and actions that affect their jobs.
- Improve communications to reduce uncertainty about career development and future employment prospects.
- Provide opportunities for social interaction among workers.
- Establish work schedules that are compatible with demands and responsibilities outside the job.

*Sources:* "Stress at Work," National Institute for Occupational Safety and Health, cdc.gov, https://www.cdc.gov/niosh/topics/stress/default.html; "Stress....at Work," DHHS (NIOSH) Publication Number 99-101, cdc.gov, https://www.cdc.gov/niosh/docs/99-101.

**Attitudes Toward the Physical Conditions of Job Design**

An additional key factor associated with stress on the job relates to the physical conditions of a job. Some jobs have physical conditions that may lead to heightened levels of employee stress. For example, a job may require performing tasks in unpleasant conditions, such as working in extremely hot or cold temperatures, working without privacy, or working with excessive noise. Some jobs require employees to perform strenuous labor that is physically demanding on the human body. Construction workers and firefighters, for example, perform jobs that require an extensive amount of physical exertion. But physical stress is not limited to extreme jobs. Manufacturing and office workers face physical stress that can lead to repetitive-motion problems such as carpal tunnel syndrome if neglected over time.

**ergonomics**

the science of understanding the capabilities of human in terms of their work requirements

In response, many companies are increasingly considering the **ergonomics** of how jobs are designed. According to the International Ergonomics Association (IEA), ergonomists contribute to the design and evaluation of tasks, jobs, products, environments, and systems in order to make them compatible with the needs, abilities, and limitations of people.[75] Topics such as posture, repetitive movements, musculoskeletal disorders, workplace layout, safety, and health are the primary focus of physical ergonomics. You may have used, or even own, an ergonomic keyboard that minimizes the physical stress of working on a computer. This type of keyboard is an example of ergonomic design to enhance working conditions and minimize physical stress. Ergonomists examine how individuals interact with machines, tools, and equipment in an attempt to minimize the physical demands of a particular job that may lead to high levels of stress, fatigue, and possibly injury.[76]

In addition to modifying the process of work, managers may use job rotation to help minimize physical stress. By allowing employees to alternate between tasks that require high and low physical exertion, job rotation may help to diminish the physical demands on employees.[77] And, as we will discuss in Chapter 8, managers may use training and development to help employees learn to cope with stressful situations on the job.

# Job Design in Practice: Regulatory Issues

In Chapter 3, we emphasized that managerial decisions must be based on job-related reasons to comply with equal employment laws and regulations. But how do you know if a reason is job related? Sound job design and job analysis play key roles in this compliance. In this section, we look at two laws that have important implications for job-design decisions: the Americans with Disabilities Act (ADA) and the Occupational Safety and Health Act of 1970.

## Importance of Identifying Essential and Nonessential Job Duties

As discussed in Chapter 3, the Americans with Disabilities Act (ADA) specifically prohibits employers from using a disability as the basis for discriminating against qualified individuals in making employment decisions. This law specifies that all individuals, including disabled individuals, are qualified for a job if they can perform the essential functions of a job, with or without reasonable accommodation. Essential functions are the job tasks, duties, and responsibilities required of a person in the job.[78]

Recall from our discussion of job descriptions that essential functions differ from marginal functions, which also may be performed in a job but are marginal or nonessential for the primary reasons that the job exists. Determining whether a specific task, duty, or responsibility is an essential function or a marginal function of a job is achieved through the job analysis process. Without conducting job analysis, companies must rely on subjective assessments of what tasks are truly essential for employees. Basing decisions on subjective assessments puts a company at risk for claims of bias or discrimination. As a result, companies increasingly turn to job-analysis techniques to ensure that job descriptions are correct and to document essential and nonessential tasks for their positions.

While job analysis provides insights into the essential tasks of a job, job design helps to address the issue of reasonable accommodation. Recall that a reasonable accommodation is a modification to how work is done or to the work environment so that someone who is qualified for a job and who has a disability can perform the job. According to the U.S. Equal Employment Opportunity Commission (EEOC), there are three general categories of reasonable accommodations: (1) changes to a job-application process; (2) changes to the work environment, or to the way a job is usually done; and (3) changes that enable an employee with a disability to enjoy equal benefits and privileges of employment (such as access to training).[79] Job design considerations play a direct role in facilitating these forms of reasonable accommodation. For example, a reasonable accommodation might include modifying a work schedule, allowing employees to share a job, modifying equipment, or making existing facilities easily accessible and usable for someone who has a disability. The reality is that most accommodations that organizations make involve modifications to how jobs are designed and do not involve substantial costs.

## Job Design and Employee Safety

In Chapter 12, we explore in depth the Occupational Safety and Health Act of 1970, which is overseen by the Department of Labor. The Occupational Safety and Health Administration (OSHA) is the primary agency for overseeing employee safety and health on the job. But it is important to note that employee safety has an important influence on the design of jobs. On its website (https://www.osha.gov/about.html), OSHA states that its mission is "to assure safe and healthful working conditions for working men and women by setting and enforcing standards and by providing training, outreach, education, and assistance."[80]

OSHA's basic premise is that companies must provide employees with an environment that does not pose recognized hazards to their safety or health. The agency guides job design in areas such as exposure to hazardous chemicals or biological agents, regulations for machine operators, requirements about protective equipment, and standards for working surfaces and environments. In the beginning of this chapter, we explored the trade-offs between pursuing efficiency and motivational approaches to how jobs are designed. Whichever job design approach you choose, you cannot compromise the safety and well-being of your employees to achieve those goals. Not only is it an ethical obligation, designing jobs to be OSHA compliant is a legal requirement.

## SUMMARY

The ultimate goal of job design is to enhance company performance. Managers achieve this goal by using job design to determine the specific tasks and responsibilities that employees should perform to maximize their individual contributions to company success. In addition, they must decide how employees will perform the specific tasks and responsibilities in each job.

There are two dominant approaches to job design that influence how tasks and responsibilities are performed. First, managers may enhance the efficiency with which employees perform their jobs, using job specification, job simplification, and repetition. Second, managers may strive to maximize employee satisfaction and motivation to work hard toward company goals. This objective is accomplished through job design techniques that change the tasks that employees perform, provide employees with more responsibilities and authority regarding the performance of their jobs, or use team-based work arrangements. Because it is difficult to maximize efficiency and motivation simultaneously, managers must make trade-offs in which approach they emphasize—decisions driven by how employees add value within their company.

*Job analysis* is the systematic analysis of the tasks that are expected to be performed within the scope of a single job. The primary goal of job analysis is to attain a clear understanding of the tasks, duties, and responsibilities expected to be performed for each job (job description) and the specific competencies that are necessary for successful performance of the job (job specifications). There are several primary sources for collecting job information: observations, diaries, interviews, questionnaires, and generic information available through O*NET. Managers may use a standardized or a customized approach to job analysis, depending on several factors.

Before companies can take action based on job design to make decisions regarding managing competencies and managing the attitudes and behaviors of employees, they need to have a clear understanding of the job descriptions and job specifications. A *job description* is a written summary of the specific tasks, responsibilities, and working conditions of a job. *Job specifications* outline the competencies—the knowledge, skills, abilities (KSAs) or other talents—that a jobholder needs in order to perform a job successfully. Job descriptions serve as a valuable tool for communicating to employees the essential tasks of their job, and they help managers make important decisions related to recruiting, hiring, evaluating, and paying employees. Job analysis provides the information to include in the job description and job specifications.

Decisions regarding job design are influenced by the three HR challenges—organizational demands, environmental influences, and legal compliance. Strategy, company characteristics, and culture guide which job-design approach is likely to be most effective to achieve company goals and to reinforce cultural values. They also influence which job design options are feasible given organizational resources. Employee concerns about work/life balance also play a role in managers' job design decisions.

Environmental influences—labor-force trends, globalizations, technology, and ethics—affect job design in several ways. They influence the feasibility of using different approaches to job design, the viability and need for telecommuting and virtual teams, and the level of stress that employees experience on the job. Many companies use tactics such as ergonomics and job rotation to help employees cope with physical and psychological job stress. Finally, the legal environment has a strong influence on job design and job analysis, requiring that managers have a clear understanding of what tasks and responsibilities are essential for job success. Managers also must ensure that jobs are designed with consideration of the safety and well-being of employees.

# KEY TERMS

| | |
|---|---|
| compressed workweek | empowerment |
| critical incident | ergonomics |
| diary | flextime |
| Dictionary of Occupational Titles (DOT) | growth need strength |

job analysis
Job Characteristics Model
job description
job design
job enlargement
job enrichment
job rotation
job sharing
job simplification
job specialization
job specifications

Occupational Information Network
    (O*NET)
participation
role ambiguity
role conflict
role overload
role underload
self-managed team
telecommuter
time and motion studies
voice

## DISCUSSION QUESTIONS

1. Compare and contrast job analysis and job design. Why is it important for a manager to understand both concepts?

2. Discuss the difference between job design in a manufacturing environment and job design at a high-tech firm.

3. Call centers often experience high turnover, which is quite costly. These centers, which handle everything from computer help-desk functions to the processing of mortgage applications, have been described as white-collar factories. Large numbers of employees work in cubicles, responding to phone calls all day, often from upset customers. Often, they have quotas for the volume and types of calls that they handle each day. Is it more important to design these jobs to increase efficiency or motivation? As a manager, how might you make such a change?

4. Which of the environmental considerations do you think will have the greatest impact on how companies design jobs in the next 5 to 10 years? Why? What types of implications do you think this environmental consideration will have?

5. The choices you make in how you analyze jobs have a direct impact on the results of your analysis. Compare and contrast the different job-analysis approaches and provide an example of when each type would be appropriate.

6. Identify three job-design issues that would be affected by the extensive use of virtual teams. How would you manage these issues?

7. An employee who is your firm's only accountant tells you that due to an illness, he will be able to come to work only half-days from now on. Are you legally required to accommodate this request? Why or why not? If you are, as his manager, how could you redesign the job to retain this valuable employee? If you are not required to accommodate him, would you do so? Why or why not?

## LEARNING EXERCISE 1

Research the relationship between job design and a topic related to either employee stress or work/life balance. Using information from this text, from class lectures, and from your research, prepare a one-page summary of best practices that companies have used to manage stress or work/life issues.

1. How does job design affect either employee stress or work/life balance?

2. Are certain job-design approaches better than others for addressing employees' stress or work/life balance? Why?

3. What organizational or environmental factors might prevent managers from implementing the job-design options you noted in your response to question 2?

## LEARNING EXERCISE 2

Obtain a job description and job specifications. Critique the content of the job description and specifications.

1. Does the job description appear to be complete? If not, what is missing?
2. Do all relevant competencies (KSAs) appear to be included? If not, what would you recommend be added?
3. Is any information missing? Be specific in listing areas for improvement.

## LEARNING EXERCISE 3

Decide on a job that you think you would like to have when you graduate. Develop a structured job-analysis questionnaire for that job. Arrange to interview someone who is currently employed in the type of job that you selected.

Use the information that you collect to prepare a job description following the job-description checklist in Exhibit 4.9. Be sure to include tasks, duties, responsibilities, job specifications, and working conditions. Now consider how this job adds value to the company. Is it through efficiency or differentiation? Are the tasks, duties, and responsibilities consistent with how this job adds value?

## CASE STUDY 1: HOMESOURCING AT SYKES HOME

Sykes Home is part of Sykes, a 55,000-employee company that is a digital marketing and customer-service global outsourcer headquartered in Tampa, Florida. The company has over 65 locations in 20 countries, and its employees speak over 30 languages.

Sykes's Work at Home program hires customer service representatives in the United States and Canada to serve Sykes company clients around the globe while working from their home. Sykes has been offering this Work at Home program for over 20 years, and it is the most experienced and largest employer to provide this type of work arrangement. In fact, Sykes Work at Home is a pioneer in this virtual contact-center industry.

Using cloud-based technology allows Sykes Work at Home to meet client needs without geographic limitations. The company's well-designed operational delivery platform ensures increased collaboration and consistent support, regardless of the physical location of the over 7,000 home-based locations across 40 states in the United States, as well as in Canada. The company employs email, phone, chat, Web, social media, and digital self-service to communicate with customers. Results reported by the company show a 20% improvement in performance management, and the ability to cut down on recruiting time for new employees by one-to-two weeks over the traditional brick-and-mortar process, thus ensuring better productivity and quicker scale-up to meet client needs. The average age of employees is 41, and the training program is intensive and ongoing.

*Sources:* "Sykes Expanding Sykes Home Virtual Call Center Model," *Computer Workstations*, 25 (2012): 2, Retrieved from https://search.proquest.com/docview/918654391?accountid=11667; "Christopher S.D. Rogers – Global VP, IT, Sykes Enterprises, Incorporated," Boardroom Insiders Profiles (May 13, 2013), Retrieved from https://search.proquest.com/docview/1657237245?accountid=11667; "Work at Home," Sykes.com, https://www.sykes.com/how-we-help/outsourcing/work-at-home-solutions/.

### Discussion Questions

1. What types of jobs are best suited for home-sourcing arrangements?
2. As a manager, what challenges would you anticipate for designing jobs for individuals who work off site, in their own homes? As an employee, what challenges would you anticipate to experience working from home?

3. What are the greatest risks associated with this job-design approach? What are the greatest benefits associated with this job-design approach? As a manager, what would you do to overcome those risks?

4. Visit the Sykes Home website and other articles you can find about this company (include your reference list with your answer). Would you want to work in a homesourcing arrangement for Sykes Home? As an employee, what challenges and opportunities would doing so present?

## CASE STUDY 2: RETHINKING JOBS AT ELLERS TECHNICAL SUPPORT PROFESSIONALS (ETSP)

Ellers Technical Support Professionals (ETSP) is a young company that was started five years ago by William "Bill" Ellers. Bill created the company to serve a relatively small but growing need among companies in the Washington, DC, area, including nearby Reston, Virginia, and Columbia, Maryland. ETSP provides technical support and administrative oversight for the computing needs of a variety of small to midsize public organizations. Approximately 60% of ETSP's business is supportive in nature. When clients experience computer problems or require the development of new computer programs, Bill's staff provides these services on an as-needed basis. The remaining 40% of ETSP's business involves serving as an outsourcing partner for clients to oversee the administrative aspects of their computer-related activities completely. In these relationships, Bill's staff members are responsible for the design, implementation, and maintenance of all computer systems.

Because the ETSP client base is not-for-profit organizations, clients are typically unable to pay a high cost for computer support. As a result, the company's primary source of competitive advantage is the delivery of these services at an acceptable level of quality for low cost. To achieve this objective, ETSP focuses on cost containment throughout its organization. For example, to increase efficiency, programmers typically perform a fairly narrow array of programming activities across the client organizations. Each programmer is an expert in a particular technological domain, and each works independently on relatively standardized problems.

While the potential for high growth at ETSP is strong, Bill has not been able to devote as much attention to generating new business as he would like. Instead, he has been spending a good amount of his time dealing with relatively high turnover among his programmers. ETSP currently employs 20 programmers, but it is averaging about 50% turnover per year. While there is a wide supply of entry-level programmers in the labor market, the process of recruiting, hiring, and training each programmer requires a fair amount of cost, time, and effort.

In an attempt to reduce the turnover problem, Bill decided to meet with the current employees to ask what changes he can make to improve employee retention so that he can focus on growing the business. After an extensive discussion, the employees suggested that Bill consider redesigning the jobs. Now Bill has to decide what to do.

### Discussion Questions

1. In your opinion, what are the primary causes of turnover?
2. What job-design options might help Bill reduce turnover among the employees?
3. What are the advantages and disadvantages of these options?
4. What job-design changes would you recommend that would allow ETSP to focus on low costs and quality service for public organizations?

## APPENDIX

# Standardized and Customized Approaches to Job Analysis

## Standardized Approaches to Job Analysis

As noted earlier in this chapter, a standardized job-analysis approach uses a single instrument to evaluate multiple jobs within a single company or across many companies. This type of standardized approach requires identifying underlying job dimensions that are applicable to a variety of jobs, allowing for comparisons of dissimilar jobs in meaningful ways. The two most common standardized approaches that companies use are Functional Job Analysis (FJA) and the Position Analysis Questionnaire (PAQ).

### Functional Job Analysis (FJA)

FJA was designed in an attempt to create a single job-analysis instrument that might be used to evaluate a wide array of dissimilar jobs. As described in this chapter, the FJA is based on the notion that it is possible to systematically compare jobs that are dissimilar in the tasks that they perform by focusing on several job dimensions or functional categories of job tasks rather than on actual tasks.[81] Functional categories are broad categories of work-related activities that are applicable to all jobs and that focus on three distinct work domains related to *data*, *people*, and *things*. According to this approach, all jobs comprise these three job dimensions and vary in the functional levels or levels of difficulty associated with these dimensions.

Procedurally, an FJA requires that a job analyst study each job to evaluate the difficulty level for each of these three dimensions and the percentage of the time the job incumbent would be expected to perform at a particular difficulty level for each dimension. For example, when evaluating jobs along the *people* dimension, jobs may range from simply taking instructions to supervising others to mentoring subordinates. Similarly, when evaluating jobs along the *things* dimension, jobs may range from handling to setting up. The more difficulty associated with each job on a dimension, the lower the score. Each job is given a numeric score that facilitates comparisons across jobs and that serves as the basis for subsequent HR activities, such as establishing job groupings for compensation decisions.

***Dictionary of Occupational Titles (DOT)***

a list of concise job definitions created by the Employment and Training Administration and published by the U.S. Department of Labor

A popular form of the FJA approach was the ***Dictionary of Occupational Titles* (DOT),** a list of concise job definitions created by the Employment and Training Administration (ETA) and published by the Department of Labor.[82] First published in 1939, and based on data that were collected by occupational job analysts, the DOT contained thousands of job definitions organized alphabetically by title, with a coding arrangement for occupational classification. Exhibit A4.1 (on the following page) shows the functional levels for the three job dimensions in the Department of Labor's approach to classifying jobs.

The DOT was eventually replaced by the Occupational Information Network (O*NET) in the 1990s. The O*NET system can be accessed online or through a variety of public- and private-sector career and labor market information systems.[83] Under the sponsorship of the Department of Labor's Employment and Training Administration (ETA), O*NET data collection activities are conducted by the National Center for O*NET Development, located in Raleigh, North Carolina. Data are collected directly from incumbent workers in targeted occupations at businesses statistically selected from a random sample. These workers complete standardized questionnaires that are analyzed and incorporated into the O*NET database

**EXHIBIT A4.1**

The Department of Labor Version of FJA

| Data | People | Things |
|------|--------|--------|
| 0 Synthesizing | 0 Mentoring | 0 Setting Up |
| 1 Coordinating | 1 Negotiating | 1 Precision Working |
| 2 Analyzing | 2 Instructing | 2 Operating–Controlling |
| 3 Compiling | 3 Supervising | 3 Driving–Operating |
| 4 Computing | 4 Diverting | 4 Manipulating |
| 5 Copying | 5 Persuading | 5 Tending |
| 6 Comparing | 6 Speaking–Signaling | 6 Feeding–Offbearing |
| | 7 Serving | 7 Handling |
| | 8 Taking Instructions–Helping | |

periodically. The new occupational information is made available through the O*NET Online application and in the downloadable O*NET database files.[84] The O*NET database is a comprehensive source of information for more than 1,000 occupations. Exhibit A4.2 provides a sample excerpt from the O*NET website (http://online.onetcenter.org) for the job of an accountant.

As mentioned earlier in this chapter, one of the primary advantages of O*NET is that it serves as an online resource to help managers with the job-analysis process. Managers can look to O*NET as a starting point for job descriptions and an understanding of the specific KSAs to seek when filling a position, especially for jobs that might not have existed in the company previously.

## Position Analysis Questionnaire (PAQ)

The second common standardized job-analysis technique is the Position Analysis Questionnaire (PAQ), which is a 194-item survey that measures a number of different employee work-related behaviors necessary to perform a variety of tasks in different jobs. Of these survey items, 187 relate to worker behaviors that employees must display to successfully perform the required tasks of a job (e.g., estimating sales or analyzing information).[85] The remaining items focus on documenting the type of compensation employees receive in their jobs. These 187 survey items are designed to measure the extent to which six broad job domains are representative of a particular job:

1. *Information input*—Where and how do employees get the information that they need to perform the job?
2. *Mental processes*—What reasoning, decision-making, planning, and information-processing activities do employees perform in the job?
3. *Work output*—What physical activities are required to perform the job, and what tools are used?
4. *Relationships with other persons*—What relationships with other people are required to perform the job?
5. *Job context*—What are the physical and social aspects of the work environment in which the job is performed?
6. *Other characteristics*—What activities, conditions, or characteristics, other than the previous five, are relevant to the job?

The underlying logic of this approach is that while the specific tasks performed across jobs may differ, certain *work behaviors* are common in the performance of

## EXHIBIT A4.2

### Excerpt from O*NET for the Job of an Accountant

Analyze financial information and prepare financial reports to determine or maintain record of assets, liabilities, profit and loss, tax liability, or other financial activities within an organization.

**Sample of reported job titles:** Accountant, Accounting Manager, Accounting Officer, Accounting Supervisor, Business Analyst, Certified Public Accountant (CPA), Cost Accountant, General Accountant, Project Accountant, Staff Accountant

#### TASKS
- Develop, maintain, and analyze budgets, preparing periodic reports that compare budgeted costs to actual costs.
- Prepare, examine, or analyze accounting records, financial statements, or other financial reports to assess the accuracy, completeness, and conformance to reporting and procedural standards.
- Review accounts for discrepancies and reconcile differences.
- Prepare adjusting journal entries.
- Establish tables of accounts and assign entries to proper accounts.
- Analyze business operations, trends, costs, revenues, financial commitments, and obligations, to project future revenues and expenses or to provide advice.

#### TECHNOLOGY SKILLS
- **Accounting software**—Fund accounting software; Intuit QuickBooks; Intuit QuickBooks Premier; Sage 50 Accounting
- **Database user interface and query software**—Best Software CPAPayroll; FileMaker Pro; Microsoft Access; Yardi Systems Yardi Enterprise
- **Enterprise resource planning ERP software**—Microsoft Dynamics GP; NetSuite ERP; Oracle PeopleSoft Financials; SAP Business Objects
- **Financial analysis software**—Brentmark Estate Planning Quickview; Cartesis Magnitude iAnalysis; Delphi Technology; Oracle E-Business Suite Financials
- **Tax preparation software**—ATX Total Tax Office; CCH ProSystem fx TAX; Intuit Lacerte; Orrtax Software IntelliTax Classic

#### KNOWLEDGE
**Economics and Accounting**—Knowledge of economic and accounting principles and practices, the financial markets, banking, and the analysis and reporting of financial data.
**Mathematics**—Knowledge of arithmetic, algebra, geometry, calculus, statistics, and their applications.
**Clerical**—Knowledge of administrative and clerical procedures and systems such as word processing, managing files and records, stenography and transcription, designing forms, and other office procedures and terminology.
**English Language**—Knowledge of the structure and content of the English language, including the meaning and spelling of words, rules of composition, and grammar.
**Law and Government**—Knowledge of laws, legal codes, court procedures, precedents, government regulations, executive orders, agency rules, and the democratic political process.

*Source:* O*NET OnLine, Summary Report for: 13-2011.01 – Accountants, https://www.onetonline.org/link/summary/13-2011.01.

most jobs. Procedurally, this approach follows a simple format. First, a job analyst assesses the extent to which various elements are involved in a job. This process is usually done through observation of the job and interviews with current jobholders and job supervisors. Then, the job analyst rates the applicable job elements in terms of their importance to the job, the amount of time spent on the tasks, their extent of use, their possibility of occurrence, and any other special codes.[86] Finally, these ratings are sent to PAQ corporate headquarters, where they are scored and a report is generated regarding the job's scores on each of the dimensions.

Because the PAQ is widely used for job analysis across many companies, results that are submitted to the PAQ headquarters may be used to identify comparisons among similar jobs in different companies. In addition to identifying the specific job behaviors that are performed in a job, the PAQ approach may be extended to provide insights into the job specifications or KSAs required to perform the job (www.erieri.com/paq). For example, research has shown that the PAQ is related to the General Aptitude Test Battery (GATB), a standardized ability test. This relationship facilitates a link between dimension scores on the PAQ and estimates of the KSAs needed to perform a job.[87]

Of course, as with all other standardized techniques, the PAQ has trade-offs. The disadvantages of the PAQ are that it is fairly complex, sophisticated, time consuming, and potentially quite costly. And, due to the complexity of the evaluation process, it is recommended that the PAQ be administered by trained analysts. In addition, the PAQ is believed to be more suited for blue-collar jobs than for professional, managerial, and some technical jobs.[88] Due to these limitations, the PAQ approach is not the most appropriate for analyzing every situation, but it does provide an excellent method for classifying different jobs into a coherent structure that is useful for other HR activities, such as administering pay and benefits programs. Finally, because the work behaviors may be linked to necessary job specifications, the PAQ may prove useful for staffing and training purposes as well.

## Customized Approaches to Job Analysis

While standardized approaches focus on job dimensions that are represented in most jobs, customized techniques allow managers to develop a job description and job specifications that reflect the unique attributes of a particular job. We will look at three approaches for customized job analysis: the critical-incidents approach, the task inventory approach, and the job element approach.

### Critical-Incidents Approach

The critical-incidents approach obtains specific, behaviorally focused descriptions of work activities. **Critical incidents** are specific behaviors that distinguish exceptionally good performance in a particular job from exceptionally poor performance in the same job. For example, the critical-incidents approach may be used to develop indicators of good or poor performance for the professor teaching this course in terms of how he or she responds to student questions. An example of exceptionally good performance for this job dimension might be, "When students have questions about course material, the professor listens carefully and takes the necessary time to completely answer the questions." In this same context, an example of poor performance on the same job dimension might be, "When students have questions about course material, the professor dismisses the questions as disrupting the flow of the class and continues to present new material to the class."

**critical incident**

a statement or example of exceptionally good or exceptionally poor performance that employees display over in the performance of their job

The process of conducting a critical-incidents analysis is fairly straightforward. First, individuals familiar with a job, such as supervisors, employees, or subject-matter experts, identify the major dimensions of the job. Next, they specify behaviors that, when displayed on the job, lead to high or low performance on those dimensions. These behaviors (critical incidents) are then reviewed by all knowledgeable individuals to ensure that all relevant job dimensions are captured and that all critical incidents for those dimensions are identified.

The primary benefit of the critical-incidents approach is that it focuses specifically on job behaviors that are critical for job success. Managers can use these behaviors as the foundation for other HR activities, such as training programs and performance evaluations. To be effective, however, the critical incidents that are identified should be specific and should focus on behaviors that are observable in the performance of a job. In addition, critical incidents must be detailed enough so that different individuals viewing the critical incidents will be able to understand the specific behaviors that drive successful or unsuccessful job performance.[89]

## Task Inventory Approach

Whereas the critical-incidents approach focuses on specific behaviors that drive job success, task inventories focus on the tasks that are necessary for job success. The task inventory method of collecting information generally involves asking current jobholders or their supervisors to evaluate the extent to which different tasks are performed.[90] After tasks are identified, they are rated in terms of their importance for job success, the amount of time devoted to each task, the difficulty of the task, and the time needed to learn how to perform the task.

Although typically focused on the tasks required to execute a job, task inventories may be extended to also identify the job specifications (competencies) necessary to perform the job successfully.[91] For example, after the tasks performed in a job are identified, subject-matter experts, supervisors, and jobholders may identify the specific KSAs needed to perform each specific job task. After compiling the data, the result of this process is a specific listing of the job specifications necessary to complete each of the tasks in the job.

## Job Element Approach

The third customized approach to job analysis is the job element approach. This approach is distinct because it focuses *solely* on analyzing the employee competencies that are necessary for successful job performance rather than focusing on the tasks to be performed in a job. With this approach, people who are familiar with a job evaluate the specific skills necessary to perform the essential tasks. The essence of this approach is that it focuses on job elements—specific worker requirements that are necessary to perform a job. Job elements can be cognitive abilities, such as reading blueprints or understanding statistics; psychomotor elements, such as driving a car or operating machinery; or work habits, such as willingness to work long hours. For example, some specific job elements for a firefighter might be good physical stamina and the ability to work well under pressure.[92]

After the job elements are identified by job analysts or subject-matter experts, they are collected and evaluated along four dimensions:

- *Barely acceptable*—The number of barely acceptable employees who have this element
- *Superior*—The degree of how useful an element is for distinguishing superior workers from average workers
- *Trouble likely if not considered*—The probability of trouble occurring in the performance of a job if employees do not have this element
- *Practical*—The extent to which job applicants are likely to possess this element.[93]

Each element is then rated 0 (element has minimal value), 1 (element has some value), or 2 (element has high value). Rating the usefulness of each element for each dimension provides additional information regarding which predictors are particularly important. For example, using the firefighter example, ability to work under high pressure would likely score high for the *superior, trouble likely if not considered*, and *practical dimensions*. But this job element would likely score low for the barely acceptable dimension. In other words, in this example, the ability to work under high pressure is a trait that not all people possess, but it is an important distinguishing factor for high performers, an important element for job success, and a practical tool for evaluating job applicants.

# NOTES

[1] F. Taylor, *Principles of Scientific Management* (New York: Harper, 1911); and F. Taylor, *Scientific Management* (New York: Harper & Brothers, 1947).

[2] W. R. Scott, *Organizations: Rational, Natural, and Open System,* 5th ed. (Englewood Cliffs, NJ: Prentice Hall, 2003).

[3] M. Witzel, "A Short History of Efficiency," *Business Strategy Review* 13 (2002): 38–47.

[4] M. Krebs, "The Starting Line," *Automotive News* 77 (2003): 16.

[5] F. P. Morgeson and M. A. Campion, "Minimizing Trade-offs When Redesigning Work: Evidence from a Longitudinal Quasi-experiment," *Personnel Psychology* 55 (2002): 589–612.

[6] G. R. Oldham and Y. Fried, "Job Design Research and Theory: Past, Present, and Future," *Organizational Behavior and Human Decision Processes* 136 (2016): 20–35; J. R. Hackman, G. Oldham, R. Janson, and K. Purdy, "A New Strategy for Job Enrichment," *California Management Review* 17, no. 4 (1975): 57–71.

[7] Ibid.

[8] R. W. Renn and R. J. Vandenberg, "The Critical Psychological States: An Underrepresented Component in Job Characteristics Model Research," *Journal of Management* 21 (1995): 279–303.

[9] Oldham and Fried, "Job Design Research and Theory"; Past, Present, and Future," *Organizational Behavior and Human Decision Processes* 136 (2016): 20–35; J. Hackman, "Work Design," in *Improving Life at Work,* ed. J. Hackman and J. Suttle (Santa Monica, CA: Goodyear, 1976), 96–162.

[10] W. E. Gallagher, Jr. and H. J. Einhorn, "Motivation Theory and Job Design," *Journal of Business* 49, no. 3 (1976): 358–373. Oldham and Fried, "Job Design Research and Theory"; Past, Present, and Future," *Organizational Behavior and Human Decision Processes* 136 (2016): 20–35

[11] Anonymous, "Energize and Enhance Employee Value with Job Rotation," *HR Focus,* January 2008, 6–10; and M. A. Campion, L. Cheraskin, and M. J. Stevens, "Career-Related Antecedents and Outcomes of Job Rotation," *Academy of Management Journal* 37 (1994): 1518–1542.

[12] N. Slack, C. L. Cooper, and C. Argyris, "Empowerment," *Blackwell Encyclopedic Dictionary of Operations Management* (Boston: Blackwell Publishers, 1997), 44.

[13] G. Lee, P. B. Kim, and R. R. Perdue, "A Longitudinal Analysis of an Accelerating Effect of Empowerment on Job Satisfaction: Customer-Contact vs. Non-customer-contact Workers," *International Journal of Hospitality Management* (2016), 571–578. C. R. Leana, "Predictors and Consequences of Delegation," *Academy of Management Journal* 29 (1986): 754–774; and Z. X. Chen and S. Aryee, "Delegation and Employee Work Outcomes: An Examination of the Cultural Context of Mediating Processes in China," *Academy of Management Journal* 50 (2007): 226–238.

[14] Hackman et al., "A New Strategy for Job Enrichment."

[15] Lee et al., "A Longitudinal Analysis of an Accelerating Effect of Empowerment"; S. E. Seibert, S. R. Silver, and W. A. Randolph, "Taking Empowerment to the Next Level: A Multiple-Level Model of Empowerment, Performance, and Satisfaction," *Academy of Management Journal* 47 (2004): 332–349.

[16] W. H. N. Thomas and Daniel C. Feldman, "Employee Voice Behavior: A Meta-analytic Test of the Conservation of Resources Framework," *Journal of Organizational Behavior* (2012), 216; P. Holland, A. Pyman, B. K. Cooper, and J. Teicher, "Employee Voice and Job Satisfaction in Australia: The Centrality of Direct Voice," *Human Resource Management* 50 (January/February 2011): 95–111.

[17] Justin M. Berg, Jane E. Dutton, and Amy Wrzesniewski, "What Is Job Crafting and Why Does It Matter?" Theory-to-Practice Briefing, Center for Positive Organizational Scholarship, Michigan Ross School of Business, positiveorgs.bus.umich.edu, revised August 1, 2008, https://positiveorgs.bus.umich.edu/wp-content/uploads/What-is-Job-Crafting-and-Why-Does-it-Matter1.pdf.

[18] S. G. Cohen and D. E. Bailey, "What Makes Teams Work: Group Effectiveness Research from the Shop Floor to the Executive Suite," *Journal of Management* 23 (1997): 239–290; and B. L. Kirkman et al., "Five Challenges to Virtual Team Success: Lessons from Sabre, Inc.," *Academy of Management Executive* 16 (2002): 67–79.

[19] C. Zarraga and J. Bonache, "Assessing the Team Environment for Knowledge Sharing: An Empirical Analysis," *International Journal of Human Resource Management* 14 (2003): 1227–1245.

[20] M. A. Campion, G. J. Medsker, and A. C. Higgs, "Relations Between Work Group Characteristics and Effectiveness: Implications for Designing Effective Work Groups," *Personnel Psychology* 46 (1993): 823–850.

[21] E. L. Deci, J. P. Connel, and P. M. Ryan, "Self-Determination in a Work Organization," *Journal of Applied Psychology* 74 (1989): 580–590; E. E. Lawler, III, *High Involvement Management* (San Francisco: Jossey-Bass, 1986); C. C. Manz, "Self-leading Work Teams: Moving Beyond Self-Management Myths," *Human Relations* 45 (1992): 7–22; and C. C. Manz and H. P. Sims, Jr., *Business Without Bosses: How Self-managing Teams Are Building High-Performance Companies* (New York: Wiley, 1993).

[22] J. Tata and S. Prasad, "Team Self-Management, Organizational Structure, and Judgments of Team Effectiveness," *Journal of Managerial Issues* 16, no. 2 (2004): 248–265; and R. S. Wellins et al., *Self-Directed Teams: A Study of Current Practices* (Pittsburgh: DDI, 1990).

[23] R. Batt, "Work Organization, Technology, and Performance in Customer Service and Sales," *Industrial & Labor Relations Review,* 52(4) (1999): 539–564.

[24] B. L. Kirkman, B. Rosen, P. E. Tesluk, and C. B. Gibson, "The Impact of Team Empowerment on Virtual Team Performance: The Moderating Role of Face-to-Face Interaction," *Academy of Management Journal* 47 (2004): 175–192; and G. Brown, C. Crossley, and S. L. Robinson, "Psychological Ownership, Territorial Behavior, and Being Perceived as a Team Contributor: The Critical Role of Trust in the Work Environment," *Personnel Psychology* 67 (2014): 463–485; J. Kahnweiler, "Have We Gone Too Far in Promoting Collaboration? All Teamwork—and No Individual Play—Can Make for Dull Employees," *HR Magazine,* 63(2) (2018): 26–27.

[25] Greg R. Oldham and Yitzhak Fried, "Job Design Research and Theory: Past, Present and Future," *Organizational Behavior and Human Decision Processes,* 136 (2016): 20–35.

[26] M. A. Campion, "Ability Requirement Implications of Job Design: An Interdisciplinary Perspective," *Personnel Psychology* 42 (1989): 1–24; and Gallagher and Einhorn, "Motivation Theory and Job Design."

[27] F. P. Morgenson and M. A. Campion, "Minimizing Trade-offs When Redesigning Work: Evidence from a Longitudinal Quasi-experiment," *Personnel Psychology* 55 (2002): 589–612.

[28] Ibid.

[29] M. A. Campion, "Interdisciplinary Approaches to Job Design: A Constructive Replication with Extensions," *Journal of Applied Psychology* 73 (1988): 467–481; and M. A. Campion and P. W. Thayer, "Development and Field Evaluation of an Interdisciplinary Measure of Job Design," *Journal of Applied Psychology* 70 (1985): 29–43.

[30] H. Risher, "Job Evaluation: Validity and Reliability," *Compensation and Benefits Review,* January—February 1989, p. 24.

[31] O'NET Resource Center, https://www.onetcenter.org/overview.html.

[32] R. J. Harvey, "Book Review, *Functional Job Analysis* by Sidney A. Fine and Steven F. Cronshaw," *Personnel Psychology* 55 (2002): 202–204; R. J. Harvey, "Job Analysis," in *Handbook of Industrial and Organizational Psychology,* ed. M. D. Dunnette and L. Hough (Palo Alto, CA: Consulting Psychologists Press, 1991), 2, 71–163.

[33] S. A. Fine and W. W. Wiley, *An Introduction to Functional Job Analysis* (Kalamazoo, MI: W.E. Upjohn Institute for Employment Research, 1971).

[34] B. Becker and M. Huselid, "SHRM and Job Design: Narrowing the Divide," *Journal of Organizational Behavior,* (2/3) (2010): 379–388; S. E. Jackson, R. S. Schuler, and J. C. Rivero, "Organizational Characteristics as Predictors of Personnel Practices," *Personnel Psychology* 42 (1989): 727–786; R. Miles and C. C. Snow, "Designing Strategic Human Resource Systems," *Organizational Dynamics* 13 (1984): 36–52; and J. E. Delery and D. H. Doty, "Modes of Theorizing in Strategic Human Resource Management: Tests of Universalistic, Contingency, and Configurational Performance Predictions," *Academy of Management Journal* 39 (1996): 802–835.

[35] Women's Bureau of U.S. Department of Labor Issue Brief. *Workplace Flexibility: Information and Options for Small Businesses.* Department of Labor Online, https://www.dol.gov/wb/WorkplaceFlexibility_508_FINAL.pdf.

[36] K. Matos, E. Galinksy and J. Bond, "2016 National Study of Employers," sponsored by Families and Work Institute, Society for Human Resource Management, and When Work Works, http://www.whenworkworks.org/be-effective/guides-tools/2016-national-study-of-employers.

[37] Anonymous, "Optimised Flexible Working Could Add Billions to the UK Economy," *RSA 21st-Century Enlightenment*, July 15, 2013, http://www.thersa.org/large-text/about-us/media/press-releases/optimised-flexible-working-could-add-billions-to-uk-economy.

[38] R. H. Hall, *Organizations: Structures, Processes, and Outcomes*, 8th ed. (Upper Saddle River, NJ: Prentice Hall, 2002).

[39] J. D. Kok and L. M. Uhlaner, "Organization Context and Human Resource Management in the Small Firm," *Small Business Economics*, December 2001, 273–291.

[40] J. H. Harris and L. A. Arendt, "Stress Reduction and the Small Business: Increasing Employee and Customer Satisfaction," *SAM Advanced Management Journal* (Winter 1998), 27–34.

[41] K. M. Kacmar, D. S. Carlson, V. K. Bratton, and M. C. Andrews, "An Integrated Perspective of Antecedents to Ingratiatory Behaviors," paper presented at the National Academy of Management Meetings, Seattle, August 2003; N. A. Bowling, S. Khazon, G. M. Alarcon, C. E. Blackmore, C. Bragg, M. R. Hoepf, et al., "Building Better Measures of Role Ambiguity and Role Conflict: The Validation of New Role Stressor Scales," *Work & Stress*, 31(1) (2017): 1–23.

[42] Kahn et al., *Organizational Stress*; see also G. D. Walls, L. M. Capella, and W. E. Greene, "Toward a Source Stressors Model of Conflict Between Work and Family," *Review of Business* 22 (2001): 86–91.

[43] Matos et al., "2016 National Study of Employers."

[44] J. Horn, "Happy Qualcomm Workers Earn Best Employer Nod," *UT San Deigo*, August 23, 2013, http://www.utsandiego.com/news/2012/aug/23/tp-happy-qualcomm-workers-earn-best-employer-nod/.

[45] Matos et al., "2016 National Study of Employers."

[46] J. C. Latack and L. W. Foster, "Implementation of Compressed Work Schedules: Participation and Job Redesign as Critical Factors for Employee Acceptance," *Personnel Psychology* 38 (1985): 75–93.

[47] S. Ronen and S. B. Primps, "The Compressed Work Week as Organizational Change: Behavioral and Attitudinal Outcomes," *Academy of Management Review* 6 (1981): 61–74.

[48] P. A. Smith and A. A. I. Wedderburn, "Flexibility and Long Shifts," *Employee Relations* 20 (1998): 483–489.

[49] "Have You Considered Job Sharing as a Retention Tool?" *HR Focus* 83, no. 9 (September 2006): 10–11.

[50] S. Nollen, "Job-Sharing," *Blackwell Encyclopedic Dictionary of Human Resource Management* (Oxford, UK: Blackwell Publishing, 2005), 213.

[51] Matos et al., "2016 National Study of Employers."

[52] M. Mills, R. A. Mathews, J. B. Henning, and V. A. Woo, "Family-Supportive Organizations and Supervisors: How They Influence Employee Outcomes and for Whom?" *International Journal of Human Resource Management* 25 (2014): 1763–1785; and M. M. Arthur, "Share Price Reactions to Work-Family Initiatives: An Institutional Perspective," *Academy of Management Journal* 46 (2003): 497–505.

[53] K. Hannon, "Reaping the Benefits of an Aging Work Force," *The New York Times*, March 2, 2018, https://www.nytimes.com/2018/03/02/business/retirement/aging-workers-opportunity.html.

[54] J. Mullich, "They Don't Retire Them, They Hire Them," *Workforce Magazine*, December 2003, 49–54. W. W. Heisler and D. B. Bandow, "Retaining and Engaging Older Workers: A Solution to Worker Shortages in the U.S.," *Business Horizons*, 61(3) (2018): 421–430.

[55] L. L. Colangelo, "Job Fair Aims to Connect Workers over the Age of 50 with Employment Opportunities," May 19, 2014, http://www.nydailynews.com/new-york/queens/job-fair-aimed-people-age-50-article-1.1810546.

[56] Heisler and Bandow, "Retaining and Engaging Older Workers."

[57] Ibid., also see Mullich, "They Don't Retire Them, They Hire Them."

[58] Brethren Village website, "Employment Benefits at Brethren Village," http://www.bv.org/careers/benefits.asp.

[59] Mullich, "They Don't Retire Them, They Hire Them."

[60] M. C. Noonan and J. L. Glass, "The Hard Truth About Telecommuting," *Monthly Labor Review*, June 2012, 38–45.

[61] Bureau of Labor Statistics, American Time Use Survey Summary, bls.gov, June 27, 2017, http://www.bls.gov/news.release/atus.nr0.htm.

[62] Society for Human Resource Management Press Release, "Telecommuting Has Increased Threefold in 20 Years, SHRM Survey Shows," July 13, 2016, https://www.shrm.org/

about-shrm/press-room/press-releases/pages/telecommuting-up-over-past-20-years.aspx; Society for Human Resource Management, "2017 Employee Benefits," https://www .shrm.org/hr-today/trends-and-forecasting/research-and-surveys/documemts/2017 %20employee%20benefits%20report.pdf.

[63] GlobalWorkplaceAnalytics.com, *Latest Telecommuting Statistics*, http://globalworkplace-analytics.com/telecommuting-statistics, updated July 2018.

[64] P. J. Mateyka, M. A. Rapino, and L. C. Lanivar, "Home-Based Workers in the United States: 2010," *Current Population Reports*, October 12, 2010, https://www.census.gov/ library/publications/2012/demo/p70-132.html.

[65] Telework Enhancement Act of 2010, https://telework.gov/guidance-legislation/telework-legislation/telework-enhancement-act/.

[66] Rebecca J. Thompson, Stephanie C. Payne, and Aaron B. Taylor, "Applicant Attraction to Flexible Work Arrangements: Separating the Influence of Flextime and Flexplace," *Journal of Occupational & Organizational Psychology*, 88(4) (2015): 726–749.

[67] Kirkman et al., "The Impact of Team Empowerment on Virtual Team Performance"; and J. Lipnack and J. Stamps, *Virtual Teams: People Working Across Boundaries with Technology*, 2nd ed. (New York: Wiley, 2000).

[68] F. Seibdrat, M. Hoegl, and H. Ernst, "How to Manage Virtual Teams," *MIT Sloan Management Review*, July 1, 2009, http://sloanreview.mit.edu/article/how-to-manage-virtual-teams/ and K. Ferrazi, "Virtual Teams Can Outperform Traditional Teams," *HBR Blog network*, March 20, 2012, http://blogs.hbr.org/2012/03/how-virtual-teams-can-out-perfo/.

[69] Michael D. Watkins, "Making Virtual Teams Work: Ten Basic Principles," *Harvard Business Review*, June 27, 2013, https://hbr.org/2013/06/making-virtual-teams-work-ten.

[70] A. Malhotra, A. Majchrzak, and B. Rosen, "Leading Virtual Teams: Table 1: Practices of Effective Virtual Teams," *Academy of Management Perspectives* 21 (February 2007): 61–70.

[71] "Flexible Working," *Gov.UK*, June 30, 2014, https://www.gov.uk/flexible-working/overview; "Next: Flexible Upper Lips," *Monthly Labor Review* 127, no. 5 (May 2004): 44.

[72] Harris and Arendt, "Stress Reduction and the Small Business."

[73] CareerCast.com, "The Most Stressful Jobs in 2018," CareerCast.com, https://www.career-cast.com/jobs-rated/2018-most-stressful-jobs.

[74] "Coping with Stress at Work," *American Psychological Association*, apa.org, http://www. apa.org/helpcenter/work-stress.aspx.

[75] Stephanie Denning, "How Stress Is the Business World's Silent Killer," *Forbes*, May 4, 2018, https://www.forbes.com/sites/stephaniedenning/2018/05/04/what-is-the-cost-of-stress-how-stress-is-the-business-worlds-silent-killer/#3d0149516e06.

[76] International Ergonomics Association, "What Is Ergonomics?" http://www.iea.cc/whats/.

[77] J. Croasmun, "Office Workers Choose Egonomics Over Morale," June 30, 2004, https:// ergoweb.com/office-workers-choose-ergonomics-over-morale/.

[78] P. Paull, F. M. Kuijer, B. Visser, and H. C. G. Kemper, "Job Rotation as a Factor in Reducing Physical Workload at a Refuse Collecting Department," *Ergonomics* 42 (1999): 1167–1178.

[79] U.S. Equal Employment Opportunity Commission, "Disability Discrimination," http:// www.eeoc.gov/laws/types/disability.cfm.

[80] U.S. Equal Employment Opportunity Commission "Small Employers and Reasonable Accommodation," https://www.eeoc.gov/facts/accommodation.html.

[81] Occupational Safety and Health Administration, "OSHA's Mission," https://www.osha .gov/about.html.

[82] Fine and Wiley, *An Introduction to Functional Job Analysis*.

[83] Informational Technology Associates, "Dictionary of Occupational Titles," https:// occupationalinfo.org/.

[84] U.S. Department of Labor, "The O*NET Data Collection Program," http://www.doleta .gov/programs/onet/datacollection.cfm.

[85] L. Friedman and R. J. Harvey, "Can Raters with Reduced Job Descriptive Information Provide Accurate Position Analyses Questionnaire (PAQ) Ratings?" *Personnel Psychology* 39 (1986): 779–789.

[86] M. T. Brannick and E. L. Levine, *Job Analysis: Methods, Research, and Applications for Human Resource Management in the New Millennium* (Thousand Oaks, CA: SAGE Publications, 2002), 41.

[87] E. J. McCormick, P. J. Jeanneret, and R. C. Mecham, "A Study of Job Characteristics and Job Dimensions as Based on the Position Analysis Questionnaire (PAQ)," *Journal of*

*Applied Psychology Monograph* 56 (1972): 347–368; and R. D. Arvey, E. Salas, and K. A. Gialluca, "Using Task Inventories to Forecast Skills and Abilities," *Human Performance* 5, no. 3 (1992): 171–190.

[88] E. T. Cornelius, III, A. S. DeNisi, and A. G. Blencoe, "Expert and Naive Raters Using the PAQ: Does It Matter?" *Personnel Psychology* 37 (1984): 453–464.

[89] D. Bownas and H. J. Bernardin, "The Critical Incident Method," in *The Job Analysis Handbook for Business, Industry, and Government*, vol. II, ed. S. Gael (New York: Wiley, 1988), 1120–1137.

[90] Arvey, Salas, and Gialluca, "Using Task Inventories to Forecast Skills and Abilities."

[91] Ibid.

[92] Brannick and Levine, *Job Analysis*.

[93] Ibid.

# Chapter 5

# Workforce Planning

## Learning Objectives

**AFTER READING THIS CHAPTER, YOU SHOULD BE ABLE TO:**

1 Explain why workforce planning is an important activity of managers.

2 Describe the internal and external factors that affect labor supply and demand.

3 Discuss the tactics that managers use to remedy labor shortages and labor surpluses.

4 Discuss the advantages and disadvantages of various workforce planning tactics.

5 Describe how a firm's organizational demands affect its workforce planning decisions.

6 Explain the impact that environmental factors have on a firm's workforce planning decisions.

7 Discuss the legal aspects of the workforce planning tactics that companies use.

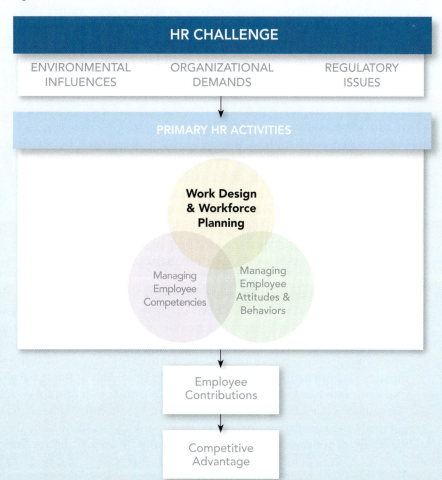

# The Importance of Workforce Planning

During the twentieth century, Ford and General Motors (GM) were two of the most successful companies in the automobile industry. At one point, GM garnered almost 51% of the global automotive market share.[1] Ford's introduction of assembly-line technologies reduced the company's production costs to a point where nearly every American family could afford to own an automobile (or multiple automobiles).[2] Over the years, however, these two companies have faced tough times. In 2006, for example, both companies experienced escalating fixed costs, negative profits, and diminished consumer demand for their products.[3] Both companies responded by closing plants and laying off employees.[4]

Ford cut thousands of jobs to match its workforce capacity with the demand for its products.[5] The company's workforce went from 283,000 employees in 2006 to 165,968 in 2012, and then to 171,000 in 2013.[6] Ford offered 90,000 of its retired engineers and office workers the option to accept a large lump-sum payment to give up their regular monthly pension check for the rest of their lives in 2012.[7] As its performance steadied, Ford was able to expand its workforce once again. The company reported 202,000 employees on the payroll in December 2017. In April 2018, Ford's new chief executive officer (CEO), James Hackett, announced that by 2020 the company was going to get out of the car business in North America except for continuing to produce the Mustang and a new Focus crossover in order to focus on the more lucrative sport utility vehicle (SUV) and pickup truck market. This significant shift in business meant that Ford had to once again make decisions about the type and number of workers needed across its business units.[8]

Similar to how Ford addressed the downturn in the economy, GM announced in 2008 that it would extend a buyout option for 78,000 employees and provide special incentives for its 40,800 workers who were eligible for retirement. The goal of the plan was to incentivize these workers to retire sooner rather than later in order to reduce the company's workforce.[9] GM also made an incentive offer to 42,000 of its 118,000 former white-collar workers and surviving spouses in 2012 to reduce the company's ongoing legacy expenses.[10] In 2013, GM offered additional buyouts to its skilled workers.[11] Following these reductions in force, GM made a significant recovery and hired more workers. In June 2018, GM reported having 180,000 employees on its payroll, but by that time there were predictions that the hiring trend had peaked.[12]

Major decisions such as these are most often made by a firm's top managers. However, managers at all levels provide input into how the plans will be implemented. Decisions have to be made about which parts of the organization to close, which employees will be let go in units that remain open, or both. In smaller companies, managers have even more direct input into workforce planning decisions and implementation. Even in companies where the human resources (HR) department is able to provide assistance in workforce planning decisions, managers should play an active role in the process. After all, managers are ultimately responsible for the success of the groups of individuals they supervise. Thus, the quality of a firm's workforce planning decisions directly affects the performance of a manager's staff.

If, as a manager, you do not have the right number of employees with the right skill sets, you will find your unit unable to take advantage of potential business opportunities. Alternatively, operating in excess of your staffing requirements or employing people who are not adding a sufficient amount of value to the activities that they do is an inefficient use of your firm's financial capital. A surplus of employees translates into bloated payroll levels, benefits, and other employee-related expenses. The greater your labor costs, the lower your profitability is likely to be.

Finally, the effectiveness of the people you manage is likely to be directly affected by the quality of your workforce planning decisions. As we will discuss later in this chapter,

**EXHIBIT 5.1**

Framework for the Strategic Management of Employees

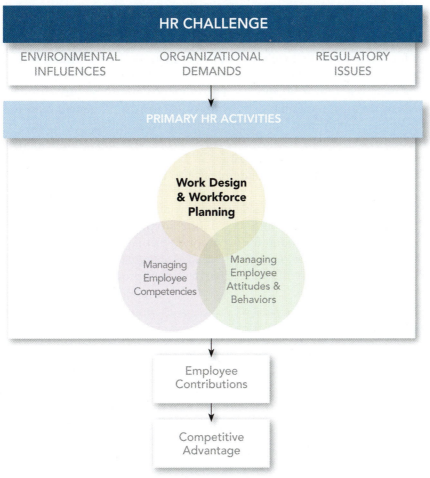

if your staff members operate short-handed for any length of time, or lack the skills they need, they are likely to feel overworked and experience burnout. This situation, in turn, can lead to higher turnover and diminished performance on their part.[13]

In Chapter 4, we discussed job design. Remember that job design does the following:

- Focuses on decisions about how jobs should be structured
- Ensures that job-related tasks and activities are performed in a way that has the most potential to add value to the company and its customers

The best-designed jobs in the world add no value if people are not in a position to perform them, however. As Exhibit 5.1 shows, work design and workforce planning require managers to pay equal attention to how jobs are designed and to workforce planning.

The focus of this chapter is workforce planning. We first discuss how a firm's internal demand for labor relative to its internal supply dictates whether managers experience labor shortages or surpluses among their workforces. We then explore how external factors put pressure on a company's supply and demand for labor. Third, we discuss the tactics that you, as a manager, can use to remedy labor shortages and surpluses. Finally, we wrap up the chapter with an examination of workforce planning in the context of coping with organizational demands, environmental considerations, and regulatory issues.

**workforce planning**

the process of making sure that individuals with the right skills are where they need to be, at the right time, to meet a firm's current and future needs

**labor demand**

the number and types of employees the company needs to meet its current and future strategic objectives

**labor supply**

the availability of current or potential employees to perform a company's jobs

**labor shortage**

exists when the demand for labor exceeds the available supply of it (demand > supply)

**labor surplus**

exists when the supply of labor is greater than the demand for it (supply > demand)

# Workforce Planning

Exhibit 5.2 provides a visual framework for **workforce planning**—the process of making sure that individuals with the right skills are where they need to be, at the right time, to meet a firm's current and future needs. In many ways, workforce planning is an ongoing balancing act. Companies must balance the demand for labor with the available supply of labor. **Labor demand** refers to the number and types of employees that a company needs to meet its current and future strategic objectives. **Labor supply** refers to the availability of current or potential employees to perform a company's jobs. In other words, managers have to look at both the labor supply and the labor demand within their company (internal considerations), and they also need to anticipate and plan for factors outside their company (external considerations).

Understanding the supply and demand for labor is only half the equation, though. Managers also must take action to address labor shortages and surpluses. A **labor shortage** exists when the demand for labor exceeds the available supply of it (demand > supply). In contrast, a **labor surplus** exists when the supply of labor is greater than the demand for it (supply > demand). Overtime, outsourcing, and offshoring are examples of tactics that a manager can use to cope with a labor shortage. Tactics such as layoffs and early-retirement programs can be used to cope

## EXHIBIT 5.2

### The Framework for Workforce Planning

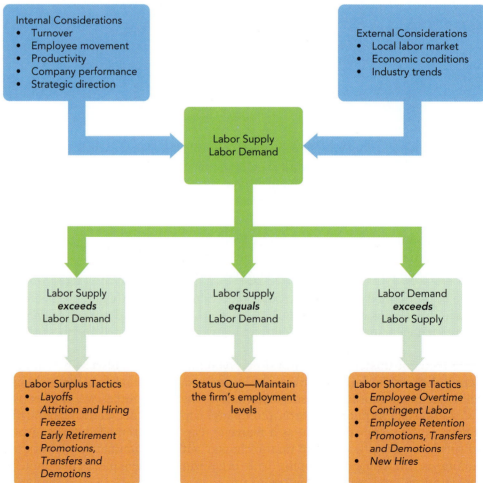

with a labor surplus. Knowing which tactic to use requires that you have some insight into your company's actual labor supply and demand.

# Forecasting Labor Supply and Labor Demand

A variety of factors affect the relative supply and demand for labor in companies. As noted previously, managers must examine both the internal and external environmental factors that exert pressure on the labor supply relative to its demand. We next discuss these two types of factors.

## Internal Factors

The number of employees in different parts of an organization is always changing due to a variety of factors. Employee turnover is one factor. The productivity of the firm's employees, the company's performance, and changes in the firm's strategic direction also affect the demand for different jobs in different parts of a company. Companies also must allocate employees via promotions, transfers, and demotions to areas in the firm where these people can make the biggest contributions. At any point in time, some parts of a company may be facing shortages of employee talent, whereas others may have surpluses. Let's now discuss these internal factors in more detail.

### Turnover

Managers consider the internal labor force (the company's current employees), when reviewing current and long-term workforce needs. However, the internal labor force is not static; rather, it changes over time. Employee **turnover**, which directly affects a firm's labor demand, includes the voluntary and involuntary termination of employees within an organization. The primary difference between the two types is whether the turnover is initiated by the company (involuntary turnover) or by the employee (voluntary turnover).[14] Industries vary in their total rate of separation (voluntary plus involuntary turnover). Service industries, such as accommodation, food and beverage, the arts, entertainment, and recreation, as well as retail/wholesale, tend to have higher turnover rates than high-tech, education, government, and professional trades.[15] According to the National Restaurant Association, the turnover rate for the hospitality industry is greater than 70%. In thinking about this high percentage, keep in mind that many workers in the hospitality industry, especially in restaurants, are students who may work only part of the year, and the industry has seasonal needs in many locations. Thus, this turnover rate must be interpreted while considering both voluntary and involuntary turnover.[16]

Turnover has a significant impact on companies. The most obvious impact occurs when a company loses a talented employee. Another problem occurs when an employee's former coworkers—those who remain with the firm—must pick up the slack to make sure that the work still gets done. Even when a replacement employee is eventually hired, his or her coworkers are still likely to experience stress until the newly hired person gets fully up to speed.

In addition, both costs and time demands are associated with filling open positions. Other companies have realized great gains by addressing high turnover. Facing a 213% crew turnover, compared to an industry average of just over 125%, managers at Steak 'n Shake realized that profitability, employee morale, and customer service at its restaurants were suffering. Steak 'n Shake estimated that it could save up to $4 million per year if it could reduce its turnover. The company subsequently took steps to do so.[17]

Managing turnover involves time demands for managers. Imagine working in a company with 1,000 employees. If your company has a turnover rate of 10%, this

**turnover**

the voluntary and involuntary termination of employees within an organization percentage means that you are losing 100 people each year. To remain competitive, you have to make sure that those 100 jobs get filled and their associated tasks and responsibilities are completed. If your company is losing 20 people per month, or 240 per year, maintaining sufficient staffing levels will be that much more difficult. When employees leave, there are fewer individuals who can move to other positions in the company. Although this might improve the promotional prospects of the employees who remain with the firm, it diminishes the potential internal labor supply available for higher-level openings in the long term. This concern is related to the second component of the internal workforce framework, the actual and potential movement of employees throughout companies.

## Employee Movements

Even without turnover, the profile of a company's workforce changes over time as employees move into different jobs. Companies use promotions, transfers, and demotions to move employees from one job to another. **Promotions** involve moving employees to higher-level positions, which often are associated with increased levels of responsibility and authority. Employees also can **transfer** to other jobs with similar levels of responsibility. Most transfers within a company are viewed as lateral moves. Employees also can be **demoted**, or moved to lower-level positions within their companies. Of course, moving people throughout an organization should be a strategic decision. Additionally, managers can use several tools to help track employee movements: replacement charts, succession planning, and transition matrices.

Companies use **replacement charts** to identify potential replacement employees for positions that could open up within their organizations. Essentially, a replacement chart shows the employees who potentially could be moved from one job to another if vacancies occur. With such a system in place, a company is ready to make personnel changes on short notice.

**Succession planning** is similar to using replacement charts but it focuses on identifying employees who might be viable successors for top managerial positions—that is, for key jobs that could become vacant. As the name implies, succession planning involves identifying who is next in line for higher-level jobs. It also requires the company to fill in information about any skill that a potential successor needs to develop. A well-defined succession process is important for a variety of reasons. First, the existence of a plan is more likely to lead to appropriate development of employees for advancement opportunities. Second, a succession plan ensures that someone who has the right experience is ready at all times to step into a critical but vacant higher-level job. Kevin Johnson became the CEO of Starbucks when Howard Schultz, the highly regarded longtime leader of the company, announced he was stepping down from that role. Johnson had been the company's chief operating officer (COO) since 2015 and worked closely with Schultz. Schultz had brought Johnson onto the Starbucks board in 2009. The two had worked together to craft the company's strategy for the future. Thus, Schultz had ensured that there was a successor ready when he made his decision to leave the company that he had been with for many decades.[18] Similarly, Kathy Warden had been groomed to become the CEO of Northrop Grumman, a major defense contractor, when Wes Bush announced his plans in 2018 to retire on January 1, 2019. Warden, who had worked at Northrop Grumman since 2008, had been moved into the President and COO role a year earlier and been in charge of overseeing a major acquisition for the company.[19]

Once identified, successors undergo development activities and experiences to prepare them for jobs that they could potentially fill. Depending on the position and the length of time that it would take a potential successor to get up to speed, companies sometimes realize that they need to begin recruiting immediately to fill positions that may not become vacant for months or even years. However, without

---

**promotion**

moving employees to higher-level positions, which often are associated with increased levels of responsibility and authority

**transfer**

moving employees to other jobs with similar levels of responsibility

**demotion**

moving employees to lower-level positions within the company

**replacement charts**

method of tracking information about potential replacement employees for positions that could open up within organizations

**succession planning**

the process of planning for future leadership of the company by identifying and developing employees to fill higher-level jobs within the company as they become available

engaging in succession planning, firms might not be aware of this need. In addition to helping companies identify their long-term workforce planning needs, the process of identifying replacement employees for positions can reveal that a firm could face a shortage of employees to fill its lower-level jobs if its upper-level jobs became vacant and workers are promoted into them.

A third tool that managers can use to understand the internal movement trends of their workforces is a **transition matrix**. A transition matrix provides a model for tracking the movement of employees throughout an organization, rather than for a single job, over a certain period of time. Exhibit 5.3 shows an example of a transition matrix for a hypothetical company for a one-year time period.

The data in the completed matrix in Exhibit 5.3 provide a wealth of useful information. For example, we can see that the turnover rate is highest among managers (40%) and lowest among employees (20%). Knowing the average turnover rate of different groups of employees provides some insight about the number of employees a company needs to hire for each position.

A transition matrix also highlights the movement of employees throughout the organization, which, as we have explained, further affects a firm's internal demand and supply of labor. Each row in the transition matrix shows where the employees who started at the beginning of the year ended up a year later. For example, in Exhibit 5.3, we can see that two managers were promoted to vice president, three managers remained in their positions, one manager was demoted to a supervisor, and four managers left the organization. After completing the data for all the positions, the columns in the table highlight the anticipated labor shortage or surplus of internal labor for each position. Looking at the column for managers, we can see that the internal labor supply of managers was 5—the 3 managers who remained in their positions and the 2 supervisors who were promoted to manager positions. Given the starting number of 10 managers in 2018, this information suggests that there will be a labor shortage of 5 managers for 2019. In contrast, the data show that there will be the required number of supervisors, with 7 nonmanagerial employees promoted to the job of supervisor. There may have been more nonmanagerial employees eligible for promotion, but it only makes sense to promote employees into positions that are available; otherwise, a labor surplus is created.

One of the primary benefits of a transition matrix is that it provides data to help prepare for workforce demands in the future. Hiring now for anticipated labor shortages, for example, can help a firm avoid the unnecessary stress and costs associated with its current employees having to work overtime. To truly understand your firm's internal labor supply and demand, however, you also have to have a firm grasp of the productivity of your workforce—that is, how well employees will

**transition matrix**

a method for tracking the internal movement of employees throughout an organization over a certain period of time

## EXHIBIT 5.3

### An Example of a Transition Matrix

| 2018 | 2019 | | | | |
|---|---|---|---|---|---|
| | Vice President | Manager | Supervisor | Non-Managerial Employees | Exit the Company |
| 3 Vice Presidents | 2 (67%) | | | | 1 (33%) |
| 10 Managers | 2 (20%) | 3 (30%) | 1 (10%) | | 4 (40%) |
| 20 Supervisors | | 2 (10%) | 12 (60%) | | 6 (30%) |
| 200 Employees | | | 7 (3.5%) | 153 (76.5%) | 40 (20%) |
| Anticipated Labor Supply | 4 | 5 | 20 | 153 | 51 (out of 233) |

be able to meet the anticipated growth or decline in the demand for your products, services, or both. We discuss this aspect next.

### Employee Productivity

**productivity**

the level of a firm's output (i.e., products or services) relative to the inputs (i.e., employees, equipment, materials, and so forth) used to produce the output

**productivity ratio**

the employees (i.e., labor demand) needed to achieve a certain output level (i.e., level of sales, production, and so forth)

**Productivity** refers to the level of a firm's output (i.e., products or services) relative to the inputs (i.e., employees, equipment, materials, and so forth) used to produce the output.[20] A **productivity ratio** reflects the *number* of employees (i.e., labor demand) needed to achieve a certain output level (i.e., level of sales, production, and so forth). You can calculate these ratios by collecting data on your firm's output levels versus the number of employees in prior years, and taking into account any new resources designed to increase production. Sales data and number of products produced in previous years are examples of the types of output that data firms use to calculate their productivity ratios.

Exhibit 5.4 shows a hypothetical productivity ratio for a manufacturing plant for assembly-line employees. In this case, you can see that the productivity ratio for 2013 was 40 (5,000 units / 125 employees). Once the ratio is calculated each year prior to the years for which an estimate is needed, an average productivity ratio is established. In this case, the average is 42.86 units per employee. To use this information as a forecasting tool, managers simply need to project the output that they anticipate their firms will produce in future years. For example, in Exhibit 5.4, the estimated productivity output is 7,250 units. If you divide 7,250 by the productivity ratio (42.86), you get a forecasted labor demand of 169 employees. Based on this information, the company will need to hire 9 more assembly-line employees to maintain its current level of productivity.

One of the benefits of understanding the productivity ratio is that it allows you to plan for different potential scenarios that reflect the growth or decline in the demand for your products. For example, if your company anticipates the demand for its products to increase by 10%, it can simply adjust the output level and calculate a revised labor-demand figure. The same process can be used to forecast your labor demand if you are experiencing a decline in the demand for your products. Moreover, the calculations can be performed in a variety of industries. For example, depending on the type of businesses they are in, companies can use sales figures, phone volumes, Internet volumes, or customer interactions. In other words, so long as there is some quantifiable output measure, managers can calculate their productivity ratios and the associated number of employees that they will need.

## EXHIBIT 5.4

### Calculating Productivity Ratios

| Year | Productivity Output (units per month) | Number of Employees | Productivity Ratio (output/employees) |
|------|---------------------------------------|---------------------|---------------------------------------|
| 2013 | 5,000 | 125 | 40 |
| 2014 | 5,500 | 125 | 44 |
| 2015 | 6,000 | 135 | 44.44 |
| 2016 | 6,000 | 140 | 42.85 |
| 2017 | 6,250 | 150 | 41.67 |
| 2018 | 6,500 | 150 | 43.33 |
| 2019 | 7,000 | 160 | 43.75 |
| 2020* | 7,250 | X = 169 employees needed | Average Ratio = 42.86 |
| 2021* | 7,500 | X = 175 employees needed | Average Ratio = 42.86 |

*Estimates

Of course, companies can intervene in ways that directly affect their productivity ratios. As we discuss in Chapters 6 through 8, more extensive recruitment, better selection decisions, and even more comprehensive or effective training can change a firm's productivity ratio. With a more talented workforce, for example, a firm could anticipate its level of productivity per employee to increase.

### Company Performance

As our discussion of Ford and GM at the beginning of this chapter highlighted, the overall performance of a company influences its labor supply and demand. Facing diminishing customer demand, Ford and GM realized that their demand for labor was not at the same level as it had once been. In fact, they were facing a labor surplus. This is a common problem among companies that are performing poorly; they simply do not need or cannot afford the same number of workers as they had in the past.[21] In contrast, when companies excel in terms of their performance, they often realize that their demand for labor is outpacing their current supply. Moreover, all other things being equal, better-performing companies are more likely to have the financial resources to employ a greater number of employees, as well as offer high pay for top-notch employees.

### Strategic Direction

One limitation to solely tracking the actual or potential movement of employees through your firm via replacement charts, succession planning, and transition matrices is that this approach is often based on maintaining the status quo.[22] Productivity ratios are also limited to some extent because they assume that a firm's current processes and procedures will remain intact for the foreseeable future. However, companies evolve. They take steps to improve their performance by continually making decisions about whether they should strive for growth, maintain the status quo, retrench, or refocus their operations.[23]

Of course, all these changes directly affect whether a company will experience a shortage or surplus of labor. Companies that are planning to expand their operations to facilitate growth are likely to try to increase their productivity in an attempt to capture more market share. As a result, they are likely to face labor shortages. In contrast, companies that are planning on reducing the scope of their operations are likely to try to curtail their output levels. These companies are more likely to experience labor surpluses.

Companies also engage in mergers and acquisitions that affect their supply and demand for labor and the tactics they use to balance the two. For example, when two companies merge, their goal is to achieve greater efficiencies or leverage some corporate know-how across units to realize a competitive advantage. One of the major implications of a merger or an acquisition relates to the overlapping skill sets the employees of the two companies are likely to have. When two companies become one, there are likely to be some redundancies across positions. For example, both companies are likely to employ workers doing similar activities, such as accounting, marketing, production, grounds maintenance, mail service, and management activities. When the companies merge, they are forced to deal with these redundancies. Oftentimes they do so by laying off employees.

## External Factors

To some extent, managers can control internal labor factors. Managers also have to evaluate factors in the external environment over which they have less control. These factors relate to the local labor market, economic conditions, and industry trends that affect the supply and demand for goods and services.

### Local Labor Market

People in the local labor market represent a potential external labor supply for firms. One of the major drivers of the size and composition of the local labor market available to a firm is its location. As we will discuss further in Chapter 6, local labor markets vary dramatically in terms of the number and types of individuals within them available for work. A company located in New York City will have access to a much larger pool of potential workers than a company located in rural South Dakota, for example. Similarly, in certain geographic areas, employees will lack the types of skills that an employer needs. In this case, the availability of the local labor supply might not be sufficient to meet a company's labor demand. In contrast, college towns generally have a relatively large supply of highly educated people available to do a variety of types of work. Clearly, the relative size and composition of a local labor market, with individuals with different skill sets, directly affect the labor pool's potential to serve adequately as a viable source of labor for companies.

### Economic Conditions

The general health of the economy—particularly the unemployment rate—has a big impact on the availability of workers. As the unemployment rate rises, firms find it easier to hire qualified individuals in the external labor market. In contrast, when the unemployment rate drops, hiring qualified individuals becomes more difficult. Companies competing on a global basis face a particular challenge with unemployment. For example, in October 2018, the unemployment rate in the United States was around 3.7%.[24] At the same time, the unemployment rate in Italy was significantly higher, at 10.1%.[25] That same month, Greece and Spain had much higher rates (19.9% and 14.55%, respectively).[26] As you can imagine, with a greater supply of available labor, companies in Italy, Greece, and Spain would likely have an easier time finding employees than would companies in the United States.

Beyond unemployment figures, the general health of the economy also affects a firm's workforce planning. When the economy is stagnant or in a recession, the demand for many products drops. In contrast, during periods of high economic growth, the demand for many products increases. The level of consumer demand—whether it is growing or declining—directly affects the amount of labor that companies demand to meet their customers' needs. Take, for instance, the coal industry. As the push for cleaner energy continues to grow, the need for coal to produce energy has declined, leaving many coal miners unemployed. State and local economic development efforts in Virginia have helped attract call and data centers to the state's coal-mining areas in southwest Virginia. Call and data centers are growing industries with good-paying jobs, strong training programs, and high need for workers.[27]

### Industry Trends

Many industries experience predictable purchasing patterns that fluctuate over time and directly influence when they experience labor shortages or surpluses. Retail establishments are a prime example of this. Although retailers such as Bath & Body Works and Macy's operate their stores on a year-round basis, their sales follow a predictable pattern: Their highest sales occur in the weeks and days leading up to Christmas. As a result, these firms demand a greater amount of labor during this time of the year. Understanding cyclical patterns such as these helps managers ensure that they don't have too many employees during slow times and have enough employees during busy times.

Many companies are also suppliers to other companies. In other words, they don't sell to individual consumers but to firms. To some extent, the labor demand of supplying firms such as these is a function of the success of their customers. Consider the computer industry. Computer manufacturers such as Dell, HP, and

Asus rely on suppliers for many of the components that make up the computers that they sell, including computer monitors, storage devices, and processing chips. Consequently, the amount of labor these suppliers demand is directly influenced by the relative success—or failure—of the computer manufacturers that purchase their products. If a company is a direct supplier of monitors for Dell, for example, it can estimate its demand for labor based on the computers that Dell anticipates selling. For instance, if Dell expects to sell 5% more computers in the coming year than it sold this past year, the supplier can expect to be asked to provide 5% more monitors as well.

Although an economy's leading indicators—such as its unemployment rate and inflation rate—are often fairly predictable, sometimes labor-demand patterns are subject to industry shocks. *Shocks* are dramatic changes in the nature of the products or services offered in the economy or dramatic changes in how companies compete. Do you own an iPad, produced by Apple? Perhaps you do. Depending on the type of iPad, you can hold nearly 60,000 photos, over 18,000 songs, over 5,000 apps, and more.[28] That's a lot — much more than a CD or cassette tape can hold.

Now, take a second to think about how the introduction of the iPod and other MP3 players revolutionized the way we access music and affected labor supply and demand. The relationship is more straightforward than you might think. Prior to the sudden popularity of the MP3 player in the consumer market, consumers generally had to rely on portable CD or cassette players, such as the Sony Walkman. As the demand for digital music grew, the producers of CDs and CD and cassette players watched the demand for their products drop, much like what happened with the manufacturers of record players when 8-track tapes, and then cassette tapes, took the place of vinyl records. (On a side note, vinyl albums are now back in vogue and there is a renewed demand for record players.) Many of these firms surely realized that the number of employees they had on staff was too high. In contrast, companies that produced MP3 players surely realized that they would have a labor shortage on their hands. As you can see, the actions of other companies and how they affect consumers' preferences for products or services directly affect the labor demanded by other companies.

## Tactics Firms Use to Balance Their Supply and Demand for Labor

Based on our discussion to this point in the chapter, it should be evident that the supply and demand for employees within companies is constantly shifting. Effectively managing the workforce involves anticipating where employees will be needed (or not) within the firm and balancing the demand with the available supply. Once you have a good idea about where labor surpluses and shortages exist within a company, the next step is to take action to balance those pressures.

### Labor Shortage Tactics

When faced with a labor shortage, most people initially think about recruiting new employees. Although this is certainly a viable option, other tactics can be used to address labor shortages, too. Some of the typical methods are using overtime, outsourcing, and contingent labor; increasing employee retention rates; strategically using employee promotions, transfers, and demotions; and hiring new employees.

#### Employee Overtime

One of the quickest ways to handle a labor shortage is through the use of overtime. *Overtime* refers to employees working additional hours beyond their standard schedules. Most full-time employees work a 40-hour workweek. To address a labor shortage, managers may require their employees to work additional hours to meet a company's needs. Retailers often ask their current employees to work extra hours around the holidays, for example.

Although federal and state laws regulate how much overtime employees are allowed to work (an aspect we will discuss in Chapter 10), using overtime is a viable way for a company to cope with a labor shortage quickly. The tactic is very useful when a labor shortage is expected to be of short duration. As the length of the anticipated labor shortage increases, however, paying overtime might prove too costly. (Hourly employees are generally paid 1.5 times their hourly wage for working overtime.) Another potential downside is that when employees work too many overtime hours, they can become dissatisfied, experience burnout, or both. Eventually, overtime can lead to increased employee turnover, creating further labor shortages.

### Outsourcing and Contingent Labor

In addition to overtime, a second tactic that you can use to remedy a labor shortage is to arrange for external, or outsourced, workers to produce your goods and services. **Outsourcing** is the practice of sending work to other companies. Companies often outsource activities such as the maintenance for their grounds, food service for their cafeterias or vending machines, and payroll management. Companies also outsource jobs like those found at a call center that provides customer service. Remember the Company Spotlight in Chapter 4 about the Sykes Work at Home program? Sykes serves as a business process outsourcer for many companies around the globe. Moreover, because external service providers like Sykes often focus on a single or limited number of services and provide their services to many companies, they are often able to do them more efficiently. Besides saving money, outsourcing allows companies to focus on the activities that they do best—the ones that give them a competitive advantage.

In addition to outsourcing, companies hire contingent labor to remedy labor shortages.[29] **Contingent labor** refers to employees who have no implicit or explicit expectation for ongoing employment. **Alternative employment arrangements** include independent contractors, temporary help agency workers, on-call workers, and workers provided by contract firms. In May 2017, the Bureau of Labor Statistics (BLS) conducted an extensive survey of contingent and alternative work arrangements. The results of this survey in terms of number of workers in each category are in Exhibit 5.5. The survey found that contingent workers were twice as likely as noncontingent workers to be under age 25, to work part time, and to be more likely to be enrolled in school. However, 55% of the contingent workers would prefer to be working in a permanent job.

**outsourcing**

the practice of sending work to other companies

**contingent labor**

employees who have no implicit or explicit expectation for ongoing employment

**alternative employment arrangements**

independent contractors, temporary help agency workers, on-call workers, and workers provided by contract firms.

### EXHIBIT 5.5

Contingent and Alternative Work Arrangement Percentages and Numbers of Workers

| Category of Worker | Percentage of Total Employment | Number of Workers |
|---|---|---|
| Contingent | 3.8% | 5.9 million |
| Alternative Work Arrangements | | |
| • Independent Contractors | 6.9% | 10.6 million |
| • On-call Workers | 1.7% | 2.6 million |
| • Temporary Help Agency Workers | .9% | 1.4 million |
| • Workers provided by Contract Firms | .6% | 933,000 |

*Source:* Bureau of Labor Statistics, "Contingent and Alternative Employment Arrangements—May 2017," bls.gov, June 7, 2018, https://www.bls.gov/news.release/pdf/conemp.pdf.

Among the alternative employment arrangement workers, the independent contractors were likely to be older. The temporary help agency workers were more likely to be Black, Hispanic, or Latino. Contract workers were more likely to be men.[30] Like outsourcing, hiring contingent labor or using alternative employment arrangements also can help a firm save money and hone its strategic focus.

Contingent labor and alternative work arrangements also provide companies with both numerical and functional flexibility. **Numerical flexibility** refers to the number of employees working for a company. Using contingent workers gives companies the flexibility to adjust their number of employees relatively quickly. This ability can be a major benefit for companies that face predictable variations in the demand for their services. As Company Spotlight 5.1 shows, Target relies extensively on contingent workers to cope with the busy holiday shopping season.

**Functional flexibility** refers to the ability of the firm to adjust the types of skills available in its workforce. Because companies can readily adjust which contingent workers they use, they can quickly modify the composition of the knowledge, skills, and abilities of their workforces. As a result, the companies don't have to make long-term investments to develop or hire workers for particular skills that are needed for only a short period of time. At the same time, however, relying too heavily on contingent labor can prevent companies from investing in the employee competencies they need for their long-term success.[31]

> **numerical flexibility**
> a form of flexibility related to the ease of adjusting the number of individuals working for a company
>
> **functional flexibility**
> the ability of the firm to adjust the types of skills available in its workforce

### Employee Retention

As noted previously, turnover is a significant cause of labor shortages. The average employee turnover rate in retail is around 60%. As employees have more choices of

## COMPANY SPOTLIGHT  5.1

### Gearing Up for the Holidays at Target

What do you do if a considerable portion of your yearly business happens in only the last few months of the year? That is precisely the scenario that occurs at retail establishments such as Target stores every holiday shopping season. The answer? You need to understand trends in the consumer demand for the products you sell and take advantage of a seasonal workforce.

Although Target has a large full-time workforce, during the holiday season the size of its workforce swells with contingent, or seasonal, workers. By mid-September in 2018, Target had already advertised in its company newsletter that it would be hiring approximately 120,000 seasonal team members for its 1,839 stores across the U.S. This number represented a 20% increase over the year before. But that 120,000 team members wasn't all Target needed for the 2018 holiday shopping season. Target needed another 7,500 seasonal workers at its distribution and fulfillment centers to fill online orders and replenish products in its retail stores.

In attempt to have better luck at attracting workers in an already tight labor market, Target advertised that it would be paying a minimum hourly wage to start of $12 an hour, providing a 10% merchandise discount with an additional 10% for wellness merchandise (e.g., fruits, workout gear), flexible schedules, opportunities for extra pay on Thanksgiving and Christmas, and more.

*Sources:* Target, "Target's Hiring 120,000 Team Members for the Holidays Starting at $12 an Hour," A Bullseye View, corporate.target.com, September 13, 2018, https://corporate.target.com/article/2018/09/seasonal-hiring-2018; Lauren Thomas, "Target to Hire 20% More Workers This Holiday Season, Doubling the Number of Jobs Dedicated to Online Orders," CNBC, cnbc.com, September 13, 2018, https://www.cnbc.com/2018/09/13/target-to-hire-20percent-more-workers-this-holiday-season.html.

places to work in a tight labor market, companies are searching for ways to retain employees and avoid the costs associated with recruiting, onboarding, and training new workers. One approach taken by Walmart is to shorten the length of a training program tied to raises so that employees get raises faster. Walmart also provides an associate education benefit that includes affordable access to associate and bachelor's degrees.[32] At a basic level, reducing turnover lowers a firm's recruitment and selection costs, reduces its need to train new employees, and helps ensure that productive employees remain with the company. It is not surprising that companies such as Southwest Airlines, Lincoln Electric, and Wegmans, which have lower turnover rates than other firms in their industries, also lead their industries in terms of employee productivity and corporate performance.

Knowing that you will be able to retain a steady number of your employees also will improve your workforce forecasting, at least on the internal supply side of the equation. Employee satisfaction is a key predictor of turnover, and in the remaining chapters of the book, we will look at how to improve it.[33]

### Employee Promotions, Transfers, and Demotions

Rather than rely on your current employees to work longer hours, as a manager you might opt to move employees from one area of a company into another area that has a labor shortage. This can be a very effective way to deal with the situation, especially because it can be done quickly. Because companies are already familiar with their current employees, managers are also likely to be better informed about the potential of these employees to succeed in their new jobs. Of course, one of the disadvantages of relying on employee transitions is that you're simply shifting the labor shortage from one area of your company to another. Every employee who is promoted, transferred, or demoted to another job leaves behind a vacant job with tasks, duties, and responsibilities that someone else must take on.

### New Hires

The final tactic for addressing a labor shortage is to recruit and hire new, full-time employees. While overtime and employee transitions focus on addressing labor shortages with current employees, hiring new employees increases the size of your workforce. One of the primary benefits of full-time hires is that this approach provides a more permanent solution to a labor shortage instead of a temporary one. At the same time, however, hiring new employees involves making a long-term commitment to their employment. As a manager, it is important that you understand whether your labor shortage is permanent or temporary before hiring new full-time employees. If the shortage is temporary, hiring new employees could, of course, result in a labor surplus down the road.

There is no single best solution for how to deal with a labor shortage or surplus. Each of the tactics discussed here has advantages and disadvantages that must be considered, including how long you expect a shortage or surplus to last. As we have indicated, using overtime and contingent labor can remedy a shortage very quickly. In contrast, improving employee retention to remedy a shortage takes more time to accomplish, as does hiring new employees and getting them up to speed.

## Labor Surplus Tactics

As noted earlier, employing surplus labor is likely to be financially prohibitive for many companies, particularly when the surpluses are anticipated to be permanent (or at least last for a long time). Layoffs, attrition, hiring freezes, early-retirement programs, and movement of employees (either temporarily or permanently) to other work areas are some of the common tactics that managers use to address labor surpluses. Let's now examine each of these tactics.

## Layoffs

A layoff involves quickly reducing the number of workers you employ. For many years, the Bureau of Labor Statistics (BLS) reported information about mass layoffs. Information for the last years that data were collected is shown in Exhibit 5.6 to demonstrate how extensive mass layoffs can be over time. As you will see, the year with the largest number of mass layoffs was during the Great Recession. In 2009, there were 28,030 mass layoff events by companies, which affected over 2.75 million people.[34] These trends are not limited to the United States. Weatherford International announced a worldwide layoff, with plans to cut 7,000 jobs to save $500 million in 2014,[35] and in an ongoing effort to cut costs at Volvo, 4,400 jobs were eliminated that same year as profits slipped.[36]

Some states have their own version of the Worker Adjustment and Retraining Act (WARN Act). For instance, the Illinois Worker Adjustment and Retraining Notification Act requires employers with at least 75 employees to notify the state 60 days prior to a plant closing or a mass layoff. The Act defines a mass layoff as one affecting at least a third of the workforce, or at least 250 workers at a company of any size. In the spring of 2018, Allstate announced that by the end of the year, it would close its printing plant in Wheeling, Illinois, and shift the work to an outside vendor. Around the same time, Siemens Medical Solutions announced it would be making 104 job cuts through closing a Hoffman Estates facility in Illinois. This closure resulted from the consolidation of research and development facilities. Both companies were required by Illinois law to notify the state in advance of these changes.[37] We discuss the WARN Act in more detail later in this chapter.

### EXHIBIT 5.6
### Mass Layoffs, 1996–2012

| Year | Layoff Events | Initial Claimants for Unemployment Insurance |
|------|--------------|----------------------------------------------|
| 1996 | 14,111 | 1,437,628 |
| 1997 | 14,960 | 1,542,543 |
| 1998 | 15,904 | 1,771,069 |
| 1999 | 14,909 | 1,572,399 |
| 2000 | 15,738 | 1,835,592 |
| 2001 | 21,467 | 2,514,862 |
| 2002 | 20,277 | 2,245,051 |
| 2003 | 18,963 | 1,888,926 |
| 2004 | 15,980 | 1,607,158 |
| 2005 | 16,466 | 1,795,341 |
| 2006 | 13,998 | 1,484,391 |
| 2007 | 15,493 | 1,598,875 |
| 2008 | 21,137 | 2,130,220 |
| 2009 | 28,030 | 2,796,456 |
| 2010 | 19,564 | 1,854,596 |
| 2011 | 18,521 | 1,808,451 |
| 2012 | 17,080 | 1,666,931 |

Each action (layoff event) involved at least 50 persons from a single establishment.

*Source:* Bureau of Labor Statistics, "Mass Layoffs (Monthly) Archived News Releases 1996–2013," August 13, 2014, http://www.bls.gov/schedule/archives/mmls_nr.htm#2007.

The primary advantage of layoffs is that a company can use them to relatively quickly adjust the size and composition of its workforce. When carried out effectively, a layoff can be an isolated event that results in a good balance between an organization's needs and the capabilities of its employees. However, layoffs are associated with several disadvantages as well. Companies sometimes focus solely on short-term cost-containment efforts when making layoff decisions rather than their long-term objectives. When this happens, they often lose employees who are critical to their future success. In other words, although layoffs lower a company's immediate expenses, they don't always generate future business improvements or operational efficiencies.[38] Announcing a layoff can also produce feelings of job insecurity in a firm's employees, which in turn can lead to higher turnover and lower employee commitment and loyalty.[39] A firm that engages in layoffs is likely to have a harder time attracting new employees in the future than one that does not.

### Attrition and Hiring Freezes

**attrition**

a decision not to fill vacant positions that emerge as a result of turnover or other employee movements in a company

**hiring freezes**

a temporary ban on the hiring of new employees for a specified period of time

Two tactics that companies may turn to for coping with a labor surplus focus primarily on delaying the hiring of new employees. **Attrition** refers to a decision not to fill vacant positions that emerge as a result of turnover or other employee movements in a company. **Hiring freezes** put a temporary ban on the hiring of new employees for a specified period of time. One of the advantages of using attrition and hiring freezes to "right-size" the workforce is that they create lower levels of stress among employees than layoffs do. The downside of attrition and hiring freezes, however, is that the employees who are not laid off often find themselves performing extra duties to make up for staffing shortages.[40] Furthermore, it can take a long time to reach a firm's desired employment levels when a freeze or an attrition period is over.

### Early Retirement

Early-retirement programs are an additional tactic that companies turn to in order to address their labor surpluses. The goal of these programs is to provide employees with a financial incentive to retire early, thereby lowering the number of a firm's employees and the company's labor costs. Recall our discussion at the beginning of this chapter about GM and Ford. Here are a few more details about the GM actions. In 2006, GM said that employees who had 30 years of service could have $35,000 and full pensions if they retired.[41] In 2013, the automaker offered lump sums of up to $65,000 for hourly skilled trades employees to take early retirement.[42] In 2018, GM offered $20,000 cash and a $25,000 car voucher to nearly all of its United Auto Worker (UAW) employees to encourage them to retire early or simply leave the company.[43] Although there are certainly costs associated with early-retirement programs, companies can use them to trim the size of their workforce without having to resort to layoffs. However, if an early-retirement program is too enticing, it can result in a greater exodus of employees than a company desired to have happen. For example, in 2003, Verizon Communications initiated an early-retirement program in an attempt to trim about 12,000 workers from its payroll. More than 21,000 employees accepted the offer, leaving Verizon with a labor shortage.[44] Clearly, there are downsides to early-retirement incentives. As happened with Verizon Communications, when the offer is too attractive, companies tend to lose a lot of employees that they would rather not lose and spending more money for the initiative than planned.

### Employee Promotions, Transfers, and Demotions

A final tactic for addressing labor surpluses is to use employee promotions, transfers, and demotions. Just as these practices can remedy labor shortages, they also can remedy labor surpluses. For example, rather than reduce the size of a group of employees through layoffs or early retirements, a company might move some employees to other areas in the firm that are facing labor shortages. This way, employees don't lose their jobs and the company doesn't have to bear any layoff-related costs. The major disadvantage of this tactic is that there may be no area of the company that is experiencing a labor shortage. Even if there is, the employees in the surplus labor areas might not have the needed skills to succeed in the new jobs.

# Workforce Planning in Practice: Organizational Demands

Different companies are likely to use different workforce-planning tactics. As shown in Exhibit 5.7, the tactics that firms use are likely to vary as they cope with different organizational demands, environmental influences, and regulatory issues.

## Strategy and Workforce Planning

A firm's strategy affects its workforce planning in several ways. First, it affects how quickly the company is likely to need to respond to labor shortages or surpluses. Second, it affects how critical different skill sets are in the organization, which in turn determines the workforce planning tactics that managers are likely to use.

### Required Speed to Deal with Shortages and Surpluses

As noted in Chapter 2, some companies focus on low costs as a key source of their competitiveness. Others attempt to differentiate themselves from their competitors

---

**EXHIBIT 5.7**

Workforce Planning in Practice

| Context | Practice Issues |
|---|---|
| **Organizational Demands** | |
| *Strategy* drives . . . | • Required speed to deal with shortages and surpluses<br>• Criticality of employee groups |
| *Company characteristics* determine . . . | • The relative impact of labor shortages and surpluses<br>• Who carries out workforce planning |
| *Culture* establishes . . . | • Likelihood of firms using different tactics<br>• Employee reactions to workforce planning tactics |
| *Employee concerns* include . . . | • Employee stress and work/life balance issues<br>• Perceptions of procedural and distributive justice |
| **Environmental Demands** | |
| *Labor force* influences . . . | • Availability of internal and external workers<br>• Which tactics to use |
| *Technology* affects . . . | • The number of employees needed<br>• The types of workers that are needed<br>• The quality of workforce planning |
| *Globalization* impacts . . . | • Where the workers are<br>• Which workforce planning tactics to use |
| *Ethics/social responsibility* shapes . . . | • Community reactions to workforce planning tactics<br>• How companies help employees cope |
| **Regulations** | |
| **Regulations** *guide* . . . | • Requirements for mass layoffs and plant closing<br>• Determining who is an employee versus an independent contractor |

in terms of the quality, types of products, and/or services they offer. In other words, they try to offer products, services, or features for which customers are willing to pay a premium. Different business strategies such as these affect how quickly firms must cope with labor shortages and surpluses. Companies focused on keeping their costs low will view a labor surplus as particularly problematic. These companies are likely to reduce a surplus by using tactics that can be carried out quickly (e.g., layoffs). In contrast, firms that pursue a differentiation strategy might have a bit more cushion to absorb the costs of a labor surplus. These firms are likely to be more willing to rely on labor reduction tactics such as early retirements and attrition—tactics that are slower but less stressful for employees. Some firms even have policies preventing the use of layoffs. Southwest Airlines, NuStar Energy, The Container Store, Nucor, and Publix all have long had no-layoff policies, and all are highly regarded companies in their industry and beyond.[45]

### Criticality of Employee Groups

A firm's strategy affects which of its employees are most critical to its success. Firms focused on differentiation strategies related to product leadership and innovation, such as SAS and SAP, are likely to depend more heavily on research and development (R&D) skills. Firms competing in terms of customer service, such as Nordstrom, are likely to be particularly dependent on their sales and customer relations staff. In contrast, cost leadership firms are likely to depend on employees with efficiency-related competencies, such as operation management skills. The criticality to the company of the employee group affects the workforce-planning tactics that managers of different firms are likely to use. The greater potential strategic impact certain positions in a firm have, the more reluctant a company will be to outsource, offshore, or turn to contingent workers to fill them.[46] Instead, the firm will tend to hire and retain permanent employees for these positions to keep them staffed.

## Company Characteristics and Workforce Planning

As noted in Chapter 2, every company is unique in many ways. These differences place pressures on the relative labor demand and supply, as well as the tactics they use to cope with surpluses and shortages. In particular, a company's size and stage of development will affect the relative impact of labor shortages and surpluses, as well as who will carry out the company's workforce planning activities.

### The Relative Impact of Labor Shortages and Surpluses

In particularly small companies, the relative impact of labor shortages or surpluses is likely to be greater than in larger companies. Imagine that you are a manager in a company that employs 20 people, and you are short 5 employees. Trying to cover the tasks and responsibilities of 5 people in a firm such as this will be more difficult than covering the tasks formerly performed by 5 people in a company that has 50,000 employees. Smaller companies, or companies that are in much earlier stages of development, usually have considerably less labor slack, meaning they have excess labor capacity. Because they generally have leaner workforces, the internal labor supply available for covering these tasks or for filling new or vacant positions in these companies may be limited. In contrast, larger companies have more employees. Their managers have more options to transfer, promote, or demote people to fill positions internally.

Now suppose that your company of 20 employees loses a client and needs only 15 employees. The labor costs of employing 20 versus 15 people might prove unmanageable. As you can see, the pressure to deal with a labor shortage or surplus quickly will make certain workforce tactics less feasible than others. If labor shortages must be addressed quickly, relying on new hires may take too long compared to relying on overtime or using contingent workers. Similarly, attrition or hiring freezes might not work quickly enough to adjust labor costs so that they are sustainable. Rather, a quicker response, such as a layoff, may be needed in a smaller company facing a labor surplus.

## Who Carries Out Workforce Planning

Your responsibility for carrying out workforce planning activities will vary depending on the size and stage of development of your company. Larger companies are likely to have greater resources, support staff, and perhaps a formal HR department to devote to these activities.[47] Also, larger companies are likely be in a better position to invest in technology that helps them track labor force trends and the labor supply throughout their organizations.[48] In smaller companies, however, workforce planning activities often fall directly on the managers responsible for supervising the employees who need to be hired. As a manager in a firm such as this, you will have to keep track of the movement of people throughout your unit, the availability of replacement employees to fill open positions, and the viability of using outsourcing or contingent labor, if it's needed.

A similar pattern is likely to exist in younger, start-up companies than in more established organizations. Companies in the early stages of development are often understaffed, particularly in terms of support staff. As a result, managers in these companies often find that they have to wear many hats and perform a wide array of activities, including making sure they are able to tap both internal and external sources of talent. As companies grow and become more mature, they are in a better position to add more support activities, including formal HR processes, to accomplish these tasks.

## Corporate Culture and Workforce Planning

A company's corporate culture affects the different tactics that firms use to deal with labor shortages and surpluses, as well as how their employees will react to those tactics.

### Likelihood of Firms Using Different Tactics

As discussed earlier, the tactics for dealing with labor shortages or surpluses vary in terms of how fast they address the problem, as well as the degree of stress and overload that employees feel during the process. Some companies have cultural values that prevent them from fully pursuing a particular course of action. Companies that are very paternalistic or extremely loyal to their employees might be hesitant to implement layoffs, even if doing so makes sense.[49] The Container Store, S. C. Johnson, Lincoln Electric, and Southwest Airlines are examples of companies that have long-standing traditions of fighting for the job security of their employees.[50] For example, when serving as the CEO of Southwest Airlines, James F. Parker stated, "We are willing to suffer some damage, even to our stock price, to protect the jobs of our people."[51] In contrast, some companies are driven by highly competitive environments (or cutthroat cultures). In firms with cutthroat cultures, managers may be more willing to take drastic measures to remedy labor surpluses and shortages—even if those measures create a lot of stress for employees.

### Employee Reactions to Workforce-Planning Tactics

Any discrepancy between the corporate culture of a firm and the workforce tactics that its managers use is likely to result in a negative reaction by the company's employees. For example, if your company has a culture of attending to the long-term well-being of its employees and rewarding their loyalty, a decision to lay off a large number of employees swiftly is likely to be poorly received. Similarly, using contingent labor, outsourcing, or offshoring to deal with a labor shortage might run counter to a corporate culture that puts a priority on the long-term job security of employees. In contrast, using tactics that are consistent with your cultural values is more likely to strengthen those values and increase the bond between employees and the company.

While there are a variety of workforce planning tactics that you may use to balance labor supply and demand, it is important that you consider how well the tactic you choose fits with the cultural values in your company. If the choice you make is inconsistent with the company's cultural values, it may lead to lower employee morale and commitment, and possibly to greater turnover.

## Employee Concerns and Workforce Planning

The final organizational demand, employee concerns, is particularly important to consider in the context of workforce planning. After all, discussions about labor shortages and surpluses, and the tactics that you use to deal with them, directly affect your employees. As a manager, you need to understand that your choices affect not only the level of stress employees experience, but also their perceptions of justice and fairness.

### Employee Stress and Work/Life Balance Issues

When the term *workforce planning* is brought up, many people automatically think about layoffs. Although they can quickly "fix" a labor surplus, layoffs create a considerable amount of stress and turmoil, not only for the people who lose their jobs, but for their families and the communities in which they live. Even employees who survive a layoff are likely to experience a great deal of stress.[52] While layoffs are certainly logically linked to employee stress, other labor surplus tactics may create stress for employees as well. Anytime companies engage in activities that actively or passively try to reduce the number of employees, other employees are affected due to having valued coworkers removed, having to perform additional tasks to make up for the missing employees, and simply being exposed to a change in the work environment.

Workforce planning tactics that are geared toward dealing with labor shortages also may create stress for employees, albeit for different reasons. When experiencing a labor shortage, current employees may have to work harder or work extra hours to make sure that their additional tasks and responsibilities are performed. If prolonged overtime is used to deal with the labor shortage, employees may experience heightened stress, fatigue, or even injuries from trying to do more than they should do in their jobs.[53] In addition, stress can result from employee promotions, transfers, or demotions. For example, transferring an employee from one unit to another puts the employee in a new work environment, with new colleagues and new tasks and responsibilities to perform. Job change is likely to create stress for the employee until the person achieves a certain level of proficiency and feels comfortable in the job. Beyond how employees cope with stress on the job, workforce planning tactics may affect how well employees can achieve a desirable work/life balance. Working overtime forces employees to spend less time relaxing at home or enjoying other personal activities. Similarly, attrition and hiring freezes may require employees to work harder and perhaps longer hours to perform the tasks that their former coworkers used to do.

The way companies schedule workers is also an issue that causes stress and interferes with work/life planning for employees. This issue is particularly important in the retail and food service industries where hourly workers may have a different schedule week to week. To address this issue, the state of Oregon and cities of San Francisco, Seattle, New York City, and Emeryville, California, have all passed legislation requiring the use of **predictive scheduling**, and some companies voluntarily are adopting this process. Predictive scheduling protects employees from last-minute scheduling changes and inconsistent schedules that make it hard to manage activities such as scheduling medical appointments or childcare. Walmart began using predictive scheduling in U.S. stores in November 2018. Using a Walmart Schedule app, employees can see their schedules, select unfilled shifts to work, and even swap shifts with other workers. Walmart managers note that this new process saves them

**predictive scheduling**

a set of laws that place obligations on employers to provide employee schedules ahead of time

up to eight hours a week that can be used for other management activities. One of the best parts of predictive scheduling at Walmart is that employees have a core-hour schedule that ensures they work the same shifts for at least 13 weeks, thus making life management a whole lot easier.[54]

### Perceptions of Procedural and Distributive Justice

The extent to which employees understand and accept the workforce planning tactics that managers use is influenced by their perceptions of procedural and distributive justice. As noted in Chapter 2, the term *procedural justice* refers to whether employees view the processes used to make a decision as being fair. *Distributional justice* refers to whether employees believe the actual decision that was made is fair. When you make workforce planning decisions, it is important that your employees understand the rationale behind them. For example, a company facing a major performance problem for several years might be in a better position to present a layoff announcement to employees than a company that has been profitable for many years. When employees believe that your decisions were made fairly, the survivors of a layoff are likely to be less negative.[55] They also will be more willing to regroup and help work toward the company's goals.[56] In contrast, employees who disagree with the decisions or tactics used are less likely to be committed to helping the company move forward.

Even if employees agree with a course of action, they may disagree with how the practice is carried out. For example, identifying which employees are to be targeted for layoffs is typically based on individual performance, seniority, or some combination of the two. One approach is to lay off people based on their organizational tenure, with an emphasis on seniority. With last in, first out (LIFO), those with shorter tenures at a company are let go first. This approach is often how layoffs occur in union environments, a topic that you will learn more about in Chapter 13. In other organizations, performance ratings may be used, rather than simply seniority, to target the lower-performing individuals to lay off first. Obviously, how employees view a company's decisions regarding who is targeted for layoffs, transfers, demotions, promotions, overtime, and the like will be a function of what they believe the criteria should be, not necessarily the criteria actually used by the company. An employee with many years on the job might believe that seniority should be the primary criterion for layoff and promotion decisions. In contrast, an employee with only a few years on the job might believe that performance should be the primary criterion. Employees hold justice perceptions, and the best way for a manager to maintain positive justice perspectives is to keep open lines of communication with employees to maximize their involvement and acceptance of the tactics chosen.

## Workforce Planning in Practice: Environmental Influences

As you might guess, the external environment—in particular, labor-force trends, technology, globalization, and ethical considerations—acutely affects the workforce decisions that managers make. Next, we look at each of these factors.

### Labor-Force Trends and Workforce Planning

Earlier in this chapter, we referred to the external labor force as an essential part of the workforce planning process. In addition to considering your current employees, as a manager, you have to consider the individuals in the labor market outside your company who are available for work. But the external labor force is not static— it continues to evolve. Effective workforce planning requires you to stay on top of emerging labor force trends that are likely to affect your company, both in the near term and in the long term. Two trends—occupational trends and demographic trends—have a huge impact on the supply of and demand for employees, as well as the workforce planning tactics that managers will be able to use effectively.

### Availability of Internal and External Workers

As discussed in Chapter 2, the United States is facing an aging workforce due to the boom of individuals in the workforce born between 1946 and 1964—the generation known as the *baby boomers*. As this group of individuals gets older, companies are beginning to realize that they have to start planning for "the graying of the workforce."[57] Mass numbers of baby boomers are entering their retirement years. Because there are fewer younger workers to replace them, many companies are increasingly competing with other companies for the limited supply of workers.[58] Company Spotlight 5.2 shows how REI is coping with this problem.

Occupational trends also have a big impact on the availability of internal and external workers. In our discussion of job design in Chapter 4, we emphasized the importance of clearly understanding the competencies that individuals must possess to successfully do certain jobs. If certain occupations experience a decrease in the number of individuals who enter that occupation or there is a large increase in the demand for an occupation without adequate resources (such as university seats) to prepare individuals for that occupation, over time the change will significantly reduce the level of external labor supply for that job. The nursing industry, for example, is projected to experience this problem. The number of people entering the nursing field is not on pace to meet the demand.[59] In fact, hospitals are expected to realize a labor shortage of over 1 million nurses due to an increase in demand and a lack of labor supply by 2022.[60] To compound the problem, hospitals cannot simply hire people and train them on the job to become nurses because nursing professionals require specific qualifications and training. China is facing a related problem due to demographic trends and increases in demand for their labor. China's compulsory retirement age of 50 for women and 60 for men will likely go up in 2020 to help deal with the labor shortages.[61] Hong Kong will likely face a shortage of less educated workers by 2022 due to a sharp drop in labor supply resulting from retirements, which will affect employer ability to fill positions in childcare and other jobs not requiring a university degree.[62]

## COMPANY SPOTLIGHT  5.2

### REI Named Top Company Where Older Workers Are Appreciated

The employer review website kununu ranked companies based on 500,000 reviews from current and former employees over a year to identify the companies where workers over 45 felt appreciated. The top-ranked company was REI, the company that caters to outdoor enthusiasts. REI, actually Recreational Equipment, Inc., but known as REI or REI Co-op, is consistently ranked among the "100 Best Companies to Work For" by *Fortune* magazine. Glassdoor, another employer review website, also identified REI on their "Best Places to Work Employee's Choice" list. Thus, given the accolades the company already has received, it isn't surprising that REI would be at the top of the list for older workers.

REI benefits include a retirement plan fully paid by the company, health-care benefits even for some part-time workers, incentive pay, and more. The company is also committed to environmental stewardship and giving back to the community.

*Sources:* Jeff Kauflin, "The 10 Companies Where Workers Ages 45+ Feel Most Appreciated," Forbes.com, August 11, 2017, https://www.forbes.com/sites/jeffkauflin/2017/08/11/the-10-companies-where-workers-ages-45-feel-most-appreciated/#4d47d647c0c; "REI Is a Best Place to Work," rei.com, https://rei.com/about-rei/100-best-companies.

In contrast, if certain occupations experience growth, companies will have a larger external labor supply from which to find workers. The increasing number of jobs in the U.S. service sector is an example. Many of these jobs are very standardized and have few requirements pertaining to the particular occupational backgrounds or training that workers must have. Companies with jobs such as these are likely to have a much greater external labor supply available to them.

The key point here is that, as a manager, you need to be aware of the emerging demographic and occupational trends that are affecting and will affect your supply of workers. A good source to consult for labor force trends is the Bureau of Labor Statistics (BLS) of the U.S. Department of Labor (www.bls.gov).

### Which Tactics to Use

Labor force trends affect the tactics managers can feasibly use to address labor shortages. For example, if there is a shortage of workers in the labor force, companies might have to draw on the abilities of their current employees to cope with the labor crunch. Tactics such as overtime and employee transitions will likely be more feasible in such a case. Some companies have taken more active steps toward retaining their employees to prepare for pending labor shortages. For example, Home Depot, CVS, and Walmart are coping with the aging of their workforces by modifying the nature of jobs to accommodate older employees and to encourage them to keep their jobs beyond the typical retirement age.[63] Other organizations are working actively to recruit older employees. For example, after the terrorist attacks on the World Trade Center on September 11, 2001, the Federal Bureau of Investigation (FBI) hired retired agents to work as intelligence analysts and evidence examiners.[64] Of course, companies sometimes have to retrain older workers to ensure that their skills are comparable to those of younger employees. The increasing costs of the health-care benefits provided to older employees also can be an issue for some companies.[65] Despite these issues, many companies are realizing that the older workforce represents a talented, and available, labor force to staff their organizations.

## Technology and Workforce Planning

Technological changes affect the numbers and types of workers firms need, as well as the quality of managers' workforce-planning forecasts. We discuss these two aspects next.

### The Number of Employees Needed

When you think about the use of technology in organizations, perhaps you think about **automation**—using machines to perform tasks that otherwise could be performed by people. Automated kiosks, for example, are all around us. When you need to check your bag at the airport, you usually have to start at a kiosk. That machine is performing the tasks that a person once had to do. The self-checkout kiosks at Whole Foods and the self-order and pay kiosks at Panera Bread are additional examples. Technological changes such as these can create a situation in which companies simply have more employees than they need to remain competitive, or technology can help the company keep up production when there is a labor shortage.

**automation**
using machines to perform tasks that otherwise could be performed by people

Similarly, companies often implement technological improvements or engage in process redesigns that improve their productivity ratios. Improving your manufacturing technology will generally allow your employees to be more productive. If fewer employees are needed to sustain a certain level of productivity, managers can end up with a surplus of labor, or workers can be deployed to handle tasks that don't lend themselves to automation. Understanding how these types of company interventions affect the level of productivity among employees helps improve the accuracy of basing labor-demand forecasts on productivity levels.

### The Types of Workers Needed

Technological changes are not solely used to replace employees; they also can be used to complement or change how employees do their jobs, thereby affecting the types of workers that firms need. Depending on the nature of the technology in place, technological upgrades and automation may lead to an increase or a decrease in the level of skills needed to perform tasks or the need for fundamentally different skill sets.[66] The increasing popularity of the Internet is a good example. As customers increasingly rely on the Internet for shopping, what impact does this have on the labor demand for salespeople in stores? As more customers who previously would have gone to a store to purchase an item choose to shop via the Internet, the demand for salespeople to work in a physical store will continue to diminish. Over time, this shift will result in a labor surplus of salespeople. At the same time, the need for people to design, support, and manage Internet sites continues to increase. The net effect is a change in the types of skills that companies need to service their customers. In addition, the introduction of sophisticated computer technologies has required workers to have a heightened level of knowledge to do their jobs,[67] including greater technical, conceptual, analytical, and problem-solving skills.[68] For example, did you know that today's railroad employees check the safety of railcar wheels using infrared technology and acoustical listening devices while the trains are moving? Clearly, this requires these employees to have different skills than they had in the past, when they visually inspected the wheels. It is critical that you, as a manager, consider how technological changes such as the ones described here can affect your workforce plans.[69]

### The Quality of Workforce-Planning Forecasts

Technology clearly has had an impact on the demand for labor throughout organizations. Specifically, data analytics is also helping managers better predict their future workforce needs and talent gaps.[70] Recall our discussion of replacement charts and succession planning, which can be used to track a firm's internal workforce. In a very small company, it might be easy to map out all the viable positions and people able to move into them. However, as companies grow in size and employ more people with different qualifications, this task is likely to become overwhelming. Using technology, companies of all sizes can track the skill sets of their employees and identify potential matches for jobs that become vacant. When a client working with IBM needed candidates with particular backgrounds, IBM's Watson Candidate Assistant, an artificial intelligence driven solution, was able to immediately target workers who perfectly fit the needs of the client.[71] That type of responsiveness certainly helps keep customers happy.

The potential to identify and track future replacements also greatly increases the accuracy and effectiveness of succession planning in organizations.[72] When coupled with projections of labor force trends, the firm's strategic direction, or long-term productivity prospects, having a sound information system that facilitates skill inventories and tracking allows managers to know that the right individuals are where they need to be within the organization. And the more accurate a firm's forecasts, the less likely that the company will need to resort to tactics or extreme measures to manage labor shortages or surpluses.

## Globalization and Workforce Planning

**offshoring**

moving jobs out of the company's home country to another country to tap into lower-cost labor or labor with needed skillsets

The continued presence of globalization affects workforce planning in several ways. First, it highlights the importance of understanding that labor force trends vary across countries, as well as within countries. Second, the option of employing a global workforce has fueled the trend toward **offshoring**, which is moving jobs out of the company's home country to another country to tap into lower-cost labor or labor with needed skillsets.[73] Infosys Technologies Ltd. and Tata Consultancy Services Ltd., two prominent offshoring companies to which jobs are sent in India, have experienced tremendous growth in recent years as the offshoring movement has picked up steam.[74]

### Where the Workers Are

As noted previously, the aging workforce is particularly problematic for a number of developed countries such as Japan, Italy, and the United States. And despite the growing trend to send work to India, India is actually experiencing a labor shortage for professionals such as project managers, manufacturing professionals, retail managers, salesclerks, and pilots.[75] Countries vary in the quality of their human capital, as well as the relative supply of labor. For example, according to the International Labour Organization (ILO), 66% of the global population of working age people (roughly 4.7 billion) was employed in 2007.[76] That rate is expected to be 62.6% by 2020. Unemployment rates vary significantly around the world. In South Africa, for instance, the unemployment rate was 27.9% in 2018, as compared to 3% in the Czech Republic.[77] Given differences in the demographics and supply of global labor forces, companies are often forced to engage in different tactics for parts of their business in different global locations to respond to their unique labor force trends.

Workers are becoming increasingly aware of their global opportunities. Some individuals, for example, have sought out opportunities in countries experiencing high global demand for their labor, such as in India and China.[78] Many companies are increasing their investments in their overseas operations. Consequently, it's not surprising that some individuals are relocating from the United States to countries with the best prospects for job growth.[79] The political climate in a country also has a lot to do with where expatriates want to work.

### Which Workforce-Planning Tactics to Use

As a result of offshoring, countries around the world are being evaluated as potential locations for establishing offshore operations. In the past, both U.S. manufacturing jobs and professional and white collar jobs have been offshored. For example, many information technology (IT) jobs, call-center positions, and back-office operations have been offshored to India, eastern Europe, and the Philippines.[80] By viewing the external workforce at a global level, rather than at a local or domestic level, companies have a significantly larger labor pool to choose from.

Countries vary dramatically with regard to their labor costs, and these differences have fueled the offshoring trend. For some firms, the availability of a large labor supply in another country, coupled with potentially lower labor costs in those nations, is a very attractive option. Even the wages in countries in close proximity to one another range widely. Indeed, the wages in Norway and Sweden are much higher for manufacturing than in Estonia, the Czech Republic, and Slovakia. For instance, in 2016, the hourly wage for manufacturing in Norway was $25.88, as compared to $3.25 in the Czech Republic.[81]

Although offshoring may present challenges in terms of distance, it also presents an opportunity for operating a firm 24/7—without any downtime. A partner of a U.S. firm in India, for example, may conceivably start its workday just as the employees in the United States are completing their workday. By taking advantage of this situation, companies have been able to decrease the time that it takes to create products or services while dramatically increasing their firms' labor pools. Given the continual pressures that firms are under to bring out new products faster than their competitors and at lower costs, it is logical that companies such as General Electric (GE), Citigroup, and American Express will continue to expand their offshoring operations.[82]

There are, nonetheless, risks associated with adopting a global workforce planning approach. Companies must balance their cost savings against the strategic objectives they are trying to achieve, including improved product quality and operational performance, greater market access, and better customer service.[83] It is imperative that managers ensure that offshoring their business processes and activities will not compromise the quality of their operations. Saving costs at the expense of other performance outcomes is unlikely to be a sustainable strategy over time.[84] Thus, it is not surprising that companies have increasingly begun to reshore their work. **Reshoring** involves returning jobs to the country of origin. Reshoring happens for many reasons, including concerns over low quality at offshored manufacturing operations, intellectual property theft, unapproved suppliers or components, and government incentives to return work to the U.S. or other home country.[85]

**reshoring**
returning jobs back to the country of origin

## Ethics and Workforce Planning

In addition to their business implications, workforce planning decisions can be viewed from an ethical perspective. To be sure, these decisions affect the viability of a company's operations. However, as indicated earlier, workforce planning decisions also affect individuals, their families, and the communities in which companies operate. As a result, one of the challenges that you must consider when making workforce planning decisions relates to how these activities are viewed from an ethical perspective.

### Community Reactions to Workforce-Planning Tactics

Layoffs, contingent labor, outsourcing, and offshoring are certainly viable workforce planning options for firms. However, they are not without controversy. Many people believe that not only does offshoring take jobs away from domestic employees, but companies use it as a way to exploit low-cost labor and avoid complying with domestic labor laws and regulations that are designed to protect employees.[86] As highlighted in Chapter 2, Nike is a company that experienced backlash due to rumors of poor working conditions and the use of child labor among its international suppliers. In response, Nike has done an admirable job turning around that image by instituting a rigorous process for identifying and managing its international supplier network.

Decisions related to workforce planning are often about emotionally charged topics. These decisions directly affect whether people are able to keep their jobs, how hard they have to work, and whether they enjoy the benefits of full-time employment. In many cases, these issues have social, political, and competitive implications. Managers would be well advised to be fully informed about how the relevant stakeholders of their organization are going to view the workforce planning decisions they make. The ethical vantage points of different groups will influence how they react to workforce planning actions. Communities with high unemployment rates, for example, are likely to be particularly sensitive to a firm's decisions to outsource or offshore jobs.

### How Companies Help Employees Cope

In light of the impact that the different workforce planning tactics have on individuals, many companies take steps to help their employees cope with these changes. Some companies provide employees with extra breaks to help them cope with the extra tasks they have to do during a labor shortage, for example. Similarly, managers can make sure the employees transitioning to new jobs are trained properly. Many companies that resort to layoffs establish **outplacement assistance programs** to help employees who are being laid off find new jobs. Outplacement services often

**outplacement assistance programs**
help employees who are being laid off find new jobs

help individuals cope with the reality of losing a job, prepare individuals to transition to a new career opportunity quickly and successfully, and provide a sounding board or a channel for emotional support during the transition. Sometimes managers or individuals within the company provide this counseling, but often it is better left to outside service providers who are specifically trained to provide the counseling and support that individuals need.

# Workforce Planning in Practice: Regulatory Issues

Ethical considerations revolve around many of the workforce planning decisions companies make. However, there are also several legal requirements that are important to consider for workforce planning. Two specific issues that have garnered considerable attention in recent years relate to the legal requirements associated with mass layoffs and plant closings, and properly classifying workers as either employees or independent contractors. We discuss these issues next.

## Requirements For Mass Layoffs and Plant Closings

The **Worker Adjustment and Retraining Notification (WARN) Act**, passed in 1989, mandates the amount of notice that workers, their families, and their communities must receive prior to a mass layoff. The act covers the following companies:

- Companies with 100 or more employees, not counting part-time employees
- Companies with 100 or more employees, including part-time employees who in the aggregate work at least 4,000 hours per week

A company that meets one of these qualifications is required to provide 60 calendar days' notice in advance of a plant closing or mass layoff.[87] According to the act, a plant closing is a situation in which a single employment site (or one or more facilities or units within a site) will be shut down, with loss of employment for 50 or more employees during a 30-day period. A mass layoff, in contrast, does not result from a plant closing but rather is an employment loss during a 30-day period of 500 or more employees, or 50–499 employees if those targeted for the layoff make up at least one-third of the company's workforce.[88] The intention of this act is to provide workers and their families with a transition period during which to adjust to an impending layoff in order to obtain other employment or begin training to become competitive for new jobs.[89]

**Worker Adjustment and Retraining Notification (WARN) Act**

passed in 1989, mandates the amount of notice that workers, their families, and their communities must receive prior to a mass layoff

## Determining Who is an Employee Versus an Independent Contractor

As shown in Exhibit 5.8, determining whether an individual should be considered an employee or an **independent contractor** is based on three primary considerations: behavioral control, financial control, and the relationship of the parties. *Behavioral control* focuses on the extent to which there is a right by the company to direct or control how the individual performs the work. *Financial control* considers the extent to which the individual has control over the business side of the work and the degree of investment that the person makes in the work—that is, whether the person is reimbursed for his or her business expenses and has the opportunity to realize a profit or loss on the work. The *relationship of the parties* examines how the company and the individual perceive their work relationship and considers two factors: the presence or absence of employee benefits and the terminology of any existing written contract.

**independent contractor**

external worker who performs work for an organization but maintains substantial control over the means and methods of their services

## EXHIBIT 5.8
### Employee or Independent Contractor: Which Are You?

**General Rule:** An individual is an independent contractor if the payor controls the outcomes of the work and not *what* will be done and *how* the work will be done.

**Categories to Use to Classify Workers Properly**

**Behavioral Control:** The more that the company directs and controls the work, the more likely the person is an employee
- Type of instruction given
- Degree of instruction
- Evaluation systems to measure details of how work is done
- Training a worker on how to do the job

**Financial Control:** The more likely the business is to direct or control the financial and business aspects of the worker's job, the more likely the person is an employee
- Significant investment in equipment used by worker
- Unreimbursed expenses
- Opportunity for profit or loss
- Services available to the market
- Method of payment

**Relationship:** The greater the extent to which the relationship is embedded into the business and the person benefits from the business, the more likely the person is an employee
- Written contracts
- Benefits paid for worker
- Permanency of relationship
- Services provided are key activity of business

*Based on:* "Understanding Employee vs. Contractor Designation," IRS, irs.gov, https://www.irs.gov/newsroom/understanding-employee-vs-contractor-designation.

In general, the key distinction between an employee and an independent contractor revolves around the issue of control. If you can control the details of what and how an individual performs services for you, the individual is most likely an employee. In contrast, independent contractors typically maintain control over the means and methods of their services. You may control the result of their work, but not the details regarding how that work is completed. The notion of control spans many aspects of employment.

The Internal Revenue Service (IRS) provides helpful information for organizations to use in determining if someone performing work for the company is an independent contractor or an employee. One useful website is https://www.irs.gov/forms-pubs/about-form-ss8.

As a manager, you are responsible for withholding income taxes, withholding and paying Social Security and Medicare taxes, and paying unemployment taxes on the wages paid to your employees. You are not responsible for withholding or paying taxes for independent contractors. However, organizations are required to provide Form 1099-MISC to independent contractors who receive more than $600 in payment for services during the year. By not providing independent contractors with other employment benefits, such as retirement benefits, access to incentive systems and stock option plans, or medical insurance, companies can realize considerable cost savings. Given these cost savings, the appeal of hiring independent contractors is understandable. An important caveat is worth noting: Misclassifying employees as independent contractors is not without costs. Some of the potential costs that a firm can be forced to pay for misclassifications are back payroll taxes, overtime pay, retirement, or other employment benefits such as incentive pay, and medical coverage for injuries an employee incurred during the contractual arrangement.[90] In a now classic case, Microsoft learned that the costs of misclassifying employees

## COMPANY SPOTLIGHT   **5.3**

### Microsoft's Lesson Learned

During the 1989–1990 tax year, the IRS audited Microsoft and found that the company had misclassified as independent contractors thousands of software testers working alongside its full-time employees between 1987 and 1990. The IRS determined that despite these employees' classification as independent contractors, Microsoft exercised a substantial amount of control over the services they provided. Microsoft complied with the IRS's decision and paid the employment taxes it owed and the wages the workers would have made had they been properly classified as employees. However, several of the misclassified employees filed a lawsuit to gain access to the benefit plans they were denied due to their misclassification. In 1996, the courts ruled that the individuals were eligible to participate in Microsoft's stock purchase and "Savings Plan-Plus" programs. After several failed attempts to reverse this decision, Microsoft agreed to settle the lawsuit for $97 million.

*Sources:* W. G. Mister, D. M. Rose, B. J. Rowe, and S. K. Widener, "The Contingent Workforce," *Internal Auditor*, April 2003, pp. 42–47; G. Flynn, "Temp Staffing Carries Legal Risk," *Workforce*, September 1999, pp. 56–62; A. Bernstein, "Now Temp Workers Are a Full-time Headache," *BusinessWeek*, May 31, 1999, p. 46; D. Foust, "The Ground War at FedEx," *BusinessWeek*, November 28, 2005, pp. 42–43; and T. Bishop, "Former Microsoft Temps Still Waiting To Be Paid," *Seattle Post Intelligence Reporter*, May 3, 2004, http://seattlepi.nwsource.com/business/171664_msfttemps03.html

can be substantial, as Company Spotlight 5.3 explains. The Internal Revenue Service (IRS) estimates that employers have misclassified millions of workers nationally as independent contractors.[91]

## SUMMARY

Companies engage in workforce planning to ensure that employees with the right skills are where they need to be, at the right time, to meet their firms' current and future needs. The key challenge with workforce planning is that the composition of a company's workforce is constantly changing. Employee turnover, the movement of employees via promotions, transfers, and demotions to other parts of the organization, the level of employee productivity, company performance, changes in strategic direction, economic conditions, and industry trends all affect the relative supply and demand for labor within companies.

A *labor shortage* is a situation in which a firm's demand for employees exceeds its supply. There are a variety of tactics that managers may use to address a labor shortage. Managers can ask their employees to work overtime, hire contingent workers, try to reduce employee turnover, move current employees, or hire new full-time employees. A *labor surplus* is a situation in which a firm's demand for employees is less than the supply of employees it currently has. To address a labor surplus, managers can implement layoffs, rely on attrition and hiring freezes, implement early-retirement programs, or move employees to other parts of the company.

The specific choices that managers make regarding workforce planning decisions are influenced by the three HR challenges. Organizational demands (strategy, company characteristics, culture, and employee concerns) influence how quickly a labor shortage or surplus must be addressed, which tactics are most likely to be used, which employees are likely to be affected, who is involved in the

workforce planning process, and how the firm's workforce planning decisions will affect employees.

Environmental influences—labor force trends, globalization, technology, and ethics and social responsibility—also affect the workforce planning process. Labor force trends affect the availability of internal and external workers available to firms, as well as the tactics that managers can effectively use to address a shortage or a surplus. Technology affects the number of employees that firms need, the types of skills they must possess, and the quality of the firm's workforce planning forecasts. Globalization has provided companies with the opportunity to view the workforce from a worldwide perspective rather than a purely domestic perspective. Thus, globalization is affecting where work is performed and where the workers are locating. From an ethical perspective, managers must be aware of how their communities will react to their workforce planning tactics, as well as how they can help employees cope with their workforce planning decisions. Finally, the legal environment requires that managers provide fair notice to workers, their families, and the community in the case of plant closings and mass layoffs. In addition, managers are legally responsible for classifying individuals as independent contractors or employees.

## KEY TERMS

alternative employment arrangements
attrition
automation
contingent labor
demotion
functional flexibility
hiring freeze
independent contractor
labor demand
labor shortage
labor supply
labor surplus
numerical flexibility
offshoring
outplacement assistance program

outsourcing
predictive scheduling
productivity
productivity ratio
promotion
replacement chart
reshoring
succession planning
transfer
transition matrix
turnover
Worker Adjustment and Retraining Notification (WARN) Act
workforce planning

## DISCUSSION QUESTIONS

1. Define workforce planning and describe why it is an important activity for organizations of all types and sizes.
2. Explain the primary factors that affect labor supply and labor demand. Which factors are most important to consider? Why are those factors important?
3. Your midsize graphic design company is experiencing a labor shortage. What options are available to you, and how will you decide which to use?
4. Why do you think many companies immediately implement a layoff when faced with a labor surplus?
5. Describe the impact of the four organizational demands on planning for future workforce needs.
6. Explain the impact of environmental factors on managers' workforce planning decisions. Which environmental influences do you think will have the greatest impact on workforce planning in the next five years?

7. You have been asked to assist a chain of boutique home design stores in identifying ways technology can assist the customer experience. The goal of this project is to reduce the number of employees needed in each store. What suggestions will you offer?

8. What ethical and legal considerations must you consider when making the decision to offshore or outsource work from your company?

# LEARNING EXERCISE 1

As a manager, you have a number of tactics to choose among to cope with a labor shortage or surplus. Relying on overtime, hiring contingent labor, focusing on employee retention, using promotions, transfers, and demotions, and hiring new full-time employees are tactics you can use to remedy a labor shortage. When faced with a labor surplus, you might consider implementing layoffs, focusing on attrition and hiring freezes, developing early-retirement programs, or using promotions, transfers, and demotions to move employees to other areas of the company.

1. What are the advantages of each of these tactics?
2. What are the disadvantages of each of these tactics?
3. Considering the advantages and disadvantages of each tactic, develop a strategy for when each should be used and should not be used. Which organizational demands and environmental considerations are particularly important in your strategy?

# LEARNING EXERCISE 2

Many companies experience conflicting pressures when they consider offshoring work to other countries. On the one hand, a company knows it will be able to save on costs, as well as access a wider labor pool to meet the company's needs. A larger labor pool enables the company to hire higher-quality workers, often while still paying lower wages than in the home country. This opportunity can lead to greater operational efficiencies, help improve the bottom-line performance of a firm, and satisfy company shareholders.

At the same time, however, firms know that offshoring is taking jobs away from domestic workers and providing them to foreigners. This situation, in turn, can have a negative trickle-down effect on the families and communities of people who used to hold these jobs. Moreover, according to the World Bank, in 2013, approximately 767 million people around the world—or 10.7% of the world's population— lived on less than $1.90 a day. Considering that one of the benefits of offshoring is that a company can use it to pay lower wages, critics have expressed concerns over the abuse of international workers. Given these concerns, is the practice of offshoring unethical?

1. What are the greatest risks associated with offshoring? What are the greatest benefits?
2. What criteria would you use to decide whether to offshore work to a company in another country?
3. What types of jobs are best suited for offshoring? Be specific in your rationale.
4. How do you reconcile the financial and operational benefits that companies realize from offshoring with the perspective that offshoring is damaging to the country and potentially exploitive of international labor?

*Source:* "Understanding Poverty: Poverty," The World Bank, worldbank.org, www.worldbank.org/en/topic/poverty/overview.

# CASE STUDY 1: PLANNING FOR THE FUTURE AT EAST COAST BANK

Paula Mason is one of three new assistant regional managers of East Coast Bank (ECB). Her position was recently created to provide administrative support and advice for the regional manager in charge of the southwest region, Ian Swartz. In their first meeting as a team, Paula and the two other assistant regional managers met with Ian to discuss areas throughout their branches that might be addressed in order to lower costs and raise profitability. Each of the assistant managers was given different aspects to emphasize, and Paula was asked to focus on ways to reduce labor costs, increase labor productivity among employees, or both throughout the eight branches. In part, this request was a response to feedback from the branches regarding an increase in recruitment and training expenses as well as a decrease in employee morale.

Paula's first course of action was to evaluate some direct and indirect labor costs related to turnover and retention, as well as areas of bloated labor (labor surpluses) through the southwest region. Based on her analysis, Paula arrived at some basic points of information for the branches. First, ECB is organized into several broad regions throughout New Jersey, Pennsylvania, and Delaware. Each region comprises 8–12 bank branches. Each branch consists of 4 primary jobs: branch manager, assistant manager, loan officer, and teller/customer service agent. On average, each bank has 1 branch manager, 3 assistant managers, 4 loan officers, and 15 tellers/customer service agents.

Beyond the average staffing levels, Paula also was able to gather some information regarding the movement of employees within and out of the organization. As shown in the following transition matrix, ECB averages 26% turnover, with turnover among the tellers/customer service agents slightly higher, at 33%, and turnover at the assistant manager level the lowest, at 17%.

**Transition Matrix for Southwest Region**

| 2019 | 2020 | | | | |
| --- | --- | --- | --- | --- | --- |
| | Branch Managers | Assistant Managers | Loan Officers | Tellers/ Customer Service Agents | Exit the Company |
| 8 Branch Managers | 6 (75%) | | | 2 (25%) | |
| 24 Assistant Managers | 2 (8%) | 16 (67%) | 1 (4%) | 1 (4%) | 4 (17%) |
| 36 Loan Officers | | 2 (6%) | 26 (72%) | 8 (22%) | |
| 120 Tellers/ Customer Service Agents | 14 (12%) | 2 (2%) | 64 (53%) | 40 (33%) | |
| Anticipated Labor Supply | 8 | 32 | 29 | 65 | 29% (54 out of 188) |

## Discussion Questions

1. Based on the transition matrix for ECB, which positions are experiencing a labor surplus or a labor shortage?
2. What tactics would you use to address the labor shortages? Why?
3. What tactics would you use to address the labor surpluses? Why?
4. When you look at the overall pattern of employee movement, do you see any areas that are of particular concern?
5. What plan would you recommend for the future to prevent ECB from having excess surpluses and shortages?

# CASE STUDY 2: THE TURNAROUND AT FORD

Ford has been going through difficult times and recovered more than once. The company's share of the automobile market continues to shrink, and its cost structure has contributed to financial losses. In 2006, following a shrinking share of the automobile industry and a cost structure that contributed to financial losses, Ford lost $12.6 billion. In 2007, Ford did better, posting losses of only $2.7 billion. At the same time, however, Ford's market shares dwindled and in 2007, its share was 14.8%—down from 26% in the 1990s. In an effort to match its production with the demand for its products, as well as address concerns with its high labor costs, Ford has focused on trying to get smaller to achieve long-term success in the automobile industry.

One of the primary ways for Ford to achieve this goal is to take further steps to reduce the size of its workforce. Ford's workforce went from 283,000 employees in 2006 to 171,000 in 2013. Ford then announced a new round of buyouts and early-retirement packages to its workers in an effort to cut costs and replace those leaving with lower-paid workers. Some of the offers made to reduce the labor supply in 2013 included:

- Workers who were eligible for retirement would receive a $50,000 offer, higher than the $35,000 in the previous round of buyouts.
- Skilled-trade workers, such as maintenance workers, would get an additional $20,000, bringing the total potential payout for such a worker to $70,000.

Following the 2013 round of buyouts, Ford extended its tactics to reduce the size of its workforce and ongoing expenses further through means such as the following:

- Extending a buyout option for its 78,000 employees and special incentives for its 40,800 workers who are eligible for retirement to retire sooner rather than later.
- Offering a lump sum payment for 90,000 retired engineers and office workers to forgo their regular monthly pension check for the rest of their lives.

The automaker's goal in offering the company-wide buyouts was to cut jobs, reduce its ongoing pension expenses, to position itself to be more competitive in the market, and to align its labor capacity with the demand for its products.

In 2018, Ford announced that by 2020 around 90% of Ford's sales in North America would be trucks, SUVs, and commercial vehicles. The only two cars to be manufactured in North America would be the Mustang and the Focus Active Crossover. The company has reallocated $7 billion of its research funds from cars to trucks and SUVs.

## Discussion Questions

1. What factors have contributed to the large-scale labor surplus at Ford?
2. What impact is the most recent strategic plan at Ford likely to have on the company's labor supply?
3. Over the years, Ford has decided to pursue employee buyouts and attrition in an attempt to shrink its workforce to match its productivity demands. Why do you think Ford uses these two tactics? Do you think these are the best options for Ford to achieve its goals?
4. What are the downsides of these two approaches? Are there any other approaches that you might recommend to address its labor surplus?

*Sources:* J. Muller, "Ford Offers Retirees a Bag of Cash to Go Away," *Forbes,* April 27, 2012, http://www.forbes. com/sites/joannmuller/2012/04/27/ford-offers-retirees-a-bag-of-cash-to-go-away/; M. Wayland, "Ford Close to Completing US Salaried Retiree Pension Buyouts," Mlive, October 25, 2013, http://www.mlive.com/auto/index. ssf/2013/10/ford_nearing_end_of_us_salarie.html; M. Spector, "Ford Looks to Trim up to 13,000 More Jobs: Buyouts Could Pave the Way for Lower-Paid Replacements; Packages Get More Generous," *Wall Street Journal,* January 24, 2008, p. B1; Associated Press, "Ford Offering Buyouts to All Hourly Workers. Automaker Lost $2.8 Billion Last Year, Sees Grim Sales Outlook for 2008," January 24, 2008, http://www.msnbc.msn.com/id/22819848; and M. Maynard, "Ford Chief Sees Small as Virtue and Necessity," *The New York Times,* January 26, 2007; Jackie Wattles, "Ford Dropping All But 2 Cars From Its North American Dealerships," CNN Money, money.cnn.com, April 25, 2018, money.cnn.com/2018/04/25/autos/ford-cars-north-america.index.html.

## NOTES

1. "Should the Dow Ditch General Motors?" *Bloomberg BusinessWeek*, January 9, 2006, p. 34; https://www.bloomberg.com/news/articles/2006-01-08/should-the-dow-ditch-general-motors.

2. A. Harrington, "The Big Ideas," *Fortune* 140 (November 22, 1999): 98–103.

3. D. Welch, "What My Dad Taught Me About GM and the Auto Workers," *BusinessWeek*, November 7, 2005, p. 48; "Should the Dow Ditch General Motors?"; and H. David, "Can GM Stop Blowing Cash?" *BusinessWeek*, November 21, 2005, pp. 50–52.

4. H. Maurer, "Downsizing in Detroit," *BusinessWeek*, December 5, 2005, p. 32.

5. N. Maynard, "Ford Eliminating up to 30,000 Jobs and 14 Factories," *The New York Times*, January 24, 2006, http://www.nytimes.com/2006/01/24/automobiles/24ford.html?_r=1&pagewanted=2&oref=slogin.

6. Ford.com, "Engagement and Community," http://corporate.ford.com/microsites/sustainability-report-2011-12/people-data-engagement.

7. J. Muller, "Ford Offers Employees a Bag of Cash to Go Away," *Forbes*, April, 27, 2012, http://www.forbes.com/sites/joannmuller/2012/04/27/ford-offers-retirees-a-bag-of-cash-to-go-away/.

8. Bloomberg, "Ford Will Stop Making Cars—Except These 2 Models," fortune.com, April 26, 2018, http://fortune.com/2018/04/25/ford-stop-making-cars-sedans.

9. R. Haglund, "GM Offers Early Exit," *The Saginaw News*, January 18, 2008, http://blog.mlive.com/tricities/2008/01/gm_offers_early_exit.html.

10. M. M. Chapman, "Retirees Wrestle with Pension Buyout from General Motors," *The New York Times*, Business Day, July18, 2012, http://www.nytimes.com/2012/07/19/business/retirees-wrestle-with-pension-buyout-from-general-motors.html?pagewanted=all.

11. M. Kotakis, "GM to Offer Buyouts to Skilled Trade Workers," *GM Authority*, April 8, 2013, http://gmauthority.com/blog/2013/04/gm-to-offer-buyouts-to-skilled-trade-workers/.

12. "Our People," gm.com, https://www.gm.com/company/about-gm.html.

13. S. Bates, "Expert: Don't Overlook Employee Burnout," *HR Magazine* 48 (August 2003): 14; and "Enterprises Struggle to Combat IT Burnout," *Business Communications Review* 33 (May 2003): 6.

14. J. D. Shaw, J. E. Delery, G. D. Jenkins, Jr., and N. Gupta, "An Organization-Level Analysis of Voluntary and Involuntary Turnover," *Academy of Management Journal* 41 (1998): 511–525.

15. SHRM Executive Brief, "Differences in Employee Turnover Across Key Industries," December 2011, http://www.shrm.org/research/benchmarks/documents/assessing%20employee%20turnover_final.pdf.

16. "Hospitality Employee Turnover Rate Edged Higher in 2016," National Restaurant Association, restaurant.org, https://www.restaurant.org/News/Hospitality-employee-turnover-rate-edged-higher-in.

17. R. King, "Turnover Is the New Enemy at One of America's Oldest Restaurant Chains," *Workforce*, April 2004, http://www.workforce.com/section/06/feature/23/68/40.

18. Kate Taylor, "Starbucks' New CEO Tells Us He'll Never Be Howard Schultz—And That's Great News for the Brand," *Business Insider*, businessinsider.com, April 3, 2017, http://www.businessinsider.com/interview-with-starbucks-new-ceo-kevin-johnson-2017-4.17 H. A. Mahoney, "Productivity Defined: The Relativity of Efficiency, Effectiveness, and Change," in *Productivity in Organizations*, ed. J. P. Campbell, R. J. Campbell, and Associates (San Francisco: Jossey-Bass, 1988), 13–39.

19. Natasha Bach, "The Fortune 500 Is Set to Get Another Female CEO," fortune.com, July 13, 2018, http://fortune.com/2018/07/13/new-northrop-grumman-ceo-kathy-warden-fortune-500-women/.

20. H. A. Mahoney, "Productivity Defined: The Relativity of Efficiency, Effectiveness, and Change," in *Productivity in Organizations*, ed. J. P. Campbell, R. J. Campbell, and Associates (San Francisco: Jossey-Bass, 1988), 13–39.

21. J. Brockner, J. Greenberg, A. Brockner, J. Bortz, J. Davy, and C. Carter, "Layoffs, Equity Theory, and Work Performance: Further Evidence of the Impact of Survivor Guilt," *Academy of Management Journal* 29 (1986): 373–384.

22. W. F. Cascio, *Applied Psychology in Personnel Management* (Englewood Cliffs, NJ: Prentice Hall, 1991).

23. M. A. Hitt, R. D. Ireland, and R. E. Hoskisson, *Strategic Management: Competitiveness and Globalization*, 6th ed. (Cincinnati: Thomson, South-Western, 2005).

[24] Bureau of Labor Statistics, "Labor Force Statistics from the Current Population Survey," bls.gov, November 5, 2018, https://data.bls.gov/timeseries/LNS14000000.

[25] "Italy Unemployment Rate, 1983–2018," Trading Economics, tradingeconomics.com, https://tradingeconomics.com/italy/unemployment-rate.

[26] "Greece Unemployment Rate, 1998–2018," *Trading Economics,* tradingeconomics.com, https://tradingeconomics.com/Greece/unemployment-rate; "Spain Unemployment Rate, 1976–2018," *Trading Economics,* tradingeconomics.com, https://tradingeconomics.com/Spain/unemployment-rate.

[27] Tim Thornton, "Wired for Jobs," Virginia Business, virginiabusiness.com, February 28, 2017, http://www.virginiabusiness.com/news/article/wired-for-jobs.

[28] Brownlee, J., January 29, 2013. "This Is How Many Apps, Songs, Videos, Photos, and Games You Can Fit on a 128GB iPad." *Cult of Mac.* http://www.cultofmac.com/213073/this-is-how-many-apps-songs-videos-photos-games-you-can-fit-on-a-128gb-ipad/.

[29] S. N. Houseman, "Why Employers Use Flexible Staffing Arrangements: Evidence from an Establishment Survey," *Industrial and Labor Relations Review* 55 (2001): 149–170.

[30] Bureau of Labor Statistics, "Contingent and Alternative Employment Arrangements—May 2017," bls.gov, June 7, 2018, https://www.bls.gov/news.release/pdf/conemp.pdf.

[31] J. David, "The Unexpected Employee and Organizational Costs of Skilled Contingent Workers," *Human Resource Planning,* June 2005, pp. 32–41; D. P. Lepak and S. A. Snell, "The Human Resource Architecture: Toward a Theory of Human Capital Allocation and Development," *Academy of Management Review* 24 (1999): 31–48; and J. Zappe, "Tracking the Cost-Benefit of Using Contingent Employees," *Workforce* online, May 2005, http://www.workforce.com/archive/article/24/05/46.php.

[32] Phil Wahba, "How Walmart Is Helping New Employees Get Raises Faster," fortune.com, January 27, 2017, fortune.com/2017/01/26/walmart-raises-salaries-wages/; "Walmart's New Education Benefit Puts Cap and Gown Within Reach for Associates," walmart.com, May 30, 2018, https://news.walmart.com/2018/05/30/walmarts-new-education-benefit-puts-cap-and-gown-within-reach-for-associates.

[33] C. O. Trevor, "Interactions Among Actual Ease of Movement Determinants and Job Satisfaction in the Prediction of Voluntary Turnover," *Academy of Management Journal* 44 (2001): 621–638.

[34] "Mass Layoffs—May 2013," Bureau of Labor Statistics, June 21, 2013, http://www.bls.gov/news.release/pdf/mmls.pdf.

[35] M. Ryan, "Weatherford to Cut 7,000 Employees," *Houston Business Journal*, January 31, 2014, http://www.bizjournals.com/houston/news/2014/01/31/weatherford-to-cut-7-000-employees.html.

[36] C. Zander, "Volvo to Cut 4,400 Jobs as Fourth-Quarter Profit Slides," European Business News, *Wall Street Journal*, February 6, 2014, http://online.wsj.com/news/articles/SB10001424052702304680904579366043117729428.

[37] Alexia Elejalde-Ruiz, "Allstate, Siemens Among Employers Notifying State of Mass Layoffs," *Chicago Tribune*, chicagotribune.com, June 12, 2018, www.chicagotribune.com/business/ct-biz-allstate-print-center-layoffs-0613-story.html.

[38] Hitt, Ireland, and Hoskisson, *Strategic Management*.

[39] L. Greenhalgh, L. T. Lawrence, and R. I. Sutton, "Determinants of Work Force Reduction Strategies in Declining Organizations," *Academy of Management Review* 13 (1988): 241–254; J. Brockner, J. Davy, and C. Carger, "Layoffs, Self-esteem, and Survivor Guilt," *Organizational Behavior and Human Decision Processes* 36 (1985): 229–244, 1985; R. I. Sutton, "Managing Organizational Death," *Human Resource Management* 22 (1983): 391–412; and B. M. Staw, L. E. Sandlelands, and J. Dutton, "Threat-Rigidity Effects in Organizational Behavior: A Multilevel Analysis," *Administrative Science Quarterly* 26 (1981): 501–524.

[40] D. M. Ihrke and T. L. Johnson, "Regional Variations in Burnout Rates in a Natural Resources Agency," *Journal of Health & Human Services Administration*, Summer 2002, pp. 48–74; and C. A. Lindquist and J. T. Whitehead, "Burnout, Job Stress, and Job Satisfaction Among Southern Correctional Officers: Perceptions and Causal Factors," *Journal of Offender Counseling: Services and Rehabilitation* 10 (1986): 5–26.

[41] Haglund, "GM Offers Early Exit."

[42] S. Byron, "UAW Members Offered $65K Lump Sum Buyout by GM, According to Investment Firm," Mlive, January 23, 2013, http://www.mlive.com/business/mid-michigan/index.ssf/2013/01/uaw_members_offered_65k_lump_s.html; "GM Offers Early Exit," January 24, 2008, http://blog.mlive.com/tricities/2008/01/gm_offers_early_exit.html.

[43] Tom Krisher, "GM, Chrysler Offer New Retirement, Buyout Packages," *ABC News,* https://abcnews.go.com/Business/story?id=6790105&page=1.

[44] P. J. Kiger, "Early-Retirement Offers That Work Too Well," *Workforce Management,* January 2004, 66–68.

[45] Sam Becker, "Job Search? These 5 Companies Have Policies That Prevent Layoffs," *Money & Career CheatSheet,* cheatsheet.com, January 8, 2017, https://www.cheatsheet.com/money-career/job-search-these-companies-have-policies-that-prevent-layoffs.html/?a=viewall.

[46] D. P. Lepak and S. A. Snell, "Examining the Human Resource Architecture: The Relationships Among Human Capital, Employment, and Human Resource Configurations," *Journal of Management* 28 (2002): 517–543.

[47] D. Robb, "Succeeding with Succession," *HR Magazine,* January 2005, 89–95.

[48] Ibid.

[49] Greenhalgh, Lawrence, and Sutton, "Determinants of Workforce Reduction Strategies in Declining Organizations."

[50] M. Schnurman, "Secret to Container Store Success: Invest in People First," *Dallas News Business,* November 4, 2013, http://www.dallasnews.com/business/columnists/mitchell-schnurman/20131104-secret-to-container-stores-success-invest-in-people-first.ece; SCJohnson Website, "Best People, Best Place," http://www.scjohnson.com/en/Careers/overview.aspx; and "Southwest Airlines One Report 2010," http://www.southwestonereport.com/_pdfs/People.pdf.

[51] M. Conlin, "Where Layoffs Are a Last Resort: Treating Them as Unthinkable Can Have Big Benefits," *BusinessWeek,* http://www.businessweek.com/stories/2001-10-07/where-layoffs-are-a-last-resort.

[52] A. K. Mishra and G. M. Sprietzer, "Explaining How Survivors Respond to Downsizing: The Roles of Trust, Empowerment, Justice, and Work Redesign," *Academy of Management Review* 23 (1998): 567–588.

[53] S. P. Proctor, R. F. White, T. G. Robins, D. Echeverria, and A. Z. Rocskay, "Effect of Overtime Work on Cognitive Function in Automotive Workers," *Scandinavian Journal of Work, Environmental, and Health* 22 (April 1996): 124–132.

[54] Valerie Bolden-Barrett, "Walmart Announces Predictive Scheduling for All US Stores," HRDive, November 14, 2018, https://www.hrdive.com/news/walmart-announces-predictive-scheduling-for-all-us-stores/542188/.

[55] J. Brockner, M. Konovsky, R. Cooper-Schneider, R. Folger, C. Martin, and R. J. Bies, "Interactive Effects of Procedural Justice and Outcome Negativity on Victims and Survivors of Job Loss," *Academy of Management Journal* 37 (1994): 397–409.

[56] Greenhalgh, Lawrence, and Sutton, "Determinants of Work Force Reduction Strategies in Declining Organizations"; J. Brockner, "Why It's So Hard to Be Fair," *Harvard Business Review,* March 2006, 122–129.

[57] M. Toosi, "Labor Force Projections to 2012: The Graying of the Workforce," *Monthly Labor Review,* February 2004, 37–57.

[58] N. R. Lockwood, "The Aging Workforce: The Reality of the Impact of Older Workers and Eldercare in the Workplace," *HRMagazine,* December 2003, http://findarticles.com/p/articles/mi_m3495/is_12_48/ai_n5989579.

[59] A. Weintraub, "Nursing: On the Critical List," *BusinessWeek,* May 28, 2002, http://www.businessweek.com/stories/2002-05-27/nursing-on-the-critical-list.

[60] "Nursing Shortage," American Association of Colleges of Nursing, http://www.aacn.nche.edu/media-relations/fact-sheets/nursing-shortage; and C. Courchane, "With Nurse Shortage Looming, America Needs a Shot in the Arm," *Washington Times,* June 6, 2011, http://www.washingtontimes.com/news/2011/jun/6/with-nurse-shortage-looming-america-needs-shot-in-/?page=all.

[61] "China Confronts Workforce Drop with Retirement-age Delay," *Bloomberg News,* December 25, 2013, http://www.bloomberg.com/news/2013-12-24/china-confronts-workforce-drop-with-retirement-age-delay.html.

[62] P. Siu, "Labour Shortage: Retirement Blamed," South China Morning Post—Hong Kong, May 14, 2014, http://www.scmp.com/news/hong-kong/article/1516669/labour-shortage-retirement-blamed.

[63] A. Canik, C. Crawford, and B. Longnecker, "Combating the Future 'Retirement Gap' with Tailored Total Rewards," *IHRIM Journal,* September/October 2004, 32–37, http://www.ntcassoc.org/assets/2005/Combating%20Retirement%20Gap-IHRIM_BLongnecker.pdf.

[64] J. Mullich, "They Don't Retire Them, They Hire Them," *Workforce Management*, December 2003, 49–54, http://www.workforce.com/articles/they-don-t-retire-them-they-hire-them.

[65] D. M. Cutler and B. C. Madrain, "Labor Market Responses to Rising Health Insurance Costs: Evidence on Hours Worked," *RAND Journal of Economics* 29 (Autumn 1998): 509–530.

[66] J. W. Dean, Jr., and S. A. Snell, "Integrated Manufacturing and Job Design: Moderating Effects of Organizational Inertia," *Academy of Management Journal* 34 (1991): 776–804; Ravin Jesuthasan and John Boudreau, "How Automation Will Affect Your Workforce," SHRM, shrm.org, June 12, 2018, https://www.shrm.org/resourcesandtools/hr-topics/technology/pages/how-automation-will-affect-your-workforce.aspx.

[67] T. Aeppel, "Firms' New Grail: Skilled Workers. U.S. Manufacturers Report Shortages Are Widespread; Critics Cite Training Cuts," *Wall Street Journal*, November 22, 2005, p. A2.

[68] S. A. Snell, D. P. Lepak, J. W. Dean, Jr., and M. A. Youndt, "Selection and Training for Integrated Manufacturing: The Moderating Effects of Job Characteristics," *Journal of Management Studies* 37 (2000): 445–466; J. P. MacDuffie, "Human Resource Bundles and Manufacturing Performance: Organizational Logic and Flexible Production Systems in the World Auto Industry," *Industrial and Labor Relations Review* 48 (1995): 197–221; S. Zuboff, *In the Age of the Smart Machine: The Future of Work and Power* (New York: Basic Books, 1988); and R. E. Walton and R. I. Susman, "People Policies for the New Machines," *Harvard Business Review* 65 (1987): 98–106.

[69] L. M. Lynch, "Job Loss: Bridging the Research and Policy Discussion," *Economic Perspectives*, 2nd Quarter 2005, 29–37.

[70] A. R. Hendrickson, "Human Resource Information Systems: Backbone Technology of Contemporary Human Resources," *Journal of Labor Research* 24 (2003): 381–394.

[71] C. Lamb, "HR Transformation: It's All About the Skills," June 25, 2018, https://www.ibm.com/case-studies/buzzfeed

[72] B. Patterson and S. Lindsey, "Weighing Resources: Technology Can Streamline Workforce Planning and Cost Analysis," *HRMagazine*, October 2003, pp. 103–108.

[73] C. M. Solomon, "Managing Virtual Teams," *Workforce* 80 (June 2001): 60–65; and R. B. Reich, "Plenty of Knowledge Work to Go Around," *Harvard Business Review*, April 17, 2005.

[74] P. Thibodeau, "Offshoring Fuels IT Hiring Boom in India," *Computerworld*, October 18, 2004, p. 8, http://www.computerworld.com/s/article/96710/Offshoring_Fuels_IT_Hiring_Boom_in_India; and K. Rapoza, "Offshoring Trend to India, Elsewhere, Has a Decade Left," March 21, 2013, http://www.forbes.com/sites/kenrapoza/2012/03/21/offshoring-trend-to-india-elsewhere-has-a-decade-left/.

[75] M. Kripalani, "India's Skills Crunch: As the Economy Booms, Companies Scramble to Find Trained Workers," *BusinessWeek*, November 7, 2005, pp. 54–55; and "The Perils of Unskilled Labor," *BusinessWeek*, November 7, 2005, p. 148.

[76] World Development Indicators, "Population Dynamics 2014," The World Bank, http://wdi.worldbank.org/table/2.1.

[77] "Unemployment Rate," IMF DataMapper, World Economic Outlook, International Monetary Fund, imf.org, April 2018, www.imf.org/external/datamapper/LUR@WEO/OEMDC/ADVEC/WEOWORLD.

[78] "Unemployment Rate in Selected World Regions in 2012 and 2013," Statista, http://www.statista.com/statistics/279790/unemployment-rate-in-seclected-world-regions/; and International Labour Organization, "ILO Projects Global Economic Turbulence Could Generate Five million More Unemployed in 2008," January 23, 2008, http://www.ilo.org/global/about-the-ilo/media-centre/press-releases/WCMS_090085/lang--en/index.htm.

[79] Paragon Relocation Press Release, "New Report Shows Record Number of Expats Worldwide," February 4, 2014, http://www.paragonrelocation.com/relocation-news/index.php/new-report-shows-record-number-of-expans-worldwide/.

[80] V. Patel, "India, Inc.," *Newsweek*, December 14, 2005.

[81] "International Comparisons of Hourly Compensation Costs in Manufacturing, 2016–Summary Tables," The Conference Board, conference-board.org, https://www.conference-board.org/ilcprogram/index.cfm?id=38269.

[82] J. Ewing, "Based in New Jersey, Thriving in Bulgaria," *BusinessWeek*, December 12, 2005, p. 54.

[83] B. Kavoussi, "General Electric Avoids Taxes by Keeping $108 Billion Overseas," *Huffington Post*, March 11, 2013, http://www.huffingtonpost.com/2013/03/11/general-electric-taxes_n_2852094.html; P. Thibodeau, "Citigroup Cutting IT Jobs, Shifting Some Work

Offshore," *Computerworld*, December 5, 2012, http://www.computerworld.com/s/article/9234382/Citigroup_cutting_IT_jobs_shifting_some_work_offshore; J. Solomon, "India Becomes Collection Hub: Low-Cost Workers Help U.S. Firms Pursue Debtors; Local Companies Go Abroad," *Wall Street Journal*, December 6, 2004, p. A13.

[84] R. Aron and J. V. Singh, "Getting Offshoring Right," *Harvard Business Review*, December 2005, 135–143; and D. P. Lepak and S. A. Snell, "Employment Sub-systems and Changing Forms of Employment," in *Oxford Handbook of Human Resource Management*, ed. P. Boxall, J. Purcell, and P. Wright (Oxford, UK: Oxford University Press), 210–230.

[85] Leigh Buchanan, "Why U.S. Manufacturers Are Turning Their Attention to 'Reshoring'," Inc., inc.com, October 26, 2017, https://www.inc.com/leigh-buchanan/how-american-manufacturers-are-reshoring.html.

[86] M. Kripalani, "Five Offshore Practices That Pay Off," *BusinessWeek*, January 30, 2006, pp. 60–61.

[87] Lepak and Snell, "Employment Sub-systems and Changing Forms of Employment."

[88] U.S. Department of Labor, "Worker Adjustment and Retraining Notification (WARN) Act Compliance Assistance Materials," April 27, 2009, http://www.dol.gov/compliance/laws/comp-warn.htm.

[89] C. J. DeGroff, "Desperate Measures: Invoking WARN's Unforeseeable Business Circumstances," *Employee Relations Law Journal* 28 (Winter 2002): 55–73.

[90] Internal Revenue Service, "Independent Contractors (Self Employed) or Employee?" http://www.irs.gov/Businesses/Small-Businesses-&-Self-Employed/Independent-Contractor-Self-Employed-or-Employee; and M. L. Stumpj and H. Sprohge, "Independent Contractor or Not?" *Journal of Accountancy*, May 2004, 89–95.

[91] Stumpj and Sprohge, "Independent Contractor or Not?"

# Part 3

# Managing Employee Competencies

# Chapter 6

# Recruitment

## Learning Objectives

**AFTER READING THIS CHAPTER, YOU SHOULD BE ABLE TO:**

**1** Define *recruitment* and explain its importance for gaining a competitive advantage.

**2** Describe the components of a successful recruitment strategy.

**3** Identify multiple sources for recruiting employees and discuss their advantages and disadvantages.

**4** Prepare a recruitment advertisement.

**5** Discuss the role recruiters play in the recruitment process.

**6** Explain several ways to evaluate recruitment success.

**7** Distinguish between effective recruiting strategies based on organizational demands.

**8** Understand the impact environmental factors have on a firm's recruiting strategy and the outcomes the organization achieves as a result.

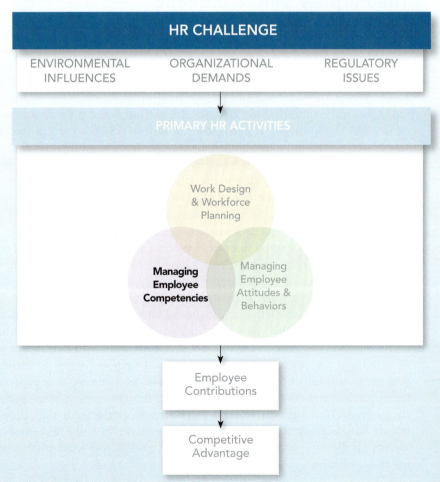

A company can have the best-designed workforce planning process and still not have the right talent in place to achieve organizational goals. The company must take the next step and craft a recruitment strategy focused on attracting the right talent to ensure organizational success. This chapter introduces the concept of employee recruitment and addresses the questions introduced in Chapter 1:

- For what competencies do you recruit?
- What groups do you target with your recruitment message?
- Do you recruit internally, externally, or both?
- How do you ensure that you offer an employee-value proposition that will attract the right applicants?

In this chapter, we also describe what your role as a manager will be in the recruitment process. We start the discussion by describing the general process of recruitment and what research has shown about best practices. We follow that with a discussion of how organizational and environmental demands, including legal issues, affect the decisions managers need to make when they are recruiting employees.

If you have ever applied for a job, already you have been engaged in a recruitment process. If not, you will be involved in the recruitment process as an applicant at some point. What you are learning now will give you an edge as a manager and as a recruitee. Managers who are the most successful at recruitment understand its importance and how to do it well—one aspect of the Managing Employee Competencies circle shown in Exhibit 6.1. Successful recruitment makes the manager's job easier because she has competent employees in place to do what is required to achieve and sustain a competitive advantage.

## The Purpose of Recruitment

**recruitment**

the process of identifying potential employees, communicating job and organizational attributes to them, and convincing them to apply for available jobs

The term **recruitment** refers to the activities companies engage in to identify potential employees, communicate job and organizational attributes to potential hires, and convince qualified individuals to apply for existing openings in the company.[1] When we discussed the Americans with Disabilities Act (ADA) in Chapter 3, you learned the importance of understanding what it means for an employee to be qualified to do a job. Recall that when an individual is *qualified*, he or she has the knowledge, skills, and abilities (KSAs)—the competencies, in other words—to do the job and help the firm achieve its organizational goals.

Recruitment is a process that begins when a manager needs to fill a job and continues until the job is filled. As you learned in Chapter 5 when you studied workforce planning, job openings occur for a number of reasons. An employee may choose to voluntarily leave a job for a job at another company. A company can promote an employee from one job to a higher-level job. Alternatively, an employee may make a lateral move within the company, thus vacating the prior position. Companies also create new jobs to cope with growth, new corporate strategies, and reengineering of the workplace.

The importance of recruitment is considerable. Think for a minute about what would happen if you had an employee quit and it took several months to find a replacement. If the work the employee did was critical to your organization's success (and it should be, otherwise, why did you need the employee in the first place?), then someone is going to have to do the work until you can hire a new employee. As a manager, you may have to pitch in and help—or even do most of the work if you are in a small company. We will discuss more about how company size affects recruitment later in this chapter. Overall, if managers cannot attract employees, they have to find alternative ways of getting work done, or they have to change the nature of the work that is done. They may have to raise the salary for the job to attract applicants, even though it results in additional and often unexpected costs for the company.

**EXHIBIT 6.1**

Strategic Human Resources Framework

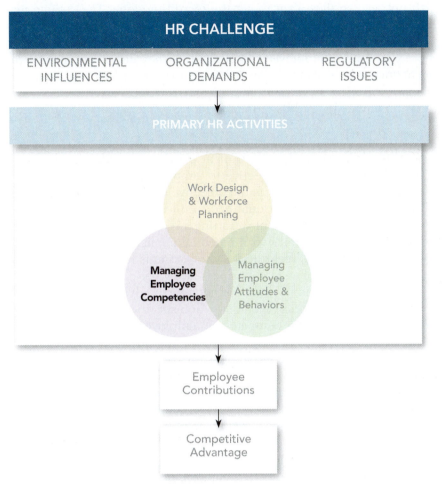

The importance of aligning a firm's recruitment to its organizational goals cannot be overstated.[2] When a company and its managers recruit well, the rest of the firm's employee management activities will require less time and effort, and time and effort saved equals money saved. Thus, talent acquisition is a critical part of talent management.

## The Recruitment Process

A successful recruiting process results from understanding why you are recruiting employees and the type of employees you need.[3] Too often, managers have an opening and immediately pull together a recruitment advertisement to send to the local newspaper or to post on the Internet. They do this without giving much thought to what they are doing or why they are doing it. "Have an opening, fill it," seems to be the mentality. Here's an example. A dentist office in a small town had a stable workforce for years until several employees retired. The manager's approach to filling openings was simply to put an ad in the local paper without giving much thought to the job requirements. The advertisement resulted in applications and new employees were hired, but over and over again the new employees had to be terminated during the probationary period for not being able to perform the job. This strategy for recruitment was ineffective.

To be sure, managers are often under pressure to fill job vacancies as quickly as possible. They generally do not want to overwork other employees who are performing necessary tasks, and they do not want to let critical work slow down or be left undone, so they want to get the recruiting done. These same managers would never consider spending a large sum of the organization's money for new equipment without careful planning. Shouldn't they spend just as much time and effort planning for employee recruitment as they do for purchasing the right equipment? Actually, recruitment probably deserves more time and attention. After all, employees hired today will be the employees making decisions tomorrow about how the company will spend its money! Of course, many managers *do* understand that spending some time developing a recruiting strategy will save their firms time and money later.

The first step in a successful recruitment plan is to decide on the objective for the recruiting process.[4] Is the objective to simply generate a few applicants and make a quick hiring decision? Or is the objective simply to recruit a large number of applicants and hope some are qualified to fill the openings? Knowing the best sources for recruitment and carefully crafting a recruitment message are parts of a solid plan. The person who talks with potential applicants also plays a key role in the outcome of the process, regardless if the person is formally a recruiter for the company or the manager of a small business doing her or his own hiring.

In Chapter 4, you learned how to conduct a job analysis and how to write a job description. The job description includes a "job specifications" section, which is a detailed account of the specific competencies employees must possess to succeed in the job. You can prepare a job description yourself or use one prepared by someone else. Either way, having a good grasp of a position's job duties and requirements is essential.[5] Even if the hiring manager has someone else prepare the ad copy, he has to give the preparer the information to include. This information, coupled with knowledge of the firm's goals and values, lays the foundation for the recruitment plan. In other words, before you can really look for ways to generate interest in job vacancies and identify high-potential individuals, you have to know what specific knowledge, skills, and/or abilities (KSAs) are needed to succeed in the job.

When you understand the required competencies, how do you recruit employees who have them? As the hiring manager, you are in the best position to know what type of employee will fit with the job and with the organization. Therefore, you need to be able to make strategic decisions during each step in the recruitment process. One of these strategic decisions relates to where you look to find employees.

A successful organization recognizes that it is important to recruit both internally (within the organization) and externally (outside the organization). As you read the following sections, think about an organization with which you are familiar and how that organization would likely go about recruiting employees. Think, too, about the advantages and disadvantages of using the various approaches described. Knowing these advantages and disadvantages will give you an opportunity to make informed decisions when you are recruiting employees.

## Internal Recruitment

Many organizations recognize that the best place to find employees for job openings is within the organization itself. Cintas, the largest uniform supplier in North America, makes sure that employees throughout the organization know about any open management positions. This company knows that it makes good business sense to retain current employees by giving them an opportunity for new challenges and promotions.[6] Also, employees who have greater opportunities within their organization are more satisfied than employees with fewer opportunities. Exhibit 6.2 provides suggested guidelines for ensuring that internal recruitment is successful.

**EXHIBIT 6.2**

## Guidelines for Successful Internal Recruiting

1. Develop and communicate job pathways for promotions and lateral moves within the company.
2. Develop a process for job posting that is accessible to all employees.
3. Ensure job advertisements clearly communicate job requirements and expectations.
4. Use employee records to identify potential candidates for open positions and invite them to apply.
5. Follow up with all internal applicants to acknowledge their applications and keep them informed of the progress of the search.
6. Treat internal candidates with the same level of care that you treat external candidates.

### Internal Recruitment Methods

Now let's take a look at some of the ways companies and managers inform employees about current job openings. As a manager, you need to be familiar with these methods so that you can decide how to conduct **internal recruiting**. Even if you have a staffing department, you need to ensure that the appropriate methods are used to identify the best applicants for you; your role in recruitment should not be a passive one. Company Spotlight 6.1 provides an example of how one company is working to use internal recruiting to help achieve a competitive advantage.

**internal recruiting**

the process of seeking job applicants from within the company

## COMPANY SPOTLIGHT   **6.1**

### Retaining Top Talent Through Internal Recruiting at Staples

Using exit interviews and employee engagement surveys, Staples, the office supply superstore, realized the main reason employees were leaving the company was lack of career mobility. They decided to do something about it.

Lisa Pueschel, vice president for talent acquisition and workforce planning, knew there were lots of opportunities at Staples for employees to advance. She knew this well because she herself had held eight jobs at Staples in her 18 years with the company. She realized, however, that there were a number of reasons employees didn't always know about the career mobility opportunities that did exist. The reasons identified include:

1. **Lack of information:** Job websites show open jobs but don't make it easy for employees to connect their skills and experience to those jobs.
2. **Unclear career paths:** Employees with interests outside their current department have difficulty moving to a department with a better fit.
3. **Talent hoarding:** Managers may be reluctant to "give up" a good employee, even if it would mean a promotion for that person.

Using this information, VP Pueschel encourages managers to think about "talent exporting" and "talent importing." The idea is to open up more opportunities to recognize the talent within the organization rather than focusing on external recruiting. To achieve this goal, Staples focuses on supporting internal mobility through stakeholder buy-in, using a proactive process, and making career paths visible. Senior leadership was easier to convince to take this new approach than hiring managers, so tools were developed to help hiring managers become more comfortable with the process. These tools focus on developing talent, and use of a career platform called Career Pro to help employees more easily match their knowledge, skills, and abilities (KSAs) with available opportunities. The company's ultimate goal is to fill more positions internally than externally at the higher levels.

*Sources:* Pueschel, Lisa, "The Business Impact of Recruiting Your Own Employees," blog.smashfly.com, September 11, 2017, blog.smashfly.com/2017/09/11/internal-recruiting-strategies-from-staples-business-impact-of-recruiting-employees/; Maurer, Roy, "Staples Encourages Internal Mobility to Retain Top Talent," shrm.org, July 6, 2017, https://www.shrm.org/resourcesandtools/hr-topics/talent-acquisition/pages/staples-internal-mobility-retain-top-talent.aspx .

Perhaps the simplest way internal applicants are recruited is through word of mouth. A manager has a job opening and talks to other managers or employees to find out about possible internal candidates. This technique is not always the most effective, though. More formal techniques will ensure that managers are identifying the most qualified candidates. Formal techniques also ensure that employees have an equal opportunity to find out about openings and apply for them.

A job posting system is the most frequently used approach to notify current employees about job openings. This approach can be as informal as posting a note on the cafeteria bulletin board or as formal as having job announcements listed in the company newsletter and posted on the company intranet. The goal of **job posting** is straightforward—to get word of a job opening out to as many employees as possible within the company. An intranet, an internal website for employees, allows a company to access a wide internal applicant pool. When using an intranet for job postings, managers need to make sure that it is just as easy for employees to find jobs within the company as it is to find jobs at other companies.

Companies that use a human resource information system (HRIS) have an added way to identify internal candidates for job openings. These companies create a searchable database referred to as an **employee inventory**, which can be used to identify employees who meet certain job requirements. Employees who match the posted job criteria can be automatically notified about the opening, and managers can receive lists of names of qualified candidates. Managers can then contact these employees and encourage them to apply for the job. If a company needs an electrical engineer with three to five years of experience in Asia, for example, a search of the employee inventory produces a list of employees within the company who meet those job requirements. The hiring manager can review recent performance appraisals and talk to supervisors rather than having to solely rely on references for performance-related information. This internal information puts the hiring manager in a much better position to determine how well a particular employee will perform in the new job. After all, past performance is generally the best predictor of future performance.

Many companies have embraced the idea of having an employee inventory as part of their HRIS. Companies have found, however, one critical challenge related to using such a system. For the inventory to be effective, the information must be kept up to date. That sounds like it shouldn't be a problem, but often it is. Some companies request their employees to enter the data themselves through an intranet portal; other companies maintain the data through the company's human resources (HR) department. If employees fail to enter the data, or if the HR department doesn't get the information for updates, the usefulness of the inventory is limited.

### Advantages and Disadvantages of Internal Recruitment

Organizations realize that there are tangible and intangible advantages to recruiting internally. Internal recruitment can be more cost-effective than running ads or engaging in external recruiting. Existing employees are already familiar with the company's operations, which cuts down on the time and money it takes to train them. In addition, current employees like being given opportunities for advancement. Employees want to know that their employer recognizes their value to the company. When employees are given opportunities for jobs they want, such as through promotions, they are more likely to be committed to the company, more loyal, and more productive. And, as we have mentioned, the firm's hiring managers also have access to applicants' performance appraisals and can talk to the employee's supervisors. Internal candidates also are more likely to fit the company's culture.

**job posting**

the most frequently used technique for notifying current employees about job openings within the company

**employee inventory**

a searchable database that can be used to identify employees who meet certain job requirements

Sometimes companies need new ideas or want to change their corporate culture, or they need to increase the diversity of their workforce. These companies know that the best way to reduce "inbreeding" and to increase diversity is to bring in new employees rather than promote current employees who are already entrenched in the company's way of doing things, especially when there is little diversity in terms of demographic and/or personality attributes in the existing workforce. Bringing in "new blood" (new employees) does not come without a cost, however. Managers need to be aware that employees who apply for openings and aren't selected may become disgruntled, be less productive, or leave the company. Of course, promoting or transferring an employee internally creates a new vacancy elsewhere in the organization. Consequently, even when companies recruit internally, they need to look externally to build their workforces at some point. In the next section, we examine the options for external recruitment.

## External Recruitment

An organization that cannot fill jobs internally, or that has decided "new blood" is needed, can choose from a wide range of sources for recruiting job applicants from outside the organization. When we think about **external recruiting**, we often think about advertisements, job fairs, and the Internet. Choosing an external recruitment source is often dictated by several factors, including the nature and location of the job.

**external recruiting**
the process of recruiting employees from outside the organization

A sign observed on the back of a pickup truck traveling down the Beltway in Washington, D.C., read: "Plumbers and Foremen Wanted." The message included a telephone number. Clearly, someone believed that this advertisement would attract workers. What were the underlying assumptions in this approach? First, someone had assumed that the truck would be driven and/or parked in locations frequented by plumbers and foremen or plumber and foremen "wannabes." The second assumption was that those individuals would be the kind of employees needed by the company; that is, they would have the required competencies and fit the company's culture. (It is important also to add here that we are assuming that the recruiter was using "foremen" as a generic term like "chairman" and not in an attempt to limit recruitment to only male applicants!)

In general, two factors have the greatest impact on where recruiting should take place. First is the skill level of the job. The higher the skill level, the harder it may be to find qualified candidates. This second factor is related to the first: The harder it is to find qualified candidates, the broader the geographic area in which you must search. If you are recruiting a vice president of operations for a multinational company and you either don't have someone internally who is qualified or you want some fresh ideas and perspectives, the search will likely need to be far and wide. In contrast, recruiting for a plumber would not likely require a large, national recruitment campaign. An advertisement in a local paper or a sign on a truck would be sufficient. The two factors together—skill level of the job and geographic location—are used to identify the relevant labor market for the recruitment campaign. To summarize, the **relevant labor market** is the location in which one can reasonably expect to find a sufficient supply of qualified applicants. Going back to the advertisement for plumbers and foremen, we see that the relevant labor market was presumed to be the area in which that truck was being driven—the metro D.C. area.

**relevant labor market**
the geographic location in which one can reasonably expect to find a sufficient supply of qualified applicants

Let's take a more detailed look at external recruitment methods. In some organizations, a manager will have assistance for developing and implementing an external recruitment strategy. In other organizations, the manager will have to do all of the external recruitment alone.

## Advertising

The newspaper has been the most popular place to advertise jobs over the years. Newspapers still are a viable advertising option, but the advent of the Internet has dramatically changed where people go to look for jobs. Employers, especially large corporations, now use the Internet more than they use newspapers to post jobs. However, in smaller towns and for smaller companies, the local newspaper can still be an important place for job advertisements. If the job requires high competency levels, is unique, or requires an in-demand skill set, large employers might advertise in regional, state, or national papers. The *Wall Street Journal* and *USA Today* are two popular, broadly distributed newspapers in which firms advertise high-level finance and corporate jobs.

The downside to newspaper advertising is the expense. In 2018, the cost of advertising a job in the *Washington Post* print edition ranged from $32.10 per line for a minimum three-line, single-column ad to run in the Sunday paper plus seven days on washingtonpost.com, to $39,000 for a full-page, color ad running one time. Compare those one-time costs to the $250 charge for a job ad to run for 35 days online at the *Post*. The online ad package includes the job listing, the employer's logo, and access to a résumé database.[7]

Over the past 10 years the number of job boards and other online resources for finding a job has increased. Company Spotlight 6.2 describes one extensively used online resource for finding new jobs, LinkedIn. Other well-known job boards are CareerBuilder.com, Monster.com, and indeed.com. Indeed.com is a search engine for jobs that aggregates job listings from multiple job posting sites. Users can filter job postings by location, salary range, and key words.

Log on to most company websites and you will find a "Careers" or "Job Opportunities" link there. The use of company websites to recruit job applicants has become a common practice. More sophisticated technology has made it easier to develop and use these sites. A typical company recruiting website will include a drop-down menu for career paths and another for location, or some variation of these menus that make it easy for the applicant to narrow the list of information about job openings. The design and content of employer sites are important to applicants, as is making the site mobile-optimized. Visitors to the sites form more favorable perceptions of a company when its recruitment website is attractive and contains information about career paths within the firm, along with detailed job descriptions. In fact, one survey of job seekers found that 78% of respondents agreed that the feel and the look of the prospective employer's career website was "moderately" to "highly important" in their decision to apply for a job.[8] Job seekers using online websites tend to pay attention to information with hyperlinks that include more text than graphic images or navigation tools. They also pay more attention to site content, especially on job openings, than site design, but content, design, and communication features all matter in attracting applicants.[9]

Companies often include on their career websites short videos of interns and employees talking about their work at the company or even videos of employees discussing their outside interests. Northrop Grumman is a leading innovative global security company that offers government and commercial customers technologies for applications related to cyberspace, undersea, and outer space. They provide a dynamic and interactive careers website that opens with the heading "Work on What Matters." Interested job applicants learn about the company culture and values, core capabilities, history of the company, and types of careers, and can listen to current employees talk about their experiences.[10] Recruitment websites such as this one are a better resource than most other types of advertisements for disseminating job and organization information. They present large amounts of information 24/7, and in an easy and convenient manner to anyone around the world.

# COMPANY SPOTLIGHT  6.2

## LinkedIn

LinkedIn is considered the top online site for professional networking. The company site boasts more than 562 million users from more than 200 countries and territories, and bills itself as a resource to connect the world's professionals, making them more successful and productive. LinkedIn provides a truly global professional network for finding jobs anywhere in the world.

The company was founded in 2002 and launched in 2003. Since 2016, the company has been owned by Microsoft. The company has multiple revenue streams and one of those is Talent Solutions. Through Talent Solutions, LinkedIn provides a platform to link jobs with job seekers, to help companies source active and passive talent, and to assist employers in building their brand. LinkedIn also provides other related resources. Companies can receive jobs reports and employees can see an annual ranking of the companies most sought after by professionals.

One company that has found LinkedIn to be an important source of talent is Zillow Group, an online real estate and rental marketplace that includes websites such as Trulia, HotPads, and RealEstate.com. The company credits LinkedIn with helping improve name recognition and serving as a central sourcing channel for acquiring talent, especially for finding passive talent.

*Source:* LinkedIn.com, https://about.linkedin.com/; "Zillow Group, a LinkedIn Talent Solutions Success Story," linkedin.com, https://business.linkedin.com/talent-solutions/case-studies/real-estate/zillow-group-linkedin-talent-solutions-success-story.

In addition to paying to advertise on job bulletin boards and using their own websites, organizations use online job posting bulletin boards at colleges and universities, and sites such as CareerOneStop.org, a U.S. Department of Labor website, or USAJobs.gov, the federal government's official job list. These publicly available online sites help employers provide information on job openings to large groups of potential applicants in a timely manner.

Professional organizations typically have their own job search websites. Members can post jobs for their companies and view and apply for jobs at other members' companies. The American Institute of Certified Public Accountants (AICPA), for example, provides specialized recruitment and career-management services targeted at professionals in the accounting field. Professionals can post confidential résumés online, view current job listings, and complete job applications on the site. Employers can post job listings, review the résumés of job seekers, and have background checks conducted on candidates who interest them. The AICPA resource is just one example of the specialized recruitment services available online. Some of these services are fee based.[11]

A company should not, however, just advertise online. Recruiting for certain jobs on the Internet might be less effective than recruiting through other sources. The Internet makes it easy for individuals—qualified or not—to apply for jobs, which increases the cost in terms of personnel time to review applications. Also, recall our discussion from Chapter 3 about what it means to be an affirmative action employer. To ensure that you reach the most diverse audience possible with your recruitment message, you should use multiple sources for advertising. After all, not everyone has a computer or has easy access to one. One last note about posting jobs online: Make sure the listings are kept up to date. Outdated listings signal to potential applicants that the company is not really invested in its human resources.[12]

## Educational Institutions

Along with newspaper advertisements, one of the oldest forms of employee recruitment is listing job openings on college campuses and sending recruiters to those campuses. Many companies like to recruit new, entry-level hires right out of college. Why do you think that would be the case? If you answered that these companies want younger workers, you are only partially right, and don't forget that age should not be a basis for recruiting employees. Some companies prefer new college graduates because they have less work experience and can be trained more easily to fit in with the company's culture. It is much easier to train someone to do things your way when you don't first have to "untrain" them if they have already learned to do things a certain way in another company.

When the economy is doing well, companies typically are more willing to spend money to send recruiters to college campuses. Recruiters are often looking for applicants for multiple jobs. The goal of recruiters is to identify individuals who are most likely to fit in with the corporate culture and who have the KSAs to do the job. The college degree serves as a baseline indicator that the applicant meets minimum requirements and can get up to speed fairly quickly to perform the jobs for which they are hired.

The typical college recruiting seasons run from September through November and from February through April. The fall recruiting season is increasingly the most important for many jobs. Companies often spend a great amount of resources to develop ongoing relationships with their preferred recruiting schools to ensure that the short recruiting periods are used most effectively. In addition to participating in campus interviewing sessions and career fairs, EY, a global leader in tax, assurance, and advisory and transaction services, offers leadership development opportunities to second- and third-year students to build brand awareness early.[13] Recruiters often speak to student professional organizations while on campus, are involved with alumni groups, provide students with internships, and build relationships with faculty. All these activities are geared toward networking to build the company image and to ensure the company can recruit the best and brightest talent available.

Companies that do not have the resources to send recruiters to campus or do not have a particular school on their preferred recruiting list often will accept résumés from students on a limited basis, conduct Skype or other virtual interviews with prospective job candidates, or both.

**externships and internships**

ways for employers to connect with students in the workplace who could become future employees

**Externships and internships** are particularly good ways for employers to connect with students who could become future employees. They bring prospective employees on site to consider a company's career opportunities. *Externships* are brief experiences (maybe as short as a few days or just a week) that expose students to a company and its jobs without students necessarily doing any work for the company. An externship is basically a job shadowing program, and students typically receive neither pay nor academic credit. However, they do receive excellent exposure to careers and companies.[14]

Internships are usually a month or longer, involve hands-on-work, and students receive college credit and/or pay.[15] They also give an employer more time to evaluate prospective employees for future opportunities. Internships should provide students with structured work activities, training programs, and mentoring opportunities.[16] In 2018, the National Association of College and Employers (NACE), reported that the average bachelor's level intern made $18.73 an hour.[17]

**career fair**

an opportunity for employers to interact with a large number of potential applicants at one time

## Career Fairs

**Career fairs**, or job fairs, provide an opportunity for employers to interact with a large number of potential applicants at one time. These fairs are often held on college campuses as part of the college recruitment activities, but can also be held in more public venues. Typically, employers set up booths where potential applicants can stop by, talk to recruiters, drop off résumés, and pick up information about the company. The recruiters have an opportunity to talk with the applicants and begin to gauge their fit with the company and job.

A newer approach to the job fair concept is the use of online resources to hold virtual career fairs. Like more traditional in-person career fairs, virtual career fairs can be open to multiple types of jobs and applicants or limited to certain types of companies or professions or selective types of applicants. AICPA, which we mentioned earlier in this chapter, hosts a virtual career fair through its CPA Career Center. Job seekers can explore job postings, learn about the companies, and engage in one-on-one conversations with representatives from the participating employers.[18] Virtual career fairs can be cost effective and allow companies to have access to a global talent pool. Company Spotlight 6.3 provides information about a company that uses virtual career fairs to connect veterans and their spouses with potential employers.

## COMPANY SPOTLIGHT 6.3

### Connecting Jobs with Veterans Through Virtual Career Fairs

VR, a division of Astound Virtual, uses virtual job fairs to help veterans find work. The goal of the company is to provide virtual recruitment solutions that make it easy for veterans and their spouses to connect with employers. Major companies such as Penske, Accenture, Chase, Travelers, and Verizon participate in these virtual career fairs.

According to the company website, more than 212,000 veterans and military spouses have found jobs through VR since 2011. During the career fairs, employers log in and interact with career fair participants. A military skills translator developed by the company assists veterans in translating what they did and what they learned in the military into civilian-sector language.

The company works with recruiters to design a virtual booth that can be accessible to applicants before, during, and after the actual career fair. Candidates apply in real time as they talk with the recruiters, and social networking can be integrated into the process. The virtual career fair saves both the employer and applicants the cost and time of traveling to a traditional career fair. Finally, it saves companies the expense of having to rent and set up space in a physical location.

*Source:* "About Us," Astound Virtual, http://www.veteranrecruiting.com.

### Employment Agencies and Employee Search Firms

Companies choose to seek outside assistance to find job applicants for a variety of reasons. The company might have a small HR department with limited time to conduct recruitment activities. The organization might decide that using a search firm specializing in a particular profession will provide access to more qualified applicants and reduce the time spent in the initial screening, thus making the search more efficient and productive. Several types of employment agencies and search firms exist: public agencies, private agencies, and executive search firms. Exhibit 6.3 provides a summary of the types of employment agencies and search firms.

**Public employment agencies** are not-for-profit agencies affiliated with the Department of Labor's Training and Employment Services. They are located in cities and counties throughout the country. In addition to processing unemployment claims, public agencies assist job seekers by providing career guidance, testing, training, and placement activities. They assist employers by giving them access to a

**public employment agencies**

not-for-profit employment agencies affiliated with local, state, or federal governments

## EXHIBIT 6.3

### Employment Agencies and Search Firms

| Type of Agency or Search Firm | Process and Payment |
|---|---|
| Public employment agency | Assists job seekers with career services and placement, and employers with finding applicants; services are affiliated with Department of Labor and offered at no charge |
| Private employment agency | Provides job search assistance for a fee paid either by the company or the individual |
| Contingency recruiting agency | Provides job search assistance to employers with payment made as a flat fee or a percentage of the first year's salary if the employer hires a candidate recommended by the agency |
| Retained agency (also referred to as *executive search firm* or *headhunter*) | Conducts searches for an employer on a retainer basis with the fee paid at the conclusion of predetermined steps; searches are usually for high-level executives |
| On-demand recruiting service | Provides search services to employers on a contract basis for actual time expended rather than receiving a set payment per search or hire |
| Recruitment process outsourcing (RPO) | Delivers specified recruitment services to employers on a contractual basis for one to four years; base monthly fee under contract is determined by the number of searches and related services provided |

**private employment agency**

an agency that provides job search assistance for a fee, and often to select professions only

**contingency recruiting agency**

an employment agency used by employers with payment made as a flat fee or percentage of the new hire's first-year salary, and paid only if the search is successful

**retained search agency**

an agency used for recruiting high-level positions, such as CEOs and vice presidents, with the agency paid a retainer for the work it does

**executive search firm, or headhunter**

see retained search agency

**on-demand recruiting service**

an agency that charges based on the time it spends recruiting rather than paying an amount per hire

large pool of skilled and unskilled workers. A nationwide database at CareerOneStop.org matches employers with potential employees. The best part for many employers and job seekers is that the services of these agencies are free.[19] Federal contractors are required by law to post many of their jobs with such government run agencies.

**Private employment agencies** provide job search assistance for a fee, and often to select professions only. The fees can be paid by companies listing jobs and/or by individuals using the agency's services to find jobs, although increasingly the latter arrangement is less common. **Contingency recruiting agencies** are paid by the company at the conclusion of a successful search. The recruiter conducts the initial recruiting, screening, and interviewing, and sets up the interview with the company. The agency is paid a flat fee or a percentage of the first year's salary of a hire recommended by the agency. **Retained search agencies** are often used for recruiting high-level positions, such as CEOs and vice presidents. The main difference between this type of agency and a contingency agency is when the fee is paid. In a retained agency, the employer pays a retainer for the agency to conduct the job search rather than paying upon completion of the search.[20] Retained agencies are often referred to as **executive search firms**, or **headhunters**. In working with these firms, it is important to ensure that they adhere to a code of ethics such as that developed by the Association of Executive Search Consultants (AESC). These firms deal with sensitive company information and sensitive information about candidates who may not want their current employers to know that they are considering other opportunities.[21]

A third type of recruiting agency is **on-demand recruiting services.** This type of firm charges based on the time it spends recruiting rather than charging per hire. The services of these organizations can be purchased weekly or monthly, and they are often a cost-effective alternative to contingency or retained agencies. Access to an on-demand recruiting service is particularly useful when a firm expands rapidly and needs a large number of new employees quickly. Such was the case for the biotech manufacturer Centocor, a subsidiary of Johnson & Johnson, when the U.S. Food and Drug Administration (FDA) gave approval for expanding production of one of its drugs. Centocor didn't want to hire more recruiters to find and screen hundreds of applicants for manufacturing and scientific jobs, and the company did not have the budget to outsource the work to a traditional recruiting agency. Outsourcing would have cost 20%–30% of the annual salary for each new hire. What the company needed was a temporary solution. Centocor turned to an on-demand recruiting service agency and was pleased with the results.[22]

During the economic downturn after 2008, many companies cut back on their recruiting staff to save money. As the economy improved, and not wanting to add fixed costs in the form of recruiting staff, companies started using a new type of recruiting resource known as **recruiting process outsourcing (RPO)**. This type of recruitment service works well for both large and small companies that have a steady demand for hiring. Contracts with outsourcers last for one to four years, with the outsourcer receiving a base monthly fee determined by the number of searches and related services provided. RPOs administer some or all recruitment functions for a firm.[23] Many RPOs include advanced analytic services as part of a bundle package of services for employers. Technology allows RPOs using talent analytic tools to measure long-term outcomes for employees placed in companies.[24]

**recruiting process outsourcing (RPO)**
an agency that contracts with an employer to administer some or all of the employer's recruitment functions

### Professional Associations

Most professions have one or more organizations or associations that individuals in the profession can join; some even have student chapters. These organizations provide a variety of services to members, such as access to resources about the profession, opportunities to network with others in the same field, information about job openings, and access to specialized research. A placement service is often a feature at annual meetings, providing an opportunity for members to interview for jobs. The jobs may also be listed on the association's website, as was described earlier for the AICPA.

### Temporary Employees

Hiring temporary workers is often a great method for recruiting permanent employees. Often, temporary positions are truly temporary in nature. However, many temp positions are considered **temp-to-hire**, meaning the employee comes in for a short period of time but may become a permanent employee. This approach to recruiting enables the company to learn about the capabilities of temp workers through observing how well they perform in the actual jobs they would be doing. The arrangement also gives temp employees the opportunity to evaluate the company and determine whether or not they want to work there.

**temp-to-hire**
a person hired to work for the company for a short period of time but who may become a permanent employee

**Gig workers** are independent contractors, also known as *freelancers*, who are hired by employers to perform specialized work. These workers are found across industries, but most often work in knowledge intensive industries and creative occupations where workers can work remotely. There may be as many as 150 million gig workers in North America and Western Europe. Many of these workers were once employed as full-time employees of organizations, often possess strong skills and abilities, and may or may not have chosen to be gig workers. Just as much care needs to go into recruiting workers from the gig economy as goes into recruiting other temporary or full-time employees.[25]

**gig worker**
an independent contractor, also known as a *freelancer*, hired by an employer on a temporary basis to perform specialized work

### Employee Referrals

Many companies rely on employee referrals to identify potential job candidates. This trend seems to have grown in recent years as a pushback to the sheer volume of applications received through job boards and the need to be more efficient in hiring talent. Some firms have even set goals for the proportion of hires desired from internal referrals. Further, some companies provide prizes and cash incentives to employees who make referrals that result in new hires once the firm is sure that a good hire has been made.[26]

Research has shown that recruiting programs such as these are among the most effective ways to recruit employees. Moreover, employees hired as a result of referrals tend to have lower turnover and experience greater job satisfaction than employees recruited through more formal approaches.[27] A study by researchers at the Federal Reserve Bank of New York reported that candidates referred by current employees of companies were twice as likely to get an interview and 40% more likely to be hired.[28]

This practice works because employees tend to refer people they already know and who they think will fit in with the company and be able to do the job. Referral programs also have the benefit of tapping people who might not be formally looking for a job, but who are friends or acquaintances with a current employee who has encouraged them to explore the opportunity.

The practice is not without its problems, however. The Federal Reserve Bank study noted earlier found that 71% of employee recommendations were of the same race or ethnicity, and 63% were of the same gender.[29] These data suggest that relying largely on employee referrals is likely to limit diversity in the company.

### Sourcing Applicants

**sourcing**

the process of identifying, attracting, and screening potential applicants who are not actively in the market for a new job

Over the past 20 years, companies have begun to use skilled researchers to identify, attract, and screen potential applicants who are not actively on the market. This process of finding passive job candidates is known as **sourcing**. It was first used in the United States during the late 1990s due to a shortage of skilled labor at the time.[30] As previously noted, social networking sites such as LinkedIn provide an excellent resource for sourcing passive candidates. Often, the recruiters in charge of sourcing applicants are very good at identifying people who appear to be good matches with a job and a company, even when the individuals aren't looking for jobs. These recruiters know how to acquire and use Web search tools that help them find passive applicants. Companies such as Oracle are increasingly expecting their recruiters to be adept at strategically sourcing and attracting passive job candidates.[31] Technology has made doing so much easier.

### Re-recruiting

**re-recruiting**

the process of enticing qualified former employees to return to the company to work

In a tight labor market, firms may decide to try to entice qualified former employees to return to their companies. This process is known as **re-recruiting**. These employees may have left for better opportunities, or they may have been downsized in a company restructuring. They are already knowledgeable about the firm's business, so they are able to get up to speed easily and quickly.

### Advantages and Disadvantages of External Recruitment

External recruitment is generally more costly than internal recruitment. There are media fees to pay to get an ad printed or posted, and there are agency fees to pay if an employment agency is used. Consequently, it is important to understand what may make the benefits outweigh the financial costs.

One clear advantage of external recruitment is the opportunity for a company to bring in employees who have a fresh perspective. Whether they are new college grads or employees with work experience at other companies, "outsiders" can help the company see new ways of doing business. In addition, recruiting externally allows companies to target specific competencies that their current employees might not possess. If a company is implementing new technologies or changing its

## EXHIBIT 6.4

Advantages and Disadvantages of Internal and External Recruiting

| Internal Recruiting | | External Recruiting | |
|---|---|---|---|
| **Advantages** | **Disadvantages** | **Advantages** | **Disadvantages** |
| More cost effective | Creates a new vacancy | Brings new ideas into the company | More expensive than internal recruiting |
| Existing employees know company operations and culture | Employees too entrenched in current operations and culture to make needed changes | Employees who will help change the culture can be recruited | New hires have to learn company operations and culture |
| Advancement opportunities motivate employees | Employees not selected may become problematic and/or leave | Can bring in needed skills | Lack of performance data |
| Performance data available for applicants | Existing employees may not have needed skills | Opportunity to change diversity profile of the firm | Existing employees not selected may be resentful |

strategic priorities, it might have to look outside for people with the skills it needs. To be successful, however, managers must understand which external recruitment source is optimal for filling a particular position. Managers should be cautious when recruiting externally. Bringing in outsiders can upset internal applicants who didn't get the job, resulting in lowered morale and productivity on their part. Exhibit 6.4 summarizes the advantages and disadvantages of internal and external recruiting. The appendix to this chapter discusses how to measure the effectiveness of recruiting methods.

# Maximizing Recruitment Effectiveness

A number of factors influence the effectiveness of a firm's recruiting efforts. These factors include the message conveyed in the recruitment advertisement, the personality and knowledge of the recruiter, and the willingness of the company to continually evaluate its recruiting activities. We will now give you some guidance on how these and related activities should be managed. As you study this information, keep in mind what recruiting is all about: identifying and attracting individuals who have the competencies needed for an organization to achieve its goals. Also, consider what your role as a manager would be in each activity.

## Preparing Recruitment Advertisements

Effective recruitment advertisements are no different from effective advertisements for products or services. Successful product ads first attract the attention of the consumer and then compel them to buy the product. Likewise, successful recruitment ads attract potential applicants and then convince them to apply for the job advertised. Even if a company is using the services of an employment agency, it is still up to the company, and generally the hiring manager, to identify the information that needs to be included in communications designed to attract potential applicants.

## Developing a Recruitment Value Proposition

In the late 1990s, employers were having a hard time attracting employees. As a result, they started paying more attention to how marketers persuaded customers to buy goods and services. Employers subsequently adopted and applied marketing concepts such as *creating a value proposition* and *branding* to recruit employees. Now, recruiters talk about creating a value proposition for recruiting employees, especially for recruiting top talent. A **recruitment value proposition** helps potential applicants differentiate what one company offers to its employees versus what other companies offer.

According to J. W. Marriott, Jr., the CEO of the Marriott hotel chain, people looking for jobs are just as conscious of value as consumers shopping for products or services.[32] Marriott and other companies that offer successful value propositions have designed both their jobs and corporate cultures to attract the talent they need now and in the future.[33] These companies focus on aligning all their HR management activities with their recruitment activities. They know what sets them apart, and they communicate this message throughout the recruitment process. Communicating their corporate culture is just as important as communicating their job openings.[34]

The recruitment value proposition conveyed to potential employees includes information about a job's duties and associated working environment, total rewards offered by the firm, and the company's corporate image. In fact, the information found in most recruitment ads can be grouped into these three categories.[35] The nature of the information presented makes the difference: Unlike traditional recruitment communications, a value proposition lets prospective employees know what they will experience when working for the company. The experience can include everything from the level of compensation and type of leadership development opportunities the position affords to the nature of the work environment. The critical component is to know what your target audience is looking for and to let the potential employees know what the company can offer relative to that.

The value proposition is different for each company. It helps a potential applicant understand what day-to-day life in the firm would be like and compare jobs across companies.[36] A well-designed value proposition and accompanying brand can help a potential applicant decide whether there is likely to be a good person–organization fit. Those who perceive a better fit are more likely to want to work for the organization.[37] Therefore, as a manager, you need to carefully consider what you are communicating to prospective employees throughout the recruitment process, both in printed form and in person. If your advertisements imply certain values, but your actions and words (or those of other employees during the interview process) convey something else, you have a very real problem to address.

Once a company has specified its value proposition, it can turn its attention to developing a brand to embody that proposition and help the company become an employer of choice.[38] **Employer branding** involves developing a long-term strategy to manage how a firm's stakeholders, including its current and future employees, perceive the company. Like product branding, employer branding is about creating a connection. In this case, the connection is between the potential applicant (either external or internal) and the employer rather than between the customer and the product.[39]

In 2017, B&CE, a not-for-profit organization that provides employee benefits products, was recognized with the Personnel Today Employer Branding Award. When the organization wanted to create a more cohesive workplace culture, it did so by focusing on creating simplicity, showing compassion, and keeping promises. These values became embedded in recruitment activities such as job ads, employee onboarding, and recognition programs. This branding effort is credited with helping reduce employee turnover, receiving high marks as a great place to work, and winning two local business awards.[40]

---

**recruitment value proposition**

a marketing concept used to design the advertising message in such a way that potential applicants can differentiate what one company offers to its employees from what other companies offer

**employer branding**

developing a long-term strategy to manage how a firm's stakeholders, including its current and future employees, perceive the company

# Writing a Recruitment Message

A recruitment advertisement should be written to convey the value proposition and the brand, as well as other basic job and company-related information. Recruitment advertisements that provide visual cues and specific information about the job and the company, along with personally relevant information, will generate more applicants.[41] Individuals are more attracted to jobs for which they have more information, especially when that information is specific about job or company attributes such as benefits, location, culture, and job requirements.[42] The information reduces the amount of uncertainty job seekers have about a particular job opportunity. When writing an advertisement, it is useful to think in terms of why a highly talented person would want to work at the company.[43] Providing little information in the advertisement tends to reflect poorly on a company and signals to potential applicants that the company does not value its employees highly enough to create a persuasive, informative ad designed to attract good workers.[44] Using more gendered wording (e.g., masculine- versus feminine-oriented language) in job advertisements can result in gender inequality. Using words such as *ninja* and *dominate* have a masculine connotation and may result in fewer women applying for the jobs, while *supportive* and *collaborative* are still widely associated with femininity which may keep men from considering whether or not to apply.[45]

Exhibit 6.5 provides tips on writing successful print ads. At the very least, it is important to include a brief description of the job and its minimum requirements, as well as information about how to apply for the job and any deadlines. Most of the research about successful recruitment ads has focused on newspapers and similar media, such as trade journals. Unfortunately, because of the costs involved, ads placed in print publications such as these are often limited to the bare essentials.

As already noted, online advertisements can be much more detailed than print advertisements. Printed ads are typically presented in a linear manner so individuals are passively exposed to the information in them. Online ads, on the other hand, allow individuals to actively search for information and find the information of most interest to them. If an advertisement is posted on a company's website, various links to other pages of content can be included. Many companies include links to streaming video of current employees talking about working for the company. Regardless of the format, the ads must focus on the target audience's needs and communicate the information in an easily understood and accessible manner. Sometimes providing straightforward information is still the best route, as is inclusion of diversity cues such as pictures of diverse organizational members. Research has shown that including diversity cues encourage both Blacks and Whites to be more attentive in processing the information on recruiting websites.[46]

---

## EXHIBIT 6.5

### Minimum Requirements for a Successful Job Advertisement

- Job title
- Brief description of the duties
- Required education, experience, and skill level, as well as preferred levels if appropriate
- Work conditions (e.g., travel, standing for long periods of time, working outdoors)
- Compensation and benefits
- Information about company
- Equal Employment Opportunity (EEO)/Affirmative Action Disclosure
- Where and how to apply
- Application deadline

The requirements for a successful recruitment video are the same as for other recruitment messages. They need to be geared to the target audience, reflect the culture of the organization, and be of high quality. The content and quality, just as with other recruitment techniques, will be perceived as a reflection of the company and will affect the willingness of potential applicants to pursue job opportunities. Technology advances, such as artificial intelligence (AI) and omnichannel solutions, make it possible to personalize recruiting messages with a goal of reaching higher-quality candidates. These approaches enable the employer to collect data at every point of contact with applicants, allowing for even more personalized experiences and longer-term measurement of recruiting outcomes.[47]

## Recruiters

The recruiter plays a key role in the success of the firm's recruitment efforts. Generally, there are two categories of recruiters: professional recruiters and hiring managers. Professional recruiters find applicants to fill open positions. They can be company employees or work for employment agencies. Hiring managers are involved in identifying and attracting potential employees. If you are working in a small company, you may have responsibility for the entire recruitment process. As a manager in a larger company, your role will be to ensure that the professional recruiters have the information they need to assist in filling open positions and to provide your input on applicants of interest.

Research has consistently shown that how the recruiter is perceived and the ability of the recruiter to convey information about the job and the company affect the willingness of individuals to apply for jobs.[48] The warmer the personality of the recruiter and the more the recruiter knows and conveys about the job and the company, the better.

Professional recruiters and hiring managers need to be trained to convey the company's value proposition and brand in an effective manner. They should be trained on equal employment opportunity (EEO) issues so that they do not discriminate in the recruitment process, either intentionally or unintentionally. The training should also address issues such as false representation. Telling a recruit that the job will provide certain benefits that it does not, and inflating the firm's financial position, are examples of possible false misrepresentations that can lead to the company being sued.[49] We will discuss more about legal issues such as these later in the chapter.

## Realistic Job Previews

Recruiting is a form of marketing. Decisions have to be made about what and how much information to give to job applicants. One line of research suggests that a balanced recruitment message will have the best long-term results for the company. A balanced recruitment message provides positive information about the job and company, as well as information that is likely to be less favorable to some potential applicants. Such a message is referred to as a **realistic job preview (RJP)**. One outcome of providing a realistic job preview is that individuals will screen themselves out of the application process when they realize that some aspects of the job or aspects of the company are not attractive to them. This outcome seems even more likely to occur when that information is presented by an interviewer rather than in written form.[50] Applicants who accept jobs with the company after being provided with an RJP are more likely to have accurate

**realistic job preview (RJP)**
a message that provides positive information about the job and company, as well as information that is likely to be less favorable to some potential applicants

expectations (which may be lower expectations) and are more likely to stay with the company longer.[51]

Like many hotels, Hilton and Aloft BWI airport properties had a significant turnover rate among housekeeping staff. When the regional HR director learned about RJPs, she decided to give the idea a try. The result was noticeable. Turnover that was at about 100% before the company started using the RJPs dropped by 30%. The RJP is rigorous. Applicants participate in a four-hour exercise in which they have to make a half-dozen beds. They sign a statement acknowledging that the exercise is a voluntary job tryout, but they do get a lunch provided by the company.[52]

## Recruitment Follow-Up

All too often, people apply for jobs and wait a long time to hear back from companies, or never hear from them at all. Remember that the recruitment process is concerned with generating interest in the company. Maintaining communication with prospective employees is an effective way to signal that you and your company value them. You may not have a job for an applicant now, but he may be just the right person for a future job, or may become a customer in the future.

At a minimum, a recruiter or manager should prepare and send a standardized, but personalized, letter to each applicant to let her know the status of the application, even if it is a rejection. Sending personalized responses is made easier with software designed to aid in the recruitment process. A well-done rejection letter can actually leave a favorable impression of the company with the applicant. Later, the applicant will be more likely to consider the company as an employer and will speak more positively of the company to others. In other words, it's important to always leave the prospective employee with a good impression of the company. You never know when you are going to need this person to come to work for you.

## Recruitment Effectiveness

The appendix to this chapter discusses a number of metrics that companies use to evaluate recruitment effectiveness. Yield ratios, cost-per-hire, time-to-fill, and managers' feedback are all techniques designed to measure the success of a recruitment program. The appendix also includes a discussion of benchmarking as a way to evaluate how well a company is doing with regard to its recruitment.

Principles

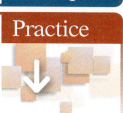

Practice

# Recruitment in Practice: Organizational Demands

Let's now take a look at the organizational, environmental, and regulatory factors that affect recruitment decisions, as described in Exhibit 6.6. As you will see, recruitment can play a key role in how well a company attains and maintains a competitive advantage. Without the right people in the right place doing the right things, a firm cannot be successful.

All companies need to recruit employees, but organizational demands and environmental influences differ. All effective recruiting starts with a clearly defined description of the job requirements. Recruiting cannot be effective unless a manager first has a solid understanding of what the person hired will be doing and how the job fits into the overall goals of the company. Without this information, a manager is likely to make decisions based on incomplete and/or nonrelevant criteria, resulting in less-than-optimal outcomes.

## EXHIBIT 6.6
## Recruitment in Practice

| Context | Practice Issues |
|---|---|
| **Organizational Demands** | |
| Strategy drives . . . | • Content of recruitment message |
| | • Choice of recruitment methods |
| Company characteristics determine . . . | • Use of internal versus external recruiting |
| | • Who does recruitment |
| Culture establishes . . . | • Recruitment value proposition |
| | • Balance of internal versus external recruiting |
| Employee concerns include . . . | • Appraisal of recruitment message |
| | • Perception of the fairness of the process |
| **Environmental Demands** | |
| Labor force influences . . . | • Who is targeted for recruitment |
| | • How much recruitment is needed |
| Technology affects . . . | • How recruitment is managed |
| | • Skills recruited |
| Globalization impacts . . . | • How recruiting is done |
| | • Where recruiting is done |
| Ethics/social responsibility shapes . . . | • Response to value proposition |
| | • Truth-in-hiring |
| | • Target of recruitment |
| **Regulations** | |
| Regulations guide . . . | • Content of recruitment message |
| | • Recruiter words and actions |
| | • Recordkeeping |

## Strategy and Recruitment

To illustrate how the strategy of a firm affects recruitment, we focus on two aspects of the recruitment process—the content of the recruitment message and the recruitment methods selected. Once again, we will focus on low-cost versus differentiation strategies. Keep in mind that there are other strategies that firms pursue, but these two are particularly important to consider during the recruitment process, and serve to illustrate why strategy matters.

### Content of a Recruitment Message

A central goal of a recruitment message is to attract applicants who will be the best fit with the job and the organization. The information conveyed to prospective applicants should address the advantages of working for the organization, such as relocation allowances and other special perquisites, as well as the nature of the competencies sought. The recruitment message needs to tell a positive story about why employees would want to work for the company. Remember that the goal for the company is to stand out during the recruitment process in order to attract top talent; recruitment is marketing, after all. At a minimum, the specific content of the recruitment message should reflect the types of people and competencies needed to ensure that the firm achieves and retains a competitive advantage in the marketplace for its products and services.

Here are two examples that help to illustrate how differentiation of a firm affects its recruitment message. A hotel focused on customer service will want to ensure that guests will return and will tell others to use that hotel. If you were a manager in this hotel, what would you want to focus on in the recruitment message? Most likely, you would emphasize that prospective employees should be customer service–oriented and have the ability to take initiative—two characteristics critical to providing hotel guests with a high level of service during their stay.

As another example, consider a biotech firm focused on innovation. How might the recruitment message you craft for this firm differ from the hotel recruitment message? Perhaps you would tell future employees about the firm's focus on adventure, change, learning, and discovery. You might also highlight major advances the company is known for in its field. The target audience for this firm will be very different from the target audience for the hotel, and the recruiting messages will reflect these differences.

Now let's take a look at the recruitment message for a firm that uses a cost leadership strategy. This strategy suggests focusing on outperforming competing firms by offering the lowest costs for products or services.[53] Issues related to efficiencies and cost reductions dominate. As discussed in Chapter 4, in these work environments, employees are typically expected to perform jobs that are narrow in focus and that involve standardized and repetitive actions. Think about how the recruitment message for Target, a retail store that sells a wide range of household, clothing, and other products, would differ from the recruitment message for Tiffany & Co., a high-end jewelry store. Both companies are in the retail industry, and both sell jewelry, but the similarities both begin and end there. Target wants to hire people who are willing to work at a minimal rate of pay, keep merchandise stocked efficiently on its shelves, and scan customer purchases at the checkout. Tiffany & Co. wants people who can provide a luxury shopping experience for its customers. These differences affect the recruitment message. Target has a low-cost strategy, while Tiffany & Co. has a differentiation strategy that focuses on customer service.

### Choice of Recruitment Methods

The type of strategy affects which recruitment methods a company is most likely to use. The recruitment methods emphasized by companies pursuing a low-cost strategy are likely to emphasize low-cost approaches. Word of mouth (employee referrals) is a low-cost method for identifying potential employees. Showing current employees talking about how much they like working at the company and emphasizing the benefits offered to them doesn't cost a lot and can add to a firm's value proposition as an employer.

Companies pursuing differentiation, in contrast, may have to be more focused in how they reach the targeted audience. Depending on the source of differentiation, they have to use the method that attracts individuals with the specific competencies required to achieve company goals. Trade publications and Web sources are two methods managers can use to target individuals with particular backgrounds or occupational skills. And because employees often associate with people with similar backgrounds and interests, employee referrals may prove to be a good approach to identifying people with special skill sets.

## Company Characteristics and Recruitment

The size of a company and its stage of development affect the extent to which internal recruiting is used, where recruiting is done, and who manages the process. Larger companies generally have more resources and a greater need for more formal processes than smaller firms. Older, more established firms are also more likely to have formalized recruitment processes. The size and stage of a company's development affect the extent to which internal recruiting is used versus external recruiting, as well as who does the recruiting.

### Use of Internal Versus External Recruiting

Unlike small businesses, large companies have a ready supply of labor from which to recruit new employees. As discussed in Chapter 5, larger companies are more likely to have **succession planning** activities in place and other tools, such as

**succession planning**
a process of planning for the future leadership of the company by identifying and developing employees to fill higher-level jobs within the company as they become available

**replacement chart**

a method of tracking information about employees who can move into higher-level positions within the company in the future

**replacement charts**, to identify employees who can move into vacant positions within the company. They are also more likely to have employee inventories and formal job posting systems that provide information relative to job openings for current employees. Small businesses do many of the same things, but they do so in a more informal manner. The owner of a small business might promote a current employee into a higher-level position because she or he knows the employee is capable of performing the new responsibilities. At other times, smaller organizations might lack employees with the needed competencies, leaving the manager no choice but to recruit externally.

### Who Manages Recruitment

A manager working in a large, established, multinational company will have different recruiting responsibilities than a manager working in a small, or even medium-sized, business. The large multinational company will have a formal recruiting staff responsible for creating advertisements, selecting recruitment methods, and managing the process. As noted earlier, your role as a manager is to work with the recruiting staff so they understand your needs and have your input on where to recruit for the job. Depending on your role in the organization, you might even be asked to make a recruiting trip to a college to talk to prospective applicants. In fact, a lot of organizations are sending employees to their alma maters to recruit students for internships and permanent positions.

In a smaller enterprise, you may be the recruiter. You would have to write the recruiting message, decide which methods to use to recruit, and manage the entire process. Unlike in a larger organization, you will not have a formal recruiting department to handle the details for you. More than likely, you will advertise in only a few places, and only locally, for most job openings. The local newspaper and a company website may be the recruiting media you use most frequently. Your recruiting responsibilities in a start-up company will be similar to those in a smaller business. As the company grows, more formalized processes and specialized staff will be needed to assist with recruitment. If the company stays small, you may remain responsible for many of the recruiting activities.

## Culture and Recruitment

Early in this book, we began talking about the need for alignment between how a firm manages its HR activities and its corporate culture. You should consider your firm's organizational culture in terms of all your recruiting activities, including the value proposition you offer and the balance you strike between recruiting candidates internally versus externally.

### Recruitment Value Proposition

A company should focus on communicating information about the specific job available, the reputation of the company, how the company positions itself in the marketplace, and the compensation and benefits that go along with the job and with working at that company. How the company presents this information will signal a lot about its organizational culture to prospective applicants. A company that emphasizes compensation and benefits in its recruitment message suggests to applicants that the culture values employees and rewards them accordingly. A company that emphasizes growth and opportunity in its recruitment message may be signaling that financial rewards are not as great, but that its cultural values provide more intrinsic rewards. Or a company could emphasize both a job's financial rewards and opportunities for growth and signal through the recruitment process that employees are highly valued and that the firm aims to be an employer of choice.

In addition, the people chosen to do the recruiting will communicate a lot about the company's value proposition. If a firm's recruitment activities are handled primarily by the company's staffing department, applicants are likely to perceive that a formal culture exists. If more employees are involved at various levels, the applicant is more likely to get a realistic view of the organization and believe that the firm's culture is more open. As a manager, your involvement in the recruiting process and what you do as you interact with prospective applicants will signal a lot about the culture of your company, whether you intend it to or not.

### Balance of Internal Versus External Recruiting

In many companies, every effort is made to fill a position internally before recruiting externally. Employees are groomed to move up in the organization. In other organizations, finding the best person for the job is most important, regardless of whether that person is internal or external. In still other organizations, key positions are almost always filled externally because these companies are seeking change.

As we have already noted, there are pros and cons to each type of recruitment strategy. A company should carefully consider the balance between its external and internal recruiting and decide how that balance affects the culture of the organization. If there is too much focus on internal recruitment, the company might become insular and lose its competitive edge. If there is too much external recruitment, employees will feel less valued and seek opportunities outside the firm. Thus, as a recruiting manager, it is important for you to understand your company's objectives and policies about internal recruitment and seek to ensure that you help maintain the appropriate balance.

## Employee Concerns and Recruitment

From an employee perspective, two issues are important during the recruitment process: how the employee/applicant appraises the recruitment message and the fairness exhibited during the process.

### Appraisal of Recruitment Message

When you look for a job, what attracts you most? The compensation or the benefits? The location? The culture of the company? We have already spent some time discussing the type of information that needs to be included in a recruitment message. Now, we want to turn to the importance of considering how prospective employees are likely to view that message. Certainly, not everyone is looking for the same things when seeking a new job. Some applicants will focus most on a company's culture. They may be interested in the development of their careers or opportunities to create innovative new products or services. Or they may be drawn to a company that values the work/life balance of its employees. Other applicants may focus on the tasks of the job itself. They want to know what they will be doing to see if that fits with their interests and competencies. Still other applicants will focus on the job's benefits and compensation level. Of course, there are applicants who pay attention to all three of these issues.

By emphasizing one aspect more than another, the company is sending a message about what it values most or what it believes the employees it wants to recruit will be looking for. Applicants are likely to evaluate different aspects of the recruitment message to discern whether they are interested in the job and whether they are a good fit with the company.

### Perception of Fairness of the Process

As a manager, you want to make sure that information in print and in other media, as well as direct recruiter communications, represents the job fairly and accurately. Overselling a job will have short- and long-term consequences for the company. Word travels quickly about an employer that is found to be less than honest in its recruitment activities—especially in small, local labor markets and highly specialized labor markets. If you engage in such practices, fewer applicants will respond to your firm's future recruitment efforts. In addition, as a manager, you will be put in the position of having to deal with unhappy new employees who feel they were misled in the recruitment process. In contrast, a credible employer will attract a large applicant pool and employees who feel they were fairly treated.

As noted earlier, realistic job previews (RJPs) are one way to try to increase perceptions of fairness. Describing both the positive and negative aspects of a job will reduce the size of your applicant pool. However, applicants who accept jobs with the company after being given an RJP are more likely to view the recruitment process as fair and stay with the company longer.[54]

# Recruitment in Practice: Environmental Influences

Along with organizational demands, companies must account for environmental influences when conducting a recruitment campaign. The labor force, technology, globalization, and ethical and corporate social responsibility issues all affect what employers do to recruit employees.

## The Labor Force and Recruitment

By now, you should be well aware that a critical element of a successful recruitment plan is directing your message to the right audience. The nature of the targeted labor force also affects how much recruiting you will have to do to yield the number of employees required to achieve the company's goals. Let's now look at both of these aspects.

### Target of Recruitment

When companies are recruiting, they naturally want to target employees who have the competencies they need. In addition, most companies understand the importance of targeting a diverse applicant pool. The changing demographics of the labor force in many parts of the world—not just the United States—mean that companies have to be open to diversity to recruit the most qualified workers.

Employers limit their ability to attract needed workers when they either intentionally or unintentionally target their recruitment messages to a young or nondiverse population. Older workers, minorities, and individuals with disabilities are often highly qualified potential employees. In 2018, older workers represented 23.1% of the U.S. workforce, up from 13.4% in 2000. Goldman Sachs and Massachusetts General Hospital are companies that have recognized the value of hiring older employees by actively recruiting them.[55] As a manager, you have a particular responsibility to oversee the recruitment process to ensure that it is managed in a nondiscriminatory manner. Let's take a look at some of the groups you might target with your recruitment efforts.

We have already noted that baby boomers represent the largest segment of the workforce. This generation is now reaching retirement age at the same time as there are fewer new entrants into the workforce.[56] And this is not limited to the workforce in the United States. Other countries around the world, such as Canada and Japan, are addressing similar issues. To cope with this trend, companies need to take a proactive stance and develop recruiting plans targeted at these older workers.[57] Many older workers actually need to and want to work, and they want to know that their contributions are valued.

Companies that target this age group recognize their strong work ethic, willingness to work nontraditional hours, reliability, and invaluable experience. KPMG, an auditing, tax, and advisory firm, has found older workers to be more dedicated and to bring credibility to client relationships because of their experience and dedication to the company, unlike younger workers who plan to move from company to company.[58] UPS, a large packaging and delivery business, actively recruits its retirees, especially to help meet the holiday rush.[59]

Recruiting minorities is a plus for the reputation of businesses as well. For many years, Avon Company, a global leader in the beauty-products market, was selected as one of *Fortune*'s "50 Best Places for Minorities." The company has also been recognized as a best company to work for by *Working Mother* magazine, *Latina Style Magazine*, and *Hispanic Magazine*. These honors result in part from the company's efforts to recruit more minorities to its workforce in the past 10 years.[60] Many other companies actively recruit minorities as well. After all, if the company's customer base is going to be diverse, shouldn't the employee base be the same?

Individuals with disabilities make up a large segment of the workforce and are excellent candidates for many job openings. Cisco Systems, a computer networking company, regularly recruits disabled individuals. The company knows that doing so makes good business sense and increases the diversity of its workforce. Additionally, Cisco is committed to creating technology tools that enable more individuals with disabilities to engage in meaningful work. Company Spotlight 6.4 describes Cisco's Project LifeChanger, designed to empower workers with disabilities.[61] AT&T and Pepsico also emphasize empowerment and success for their disabled employees.[62]

All is not rosy, however, for disabled workers. Recall that in Chapter 3, we noted both the increase in the number of disability claims against employers and the even larger increase in monetary awards made to settle claims. While the opportunities have increased, there is still much work that needs to be done to identify and provide opportunities for this segment of the population. In 2017, the unemployment rate was 4.2% for people without disabilities, but 9.2% for people with disabilities. Many employers continue to perceive that individuals with disabilities do not have the skills to do the work required or would not be productive, and so do not even give them a chance to demonstrate otherwise.[63]

## COMPANY SPOTLIGHT 6.4

### Project Life Changer—Cisco Focuses on Empowering People with Disabilities

In 2016, Cisco launched Project LifeChanger. This initiative came out of Cisco's Innovation Challenge and was the result of a collaboration among the company's employees, the National Council for Vocational Rehabilitation, technology companies, not-for-profit employment service agencies, and the state of California. Cisco recognized that individuals with disabilities face physical barriers to working and issues related to technical accommodations, transportation, and bias about their capabilities.

Now, as a result of Project LifeChanger and the innovative work of volunteers, people with disabilities can join and contribute to work teams at Cisco. Included in the resources that enable individuals to transcend barriers are Cisco's Video and Collaboration technologies.

This award-winning program is available at Cisco locations in California, India, Belgium, and Brazil. As a result of the program, around 100 people with disabilities who otherwise might not have been hired are now part of the Cisco workforce. The value to the company of hiring these talented workers with disabilities and providing the resources for them to overcome barriers has been tremendous. Outcomes include high retention, low error rates, low absenteeism, and twice the productivity of their peers.

*Source:* "Cisco LifeChanger," https://www.cisco.com/c/dam/en_us/about/inclusion-collaboration/life-changer.pdf; Cisco— Project LifeChanger," *Diversity Journal*, February 25, 2017, http://www.diversityjournal.com/16576-cisco-project-lifechanger/.

### How Much Recruitment Is Needed

In September 2018, the unemployment rate in the United States was only 3.7%.[64] When the unemployment rate reaches this low, companies have to recruit extensively to attract potential employees. Keep in mind, however, that the labor market is seldom tight for all jobs in all locations. Nor does a tight labor market mean that all qualified workers obtain employment. Thus, as a manager, you may find yourself having to heavily recruit for some jobs at the same time that you have a large number of applications for other jobs. The overall unemployment rate and nature of the relevant labor market in terms of skills and location will determine how much recruiting has to occur. How you define your target group also influences how much recruitment is needed. In general, the broader the targeted recruitment pool, the less recruitment effort needed.

## Technology and Recruitment

We noted earlier in the chapter that technology has heavily influenced how recruiting is done. Technology also influences how companies manage the recruiting process and the types of skills for which they recruit. The choices you make about how to use technology in the recruiting process can make your job as a manager both easier and more difficult. The use of technology can make your job easier by automating many of the processes, such as résumé collection, and more difficult because you are likely to have more résumés to review.

Additionally, companies are using social media in two ways to recruit applicants. For college students, one campus recruiter suggests using mobile-optimized career websites, conveying information via text, and using mobile and geotargeted ads.[65] Further, social media sites such as LinkedIn and Facebook enable recruiters to discover who in the company an applicant may already know, allowing the recruiter to gather additional information from that person about the applicant's fit with the company.[66]

### How Recruitment Is Managed

Online job posting and sourcing of passive applicants are two recruiting approaches that we have discussed that didn't exist prior to 1991, the year the Internet became readily available. Technology affects recruiting in other ways as well. Companies with an *enterprise resource planning (ERP)* system—a system that integrates information from different functional areas across a company--can use the Web recruitment function included with that program. Another option is to purchase a *recruitment application package* from a software vendor. These programs are often tailored to a particular industry or target businesses by size. Such a program can link to a company's human resource management system (HRMS) or stand alone. The third option involves using a Software-as-a-Service (SaaS) provider, a company that hosts software in the cloud so your company doesn't have to manage it. The decision about which route to take should be driven by the strategy and the resources of the organization. A company with a low-cost strategy may choose to go with an SaaS to avoid investing heavily in computer hardware and software and having to recruit software and personnel to manage their upkeep.

Some of the software available for posting jobs and collecting applications online can track and screen applications and résumés, reducing the time-consuming résumé-review process. Previously, managers and recruiters had to personally review each résumé and application to determine who should be considered for job opportunities. Now, résumés and applications can be entered online or scanned into résumé tracking programs. The programs use search criteria to determine whether applicants have the key KSAs the job and organization require. Additionally, companies are using data analytics and predictive modeling in the recruiting function. Such processes will enhance the firm's ability to optimize its search for talent and its ability to match applicants with jobs.[67] However, firms need to exercise caution when employing technology for job searches. Amazon recently had to quit using an AI tool to help with recruiting when it was consistently shown to lead to bias against women. The problem resulted from the AI tool reviewing male-dominated resumes from the past 10 years at Amazon to come up with its algorithms.[68]

Online recruiting on company websites has given employers a unique opportunity to aim their recruitment efforts at a more diverse workforce. Visuals can be used to communicate the company's focus on diversity. For instance, the career section for many company websites includes a number of photographs representing employees. Generally, these pictures show a diverse group of people in terms of race, ethnicity, color, gender, and age. It is not uncommon for a site to include a picture of someone in a wheelchair to show the company's commitment to employing individuals with disabilities. Research has shown that this approach works.[69]

Beyond enhancing a firm's diversity efforts, technology has provided managers with many new tools for managing their recruitment efforts. A SHRM survey found that 84% of organizations used social networking sites to recruit potential job candidates, up from 56% in 2011. Kroger has found that use of social media enables the company to target recruiting campaigns more narrowly by focusing on zip codes in proximity to their stores needing to hire employees. The company has found that social media works well for reaching potential job applicants who might not see in-store or Web ads. They use social media recruiting for in-store hourly positions and some hard-to-fill jobs like loss prevention. The company can view where people tag other people they know who are looking for work. Social media recruiting basically acts as a word-of-mouth referral program.[70] Care must be exercised, however, to ensure that a reliance on social networks for recruiting does not eliminate older workers as they may be less likely to be "linked in." Additionally, as we noted in Chapter 3, use of social media may exacerbate the potential for discrimination against other protected classes because of the information available to prospective employers.[71]

### Skills Recruited

Technology has changed the skills required for many jobs and changed where employees work. Most people use some computer technology on the job but the nature and extent of that use varies considerably. Manufacturing plants, for example, increasingly rely on computers to help workers design and manufacture products and control the quality of their production. As a result, the individuals recruited to work in these plants are likely to need computer skills they would not have needed in years past. As a result, managers must ensure that the recruitment message accurately portrays the level and type of technological skills the firm needs.

Also, many jobs that require computer skills do not have to be performed in a specific location. As a result, the recruitment pool can be expanded. Many stay-at-home moms and dads, who often are highly computer literate, find jobs such as these very attractive. They are good potential targets to recruit for jobs where location doesn't matter but computer skills do.

## Globalization and Recruitment

Globalization affects employee recruitment in a number of ways. First, multinational companies have to consider the impact of national origin norms and values, as well as country laws, when recruiting globally. A single recruitment message will not work in multiple countries. Second, technology enables companies to recruit a larger pool of applicants. This larger pool gives a company the opportunity to select employees from a larger labor pool; however, it also allows many other companies to vie for the same group of skilled employees. Let's now look closer at how globalization affects how and where recruitment is done.

### How Recruiting Is Done

Recruiting on a global scale complicates the recruiting process because people from different parts of the world have different values and needs.[72] Thus, the recruiting message may have to be crafted in multiple ways in order to be viable for different target audiences. China provides a good example. Recruiting methods in China are similar to those in the United States. (The methods include advertising in newspapers, making campus visits, employing search firms, and so forth.) It is the value proposition that must be tailored differently to attract workers. Seldom is housing a job benefit in the United States. In China, where there is often a shortage of qualified workers for professional jobs and also a shortage of housing, companies that include housing as part of the value proposition have an advantage over companies that do not, especially when recruiting for senior positions, where such a perk is expected.[73]

To try to increase the effectiveness of the recruiting process, some multinational companies hire individuals as recruiters from the country where employees are needed. These host country nationals (HCNs) know the expectations and needs of the potential applicants, as well as what is and is not allowed during recruitment in the country. Other companies use a search firm that specializes in identifying talent globally or in a particular country. QualiFind is one such search firm. This company services the U.S. and Mexican markets but is part of a global network.[74] Honeywell Aerospace turned to QualiFind when it built a new *maquiladora* in Mexicali, a town in northern Baja. A *maquiladora* is a factory that imports equipment and materials and turns them into finished products to ship back across the border. QualiFind helped the manufacturer identify the 300 engineers it needed for the new plant, and it received approximately 25% of the first year's salary for each employee placed.[75]

Differences also exist internationally in terms of preferred recruitment methods. In some countries, newspapers would be effective; in other countries, word of mouth may be the best recruitment method. Managers need to remember that the Internet is still not available in every part of the world. Consequently, relying solely on Web postings might not yield a sufficient number of employees needed in some locales, especially in less developed countries. In fact, utilizing only that method might cause a company to miss out on identifying some highly qualified workers.

### Where Recruiting Is Done

As we have explained, the Internet certainly has broadened the ability of firms to find the employees they need anywhere in the world, and vice versa. If you need an employee in Bangkok, you can post the job on any number of international job sites and on your own corporate website, and you are likely to receive applications from all over the world. A number of restaurant firms, for instance, use the Web to attract the best job candidates from around the globe.[76]

In cases where the work can actually be done virtually, you can advertise in India for employees to work on a project with employees in two or three or more other countries. Technology, thus, opens up the labor market for many jobs. There is a caveat to all this good news about having access to workers all over the globe: More and more employers are looking for employees in the same world labor pool—a pool that at times is geographically dispersed, but not very large.[77]

## Ethics, Corporate Social Responsibility, and Recruitment

Companies have a great opportunity during the recruiting process to showcase their ethical practices and social consciousness. The value propositions they offer, truth-in-hiring, and the groups they target send signals not only to potential employees, but also to the world at large.

## Value Proposition Offered

Recall that one aspect of a value proposition is a firm's corporate image. *Fortune* magazine publishes a list of the 100 best companies to work for each year. The list includes companies such as Salesforce, Wegmans, Deloitte, and USAA. The survey used to develop the rankings includes information about trust, pride in the work, credible and respectful leadership, and camaraderie.[78]

Recruitment research also shows that the applicants' perceptions of the firms' corporate social responsibility is most influenced by the perceived ethical behavior of the firm.[79] If applicants perceive during the recruitment process that the firm is more ethical, they will find it more attractive as a potential employer. Thus, managers and other recruiters need to pay attention to both the specific ethical information the applicant receives during recruitment and what the recruitment process itself signals about the ethics of the company.[80]

## Truth-in-Hiring

What message is being sent by the recruitment tactics you use? For instance, is it okay to exaggerate claims about what the job candidate will get if he or she accepts the job? A judge in Texas ruled in favor of two diving students who were able to argue that they had been recruited under false pretenses. The divers were enticed to work for a Texas offshore oil company by being told they would get "plenty of diving work" and "get in the water immediately." Instead, the two were given land jobs. The judge ordered the payment of damages to them because there was enough evidence to indicate that the promises made were not true.[81] The number of lawsuits over lack of truth-in-hiring is increasing. This increase results primarily from two issues: (1) aggressive efforts of employers to attract employees in a tight labor market and (2) employees who are terminated and now seek recourse against their former employers. Often, these truth-in-hiring lawsuits, which are tort claims, occur when a job candidate has been lured from an existing, high-paying job by promises of great opportunities at the new firm and those promises fail to come through. Exhibit 6.7 provides guidance on preventing truth-in-hiring lawsuits. These lawsuits can be expensive because courts may award both compensatory and punitive damages.[82]

---

### EXHIBIT 6.7

### Guidance for Preventing Truth-in-Hiring Lawsuits

1. Don't exaggerate information about the company or job.
2. Be honest and give the candidate a realistic job preview (RJP).
3. Include disclaimer language in the offer letter to make it clear that conditions addressed in the letter represent only the company expectations.
4. Make sure the offer letter includes a statement that the offer is contingent upon a clean background check.
5. Include employment-at-will language in the offer letter.
6. Spell out any contingencies.
7. Specify compensation and benefits information on a pay-period basis rather than on an annual basis to avoid implying that the job is guaranteed for a year, and do not state amounts anticipated for commissions or variable pay.

*Source:* Based on Hansen, Fay, "Avoiding Truth-in-Hiring Lawsuits," *Workforce Management,* last modified December 11, 2007, http://www.workforce.com/articles/avoiding-truth-in-hiring-lawsuits.

**Targets of Recruitment**

Ethical and socially responsible companies convey their beliefs in the value propositions they offer, and they go a step further by actively recruiting employees who can live by the company's code of ethics. By focusing on finding the right people during the recruiting process, a company will have fewer violations of the code. In fact, a company code of ethics should be shared with applicants during the recruitment process and should include a statement about the values that are important to the company and the behaviors it expects of its employees.[83] Additionally, an ethical culture is related to the intent of employees to recommend their organization to others, which has significant implications for employee referrals.[84]

An ethical issue may arise when companies choose to poach employees from other companies, although that issue is debatable. Poaching, also referred to as *lateral hiring*, often occurs when there is a labor shortage for a particular type of worker. Before engaging in this practice, managers need to think carefully about what they are doing and how they are doing it. Companies need to realize that the employees that they recruit in this way are just as likely to go with the next good offer that comes along. One of the best ways to prevent employees from leaving is to create a strong sense of loyalty with them.[85] Poaching more clearly becomes an ethical problem when the primary reason for its occurrence is to garner trade secrets or other proprietary information about the employee's former company.

# Recruitment in Practice: Regulatory Issues

A business owner decides that he wants a cute, female college student to work in his hardware store as a sales associate. After all, someone who is young, attractive, and female might just bring in more customers. Doesn't he have the right to hire whomever he wants? Well, not exactly. He cannot target his recruitment activities in such a way that he discriminates or gives the appearance that he would discriminate against anyone on the basis of their race, color, religion, sex, or other protected classification unless he can show that the criterion is essential for the performance of the job. In this example, the owner would have a hard time showing that males and older workers cannot be effective as sales associates. Recruitment content, words and actions, and recordkeeping can all become problematic if not properly managed.

## Content of a Recruitment Message

When writing a recruitment message, it is very important to think about what is said. A seemingly innocent comment such as "Young, energetic workers sought for part-time opportunity" immediately tells older workers that they are not wanted. As we have explained, limiting entry-level positions to recent college graduates can be problematic and has the potential to lead to charges of age discrimination as well. A technology company, Textio, has a tool for improving how job postings are written and it employs an important feature: the software can identify biased language and suggest more appropriate wording. A research project by the company actually found that the average job post had twice as many masculine-tone phrases as feminine with the result that more men apply for the advertised jobs. Australian software company Atlassian used Textio's software and in one year increased the number of females being hired for technical jobs by 80%.[86] If your organization comes under an affirmative action plan (discussed in Chapter 3), you are required to indicate as part of the ad that the company is an EEO company. Often, a company that voluntarily has an affirmative action plan will include this information as well, hoping to attract a more diverse applicant pool.

Always keep in mind that all recruitment activities have to be nondiscriminatory. To foster affirmative action, part of a company's recruiting strategy has to be a desire to reach as many qualified applicants in underrepresented groups as possible. Recruiting managers often do this by advertising open positions at historically Black and historically Hispanic universities and at women's colleges. They also make sure that they advertise both in newspapers and on the Internet, and they list job openings with public employment agencies.

## Recruiters' Words and Actions

Employment recruiters need to understand the importance of not discriminating, either intentionally or unintentionally. As a manager, you will often be the recruiter. Even seemingly innocent comments to an applicant or to someone else about an applicant can be construed as discriminatory. Statements such as "We are really looking for a younger person," asking women if they intend to have children, and making offensive comments can be perceived as discriminatory. The first example suggests that age discrimination is occurring. The second example seems innocuous enough—like you are just making conversation. However, it might be construed that you believe that having children will disrupt a woman's work and career.

A research study conducted at one university in the U.S. found that the examples, words, and actions of recruiters from technology companies created a "chilly" environment for women, much like the job ads mentioned earlier. This environment served to discourage the women from applying for jobs at these companies.[87] Finally, making offensive remarks, such as telling an off-color joke or making suggestive comments sends a very negative message about your company's work culture and suggests that you might engage in discriminatory behaviors.

## Recordkeeping

A final concern regarding regulatory issues and the recruiting process is the need for careful recordkeeping. Employers need to retain résumés and applications as required by local, state, and federal laws. The ADA and Title VII require that résumés and applications be kept for at least one year. Other laws have similar provisions. And, if a company is required to be an affirmative action employer, it must document its recruitment activities to demonstrate that it has actually targeted underrepresented groups. We will elaborate more on recordkeeping requirements in Chapter 7 when we define the term *job applicant*.

## SUMMARY

Employee recruitment is a process that involves identifying and attracting potential applicants for available jobs within the organization. In essence, recruitment involves marketing the organization and the open jobs such that prospective employees want to work for the company. Creating a value proposition that communicates the vision and values of the company helps differentiate it from competitors and allows it to attract a larger pool of qualified applicants.

Before a company begins the recruiting process, it must develop a recruiting strategy. The first step in doing so involves reviewing the goals and objectives of the organization and understanding how jobs help it achieve those goals and objectives. A well-prepared job description provides managers and recruiters with the information they need for the next step—deciding where and how to recruit.

The company may decide to recruit internally and use a job posting process, employee inventories, or both to identify potential applicants. Some companies

have well-defined succession plans and executive development programs, which can be used to identify potential applicants for open positions. Internal recruiting programs such as these give the company a way to communicate how much it values its current employees. Internal recruiting is also cost effective because the employees are already familiar with many aspects of the organization; advertising jobs internally is also relatively inexpensive, especially compared to the high costs associated with some external recruitment activities.

Sometimes organizations want to hire people with new ideas. Firms can do so by using a variety of external recruitment sources, including advertising in newspapers and on the Internet, recruiting at colleges and other educational institutions, and engaging placement agencies to handle the recruitment activity. Along with fresh ideas, employees recruited externally bring with them the knowledge and experience they have gained from their previous jobs. They will have to be trained and oriented to the company culture, however. Also, current employees may be unhappy when external applicants are hired to fill the openings for which they applied.

A recruitment message must be informative and communicate information about both the job and the company. A recruitment message is like any other marketing message: It must attract the attention of those to whom it is targeted so that they will want to take action.

Recruiters play a key role in the success of the recruitment process. Ensuring that recruiters are warm, personable, and knowledgeable about the company and the openings it has will increase the likelihood that potential applicants will follow through and apply with the company. A realistic job preview (RJP) can help balance an applicant's positive and negative impressions of the job and the company. RJPs have been found to lead to higher satisfaction and better-met expectations on the part of applicants who continue in the recruitment process.

An organization's demands, including its strategy, culture, and financial resources, all affect what the firm does and how it does it during the recruitment process. Environmental influences such as technology, globalization, and the labor market also need to be considered when a company is designing a strategy. Host country nationals (HCNs) and global search firms are used in addition to the Internet for global recruiting, but it is important to remember that applicants in developing countries often do not have access to the Internet. Firms recruiting in those countries have to use other techniques as well.

A firm should ensure that its recruitment advertisements and other recruitment activities communicate to potential applicants that the company values diversity and supports EEO.

## KEY TERMS

| | |
|---|---|
| career fair | internships |
| contingency recruiting agency | job posting |
| cost-per-hire | on-demand recruiting services |
| employee inventory | private employment agency |
| employer branding | public employment agency |
| executive search firm | realistic job preview (RJP) |
| external recruiting | recruiting process outsourcing (RPO) |
| externships | recruitment |
| gig worker | recruitment value proposition |
| headhunter | relevant labor market |
| internal recruiting | replacement chart |

re-recruiting
retained search agency
sourcing
succession planning

temp-to-hire
time-to-fill rate
yield ratio

## DISCUSSION QUESTIONS

1. Earlier in this chapter, you read about a dentist in a small town who was having trouble hiring the right staff. When an opening occurred, the manager would place an ad in the local paper, but over and over again, the individuals hired didn't work out. What recommendations would you make to the manager to improve his recruiting strategy and gain a better outcome?

2. What is the relationship between job analysis and employee recruitment?

3. What are the challenges a company needs to consider when filling open positions externally? How can a company mitigate the possible consequences of external recruitment?

4. Define what is meant by the term *recruitment value proposition* and discuss whose responsibility it is to create this value proposition.

5. Your company has just undergone a great deal of growth and used a variety of recruitment methods to identify new talent to hire. What metrics would you use to decide which recruitment methods were the most successful?

6. A small, boutique hotel in Paris, France, and an international hotel chain headquartered in New York City are both looking for housekeepers. Describe the organizational demands for each company and how the demands would affect recruiting decisions.

7. The demographics in the neighborhood around the retail store you manage have changed greatly in the past five years. Instead of a primarily Caucasian and Black population, there are now large numbers of Hispanics and Asians. How would these demographic changes likely affect your recruiting strategy, and why?

8. Research how companies are recruiting gig workers. Develop a short slide show of best recruiting practices for these workers to share with your classmates. Be sure and include proper citations for resources used.

## LEARNING EXERCISE 1

Choose two companies in the same industry that have career information posted on their company websites. Review the information on their websites, using both a computer and a mobile device, and prepare a critical evaluation of each. Consider the following questions as you conduct your review.

1. How much detail is provided? Do the companies simply list their available openings, or do they provide an overview of what it is like to work at the company? What information is not included that you wish had been included?

2. What is the process for applying for jobs at each company?

3. Did you leave each website thinking that you had a good understanding of what it would be like to work for the company?

4. Did the company make it easy to use a mobile device to apply for a job? Why or why not?

5. Discuss how these websites increased or decreased your interest in working for these companies.

6. As a manager, what recommendations would you make to improve the quality of the sites, and why? Reference what you learned in this chapter about recruitment messages and advertising.

## LEARNING EXERCISE 2

Find a job description for a job of interest to you and develop an advertising recruitment strategy for that job.

1. Write the content for the advertisement.
2. What aspect of the ad do you think is most important, and why?
3. If you were a manager preparing to recruit for this position, what information other than the job description would you use to decide what to include in the ad?
4. Show the advertisement to at least two other people and ask them to give you feedback to improve the ad. Describe their comments and ideas and whether you agree with them or not, and why.
5. Discuss where you would advertise, and why you made the choices you did.
6. How would you measure success of your recruitment strategy?

## CASE STUDY 1: BOOZ ALLEN HAMILTON: DOES SOCIAL GOOD MATTER IN RECRUITING?

Did you know that each day in the United States, 1,500 people are diagnosed with heart failure? A key early indicator of heart disease is a decline in cardiac function. What do those two facts have to do with employee recruiting? For Booz Allen Hamilton, a management consulting, technology, and engineering services firm, a lot.

Along with cosponsor Kaggle, the world's largest online data science competition community, Booz Allen Hamilton invited data scientists from around the globe to help change how heart disease is diagnosed by participating in the second annual Data Science Bowl in 2016. Participants used data from the National Institutes of Health (NIH) and Children's National Medical Center to create algorithms to automate the process of assessing heart function. Three teams took home a total of $200,000 as a result of their participation in the 90-day competition.

Creating competitions such as this one addresses a recognized motivator for millennials: making an impact on their world. In fact, the idea at Booz Allen Hamilton started with a competition at one university focused on using analytics to address social issues. Expecting a few dozen participants, Booz Allen Hamilton was surprised when more than 150 participants from 11 universities showed up.

The 2018 competition invited competitors to participate in a 90-day event focused on creating algorithms designed to identify nuclei in cell images that will expedite the detection of deadly diseases. Winners split $170,000 in cash and prizes, including a personal AI supercomputer. In 2015, the first year of the competition, more than 1,000 teams from 70 countries signed up. The focus that year was on developing an algorithm to use underwater photos to monitor ocean health. The client was the Hatfield Marine Science Center.

Booz Allen Hamilton has found that the competition not only helps a social cause, but also attracts high-quality applicants to the firm. Participants in the Data Science Bowl are encouraged to apply for jobs at the company, resulting in hundreds of qualified applicants sending in their résumés. The company believes that the

competition sets it apart from its competitors. Participants recognize that Booz Allen Hamilton believes in making a difference, and that provides a competitive advantage to the company in recruiting data scientists in a highly competitive marketplace for such employees.

### Discussion Questions

1. Visit the website for the Data Science Bowl and Kaggle.com to learn more about the competition.

2. Critique the use of this competition as a recruiting strategy. What are the advantages and disadvantages? Are there any possible EEO issues with such a recruiting strategy?

3. Besides the opportunity to obtain a job with Booz Allen Hamilton, why do you think the competition has such worldwide appeal, especially for millennials?

4. Discuss whether you would participate in an activity such as this one in order to obtain a job at a company.

5. Find an additional example of how a company is engaged in corporate social responsibility activities that would attract millennials and Generation Z to apply for jobs at the company. Describe why the activity would entice applicants to want to work for the company.

*Sources:* Data Science Bowl, http://www.datasciencebowl.com; "Crowdsourced Solutions from the Second Annual Data Science Bowl Result in Algorithm That Could Transform Heart Disease Diagnosis," March 30, 2016, https://www.boozallen.com/e/media/press-release/booz-allen-kaggel-announce-2nd-data-science-bowl-results.html; "Booz Allen and Kaggle Launch Annual Data Science Competition," https://www.boozallen.com/e/media/press-release/booz-allen-and-kaggle-launch-annual-data-science-competition.html; "Booz Allen & Kaggle's Annual Data Science Competition Puts Artificial Intelligence to Work Accelerating Life-Saving Medical Research," 3BLMedia, January 16, 2018, https://3blmedia.com/News/Booz-Allen-Kaggles-Annual-Data-Science-Competition-Puts-Artificial-Intelligence-Work

## CASE STUDY 2: FASTER RECRUITING NEEDED AT INTUIT

Intuit is a software company that produces four products: TurboTax, QuickBooks, ProConnect, and Mint. The company's mission is "powering prosperity around the world." To accomplish its mission, Intuit needs to attract top talent, the majority of whom have strong technical skills. Until recently, the company could advertise for employees, bring them in for multiple interviews, and then make a decision about who to hire. With the lower unemployment rate overall in the United States and the higher demand for technology workers around the world, Intuit now finds itself needing to put candidates through one day of tests and interviews and make a quick decision—sometimes even making the offer the same day as the interview.

Founded in 1983, the company now has 8,300 employees worldwide and has received accolades, including being named a Fortune 100 "Best Company to Work For" for 16 consecutive years. The company also has been named a "Best Workplace for Diversity" and a "Best Workplace for Women." In fiscal year 2017, Intuit's revenue was $5.2 billion. The employee culture is one of innovation, action, and passion about the work that employees perform.

The company believes strongly in corporate social responsibility. With each Intuit Prosperity Bundle of TurboTax and QuickBooks purchased, the company donates $25 to a Kiva entrepreneur. (Kiva is an international non-profit focused on connecting people through lending and has a goal of reducing poverty). Overall, Intuit has donated 30,000 employee hours to charity, reduced their building carbon footprint by 64%, and made product donations worth $42 million.

### Discussion Questions

1. From all reports, Intuit provides a great work environment for its employees. Review the recruiting website of Intuit and read about the company at review sites such as Glassdoor.com and indeed.com. Based on what you have learned about effective recruiting strategies, what employees are saying about Intuit, and what the company says about itself, evaluate how well the website succeeds at creating a compelling recruitment message.

2. Based on your research to answer Question 1, discuss the value of websites that review companies from both an employer and potential employee perspective.

3. How would you describe Intuit's value proposition?

4. Discuss why you would or would not want to work for a company like Intuit if you had the type of skills for which they were recruiting.

*Sources:* Based on Colvin, Geoff, "Ready, Set, Jump!" *Fortune* (serial online). February 2018, 177(2), 44–52; available from: Business Source Complete, Ipswich, MA, https://www.scribd.com/article/369570093/Ready-Set-Jump; Donnelly, Grace, "These 'Best Companies to Work For' Are Hiring for More than 110,000 Jobs," *Fortune*, February 15, 2018, http://fortune.com/2018/02/15/best-companies-hiring-jobs/; "Careers," https://www.intuit.com/company/.

# APPENDIX

# Metrics Used to Evaluate an Organization's Recruiting Effectiveness

Companies frequently engage in activities without stopping to evaluate what is working and why or how the activities can be improved. Recruitment is one such activity. Companies often continue to advertise jobs in the same publications year after year, without evaluating the usefulness of doing so. Recruiters are tasked with identifying and attracting one of the most precious resources that the company will ever have. Yet, often recruiters are not held accountable for the number of employees they bring in to the organization—nor the quality of those employees.

Exhibit A6.1 provides examples of some of the metrics used to measure a firm's recruitment success. We will take a closer look at some of the metrics that companies typically track, including yield ratios, cost-per-hire, time-to-fill, and managers' feedback.

## Yield Ratios

We have already talked about some of the costs associated with various recruiting sources. Because these costs are so varied, evaluating the outcomes of each in terms of new hires made per source and retention per source provides valuable information to the company. Just because a recruitment source is cheap or expensive doesn't mean that it is effective. **Yield ratios** provide a metric of the effectiveness of recruitment sources. A yield ratio measures the outcome from using a specific recruiting source compared to the number of applicants generated by the source. An example of how yield ratios are computed is shown in Exhibit A6.2.

Based on the yield ratios shown in the last line of Exhibit A6.2, the online job posting was the better source of applicants who met the requirements to be interviewed.

**yield ratio**

a tool that provides a metric of the effectiveness of recruitment sources

---

**EXHIBIT A6.1**

## Commonly Used Recruiting Metrics

**Cost-per-hire:** Total recruiting costs—advertising, travel, office rent, equipment, staff salaries, search-firm fees, background checks, and more—divided by the number of new hires; focus is recruiting expenses

**Staffing efficiency ratio (recruiting efficiency index):** The firm's total recruiting costs divided by the total starting compensation of new hires; more precise than cost-per-hire because it accounts for the different pay levels of new employees

**Time-to-fill/start:** The average number of days from the day a manager requests a job be filled to the day a candidate accepts an offer, or the average number of days from the requisition to the employee starts work; measures how quickly jobs are filled; indicator of company's ability to hire

**Quality of hire:** Gauges performance of the employee and is a way to measure employee contribution to the company; typically, the performance review process will provide this data with assessment done three, six, or more months after the person starts the job

**Hiring manager satisfaction:** The hiring manager's satisfaction with the performance of the firm's recruiters and his or her new employees; managers can complete a survey using a ratings scale to measure a recruiter's timeliness of contacts, sourcing, quality of referred candidates, scheduling, and other factors

**First-year turnover:** The number of employees who leave a firm divided by the firm's total number of employees in a year; rough indicator of the quality of a firm's hires; can be gauged for each recruiter

**Referral rates from various sources:** Captures information about where applicant learned about job and which sources result in most and highest quality hires

*Sources:* Based on Hirshman, Carolyn, "Incentives for Recruiters?" *HRMagazine* 48 (2003): last modified November 1, 2003, http://www.shrm.org/publications/hrmagazine/editorialcontent/pages/1103hirschman.aspx; Earle, David, "Recruiting Analytics: 5 Ways to Benchmark Success," Jobvite, www.staffing.org/documents/recruitingintelligence.pdf; "Give Recruiting Metrics a Greater Role," https://www.careerbuilder.ca/jobposter/staffing-recruiting/article.aspx?articleid=atr_0013recruitingmetrics

## EXHIBIT A6.2

### Yield Ratios for the Job of Systems Engineer

| Job Title: Systems Engineer | | |
|---|---|---|
| Recruitment Sources | Trade Journal | Company Website |
| Résumés received | 150 | 255 |
| Applicants selected for interviews | 35 | 89 |
| Yield ratio | 35/150 = 23% | 89/255 = 35% |

Yield ratios should be calculated at each step of the hiring process and over time in order to evaluate which recruiting source leads to the hiring of employees who are retained longer and perform better in the organization. Yield ratios tell that story.

## Cost-per-Hire

**cost-per-hire**

the costs related to the recruitment part of hiring a new employee

Calculating the **cost-per-hire** involves first identifying all the factors that affect a firm's cost-per-hire. Exhibit A6.3 shows examples of some of the costs related to just the recruitment part of hiring a new employee. Both direct and indirect costs have to be considered. By comparing the costs of different sources and then comparing that information to the yield ratios for those sources, you can make an informed decision about where the firm should best spend its limited recruiting dollars.

## Time-to-Fill Rate

**time-to-fill rate**

a measure of the length of time it takes from the time when a job opening is announced until someone begins work in the job

The **time-to-fill rate** is a measure of the length of time it takes from the time when a job opening is announced until someone begins work in the job. Johnson Controls, which manufactures products ranging from heating and air conditioning systems to car batteries, and also manages commercial office space, used data analytics to reduce its time-to-fill rate. The company has 170,000 employees worldwide. By using data already in its applicant tracking system, Johnson Controls reduced the time-to-fill manufacturing supervisor positions from 54 days to 37 days.[88] The importance of the time-to-fill rate for recruitment is considerable in many cases. Taking a long time to fill a position can result in increased stress and diminished productivity for employees who have to make up for the staff shortage.

## EXHIBIT A6.3

### Components of Recruitment Costs

The following are examples of the types of costs that must be considered when computing cost-per-hire:
- Advertising costs (printing materials, posting, etc.)
- Agency fees (if applicable)
- Employee referral bonuses
- Recruiters' salaries
- Recruiters' assistants' salaries
- Cost of operations not included in above (overhead)
- Travel for recruiters and/or applicants

## Manager Feedback

A firm's cost-per-hire and time-to fill rate are important. However, they tell only part of the story; they don't measure the quality of the people the firm

hires. To obtain this information, you need to gather ongoing feedback from the new hire's manager and performance feedback on criteria identified as critical to successful job performance. If outdated job descriptions are being used in the hiring process, applicants might be hired quickly and at a low cost, but then not succeed on the job. As a manager, you should work with your recruiting staff so they can decide what to continue to do or what to do differently. If you function as the recruiting staff, it is just as important to try to gauge the quality of your firm's new employees hired and what you can do to improve on that quality, if necessary.

## Benchmarking Best Practices

Companies use benchmarking as another way to evaluate their recruitment practices. *Benchmarking* involves identifying the strategies used by other organizations in your industry that are similar in size and location. Why do you think that benchmarking recruitment practices is necessary to achieve a competitive advantage? It is important to know what your competition is doing so you can match and exceed it. In a tight labor market, companies that benchmark against their competitors are more likely to be able to hire an ample number of qualified employees because they are leaders in their industry. Often, industry or professional associations publish their best practices.

Of course, benchmarking should be done with caution because each company has its own unique organizational demands and environmental influences. As a result, not every company will engage in the same recruitment activities, nor should they.

## NOTES

[1] For more comprehensive discussion of the recruitment process, see James Breaugh and Mary Starke, "Research on Employee Recruitment: So Many Studies, So Many Remaining Questions," *Journal of Management* 26 (2000): 405–434; James Breaugh, "Employee Recruitment: Current Knowledge and Important Areas for Future Research," *Human Resource Management Review* 18 (2008): 103–118; and James Breaugh, "Employee Recruitment," *Annual Review of Psychology* 64 (2013): 389–416.

[2] Lynne Morton, *Integrated and Integrative Talent Management: A Strategic HR Framework* (New York: The Conference Board, 2004).

[3] Breaugh and Starke, "Research on Employee Recruitment."

[4] Ibid.

[5] Ibid.

[6] "Career Development," cintas.com, https://www.cintas.com/careers/why-work-at-cintas/.

[7] "Jobs Ad Rates 2018," *Washington Post*, https://www.washingtonpost.com/wp-stat/ad/public/static/media_kit/2018-Jobs-rate-card.pdf; *Washington Post Jobs*, https://employers.washingtonpost.com/pricing/.

[8] Ian Williamson, Dave Lepak, and J. King, "The Effect of Company Recruitment Website Orientation on Individuals' Perceptions of Organizational Attractiveness," *Journal of Vocational Behavior* 63 (2003): 242–263; Colin Day, "Reaching Your Other Customers: Why Recruiting Needs to Be an Extension of Marketing," *Forbes/Entrepreneurs Online*, May 12, 2015, http://www.forbes.com/sites/groupthink/2015/05/12/reaching-your-other-customers-why-recruiting-needs-to-be-an-extension-of-marketing/#2df7fc9f18a7.

[9] David Allen, Jonathan Biggane, Mitzi Pitts, Robert Otondo, and James Van Scotter, "Reactions to Recruitment Web sites: Visual and Verbal Attention, Attraction, and Intentions to Pursue Employment," *Journal of Business and Psychology* 28 (2013): 285.

[10] "Work on What Matters," Northropgrumman.com, http://www.northropgrumman.com/Careers/Pages/default.aspx.

[11] "Career Resources," AICPA, http://www.aicpa.org/CAREER/JOBBOARDS/Pages/Job-Boards.aspx.

[12] Martha Frase-Blunt, "Make a Good First Impression," *HRMagazine*, April 2004, https://www.shrm.org/hr-today/news/hr-magazine/pages/0404f-b.aspx.

13 "Emerging Leaders Program," EY.com https://www.ey.com/us/en/careers/students/your-role-here/students---programs---emerging-leaders-program.

14 Jacquelyn Smith, "Externships: What They Are and Why They're Important," *Forbes*, last modified May 30, 2013, http://www.forbes.com/sites/jacquelynsmith/2013/05/30/externships-what-they-are-and-why-theyre-important/

15 Ibid.

16 "Internships: 15 Best Practices for Internship Programs," National Association of Colleges and Employers, http://www.naceweb.org/recruiting/15_best_practices/.

17 "Current Benchmarks," National Association of Colleges and Employers, naceweb.org, http://www.naceweb.org/job-market/compensation/current-benchmarks/.

18 "Find Talent Without Leaving the Office," aicpa.org, https://www.aicpa.org/interestareas/privatecompaniespracticesection/humancapital/teamrecruitment/find-talent.html

19 "Business Center," http://www.careeronestop.org/BusinessCenter/index.aspx.

20 Ken Sundheim, "A Guide to Hiring Recruitment Firms," *Forbes.com*, last modified September 19, 2013, http://www.forbes.com/sites/kensundheim/2013/09/19/331/.

21 Stephenie Overman, "Searching for the Top," *HRMagazine* 53 (2008): 53.

22 Martha Frase-Blunt, "A Recruiting Spigot," *HRMagazine*, last modified April 1, 2003, http://www.shrm.org/publications/hrmagazine/editorialcontent/pages/0403frase.aspx.

23 Robert Grossman, "How to Recruit a Recruiter Outsourcer," *HR Magazine* 57 (2012): 51–54.

24 Roy Maurer, "More Employers Embrace RPO as Hiring Battles Heat Up," *SHRM.org*, January 11, 2017, https://www.shrm.org/resourcesandtools/hr-topics/talent-acquisition/pages/employers-embrace-rpo-hiring-battles.aspx,

25 Gianpiero Petriglieri, Susan J. Ashford, and Amy Wrzesniewski, (2018), "Thriving in the Gig Economy," *Harvard Business Review*, March-April: 140-143, https://hbr.org/2018/03/thriving-in-the-gig-economy; Andre Lavoie, "Recruiting Tips That Will Make You Rethink the Gig Economy," entrepreneur.com, January 10, 2017, https://www.entrepreneur.com/article/286937.

26 Nelson D. Schwartz, "In Hiring, a Friend in Need Is a Prospect, Indeed," *The New York Times*, last modified January 27, 2013, http://www.nytimes.com/2013/01/28/business/employers-increasingly-rely-on-internal-referrals-in-hiring.html?pagewanted=all&_r=0.

27 James Breaugh, *Recruitment: Science and Practice* (Boston: PWS-Kent, 1992).

28 Meta Brown, Elizabeth Setren, and Giorgio Topa, "Do Informal Referrals Lead to Better Matches? Evidence from a Firm's Employee Referral System," *Federal Reserve Bank of New York Staff Reports*, no. 568, June 2013.

29 Ibid.

30 Frase-Blunt, "A Recruiting Spigot."

31 Josh Bersin, "The 9 Hottest Trends in Corporate Recruiting," *Forbes*, last modified July 4, 2013, http://www.forbes.com/sites/joshbersin/2013/07/04/the-9-hottest-trends-in-corporate-recruiting/.

32 J. W. Marriott, Jr., "Our Competitive Strength: Human Capital," *Executive Speeches* 15 (2001): 18–21.

33 Elizabeth Chambers, Mark Foulon, Helen Handfield-Jones, Steven Hankin, and Edward Michaels III, "The War for Talent," *McKinsey Quarterly* 3 (1998): 1.

34 Jim Harris and Joan Brannick, *Finding & Keeping Great Employees* (New York: American Management Association, 1999).

35 Alison Barber, *Recruiting Employees: Individual and Organizational Perspectives* (Thousand Oaks, CA: SAGE Publications, 1998).

36 Ed Michaels, Helen Handfield-Jones, and Beth Axelrod, *The War for Talent* (Boston: Harvard Business School Press, 2001).

37 Dan Cable and Tim Judge, "Person–Organization Fit, Job Choice Decisions, and Organizational Entry," *Organizational Behavior and Human Decision Processes* 67 (1996): 294–311; and Dan Turban, J. Campion, and Alison Eyring, "Job Attributes: Preferences Compared with Reasons Given for Accepting and Rejecting Job Offers," *Journal of Occupational and Organizational Psychology* 66 (1993): 71–81.

38 Kristin Backhaus and Surinder Tikoo, "Conceptualizing and Researching Employer Branding," *Career Development International* 9 (2004): 501.

39 Martin Edwards, "An Integrative Review of Employer Branding and OB Theory," *Personnel Review* 39 (2010): 5–23.

40 Jo Faragher, "B&CE Carries Off Employer Branding Award," November 23, 2017, person-neltoday.com, https://www.personneltoday.com/hr/personnel-today-awards-2017-employer-branding-award/.

41 For a more comprehensive discussion of what works and what doesn't in recruiting employees, see Breaugh and Starke, "Research on Employee Recruitment"; Breaugh, "Employee Recruitment".

42 Barber, *Recruiting Employees*; and Breaugh and Starke, "Research on Employee Recruitment."

43 Ed Michaels, Helen Handfield-Jones, and Beth Axelrod, *The War for Talent* (Boston: Harvard Business School Press, 2001).

44 Alison Barber and M. Roehling, "Job Posting and the Decision to Interview: A Verbal Protocol Analysis," *Journal of Applied Psychology* 78 (1993): 845–856; See also Steve Maurer, V. Howe, and T. Lee, "Organizational Recruiting as Marketing Management: An Interdisciplinary Study of Engineering Students," *Personnel Psychology* 45 (1992): 807–833.

45 Danielle Gaucher, Justin Friesen, and Aaron Kay, "Evidence That Gendered Wording in Job Advertisements Exists and Sustains Gender Inequality," *Journal of Personality and Social Psychology* 101 (2011): 109–128; Carmen Nobel, "How to Take Gender Bias Out of Your Job Ads," forbes.com, December 14, 2016, https://www.forbes.com/sites/hbsworkingknowledge/2016/12/14/how-to-take-gender-bias-out-of-your-job-ads/#613503f51024.

46 H. Jack Walker, Hubert Field, Jeremy Bernerth, and J. Bret Becton, "Diversity Cues on Recruitment Websites: Investigating the Effects of Job Seekers' Information Processing," *Journal of Applied Psychology* 97 (2012): 214–224.

47 Roy Maurer, "2017 Recruiting Trends Point to Technology Driving Change," shrm.org, February 23, 2017, https://www.shrm.org/resourcesandtools/hr-topics/talent-acquisition/pages/recruiting-trends-2017-technology-change.aspx.

48 Sara Rynes, R. Bretz, and Barry Gerhart, "The Importance of Recruitment in Job Choice: A Different Way of Looking," *Personnel Psychology* 44 (1991): 487–521; and Sara L. Rynes, "Recruitment, Job Choice, and Post-Hire Consequences: A Call for New Research Directions," in *Handbook of Industrial and Organizational Psychology*, 2nd ed., ed. Marvin Dunnette (Palo Alto, CA: Consulting Psychologists Press, 1991), 399–444.

49 B. Sleeper and R. Walter, "Employee Recruitment and Retention: When Company Inducements Trigger Liability," *Review of Business* 23 (2002): 17–22.

50 Alan Saks and S. Cronshaw, "A Process Investigation of Realistic Job Previews: Mediating Variables and Channels of Communication," *Journal of Organizational Behavior* 11 (1990): 221–236.

51 John Wanous, *Organizational Entry: Recruitment, Selection, Orientation, and Socialization of Newcomers*, 2nd ed. (Reading, MA: Addison-Wesley, 1992); and Stephanie Haden, "Realistic Job Previews and Performance: The Mediating Influence of Personal Goals," *Journal of Management Research* 12 (2012): 163–178.

52 Michael Tucker, "Show and Tell," *HRMagazine* 57 (2012): 51–53.

53 Michael Porter, *Competitive Advantage: Creating and Sustaining Superior Performance* (New York: Free Press, 1985).

54 Wanous, *Organizational Entry*.

55 Shelley Emling, "Good News for Job Seekers over 50," April 4, 2018, AARP.com, https://www.aarp.org/work/working-at-50-plus/info-2018/older-workers-programs.html.

56 "Time to Start Focusing on Attracting Older Workers," *HR Focus* 81 (2004): 13–14.

57 Nancy Lockwood, "The Reality of the Impact of Older Workers and Eldercare in the Workplace," *HRMagazine* 48 (2003): A1.

58 "Some Employers See Perks of Hiring Older Workers," *TimesDispatch.com*, last modified September 23, 2013, http://www.timesdispatch.com/business/some-employers-see-perksof-hiring-older-workers/article_d0630861-311c-5be0-a135-09f75f80131c.html.

59 Chris Farrell, "Hiring Older Workers is Suddenly in Season," *forbes.com*, November 17, 2017, https://www.forbes.com/sites/nextavenue/2017/11/17/hiring-older-workers-is-suddenly-in-season/#4f4bdb4fe880.

60 "Avon: Awards and Recognition," http://www.avoncompany.com/corporate-responsibility/about-cr/awards-recognition.

61 "Cisco—Project LifeChanger," *Profiles in Diversity Journal*, February 25, 2017, http://www.diversityjournal.com/16576-cisco-project-lifechanger/.

62 "Working with Disabilities," AT&T Careers, https://www.att.jobs/diversity/#working-with-disabilities; "Individuals with Disabilities," http://www.pepsico.com/About/Diversity-and-Engagement.

63 "Persons with a Disability: Labor Force Characteristics Summary," U.S. Department of Labor, Bureau of Labor Statistics, June 21, 2018, http://www.bls.gov/news.release/disabl.nr0.htm. Frank Kalman, "Employers Reluctant to Hire Workers with Disabilities Miss Top Talent," *Diversity Executive*, last modified February 14, 2012, http://diversity-executive.com/articles/view/employers-reluctant-to-hire-workers-with-disabilities-miss-top-talent May 10, 2018

64 "United States Unemployment Rate, 1948-2018" Trading Economics, tradingeconomics.com, https://tradingeconomics.com/united-states/unemployment-rate.

65 "Emerging Leaders Program," EY.com, http://www.ey.com/us/en/careers/students/your-role-here/students---programs---emerging-leaders-program.

66 Dan Schawbel, "How 2012 Graduates Can Get Jobs and Advance Their Careers," Forbes, last modified May 29, 2012, http://www.forbes.com/sites/danschawbel/2012/05/29/how-to-land-a-job-and-grow-your-career-at-ernst-young/.

67 Roy Maurer, "2017 Recruiting Trends Point to Technology Driving Change," February 23, 2017, shrm.org, https://www.shrm.org/resourcesandtools/hr-topics/talent-acquisition/pages/recruiting-trends-2017-technology-change.aspx.

68 Isabel Asher Hamilton, "Amazon Built An AI Tool to Hire People But Had to Shut It Down Because It Was Discriminating Against Women," Business Insider Nordic, October 10, 2018, https://nordic.businessinsider.com/amazon-built-ai-to-hire-people-discriminated-against-women-2018-10?r=US&IR=T.

69 L. Perkins, K. Thomas, and G. Taylor, "Advertising and Recruitment: Marketing to Minorities," *Psychology & Marketing* 17 (2000): 235–255. See also D. Avery, "Reactions to Diversity in Recruitment Advertising—Are Differences Black and White?" *Journal of Applied Psychology* 88 (2003): 672–680.

70 Drew Robb, "How Three Companies Went Social with Recruiting," https://www.shrm.org/hr-today/news/hr-magazine/pages/0914-social-media-recruiting.aspx.

71 Margaret Vroman, Karin Stulz, Claudia Hart, and Emily Stulz, "Employer Liability for Using Social Media in Hiring Decisions," *Journal of Social Media for Organizations* 3(1) (2016): 1–12, http://www2.mitre.org/public/jsmo/pdfs/03-01-employer-liability.pdf.

72 Mary Gowan, "Development of the Recruitment Value Proposition for Geocentric Staffing: Influence of Cultural Differences and Previous International Experience," *Thunderbird International Business Review* 46 (2004): 678–708.

73 Stephenie Overman, "Recruiting in China," *HR Magazine* 46 (2001): 86.

74 "Who We Are," The QualiFind Group, http://www.qualifindgroup.com/about-us/who-we-are.

75 Michael Alenn, "Recruiting in Baja California Tijuana Is a Qualified Success," *Workforce Management*, last modified May 22, 2007, http://www.workforce.com/articles/recruiting-in-baja-california-is-a-qualified-success.

76 J. Antun, S. Strick, and L. Thomas, "Exploring Culture and Diversity for Hispanics in Restaurant Online Recruitment Efforts," *Journal of Human Resources in Hospitality & Tourism* 6 (2007): 85–107.

77 D. D'Agostino, "Global Recruiting: Star Search," *CIO Insight*, last modified March 6, 2006, http://www.cioinsight.com/article2/0,1540,1940172,00.asp.

78 "Fortune 100 Best Companies to Work for 2018," http://fortune.com/best-companies/.

79 Rong-Tsu Wang, "Modeling Corporate Social Performance and Job Pursuit Intention: Mediating Mechanisms of Corporate Reputation and Job Advancement Prospects," *Journal of Business Ethics* 117 (2013): 569–582; Lu Zhang and Mary Gowan, "Corporate Social Responsibility, Applicants' Individual Traits, and Organizational Attraction: A Person-Organization Fit Perspective," *Journal of Business and Psychology* 27 (2012): 345–362.

80 Sandra DeGrassi, "Go, Stop, Yield: The Effect of Ethical Signals on Recruitment Outcomes," *Journal of Leadership, Accountability and Ethics* 9 (2012): 30–43.

81 Robert Walter and Bradley Sleeper, "Employee Recruitment and Retention: When Company Inducements Trigger Liability," *Review of Business* 23 (2002): 17+.

82 Fay Hansen, "Avoiding Truth-in-Hiring Lawsuits," *Workforce Management*, last modified December 11, 2007, http://www.workforce.com/articles/avoiding-truth-in-hiring-lawsuits.

83 Randy Myers, "Ensuring Ethical Effectiveness: New Rules Mean Virtually Every Company Will Need a Code of Ethics," *Journal of Accountancy* 195 (2003): 28+.

84 Pablo Ruiz-Palomino, Ricardo Martinez-Cañas, and Joan Fontrodona, "Ethical Culture and Employee Outcomes: The Mediating Role of Person-Organization Fit," *Journal of Business Ethics* 116 (2013): 173–188.

85 Timothy Gardner, Jason Stansbury, and David Hart, "The Ethics of Lateral Hiring," *Business Ethics Quarterly* 20 (2010): 341–369.

86 "Textio Hire," texio.com, https://textio.com/products/; Sabrina Barr, "The Language in Job Adverts That Deters Female Applicants," Independent, June 12, 2018, https://www .independent.co.uk/life-style/job-adverts-language-deter-women-applications-men-gender-employment-a8395106.html.

87 Alison T. Wynn and Shelley J. Correll, "Puncturing the Pipeline: Do Technology Companies Alienate Women in Recruiting Sessions?" *Social Studies of Science* 48(1) (2018): 149–164.

88 Toni Vranjes, "Use 'Big Data' to Guide Your Recruiting Decisions," *SHRM.org*, last modified April 29, 2014, http://www.shrm.org/hrdisciplines/staffingmanagement/articles/pages/ere-big-data.aspx.

# Chapter 7

# Selection

## Learning Objectives

**AFTER READING THIS CHAPTER, YOU SHOULD BE ABLE TO:**

**1** Describe how employee selection affects the performance of firms.

**2** Discuss the meaning and importance of person–job fit.

**3** Identify the standards required for an employee selection process to be effective.

**4** Discuss the various types of employee selection methods managers can use.

**5** Explain how managers make final employee selection decisions.

**6** Describe how organizational demands affect the employee selection process.

**7** Incorporate environmental demand factors into the employee selection process.

**8** Ensure that a firm's employee selection process is legally compliant.

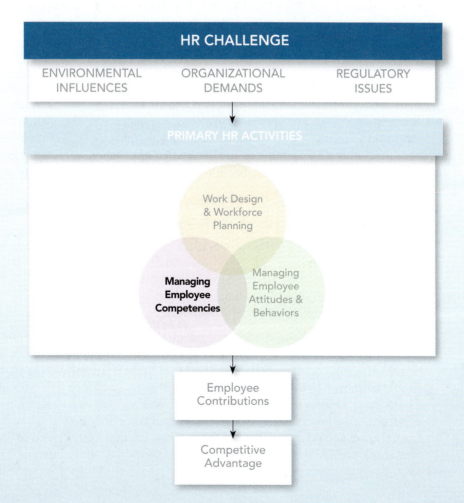

You have started your own company and it is doing well. Because of company growth, you need to hire more employees. Will you have them fill out an application? Take a test? Answer questions in an interview? How will you decide which applicants are the right ones to hire?

If you are a manager in any type of organization—public, private, for-profit, or nonprofit, you will play a role in selecting people for jobs. Many companies have human resources (HR) departments to assist with this process. However, the ultimate responsibility for selection rests with you, the hiring manager. In most companies, managers conduct the final interviews and make the final hiring decisions. Managers are the ones who work with the employees on a daily basis, so they have a vested interest in making sure that they hire the right candidates for the job.

By now, you know that job design dictates the tasks, duties, and responsibilities of a job. Job design provides the focus for the recruitment process. In this chapter, we look at the next step after recruitment: *selection*. We discuss the relationship between a firm's selection process and its performance, emphasize the importance of person–job fit, identify the standards for an effective selection process, and describe the methods used to assess applicant fit. We wrap up our discussion by describing how HR challenges affect the decisions that you, as a manager, will make when you're setting up a selection process and hiring employees.

## Selection Defined

In this chapter, we are continuing to focus on managing competencies. Remember that *competencies* are the knowledge, skills, abilities—or KSAs—and other talents employees need to perform their jobs effectively and efficiently. As shown in Exhibit 7.1, managing competencies is a central part of the strategic HR framework.

Chapter 6 focused on the recruitment component of managing competencies and emphasized the need to generate the best pool of qualified applicants for the organization. Once you have that pool, you need to decide which applicants to keep in the pool for further consideration and, ultimately, which ones to hire. This process is not always easy. For starters, some companies receive thousands of applications per month. Southwest Airlines has received as many as 90,043 résumés in one year but hired only 831 employees in that year. That means applicants had less than a 1% chance of getting hired, and Southwest had to review a lot of résumés to select those who did get hired.[1]

As mentioned in Chapter 1, managers need to consider a number of key questions during the selection process. These include:

- How do you generate the information you need to make an effective, and legal, hiring decision?
- Which tests are most effective for identifying employees with high potential?
- What questions should you ask candidates during an interview?
- Who makes the ultimate hiring decision?

**selection**

the systematic process of deciding which applicants to hire

**prediction**

making a determination about how likely it is that candidates selected will be successful in the job based on their current ability to do the job or the potential they have to be able to learn to do the job and do it well

**Selection** is the systematic process of deciding which applicants to hire. The primary decisions are: (1) which applicants should be hired as new employees, (2) which employees should be promoted to higher-level jobs, and (3) which employees should be moved to other jobs within the company that don't involve a promotion. At a basic level, selection is about **prediction**. When a manager selects an applicant for a job, she or he is predicting that the applicant can either do the job or will be able to learn the job and do it well. People think about selection most often in terms of hiring new employees. Managers may also have the option to move current employees into vacant positions—a process called *internal selection*. As we discussed in Chapter 5,

**EXHIBIT 7.1**

Strategic Human Resources Framework

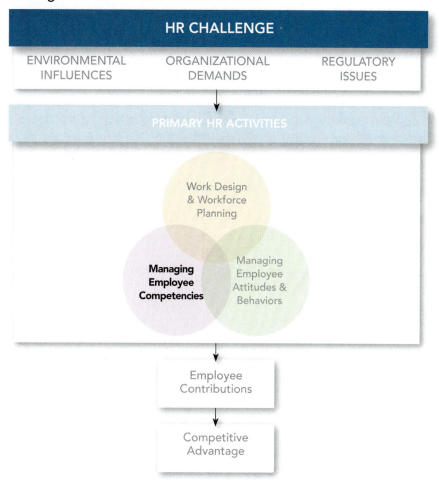

companies use promotions, transfers, and demotions to move individuals to different areas within a company. The following activities are typically part of the selection process for both new hires and internal transitions:

1. Review applications and résumés to determine which applicants best match the requirements of the job and the organization.
2. Identify and implement appropriate methods to assess the degree of fit among the job requirements, the qualifications of the applicants, and the organizational culture.
3. Make a final decision about which applicant is the most qualified for the particular job and should be offered the job.

We will discuss these concepts throughout the rest of this chapter.

## How Employee Selection Processes Affect the Performance of Firms

Employees who are not a good fit with the jobs for which they are hired and/or the culture of the organizations that hire them tend to leave their firms. Combining industry and census data, the Work Institute estimates that the cost of turnover for an employee is equal to 33% of that employee's annual salary.[2] The cost to replace workers can range from 16% of annual salary for employees making less than $30,000 a year to 213% of the annual salary for executives.[3] But these costs are just one reason why managers need to make good hiring decisions.

A second, and potentially more damaging, situation can occur when bad selection decisions don't end with turnover. If employees are not qualified to do their jobs, a company is likely to make more mistakes, experience higher production costs, and experience lower employee morale. Ultimately, the company will lose customers and money. Conversely, if a company selects the right employees, it is more likely to gain customers, have happier employees, and make more money. In short, a company realizes many benefits by hiring the right person for a job and incurs many costs by hiring the wrong person.

## Person–Job Fit

**person–job fit**

the extent to which there is a good match between the characteristics of a potential employee, such as knowledge, skills, values, and the requirements of the job

In terms of the selection process, you need to understand why **person–job fit** is crucial. Have you ever had to do something that was really difficult? Or something that just wasn't interesting? Would you want to do those tasks every day for 40-plus hours per week? Each of us has different abilities and interests, and it is unlikely that all potential employees would enjoy the tasks required for all jobs or possess the abilities to succeed in all jobs. Employees who believe there is a good

## COMPANY SPOTLIGHT 7.1

### Want to Work for the United States Antarctic Program (USAP)?

The National Science Foundation (NSF) manages the United States Antarctic Program (USAP) and deploys around 3,000 people to work in Antarctica every year. These workers maintain research stations and vessels, conduct scientific research, or provide support to the researchers. The NSF hires most of the employees through one of five contract firms. Leidos is the prime contractor for NSF's USAP program infrastructure management. The Leidos company mission is to make "the world safer, healthier, and more efficient through information technology, engineering, and science."

Leidos hires employees mainly for the months of October–February, the summer season. They have locations at either the South Pole stations or McMurdo Station. Salaries are competitive with similar positions in the United States, benefits are available, and Leidos provides room, board, and airfare from the employee's home to the work location. Applicants selected for positions must have the required job skills, provide proof of U.S. citizenship, and pass strict physical and dental exams, a pre-employment background check, and a drug screen. There are some winter season positions and applicants for those positions must pass a psychological exam.

So, think you are ready to sign up? If you are adventurous, concerned about the environment, don't mind living in a dormitory and eating in a cafeteria, and are okay working in sometimes very adverse conditions, you might want to consider applying for one of the available positions. Before you apply, you can check out some online blogs and other resources to gain a realistic job preview (RJP).

*Sources:* "Mission, Vision, and Values," https://www.leidos.com/about/mission; "Antarctic Support Contract (ASC)," https://www.leidos.com/antarctic-support-contract; "Jobs and Opportunities," United States Antarctic Program, https://www.usap.gov/jobsAndOpportunities/index.cfm?m=1#agencies.

match between their own KSAs and interests and the requirements of their jobs are going to be more satisfied with their positions.[4] As you know and research has shown, satisfied employees tend to be more productive.[5] A strong person–job fit maximizes the benefits for both employees and their organizations. In contrast, when there is a poor person–job fit, companies can expect to face higher turnover and absenteeism, along with lower employee morale and productivity.

Company Spotlight 7.1 describes a unique situation in which person–job fit is especially critical. Most employment situations aren't quite as dramatic as working in Antarctica. Making good selection decisions is important, however, regardless of the location or type of job.

## Standards for an Effective Selection Process

You already know that an effective selection process results in hiring the most qualified individual for the job. So, how does that work? A number of standards must be met for the selection process to accomplish its goals. At a minimum, all parts of the selection process need to be *reliable, valid,* and *unbiased.* On the surface, these standards might seem easy to understand and follow. In fact, they are quite complex. Selection is about measuring the degree to which each applicant possesses the competencies required to do a job. The precision of the measurement at each step will largely determine the success of the process.

The measurements would be relatively easy if we had something equivalent to a tape measure to gauge the competencies of one applicant versus another. Unfortunately, there is no instrument that measures all of a job applicant's traits and skills with complete accuracy. There are, however, tools that can help a manager predict the future job success of candidates. Before deciding which predictor to use, you have to first understand how consistent the method of prediction is, meaning the *reliability* of the method, and how well it serves as a predictor of job success, which refers to the *validity* of the method. The effectiveness of any selection tool is a function of reliability and validity.

### Reliability

**Reliability** indicates how well a selection measure yields consistent results over time or across raters. The key word here is *consistent*. We all want a reliable car to drive; just ask anyone who has had to call a tow truck on a rainy day. We want to be able to count on the car performing the same way each time we use it. We need reliable selection measures just as we need reliable transportation.

**reliability**
the extent to which a selection measure yields consistent results over time or across raters

Several types of reliability are important for selection. First, selection procedures need to be reliable *over time*. If an applicant takes a test today and then retakes it a week from now, we expect the scores to be similar. This correlation between the scores means there is *test–retest reliability*. If the applicant studied the subject matter between the two test administrations, or if the applicant remembered how he or she responded the first time and simply responds the same way the second time, the test scores will not be reliable. They won't give you a picture of the true capabilities of the person. Exhibit 7.2 shows the results of a test–retest conducted to determine the reliability of a particular selection measure. A high correlation (indicated by the *r* value) between two test administrations indicates that the test is reliable. Notice how close the scores are from one test time to the next. Most applicants had similar, though not identical scores, resulting in a high degree of correlation between the two test administrations and the conclusion that the test appears to be highly reliable.

## EXHIBIT 7.2

### Test-Retest Reliability

| Applicant | Test Score | Retest Score |
|---|---|---|
| James | 70 | 75 |
| Carlos | 95 | 96 |
| Juanita | 83 | 86 |
| Maria | 75 | 78 |
| Hui | 77 | 75 |
| Mehdi | 90 | 92 |
| Jun | 88 | 86 |
| Aaron | 91 | 91 |
| Camille | 86 | 83 |
| Dexter | 70 | 73 |
| Jie | 98 | 96 |
| | | $r = .97$ |

Second, selection procedures need to be reliable *across raters*. If three people interview an applicant for a job and are using the same questions and the same scoring mechanism, they should evaluate the interviewee in a similar manner. If they do so, we would have *high interrater reliability*. Discrepancies among interviewer scores occur when interviewers have different expectations about how the questions should be answered or what the questions mean.

The first questions to ask when purchasing a test to use for employee selection relate to the test's reliability: How was the test developed? What were the demographics of the population used to assess reliability? What is the correlation coefficient—the measure of reliability—for the test? If you are developing your own test (and keep in mind that even the interviews you conduct with candidates are a type of selection "test"), you need to make sure the test is reliable. The appendix to this chapter provides additional information about the reliability and validity of different selection methods.

## Validity

**validity**

the extent to which a selection method measures what it is supposed to measure and how well it does so

Reliability alone does not ensure that a selection method is going to predict success on the job. In other words, it is a necessary but not sufficient indicator of the usefulness of the test. Selection methods must also be valid. **Validity** is the extent to which a selection method measures what it is supposed to measure and how well it does so.[6] A personality test should measure personality. A programming test should measure programming knowledge and skill. When we talk about validity, we are really focusing on how much evidence there is to support the conclusions that are made based on the scores of the selection measures. Simply stated, we are investigating the job-relatedness of the selection measure.

As an example, a company might have developed a selection test for customer service skills that gives consistent results over time. However, if the test doesn't correlate with any other established measures of customer service skills, such as the performance of good customer service representatives, it will be reliable, but it won't be valid. Why, then, would the company want to use the test to select its employees? As you might imagine, consistently measuring the wrong KSAs, instead of those actually needed to do a job, would not result in good hiring decisions.

## EXHIBIT 7.3

## What Makes a Good Test?

An employment test is considered "good" if the following can be said about it:
- The test measures what it claims to measure consistently or reliably. This means that if a person were to take the test again, the person would get a similar test score.
- The test measures what it claims to measure. For example, a test of mental ability should in fact measure a person's mental ability, and not another characteristic.
- The test is job relevant. In other words, the test measures one or more characteristics that a person needs in order to be able to do the job.
- By using the test, more effective employment decisions can be made about individuals. For example, an arithmetic test should help you select qualified workers for a job that requires knowledge of basic math.

The degree to which a test has these qualities is indicated by two technical properties: reliability and validity.

*Source:* Based on U.S. Department of Labor, *Testing and Assessment: An Employer's Guide to Good Practices* (Washington, DC: U.S. Department of Labor, Employment and Training Administration, 2000), http://www .onetcenter.org/dl_files/empTestAsse.pdf.

Exhibit 7.3 summarizes the criteria for a selection method to be considered both reliable and valid. Selection is an art rather than a science, though. Consequently, we have to recognize that there will always be less than perfect measures in the selection process. However, that does not change the need to be as precise as possible.

## Unbiased

In addition to being reliable and valid, selection measures need to be unbiased. Unfortunately, bias often creeps in and compromises the fairness of the selection process. **Selection bias** occurs when one's personal views are allowed to affect the outcome of the decision-making process, rather than the decision being based on the results of the selection measures. Measurement bias can occur as well, but that discussion is beyond the scope of this book.

**selection bias**

when one's personal views are allowed to affect the outcome of the decision-making process, rather than basing the decision on the results of the selection measures

Consider the following situation: A company decides to use a written test, a work sample, and an interview to find the best candidate for a position. A particular candidate performs poorly on the written test and work sample. The interviewer really likes the applicant and wants to hire him, even with his poor performance on these metrics. In this case, bias has entered into the process; some factor other than the actual outcome of the selection process has affected the decision. We next discuss four common types of bias: (1) the influence of personal characteristics, (2) the contrast effect, (3) the halo/devil's horn effect, and (4) impression management.

### Candidates' Personal Characteristics

A person's attractiveness, age, and gender are examples of personal characteristics that can affect employee selection decisions due to the preferences of interviewers, stereotypes, and poorly designed selection processes. As discussed in Chapter 3, *disparate treatment* results when a selection decision is based on a personal characteristic that is also a protected classification, such as age. *Disparate impact* occurs if the personal characteristic used to select employees leads to a lower percentage of a protected class being hired than the percentage of the nonprotected class because members of the protected class are less likely to have that characteristic. Remember the example in Chapter 3, when we talked about the unintentional outcome of using height as a requirement for selection. Females tend on average to be shorter than males, so they would be less likely to be hired. Thus, a personal characteristic of a protected class would have affected the outcome of the selection process.

## Contrast Effect

The **contrast effect** happens when an evaluation of one or more job applicants is artificially inflated or deflated compared to another job applicant. For example, suppose a manager has four candidates to interview for a job opening. The first candidate is really impressive. The candidate doesn't meet the test for previous work experience, one of the main requirements of the job, but she does rate very highly on all the other requirements. If the manager judges the remaining candidates based on the first candidate's high ratings on most of the selection measures, the contrast effect has occurred. The first candidate caused the others to appear less than stellar by comparison. The contrast effect could also occur if the first candidate did poorly, causing the other candidates to appear more qualified than they really are.

## Halo/Devil's Horns Effect

A **halo effect** or **devil's horns effect** occurs when a positive or negative characteristic of a job candidate affects the evaluation of the candidate's other attributes. Based on the job description, you decide that applicants for a sales position need to be able to (1) make sales presentations, (2) work as part of a sales team, and (3) maintain accurate, detailed records of sales calls. Using interview questions and role playing, you assess the ability of the applicants to meet each criterion based on a scale of 1 to 5 (1 = poor to 5 = excellent). Candidate A really wows you with his sales presentation. You score him 5 on this criterion. He doesn't do as well on the other two criteria. You choose to ignore the negative results and rate him high anyway because of his dynamic presentation. By overlooking possible problems, you are demonstrating the halo effect. Likewise, the devil's horns effect would occur if Candidate A performed really well on the other two parts of the assessment, but you rated him low on all three parts because of his poor sales presentation.

## Impression Management

The final type of bias that we will discuss is **impression management.** Impression management occurs when a job applicant engages in actions to present himself in a positive light to the interviewer with the idea of biasing the outcome of the interview in his favor, regardless of his qualifications for the job. Self-promotion, ingratiation, and opinion conformity are typical types of behaviors.[7] If an applicant who is good at impression management thinks the employer is looking for someone who is industrious and hardworking, he will try to portray himself as industrious and hard-working during the selection process, even if he is not.[8] By *impressing* those doing the hiring, the applicant is likely to get the job, regardless of whether he is really qualified.

# Selection Methods: Initial Screening

What are the selection tools that can help a manager identify the most qualified applicant for a job? Selection methods can be grouped into two categories: initial screening methods and final screening methods. **Initial screening** involves reviewing the information provided by job applicants and collecting additional preliminary information to decide which applicants are worthy of more serious consideration for the job. **Final screening** involves taking a more in-depth look at the applicants who make it through the initial screening prior to hiring them, including reviewing references and conducting background checks. In addition to the information discussed here, the U.S. Department of Labor's Employment and Training Administration posts a free online guide, *Testing and Assessment: An Employer's Guide to Good Practices* (http://www.onetcenter.org/

dl_files/empTestAsse.pdf), to help managers and HR professionals with their selection practices.

There are several selection methods managers can use for initial screening to narrow the pool of job applicants to a manageable number of qualified candidates. Recall from Chapter 6 that a company that does a good job of recruiting will have an applicant pool that includes a large number of highly qualified applicants. However, the applicant pool is still likely to have some less-qualified applicants. Many people are not very good at self-selection and apply for jobs for which they are not qualified. Testing and interviewing everyone who applies for a job are simply not cost-effective or practical for an employer; therefore, managers use methods such as collecting and reviewing *applications* and *résumés* and *administering screening interviews* to make the first cut in the applicant pool. As you read about these methods, think about how you would ensure that each is reliable and valid, as well as how you would keep biases from affecting the outcome.

## Applications and Résumés

If you have ever applied for a job, you probably completed an application or submitted a résumé (or both). This application gave the employer a first impression of you. Applications and résumés serve similar—but different—purposes.

**Applications** are standardized forms employers use to collect job-related information about applicants. The information is reviewed and used to determine which applicants meet the minimum job requirements and should remain in the selection process. Typically, application forms inquire about a person's eligibility to work in the United States, the person's education, current and previous work experience, skills, hours available to work, and references. Applications are completed in person or online, with most companies asking for the application to be completed online. Keep in mind that younger applicants in particular are likely to be using a smart phone or other device to apply for a job, and as a result, employers need to make sure that the application is mobile accessible.

**application**

a standardized form used by employers to collect job-related information about applicants

Exhibit 7.4 provides guidelines managers can use to prepare application questions. Also, increasingly cities and states are passing laws that prohibit asking job applicants about their salary histories as a pre-employment question. In fact, according to a 2018 report from WorldatWork, the leading nonprofit professional association for total rewards managers, 37% of employers they surveyed already had implemented a ban on asking job candidates about their salary history, even if they were not legally required to forego that information.[9]

Some companies weight each application question and tally all the responses to arrive at an overall score. By using weights, managers are able to highlight which questions are more important than others in the selection decision. Having a score for each applicant makes it easier to compare applicants to determine who is most qualified for the job. This type of application is referred to as a *weighted application blank (WAB)*. WABs are also a good predictor of turnover.[10]

A job applicant usually provides a *résumé* to prospective employers, regardless of the level of the job. A **résumé** is an overview of the applicant's qualifications and typically includes contact information and information on education, previous work experience, and special skills and interests. Résumés are usually shorter for less experienced individuals than for people who have a lot of experience. However, even more experienced workers are encouraged to limit the length of their résumés because recruiters have only a limited amount of time to review résumés and cannot wade through a lot of information.

**résumé**

an overview of an applicant's qualifications including education, previous work experience, and special skills and interests

A résumé used in lieu of an application is still considered an application for equal employment opportunity (EEO) purposes. To eliminate the possibility of

## EXHIBIT 7.4
### Guidelines for Application Questions

**General guidelines:**

- Keep all questions job related.
- Ask questions about the relevant past work experience, skills and abilities, education obtained, and goals and interests of applicants.
- Don't ask personal questions or any other questions that could imply that personal characteristics unrelated to the job will be used to make the employment decision.

**Examples of questions not to ask:**

- Are you married/do you plan to marry?
- Do you have any children/do you plan to have children?
- How old are you/what year did you graduate from high school?
- What is your religious affiliation?
- Do you have a mental or physical disability?
- How many sick days did you take last year?
- Have you had any workers' compensation injuries?

**Examples of questions you can ask:**

- This job requires travel 50% of the time. Can you fulfill this requirement?
- This job requires lifting 35 pounds. Can you lift this much weight?
- Do you have the legal right to work in the United States?
- Do you have transportation available to come to work at the required times?
- Can you meet this job's attendance requirements?
- Did you have any problems in your last job/why did you leave your last job?

discrimination, care must be exercised to make sure that demographic information about an applicant obtained through social media or provided by the applicant is not used in the selection process.[11] In reviewing résumés, focus on job-related information and do not read more into the document than what is actually there.

## Behavioral Assessments

With the increase in data-analytic tools and techniques, more companies are creating online behavioral assessments to use as part of their applicant screening process. These assessments generally use information from current employees to create personality profiles for evaluating which applicants are likely to be a good fit with the culture of the company. Companies such as Seaport Hotel & World Trade Center in Boston and AMC Theatres have found these assessments critical to identifying qualified applicants and reducing turnover. Often, a company will hire a vendor to validate a series of questions and decide which questions are most relevant for the company. The validation usually involves surveying either a sample or all current employees, and may include data from performance reviews, financial data, employee engagement, and even customer service reviews of employees.[12] Company Spotlight 7.2 demonstrates how a behavioral assessment helped make big changes at AMC Theatres.

## Screening Interviews

Reviews of applications and résumés narrows the list of applicants who will receive further consideration. A screening interview can then be used to gauge an applicant's

## COMPANY SPOTLIGHT   7.2

### Improving Customer Satisfaction at AMC Theatres Through Better Employee Selection

When AMC Theatres, headquartered in Kansas City, Missouri, made the decision to focus on providing a great customer experience as a differentiation strategy to set it apart from other movie theaters, they thought improving their employee training was the answer. When that strategy did not yield the desired results, another strategy was needed.

Faced with having to sort through 1.4 million applications a year and managing a 200% turnover rate, the company decided to focus on hiring. Deciding how to sort through that many applications can seem daunting. AMC turned to Kenexa, an IBM Company, which had already helped AMC increase its applicant pool from about 250,000 to 1.4 million applications over two years.

AMC provided a list of competencies that it thought important in customer service roles: friendly, dependable, and sales oriented. Kenexa then interviewed top employees. The combined information was used to create an assessment for AMC that was valid. The results were impressive. Crew turnover dropped from 200% to below 90%, a very acceptable percentage for an industry that hires mostly teenagers and college students. Further, employee engagement and customer satisfaction scores went up.

AMC used predictive analytics to identify what success looks like, and then used the online tool to assess the likelihood of an applicant succeeding. This process provided an efficient and effective way to reduce the applicant pool to a smaller pool of higher-qualified candidates. Most important, AMC Theatres got closer to reaching its goal of providing a magical movie experience.

*Sources:* Based on "From Finding and Keeping Talent to Driving Higher Profits Through a Single Piece of Popcorn," Kenexa, http://www.kenexa.com/Portals/Downloads/AMCCaseStudy.pdf; Kruse, Kevin, "Think Traits Not Training: How AMC Theatres Increased Sales, Profits, and Engagement," *Forbes*, last modified February 14, 2013, http://www.forbes.com/sites/kevinkruse/2013/02/14/employee-engagemetn-kenexa.amc/; and Roberts, Bill, "AMC Theatres: Finding Friendly Faces," *HR Magazine* 59 (2014): 70.

fit and actual interest in the position. A typical **screening interview** consists of the manager or someone from HR calling the applicant and conducting a short telephone interview. The goal is to confirm that the person is still looking for a job and is interested in the position, as well as to verify the information the person has already provided to the firm. The screening interview also provides a clue about the person's oral communication skills. Such information is particularly useful if those skills are essential for successful job performance.

**screening interview**

a short interview, typically conducted by telephone, to confirm the applicant is still interested in the position and to verify information provided to the firm

## Selection Methods: Final Screening

A firm's final screening activities narrow the number of job candidates to the number of employees that the company actually needs. Many selection methods are available for this purpose, including various types of employment tests, interviews, and assessment centers. Reference and background checks are also used for screening. These methods are sometimes used for initial screening, but managers most often use them later in the selection process because they can be quite time-consuming and costly. It is better to reduce the applicant pool before using them. Research suggests that as high as 76% of firms with more than 100 employees use assessment tools such as those discussed when making external hires.[13]

## Employment Tests

Employment tests generally can be categorized as *ability tests*, *achievement/competency tests*, or *personality inventories*. We describe these in the following sections.

### Ability Tests

Ability tests, sometimes called *aptitude tests*, measure basic talents, or abilities, of individuals. In the context of staffing, they provide information about an individual's potential to perform the job. For example, Barclays, a 300-year-old bank based in the United Kingdom (UK), uses ability assessments to determine if job applicants have the skills and capabilities that match jobs at the bank. They have found that these measurements of numerical and reasoning skills are good predictors of job performance.[14] Cognitive ability and physical ability tests are common types of ability tests.

**cognitive ability test**

a test that measures general intelligence or levels of specific aptitudes, such as numeric fluency, general reasoning, verbal comprehension, mechanical reasoning, logical evaluation, and memory span

**Cognitive ability tests** measure general intelligence or levels of specific aptitudes, such as numeric fluency, general reasoning, verbal comprehension, mechanical reasoning, logical evaluation, and memory span. These tests are the best predictors of performance across all types of jobs, and they are also among the lowest-cost selection methods. Their predictive value increases as the complexity of the job increases.[15] Education is often used as a replacement for cognitive ability tests to screen job applicants. Research has shown that an educational level equal to at least one year of college is related to higher cognitive ability levels among applicants.[16]

There is, however, a caveat related to using employment tests, and cognitive ability tests, in particular: Minorities typically score lower than nonminorities, often because the terminology and concepts used on the tests are more familiar to nonminorities than to minorities.[17] Ford Motor Company learned this the hard way. For many years they used a cognitive ability test called the Apprenticeship Training Selection System (ATSS). This written assessment measured verbal, numerical, and spatial reasoning. The purpose of the test was to measure mechanical aptitude. The test had been validated in 1991. Even though it had been validated, it still had significant adverse impact on African American applicants. Alternative assessments were available, but Ford chose not to use them. In 2005, Ford ended up paying out $8.55 million in monetary relief to the victims of discrimination and finally replaced the ATSS.[18] Using multiple selection methods can help offset the potential discrimination that would result from using these types of tests alone.[19]

**physical ability test**

a test that focuses on physical attributes of job candidates, such as endurance, strength, and general fitness

**Physical ability tests** focus on physical attributes of job candidates, such as endurance, strength, and general fitness. Firefighters need to be able to carry people out of burning buildings and firefighting equipment into buildings. A UPS driver needs to be able to lift a certain amount of weight to deliver boxes. Employers can administer a physical ability test to candidates in the course of the selection process prior to making a job offer, but only if there is a specific, job-related reason. Clearly, a fire department and a company such as UPS would have such job-related reasons. Keep in mind that the average female will perform differently from the average male on many physical ability tests, so beware of the potential for disparate impact.[20] (Again, think "job-related.")

Dial Corporation, now a subsidiary of Henkel AG & Company, found out firsthand what happens when a physical ability test has disparate impact on women. Dial developed a strength-test for entry-level production jobs that resulted in the percentage of women being hired dropping from 46% to 15%. Dial tried to defend the test use by saying it "looked like the job" and resulted in fewer injuries. Expert testimony showed that "looking like the job" did not mean it *was* the job, and in fact, the test was harder than actually doing the job. It turned out that the number of injuries had been reduced because of training programs that occurred before the use of the test. Dial lost the case.[21]

### Achievement/Competency Tests

**Achievement tests**, or **competency tests**, measure an applicant's current knowledge or skill level in relation to the job requirements.[22] Rather than focus on a candidate's potential, these tests examine the extent to which a job candidate can actually perform the job tasks. Someone without previous work experience or training related to the job requirements would not do well on these assessments.[23]

One of the best ways to determine whether someone can perform a job is to have the person actually perform some or all aspects of that job. Job applicants view this selection method quite favorably.[24] A **work sample** may be practical for some jobs, but not for most. Having a candidate for a word-processing job prepare documents using the software that will be used on the job is relatively inexpensive and straightforward. Work samples for lots of other jobs would have to be much more complex and would be expensive to develop and use. Consequently, work samples are used more often for skilled craft jobs such as carpenter,[25] computer programmer, and food service worker, rather than for professional jobs such as manager, attorney, and doctor.

**Knowledge tests** measure the extent to which an applicant has mastered the subject matter required to do the job. Does an accountant applicant have knowledge of accounting practices? Does an HR applicant have knowledge of HR practices? Licensure exams are examples of knowledge tests. These tests have high validity,[26] especially if they are tailored to the specific job rather than an off-the-shelf version.[27] Applicants generally perceive these tests positively.

### Personality Inventories

If you are hiring someone for a job that requires selling, you probably want someone who is assertive, maybe even extroverted. During the selection process, you will need a way to assess whether applicants have these traits. When used as part of the selection process, **personality inventories** can identify the extent to which an applicant possesses certain characteristics, such as assertiveness, self-confidence, conscientiousness, motivation, and interpersonal attributes. These inventories are appropriate to use, as long as there is a job-related reason. If a job requires working as part of a team, then it is appropriate—and, in fact, necessary—to predict how well a candidate will fit into a team setting. Earlier, we noted that Barclays uses ability tests. For their most senior roles, they use an Occupational Personality Questionnaire (OPQ) designed to indicate alignment to the company's values.[28] However, care must be given to define exactly what is meant by the term *fit*, or in the case of Barclays, *alignment*. The job analysis should help you to define this and then guide the choice of personality inventory. Some job-analysis techniques (discussed in Chapter 4), such as the Position Analysis Questionnaire (PAQ), identify appropriate worker personality dimensions; others, such as the task approach, provide information about required tasks that are useful for inferring that candidates have the appropriate personality dimensions.

Of all the ways to measure personality in the context of selection, the one that has garnered the most attention is the Big Five approach. This approach suggests that all personality traits can be grouped under one of five dimensions: extroversion, agreeableness, conscientiousness, emotional stability, and openness to experience. These dimensions are defined in Exhibit 7.5. Of these dimensions, conscientiousness has been shown to be the most valid across all occupational groups. Emotional stability and extraversion are valid across some occupational groups, but not all.[29] For instance, in a study of the Big Five and sales performance, the researchers found that conscientiousness and openness predicted sales performance, but agreeableness had a negative relationship to sales performance, and extraversion and neuroticism were not related to sales performance.[30]

---

**achievement test (or competency test)**

a measure of an applicant's current knowledge or skill level in relation to the job requirements

**work sample**

a test in which the person actually performs some or all aspects of a job

**knowledge test**

measures the extent to which an applicant has mastered the subject matter required to do a job

**personality inventory**

a selection measure that identifies the extent to which an applicant possesses certain characteristics, such as assertiveness, self-confidence, conscientiousness, motivation, and interpersonal attributes

**EXHIBIT 7.5**

## Characteristics Representative of the Big Five Personality Traits

| Neuroticism | Lack of emotional stability evidenced by excessive or inappropriate anger, anxiousness, paranoia, or depression |
|---|---|
| Extraversion | Outgoing personality, positive, sociable, and active |
| Conscientiousness | Self-control, achievement oriented, dependable, and orderly |
| Openness to experience | Philosophical and intellectual, unconventional, cooperative, and likable |
| Agreeableness | Cooperative, good-natured, gentle, and cheerful |

*Source:* Adapted from Judge, Tim, Higgins, Chad, Thoresen, Carl, and Barrick, Murray, "The Big Five Personality Traits, General Mental Ability, and Career Success Across the Life Span," *Personnel Psychology* 52 (1999): 621–652.

Two concerns have surfaced with the use of personality inventories (also referred to as *personality tests*). First, like physical impairments, mental impairments are covered under the Americans with Disabilities Act (ADA). A personality inventory that could lead to the identification of a mental impairment or disorder is considered a medical examination and is subject to ADA guidelines.[31] Remember that the ADA specifically prohibits the use of medical examinations until after a job offer has been made.

Personality tests that are designed to identify deviant and other extreme behaviors are inappropriate for all but a few types of jobs. These tests are appropriate for law enforcement jobs, for instance, because hiring a deviant person for a law enforcement position could be especially problematic. Another example of the appropriate use of personality inventories is provided by the case of Overnight Transportation of Atlanta, a motor freight company. This company reduced on-the-job delinquency behaviors such as drunkenness, fighting, and damage to vehicles by 50% to 100% by using the Hogan Personality Inventory. Savings were over $1 million each year; a single trucking accident can cost $100,000.[32]

The second concern relates to privacy rights. When the wording of questions on inventories lacks *face validity*—that is, the content doesn't appear to measure job-related attributes—applicants perceive the tests as an invasion of their privacy, regardless of how valid the inventories have been shown to be.[33] However, face validity does not ensure that the test is valid. That is, a test with content that appears to match the job duties is not automatically valid. Recall the Dial Corporation example from earlier in the chapter. Overall, personality tests can be an important part of a selection process if the personality traits they evaluate are job related, and if the tests are used in conjunction with other selection methods.

### When to Use Employment Tests

Even though most HR professionals advocate identifying or developing job-related selection tests, we realize that not all organizations can afford to do so—at least not for *every* job. Here are five situations in which the cost of *not* testing is greater than the cost of using reliable and valid tests. Use tests in the following cases:[34]

1. The current selection process doesn't yield high-quality employees.
2. Turnover or absenteeism is high.
3. The current selection methods don't meet professional or legal standards.
4. Productivity is low.
5. Errors made by employees could have serious safety, health, or financial consequences.

# Interviews

Interviews are the most frequently used selection method. Following our coverage of the main types of selection interviews, we discuss some of the most significant research regarding the use of interviews. Keep in mind that each type of interview can be used by individual interviewers or by a panel. Companies sometimes use **panel interviews**—several people interviewing an applicant at the same time—as a way to increase the reliability of the interview process.

## Unstructured Interviews

A large percentage of selection interviews are **unstructured interviews**. The interviewer (often the hiring manager) will have a general idea of what a successful applicant should know and be able to do. The interviewer will ask the candidate job-related questions, but without a defined format and without asking the same questions of all applicants. Some managers claim that they are good at judging character, and they need just a few minutes with an applicant in an interview to make a good decision. The reality is that many managers are not as good as they think they are at selecting employees. A more structured process will lead to a better hiring decision. A more structured process is also more defensible should an applicant file a charge of discrimination because of the outcome of the selection process.

## Structured Interviews

The "Working at Starbucks" page on the Starbucks website includes a section to prepare applicants for a job interview at Starbucks. In addition to advising applicants to be very familiar with the company, it tells them to be prepared to answer something called behavioral-based interview questions. These questions focus on key competencies of the position of interest.[35] Starbucks incorporates these questions into a process called a **structured interview** to ensure greater job-relatedness of the interview. This type of interview also provides a more accurate means for comparing responses across applicants because the same type of information is collected from all interviewees. Next, we discuss two types of structured interviews—situational and behavioral. Properly designed situational and behavioral interviews include a rating scale and lead to better selection decisions.

In addition to the ability assessments we have already noted, Barclays uses **situational interviews** as part of its selection process. In this type of interview, an interviewer poses hypothetical situations to the interviewee and gauges the person's responses relative to how the individual would be expected to respond in a similar situation on the job. At Barclays, applicants are expected to use their past experiences to respond to the questions.[36] Situational interviews have proved to be valid in numerous research studies, and they have been shown to be accurate in predicting performance as much as 54% of the time.[37]

A situational interview for a trader on Wall Street might go something like this: What would you do if a client asked you to provide confidential information to him? Then the applicant would describe how he would typically handle this situation. His answer would be compared to the rating scale and a score determined for the interview. The problem with situational interviews is that applicants may tell you what they think you want to hear, rather than what they actually would do. Behavioral interviews provide a way to address this issue.

The premise of the **behavioral interview** is that past behavior is the best predictor of future behavior. Rather than simply asking a candidate how she *would* handle a situation, the interviewer asks the candidate how she *has* handled the situation in the past. For example, "Tell me about a time when you had to deal with an intoxicated passenger" would be a good question to ask an applicant for a flight attendant

**panel interview**

a type of interview process in which several people interview an applicant at the same time

**unstructured interview**

a type of interview in which questions are asked without a defined format, and the same type of information is not collected from all interviewees

**structured interview**

a type of interview that uses a set of predetermined questions related to the job and usually includes a scoring system to track and compare applicant responses

**situational interview**

a type of interview in which an interviewer poses hypothetical situations to the interviewee and gauges the person's responses relative to how the individual would be expected to respond in a similar situation on the job

**behavioral interview**

a type of interview based on the premise that past behavior is the best predictor of future behavior; involves asking job candidates to respond to questions about how they have handled specific job-related types of situations in the past

## EXHIBIT 7.6

### An Example of a Rating Scale for a Behavioral Interview for a Marketing Analyst Position

**Dimension:** Preparing reports to meet client deadlines; using information gathered from primary and secondary sources.

*Describe a time when you had a deadline to meet but realized you would not be able to meet it. What were the circumstances that led up to your realization? How did you handle the situation? What was the outcome? What would you do differently next time?*

**Rating Scale:** Compare the applicant's answer to the following anchors. The score for the applicant is the number with the most similar response.

| | |
|---|---|
| 5 | Describes situation in detail, including specifics about the incident itself and how it was resolved. Answer indicates applicant has a strong ability to prioritize projects and that the applicant is willing to admit when things don't go as smoothly as planned. Applicant has a clear plan for how to avoid the same situation again. |
| 4 | Describes situation in detail, including specifics about the incident, and its resolution. Answer indicates that applicant is willing to take responsibility when appropriate and understands the consequences of missing deadlines. Applicant described the basic elements of a plan for avoiding similar situations. |
| 3 | Describes situation in some detail. Answer indicates applicant realizes that missing the deadline was a problem and that a better plan of action is needed in the future. Applicant took responsibility for own role in missing the deadline. |
| 2 | Describes situation in some detail. Applicant took some responsibility for missing the deadline but primarily blamed it on other circumstances, even though description of situation suggested otherwise. Applicant did mention that perhaps better planning could have occurred. |
| 1 | Applicant had to be prompted to answer the question. Applicant gave numerous excuses for why deadline was not met, taking no responsibility for his/her role in the missed deadline even though it was obvious that poor planning had some impact on the outcome. |

position. If the applicant has limited airline work experience, the interviewer could instead ask, "Tell me about a time when you had to deal with an extremely obnoxious person. Describe what led up to the event, your involvement in the situation, and how the incident was resolved." Follow-up questions provide additional information for the interviewer about how an applicant actually has behaved in situations, as opposed to how the applicant thinks that he would behave or ought to behave in them. Starbucks, P&G, and many other companies use behavioral-based interviewing.[38]

Exhibit 7.6 provides an example of a rating scale for a behavioral interview that is designed to evaluate candidates applying for a marketing analyst position. The behaviors that represent high and low scores to each question are determined by doing a critical incident job analysis. Each interview question can be weighted relative to its importance to the job. The rating for each response is then multiplied by the weight of its associated question, and the results are summed to give an overall score for the applicant. This approach, which has proven to be very effective, ensures that the interview process is reliable and valid.[39]

Much of the research on interviewing has focused on interviewer and applicant characteristics and how they affect the outcomes of the interview process. Research has shown that pre-interview information can affect the outcome of an interview, nonverbal behaviors of applicants can affect interview outcomes, individuals good at self-promotion are likely to get higher ratings, attractive applicants are rated more highly, and personality characteristics such as extraversion can positively affect interview outcomes.[40]

# Reference Checks, Background Checks, Credit Reports, and Honesty Tests

Employers use a variety of means to perform applicant screening, with the goal of ensuring that applicants are providing complete and truthful information in the employment process and that they are not likely to steal from the company or commit some other crime. These screening methods include reference checks, background checks, credit reports, and honesty tests. Increasingly, social media is being used to collect information about applicants as well. One report indicates that 39% of 2,100 companies surveyed used social networking sites to research job candidates. Another study reported that 43% of the hiring managers that used social media to research job candidates found information that kept them from hiring a candidate.[41]

The amount and type of information collected to verify an applicant's credentials differ by the type and level of job. An entry-level job where an employee doesn't handle cash or have other access to company money might require only a reference check. The job of bank manager, though, would require a complete background check and honesty test because someone in that job would have direct access to company funds. Many organizations warn job candidates that they will be dismissed if they are hired and it is later discovered that they provided false information during the hiring process.

**Reference checks** involve contacting individuals whose names are provided by job applicants for the purpose of verifying employment information and gathering other job-related data about an applicant to use in making the hiring decision. Often, names of current or former supervisors are given for this purpose. The questions asked of the reference should be job related and typically focus on the applicant's education, work, and related experiences, and should be structured so that all reference givers for all candidates for the job are asked the same core questions. Some companies may ask the reference provider to offer a judgment about the applicant's qualifications for the open position.

Employers often find themselves in a catch-22 when it comes to reference checks: They need to conduct them to collect information about applicants; however, they are reluctant to give reference-check-related information about their own current or former employees for fear of being sued for *defamation of character*. **Defamation of character** occurs when someone makes written or verbal comments about a person and those comments are not true and the comments cause harm to the individual, such as causing the person to be rejected for the job. Consequently, it's extremely important that any information an employer gives out about a current or former employee be true and verifiable. In addition, a hiring employer should require job applicants to sign release forms granting permission for the employer to do any necessary reference checks. The hiring employer should collect only job-related information using a structured questionnaire.

Because of the risk of defamation of character, many companies have policies limiting the amount and type of information that they can provide about former employees. Some policies prohibit personnel from divulging any information whatsoever; others limit the information provided. For example, often company employees are allowed only to confirm whether the person actually works or worked for the company, the dates of the person's employment, and the individual's salary or salaries.[42] Remember, however, that some cities and states forbid asking salary history when hiring candidates. Consequently, companies need to ensure they can legally provide past salary history for former employees. Some states have passed "Good Samaritan" laws to encourage employers to provide reference information. The laws protect reference providers from being sued if they provide verifiable information in good faith.[43]

**reference check**

contacting individuals whose names are provided by job applicants for the purpose of verifying employment information and gathering other job-related data about an applicant to use in making the hiring decision

**defamation of character**

occurs when someone makes written or verbal comments about a person and those comments are not true and cause harm to the individual, such as causing the person to be rejected for the job

A number of companies have developed software to make it easier for employers to do reference checks. SkillSurvey Reference is an online reference-checking tool from SkillSurvey, Inc. Job candidates go to the designated website and enter their work references. The references are contacted and respond to a set of questions being asked of all applicants for the job. In about two days, the responses from the references are provided to the employer. This online reference-checking tool and others like it speed up the reference-checking process, increases the likelihood that employers will provide more accurate and complete references for current and former employees, ensures that reference questions are standardized, and is believed to lead to better hires.[44]

The purpose of a *background check* is to verify information provided during the application process and/or to obtain additional information about some aspect of the applicant's life from a reliable source. Approximately 99% of large companies and 92% of small and midsize companies conduct some type of background check. They either conduct the checks themselves or hire a third-party firm that specializes in background screening to do it for them. The Internet has made conducting background checks much easier and more affordable, and social media often makes information even more readily available.[45] Regardless of the type and extensiveness of the background check a company conducts, it is important to have a policy describing what will be done, who will be involved, how the information obtained will be handled, the consequences to the applicant of a negative report, and how an applicant can appeal a negative employment decision that was based on background check information.

Information collected as part of a background check can range from verification of college degrees to criminal background checks to credit reports. All employers must collect information to verify that an applicant is eligible to work in the United States. Organizations know that under the *Immigration Reform and Control Act of 1996 (IRCA)*, they can be fined for failing to verify this information. Recall that we discussed the IRCA in Chapter 3. Also, information from background checks is considered to be a consumer report and falls under the federal Fair Credit Reporting Act (FCRA), which is discussed in a following section.[46]

**negligent hiring**

a hiring process in which an employer does not conduct a background check on an employee and that person commits a crime at work similar to the crime he or she committed in the past

Companies conduct background checks to make sure they are providing a safe working environment for their existing employees and to ensure that they are not liable for **negligent hiring**.[47] Negligent hiring occurs when an employer does not conduct a background check on an employee and that person commits a crime at work similar to a crime he or she committed in the past.

Employers must be cautious in using any negative information they obtain. The information should affect the hiring status of the applicant only if the criminal behaviors identified are related to the job tasks and duties. Learning that an applicant was convicted of manslaughter because of a driving incident could affect a firm's decision to hire that person as a driver. However, the information would be less relevant for a job that didn't involve driving for the company, such as the job of an assembly-line worker. In April 2012, the Equal Employment Opportunity Commission (EEOC) issued new enforcement guidelines on the use of criminal and arrest records in employment decisions relative to Title VII. The guidelines note that when using criminal background information in selection, the employer needs to consider the nature of the crime and the time since it occurred in relation to the requirements of the job for which the individual has applied. The employer must also allow the individual not selected because of the criminal background check to indicate why that exclusion is not appropriate.

Additionally, as of April 2018, more than 150 cities and counties in the United States and 31 states and the District of Columbia have adopted "ban-the-box" laws relative to background checks for public employment opportunities. A total of 11 states, the District of Columbia, and 31 cities and counties have extended these fair-chance hiring policies to government contractors, and 17 localities have extended the policies to private employers who do business in their jurisdictions. Under these laws, employers cannot ask about criminal records until the job offer has been made. These laws may also limit how far back an employer can investigate criminal history and when in the selection process a background check can be conducted. Typically, they do allow job offers to be withdrawn if the reason for the conviction record shows a relationship to job duties.[48]

Many jobs require employees to handle cash or securities or grant employees access to corporate bank accounts. A *credit check*, or review of an applicant's credit report, is job related in such cases. The employer needs to ensure that employees are not in a bad personal financial situation that might motivate them to steal from the company. The *FCRA* permits employers to collect information about applicants' and employees' credit.[49] Applicants must be told that the information from the report may be used for employment decisions. This information must be provided clearly in writing and not be part of the employment application. The Act requires applicants or employees to provide written authorization for an employer to have permission to legally access their credit information. Further, the employer has to certify to the credit checking source that the applicant was notified and gave permission for the credit check, all FCRA requirements are met, and the information will not be used to discriminate against the applicant or employee or in any other way be misused.

Before an employer can take an **adverse action** against an applicant, such as turning the applicant down for the job based on information in the credit report, the applicant must be notified and given a copy of the consumer report the employer is using to make the decision. The employer must also give the applicant a copy of *A Summary of Your Rights Under the Fair Credit Reporting Act*. Following the process outlined therein provides an opportunity for the applicant to review the report and notify the employer of any errors. If an adverse action is taken, the Act requires that the applicant be notified orally, in writing, or electronically. The notice should include contact information for the reporting company, a statement that you, as the employer, made the adverse decision, and instructions on how the applicant can refute the information on the report. The applicant must also be told how to get an additional free report from the company providing it, and that the report must be requested within 60 days.[50] Keep in mind that the FCRA applies to virtually any information obtained by a consumer-reporting agency, including (as noted earlier) background check information. Specific types of information considered covered under the FCRA include reference checks, information about civil lawsuits, and criminal and civil records.[51]

Many employers used polygraph tests to screen job applicants until problems with inaccurate results led to the passage of the *Polygraph Protection Act of 1988*. Specifically, the problems were related to false positives and false negatives. *False-positive* results on a polygraph test indicate that the person taking the test is lying when, in fact, she is not. *False-negative results* indicate that the person taking the test is not lying when he actually is. False negatives can be just as costly to organizations as false positives, but they are less likely to occur.

After the general use of polygraphs became illegal, employers still wanted and needed a way to predict whether an applicant would engage in illegal or counterproductive behavior. For instance, the cost of employee theft worldwide in the retail industry is reported to be $50 billion annually, making it essential that employers identify ways to mitigate such theft.[52] *Honesty tests*, also called *integrity tests*, are one of the resources that serve that purpose. These tests have been found to predict employee theft, likelihood of filing and size of workers compensation claims, substance abuse, and related types of behaviors that interfere with work performance.[53] There are two basic types of honesty tests: overt honesty tests and personality tests.

**adverse action**

an action taken against an applicant, such as turning the applicant down for the job

An *overt honesty test* is just what it sounds like: a test that is designed specifically to predict honesty and integrity. This type of test measures the frequency of a person's stealing or how lenient one's attitude is toward theft. An overt honesty test might include questions such as: "Have you ever told a lie?" or "Do you think most people would steal something if they thought they wouldn't get caught?" These types of questions are written in such a way that the same belief is assessed with multiple questions, making it more difficult for the respondent to "beat" the test.

A *personality test* asks questions in a more disguised way to identify traits known to be related to counterproductive behaviors. These traits include insubordination, substance abuse, and other discipline problems. Questions on these tests are less direct and may ask the test taker to respond to questions or items about his or her relationships with parents, spouse, or coworkers, as well as about the individual's own state of being, such as "I have thought about losing my mind."[54]

Using tests of these types for prescreening applicants is preferable to using them with current employees who are likely to become upset if they feel their integrity is being challenged by their employer. Also, if an employment decision is made about current employees who score poorly on one of these tests, they might file a lawsuit against the company if their behavior is not actually counterproductive.[55]

No employment decision should be made solely on the basis of an honesty or integrity measure. Just as polygraphs result in false positives and false negatives, so too can these tests. Some states have laws that limit the use of honesty tests; it is important to check the laws in your state before administering these tests.

## Assessment Centers

**assessment center**

a process of engaging job candidates in a series of simulations designed to evaluate their ability to perform aspects of the jobs they are seeking

**Assessment centers** in companies involve a process of engaging job candidates in a series of simulations designed to evaluate their ability to perform aspects of the jobs they are seeking. Often, assessment centers are used to make *internal* promotion decisions. They are used most often for managerial or professional positions. Typical simulations include:

- *An in-basket exercise*—Candidates sort through and respond to letters, memos, and reports within a specific time frame and within a specified context.
- *A leaderless group discussion*—Candidates are given a problem to solve together without a designated leader.
- *Role plays*—Candidates play out job-related situations, usually involving solving a problem.

Trained evaluators (often managers from within the company) observe how applicants perform during these simulations and rate their performance on a defined scale for each job-related dimension. Dimensions frequently assessed include oral and written communications, decisiveness, adaptability, initiative, delegation, and planning and organization. An assessment center's selection process can last for several days and be expensive to administer. The costs include setting up the process and the time that the firm's managers must spend rating candidates. Some companies have their own in-house assessment centers; other companies send job applicants to outside assessment centers for testing. The International Congress on Assessment Centers provides guidelines and ethical considerations for assessment center operations, including considerations for the use of assessment centers in diverse cultural settings.[56]

## Biodata

**biodata**

a shortened name for *biographical data*; refers to a standardized questionnaire that asks applicants to provide personal and biographical information to be compared with the same information for successful employees

**Biodata** is a shortened name for *biographical data* and refers to a standardized questionnaire that asks applicants to provide personal and biographical information. The questions might focus on candidates' hobbies, experiences in high school or college, preferred supervisor characteristics, and so forth. Then the information that candidates provide is compared to the information provided by a firm's successful employees. The outcome is a prediction of how likely the employee is to succeed at the company and is based on the idea that past behavior is the best predictor of future behavior.[57] Biodata has proven to be one of the best predictors of employee performance, and does not have adverse impact.[58] For instance, biodata has proven to be effective in predicting performance and turnover for jobs as diverse as nurse[59] and customer service worker.[60]

Biodata questionnaires are expensive to develop, however, and extreme care must be exercised to ensure that the questions asked are job related. Many personal and biographical questions do not appear to be job related at first glance. Employers should also make every effort to verify the information candidates provide.[61]

## Drug Tests

The *Drug-Free Workplace Act of 1988* requires all federal contractors to develop policies to ensure that their employees are drug free. Since the passage of this Act, many employers have implemented policies requiring all applicants to pass a drug test before being hired, although the legislation does not require that.[62] Most employers also prohibit the use of alcohol at their workplaces and discipline employees who come to work under the influence of alcohol or drugs.

Research has shown that employees who abuse drugs are more likely to miss work, be tardy, be involved in workplace accidents, and file workers' compensation claims. In fact, the National Council on Alcoholism and Drug Dependence reports that drug abuse, including alcohol, costs employers approximately $81 billion each year.[63] Therefore, the decision of whether or not to use drug tests is a serious one.

An employer using drug testing needs to have a written policy about its use that is in compliance with federal, state, and local laws. Generally, a candidate must sign a consent form before being tested.[64] Employees who are currently using drugs or alcohol are not protected under the ADA, but recovering drug users and alcoholics are covered. Therefore, an employer can refuse to hire someone who is using illegal substances or shows up at the interview under the influence of alcohol. The employer cannot refuse to hire someone because he or she is a recovering drug or alcohol user.[65]

## Medical Examinations

Prior to the passage of the ADA, employers could require a medical examination as a condition of employment. Now, the ADA specifies that a medical examination can be required only after an offer of employment has been made. Employers requiring a medical examination of an employee should provide a copy of the job description to the examining physician for review of the job requirements. If the results of the medical examination indicate that the person cannot perform the job requirements, and there is no reasonable accommodation that would allow him or her to do so, the company does not have to employ that individual. Generally, a medical exam can lead to disqualification of an applicant if that individual would be a direct threat to the health or safety of self or others if employed in the job under consideration.[66]

# Choosing Among Selection Methods

Which selection methods should you use, and when? Companies report that interviews are the most frequently used selection method, followed by applications and résumés.[67] (Recall that interviews are more valid when they are carefully structured, and interviewers are carefully trained to ensure that interviews are correctly administered.) That said, depending on the type of position for which you're hiring, these three methods might not result in the best hiring decision. The best, most appropriate methods depend on the job for which you are hiring and the goals and objectives your organization is trying to achieve. Bottom line: Use the methods that will provide the most relevant information you need to collect from your applicants.[68] Doing so increases the likelihood that you will identify and hire the most qualified person for the job.

Before beginning the selection process, you need to make sure you know what information you need, how you can best collect it, and how you will use it to make a final selection decision. This last part is more challenging than it might appear. Each person is likely to have different strengths and weaknesses; very few individuals will excel in all areas. Some candidates will score well on one or more selection measures and lower on others. The challenge for you as a manager is to determine how to use all the information you obtain to make the best hiring decision. Several approaches are available for helping you make this determination.

## Compensatory Approach

**compensatory approach**

a process for deriving a final score for each candidate in the selection process by weighting outcomes on multiple selection measures differentially so that some items are weighted more heavily than others and a high score on one part can offset a low score on another

If you don't do well on one assignment in most of your classes, you have the opportunity to offset that grade by doing well on another assignment. This model is known as a **compensatory approach**. Theoretically, during the selection process, a candidate could score low on one measure (perhaps a written test) but do exceptionally well on another part, such as the interview. The outcome of the interview could offset the lower score on the written test or vice versa, depending on how you weight the scores. Measures that correlate more highly with on-the-job success should be weighted more heavily. Exhibit 7.7 shows an example of how the compensatory approach works. For this particular job, the organization doing the hiring has determined that the second interview should receive the highest weight (45%), followed by the written test (35%) and the initial interview (20%). Each applicant's score on each measure is multiplied by the weight assigned to the measure to arrive at a score for the measure. These scores are summed to determine a total score for the applicant. When scores are close, you can ask applicants to provide additional information or have them return for another interview.

## Multiple-Hurdle Approach

**multiple-hurdle approach**

an approach in which applicants have to pass each step (hurdle) successfully to continue in the selection process

In the **multiple-hurdle approach**, applicants have to complete each step (hurdle) successfully to continue in the selection process. Staying with the selection techniques shown in Exhibit 7.7, an applicant would have to reach a minimum score on the written test (Hurdle 1) to be scheduled for a first interview (Hurdle 2). If the applicant does well in the first interview, he or she can proceed to a second interview, which is the last step in the process (Hurdle 2). Corporate Spotlight 7.3 provides an example of how Automattic, the company that owns WordPress.com, uses a multiple-hurdle selection process.

### EXHIBIT 7.7

Example of Using the Compensatory Approach for Selection Decision-Making

| Assessment Tool | Weight x | Applicant 1 | Applicant 2 |
|---|---|---|---|
| Written test | 35% x | 70 = 24.50 | 85 = 29.75 |
| Interview 1 | 20% x | 80 = 16.00 | 75 = 15.00 |
| Interview 2 | 45% x | 90 = 40.50 | 95 = 42.75 |
| Total | 100% | 81.00 | 87.50 |

# COMPANY SPOTLIGHT  7.3

## Job Auditions at Automattic

Automattic, the company behind WordPress.com, is located in 63 countries and has 729 employees who speak 81 languages. Automattic is a distributed company with a goal to "democratize publishing so that anyone with a story can tell it, regardless of income, gender, politics, language, or where they live in the world." Along with WordPress.com, the company has WooCommerce, VaultPress, Polldaddy, Cloudup, and other platforms. Most of their work is open source.

The company has a generous benefits program. Benefits include an open vacation policy, home office setup and coworking allowances, open parental leave (fully paid for employees who have been with the company for 12 months), a two- to three-month sabbatical every five years, and more. As you can imagine, Automattic is an attractive company for prospective employees.

Visit their "Work with Us" page, and you will quickly see that they use a multiple-hurdle selection process that includes an audition. Only about 15% of applicants make it through the résumé screening. Applicants who make it through that first step and the first interview stage are invited to work on a project on contract with existing Automatticians. These projects typically run from two to six weeks and are designed to gauge how well the job candidate fits in with the company. The chief executive officer (CEO) views this process of selection as providing the candidates with an RJP and providing the company with the ability to ensure that they are hiring smart employees. The result of the process is fewer terminations and less turnover.

The company used to rely on a traditional résumé review and interviews for hiring new employees. Maybe the candidate would be given a brain-teaser question to answer and go out to lunch with existing employees. However, that approach provided only limited information about whether or not the job candidates could do the actual work required, and whether they would fit in with the company culture. The audition, or "tryout" approach, gives candidates the opportunity to demonstrate what they can do and how well they can do it. In essence, the audition provides a work sample.

The audition is tailored to the job for which the person is applying. All job candidates are paid the same hourly rate, regardless of the type of job. Criteria used to evaluate performance during the audition include self-motivation, written communication skills, how mistakes are handled, and how well the person works with others. That last criterion is among the most important of the requirements at Automattic.

The company is flexible in working with job candidates so that the tryout period fits with their personal situation (e.g., can work nights or weekends so as not to interfere with a current job). Candidates can choose to opt out before finishing the audition if they find the job not a good fit, and the company can end the tryout for the same reason.

There is one more step after the tryout in the multiple-hurdle process, which involves a text-only Skype chat or instant messaging interview between the CEO and the job candidate who has been successful in the tryout. The focus at this stage is on cultural fit and passion. The use of a text-only interview masks any demographic characteristics of job candidates, thus helping to ensure that such are not factors in the final decision. Through this process, the company identifies the most qualified candidates and is likely to be willing to hire everyone who makes it through the process. About 95% of job candidates who make it to the final stage receive a job offer.

*Sources:* Mullenweg, Matt, "The CEO of Automattic on Holding 'Auditions' to Build a Strong Team," *Harvard Business Review*, 92 (2014): 39–42; "All Around the World, Building a New Web, and a New Workplace Join Us!" https://automattic.com/about/; Bort, Julie, "Billion-Dollar Startup Automattic Hires Employees Without Ever Meeting Them or Talking to Them on the Phone," *Business Insider Australia*, January 5, 2016, https://www.businessinsider.com.au/automattic-hires-employees-automatically-2016-1.

## Multiple-Cutoff Approach

**multiple-cutoff approach**

an approach in which an applicant performs all the measures of the job assessment process and has to reach a minimum score on each one to remain in the running for a particular job

With the **multiple-cutoff approach**, an applicant has to reach a minimum score on each measure to remain in the running for a particular job. This differs from the multiple-hurdle approach in that applicants go through all steps of the process. After all the applicants have completed all the steps, those who meet the minimum score on all parts are considered eligible for the job, and the selection decision is made from that group.

## Choosing a Scoring Method

Each scoring approach has advantages and disadvantages. The compensatory model works best when there are no absolute requirements that a candidate has to meet. If you are hiring a project manager and there are six qualifications the successful candidate should have, but no one qualification is a make-or-break factor in the decision, then the compensatory approach would work well. The multiple-hurdle approach works well when there are absolutes. For example, if a candidate for a project manager's position needs to have each qualification you are measuring and you can prioritize the qualifications from most critical to least critical, then the multiple-hurdle approach would be a good choice. If all the qualifications must be met at a minimal level, then the multiple-cutoff approach would work.

For some jobs, a company might use a combination of a multiple-hurdle approach and another approach. Suppose, for example, that a company needs an accountant who is a certified public accountant (CPA). In this situation, it would be logical to use the CPA credential to make the first cut. After that cut, a compensatory or multiple cutoff, or even further hurdles, could be used.

Principles

Practice

# Selection in Practice: Organizational Demands

Now that you have a good understanding of the fundamentals of the selection process, we focus on the types of decisions managers must make on a regular basis when designing the process and selecting employees. Exhibit 7.8 outlines many of these decisions. We have already established how the requirements of a job and a firm's recruitment efforts affect the employee selection process. Let's now look at how organizational demands, environmental demands, and regulatory issues affect the decisions you will make as a manager when selecting employees to work for you.

## Strategy and Selection

By now, you clearly understand that the role of the selection process is to help you hire the "right" employees. The best widget in the world won't be designed, made, or sold without individuals coming up with a plan for the widget, developing the design, setting up a production process, and manufacturing and marketing it. However, different competencies individuals possess matter more or less for different strategies. Remember that a company's *strategy* is its plan for gaining a competitive advantage over its rivals. As a manager involved in hiring employees, you need to understand the company's strategy and the core competencies that it requires of all employees. Those competencies, along with the specific criteria to ensure that there is a good person–job fit, determine what you focus on when you are selecting which applicants to hire. Your firm's strategy also affects the choice of methods that you will use for collecting information about applicants.

**EXHIBIT 7.8**

Selection in Practice

| Context | Practice Issues |
|---|---|
| **Organizational Demands** | |
| *Strategy* drives . . . | • Core competencies needed |
| | • Selection criteria for person–job fit |
| | • Methods of selection |
| *Company characteristics* determine . . . | |
| | • Degree of structure |
| | • Substance and form of the selection process |
| *Culture* establishes . . . | • Selection criteria for person–organization fit |
| | • Practice of promotion from within |
| | • Who is involved in selection process |
| *Employee concerns* include . . . | • Perceptions of fairness/justice |
| | • Impact of job offered on work/family balance |
| **Environmental Demands** | |
| *Labor force* influences . . . | • Types of applicants available for selection |
| | • Willingness of applicants to accept jobs |
| *Technology* affects . . . | • Process of selection |
| | • Need to verify the legitimacy of credentials |
| *Globalization* impacts . . . | • Availability of foreign labor for jobs in home country |
| | • Staffing of international operations |
| *Ethics/social responsibility* shapes . . . | |
| | • Concerns about privacy |
| | • Amount and type of information given to applicants |
| **Regulations** | |
| *Regulations* guide . . . | • Procedures for using selection measures |
| | • Definition of who is an applicant |

## Core Competencies

Core competencies differ from company to company. Focusing on your company's strategic competencies when setting up the selection process helps ensure a strong match between what employees can do and what the company strategy requires. Companies that compete based on a low-cost strategy often design jobs to maximize employee efficiency and productivity. This strategy results in jobs with a narrow range of tasks and limited employee discretion. Low-cost focused companies are much less concerned about competencies such as creativity and flexibility than they are about competencies such as efficiency, dependability, and cooperativeness. Additionally, a company pursuing a differentiation strategy focused on customer service will look for different competencies than a company pursuing a differentiation strategy focused on innovation.

Certainly, there can be overlapping competencies among firms with different strategies. Trust and personal responsibility in all relationships, one of IBM's values,[69] is likely valued by all firms in one form or another, regardless of the strategic focus of other firms. The important point to remember is that the core competencies assessed during the selection process should be a function of a company's strategy. Therefore, as a manager, you need to know what those competencies are before you begin the process of hiring new employees.

### Selection Criteria for Person–Job Fit

Core competencies are usually broadly defined because they apply across jobs within a company. KSAs, on the other hand, are job specific and are determined by the design of a job. A company's strategy, like its core competencies, will determine the specific KSAs each employee needs in order to do his or her job. The cook in the fast-food restaurant needs different skills than the chef in a fine-dining establishment. Likewise, an accountant in a major accounting firm will have different job requirements than an accountant who works in a low cost retail chain. The two jobs will share some requirements, but the strategy of each organization results in additional and specific job requirements that need to be considered during the selection process.

### Methods of Selection

The type and number of selection methods used are driven by a company's strategy. If your company has a low-cost strategy, you will want to find the most efficient selection methods possible. A simple application and one short interview might be all that is used. Small businesses often have limited resources, so they would adopt this approach. Or, if the company typically needs a lot of people to do the same job, it may be more cost-effective to develop a selection test specifically for that job. Employees can be selected in an efficient manner with a standardized process. A theme park, such as Universal Studios, needs to hire a lot of employees for similar jobs and ensure they fit the company culture; thus, developing a selection test would be cost effective for the company.

A company with a differentiation strategy that focuses on high-quality service will be especially interested in how well future employees respond to situations involving others. Including role plays, situational interviews, or behavioral interviews in the selection process will provide a way to assess how well applicants respond to such situations. If the differentiation strategy is one of innovation, the selection methods might include a simulation in which the applicant has to do something unique or "think outside the box." Behavioral interviews and references can also reveal how "innovative" applicants have been in the past.

## Company Characteristics and Selection

The size and stage of development of a company are often highly correlated. These characteristics of a company will determine the structure of its selection process and the substance and form of the process for designing and implementing the process. Whether the firm is large or small, new or old, wealthy or struggling, as a manager, you will be able to use the information you are currently learning to conduct a successful selection process within those parameters.

### Degree of Structure

Selection processes range from highly structured to highly unstructured, and from a few steps to many steps. Some processes are very informal and include perhaps only an application and an interview; others are very formal and involve multiple steps and extensive, structured interviews. Larger, more-established companies, such as Lockheed Martin, generally have more resources and can afford to utilize more extensive selection methods. Many of these organizations also develop their own selection processes. They also recognize that the more applicants they have, the greater the risk that an informal and/or unstructured process will be viewed by applicants as subjective and biased. Thus, a structured and validated process is more likely to be in place.

Keep in mind that exceptions always exist. A company may have grown quickly and not taken the time to develop good selection processes, and even some long-established companies might not have good processes. Some firms—for example, JetBlue—have always understood the importance of a well-designed selection process.[70]

### Substance and Form of the Selection Process

A company's industry has a big impact on the type of employees the firm needs, as well as the selection norms it will tend to use. How a defense contractor selects employees obviously will be very different from how a restaurant selects employees: Defense contractors must conduct extensive background checks of applicants in order to meet government security regulations. A restaurant should do background checks for employees who will handle money and credit cards, but they will be less extensive than those done by the defense contractor.

An industry's norms can be either implicitly or explicitly conveyed. Major business consulting firms, such as Deloitte, Accenture, and KPMG, have similar, highly structured selection processes. They typically use extensive interviews and case studies to narrow the number of acceptable candidates for their open positions. These are large, established firms, but because of the norms of the industry, even the small boutique consulting firms use the same type of selection processes.

Specific practices also exist within occupations. Some occupations, such as accounting, law, and medicine, require licenses or certifications. Other occupations do not require certification but have it available. HR is an example of the latter. Companies use credentials as a signal of the competencies that an applicant will bring to the job. As a result, fewer additional steps may be needed during the selection process than for occupations that do not have similar credentials.

## Culture and Selection

Will the culture of a company matter to you when you are applying for jobs? Most likely, it will. When setting up a selection process, it is important for you to be familiar with your company's culture and decide how to determine the applicant's fit with the culture.

### Person–Organization Fit

A company's strategy and characteristics influence the criteria managers rely on to maximize person–job fit. **Person–organization fit** involves how well a person fits within the broader organizational culture.[71] Recall that a firm's culture is a function of the basic assumptions, values, and beliefs of the organization's members.[72] Each company's culture is unique and influences the selection process. Company Spotlight 7.4 provides an example of how the selection process at CDW was changed to better reflect the corporate culture.

**person–organization fit**
how well a person fits within the broader organizational culture

A company's culture can be another primary reason applicants accept job offers at the firm. Starbucks believes its corporate culture is the reason it attracts and retains good employees. The company's mission and vision statement emphasize a work environment that is positive and respectful. Starbucks hires employees who are adaptable, passionate, and dependable team players. The company's interview guidelines provide examples of questions interviewers can ask applicants to discern whether they have these attributes. Companies such as Starbucks know that a match between the values of their employees and those fostered by the organization increases employee productivity and contributes to success.[73]

It should be noted that some candidates might have the necessary competencies to do a particular job but still not fit into a company's culture. Other candidates might share the values and beliefs of an organization but lack the competencies to succeed in a particular job. That's why, as we have explained, both the person–job and person–organization fit are important.

## COMPANY SPOTLIGHT  7.4

### Culture and Selection at CDW

Many companies attribute their success to their corporate culture. These companies take their culture into account when they design their selection processes. CDW, a leading multibrand technology solutions provider, is one such company. The company has over 8,700 employees, and for their 2018 fiscal year generated over $15 billion in net sales. CDW has collected an impressive array of awards over the years as a best place to work. The company has been included on lists such as Forbes 2017 America's Best Large Employer, Computerworld's 2017 100 Best Places to Work in IT, and 2017 Military Times Best for Vets Employers. The company has also been recognized on Glassdoor's list of "Best Places to Interview," for two years.

CDW spent more than a year revamping its approach to HR management, reviewing and revising its recruitment and selection processes and its orientation and retention strategies. A big part of this revamping involved examining the relationship between the selection system and the desired culture to make sure that they were in alignment. This company knows that if it does a better job of hiring, turnover will go down. The new process incorporated a three-minute, RJP video to ensure that applicants understood the nature of the jobs for which they were applying. The selection approach was customized for CDW's jobs and included a behavioral interview. The manager to whom the applicant was likely to report if hired conducted the interview. This early interaction provided a way for managers to begin to build relationships with potential hires and to communicate and model key points of the corporate culture.

*Sources:* Adapted from Hansen, Fay, "Overhauling the Recruiting Process at CDW Corp," *Workforce Management,* last modified April 11, 2007, http://www.workforce.com/articles/overhauling_the-recruiting-process-at-cdw-corp; and Bazzell, Jared and Floersch, Cassie "CDW Gets IT with Realistic Job Previews," hirevue.com, August 31, 2017; https://www.hirevue.com/blog/cdw-gets-it-with-realistic-job-previews. "About CDW," https://www.cdw.com/content/cdw/en/about/overview.html; "Life at CDW," https://www.cdwjobs.com/pages/life-at-cdw.

### Promotion-from-Within Policy

Culture affects the extent to which a company has an internal versus external hiring mind-set. Many companies are quite loyal to their employees. When a job vacancy occurs, these companies promote current employees rather than look outside the organization. A firm's current employees are already familiar with the company's culture when the cultural values are continuously reinforced. Of course, there is also a downside to this practice. Without "new blood" coming into the organization on a regular basis, the company runs the risk of becoming stagnant. Therefore, carefully weighing the pros and cons of promoting from within is important before the culture becomes too entrenched.

### Who Participates in the Selection Process

The norms about who participates in the selection process are established in part by company culture. In a team environment where employee input is valued, all members of the team are likely to be involved in some aspect of the selection process. Google includes multiple Googlers (i.e., Google employees) in their selection process and usually includes Googlers who will be on the person's team.[74] In more traditional, hierarchical organizations, only employees in higher-level positions will be involved in selecting new employees.

## Employee Concerns and Selection

During the selection process, prospective employees want to be treated fairly and equally relative to other applicants. They also want to gather as much information as possible about the job so they can decide how it will affect their lives.

### Fair and Equal Treatment

The psychological contract between an employee and an employer begins to be established during the recruitment process and is reinforced during the process. How applicants are treated during this time gives them an idea about how they will be treated as employees. Reducing bias in the selection process and treating applicants in a consistent manner positively affects applicants' perceptions of the organization.

We all have personal preferences and stereotypes that can affect our decisions. Acknowledging this is the first step in preventing the use of those factors in making decisions. A well-designed selection process helps hiring managers clearly understand the factors that *should* affect their hiring decisions, as opposed to those that shouldn't. As we've explained, a structured selection process and training help reduce the likelihood of bias and ensure equal treatment of all applicants. Many companies train their employees on diversity issues and how to select employees. Providing hiring managers with a scoring key for rating candidates' answers to their interview questions will also reduce the risk of bias occurring. Also, remember that as a manager, you are ultimately responsible for ensuring that employees participating in the hiring process understand how they should go about making unbiased judgments about candidates. This should be the case whether the company you work for is large or small, new or established, affluent or struggling, your own company or part of a conglomerate.

### Impact of a Job on Work/Life Balance

In Chapter 6, we discussed the concept of realistic job previews (RJPs). Recall that RJPs provide candidates with information about the demands of the jobs for which they are applying, including time expectations, working conditions, and possible stressors related to the jobs. As a manager, you might have an applicant you really want to hire, and you may be fortunate to convince that person to come to work for you. However, if he starts work only to find that the job is going to require more travel than he was told, or longer work hours, or some other factor he perceives as negative, and if those requirements interfere with his family responsibilities, he is likely to find another job as soon as possible and not be very productive in the interim.

# Selection in Practice: Environmental Influences

A number of environmental influences directly affect the selection process. The labor market influences both who is available for employment and who is willing to work for the company. Technology affects the design and implementation of the selection process, and it creates new challenges for selection as well. Globalization affects a firm's decisions about hiring employees at home and abroad. Ethics and social responsibility concerns shape privacy issues, including what information and how much of it the organization should communicate to applicants. We discuss each of these issues in some detail.

## Labor Market and Selection

For selection purposes, we are interested in both the larger labor market and relevant labor markets for particular jobs. The labor market influences both the type of applicants available for selection and the willingness of applicants to accept jobs. As a manager, you will be confronted at some point with labor market challenges and have to decide to what extent those challenges affect the selection process you use.

### Types of Applicants Available

The applicant pool changes as the demographics of a country or region change. Age is one demographic that is having a direct impact on the hiring of employees today. Many older workers are finding themselves having to work to make ends meet after retiring, and some just prefer to keep working rather than retire. Often, these workers are highly qualified individuals who may want to work part time and bring their valuable skills and information to the workplace. Employers need to be open to what these potential employees can contribute and ensure that age doesn't become an explicit or implicit factor in selection. In fact, many companies are realizing that an aging workforce means that companies have to be proactive and embrace the employment of older workers to maintain a sufficiently large workforce.

In the past in the United States, teenagers often filled low-skilled, entry-level service jobs. Now, teens either don't have to work because of their parents' affluence or have lots of choices of places where they can work. As a result, they are less willing to work in fast-food jobs, discount retail jobs, or other service jobs that people in this age group would have more willingly accepted a few decades ago. Increasingly, the applicants for these jobs are immigrants to the United States who may need skill and language training so that they can communicate with customers. The selection process has to be modified to accommodate these applicants as well. For example, you may need to have your applications translated into various languages if your target applicants lack the ability to read and write English (and English is not an essential job requirement). Interviewers may need to speak multiple languages.

A number of occupations have experienced shifts in the size and nature of their applicant pools. School districts are using alternative measures to determine a potential teacher's qualifications in fields where there is a shortage of qualified teachers, for example. Sometimes when teachers are hired, they are given a timeline by which they must acquire certain credentials to remain employed. Hospitals have had to look outside their domestic borders to find qualified nurses as the population ages and more health-care professionals are needed. The selection process has to be modified in these situations to identify and process applicants. Managers have to recognize that the qualifications that they are looking for today might not look exactly like those they traditionally searched for in the past.

### Willingness of Applicants to Accept Jobs

A *loose labor market* presents the best of all possible worlds for employers. When there are more qualified employees available than job openings, an employer has the luxury of being very selective about who is hired. Applicants have fewer offers and are going to be less selective. But what happens when there are too few qualified employees in the labor market? In a *tight labor market*, employers don't have the luxury of being very selective. An employer actually may eliminate all but the most essential steps in the selection process (keeping application, background check, and interview) and use resources formally earmarked for selection to train new employees to do the job. Applicants may have multiple offers in this labor market, so much of the selection process becomes about selling the job.

## Technology and Selection

Technology has had a significant impact on how selection is managed. The two most prominent advances are the increased use of computer technology to perform part of the selection process and to verify candidates' credentials. We will first discuss technology's impact on the process of selection.

## Technology and the Process of Selection

Go into Target or Walmart for a job, and you will most likely find yourself completing an application at a computer kiosk. At this kiosk, applicants can be asked to complete a personality or situational judgment questionnaire, which serves the same purpose as a screening interview. The information collected supplements the information job seekers put on their applications and provides the companies with a preliminary idea of how well the applicants will fit the job and organization.[75]

In other organizations, an applicant might be directed to call a specific phone number to respond to similar questions. Computer kiosks, online applications, and phone systems used for initial screening save a lot of time and paperwork for the company, and the information entered by applicants can become part of a company's applicant-tracking system.

Software can review applications for key words quickly and provide a list of qualified candidates. Software screening, however, is only as good as the information input into the screening process. Many companies try to adapt their paper applications to online applications without taking into consideration how the software will use the entered information to identify qualified candidates for the job, but not always accurately.[76] For instance, filtering applications for someone with experience in art and décor for a home furnishings store might miss a qualified applicant who did not use those exact words but has interior design experience that matches the job requirements.

Companies are also using online selection tests, which raises questions about how equivalent these tests are to traditional paper-and-pencil versions. If the two versions are not highly equivalent, the Internet test may have to be validated separately. Testing conditions, such as whether a test is timed if it is online, may make a critical difference in terms of equivalence.[77] Employers using online selection tests face the same issues noted earlier in this chapter for employers using online applications. These tests need to be easily accessible by mobile devices.

Also as noted earlier, social media sites are playing an increasing role in selection as well, but they must be used with caution. In a research study that specifically examined the validity of recruiter evaluation of Facebook profiles, the researchers found that the ratings did not add any greater value to the selection process than traditional criteria and were not related to future job performance or turnover.[78]

## Verification of Credentials

Employers are finding it easier, faster, and more cost effective to do reference and background checking now that much of it can be done online. Applicants often fail to disclose information that paints them in a less-than-favorable light, such as information about having been fired from a previous job. Sometimes applicants omit information about their previous work experience simply because they're afraid it will make them look overqualified. Other information submitted by applicants is simply false. One survey reported that more than 50% of résumés contain false information.[79] Electronic processing of reference and background checks may make it more difficult for applicants to lie about their past. Nonetheless, employers need to exercise due diligence to ensure that the information they are collecting electronically is coming from reliable sources and is accurate. Employers also need to be aware that there is an increase in class action lawsuits under the FCRA relative to the use of background checks. Among the companies that have already experienced such lawsuits are JPMorgan, Uber, and TransUnion. These companies and others had to pay amounts ranging from $1.25 million to $60 million in 2017.[80]

Technology may be making it more difficult for applicants to conceal or falsify information, but it can make it easier, too. For example, some job applicants have gone so far as to hack into university computers and add their names to graduation lists. A candidate for a director position at Korn/Ferry, an international executive search firm, did just that. (He was found out, and not surprisingly, he didn't get the job.) In addition, technology makes it much easier for candidates to forge documents indicating that they have certain credentials when they actually lack them.[81]

Organizations need to be proactive and make sure they have clear policies that are well communicated to hiring managers and others involved in the search process about the use of information obtained online. Doing so will help ensure that employee rights are protected and reduce the use of discriminatory information found on social media sites. Employers should consider obtaining permission from job applicants to do social media searches, just as they request consent for other types of background checks and references.[82]

## Globalization and Selection

Many organizations find themselves involved in global selection activities in one of four ways:

1. Hiring increasingly larger numbers of international employees to work in their domestic operations
2. Selecting internal candidates to send to other countries to work
3. Hiring host-country nationals (HCNs) to work in their companies' operations in host countries
4. Hiring international employees to work for the company abroad

Each of these activities creates unique challenges and opportunities related to selecting employees. Next we discuss these practices.

### The Labor Market at Home

The most carefully constructed selection process is ineffective if applicants aren't available to apply for open jobs. During the end of the twentieth century and the beginning of the twenty-first century, the U.S. economy was booming, and job growth was on the rise. High-tech and other companies began to rely more and more on immigrants for their staffing needs as a result, especially given the shortage of math and science majors in the United States and the increasing need for workers with those backgrounds. However, after the terrorist attacks on September 11, 2001, the amount of information, time, and cost required to obtain visas for immigrants to work in the United States increased, and the number of available H-1B visas decreased. *H1-B* is a classification used for nonimmigrant aliens who are employed to work temporarily in very specific occupations, such as engineering, math, law, theology, architecture, physical sciences, and medicine. The need for such workers did not decrease in the same proportion, however.

For instance, the U.S. Citizenship and Immigration Services (USCIS) reported receiving 190,098 petitions for H-1B visas for fiscal year 2019 (July 1, 2018–June 30, 2019). This number significantly exceeded the cap on available visas of 85,000.[83] For the calendar year 2019, only 65,000 aliens could receive these visas. An additional 20,000 could file for a visa under an advanced degree exemption. The current cap was put in place in 2004. Employers seeking to hire workers with H1-B status have to complete a labor condition application with the Department of Labor and pay a fee. The workers can have H1-B status for six years at a time.[84]

## Labor Market Abroad

If you are staffing an international operation, you will need to decide whether to hire parent-country nationals (PCNs), host-country nationals (HCNs), third-country nationals (TCNs), or some combination of the three. The choices that you make are critical to the success of your operation.

Companies send **parent-country nationals (PCNs)** on international assignments for a variety of reasons, which can differ from country to country. In the United States, PCNs are used to fill a skill gap or to start a new operation. For companies in the United Kingdom and Japan, PCNs are used to set up a new operation, and in Germany, they are used to develop international talent.[85] Selecting the right PCN for an assignment is challenging but essential. When PCNs fail (return to their home countries earlier than planned), it is very costly for organizations.

PCNs are often selected for assignments abroad because of their technical skills. However, research suggests that companies need to focus on other factors that can affect the ability of PCNs to work successfully abroad, such as the ability of PCNs to adapt and of their family members to adapt to foreign cultures.[86] When hiring for domestic positions, most U.S. employers do not include the families of candidates in the selection process. However, because it often can be difficult for families to relocate abroad and adjust to conditions there, international selection decisions should include candidates' families. This focus can be justified as job related. Research supports the importance of the family's adjustment to PCN success. Companies in Sweden and Switzerland routinely include families in the selection process for assignments abroad.[87]

Also, remember that EEO laws apply to U.S. employees working abroad. Therefore, when selecting employees for international assignments, you need to make sure you do not discriminate. Some employers argue that they can send only men to certain countries. For instance, they might argue that women in a country like the United Arab Emirates (UAE) are limited in terms of the types of jobs they are allowed to hold in the country. The argument is that cultural forces there require women to follow a "code of modesty" and be segregated from men. However, cultural and societal changes have resulted in UAE women working in a wide range of occupations.[88]

Always remember that Title VII of the Civil Rights Act prohibits U.S. employers from discriminating on the basis of gender; however, if the host country's laws and customs actually prohibit employment of a woman in the job that your company has available, the host country's laws and customs overrule U.S. laws and customs. Employers need to make sure that what they think is true about laws and customs in another country is actually true and not merely an impression with no real basis as in the UAE example.

Some multinational organizations staff their operations abroad with **host-country nationals (HCNs)**. More senior positions are often still reserved for PCNs, especially when the cultural distance between the home and host country is greater.[89] However, staffing with HCNs makes a lot of sense too. HCNs know the local culture and resources, and they are usually much less costly to employ, at least in developing countries.

Companies that are going to be hiring HCNs need to be aware of differences in selection practices across countries. One study found that European and U.S. multinational companies (MNCs) used more structured interviews for selection than Japanese firms. The United Kingdom MNCs used more psychological tests and the Germans used more behavioral assessments.[90] Additionally, some countries have adopted quotas to increase diversity and have different protected classes than the United States. Private companies in Japan with 50 or more employees are required to hire individuals with disabilities so that they represent 2% of the total

**parent-country national (PCN)**

an employee who is a citizen of the country in which the company is headquartered but working for the company in another location

**host-country national (HCN)**

an employee who is a citizen of the country in which the company's branch or plant is located, but the company is headquartered in another country

number of employees. In Australia, political opinion is a protected classification, and in the United Kingdom, gender reassignment is specifically noted as a protected classification.[91]

When selecting HCNs for an international assignment, multinational firms often employ HCN HR directors to ensure that the selection processes used conform to local laws. If the company doesn't have a HR professional in house, it is often advantageous to hire the services of a local consultant to ensure that the selection practices are appropriate for the host country and that the company doesn't violate host country laws relative to selection.

Increasingly, employees are willing to work wherever in the world the best opportunities exist. This willingness is good news for employers because there are not always enough qualified employees from a company's home or host country to staff a new (or even an existing) operation. **Third-country nationals (TCNs)** are foreign nationals who work in countries other than their home country or their company's home country. Many of the same selection practices that apply to PCNs apply to TCNs. Ensuring that a TCN has good technical skills is not enough to ensure the person's success on the job. Attention should also be paid to the ability of the person and his or her family to adapt to the country to which he or she is relocating.

Starting May 25, 2018, the General Data Protection Regulation (GDPR) in the European Union (EU) became effective. This regulation gives EU residents more control over how data about them is managed. Basically, it strengthens privacy rules. The regulations cover data collected when recruiting and selecting employees, regardless whether the data is provided through emails or other means and regardless of whether you keep it in a spreadsheet or in the cloud. Companies should develop recruitment and selection GDPR-compliant policies. Failure to comply with this regulation can cost firms up to 4% of their annual revenue or 20 million euros, whichever is greater.[92]

> **third-country national (TCN)**
>
> a foreign national who works in a country other than her or his home country or her or his company's home country

## Ethics and Employee Selection

A number of ethical and social responsibility issues exist in employee selection. We will focus on two of these: concerns about privacy and the amount and type of information provided to applicants.

### Concerns About Privacy

Honesty tests, background checks, credit reports, drug tests, and medical exams are among the selection methods that applicants consider highly invasive.[93] Additionally, applicants may perceive that the use of social networking sites during the employment process is an invasion of privacy and perceive the selection process as unfair as a result.[94] These and related selection methods can be used only when they can be shown to be job-related and no other less-invasive alternative is available. If a drug test is needed, collecting a hair or saliva sample from a candidate is likely to be perceived as less invasive than collecting a urine or blood sample.[95] If invasive methods are used, well-defined policies should be in place to ensure that applicants are treated fairly. The tests should be administered consistently across all candidates being considered for the same job. The rationale behind the tests should be explained to candidates as well, and the reliability and validity of the tests should be established.

By far, the most invasive selection method an employer could use is genetic testing. This type of test is done to find out if an employee is predisposed to certain medical conditions or diseases that could affect work performance and cause increases in company medical insurance rates. As we noted in Chapter 3, the Genetic Information and Nondiscrimination Act of 2008 (GINA) made it illegal for employers to discriminate on the basis of genetic information, and in most cases, there is no job-related reason for an employer to conduct genetic testing as part of a selection process.

### Amount and Type of Information Given to Applicants

As a manager, you might find yourself in a dilemma about what information and how much of it you should provide to job applicants. If you're not careful, you might inadvertently omit information in order to make a job seem more attractive to applicants than it is, especially for applicants you really want to hire. Or you might inadvertently omit information about the hazards related to a job or activities your company engages in that applicants might find questionable. It is, therefore, important for you and your organization to think through what information is ethical and responsible for you to divulge before you start the selection process.

Realize, too, that you and your company will face consequences as a result of the choices that you make. Remember from Chapter 6 that RJPs have been shown to be quite effective in making employees aware of the positive and negative aspects of a job and have the added benefit of yielding more satisfied and productive employees.[96]

## Selection in Practice: Regulatory Issues

We have already addressed a number of regulatory issues related to selection throughout this chapter. In this section, we focus on two additional regulatory issues of particular importance to the selection process for managers: procedures for using selection measures and the definition of an applicant.

### Procedures for Using Selection Measures

In 1978, the EEOC, the Civil Service Commission, and the Department of Labor issued guidelines for the legal use of employee selection procedures. Those guidelines, the *Uniform Guidelines on Employee Selection Procedures*, describe in detail how organizations can legally use tests and other selection methods. Even though they were developed more than 38 years ago, the *Uniform Guidelines* are still given great deference by the courts in establishing whether or not a selection measure is job related.[97] The *Guidelines* also describes the recordkeeping procedures that employers should follow with regard to their selection activities. Required records include information on the demographics of applicants, as well as test validation information. A complete description of these *Guidelines* is beyond the scope of this book, but it is important that you know that the *Guidelines* exist. They are an invaluable reference when it comes to setting up a selection process. For instance, they offer guidance on what to do if your selection practices result in adverse impact and define what constitutes biased or otherwise unfair selection procedures.[98]

Additionally, the Society for Industrial and Organizational Psychologists (SIOP) has published *Principles for the Validation and Use of Personnel Selection Procedures*. They are provided to guide the choice, development, evaluation, and use of employee selection procedures. SIOP published the fourth edition of the principles in 2003. A fifth edition was in the works at the time of the preparation of this chapter and is due to be released in 2018.[99]

### Definition of an Applicant

You might be wondering why we even need to discuss the definition of an applicant. After all, we are at the end of this chapter. Haven't we defined the term already? Yes and no. We gave you a generic definition of the term.

The rapid growth of computer technology was accompanied with a change in how applicants and employers interacted, as we have already noted. As a result, in 2004, the EEOC provided clarity on who is considered a job applicant for Internet and related technology.[100] When it comes to electronic technologies, such as email, applicant tracking systems, employment Web pages, and the Internet, an individual is considered an applicant in the following situations:

1. The employer is acting to fill a specific position.
2. The applicant has followed the procedures described by the employer for applying for a job.
3. The applicant actually has indicated interest in a specific position.[101]

This definition is quite important in the event of a discrimination charge. Without it, an individual could just make an email inquiry about a possible job and then decide to charge the company with discrimination if he didn't get the job.

Even prior to issuing the new guidelines, many employers had already established policies for determining who was actually an applicant. The policies resulted in part from efforts by the EEOC to find employers who were discriminating. To do this, the EEOC sent testers—individuals who were not actual applicants—to apply for jobs in an attempt to identify unlawful discrimination practices.[102] Employers have responded to the use of testers by specifying that they do not accept unsolicited applications. Managers need to ensure that everyone who is involved in the selection process has been carefully trained in terms of how to conduct the process and what records to maintain.

## SUMMARY

*Selection* is the systematic process of deciding which applicants to hire to achieve your organizational goals. Selection involves making predictions about which job applicants will be able to perform a job successfully. Matching the right person to each job leads to more satisfied and productive employees.

The selection process is basically the same for external and internal hires. Job-analysis information is used to determine the required KSAs a successful job incumbent should have. This information is then used to decide on the most appropriate methods for selecting from the pool of job applicants.

Selection methods need to be reliable, valid, and unbiased. *Reliability* means that the methods used are consistent over time and across raters. *Validity* means that the methods are actually measuring what they were designed to measure. *Unbiased* means that the personal characteristics of applicants and impression management efforts by applicants do not affect the selection decision. *Unbiased* also means that selection decisions are made based on how applicants perform during the selection process, not on how well one applicant performs relative to another applicant or how well an applicant does on only one part of the selection process.

The selection process typically consists of two parts: initial screening and final screening. *Initial screening* includes reviewing applications and résumés and conducting an initial interview. *Final screening* reduces the number of job candidates to the number of employees needed for the job. Final screening methods include ability tests, achievement/competency tests, work samples, personality inventories, reference checks, background reports, credit reports, and scores on honesty/integrity tests, as well as interviews, assessment centers, and biodata. Drug tests can be used as well. A medical examination can be requested by a firm only after it has extended an employment offer to a candidate.

The final selection decision can be made in one of four ways: the compensatory approach, multiple-hurdle approach, multiple-cutoff approach, or a combination approach. Each approach has advantages and disadvantages.

From an organizational design perspective, strategy drives the core competencies candidates need and the person–job fit criteria, as well as which methods are used to select employees. Company characteristics determine how structured the selection process is, the substance and form of selection methods used, and how much discretion individual managers have in terms of designing and implementing the process. Culture establishes the person–organization fit criteria, whether there will be a promotion-from-within policy, and who participates in the selection process. Applicant concerns include the right to fair and equitable treatment and the impact of one's job on one's family life.

Various environmental demands affect the design and outcome of the selection process. The labor force influences the characteristics of applicants who will be interested in job openings and the willingness of applicants to accept jobs. Technology affects how the selection is done and the process of verifying applicants' credentials. Globalization affects the composition of domestic and foreign labor markets. Two ethical issues that have to be addressed during the selection process are concerns about privacy and what and how much information to provide to applicants. Finally, regulations guide the procedures used for selecting tests, keeping records, and defining who is an applicant.

## KEY TERMS

achievement/competency test
adverse action
application
assessment center
behavioral interview
biodata
cognitive ability test
compensatory approach
concurrent criterion-related validity
construct validity
content validity
contrast effect
criterion-related validity
devil's horns effect
defamation of character
final screening
halo effect
host-country national (HCN)
impression management
initial screening
knowledge test
multiple-cutoff approach
multiple-hurdle approach

negligent hiring
panel interview
parent-country national (PCN)
person–job fit
person–organization fit
personality inventory
physical ability test
prediction
predictive criterion-related validity
reference check
reliability
résumé
screening interview
selection
selection bias
situational interview
structured interview
subject matter expert (SME)
third-country national (TCN)
unstructured interview
validity
work sample

## DISCUSSION QUESTIONS

1. What is the relationship between employee selection and a company's performance? Can a firm be successful if it does not have a well-designed selection process? Why or why not?

2. What is meant by person–job fit, and why does it matter?

3. Describe the relationship between reliability and validity. How does each relate to the employee selection process?

4. Provide an example to demonstrate that you understand the difference between initial and final selection procedures and how they are related.

5. What are the pros and cons of a compensatory process for making a final employee selection decision?

6. Suppose you are the manager of a software company. You want to create a structured behavioral interview for the job of programmer. What role should your organization's culture play in terms of the interview questions you create? What might be an appropriate question to include? If you aren't sure what this particular job entails, visit O*NET (http://online.onetcenter.org) and read about it.

7. Identify and describe ways technology can be used to enhance the selection process. What are the possible problems that can occur because of the use of technology? How can you avoid those problems?

8. Why is it important to carefully define the meaning of *applicant* for selection purposes?

9. What would be the advantages and disadvantages of using each of the three types of global staffing: PCN, HCN, and TCN?

## LEARNING EXERCISE 1

Think about a company that you admire and would like to work for when you graduate. Research how that company handles the selection process. You can do this by visiting the company's website and through an interview. Use your networking skills (such as your LinkedIn connections) to contact someone at the company who you can interview about the selection process. As you answer the following questions, keep in mind that the list is not exhaustive, so you will want to add others:

1. How does this company select employees?

2. Is the same process used for all jobs? If not, how does the process differ, and why?

3. Does the company use initial and final screening methods?

4. How does the company incorporate technology into the selection process?

5. Based on what you have learned about the employee selection process from this chapter, discuss your perceptions of the effectiveness of the company's selection process.

## LEARNING EXERCISE 2

Jibe, Inc., is a leading recruitment-technology company. In the company's 2014 *Jibe Talent Acquisition Survey*, it found that many job seekers are frustrated because job applications online are not mobile friendly. The survey, conducted for Jibe by Kelton Global, asked more than 1,000 job seekers and 300+ HR professionals to respond to questions about technology and the job search. Among the job seekers, 20% indicated they would give up on applying for a job if it could not be done on a mobile device, and 70% said they would apply from a smart phone if that option were available. Unfortunately, the survey also found that more than 27% of the HR professionals indicated that none of their online application process was optimized for mobile applications.

1. Interview five college students not in your class who are seniors and ask them about the application processes they have experienced in their job search. Include questions about their online experience, particularly focusing on applying for jobs on mobile devices versus online or in other ways. What did they like? What do they wish was different? Prepare a one-page summary of what you learned.

2. Using the information you have learned in this chapter, develop the content for an application that would be legally compliant, achieve the goals of most employers, and be mobile friendly.

*Sources:* "Recruitment Survey Reveals Significant Disconnect between Job Seeker Expectations and Reality," September 8, 2014, https://www.jibe.com/news/recruitment-survey-reveals-significant-disconnect-between-job-seeker-expectations-and-reality/; Thygesen, Kes, "How to Make the Mobile Job Application Experience Great for Candidates," August 12, 2016, https://entrepreneur.com/article/279981).

# CASE STUDY 1: SELECTION AT SILAS MILL

Silas Mill was once known as the producer of the finest linen fabric in the world. The company, headquartered in Macon, Georgia, has had a long history of invention and innovation. That culture served the company well as the textile industry moved to China. Instead of trying to hold onto its competitive advantage in the linen industry, Silas Mill found new products to manufacture. Now, it produces a wide range of high-performance fabrics used in industrial and commercial settings. The company recently used nanotechnology to develop stain-resistant fabrics that are increasingly popular in skilled nursing facilities and hospitals because of their durability and ease of care.

The company has grown from 150 employees working at one plant in Macon to 700 employees working in three plants in the United States and one in China. Some of the corporate jobs at Silas Mill are marketing analyst, executive assistant, designer, sales representative, customer service specialist, purchasing manager, attorney, research scientist, and accountant. The company values integrity, relationships, innovation, and change. Its mission statement emphasizes the importance of putting the customer and employee first:

> At Silas Mill, we strive to be the number-one provider of high-quality, high-performance designer fabrics and the number-one employer in our industry. We believe in always putting the customer first, valuing our employees, and maintaining the highest ethical standards.

As Silas Mill has grown and continued to be a leader in textile innovation, it has grown its reputation as a preferred employer as well. The downside, however, is that the HR staff are finding it increasingly difficult to wade through all the applications to ensure they have the most qualified employees for open jobs.

The current selection process is pretty standard across jobs: HR staff members manually review the applications and résumés that come in, identify a short list of applicants for a particular job, and then invite the individuals on the short list in for an interview with the hiring manager and some of their coworkers.

## Discussion Questions

1. How might Silas Mill use technology to make its selection process more effective and efficient?

2. Discuss why it is important for Silas Mill to consider culture in the selection process. In developing your answer, specifically address how and why Silas Mill can and should assess an applicant's innovativeness as part of the selection process.

3. As Silas Mill continues to grow its business, what might be some issues related to the labor market that will need to be considered, and how will those affect the selection process?

4. What advice would you give the HR staff at Silas Mill to ensure they have the most effective selection process possible?

# CASE STUDY 2: EMPLOYEE SELECTION AT DELOITTE AUSTRALIA

Deloitte is the brand name used for Deloitte Touche Tohmatsu Limited, a UK-based private company with more than 263,900 professionals worldwide in the service areas of audit, tax, consulting, financial advisory, risk management, and related services. The firm operates in more than 150 countries and had revenues in fiscal year 2018 of $43.2 billion. Deloitte is one of the "Big Four" accounting firms and the largest professional services firm in the world.

Deloitte Australia is recognized as the number one employer-of-choice for graduates by Gradconnnection. Workplace Gender Equality Agency has recognized the firm as an employer-of-choice for women. Deloitte Australia is the only professional services firm on the Australian Center for Corporate Social Responsibility's Top Ten list. Further, the firm has invested more than $20 million in their communities through pro bono work and donations, as well as through volunteer work.

Deloitte Australia, like the rest of Deloitte, is a highly progressive company that is often on the leading edge of HR practices. The firm provides information on the company website that can serve as a guide for prospective employees. The website also includes information about the company's recruitment and selection processes for both new college graduates and experienced hires.

The application process for college students starts with completing an online application. Applicants can also read information about Deloitte and about the members of the recruitment team on the website. Recruitment team members review applications, make an assessment of fit with skills, and determine if there is a match to key selection criteria. The company tries to contact applicants in seven days with a decision about their continuation status in the selection process.

The selection process includes multiple steps. The process starts with a first interview, usually by phone with a member of the recruitment team, and continues with interviews with members of the relevant service team. The number of these interviews varies across service areas. The process ends with an in-depth interview addressing technical and motivational fit with the role, team, and company. A Deloitte partner from the service line participates in the final interview.

The selection process for some roles may also include psychometric or skills-based tests. Other roles require an assessment in the form of a case study. These assessments take place either online or face to face, within two weeks of the rest of the interviews.

Finally, if the firm is interested in making an offer, it will conduct a preemployment check of the applicant's references and work rights with the Australian government's Department of Immigration and Border Protection (DIBP).

## Discussion Questions

1. Discuss the pros and cons of providing so much information about the selection process on the company website. Would this amount of information make you more or less likely to apply for a job with Deloitte Australia, or any other company that provided this much information? Discuss your response.

2. What concerns would you have about the process if you were an applicant?

3. Describe the selection process in terms of which parts are initial screening and which are final screening. Is Deloitte Australia using a compensatory, multiple-hurdle, or multiple-cutoff approach to selection? Why do you think they have chosen this particular approach? Do you think it is logical, given the nature of the firm?

4. Research Australian hiring guidelines and discuss how they differ from U.S. guidelines and how they are similar.

*Sources:* "About Deloitte: Our Culture, People, Diversity, and Firm," http://www2.deloitte.com/au/en/pages/about-deloitte/articles/about-deloitte.html#, "About Delooitte: Learn About Our Global Network of Member Firms," https://www2.deloitte.com/us/en/pages/about-deloitte/articles/about-deloitte.html; "Recruitment Process," https://www2.deloitte.com/au/en/pages/careers/articles/interview-process-careers ; Deloitte Announces Record Revenue of US $43.2 Billion," https://www2.deloitte.com/global/en/pages/about-deloitte/articles/global-revenue-announcement.html.

# APPENDIX
# Reliability and Validity

This appendix provides you with more detailed information about the concepts of reliability and validity. As you have already learned, if selection methods are not reliable and valid, you cannot be assured that they are useful for making good selection decisions.

## Reliability

In this chapter, we defined *reliability* as how well a selection measure yields consistent results over time or across raters. But how do you really know the degree of reliability of a selection technique such as a test or an interview? Answer: By computing a reliability coefficient. The coefficient expresses the degree of relationship between two variables. A higher reliability coefficient means that the test is more reliable. Reliability coefficients can range from 0 to 1.00. The traditionally applied rule of thumb is that the reliability coefficient should be at least .85, and preferably .90, for the test to be considered reliable for selection purposes.[103]

## Validity

As discussed in the chapter, reliability alone does not ensure that the selection method is going to predict success on the job. Remember that *validity* is the extent to which a selection method measures what it is supposed to measure and how well it does so—or, simply, the job-relatedness of the selection measure. There are three ways to show that a selection method is valid: content validity, criterion-related validity, and construct validity.

### Content Validity

**Subject matter experts (SMEs)**—individuals with the skills, knowledge, and expertise related to a particular job—identify questions to include in selection tests and interviews to ensure that what needs to be measured is measured. A test developed by SMEs is considered to have **content validity,** job-relevant information that mirrors aspects of the job. For example, suppose a company has an opening for an electrical engineer. If the hiring manager decides to use a test to measure how much knowledge of electrical engineering applicants already have, she could either purchase a test designed to measure electrical engineering concepts or develop such a test. In either event, SMEs with expertise in electrical engineering should participate in the development of the test. In fact, if the company wants to purchase such a test, it is important to ask the vendor, "What was the background of the SMEs who prepared the test?" to determine whether the test content is really appropriate.

Most managers don't have to develop entire selection tests, but they may be called upon to provide questions for use on such a test based on their expertise in a particular area and their knowledge of the job for which the test will be used. Also, as mentioned earlier, managers are required to interview prospective employees. As with tests, the closer the questions reflect the job, the greater the content validity of the interview.

### Criterion-Related Validity

Content validity provides support that a test measures what it is designed to measure based on how well the information in the test reflects the job requirements it is designed to measure. **Criterion-related validity**, also referred to as *empirical validity*, provides additional evidence of the validity of the measure by establishing

**subject matter expert (SME)**

an individual with the skills, knowledge, and expertise related to a particular job

**content validity**

the extent to which the selection test focuses on job relevant information that mirrors aspects of the job

## EXHIBIT A7.1

### General Guidelines of Interpreting Validity Coefficients

| Validity Coefficient Value | Interpretation |
|---|---|
| Above .35 | Very beneficial |
| .21–.35 | Likely to be useful |
| .11–.20 | Depends on circumstances |
| Below .11 | Unlikely to be useful |

*Source:* Based on U.S. Department of Labor, *Testing and Assessment: An Employer's Guide to Good Practices* (Washington, DC: U.S. Department of Labor, Employment and Training Administration, 2000), http://www.onetcenter .org/dl_files/empTestAsse.pdf.

**criterion-related validity (also referred to as empirical validity)**

provides additional evidence of the validity of a measure by establishing a statistical relationship between the selection test and some measure of job performance

**predictive criterion-related validity**

a type of criterion-related validity that involves examining the relationship between selection measure scores taken prehire and performance scores collected at a later date

**concurrent criterion-related validity**

a type of criterion-related validity that involves administering the selection test and collecting performance measure scores concurrently

**construct validity**

how well a selection tool, such as a test, measures the job-related characteristic that it claims to measure

a statistical relationship between the selection test and some measure of job performance, such as performance-appraisal scores or quotas for production of work. Criterion-related validity is determined by correlating the selection test scores with scores on the performance measure. If there is a positive relationship, the test is said to be a valid predictor of a person's performance on the job. Consider this example: Jane, Mark, Jorge, Abbie, Jie, Aron, and Darius all took a test as part of the selection process for managerial jobs, and all were hired for these jobs. After they had worked for the company for six months, the performance of each employee was evaluated, and a correlation coefficient computed between each person's test scores and performance-appraisal scores. The results indicated that the test predicted how well each person would perform on the job. Thus, assuming that the test is reliable, it is also a valid predictor and can be used in the future to select among job applicants. Now let's look at two types of criterion-related validity: predictive criterion-related validity and concurrent criterion-related validity.

The following example demonstrates **predictive criterion-related validity**. Suppose job applicants are given a selection test that is not used to select employees. The scores on the test are filed away until the sample of test-takers who are actually hired is sufficiently large (usually well over 100 test takers; the more test-takers, the better). At that time, an evaluation of the performance of these employees is conducted and the correlation between the scores is computed.

Another approach is **concurrent criterion-related validity**. This type of validity involves administering the selection test and collecting performance measure scores concurrently. The correlation between the two—the test score and performance measure scores—are computed and correlated to determine whether the test predicts how well people will perform on the job. Instead of filing away the scores, as in the previous example for predictive criterion-related validity, the scores are correlated with performance evaluation results collected at approximately the same time.

Exhibit A7.1 provides general guidelines for interpreting validity coefficients. As you can see, validity coefficients don't have to be as high as reliability coefficients to be beneficial. And because a person's on-the-job performance depends on many factors, no single selection tool will predict one's performance perfectly.[104]

## Construct Validity

**Construct validity** is how well a selection tool, such as a test, measures the job-related characteristic—the construct—that it claims to measure. *Constructs* are abstract qualities or traits a person can possess, such as conscientiousness or a customer service orientation. An example will help to make this concept clearer. A hotel reservation center needs employees with a customer service orientation. The hotel can

use a test to select employees with this orientation as long as the test is valid. To judge the construct validity of the test, the hotel needs to do the following:

1. Define exactly what the term *customer service orientation* means within the hotel industry.
2. Show that the content of the test to be used reflects this type of customer service orientation (i.e., has content validity).
3. Provide evidence that the test correlates with other measures of the customer service orientation construct.
4. Show that the test predicts a person's job performance (empirical validation).

As with criterion-related validity, empirical evidence needs to be collected to show that the test exhibits construct validity.

## NOTES

1. Jad Mouawad, "Pushing 40, Southwest Is Still Playing the Rebel," *The* New York Times, http://www.nytimes.com/2010/11/21/business/21south.html?pagewanted=all&_r=0, last modified November 20, 2010.
2. Lindsay Sears, *2017 Retention Report: Trends, Reasons, & Recommendations,* Work Institute, 2017, www.workinstitute.com.
3. Suzanne Lucas, "How Much Does It Cost Companies to Lose Employees?" CNN Money-Watch, http://www.cbsnews.com/news/how-much-does-it-cost-companies-to-lose-employees/, last modified November 21, 2012.
4. Amy Kristof-Brown, Karen Jansen, and Amy Colbert, "A Policy-Capturing Study of the Simultaneous Effects of Fit with Jobs, Groups, and Organizations," Journal of Applied Psychology 7 (2002): 985–983.
5. David Caldwell and Charles O'Reilly III, "Measuring Person–Job Fit with a Profile Comparison Process," Journal of Applied Psychology 15 (1990): 648–657.
6. U.S. Department of Labor, Testing and Assessment: An Employer's Guide to Good Practices (Washington, DC: U.S. Department of Labor, Employment and Training Administration, 2000), http://www.onetcenter.org/dl_files/empTestAsse.pdf.
7. Rick Posthuma, Fred Morgeson, and Michael Campion, "Beyond Employment Interview Validity: A Comprehensive Narrative Review of Recent Research and Trends Over Time," Personnel Psychology 55 (2002): 1–81.
8. Winfred Arthur, Jr., David Woehr, and William Graziano, "Personality Testing in Employment Settings: Problems and Issues in the Application of Typical Selection Practices," Personnel Review 30 (2001): 657–676.
9. "Banning the Use of Salary History in Job Offers Proves Less Difficult Than Anticipated," worldatwork.com, March 20, 2018, https://www.worldatwork.org/press-room/banning-the-use-of-salary-history-in-job-offers-proves-less-difficult-than-anticipated.
10. David Allen, Retaining Talent (Alexandria, VA: SHRM, 2008).
11. Victoria Brown and E. Daly Vaughn, "The Writing on the (Facebook) Wall: The Use of Social Networking Sites in Hiring Decisions," Journal of Business and Psychology 26 (2011): 219–225.
12. Bill Roberts, "Most Likely to Succeed," HR Magazine 59 (2014): 69–71.
13. Tomas Chamorro-Premuzic, "Ace the Assessment," *Harvard Business Review*, 93 (2015): 118-121.
14. "Taking the Barclays Online Assessment Test? Here's What to Expect," Barclays News, https://www.jobs.barclays.co.uk/connect-with-us/taking-the-barclays-online-assessment-test-heres-what-to-expect/, last modified May 29, 2014.
15. Frank Schmidt and John Hunter, "The Validity and Utility of Selection Methods in Personnel Psychology: Practical and Theoretical Implications of 85 Years of Research Findings," Psychological Bulletin 124 (1989): 262–274; and Greg Chun-Yan and Steven Cronshaw, "A Critical Re-examination and Analysis of Cognitive Ability Tests Using the Thorndike Model of Fairness," Journal of Occupational and Organizational Psychology 75 (2002): 489–509.
16. Christopher Berry, Melissa Gruys, and Paul Sackett, "Educational Attainment as a Proxy for Cognitive Ability in Selection: Effects on Level of Cognitive Ability and Adverse Impact," Journal of Applied Psychology 91 (2006): 696–705.

17. Donald Gardner and Diana Deadrick, "Moderation of Selection Procedure Validity by Employee Race," Journal of Managerial Psychology 27 (2012): 365–382; and Milton Hakel, Beyond Multiple Choice: Evaluating Alternatives to Traditional Testing for Selection (Hillsdale, NJ: Lawrence Erlbaum Associates, 1998).

18. "Employment Tests and Selection Procedures," U.S. Equal Employment Opportunity Commission, http://www.eeoc.gov/policy/docs/factemployment_procedures.html.

19. Chun-Yan and Cronshaw, "A Critical Re-examination and Analysis of Cognitive Ability Tests."

20. U.S. Department of Labor, Testing and Assessment.

21. "Employment Tests and Selection Procedures," U.S. Equal Employment Opportunity Commission, http://www.eeoc.gov/policy/docs/factemployment_procedures.html.

22. U.S. Department of Labor, Testing and Assessment.

23. Schmidt and Hunter, "The Validity and Utility of Selection Methods in Personnel Psychology."

24. John Hausknecht, David Day, and Scott Thomas, "Applicant Reactions to Selection Procedures: An Updated Model and Meta-Analysis," Personnel Psychology 57 (2004): 639–683.

25. U.S. Department of Labor, Testing and Assessment.

26. Ibid.

27. Schmidt and Hunter, "The Validity and Utility of Selection Methods in Personnel Psychology."

28. "Taking the Barclays Online Assessment Test?"

29. Murray Barrick and Michael Mount, "The Big Five Personality Dimensions and Job Performance: A Meta-Analysis," Personnel Psychology 44 (1991): 1–26.

30. Adrian Furnham and Carl Fudge, "The Five-Factor Model of Personality and Sales Performance," Journal of Individual Differences 29 (2008): 11–16.

31. U.S. Department of Labor, Testing and Assessment.

32. Ariele Emmett, "Snake Oil or Science?" Workforce Management, October 2004, 90–92.

33. U.S. Department of Labor, Testing and Assessment.

34. Ibid.

35. "Working at Starbucks, Resume and Interview Tips," http://www.starbucks.com/careers/interview-tips; and Gretchen Weber, "Preserving the Starbucks Counter Culture," Workforce Management, February 2005, 28–34.

36. "A Great Experience Begins Here," Barclays News, http://www.jobs.barclays.co.uk/about-joining/tips-advice/.

37. Steven Maurer, "A Practitioner-Based Analysis of Interview Job Expertise and Scale Format as Contextual Factors in Situational Interviews," Personnel Psychology 55 (2002): 307–327; Timothy DeGroot and Donald Kluemper, "Evidence of Predictive and Incremental Validity of Personality Factors, Vocal Attractiveness, and the Situational Interview," International Journal of Selection and Assessment 15 (2007): 30–39; and Jennifer Merritt, "Improve at the Interview," BusinessWeek 3818 (2003): 63.

38. "Hiring Process, Your Steps to Success," P&G, https://www.pg.com/en_US/downloads/careers/PGHiringProcess.pdf.

39. Maurer, "A Practitioner-Based Analysis of Interview Job Expertise and Scale Format"; and Leatta Hough and Frederick Oswald, "Personnel Selection: Looking Toward the Future—Remembering the Past," Annual Review of Psychology 51 (2000): 631–664.

40. Posthuma et al., "Beyond Employment Interview Validity"; and Hough and Oswald, "Personnel Selection."

41. Steve Vaughan, "Business Column: Past Mistakes Can Haunt Job Seekers," Virginia Gazette, http://www.vagazette.com/news/va-vg-bizcolumn-0709-20140708,0,486063.story, last modified July 8, 2014.

42. Shari Lau, "When Must an Employer Respond to a Request for Verification of Employment? What Information Must or Can Be Given?" HR Magazine 59 (2014): 20.

43. Ibid.

44. Michelle Goodman, "Reference Checks Go Tech: Armed with Reference-Checking Software, Not Only Can Companies Obtain Better Feedback from References, But Also They Can Obtain More of It Per Candidate," Workforce Management 91 (2012): 26–28; "SkillSurvey Pre-Hire 360 Expands to Become SkillSurvey Reference," skillsurvey.com.

45. Robert Capwell, "Written Policy Is Biggest Tool in the Box for Ensuring Proper Screening Compliance," SHRM.org, http://www.shrm.org/hrdisciplines/staffingmanagement/articles/pages/cms_020120.aspx; and Vaughan, "Business Column."

46. Ron Holland and Jonathan Batten, shrm.org, October 20, 2017, https://www.shrm.org/ResourcesAndTools/hr-topics/talent-acquisitions/pages/fcra-avoid-risky-background-checks.aspx.

47. "Background Checking—The Use of Criminal Background Checks in Hiring Decisions," SHRM.org, http://www.shrm.org/research/surveyfindings/articles/pages/criminalbackgroundcheck.aspx, last modified July 19, 2012.

48. "What You Should Know About the EEOC and Arrest and Conviction Records," U.S. Equal Employment Opportunity Commission, http://www.eeoc.gov/eeoc/newsroom/wysk/arrest_conviction_records.cfm; Roy Maurer, "Know Before You Hire: 2016 Employment Screening Trends," *SHRM.org*, January 20, 2016, https://www.shrm.org/resourcesand-tools/hr-topics/talent-acquisition/pages/2016-employment-screening-trends.aspx. Beth Avery and Phil Hernandez, "Ban the Box: U.S. Cities, Counties, and States Adopt Fair Hiring Policies," https://www.nelp.org/publication/ban-the-box-fair-chance-hiring-state-and-local-guide/, April 20, 2018.

49. "Using Consumer Reports: What Employers Need to Know," Bureau of Consumer Protection Business Center, http://www.business.ftc.gov/documents/bus08-using-consumer-reports-what-employers-need-know; Roy Maurer, "Know Before You Hire: 2018 Employment Screening Trends," shrm.org, February 5, 2018, https://www.shrm.org/resourcesandtools/hr-topics/talent-acquisition/pages/know-before-you-hire-2018-employment-screening-trends.aspx.

50. Ibid.

51. Ron Holland and Jonathan Batten, "FCRA 101: How to Avoid Risky Background Checks," *SHRM.org*, October 20, 2017, https://www.shrm.org/ResourcesAndTools/hr-topics/talent-acquisition/pages/fcra-avoid-risky-background-checks.aspx.

52. Elaine Pofeldt, "This Crime in the Workplace Is Costing US Businesses $50 Billion a Year," cnbc.com, September 12, 2017, https://www.cnbc.com/2017/09/12/workplace-crime-costs-us-businesses-50-billion-a-year.html.

53. Celina Oliver, Maggie Shafiro, Peter Bullard, and Jay Thomas, "Use of Integrity Tests May Reduce Workers' Compensation Losses," Journal of Business and Psychology 27 (2012): 115–122; Adrian Furnham, "Can You Really Test Someone for Integrity?" August 11, 2015, http://fortune.com/2015/08/11/hiring-integrity-test/.

54. Michael Cullen and Paul Sackett, "Integrity Testing in the Workplace," in Comprehensive Handbook of Psychological Assessment, Volume 4: Industrial and Organizational Psychology, ed. Jay Thomas and Michel Hersen (Hoboken, NJ: John Wiley & Sons, 2004), 149–165; and David Shaffer and Ronald Schmidt, "Personality Testing in Employment," FindLaw, Corporate Counsel, Human Resources, http://corporate.findlaw.com/human-resources/personality-testing-in-employment.html#integ, last modified March 26, 2008.

55. U.S. Department of Labor, Testing and Assessment.

56. International Taskforce on Assessment Center Guidelines, "Guidelines and Ethical Considerations for Assessment Center Operations," *Journal of Management* 41 (2015): 1244–1273.

57. Michelle Rafter, "Candidates for Jobs in High Places Sit for Tests That Size Up Their Mettle," Workforce Management, May 2004, 70–72; and U.S. Department of Labor, Testing and Assessment.

58. James Breaugh, Kathleen Frye, Deborah Lee, Vanessa Lammer, and Jenna Cox, "The Value of Biodata for Selecting Employees: Comparable Results for Job Incumbent and Job Applicant Samples?" *Journal of Organizational Psychology*, 14 (2014): 40–51.

59. Bret Becton, Michael Matthews, David Hartley, and Douglas Whitaker, "Using Biodata as a Predictor of Errors, Tardiness, Policy Violations, Overall Job Performance, and Turnover Among Nurses," Journal of Management and Organization 18 (2012): 714–727.

60. Breaugh et al., "The Value of Biodata for Selecting Employees.

61. U.S. Department of Labor, Testing and Assessment.

62. "Drug-Free Workplace Policy Builder, Section 7: Drug Testing," elaws—Drug-Free Workplace Advisor, U.S. Department of Labor, http://www.dol.gov/elaws/asp/drugfree/drugs/screen92.asp.

63. "Drugs and the Workplace," National Council on Alcoholism and Drug Dependence, Inc., http://ncadd.org/learn-about-drugs/workplace/242-drugs-and-the-workplace.

64. U.S. Department of Labor, *Testing and Assessment*.

65. Ibid.

66. Ibid.

67. Ivan Robertson and Mike Smith, "Personnel Selection," Journal of Occupational and Organizational Psychology 74 (2001): 441–472.

68. Steffanie Wilk and Peter Cappelli, "Understanding the Determinants of Employer Use of Selection Methods," Personnel Psychology 56 (2003): 103–124.

69. "IBMer value. . .," on being an IBMer, IBM, http://www.ibm.com/ibm/values/us/.

70. Eve Tahmincioglu, "Keeping Spirits Aloft at JetBlue," Workforce Management, http://www.workforce.com/articles/keeping-spirits-aloft-at-jetblue, last modified December 6 2004.

71. Amy Kristof, "Person–Organization Fit: An Integrative Review of Its Conceptualizations, Measurements, and Implications," Personnel Psychology 49 (1996): 1–49.

72. Edgar Schein, Organizational Culture and Leadership (San Francisco: Jossey-Bass, 1985).

73. Weber, "Preserving the Starbucks' Counter Culture"; and "Working at Starbucks."

74. "How We Hire at Google," http://www.google.com/about/careers/lifeatgoogle/hiringprocess).

75. T. Shah, "Retailers Sometimes Turn to a Different Means of Screening Applicants," Knight Ridder Tribune Business News, June 21, 2004, p. 1.

76. "Recruitment Goes Virtual," Human Resource Management International Digest 21 (2013): 19–21.

77. Denise Potosky and Phil Bobko, "Selection Testing via the Internet: Practical Considerations and Exploratory Empirical Findings," Personnel Psychology 57 (2004): 1003–1034.

78. Chad Van Iddekinge, Stephen Lanivich, Philip Roth, and Elliott Junco, "Social Media for Selection? Validity and Adverse Impact Potential of a Facebook-Based Assessment," Journal of Management (2013): 0149206313515524.

79. Lindsay Olson, "The Top 10 Lies People Put on Their Résumés," Money, U.S.News.com, last modified October 3, 2013, http://money.usnews.com/money/blogs/outside-voices-careers/2013/10/03/the-top-10-lies-people-put-on-their-resumes.

80. Mary Elizabeth Burke, "2004 Reference and Background Checking Survey Report," *Society for Human Resource Management*, SHRM.org, http://www.business.uwm.edu/gdrive/Singh_R/Research%20Resources/Reference,%20background%20checking/SHRM_reference%20&%20background%20checking%20report_2004.pdf; Roy Maurer, "Know Before You Hire: 2016 Employment Screening Trends," *SHRM.org*, January 20, 2016, https://www.shrm.org/resourcesandtools/hr-topics/talent-acquisition/pages/2016-employment-screening-trends.aspx; Anonymous, "Top 5 Settlements of 2017 for FCRA Violations, Number 1 is Record Breaking! January 5, 2018, https://www.hiresafe.com/2017-top-5-settlements-for-fcra-violations/.

81. C. Mason-Draffen, "Lying on Résumé Can Cost Workers Their Jobs," Knight Ridder Tribune Business News, June 10, 2004, p. 1.

82. Margaret Vroman, Karin Stulz, Claudia Hart, and Emily Stulz, "Employer Liability for Using Social Media in Hiring Decisions," *Journal of Social Media for Organizations*, 3 (2016): 1-12.

83. SGM Law Group, "H1B Lottery 2018: Results, Process, and 2019 Chances," http://www.immi-usa.com/h1b-lottery-2016-results-chances-process.

84. "USCIS Reaches FY 2017 H-1B Cap," U.S. Citizenship and Immigration Services, April 7, 2016, https://www.uscis.gov/news/news-releases/uscis-reaches-fy-2017-h-1b-cap; H-1B Fiscal Year (FY) 2019 Cap Season, https://www.uscis.gov/working-united-states/temporary-workers/h-1b-specialty-occupations-and-fashion-models/h-1b-fiscal-year-fy-2019-cap-season.

85. Zsuzsanna Tungli and Maury Peiperl, "Expatriate Practices in German, Japanese, U.K., and U.S. Multinational Companies: A Comparative Survey of Changes," Human Resource Management 48 (2009): 153–171.

86. Rosalie Tung, "Expatriate Assignments: Enhancing Success and Minimizing Failure," Academy of Management Executive 1 (1987): 117–126; Mila Lazarova, Mina Westman, and Margaret Shaffer, "Elucidating the Positive Side of the Work-Family Interface on International Assignments: A Model of Expatriate Work and Family Performance," Academy of Management Review 35 (2010): 93–117. For a more detailed discussion of expatriate selection, see Peter Dowling, Marion Festing, and Allen Engle, International Human Resource Management, 6th ed. (Hampshire, UK: Cengage Learning, 2013).

87. Jeffrey Katz and David Seifer, "It's a Different World Out There: Planning for Expatriate Success Through Selection, Pre-Departure Training and On-Site Socialization," Human Resource Planning 19 (1996): 32–47; Lazarova, Westman, and Shaffer, "Elucidating the Positive Side of the Work-Family Interface"; Tungli and Peiperl, "Expatriate Practices in German, Japanese, U.K., and U.S. Multinational Companies."

88. Musa Shallal, "Job Satisfaction Among Women in the United Arab Emirates," Journal of International Women's Studies 12 (2011): 114–134.

89. Yaping Gong, "Subsidiary Staffing in Multinational Enterprises: Agency, Resources, and Performance," Academy of Management Journal 46 (2003): 728–739.

90. Tungli and Peiperl, "Expatriate Practices in German, Japanese, U.K., and U.S. Multinational Companies."

91. Larry Turner and Allison Suflas, "Global Diversity—One Program Won't Fit All," HR Magazine 59 (2014): 59–61.

92. Roy Maurer, "New EU Data Will Change How You Engage with Job Applicants," *SHRM.org*, February 28, 2018, https://www.shrm.org/resourcesandtools/hr-topics/talent-acquisition/pages/gdpr-eu-data-law-hr-recruiting-shrm.aspx.

93. Eugene Stone-Romero, Dianna Stone, and David Hyatt, "Personnel Selection Procedures and Invasion of Privacy," Journal of Social Issues 59 (2003): 343–368.

94. Juan Madera, "Using Social Networking Websites as a Selection Tool: The Role of Selection Process Fairness and Job Pursuit Intentions," International Journal of Hospitality Management 31 (2012): 1276–1282.

95. Stone-Romero, Stone, and Hyatt, "Personnel Selection Procedures and Invasion of Privacy."

96. Stephanie Haden, "Realistic Job Previews and Performance: The Mediating Influence of Personal Goals," Journal of Management Research 12 (2012): 163–178.

97. U. S. Department of Labor, Uniform Guidelines on Employee Selection Procedures, http://www.gpo.gov/fdsys/pkg/CFR-2011-title29-vol4/xml/CFR-2011-title29-vol4-part1607.xml; Daniel Biddle, "Are the Uniform Guidelines Outdated? Federal Guidelines, Professional Standards, and Validity Generalization (VG)," The Industrial Organizational Psychologist April (2008): 17–23.

98. U.S. Department of Labor, Testing and Assessment.

99. "Principles for the Validation and Use of Personnel Selection Procedures," Fourth Edition, SIOP, http://www.siop.org/_Principles/principlesdefault.aspx.

100. "Recordkeeping Guidance Clarifies Definition of 'Job Applicant' for Internet and Related Technologies," U.S. Equal Employment Opportunity Commission, last modified March 3, 2004, http://www.eeoc.gov/eeoc/newsroom/release/3-3-04.cfm.

101. Ibid.

102. U.S. Equal Employment Opportunity Commission, EEOC Notice Number 915.002, May 22, 1996, http://www.eeoc.gov/policy/docs/testers.html.

103. Robert Gatewood, Hubert Field, and Murray Barrick, Human Resource Selection (Mason, OH: South-Western Cengage Learning, 2011).

104. U.S. Department of Labor, Testing and Assessment.

# Chapter 8

# Learning and Development

## Learning Objectives

**AFTER READING THIS CHAPTER, YOU SHOULD BE ABLE TO:**

1 Explain the purpose of learning and development.

2 Use a needs assessment to determine training gaps.

3 Describe commonly used training methods.

4 Discuss the types of training needed in organizations.

5 Develop a way to measure the effectiveness of training.

6 Make decisions about training within the context of organizational demands.

7 Design training programs that address environmental influences.

8 Ensure that a firm's learning and development activities are legally compliant.

| HR CHALLENGE | | |
| --- | --- | --- |
| ENVIRONMENTAL INFLUENCES | ORGANIZATIONAL DEMANDS | REGULATORY ISSUES |

**PRIMARY HR ACTIVITIES**

Work Design & Workforce Planning

**Managing Employee Competencies**

Managing Employee Attitudes & Behaviors

Employee Contributions

Competitive Advantage

# The Purpose of Learning and Development

From the time you were born, you have been engaged in learning. Take a few minutes to think about everything you have learned over the years—how to dress yourself, how to get your homework done, how to drive, how to perform tasks at work... The list is endless. Now, think about how you learned to do all those things. Did you have a teacher? Did you learn in a classroom setting? Did you get it right the first time or make some mistakes and have to start over? Did you learn everything all at once or over time?

Chapter 4 introduced you to workforce planning, and in Chapter 5, you learned about job design and job analysis. Recall that job design and analysis define the tasks employees need to perform, as well as the competencies they need to successfully do those tasks. Managers use that information to determine the training their employees need and to identify or develop effective training programs for them.

In Chapters 6 and 7, we examined the first two aspects of managing employee competencies, the highlighted circle in Exhibit 8.1. These chapters addressed employee recruitment and selection, both of which also affect learning and development activities, the third aspect of managing competencies. At a basic level, learning, which includes training and development, is needed to ensure that employees recruited and selected are able to do their jobs well, and that they will be prepared for future jobs in the company. If the labor market is flush with many highly qualified workers,

**EXHIBIT 8.1**

Strategic Human Resources Framework.

managers can easily find employees with the skill sets required to be immediately productive in their jobs. As a result, these workers will need less training and development. Conversely, fewer qualified workers in the labor force will mean new employees will need more training to ensure that they can perform the work needed.

Learning and development encompasses a range of activities that enable employees to perform their jobs efficiently and effectively, now and in the future. Additionally, lack of employee development opportunities offered by the firm is a major reason that young high-achievers look for other jobs.[1] Providing the appropriate learning and development opportunities for employees will increase their satisfaction and help them perform at a higher level, better enabling the company to achieve its goals.

In this chapter, we discuss the essential components of creating a process to ensure that learning and development activities are successful. Chapter 4 discusses how the tasks, duties, and responsibilities of a job affect the amount and types of learning and development employees need to perform their jobs well. We wrap up this chapter by discussing how organizational demands, environmental factors, and regulatory issues affect the decisions managers have to make about employee learning and development.

Before we discuss the specifics of learning and development, we need to introduce two programs designed to help new employees acclimate to the organization, its culture, and their jobs. These programs are orientation and onboarding.

## Employee Orientation

**Employee orientation** ensures that new employees know and understand company policies and procedures. When done well, orientation helps employees get off to a good start. In most companies, orientation introduces new employees to the history of the company, describes the culture, and informs employees about company policies and procedures. Recent research of employee orientation has shown that managing orientation differently may have greater value for the new employee and, ultimately, the company.

**employee orientation**

a process designed to ensure employees understand the policies and procedures of the company when they first begin work, as well as understand how their job fits with the goals of the company

Collecting data at Wipro, a business process outsourcing company headquartered in Bangalore, India, and in a controlled lab study, researchers from Harvard University, London Business School, and the University of North Carolina found the following: Instead of focusing only on the company, employee orientation is most effective when it focuses on the employee's personal identity. In their research, new employees were divided into three groups: a control group that received the standard company orientation, an individual identity group focused on how working at the company would help the employees have opportunity for self-expression, and an organizational identity group where the focus was on telling the employees why the company was a good place to work. When the researchers checked back at seven months, the individual identity group had lower turnover than either of the other two groups. These findings suggest the importance of helping new employees see how they can have self-expression in their new roles. As a result of this research, Wipro redesigned its orientation to include personal identity socialization.[2]

## Onboarding

For many companies, new employee orientation is only one part of a larger program known as **onboarding,** the process used to socialize new employees to their jobs and the company, including helping them acclimate to the culture and goals of the company. Employers who recognize the critical role of human capital in organizational success pay careful attention to the onboarding process.[3]

Studies have found that 20% of employees leave the company within the first 90 days of a new job. A structured onboarding program can make a difference in

**onboarding**

the process used to socialize new employees to their jobs and the company, including helping them acclimate to the culture and goals of the company

new employees staying or leaving in both the short and long term. For instance, taking new employees through a structured onboarding experience has been found to be related to a 58% better retention rate after three years.[4] Therefore, it is no surprise that onboarding programs that create a welcoming environment and set the employee up for success are seen as critical.

Onboarding programs can be informal, but most are formal programs that help bring new employees up to speed quickly and connect them with coworkers. The onboarding process ensures that employees have the information they need (or know where to get it), have someone to go to with questions and problems, and receive the training needed to be successful on the job.

During the entire onboarding process, employees need to understand that they matter as individuals to the company. When employees know that they are valued for what they individually bring to the company and are not seen as just another employee, they are more likely to be satisfied and stay with the company longer. With those types of goals in mind, L'Oréal provides a customized induction program for each new employee. This program is described in Company Spotlight 8.1. In summary, onboarding is successful when it helps build employee self-efficacy, provides role clarity, enables social integration, and provides knowledge about the company culture.[5]

Now, let's take a close look at the process of designing and implementing learning and development programs. We start by providing some definitions of terms.

## Learning, Training, and Development Defined

**Learning** involves acquiring both tacit and explicit knowledge.[6] Employees acquire knowledge through formal and informal training activities and other experiences. **Training** is the systematic process of providing employees with the competencies—knowledge, skills, and abilities (KSAs)—required in order to do their current jobs. For instance, an employee might need to learn to use new computer software to do his job. This employee would need to be trained on the new software. Training can take many forms. Employees can obtain KSAs on the job, by attending classes either online or in a classroom setting, by participating in role plays or simulations, or through a combination of these and other methods (discussed later in this chapter).

In addition to training employees for their current jobs, companies invest a lot of resources in developing employees for other jobs. Recall that in Company Spotlight 4.2, in Chapter 4, you read about the Human Resource Leadership Development Program (HRLDP) and other similar programs at Lockheed Martin. This company invests a lot of resources in leadership development in order to prepare **high-potential employees** (employees with the greatest likelihood of being successful and making significant contributions to organizational goal achievement) for new and more significant jobs in the future. The purpose of training is to improve how well employees perform their current jobs. **Development**, in contrast, is future focused and aims to prepare employees to take on additional responsibilities in different jobs, usually at a higher level.

Both training and development help an organization equip its workforce to gain a sustained competitive advantage. Good managers make sure their employees participate in both. For example, many companies invest a lot of money in skills training and invest heavily in leadership development programs designed to prepare workers for higher-level jobs in their firms. This approach resulted in Leading Real Estate Companies of the World claiming the number one place on the 2018 Training Top 125 Winners list. Ranking number two to five on this list were New York Community Bancorp, Sonic Automotive, BNSF Railway Company, and Dollar General Corporation. Criteria for selection on the list included factors such

**learning**

the process of acquiring both tacit and explicit knowledge

**training**

the systematic process of providing employees with the competencies—knowledge, skills, and abilities (KSAs)—required in order to do their current jobs

**high-potential employee**

an employee with the greatest likelihood of being successful and making significant contributions to achieving organizational goals.

**development**

prepares employees to take on additional responsibilities in different jobs, usually at a higher level

# COMPANY SPOTLIGHT  8.1

## There's An App for That: Onboarding at L'Oréal

L'Oréal provides a customized induction program for each new employee. The program makes sure that newcomers understand not only the company culture and goals, but also how to use their talents in the organization. This program, called L'Oréal Follow-Up and Integration Track (FIT), helps ensure employees get off to a good start though a two-year onboarding program conducted in six parts. Included in the program are meetings with key insiders, on-the-job training (OJT) experiences, mentoring, and other activities designed to take employees through a sequenced set of activities. The result: New employees are more successful, more quickly.

In June 2017, the company took its onboarding a step further by releasing the Fit Culture App. L'Oréal describes this as being a one-of-a-kind app and the first mobile application designed to assist newcomers with decoding, understanding, and mastering the culture of a company. The app is part of the company's six-month strategic onboarding process, is free to download, and is designed to be a fun and easily navigable journey. Topics covered through the app include agility, entrepreneurship, collaboration, and networking. The ultimate goal of the app is to assist new employees in fully appreciating, understanding, and embodying the deep culture that L'Oréal has developed over its 100-year history, and to understand how they individually fit into the company.

The app is available in 11 languages and was designed specifically for younger employees. In fact, 50 newcomers to L'Oréal from 30 countries were involved in its design. Employees download the app from the Apple Store or the Play Store. They then engage in learning about the company through quizzes, games, employee testimonials, and real-life missions. The company recommends that employees complete the program over a one-month timeframe.

*Sources:* Bauer, Tayla, "Onboarding New Employees: Maximizing Success," *SHRM.org*, https://www.shrm.org/foundation/ourwork/initiatives/resources-from-past-initiatives/Documents/Onboarding%20New%20Employees.pdf; "Integration," https://www.loreal.sg/careers/what-we-offer/integration; "L'Oréal Launches Fit Culture App, A New Custom-Made Mobile App to Welcome New Employees," https://www.loreal.com/media/press-releases/2017/june/fit-app-launches.

as financial investment in employee development, linkage of development efforts to business goals, and effectiveness of development efforts in terms of business impact.[7] As baby boomers retire, other workers will need to be ready to step into their jobs. Further, ongoing training and development helps ensure that the members of the organization are currently learning and maintaining their relevancy within the scope of the needs of the company.

The importance of learning and development cannot be overemphasized. In fact, companies that treat learning and development as a fundamental requirement for achieving their goals have been rewarded for this philosophy. One study of 500 publicly traded companies found that the companies that invested the most in learning and development programs for their employees returned significantly higher returns to their shareholders than companies that did not.[8]

In 2018, companies in the United States spent $87.6 billion on employee training for an average of $986 per learner.[9] Companies that placed an even higher value on learning, known as **high-impact learning organizations**, typically spend even more on average per learner than other companies. These high-impact learning organizations know that performance improves through training and talent management initiatives.[10]

**high-impact learning organization**

a company that place a high value on learning

Appreciating the potential value of learning and development is only part of the equation. Effective managers understand that learning and development activities must be carried out properly to be effective. Designing an effective process requires making a lot of decisions, including deciding what training and development is needed, where it is needed, who should be trained, and how to best conduct the training. Although our discussion focuses directly on the training process, keep in mind that the same basic principles apply to designing effective orientation, onboarding, development, and any other learning programs.

## Designing an Effective Training Process

Effective training programs result from following a systematic process, shown in the flowchart in Exhibit 8.2. (As you read, keep in mind that these design guides apply to any type of learning and development activity, although we talk about them specifically in the context of training.) This process includes (1) needs assessment, (2) design, (3) implementation, and (4) evaluation. Some training process models include a fifth category that comes between design and implementation. This model, referred to as the ADDIE model, includes (1) analysis, (2) design, (3) development, (4) implementation, and (5) evaluation. Analysis is basically the same as needs assessment in the model we discuss and development is included in our model as part of implementation.[11]

Each part of the training process is critical. As a manager, the input you provide for each part will be important to its success. If your organization has a training department, you will provide job information to the department to use in designing the programs. You will also need to provide information about where training is needed, who should be trained, and the types of training that should be delivered. In addition, you will be responsible for providing your employees with on-the-job training (OJT), a type of training described later in this chapter. In smaller organizations, you may have complete responsibility for each part of the training process unless you have the resources to hire someone to provide the training for your employees. Let's take a look at each part of the process.

**EXHIBIT 8.2**

Flowchart for Designing an Effective Training Program

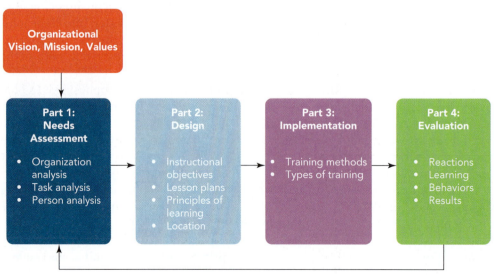

## Part 1: Needs Assessment

Training has tremendous potential to improve the performance of employees, but it is often costly and time-consuming. Consequently, wise managers conduct a training needs assessment to understand where training activities can have the most impact within their organizations. A **needs assessment** identifies where gaps exist between what employees should be doing and what they are actually doing.[12] Training is used to fill these gaps.

Remember that training should support the company's strategic goals. Rockwell Collins, an aviation electronics and communication company serving government and private-sector customers, recognizes that its customers need intensive training for their employees to be successful using Rockwell Collins' products. To assist their customers in achieving their strategic goals, the company has developed a comprehensive needs assessment as a starting point for designing and delivering training solutions. Rockwell Collins's comprehensive needs assessment form ensures that training requests from managers at the client company are in keeping with strategic goals, the training is actually needed, and no alternatives to training exist.[13] Analyses such as this one focus on ensuring that managers request training programs that will add value to their company. When done effectively, a training needs assessment involves three separate, but equally important, analyses: organization analysis, task analysis, and person analysis. As you read about each of these analyses, you will understand more about the types of data needed to identify the gaps we have described between what employees should be doing and what they are actually doing.

The needs assessment begins with an **organization analysis** to determine a firm's progress toward achieving its goals and objectives. Scanning the environment for opportunities and threats and evaluating the strengths and weaknesses internally will help you identify training gaps. Is the company doing what it set out to do? If it isn't, is it because its current employees need better training? How do the organization's performance metrics, such as meeting its production goals, look? Do these metrics suggest that there are performance gaps that could be reduced with training? By answering questions such as these, companies will know where in the organization to provide training.

Along with determining where training is needed, the organization analysis involves determining the external and internal factors that affect what a company is trying to do and how it can do it. In the external environment, the demographics of the labor market determine the availability of workers with the skill sets needed to achieve the company's goals. New technologies present an opportunity for more efficient and effective processes. However, managers will need to determine whether there is a gap between the KSAs their employees have and the ones they need to make the most of the new technologies. When new laws are passed, employees need to be trained to comply with them. New business initiatives undertaken by the firm require its managers to consider whether the company's employees have the capabilities to take advantage of those opportunities. If a downturn in the economy forces a company to lay off employees, the employees who remain often need additional training as they take on new responsibilities.

In the internal environment, employee grievances, absenteeism, turnover, and accidents can indicate a need for training. Grievances often indicate that employees' supervisors need training or that their coworkers need compliance training related to illegal behaviors such as sexual harassment. High absenteeism rates can occur when employees are highly stressed because of a lack of training—a problem that can lead to high turnover rates as well. Accidents often happen because employees have not received proper safety training. We will talk about external and internal factors in more detail in the second half of the chapter.

**needs assessment**
a means to identify where gaps exist between what employees should be doing and what they are actually doing

**organization analysis**
an assessment used to determine a firm's progress toward achieving its goals and objectives

## Task Analysis

**task analysis**

identification of the gap between (1) the KSAs employees need in order to achieve organizational objectives and (2) the KSAs the employees actually possess

After the organization analysis, the next step is to conduct a **task analysis**. The purpose of a task analysis is to identify gaps between (1) the KSAs employees need in order to achieve organizational objectives and (2) the KSAs the employees actually possess. An organization analysis focuses on identifying training gaps across a company's workforce. A task analysis focuses on identifying the specific training content needed to close the gaps between what employees know and are able to do currently and the KSAs they should possess to make actual, value-added contributions to their firms. Employees cannot be expected to perform at their highest levels until those gaps are addressed.

Gaps exist for a variety of reasons. The employees hired might not have the right KSAs. Perhaps a job was not properly analyzed before the hiring process began, and the employee was hired for the wrong skill set. Perhaps the organization itself has changed direction and the job needs to be restructured, or employees with the right skill set may not have been available in the labor market. A task analysis will reveal the discrepancies between the KSAs needed and the KSAs employees have.

KSA gaps can surface in a number of ways. For instance, problems in meeting production requirements, low levels of performance among knowledge workers, an increase in accidents, and an increase in customer complaints about service are all possible signals that employees may not have the required KSAs to perform their jobs. This gap analysis should be an ongoing process. Any time major changes are made in an organization that affect what employees do, a task analysis should be conducted to determine if employees are prepared to assume their new responsibilities.

Consider the following situation: The CEO of a midsized financial services firm decided to hire a consultant to provide his employees with customer service training. However, after the consultant conducted an organizational needs assessment, she determined that customer service was actually a key source of the firm's competitive success. What the firm really needed was more training for employees on a new computer system. The new system had some bugs that needed to be worked out, and the training on that system had been limited. As a result, employees kept going back to their old system to provide service to customers. The firm's top managers believed that the employees' preference for the old system meant that they needed more customer service training, but that was not the case. The employees already knew how to provide a high level of customer service—they were just using the system that worked for them! The moral of the story is to keep in mind that the "apparent" problem you're trying to solve might not be the actual problem—and not identifying the right gap can result in wasted training time and money.

## Person Analysis

**person analysis**

an assessment of the gap between an individual's performance and desired job outcomes

A **person analysis** involves deciding which employees actually need to participate in training programs. The information needed to make this decision can come from a variety of sources, including observations, performance appraisals, supervisor recommendations, and employee skills inventories. Individual production records and skills tests also help determine which employees need training.

Regardless of the source of the information, it is very important to make sure that training is what is needed to address any gaps between an individual's performance and desired outcomes. Employees who are unhappy at work and not performing well might actually have the right qualifications but be unwilling to use them. This highlights a key point about person analysis and training effectiveness. In general, person analysis is a great tool to use to identify situations in which employees simply are not trained properly. It does not, however, usually overcome problems of employee motivation or effort. When employees are not motivated to perform tasks that they are able to perform, performance management rather than training is the necessary course of action. In these circumstances, the resources spent to train the person are not likely to result in a high payoff; they will just increase the training costs.

Managers should also remember that when an employee is not performing well, the problem might not be a lack of skills or a lack of motivation. Rather, the person's manager might not be communicating the organization's expectations to the person. As a result, the employee might need to have his or her job responsibilities clarified.

## Part 2: Design

The information from needs analysis tells managers where in the organization training is needed (organization analysis), what the focus of the training initiatives should be (task analysis), and which employees should participate in the training programs (person analysis). And while this is critical information, training must also be designed effectively in order to be of value.

A clear understanding of the goals of the program at the beginning of the design process helps ensure that the training program is results oriented and supports the mission of the organization. Effectively designing a training program includes establishing the program's instructional objectives, developing the lesson plans for it, and incorporating principles of learning. Next, we will review each of these elements.

### Instructional Objectives

Do you like to get in your car and just drive? When you don't have to be anywhere by a specific time, doing so can be quite relaxing, especially if the traffic is light and the weather is good. But when you have to be somewhere by a certain time, you are likely to carefully plan your trip to ensure that you arrive at your destination on time. A lot of training programs aren't successful because they are more like the first journey than the latter. Take the case of the manager of a small dry cleaning establishment. He decided to put in some new dry cleaning equipment last year. He knew he would have to teach his six employees how to use the equipment. However, instead of thinking about what specifically they would need to know, he randomly relayed information to them as he thought of it. Only when customers began to complain about their dry cleaning did he realize that he wasn't doing a good job of training his employees. In large or small organizations, providing training that has clearly defined objectives saves a lot of time and energy, and it often results in superior customer service or higher-quality products.

What the manager in our story missed was an understanding of the need for a focused training plan. Writing effective instructional objectives is a first step in designing the training program. **Instructional objectives** describe the purpose of a training program and what it will accomplish. The objectives should be linked to the organization's goals and conveyed to employees so they understand what they should learn from the training and how they can use it on the job.

**instructional objective**
a statement that describes what is to be accomplished in a training program and, therefore, drives the design of the program

You probably noticed that we have listed objectives at the beginning of each of the chapters of this book. These, in fact, are instructional objectives. They served as a guide as we wrote this book so we could make sure we were providing you with the information you need relative to each topic. The objectives also serve as a guide for you as you read the chapters. Before we wrote the objectives, we thought about who our audience would be (students studying business), the level of course for which the book is targeted (college students), and what our audience would need to know relative to each topic. Had the dry cleaning manager taken the time to do the same, he likely would have had few, if any, customer complaints. Why? He would have made sure his employees were properly trained. Even OJT, as you will learn later in this chapter, needs to be well designed.

## Lesson Planning

Schoolteachers are intimately familiar with the concept of a lesson plan. They routinely map out what they will do during their class sessions to achieve their instructional objectives. Corporate training requires the same type of planning. If you work in a company that has its own training department, you likely will be asked to provide information about the content that should be covered during training. As we have already mentioned, in a small business, you may be responsible for designing and carrying out the entire training program. Having a lesson plan is critical in either case.

Instructional objectives guide the content of training. A **lesson plan** provides a map of what should be done during each training session to achieve the stated objectives. It includes what will be covered, who will cover it, how the material will be taught, where it will be taught, and how long each part will last.

## Principles of Learning

Even the best lesson plan will fail if the trainer doesn't understand that people do not all learn in the same way or at the same pace. Some people can learn how to do something by having it described to them. Others need to see it demonstrated. Many people have to actually perform the task to learn how to do it. Each of us has a preference for how we learn best, even though we can usually adapt to other teaching methods. When you're designing and providing informal as well as formal training and development programs for your employees, how you deliver the material can be as critical as the material itself. We will now discuss some principles related to learning styles, learning agility, self-efficacy, interest in learning, and training location. Attention to each of these principles can improve the likelihood that employees will learn during training.

**Learning Styles**   If you have to find your way to a new place, would you rather have someone (1) tell you the directions, (2) draw you a map, or (3) take you there the first time? **Learning styles** affect how people prefer to absorb and process new information. Research has not consistently supported the existence of learning styles, but the concept is prevalent in the training literature.

A number of ways to categorize learning styles exist. One often-cited approach categorizes learners as auditory, visual, tactile, or kinesthetic.[14] *Auditory learners* hear information and are able to process and remember it. Lectures and discussions are good training methods for these learners. *Visual learners* need to see the information, and they often prefer seeing it in a picture format, such as a map or table. They learn well in training programs using a lot of visual and audiovisual demonstrations. *Tactile learners* need to interact with the material they're learning. They are likely to underline what they are reading and take notes when listening to others. They prefer training programs that include writing activities and other experiences that keep their hands busy. *Kinesthetic learners* need to be actively involved in the learning experience by actually doing something, rather than just hearing or seeing the material. They relate well to role plays and other experiential-based training methods. We all learn in multiple ways but usually prefer one style of learning over another.

So, what does all this mean in terms of employee training? Think about your experiences in class. Have you learned better when the teacher used hands-on exercises or just lectured? Your employees, like you, are most comfortable with a particular learning style. Basically, you need to acknowledge these differences.[15] By being aware that differences exist, you will be more likely to use a variety of training approaches with your employees, and you may even learn to target your OJT style to the learning styles of the employees. The result will be better trained and more satisfied employees. For instance, visual learners will be less frustrated

**lesson plan**

a map of what should be done during each training session to achieve the stated objectives

**learning styles**

ways that people prefer to absorb and process new information

and have less difficulty learning if the learning experience includes visual as well as auditory presentations. The opposite is true for auditory learners. Incorporating all four learning styles in training programs will reduce the frustration of trainees with different styles and increase the learning that results.

**Learning Agility**   Employees high on **learning agility** seek new experiences and opportunities to learn new knowledge and skills. They are then willing and able to incorporate that information into how they perform their jobs. Employees high on learning agility are also believed to be high-potential employees.[16] While we don't recommend using learning agility as a sole selection criterion, being aware of the impact of this aspect of learning during the selection process is increasingly important.

**learning agility**

willingness to seek new experiences and opportunities to learn new knowledge and skills

**Self-Efficacy**   Having confidence that you can do something means you have **self-efficacy** with respect to that task. If you have high task self-efficacy, you are more likely to succeed at doing that task. In the context of training, employees who have higher self-efficacy with regard to the training are more likely to perform well during the training and are more likely to use that training on the job.[17] There is a possible downside, however. Employees with high self-efficacy might not be as diligent in the training process as those with low self-efficacy. High self-efficacy could lead employees to think they can rush through the training activity. Low self-efficacy can cause employees to work harder to learn the material and/or skill to overcome their lack of confidence.[18]

**self-efficacy**

having confidence that one can perform a particular task

**Interest in a Training Program**   Everything we need to learn in order to do our jobs well is not equally interesting to us. A manager needs to understand the importance of carefully choosing the right training program for employees. In general, the effectiveness of training is likely to increase when employees are genuinely interested in the content of the training and are motivated to learn.[19] Charismatic trainers and engaging and fun learning experiences heighten participants' interest in the training process. If you want to ensure that employees complete their training programs and remember what they were taught, making the training program interesting is important. But even more important is helping employees see how they can personally benefit from participating in the program. Understanding how their job performance will improve, for example, is likely to stimulate their interest in learning the material presented, as is understanding the importance of the learning to the organization's success. Exhibit 8.3 provides ideas for enhancing the learning

## EXHIBIT 8.3

### Training Adult Learners

| Adults need to: | |
| --- | --- |
| • Start with the big picture of what they are learning | • Be encouraged to explore |
| • Be intimately involved in the training activities | • Receive immediate feedback |
| • Have practice spread over time | • Experience an emotional connection to the subject |
| • Relate past and current experiences to the training | • Understand real-world benefits of the training |

*Source:* Based on Hager, P., "Lifelong Learning in the Workplace? Challenges and Issues," *Journal of Workplace Learning 16* (2004): 22–32; Pappas, Christopher, "How to Engage and Inspire Adult Learners," October 3, 2014, https://elearningindustry.com/11-tips-engage-inspire-adult-learners.

experiences of adult learners. As you will see, these ideas should work well with learners of all ages, even though they are based on research about adult learning.

**Location**    Would you learn better in a large auditorium or as part of a small group, sitting around a conference table? How about sitting at home at your computer or at a retreat center with coworkers and a dynamic trainer? Perhaps you could learn in a number of these settings. Location is important for training success. Just think about the basics such as heat, light, and comfortable seating. A room that is too warm might make trainees fall asleep; a room that is too cold will distract attendees as they try to keep warm. When deciding on the location, little things matter. Many companies take employees off-site for training programs or send them to programs sponsored by other organizations. These companies know how easily distracted employees can become by the daily routine and unexpected events related to their jobs if they are returning to their offices during breaks. Having employees in another location reduces their distractions, although with the proliferation of smart phones and tablets, this is getting more difficult. Regardless of whether it's on- or off-site, the training location should be carefully selected to ensure that the environment is conducive to learning and disruptions are minimized.

## Part 3: Implementation

We learned to feed ourselves and put on our clothes when we were toddlers. This learning took place "on the job" because our job at the time was to learn to take care of ourselves. As we entered school, we learned in the classroom, often through a variety of teaching methods. Our teachers lectured to us, led discussion groups, and had us engage in exercises to reinforce the concepts we were learning. You probably experienced different types of computer-aided learning as well. The ways you have been trained to do things in the past are not that different from how you will train your employees to do things in the future.

If you were a manager at Booz Allen Hamilton, a large professional services firm that provides consulting to private companies and government agencies, you would have a large array of learning and development resources available for your employees. They could enroll in Cyber University to learn about cyber-related technologies, take part in an internally offered course, or receive support to receive an academic degree or professional certification.[20] These examples represent different methods available for delivering training. As you read about the different methods described in the following sections, you will likely note that some of them require little to no computer or audiovisual technology and can therefore be described as "low-tech." There is minimal interpersonal interaction during the training as well, so the techniques are also "low-touch." Other methods can be classified as "high-tech" and "high-touch." Exhibit 8.4 provides a summary of the methods we discuss within the high-tech/high-touch dimensions. The content of the training determines whether it should be high-tech or high-touch, and some content calls for both. We have categorized the methods where they are most likely to fall on the chart. This list is by no means exhaustive, but it does give you a good idea of what is available and what is most commonly used.

Company Spotlight 8.2 provides an example of a "high-touch, high-tech" approach to learning. When UPS wanted to implement a safety program for drivers, it adopted a multiphase learning process that incorporated both high-touch and high-tech components.

### Training Methods

As a manager, you will constantly be making decisions about how well your employees are doing their jobs and whether additional training is needed to

**EXHIBIT 8.4**

Examples of Low-Tech/Low-Touch Versus High-Tech/High-Touch Approaches to Training

|             | Low-Tech           | High-Tech        |
|-------------|--------------------|------------------|
| **High-Touch** | OJT            | OJT              |
|             | Classroom training | Simulation       |
|             | Coaching           | Gamification     |
|             |                    | Blended learning |
| **Low-Touch**  | Printed materials | E-learning      |
|             |                    | Audiovisual      |
|             |                    | Simulation       |

*Low-tech = Limited or no use of computers and/or audiovisual technology*
*High-tech = Training depends on use of computers and/or audiovisual technology*
*Low-touch = Minimal or no interaction with others*
*High-touch = Training involves extensive interpersonal interaction*

# COMPANY SPOTLIGHT  8.2

## Increasing Driver Safety at UPS

UPS recognizes that its workers are its most important asset. With that in mind, when UPS established new goals for the company, it included two goals with associated key performance indicators (KPIs) related to workforce safety. By 2020, the company, which is already an industry leader in safety, wants to have a 1% improvement in lost time injury frequency, with fewer injuries per 200,000 hours worked, and have a 3% improvement in their already low auto accident frequency, based on the number of accidents per 100,000 driver hours.

The company already spends over $209 million on safety training courses each year out of $967 million spent overall for training. UPS employees have engaged in over 5.8 million hours of safety training. The company couples formal training with mentoring programs. UPS knows that employees can learn a lot from the experiences of others.

Drivers take part in a multiphase safety training program that runs the gamut from high-touch to high-tech experiences. Along with mentoring by experienced drivers, tractor-trailer drivers participate in 80 hours of computer-based and on-road training before starting out as drivers.

With the help of a $1.8 million grant from the U.S. Department of Labor, UPS, in collaboration with MIT, Virginia Tech, and the Institute for the Future, came up with a way to develop simulations that mirror the job of a UPS truck driver. Using a next-generation training facility known as UPS Integrad, driver trainees participate in 3-D simulations and webcasts that enable them to see their driving skills. UPS notes a significant decrease in first-year injuries and auto accidents resulting from an increase in driver proficiency from using the simulator. In 2017, UPS incorporated virtual reality (VR) into the Integrad program, taking the training to an even higher-tech, and yet more realistic, level.

*Sources:* "Employee Safety," Empowered People UPS, ups.com, https://www.sustainabilty.ups.com/committed-to-more/employee-safety/; "UPS Enhances Driver Safety Training with Virtual Reality," Globe Newswire, August 15, 2017, https://globenewswire.com/news-release/2017/08/15/1084802/0/en/UPS-Enhances-Driver-Safety-Training-With-Virtual-Reality.html.

improve or upgrade their skills and knowledge. Making sure the method of training delivery is appropriate for the content and audience will increase the value of the training. In this section we discuss the most common training methods. We provide a brief overview of each method, along with some discussion of the advantages and downsides of each. Keep in mind that there are many more methods for training than are described here. We end this section with a discussion of blended learning, an approach that many organizations are now using to reinforce learning concepts.

**on-the-job training (OJT)**

training that occurs when a manager or coworker teaches an employee how to perform some aspect of a job in the actual job location rather than in a separate training location

**On-the-Job Training (OJT)   On-the-job training (OJT)** occurs when a manager or coworker teaches an employee how to perform some aspect of a job in the actual job location rather than in a separate training location. OJT is frequently used and can be cost effective. A primary benefit is that employees are being productive while learning. The employee doesn't have to take time away from the job to attend a training program. OJT works best when the trainer is carefully selected and understands that all trainees will not learn in the same way.

On the other hand, OJT can be costly. If the person providing the training is not adequately trained to perform the job, then the new employee will not learn the right way to perform the job tasks or might not learn all the information needed to perform tasks successfully.[21] If you have ever been in a store when an employee was just learning the job on the job, you know that an employee-in-training often takes more time to assist you than an experienced employee takes. This slowness causes delays and irritates customers. And mistakes made can be costly, especially if the customer leaves and never returns.

In a more extreme example, think of the potential costs to an airline that chooses to use on-the-job training for pilots as the primary training method. You probably would not want to fly on that airline! Therefore, a manager needs to think through the costs as well as the benefits of OJT. Remember that costs include loss of productive time, loss of customers, and loss of property—at a minimum. For OJT to be effective, trainers need a framework for conducting training. Using the guidelines listed in Exhibit 8.5, along with making sure there are well-written training materials and measurable performance objectives, will enhance the likelihood of training success.

Three specific types of OJT programs are apprenticeships, internships, and cooperative education programs. *Apprenticeships* have long been an established method for teaching skilled trades. Learning a skilled trade, such as carpentry, requires "hands-on" learning under the tutelage of a master tradesperson. But there are other types of apprentice programs as well. For instance, there has been a recent push to develop apprenticeship programs for the information technology industry. In fact, the Department of Labor (DOL) has awarded the Computing Technology

---

**EXHIBIT 8.5**

Steps to Increase Effectiveness of OJT

**The trainer should:**

- Conduct an orientation to ensure trainee understands objectives of training.
- Establish rapport to reduce trainee's anxiety and increase learning.
- Demonstrate task and discuss how task is important to job.
- Coach trainee to reinforce training and address any questions.
- Observe trainee performing the task and give feedback about performance.
- Debrief trainee to further reinforce importance of training and schedule follow-ups.

*Source:* Based on Walter, D., "Training and Certifying On-the-Job Trainers," *Technical Training,* March/April (1998): 32–35.

Industry Association (CompTIA) a series of grants to put in place a nationwide apprenticeship program for information technology (IT) workers.[22]

*Internships* are a type of OJT familiar to many students. An internship involves a student working at an organization for a specified period of time for the purpose of learning what a job is like and seeing the relationship between information learned in the classroom and practice in an organization. A large number of universities have begun to require students to complete internships before they graduate in disciplines as diverse as finance and human services. These internships can be paid or unpaid, and they can be completed for college credit or not for credit. For a student, an internship provides a way to try out a job of interest. For an employer, internships provide a mechanism for recruiting the best students. Interns who do well during their time at the company often receive full-time job offers when they graduate. High school students have begun to complete internships as well.

Engineering and a few other disciplines offer *co-operative education programs* for students. These co-op programs, as they are known, are also a form of OJT. Students typically work for one semester and then attend school for a semester. A co-op also can be done while a student is taking classes. The student goes to school for part of a day and works the other part. The purpose of a co-op is the same as the purpose of internships. Students and employers get to find out if they are a good fit for each other while the student learns practical application of information being learned in school.

**Operations and Procedures Manuals**   Almost everything you buy these days comes with some kind of operations manual, whether printed or online. The same is true for many tasks that employees do on their jobs. Often, employee operations and procedures manuals outline company policies and practices as well. Because procedures and task guidelines are written down and available on the job, employees can refer to them as often as needed for clarification or if they forget something. The manuals can also be readily copied and distributed to a large number of employees or put online. The downside is that not all manuals are well written or address all potential problems or issues employees will encounter. These issues can result in frustrated employees who have trouble getting their questions answered, and frustrated customers who can't get their questions answered don't return.

**Classroom Training**   We are all familiar with **classroom training** by virtue of having been students for many years. Did you know that lecturing to employees is one of the least effective ways to train them? Why? Because, when the teacher does nothing but lecture, the employees aren't engaged. Feel familiar? Lectures can be an effective way to disseminate simple information, but lectures do not necessarily facilitate behavioral change. Including role plays, discussions, and other experiential activities as part of the classroom experience along with lectures will increase the effectiveness of classroom training.

**classroom training**

traditional learning that includes lectures, role plays, discussions, and other experiential activities

Until recently, classroom training was often an efficient and economical way to provide training for a large number of employees. Now, computer technology has made training more efficient and more economical in many cases, even allowing companies to create virtual classrooms that bring together employees from different locations. When classroom training does occur, it lasts for a shorter period of time— perhaps one day instead of five.[23]

**E-Learning**   **E-learning** involves using the Internet, computers, and other electronic tools to deliver training programs. Advances in computer technology and its accessibility have probably changed the training process more than any other innovation in history.[24] Now, training can be delivered online, on demand, 24/7, regardless of an employee's location. Companies can train more employees more efficiently, faster, and at lower

**e-learning**

using the Internet, computers, and other electronic tools to deliver training programs

cost to the company than with traditional classroom-type training programs. And companies can even use online learning to provide training for their customers. For instance, Caterpillar provides access to their Caterpillar University online training to customers. Courses are available 24/7 and include hundreds of topics ranging from safety to heavy equipment operation. The online learning includes virtual simulations, videos, interactive training, and resource libraries.[25]

E-learning can take several forms:

**web-based training**

learning experiences that are accessed through a secure website, such as online courses and webcasts

**desktop training**

a training approach in which employees access a software program housed on their computers or on a server or in the cloud

**podcast**

a digital recording that can be downloaded and played back later

- *Web-based training*—With **Web-based training**, employees can log on to a secure website and take a course or participate in a webcast.
- *Desktop training*—Employees use computer software programs to learn new information or skills. **Desktop training** differs from web-based training in that the training program is housed on the employee's personal computer, on a server, or in the cloud.
- *Podcast training*—**Podcasts** are digital recordings that can be downloaded and played back later. They have become very popular training tools due to their portability for the employee and the ease with which the company can make them widely available. Several years ago when podcasts were just becoming popular, Capital One, a financial services company, bought 3,000 iPods for its employees so that they could download more than a dozen lessons on topics the company wanted all employees to know. The goal of the program was to reduce the time employees spend in a classroom and to reduce the costs of bringing employees to Capital One's McLean, Virginia, location. The chief learning officer at Capital One reported that 87% of employees involved in this initiative felt it was a worthwhile investment of their time.[26] Of course, audio learners are the most drawn to this training approach. Today, most employees can just listen to the podcasts on their own mobile devices, making this a relatively inexpensive training resource.

Employees do not have to travel to participate in e-learning, making this type of training much more economical than many traditional training programs.[27] The downside of e-learning, however, is that employees have more control over how long and how often they practice the material—which can be bad for people who tend to skip parts or move quickly through the material.[28] Before embarking on an e-learning program, a company needs to weigh the pros and cons of this type of training and pilot the program with a small group of employees to make sure it achieves desired goals. Exhibit 8.6 lists tips that have been found to increase the likelihood of employee participation in e-learning courses.

## EXHIBIT 8.6

### Tips to Increase E-Learning Participation Rates

- Remember that e-learning is both an art and a science.
- Employ simulations to immerse the learner in the content.
- *Gamify* the e-learning by making it competitive by group, awarding points or badges, and recognizing high performers.
- Create a social experience through interactive bulletin boards, interaction with subject matter experts, and using other social tools.
- Use spaced learning rather than mass learning to break material into more easily digestible pieces.
- Develop scenarios that are relevant to the topic and the learner.
- Make it mobile so employees can participate anytime, anywhere.
- Keep it real so that employees can see a line of sight between what they are learning and what they need to do on the job.

*Source:* Based on Hughes, Andrew, "7 Tips to Expand Your eLearning Participation Rates," September 1, 2015, https://elearningindustry.com/7-tips-expand-elearning-participation-rates.

**Audiovisual Training**   **Audiovisual training** involves providing instruction on a topic to employees by having them watch a video or other visual presentation. The presentation can be stored on a DVD, or now more likely on a website. Presentations can be viewed in an individual setting or in a group setting, the choice of which should depend on the goals for the training. Using video training to teach a computer skill can be done individually. Using video training to teach team building is best done in a group setting so that the employees can practice what they are learning from the video. Group training sessions should be facilitated by an expert on the topic, who can be either a company employee or an external consultant. Video training provides an economical way to ensure that all employees receive the same information. Organizations can either prepare their own audiovisual training materials or buy programs off the shelf. The downside is that preparing a custom video for a company can be quite expensive initially. Off-the-shelf programs can also be costly because they sometimes involve a charge for each participant each time they are used.

**audiovisual training**

providing instruction on a topic to employees by having them watch or listen to a video or other visual or audio presentation

**Simulations**   **Simulations** replicate the work employees will be doing. They were first used by the military to train pilots and for weapons training. Simulations are used in a wide range of work environments to train employees on tasks ranging from driving a car to performing complicated medical procedures.[29]

Airlines use flight simulators to teach pilots to fly and to handle an airplane in typical situations and in emergency situations they are likely to encounter. This approach to training is much less expensive and much safer than waiting until a pilot actually encounters a hazardous situation and hoping that a lot of OJT happens quickly. Ask Captain Chesley Sullenberger about the value of simulation training. He will quickly tell you that he credits participating in training on flight simulators two days every six months with preparing him for much of what he encountered when he had to set his Airbus 320 down in the Hudson River—and did so safely. His simulator training focused on handling emergencies. That, coupled with his years of experience as a pilot, had trained him well to handle the situation.[30]

Good simulations are engaging, fun, and challenging. Unlike static online training programs, simulations lead to a high rate of completion by keeping the players involved in the learning process.[31] A downside, though, is the complexity involved in developing a simulation that accurately mirrors the job, especially when the job is less structured than the one in our pilot example or the UPS driver example in Company Spotlight 8.2.

**simulation**

a training activity that replicates the work the employees will be doing, without the safety and cost concerns often associated with various jobs

**Gamification**   **Gamification** involves adding game elements, game mechanics, and game design to nongame systems or turning the content into a game with business objectives. For example, badges, points, and leaderboards can be added to existing content to encourage movement through the content. Gamification is still catching on in the learning and development field, but it seems to be gaining ground.[32]

Westinghouse uses a game for safety training in their nuclear fuels division, which workers complete on their tablets or smart phones. ExactTarget, a developer of digital marketing tools, used game mechanics for training 2,000 employees when they had a new product launch.[33] SAP has used games for teaching employees about sustainability.[34] When considering the use of gamification, employers need to remember that the same process needs to be followed as for any training program: needs assessment, careful and appropriate design, well managed implementation, and evaluation. Overall, gamification shows promise for training and development since it engages employees in the learning process. One study of gamification in organizations reported a 48% improvement in employee engagement for firms from the use of games.[35]

**gamification**

adding game elements, game mechanics, and game design to nongame systems, or turning the content into a game with business objectives

**Blended Learning** Probably the most frequently used form of training now is **blended learning**. This term refers to the use of multiple modes of training to accomplish a training goal.

GC Services is a leading business process outsource provider. When the company needed a better leadership program, it tried blended learning. At first, this plan did not work well. The program format was time intensive and not well used as a result. The company's organizational design team worked to create strategic alignment between e-learning courses and facilitated workshops focused on application of what had been learned in the e-learning courses. The result: reduced costs of more than $90,000 and 75% less time away from work for participants, increased productivity, and greater participation by managers.[36]

Another global organization invested $3 million in training for 30,000 employees in North and South America, Europe, and Asia. The training on the new system technology and business processes took place over four weeks. The training was done by using a blended learning approach involving e-learning and exercises and activities in a classroom learning lab. The cost to the company was only $100 per employee—far less than the cost of classroom training alone.[37] The downside of blended learning is often the time and resources required to design the training components so they work well together; however, the payoff is generally worth the expense. A research project by the U.S. Department of Education on online learning reported that blended instruction was more effective than face-to-face classes or online learning alone.[38]

**College and University Programs** A growing number of companies are partnering with universities to provide degree completion programs for employees. Starbucks was one of the first companies to do so. The company has partnered with Arizona State University (ASU) to offer a free, online, four-year bachelor's degree to all of its 135,000 U.S. employees. The program is available to all eligible full- and part-time employees.[39] Walmart employees pay $1 per day to earn a degree once they have been with the company for 90 days. Walmart picks up the rest of the cost, including fees and books. Workers can choose between the University of Florida, Bellevue University, or Brandman University to enroll in an online degree program for working adults in business or supply chain management.[40]

Another company offering a generous tuition plan is United Technologies. The Employee Scholar Program at this aerospace and defense firm has existed since 1996. Around 38,000 of United Technologies' over 200,000 employees globally have completed a college degree. Degrees range from associate degrees to MBAs. The company has spent $1.2 billion to make this education program available.[41]

Companies that offer tuition reimbursement usually have restrictions on how much they will pay and for what kinds of education they will pay. Often, the coursework has to be directly job related, although that is not the case at Starbucks. Additionally, the amount of reimbursement can vary from full reimbursement to reimbursement of only a portion of the cost. Reimbursement can also be contingent on completing a specific number of credit hours or achieving a certain grade in a class. For instance, the firm might reimburse 100% of the cost if a grade of A is earned, but only 80% for a B grade. And, some companies, like United Technologies, pay the funds directly to the college. Other firms reimburse the employee at an agreed time.

**Coaching and Mentoring** Employee coaching is often used as a form of employee development, but there is a training element to it as well. Coaching is a billion-dollar business that started out in organizations as a way to help problem employees become better performers. Now, much of the coaching that occurs is designed to groom executives for future opportunities.[42] One of the problems with coaching, however, is that the concept is often confused with mentoring. **Coaching** is primarily about performance improvement, usually in the short term and relative to a specific skill or ability. For instance, a manager who is having trouble gaining the cooperation of his subordinates might be coached on how to better communicate with his employees.

**Mentoring** is a longer-term relationship that involves a more senior employee teaching a junior employee how the organization works and nurturing that person as she progresses in her career. ESL Federal Credit Union developed a one-on-one mentoring program when they heard from exiting employees that they did not feel supported in their jobs. After developing a formal mentoring program coupled with one-on-one coaching, turnover dropped from 3.33% to 1.09%. The industry average is 24.4%.[43] ESL has been named one of the 2018 Best Workplaces for Millennials and ranked in the Top 50 of the Small Business Administration's Most Active Lenders in the United States.[44]

Coaching is better at supporting different learning styles than a lot of other types of training and development because coaching is almost always done one on one—one coach and one employee.[45] It can be done by members of the organization, if they're appropriately trained, as well as by external coaches. One hospital in London provides 22 hours of coaching during the year for its directors and heads of departments. The head of training and development views training as an important part of the hospital's leadership and management program.[46] The growth in the coaching industry has led to the call for standards to ensure that employees and organizations are treated ethically and fairly.

Now that we have looked at some of the most frequently used methods of training, we can discuss types of training programs.

## Types of Training

Training can generally be grouped into four categories: compliance, knowledge, basic skills, and behavioral. Next, we discuss each one briefly.

**Compliance Training**   In Chapter 3, we provided a lot of information about the regulations that affect employee management. It is important for you, as a manager, to ensure that your employees, especially those with supervisory responsibility, know and abide by these regulations. Compliance training includes both legal compliance training and diversity training. **Legal compliance training** ensures that a firm's managers and employees know what they can and cannot do from a legal standpoint. Sexual harassment training and Americans with Disabilities (ADA) training are examples. **Diversity and inclusion training** helps reduce discrimination by making employees more aware of discrimination that occurs overtly and covertly in the workplace and more understanding of the importance and value of having a workplace that is open and welcoming for all employees.

Some laws specify that certain training must occur. For example, when California Assembly Bill (AB) 1825 became law, California firms with 50 or more employees were required to start providing sexual harassment training to all of their supervisors by a certain date. AB 1825 went so far as to specify the length of the training, the format in which it had to be presented, and the topics discussed—the relevant federal and state laws, remedies available to victims, and so forth. Connecticut has a similar law.[47] Even in states that do not have such laws, sexual harassment training is necessary to reduce the likelihood of such behavior occurring in the workplace and to reduce an employer's liability should it occur. The federal guidelines for reducing sexual harassment in the workplace include guidance on providing training.

The case of *Cadena v. Pacesetter Corp.*, 224 F.3d 1203 (10th Cir. 2000), highlights both the need for training and the need for employers to carefully select trainers to cover topics such as sexual harassment. In this particular case, the jury awarded

---

**coaching**

short-term training provided one on one and primarily focused on performance improvement relative to a specific skill or ability

**mentoring**

a longer-term relationship that involves a more senior employee teaching a junior employee how the organization works and nurturing that person as she progresses in her career

**legal compliance training**

ensures that a firm's managers and employees know what they can and cannot do from a legal standpoint

**diversity and inclusion training**

helps reduce discrimination by making employees more aware of the value of differences in the workplace and the need to create an open and welcoming environment for all employees

$300,000 in punitive damages to the plaintiff, and the 10th U.S. Circuit Court of Appeals upheld the award. The employer could not verify that the trainer conducting the sexual harassment training was actually qualified to do the training. Apparently, the trainer had answered some questions incorrectly during the training session, calling into question his competence.[48]

Different jobs require different types of compliance training. All supervisors need to be familiar with all the employee laws that deal with discrimination. Employees who manage compensation plans and payroll need to know the guidelines outlined by the U.S. Fair Labor Standards Act and discussed in detail in Chapter 10, as well as antidiscrimination laws. Supervisors who work in manufacturing facilities need to know about the laws related to workplace safety in their particular industry. We will discuss this topic more in Chapter 13. These are just a few of the examples of how the context of a job affects the need for compliance training.

One focus of diversity and inclusion training is helping employees to understand their biases and how those biases affect workplace outcomes. These courses are not inexpensive. A one-day program for 50 people can cost $2,000 to $6,000, but companies understand that they are important.[49]

When Starbucks made the decision to shut down all 8,000 of its shops in the United States on May 29, 2018, to provide diversity training to all of its 175,000 employees on the same day, estimates were that the loss of profits to the company would be around $12 million. So why did Starbucks make this decision? Following a racial incident involving employees and customers at one of its shops, Starbucks wanted to be bold in addressing the issue of implicit bias and stereotypes that likely led to the racial incident. They also wanted to make a clear statement that such behavior was not part of the Starbucks culture. The company also knew it was important for public relations to get out in front of the issue.[50]

In addition to making employees more aware of how stereotypes can be destructive in the workplace, diversity and inclusion training can also help employees understand that differences among people are actually good for a company that wants to be competitive. Different viewpoints lead to more and often better ideas. Diversity and inclusion training can focus on people's individual attitudes or involve major initiatives to change the corporate culture of a firm. The more comprehensive a program, the more effective it is likely to be.[51] Exhibit 8.7 provides benchmarks to use to ensure that diversity training is successful.

**Knowledge Training**    Every job has a knowledge component. Knowledge has been recognized as a key—if not *the* key—for firms that want to achieve a competitive advantage in today's global business environment. The knowledge can be either technical or practical. Examples of technical knowledge are information on how an

---

**EXHIBIT 8.7**

Benchmarks for Effective Diversity Training

| Research shows that effective diversity training requires: |
| --- |
| • Target training to both awareness and skills development. |
| • Incorporate training into a larger set of diversity initiatives. |
| • Spread training over a considerable period of time rather than all at once. |
| • Include perspective-taking activities into training program. |
| • Have participants set goals related to diversity in the workplace. |

*Source:* Based on Bezrukova, K., Spell, C. S., Perry, J. L., and Jehn, K. A., "A Meta-Analytical Integration of over 40 Years of Research on Diversity Training Evaluation," *Psychological Bulletin*, 142(2016): 1227–1274; Lindsey, A., King, E., Membere, A., and Cheung, H. K., "Two Types of Diversity Training That Really Work," *Harvard Business Review*, July 28, 2017, https://hbr.org/2017/07/two-types-of-diversity-training-that-really-work.

engine works and federal regulations that govern banking. Examples of practical knowledge are theories of what makes for good customer service and different approaches to project management. A firm's job descriptions should describe the knowledge that employees need, and training programs can then be planned to address any gaps identified.

**Skills Training** In addition to knowledge, all jobs require some type of skills. Skills can range from how to change an electrical panel for an electrician, to how to read an annual report for a financial analyst, to how to register a guest for a hotel front desk clerk. If you visit the website for the National Institutes of Health (NIH) Training Center, for example, you will find an online listing of the types of skills training available. Courses cover a wide array of topics, such as how to prepare purchase card logs and how to use computer programs.[52]

A well-written and up-to-date job description will provide information about the skills that a person needs to successfully do a job. A person analysis provides information about the extent to which employees have those skills. When both pieces of information are available, a plan can be developed to provide training to address any skills gaps.

**Behavioral Training** Employees need training on the behavioral aspects of their jobs, as well as skills training. Behavioral training focuses on the "how" of getting a job done. For example, employees whose jobs require working as part of a team might need to be taught more effective team skills.

Team training, leadership development, time management, project management, customer service, diversity, and sensitivity training are examples of training designed to change the behaviors of employees. In addition to skills training, the National Institutes of Health provides an extensive list of training opportunities related to workplace behavior. Training courses cover topics such as managing change, motivating and engaging employees, moving from conflict to collaboration, and creating a culture of service.[53] Most jobs have either some behaviors that are standardized across the organization and that can be taught, or behaviors that need to be reinforced through training.

## Part 4: Evaluation

The final component of a successful training program is evaluation. Training programs are expensive so it is critical to make sure they are delivering results. Training professionals have identified five levels of evaluation. We next discuss each level. In addition, Exhibit 8.8 provides information about the levels of evaluation for determining the return on investment (ROI) for training costs.

### Level 1: Reaction

The first level of evaluation focuses on how employees react to the training program. At the end of each term, your professors probably ask you to complete course evaluations. These evaluations usually ask you to rate on a scale of 1–5 the extent to which you learned in the course, found the course challenging, felt the instructor motivated you, and would recommend this instructor to other students. Basically, the evaluation measures your reaction to the course—how you feel about the learning experience. The same type of evaluation is also used for company training programs. The primary advantages of this level of evaluation are that the ratings are fairly easy to obtain and the information can be useful in terms of identifying problems with particular trainers or training content.

If participants only rate the trainer numerically, without providing specific feedback on the person's strengths and/or areas for improvement, the information is only

**EXHIBIT 8.8**

## Levels of Evaluation for Determining Return on Investment (ROI)

| Level | Objective of Measurement | Tool or Technique | Comments |
|---|---|---|---|
| 1. Reaction (and planned action) | Participant's reaction to and satisfaction with content and delivery of training | Participants complete evaluation forms, and/or develop action plans for implementing new knowledge | Subjective but has some usefulness. If follow-up is scheduled, participant's action plans will be more realistic |
| 2. Learning | Skills, knowledge, or attitude changes as a result of training program | Tests via paper and pencil or computerized format | Tests must be assessed for validity and reliability |
| 3. Behavior | Changes in behavior on the job as result of training | Performance reviews and observations | Assumption is that if the skills are applied, results will follow |
| 4. Results | Impact of training on business activities and processes | Cost reduction, productivity increases, improved quality, reduced labor hours, decreased production/processing time, etc. | Critical tasks are isolating the effects of training and capturing appropriate data |
| 5. ROI | Compares the costs of the training program with monetary results and is usually expressed as percentage | Detailed, comprehensive data collection and analysis of costs and benefits. Accounting expertise is helpful. The time value of money is factor | Most comprehensive and objective evaluation; process can be costly and time-consuming. |

*Source:* Adapted from Noe, Raymond, Learning System Design, SHRM Foundation's Effective Practice Guideline Series (Alexandria, VA: SHRM, 2009); Stawarski, Cathy, "What's the Difference Between Return on Expectations and Return on Investment?" October 8, 2012, https://www.td.org/insights/whats-the-difference-between-return-on-expectations-and-return-on-investment.

marginally useful. Vague questions on the evaluation form exacerbate this problem. Consider the question "How would you rate the effectiveness of this instructor?" with an accompanying scale ranging from 1 (totally ineffective) to 5 (extremely effective). Think for a minute about how you would interpret the word *effective*. Some participants might think about how the trainer conveyed the material, whether it was understandable, and whether they learned something. Other participants might think about whether the trainer was entertaining in her delivery of the material. As you can see, simply gauging participants' reactions won't tell you how much they learned, and therefore how effective the training program was; it only tells you whether they liked it.

### Level 2: Learning

The goal of training is to impart new information or skills in such a way that the trainee is then able to transfer the new knowledge or skills to the job. A pre-training–post-training assessment is the easiest way to determine whether learning has occurred during training. If the scores on the pre- and post-tests are not appreciably different, then the organization needs to review the training program. Perhaps the wrong employees were trained (they didn't need the training), the training needs assessment itself was not reliable or valid, or the trainer simply didn't deliver.

### Level 3: Behavior

Training should help employees perform at higher levels or do new things. If a firm conducted a thorough training needs analysis and the right employees were trained, their performance should improve. Employee performance is more likely to improve when there is a high degree of transfer of training. **Transfer of training** refers to the degree to which the information covered in the program actually results in job performance changes.[54]

**transfer of training**

the degree to which the information covered in the program actually results in job performance changes

Transfer of training is more likely to occur when the employee has a higher level of cognitive ability, is more conscientious, and is motivated to learn. Transfer of training is also more likely when there is a supportive work environment.[55]

Additionally, research suggests that the opportunity to actually perform the tasks learned and follow-up to the training, as well as the trainee's self-efficacy, affect the transfer of training.[56] Therefore, the more related the training content is to the tasks the employee has to perform on the job and the higher the belief by the trainee that the training will transfer to the job, the greater will be the transfer of training. The knowledge an employee acquires on how to prepare a computer spreadsheet should transfer quite well to a job that requires such work. If the training takes place on exactly the same type of software that the employee will use on the job, the transfer of training will be even greater. Not all training mirrors this closely the job tasks being taught. Nonetheless, there should be clarity about the expected outcomes of the training and a measurable improvement in how well employees perform following the training.

### Level 4 and Level 5: Results and Return on Investment

Companies have struggled for years with how to demonstrate that training really matters when it comes to a firm's bottom line. Almost everyone knows that it should, but evidence used to be hard to come by. We discussed Booz Allen Hamilton earlier in the chapter. Booz Allen Hamilton makes extensive use of many types of learning and development methods. This company has found a way to demonstrate the actual return-on-investment (ROI) of its training programs. They conducted an ROI study of an executive coaching program and found the ROI to be nearly $3 million per year. This amount equated to a 689% return on their investment in training![57]

When Farmacias del Ahorra wanted to promote the sale of their self-brand products, they turned to online learning. This Mexican pharmaceutical company trained thousands of employees after creating the infrastructure to do so. That process involved connecting the Internet in every store and creating email addresses for every employee. The result of their expense and effort: Three months after completion, 85% of employees reported that 50%–100% of content was applicable, and 95% indicated they could meet the pharmacy's objective of promoting the self-brand of the company. Turnover also decreased.[58]

Many measures can be used to evaluate the ROI of training programs. Measures can focus on collection of data about direct costs of the training program, per participant costs, savings to the company from reduction in waste, and any other measures of productivity, savings, and return on investment that make sense for the company and for which accurate data is available. Just the exercise of identifying appropriate metrics helps ensure that the goals of the training program are clearer. Studies have shown that companies that have more comprehensive measurement systems in place spend more on learning and development, while those that do not have such systems spend less or cut their programs' budgets.[59]

Exhibit 8.9 provides a checklist that managers can use when designing a training program.

## Career Development

We have noted a number of times already that many of the same principles that apply to training also apply to development. However, there are a few points we would be remiss in omitting from a discussion of employee development. We start by providing an example of some of the options available to employees

## EXHIBIT 8.9

### Checklist for Designing a Training Program

_____ Have the gaps that need to be addressed with the training program been identified?

_____ Are the objectives for the training clearly defined?

_____ Do the lesson plans support the instructional objectives?

_____ Has the audience been considered?

    _____Differences in learning styles

    _____Willingness/readiness of audience to learn

    _____Audience's belief in ability to learn the material

    _____Audience's interest in learning the material

    _____Adult learners' needs

_____ Are the training methods selected appropriate for the content of the training?

_____ Does the type of training fit with your firm's organizational needs?

_____ How will the effectiveness of the program be evaluated?

through the career development program at the National Institutes of Health (NIH), and then discuss effective career development practices.

In addition to the skills and behavioral training discussed earlier in the chapter, the NIH provides opportunities for employee career development. Employees have to meet eligibility requirements to participate and take part in a rigorous selection process. Once selected, candidates are expected to fulfill all the requirements of the program. The overall philosophy for career development at the NIH is to provide participants with a systematic approach for professional growth and self-improvement. The activities increase job-related competencies and support career planning for the employee. An example of a specific career development program is the Senior Leadership Program for senior scientists and administrators. The focus of this program is on developing competencies needed for taking on leadership roles at the NIH.[60]

Most large companies have well-designed career development programs. In small and medium-sized companies, an employee will likely have to take responsibility for his or her own career development. There are always exceptions, however. Company Spotlight 8.3 describes how a small, quick-service restaurant focuses on learning and development for its employees.

Research has found that awareness of employee development opportunities, as well as positive attitudes toward such, are related to greater likelihood of participation in voluntary employee development activities.[61] We will now take a look at a few concepts that affect the success of development activities in firms.

## Competency Analysis

We have discussed the concept of competencies a number of times already in this book. Recall that competencies are the knowledge, skills, abilities, and other characteristics that an employee needs in order to perform a job. NIH and many other organizations use the results of their competency analyses to design their career development programs. A competency analysis assists an organization in creating career paths that are logical for employees to follow, and assists in identifying what experiences employees need to acquire along the way. Individual employee performance assessments can be used to determine what gaps employees have between their KSAs and the competencies needed for jobs in their career path.

## COMPANY SPOTLIGHT  8.3

### Learning and Development Matters at Pal's Sudden Service

Fast-food restaurants have notoriously high turnover rates. That, however, is not the case at Pal's Sudden Service, a Southern quick-service restaurant founded in 1956 and located primarily in Tennessee. Pal's was the first restaurant chain in the country to earn the Malcolm Baldridge National Quality Award. Other winners of this coveted award have included companies that are probably more familiar to you, such as Federal Express and The Ritz-Carlton. A total of 90% of the 1,100-plus employees across 29 locations work part time, and 40% of that group are between 16 and 18 years of age. Given these statistics, how has the company managed to keep front-line turnover at a third of the industry level, have assistant manager turnover at a low 1.4%, and had only seven general managers leave in the company's 34 years in business?

The company believes that their success is due to a continuous learning environment. Teaching, training, and coaching are just part of the culture of the company. Take new hires, for instance. All new employees receive 120 hours of training before they can work independently. Employees go through certification and recertification processes. The CEO and other company leaders regularly spend 10% of their time mentoring promising employees. Training and development at Pal's covers a wide range of topics, from statistical process control to serving customers to making burgers. Because the company is willing to invest in them, the employees are more loyal to the company. In the end, the company, the employees, and the customers alike benefit from this focus on having a continuous learning environment as part of the company culture.

*Sources:* Hirsch, Arlene S., "Don't Underestimate the Importance of Good Onboarding," *SHRM.org,* August 10, 2017, https://www.shrm.org/resourcesandtools/hr-topics/talent-acquisition/pages/dont-underestimate-the-importance-of-effective-onboarding.aspx; Pal's Sudden Service, https://palsweb.com/about; Buchanan, Leigh, "Training the Best Damn Fry Cooks (and Future Leaders) in the U.S.," April 23, 2014, https://www.inc.com/audacious-companies/leigh-buchanan/pals-sudden-service.html.

## Career Development Activities

Managers, mentors, coaches, and career counselors play a role in assisting individual employees in acquiring the competencies needed. Employees can also take part in assessment centers (see Chapter 7), job rotation (see Chapter 4), and career workshops and related programs to gain information on where they are relative to the competencies needed to move into other jobs. Succession planning and replacement charts, discussed in Chapter 5, serve as road maps to determine which paths employees follow and what career development activities are needed.

BAE Systems, an aerospace and defense company, uses job rotation to prepare high-potential employees for leadership roles. For instance, employees selected for the Financial Leadership Development Program participate in a three-year program in which each employee switches to a new job each year and participates in challenging assignments. Employees are forced to learn new skills and information as they become knowledgeable in various functional areas within the company.[62] Successful career development plans such as this one provide clear guidelines for employees relative to participation requirements, expectations, and outcomes.

## Trends in Career Development

Careers are no longer viewed as a sequential progression from one job to another, with fairly defined skills and experiences accompanying each move up the career ladder. Instead, experiences and learning agility define careers. Artificial intelligence (AI), new business models, and robotics are leading to job redesign, which in turn requires new approaches to career development. Most organizations are struggling to keep up with these changes. The organizations that are practicing a growth mind-set are experiencing four times better retention of employees and are three times more profitable. These firms provide employees with stretch assignments and openly discuss mistakes as a way to promote learning. In other words, the firms adopt a strong learning mind-set and recognize that learning often takes place outside the standard training and development models that have traditionally existed. These types of firms are most attractive to millennials who expect ongoing feedback and frequent, new challenges in the workplace.

Further, learning and development opportunities open new doors for workers to engage in job crafting (a concept introduced in Chapter 4), and job crafting opens new needs for learning and development opportunities. As employees seek to take more ownership of their careers and work to create a career that has more meaning for themselves, they expand what they do on the job, which can lead to the desire or need for training in new areas. Consider the college professor who takes on more administrative responsibilities because he is a problem-solver and an organizer. Those traits may lead him to become a department chair, which would require developing new skills and abilities through learning and development experiences. Or consider the sales professional who participates in a negotiation seminar and then begins to expand her job in order to play an instrumental role in negotiating with clients to assist other sales professionals in closing deals. Both of these individuals may be adding value to the organization by taking on these new responsibilities that were originally not part of the jobs for which they were hired.[63]

## Learning and Development in Practice: Organizational Demands

Now that you have read about the basics of training theory and methods, we turn to a discussion of how different organizational demands require different decisions about investment and practice in training and development. Some of the decisions that have to be made are included in Exhibit 8.10. For the sake of simplicity, we once again primarily refer to training in this section, but keep in mind that the same contingencies apply to providing other learning and development opportunities. Remember that a company's mission should drive all its decisions. As an informed manager, you are the person most equipped to decide how much and what types of learning and development are appropriate for your employees to help your firm achieve its goals and have a competitive advantage. Directly or indirectly, you are held accountable for achieving results. Effective training for you and for your workforce can help you achieve those results.

### Strategy and Training

We have already noted that training and development is expensive. Resources need to be deployed where they will yield the most return on the investment while achieving the goals of the company. Considering a company's business strategy provides insight into both the level and type of investments companies should make to realize their strategic objectives.

#### Level of Investment

We noted earlier that U.S. organizations spent $87.6 billion on employee training and development in 2018. That's a lot of money for training. The decision about

**EXHIBIT 8.10**

## Learning and Development in Practice

| Context | Practice Issues |
|---------|-----------------|
| **Organizational Demands** | |
| *Strategy* drives . . . | • Level of investment in learning and development<br>• Type of investment in learning and development |
| *Company characteristics* determine . . . | • Where training is offered<br>• Who handles training<br>• Type of training needed<br>• How training is provided |
| *Culture* establishes . . . | • Focus of training (e.g., customer service, change, technology)<br>• Willingness of employees to participate in training |
| *Employee concerns* include . . . | • Access to and availability of training<br>• Focus of training (e.g., work/life balance, stress reduction) |
| **Environmental Demands** | |
| *Labor force* influences . . . | • Who needs training<br>• Type of training |
| *Technology* affects . . . | • Skills needed<br>• How training is delivered<br>• Communication of training options |
| *Globalization* impacts . . . | • Where training is delivered<br>• When training is delivered<br>• How training is delivered<br>• What training will be offered |
| *Ethics/social* responsibility shapes . . . | • Obligation to train<br>• Content of training<br>• Use of training to change behaviors |
| **Regulations** | |
| *Regulations* guide . . . | • Accessibility of learning and employee development opportunities<br>• Type of training needed |

how much to spend for learning and development will depend upon your company's strategy. If your company is pursuing a low-cost strategy, you will focus on minimizing the cost of training. Fred's, which describes itself as "The Low Price Leader," is a discount department store that started in Mississippi in 1947 and now has more than 600 stores.[64] The strategy at Fred's is to keep costs down so the company can offer lower product prices to consumers. Because cost considerations are a major component of all of Fred's organizational decisions, the firm's training approach differs from the approach taken by a company such as Nordstrom, a leading high-end retailer known for delivering a very high level of customer service.[65] Nordstrom understands that great customer service requires that all the employees of the company be extensively trained with regard to the firm's philosophy and the products it sells. As a result, the company's training costs are likely to be greater than Fred's. Nordstrom is operating on the assumption that the return on that investment will result in greater customer satisfaction and high customer retention rates.

Deciding how much money is available for training should be factored into an organizational needs analysis. If little money is available, the company will have to use other means to ensure that employees are trained to do their jobs. More selective hiring is one alternative. The company could focus on hiring employees who are already fully trained. Firms pursuing a low-cost strategy often train their employees as quickly and cost effectively as possible. This approach does not mean that training does not occur. A company might hire many unskilled employees and give them the minimum level of training needed to do their jobs. This approach costs less than paying higher wages for workers who are already trained. On the other hand, some companies view expensive training initiatives as a mechanism to actually save money in the long run via increased employee productivity and retention, increased safety, or stronger teamwork. That said, cost-oriented firms are likely to view training activities as a necessary expense that needs to be minimized. Sometimes they minimize their costs by using more mechanized systems in their workplaces, thus reducing the need to hire as many employees, although that doesn't always yield the desired results. Tesla found that some tasks were better performed by humans than by robots and ended up hiring hundreds of workers to replace the robots.[66]

In contrast, companies following differentiation strategies do not focus on cost as much as on some source of differentiation, such as innovation or customer service. These companies believe that extensively training their employees in areas directly relevant to their sources of competitive advantage is critical. This belief doesn't mean that the companies provide unlimited training to all their employees; the trade-offs in terms of costs versus benefits still have to be considered, and decisions need to be made about which employees will receive training and where.

### Emphasis of Investment

A company's strategy influences the type of investments it is willing to make in terms of training its employees. Because each company is unique, achieving its strategic objectives means a company has to train its employees in a way that adds the most value possible to the firm. The reality is that when managers have limited training dollars, they have to prioritize their training needs. For companies that try to compete by achieving high customer satisfaction levels, such as insurance agencies, training programs that focus on customer service skills, product knowledge, and teamwork are likely to have more strategic relevance. A company emphasizing high levels of employee productivity and efficiency, such as a manufacturing firm, might gain more from training initiatives that focus on helping employees improve their individual talents and expertise in their particular jobs. Moreover, some employees are less critical to train on the core competencies of the business than others. Support staff who do not interact with customers might need less, or different, training than frontline employees.

Of course, many training programs aren't optional for companies because *not* delivering training can actually result in increased costs and other problems. Failing to provide a sufficient amount of safety training for employees is likely to result in more employee injuries, higher medical costs for the firm, and government fines. These are the direct costs of failing to train employees. Indirect costs can include recruiting and hiring expenses related to replacing employees who are injured and can no longer work, or who quit because they believe their workplace isn't safe.[67] Similarly, ensuring that employees understand any regulatory restrictions or requirements they must adhere to will dramatically decrease a firm's long-term legal problems. Therefore, managers need to remember that no matter what the company strategy, certain types of training have to occur, regardless of the cost.

## Company Characteristics and Training

In addition to strategic and financial resources, other organizational factors influence training. The size and stage of development of a company influence where training is done, who does the training, the type of training needed, and how the training is provided.

## Where Training Is Done

An increasing number of companies have created their own training centers, known as corporate campuses or corporate universities. They bring their employees to these locations for much of their training and professional development activities because they want to ensure that all employees have the same training experience. They also want to maintain control over the content and delivery of the training programs, see a need that can be filled in house, or both. Walgreens spent more than three years planning its corporate university before it launched. The company's goal in starting Walgreens University was to create a diverse, innovative, and agile talent pool. Participants can select from over 200 courses offered in a wide range of formats, from classroom learning to e-learning. Some of the training programs even offer undergraduate college credit.[68]

Younger and smaller companies might need to use more OJT in order to maximize the productive time of employees. As companies become older and grow, they often have more resources and can invest in other methods of training, including sending employees to training programs or investing in e-learning that can be done in house. These companies also have more employees to train and may be more concerned about the consistency of their training and development activities.

## Who Handles Training

A company's stage of development influences who does the training. Managers in small businesses are likely to have to do much of the training or else make a strong case for why resources should be used to send employees to special training programs. Larger and more mature companies are more likely to have training departments that can help identify appropriate training opportunities and resources. As a manager in such a firm, you will be responsible for providing information to your training department about the type of training your employees need to perform at a high level.

## Type of Training

In small businesses, employees may wear many hats. The server in a small restaurant may also be the hostess or bartender. These employees are often hired for one particular role but take on additional duties as the company begins to grow or as necessity requires. In more established, larger organizations, such as Deloitte, a major consulting firm focused on audit, financial advisory, tax, and consulting services, jobs are likely to be more specialized. Managers of employees with expanding job responsibilities need to ensure that these employees receive the type of training needed to perform the new roles well. All employees, regardless of the stage of development and size of the company, need training on topics such as sexual harassment, the company pension plan, and other issues that could lead to liability for the company. Managers have an obligation to the company and to their employees to make sure this training occurs, preferably in a formal manner so that participation can be documented in case a problem occurs—especially in case of a legal challenge.

In newer, fast-growing companies, employees are being added quickly and some of the training that should occur doesn't. As a manager, you have a responsibility to ensure that the training is done no matter what. Remember that employees who are well trained add greater value to the organization because they are more effective, more efficient, and more satisfied. Unfortunately, managers today are often so busy that they fail to pay attention to how well their employees are performing until there is a problem. Many times, problems result from lack of training. For instance, expecting an employee to be able to troubleshoot a customer concern with a product can lead to a difficult customer/employee experience if the employee has not been trained on how to do the troubleshooting. The issue is not that the employee can't do the job but rather that the employee has not been trained on how to do the job.

### How Training Is Provided

In very large companies, many employees perform the same type of job. Consider large retail chains such as Michaels, Target, and Safeway. A considerable number of employees in these organizations serve as cashiers or customer service representatives. Efficiency in training these employees is easier to achieve than in smaller organizations due to economies of scale. A standardized training program can be designed for a large number of employees at a lower cost because one set of materials is developed and used many times. If you have to train only one employee or a few employees, as is usually the case in small businesses and start-up companies, the cost per employee is greater. Therefore, companies with a lot of employees who have to receive the same training will gain more return on their training investment by developing materials in-house—and they have both the human capital and financial capital to do so. Companies with few employees might be forced to send them to outside training programs because doing so is less expensive than developing their own programs, or these companies might simply resort to OJT. E-learning has made external types of training more accessible, but, again, cost and time are factors that can limit the use of e-learning.

## Culture and Training

Some companies have a culture of training and development. Employees in these companies understand the importance of continuous learning. Remember from Chapter 2 that culture is about shared values and meanings. A company's culture influences the decisions it makes about the focus of its training programs and affects the willingness of its employees to participate in training. Managers who appreciate the value of training and development are more likely to provide the resources needed for these activities. They know that the result of doing so leads to higher employee performance and higher level employee performance leads to higher firm performance.

### Focus of Training

We have already noted that Nordstrom is known for its high level of attention to customers. Ameriprise Financial also believes that it is better to keep customers satisfied than to have to find new ones. This philosophy infuses the company's corporate culture, both in terms of how employees treat customers and how it treats its employees.[69] Both companies have a customer service culture and provide training to support that culture. A company that values innovation will have a different training focus than these companies.

A change in the strategic direction of a company can also lead to a change in the culture, which leads to new training initiatives. For instance, when MasTec's Utility Services Group gained new leadership, this utility construction company decided to create a culture of learning. The company developed programs to tie learning to safety and compliance and to career opportunities and pay. These initiatives sent a clear signal to employees that learning matters at the company.[70] Training can be used to change from a culture that doesn't value diversity to one that does, from a culture that doesn't understand quality to one that does, and from a culture that doesn't appreciate the importance of being frugal to one that does. However, getting buy-in from your employees is essential to making the change happen, otherwise no amount of training will change behavior or performance. If employees believe that the changes are simply the "flavor of the month," they may go through the motions during training but transfer very little of it to their jobs.

### Employees' Willingness to Participate in Training

A firm's reward structure is a very important part of its culture. What it signals to employees about the importance of training and development may be the chief motivator that determines whether employees are willing to participate in the programs.

In companies where rewards can be obtained easily without participating in training, employees are much less likely to seek out or participate in training, especially if it means that they have less time to do those things that are rewarded. Also, as noted earlier, when employees undergo training, they are more likely to transfer what they learned if they understand that the behaviors matter.[71] For example, the University of California, Berkeley, teaches managers the importance of discussing with employees the reason why their job exists within the university, along with ensuring employees have the skills and abilities to perform their jobs. The university understands that this direct line of sight from an employee's job to the mission and goals of the university does matter.[72]

Small businesses and start-up companies are less likely than larger, more established companies to spend money for formal employee development activities. Small businesses have few opportunities for employees to move upward in their organizations or even to move vertically. When openings do exist, they are usually given to employees who have been at the company the longest. Any new knowledge needed to perform a higher-level job is acquired by employees on the job or via training and education they pay for themselves.

Many small businesses also miss the boat with regard to employee development. Often, they fail to prepare a successor to take over if the owner dies or is otherwise unable to continue operating the business. So, although employee development is very important in small firms, it is not as likely to occur there as it is in larger, more mature firms. In start-up companies, the speed with which change occurs often precludes time and resources being set aside for employee development. As these companies grow, employee development becomes more important because more job opportunities are created, and employees need to be ready to step into new roles.

## Employee Concerns and Training

As with other employee management areas, employees want to be treated fairly and equitably in terms of training opportunities.

### Fairness and Equity

In Chapters 6 and 7, we talked about the importance of fairness and equity in making selection decisions. Employees also evaluate training and development opportunities and requirements in terms of these factors. Consider a situation in which you, as a manager, have to decide which of two employees to send to a training program. Both employees hold the same position. One employee is in his 50s and has been a solid performer at the company for 10 years. Another employee is in her 30s and has been with the company for 5 years. She has been a solid performer as well. Which employee should you send if you can send only one? What factors would you consider? If the training will be seen as a reward or as a signal of future opportunities, what factors do you need to consider? As a manager, you need to have a job-related reason for deciding who participates in training. You might consider which employee has most recently been given a training opportunity, future job changes anticipated for each employee, and a host of other job-related reasons. Even if the employees were the same age, you would need to have a logical reason for selecting one for training over the other, and then be prepared to defend that decision.

Employees pay attention to situations where perceived equity issues exist. They expect you to honor the agreements you make to provide them with training and development; if you don't, they are less likely to exhibit good citizenship behaviors. Employees also expect to be paid commensurate with the training they received and perceive anything less as unfair and not equitable.[73]

### Work/Life Balance

Training can affect the work/life balance of employees in a number of ways. Some employers offer training to help their employees find a better balance between their work and personal lives. Stress- and time-management training are two such programs. More and more companies (mostly larger ones) are able to offer a telecommuting option to employees because of technology. The option has become so popular that a company called FlexJobs has started identifying the 100 top companies for remote work. In 2018, VIPKID, Appen, Conduent, Rev, and LiveOps were the top 5 companies on the list.[74] Providing opportunities for telecommuting helps address the work/life balance needs of some employees, especially in areas where commutes tend to be long. If telecommuting is a viable option, it is important to make sure supervisors are trained to manage employees who telecommute, and that these employees receive equal opportunities for training and development experiences.

Companies also have to consider work/life balance issues with regard to participation in their training programs. Employees might be required to travel away from home to take part in a training or development program. For employees with children or elder-care responsibilities, the required travel can present several challenges, including lack of child or elder care. Companies need to work with employees to assist them with these challenges. For example, a company might allow an employee to postpone training because of child-care obligations, but only if the required training can be obtained at a later time. Or the company might allow the family to travel with the employee, as long as doing so will not interfere with the employee's focus during the training activities.

## Learning and Development in Practice: Environmental Influences

In this section, we explore how environmental factors relate to training and development. Managers have to constantly scan the environment to make sure that their plans for employee training and development take into account changes in the labor market, technology advances, increased globalization of the company, and the growing need for ethics training. Company Spotlight 8.4 describes why Marriott International won an organizational excellence award for its understanding of how environmental influences affect the need for training and development.

### Labor Market

The labor market influences the decision about which employees need to be trained, as well as the type of training needed. Changes in the labor market also affect an organization's training requirements.

#### Who Needs Training

Employers are increasingly concerned with their inability to attract a sufficient number of employees with the required skill sets as skill levels needed in growth economies continue to rise.[75] Consequently, employers have to be prepared to provide more training for employees. Recall that in a loose labor market, companies have more flexibility in making decisions about which applicants to hire and are more likely to find employees with the skill sets they seek. In such a market, there would be no need to provide training to bring these new employees up to the minimum job standards. In contrast, in a tight labor market, individuals who don't meet all of a job's requirements are more likely to be hired. In that case, either the job requirements will need to be changed or training will have to be provided to the new employees, absent any other method of accomplishing the required work.

## COMPANY SPOTLIGHT  8.4

### Training and Development at Marriott International, Informed by Research and Theory

With 700,000 employees on six continents, how do you even begin to help all of them achieve everything they desire? Marriott International has it figured out. In recognition for their training and development program, a program led by industrial/organizational (I/O) psychologists and informed by psychology research and theory, Marriott received the 2018 Organizational Excellence Award from the American Psychological Association (APA).

Marriott's program takes an individualized approach to training and development. The personalized learning takes into account the needs of the employees, known to the company as *associates,* and includes digital, shorter microlearning activities. There are also learning events that are companywide, such as a recent effort to educate employees about how to identify and respond to signs that human trafficking activities are taking place on company property.

Marriott's I/O psychologists incorporate evidence-based learning modalities, data-driven information, and psychological research to assess and design training and development programs. The company knows that taking a holistic approach to learning and recognizing that training and development needs differ among employees results in more successful outcomes for the employees and the company. In fact, Marriott views its training and development program as part of an overall well-being program for employees. When employees feel valued, they are going to be more committed to the company. Part of feeling valued is knowing the company is willing to invest in their learning and growth as an associate. For Marriott, employing an evidence-based approach, drawn from psychology research and theory, ensures that the training and development activities will affect the company's competitive advantage in the industry.

*Source:* "Using Psychology to Give People and Business Room to Grow," 2018 Organizational Excellence Award Winner, Marriott International, The Awards, American Psychological Association Center for Organizational Excellence, https://www.apaexcellence.org/awards/organizational-excellence/oea2018l; "APA Recognizes Five Organizations for Healthy Workplace Practices," American Psychological Association, March 14, 2018, https://www.apa.org/news/press/releases/2018/03/healthy-workplace.aspx.

## Type of Training

A diverse labor market requires employers to think about the type of training needed. Employees might be functionally illiterate and/or immigrants with little English-speaking ability, for example. In both of these cases, employers will most likely have to provide basic English reading and writing training. This type of training is also good business. By providing literacy and English-language skills to employees, a company is not only equipping them to do their jobs, but also helping improve their lives. As a manager, you can be instrumental in determining which employees need these basic skills and identifying ways to provide them. The training can come through company programs or through community-based programs that you identify.

Wyndham Hotels was the first hospitality company to use a program called *Sed de Saber* ("Thirst for Knowledge") to teach its non-English-speaking employees how to speak English. The training was geared for employees who did not have a lot of guest contact and was done through battery-operated LeapPads, devices that resemble talking books. The interactive tutorial included pictures, sounds, and activities. The company also used LeapPads to teach Spanish to its English-speaking employees.[76]

TDIndustries is another company that understands having a diverse labor pool means you need to take that into consideration in designing training programs.

To help their Spanish-speaking employees advance, the company offers training courses in Spanish. Hispanic and Latino workers account for 37% of the total workforce at this contracting services company, which has made the *Fortune* 100 Best Companies to Work For list every year since the ranking started in 1998.[77]

## Technology

Changes in technology have made it easier to keep track of who has taken part in various training and development opportunities. Advances in technology have also changed training methods and affected how training information is communicated to employees.

### Skills Inventories

Given the cost of training, it is important to be selective about who really needs training. However, keeping track of employee training participation is a big job. Software has made that job much easier. Managers can search skills inventories databases and identify employees with needed skills and experience for open positions. Managers also can search the inventories to identify employees who have completed training that would make them eligible for job openings. This tracking process expands the options for employees and makes the manager's job easier when seeking employees internally. Skills inventories also reduce the likelihood of selecting employees for training that they don't need. A large number of companies offer tracking software, and most ERPs have that capability as well.

### Method of Delivery

Technology has had a great impact on how training is delivered. Earlier in the chapter, we discussed the various methods for delivering training and how Wyndham Hotels used LeapPads to teach English to its workers. Not all organizations have the same technology capabilities, however, and not all employees have equal access to technology for training purposes. For instance, employees working on an assembly line are not likely to have ready access to complete e-learning training sessions on the job. Companies can set aside lab space and provide time away from the factory floor for the employees to do such training. Before doing so, managers have to determine whether the employees have the computer skills needed to participate in the e-learning and make sure those skills are provided, if needed. Other companies, such as UPS (as highlighted in Company Spotlight 8.2), make extensive use of the latest technology like VR to train drivers on safety issues.

### Communication of Options

Technology also has enhanced the ability of firms to provide information about their training and development programs to their employees. For example, managers and employees can request that they be contacted by their firm's training department when certain types of opportunities are going to be offered. This notification can be done easily thanks to advances in software programs that can automatically notify individuals when specific information is input into the system. Employees can select programs that would be beneficial to them, and managers can identify training programs to which they need to send employees. They can also use the Internet to identify external training options and to keep track of the training they have completed.

## Globalization and Training

Companies doing business globally have to recognize that a "one size fits all" training program is not likely to work. Sure—the process of determining where training is needed will be the same: Conduct an organization analysis, a task analysis, and a person analysis. Even the content of the training program may be the same. What will differ is the design and implementation. Think about the challenges of designing training programs in a developing country such as Bangladesh. Access to technology will be limited, training materials will have to be translated into the appropriate languages, and the values of the Bangladeshi culture must be considered. Where training will be offered, when it will be offered, how it will be offered, and who will be trained are all considerations in a global economy.

### Where Training Will Be Offered

Companies used to have two choices of where to train employees on global assignments: bring them back to the headquarters or send a trainer to them in their location abroad. These are still the best choices for some types of training, such as OJT. Increasingly, however, by using online and other technology-oriented training programs, employees can complete a training program sitting on the beach in Hawaii rather than back in the office in Minneapolis or Hong Kong. Costs will be a major consideration in where and how you do training. For example, if you are training many host country nationals (HCNs), sending a trainer to where the employees are located will likely be less expensive than bringing the employees to the trainer. On the other hand, if the training can be done online, that may be the least expensive alternative.

### When Training Will Be Offered

Employees need training to bring them up to speed when they're hired, and they need training when their job tasks change. Because the cost to the firm when expatriates return early from assignments is high—estimated to be well over $300,000 per employee[78]—making sure these expatriates receive needed training is critical, as is ensuring that expats receive equal access to career development opportunities. For expatriates, there are three time frames in which training needs to be offered: before departure, in the assignment, and as part of repatriation.

Pre-departure training sets the stage for an expatriate's experience abroad. In addition, given the extensive research showing that a main cause of expatriate failure is inability of the expat's family to adjust to the location, including the family in the pre-departure training is important. A lot of research has focused on the pre-departure training needs of expats and has concluded that it should include setting realistic expectations for them in terms of both the living conditions abroad and how a nation's culture affects what goes on in the workplace. Pre-departure training should address issues related to language, religion, culture, business practices, and safety. Training can be done by a former expatriate or a consulting firm that specializes in expatriate pre-departure training. Numerous websites and training videos are also available to address issues related to living abroad and can be incorporated into the training program. For instance, the U.S. Department of State offers extensive information on its website (https://www.state.gov/e/eb/cba/) to help employees prepare for doing business and living abroad.

Once an expatriate is on assignment, the training should focus on what the employee needs to know to do the job. If you are the manager of an expatriate at your firm's corporate headquarters, it can be easy not to realize that the person doesn't have some of the KSAs needed to successfully complete his or her assignment abroad. Therefore, developing an ongoing communication process and having an open exchange of dialogue to encourage the expatriate to share such information earlier rather than later are important. Ensuring that career development opportunities continue is also important during this time frame.

When an employee is repatriated (brought back to the firm's headquarters on a permanent basis), she and her manager need to assess whether she should have additional training and development for her new job assignment. Forgoing this assessment sets the expatriate up for failure at a time that is stressful anyway. The expatriate already has to adjust to being in a different culture than the one she has known in her assignment abroad. Consequently, her manager needs to make sure that further stress does not result from a lack of training and development opportunities.

### How Training Will Be Offered

Before beginning the training process for HCNs, managers need to consider factors such as how the country views education in general, the role of teachers in the culture, the extent to which status matters, and willingness to take risks and experiment. Dennis Briscoe and Randall Schuler have researched the type of training methods that work best in different cultures based on two cultural dimensions (power distance and uncertainty avoidance), along with a third dimension (preferred learning format). They found, for instance, that Guatemala, Greece, and Portugal, countries that are high in power distance (hierarchy matters), strong in uncertainty avoidance (don't like risk), and prefer a more didactic learning format (classroom setting), prefer training that involves assigned readings and lectures. Switzerland, Australia, and Singapore, countries that are nearer the other end of these three continua and are therefore lower in power distance, are lower in uncertainty avoidance, and prefer a more experimental learning format, prefer training that includes simulations, role play, and structured exercises.[79]

If OJT is used, decisions have to be made about whether an HCN will be the trainer or whether an expatriate can fill that role. One particular element of culture to consider is whether employees are comfortable giving feedback and asking questions.[80] In addition, the training materials may have to be translated into multiple languages and adapted in other ways to fit the local culture in which the training will occur.

### What Training Will Be Offered

Much of the training content and development issues for expatriates and HCNs will be little different than what we have already discussed. After all, the content of training is derived from the organization, task, and person analyses. A few additional types of training and development may need to be added, however. Cross-cultural training may be necessary to ensure that problems in the workplace are not the result of either the expatriate or HCN misunderstanding why things are done a certain way. Training creates an environment in which employees can openly exchange their concerns about cultural differences. For instance, Sony Corporation has used cross-cultural training to overcome misunderstandings among employees in their global workgroups. Expatriates are also likely to need ongoing training on changing host country laws and regulations, as well as development opportunities to prepare them for new assignments.[81]

## Ethics and Training

A growing concern for firms today is how they can ensure that their employees understand what is and is not ethical behavior. To help answer this question, we discuss the fact that firms have an obligation to train employees about ethical issues, the content of the training, and the use of training to change behavior.

### Obligation to Train

Creating an ethics statement alone is not sufficient for ensuring ethical behavior occurs.[82] Employers have an obligation to train employees about ethical behavior. Corporate scandals, such as those at Enron and the accounting firm Arthur Andersen, have underscored this obligation, as has legislation in the United States, such as the Sarbanes-Oxley Act. In reality, companies need to train their employees about what constitutes ethical behavior, even absent corporate scandals and regulations.

A company that wants to ensure that all its stakeholders—employees, customers, and shareholders—are treated ethically can't just issue a statement about ethics and believe that all employees will live by it because of the varying values and beliefs of a diverse workforce. The company must be proactive in providing the right environment for ethical behavior to be valued.

### Content of Training

The content of ethics training can range from orientation to the company's values and beliefs to intensive training on the topic of ethics relative to one's profession. Accountants need to understand what are and are not acceptable practices, just as physicians need to understand what constitutes ethical medical practices. Often, ethics training is combined with other training programs. However, it should always be a part of the company orientation process for new employees. A one-time training course on ethics is not likely to be sufficient, though. In fact, most, if not all, employee training programs should touch on related ethical issues. Obviously, there are ethical issues related to diversity training. But what about leadership development and safety training programs? The reality is that there is just as great a need to incorporate discussions about ethical issues in these types of training as anywhere else. The more employees hear about the company's view on ethical behavior and see it modeled by management, the more likely they are to comply.

Organizations have several additional ethical issues to address relative to training. First, they have an ethical obligation to ensure that supervisors and coworkers don't discriminate. Second, they have an ethical obligation to ensure that all employees have equal access to the training appropriate for their jobs and roles in the company. This issue is especially important given that greater training is often associated with higher wages. Finally, companies have an ethical obligation to ensure that employees have the training needed to do their jobs effectively and safely. Recall that we discussed regulations related to the fair treatment of employees in Chapter 3; therefore, we don't elaborate further on that topic here, other than to remind you of its importance from an ethical standpoint.

We have not yet discussed the obligation to train employees to do their jobs. A number of court cases have involved charges by clients or customers that they were harmed in some way because employees lacked training. For instance, a precedent-setting case relative to the failure to train police officers is *City of Canton v. Harris*. In this case, Harris was arrested by the Canton, Ohio, police and taken to lockup. She fell several times during booking and responded incoherently to a query about the need for medical attention, which she did not receive. The U.S. Supreme Court ruled that a municipality can be held liable for failing to adequately train employees. In other words, had the police officers been appropriately trained, they would have made sure that Harris received the medical attention that she needed.[83] The ruling in this case applies to nongovernmental organizations (NGOs) as well.

### Use of Training to Change Behavior

A former dean of the Yale School of Management once noted that business schools will not be able to turn a dishonest person into an honest one. All schools can do is teach students about making appropriate value judgments in situations that are obviously right or wrong.[84] The same is true of companies. Unfortunately, many companies that have been found to be in violation of ethical practices had ethics programs in place, including codes of ethics.

If employees see their managers behaving ethically, they are more likely to do so. In your role of manager, you can't change a dishonest person into an honest one, but you can clearly set the expectations for how you expect the firm's employees to behave and hold them accountable for their behavior.

Raytheon is a company that does just that and has been recognized for its ethics training. This company requires every employee, including the CEO, to participate in ethics training, a common business practice since the passage of Sarbanes-Oxley.[85] Training mandates such as Raytheon's signal to employees that the company is concerned about ethics. In addition, if the firm's top leaders model the behavior the company seeks, employees are more likely to follow suit.

# Learning and Development in Practice: Regulatory Issues

As we have already noted, companies spend a lot of training resources on compliance issues to reduce or avoid liability. Because information covered in compliance training is fairly standard across organizations, this type of training lends itself particularly well to off-the-shelf purchases of training materials. E-learning also works well for compliance training.[86] Just remember that if your firm is involved in a lawsuit, the courts will look at whether the training is designed and delivered by trainers qualified to teach the topic.

As you learned earlier in the chapter, managers cannot discriminate when it comes to deciding who should or should not receive training: An employer cannot provide training just to women or just to Asians. Likewise, it would be inappropriate to require only men to take part in a training program with an outdoor physical component. (If outdoor training is necessary, then women need to be required to participate as well.) In other words, employees should be selected for training programs based on job-related reasons, and individuals should be treated equally, regardless of their race, color, religion, sex, national origin, age, disability, or veterans' status, unless laws specifically provide for doing so.

## Accessibility of Training and Employee Development Opportunities

Because firms have to make their training programs available to all qualified employees, this requirement effectively means that managers have to ensure that all employees have access to the training they need to do their jobs. For example, intentionally or not, managers might believe that younger employees deserve more opportunities for training. They may rationalize that younger workers will be around longer so the training investment will be more worthwhile and spending training resources on the old guys who are closer to retirement is a waste of resources. There are a couple of flaws in such a plan, not to mention the fact that it violates the Age Discrimination in Employment Act (ADEA). First, there is no guarantee that the younger workers will stick around after they complete the training and development programs they receive. Second, an underlying presumption is that older workers are not as capable of learning, are not interested in training and development, or both. This thinking is based on generalizations with little if any basis in reality.

Another accessibility issue relates to the ADA, which requires employers to make reasonable accommodations for employees with disabilities. This requirement includes making reasonable accommodations for employers' training programs. The accommodations might include changing the training location to make it accessible to disabled employees or providing special computer equipment so that disabled employees can participate in e-learning activities. In some cases, a signer for the hearing impaired might be required.

## Type of Training Needed

As regulations are passed or amended, government agencies develop new guidelines to help managers interpret the laws. Companies have an obligation to provide that information to their employees and to make sure they know what it means. Managers in particular need to understand the roles they need to play to ensure that their employees comply with the laws. This expectation includes training their new employees, as well as their current employees, when laws change.

IBM's annual Corporate Responsibility Report includes descriptions of the types of compliance programs in place at the company and training initiatives related to compliance. For instance, in 2017, as in previous years, all active IBM employees around the world participated in the company's online Business Conduct Guidelines (BCG) course and certification. The course is available in 24 languages, making it readily accessible to a global workforce. The course is revised each year and takes employees through business situations they might face. Additional compliance and ethics training is provided to targeted groups by the IBM trust and compliance officers, management, and lawyers.[87]

Compliance has become such an important topic for businesses, especially banks, that one *Wall Street Journal* article asked if the job of compliance officer had become a dream career. Banks alone have been hiring thousands of compliance officers over the past few years.[88]

## SUMMARY

Learning and development prepare workers for success on the job, which leads to success for a company. Learning involves acquiring tacit and explicit knowledge; training prepares employees to do their current jobs; and development prepares employees for future jobs. The three activities together ensure that employees can help their organization achieve its goals in the present and in the future. Some companies view learning and development as critical to their success and invest money in the programs accordingly. Other organizations do not value learning and development as highly and spend little money on the two activities.

Effective learning and development programs are systematic. They begin with a needs assessment of the organization, its tasks, and personnel. This process identifies gaps between what the firm's employees are doing and what they should be doing for the company to be successful. At this point, managers can begin to identify which employees need training or development.

Successful learning and development programs are built around solid learning strategies: clearly identifying instructional objectives for the programs, creating appropriate lesson plans, understanding the principles of learning, appreciating the impact of learning agility, and getting learners interested in the material. Learning self-efficacy affects outcomes as well. Also, trainers need to understand the nuances associated with adult learners. Finally, conducting the programs in the most appropriate location plays a part in ensuring successful outcomes.

Managers have a number of training delivery methods from which to choose. The methods include OJT, using printed materials, classroom training, e-learning, audiovisual training, simulations, blended learning, college and university options, and coaching. Employee orientation and onboarding programs help new employees learn a company's policies and procedures and understand how their positions fit in with the firm. Employee-development programs provide employees with new KSAs that will help them successfully move into lateral jobs or be promoted.

The last part of the learning and development process is to assess how well the programs have worked. Learning and development evaluations gauge participants'

reactions to the training program, the extent to which learning occurred, whether the training led to behavior changes on the job, and how the training affected the company's bottom line.

A firm's organizational strategy determines the amount and type of investment the company makes in its programs. The size and age of the company affect where learning and development occurs, as well as the type and how it is provided. The firm's organizational culture influences the focus of learning and development, and whether employees are willing to participate in it. Employees need to perceive that their firm's learning and development opportunities and activities are managed in a fair and equitable manner.

The same environmental factors that affect other employee management activities affect learning and development decisions. The nature of the labor market affects who needs the programs when they are hired and the type of programs they need. Of all the environmental factors, technology has perhaps had the greatest impact on the learning and development activities of organizations. Computer technology advances have provided a way for companies to track the activities of their employees, changed how programs are delivered, and made it easier to involve more employees and make them aware of opportunities available to them. Technology also has made it easier to provide standardized learning and development opportunities to employees scattered around the globe and affected where and how programs are offered.

Companies have an ethical obligation to ensure that their employees are prepared properly to do their jobs, especially when safety or legal concerns exist. Ethics training is becoming more commonplace. Overlapping with ethical concerns are regulatory issues such as making learning and development opportunities accessible to employees based on job-related reasons and the type of training they must have to comply with the law.

## KEY TERMS

audiovisual training

blended learning

classroom training

coaching

desktop training

development

diversity training

e-learning

employee orientation

gamification

high-impact learning organization

high-potential employee

instructional objective

learning

learning agility

learning style

legal compliance training

lesson plan

mentoring

needs assessment

onboarding

on-the-job training (OJT)

organization analysis

person analysis

podcast

self-efficacy

simulation

task analysis

training

transfer of training

web-based training

## DISCUSSION QUESTIONS

1. What is the difference between learning and development? How are these two activities related to a firm's competitive advantage?

2. Explain the difference between an organization analysis, a task analysis, and a person analysis. How are the three related? Why should all three types of analyses

be conducted to determine a firm's learning and development needs, no matter how large or small the organization?

3. Your new entrepreneurial venture is just starting to grow, and you have recently hired three new sales reps to help you develop new business. What do you think will be the greatest challenges in training the sales staff? How would you overcome these challenges? How would you assure alignment between training and company goals and values?

4. How would you measure the effectiveness of a training program designed to increase the accuracy of a company's audits? How would you measure the effectiveness of a training program designed to improve loan processing in a financial services institution? What would be similar and what would be different about the two training programs?

5. Why is having defined career paths with accompanying professional development plans important to millennials? To respond to this question, you will need to read articles from the professional business press on this topic. Consult at least two articles and include citations for each.

6. Your firm has a culture that values integrity and collaboration. What role would training play in terms of ensuring that these two values are instilled in all employees?

7. Research topics that should be covered in a pre-departure training session for expatriates being assigned to work in a specific country that you would like to visit or in which you would like to someday work. What type of training experiences would be best to cover each topic on your list, and why?

8. What is the relationship between ADA requirements and training and development programs? Why does this matter?

## LEARNING EXERCISE 1

Choose an activity that you are good at doing. The activity can be related to sports, music, a hobby—virtually anything. Prepare a plan for teaching someone how to do that activity. Apply the concepts you have learned in this chapter about effective training in putting together your plan.

1. What type of assessment will you use to prepare for this training?
2. What methods and types of training will you use?
3. What role will principles of learning play in your training program?
4. How will you determine whether the training has been successful?

## LEARNING EXERCISE 2

Develop a skills or behavioral-based training program for a job with which you are familiar. Work through the following steps to prepare your training program:

1. Obtain a copy of a job description for the job, or prepare one.
2. Include a description of the organization in which the job is done and the mission statement for the organization.
3. Identify the competencies (KSAs) that should be the focus of training, and describe why you selected each of them.
4. Describe the specific types of training that will be used, including the training content, how the content supports the company's organizational goals, who will deliver the training, when and where it will occur, and the specific methods that will be used.
5. Discuss the outcomes the company can expect the training to produce.

# CASE STUDY 1: CHANGING CULTURE AT TENARIS

Consider the following: 17,000 hourly employees and 1,200 supervisors from 20 cultures needed to be integrated into one company and share a common focus. Such was the situation facing Tenaris, a global industrial company that had grown through acquisitions and became a leader in its sector. The company manufactures and supplies tubular products and services used for drilling and production of oil and gas, as well as tubular products and services for process and power plants, automotive applications, and specialized industrial applications. Founded in 2002, Tenaris grew through acquisitions of plants and green-field projects around the world, including Canada, Colombia, Thailand, Indonesia, Saudi Arabia, and other countries. The company was recognized in 2016 as number 8 on the Training Top 125 list, selected by *Training* magazine in recognition of its commitment to employee training.

A major challenge for the company in achieving its goal was standardizing the work of the hourly employees in their mills. The company understood that it needed to provide the same high quality products and services regardless of where they were made or used. To achieve this goal of standardizing industrial processes in all mills, Tenaris created a project called 00100 in 2008. This global project name translated as 0 accidents, 0 defects, and 100 percent compliance.

## Discussion Questions

1. Identify the steps that Tenaris should have taken to ensure it could reach its goal.
2. What role would a needs assessment play in the process of developing a training program?
3. Why would Tenaris have decided to use training to change culture?
4. Discuss how training would have been different had Tenaris been a smaller company.
5. Visit the Tenaris company website and read about its Global Trainee Program. Why is this program important for helping Tenaris maintain a competitive advantage?

*Adapted from:* "L&D Best Practices: Strategies for Success (July/August 2016), *trainingmag.com*, https://trainingmag.com/trgmag-article/ld-best-practices-strategies-success-julyaugust-2016; Friefeld, Lorri, "Training Magazine Ranks 2016 Training Top 125 Organizations," February 11, 2016, https://trainingmag.com/training-magazine-ranks-2016-training-top-125-organizations; and "Global Trainee Program," http://www.tenaris.com/en/Careers/StudentsandGraduates/GlobalTraineeProgram.aspx.

# CASE STUDY 2: MAKING TRAINING A COMPETITION AT SONIC

For more than 60 years, Sonic has been America's Drive-In. With over 3,500 locations, it is also the largest chain of drive-in restaurants in America. The fast food chain sells made-to-order classics and signature menu items delivered by friendly, roller-skating carhops. Sonic created the Dr. Pepper Sonic Games, an extensive nine-month training program, with a goal of ensuring that employees across all of those locations had the same training. The company also saw it as a way to motivate employees to learn and improve their performance. For over 20 years, employees across the chain have been given the opportunity to participate in this competition. A dozen crews participate in the final competition to become the Best Crew in the Country.

The training program includes location-based sessions, team challenges, quizzes, secret shoppers, and individual competitions. The training is relevant to the work that the crews do each day so transfer of training is readily apparent. One goal of the program is to ensure that employees understand every part of the drive-in so that they can provide exemplary service to the customers and have fun while doing so. The company has found that by incorporating a gamification feel employees get excited and energized about participating in the training. An online portal provides digital training modules that help employees move to the next level. The competition involves crews competing against crews from other locations. As a result, the importance of working together as a local team (crew) is reinforced.

The company believes the training program is successful and has data to support that belief. It has seen improvements in everything from food quality to overall employee performance. Employees have a chance to build their skills and the teams have motivation to work collectively for the good of the business. In the end, members of the 12 winning teams receive an all-expense paid trip to Washington, DC, for the final competition. That event marks the first time many of the participants will have been on an airplane and, for some, even the first time to leave their home state. Those are pretty good incentives to participate in the training program, making the experience a win-win for employee and company.

### Discussion Questions

1. Visit the website for the Dr. Pepper Sonic Games (drpeppersonicgames.com) and review some of the videos posted in the Gallery on the website to learn more about Sonic and this training program.

2. Based on what you have learned about learning and development in this chapter and the information presented here and on the videos, prepare a critique of the learning and development program at Sonic.

3. What is your reaction to a training program of this type? Would you be motivated to participate? Why or why not?

4. In what other industries might this type of training program work? List the industries and justify your response.

*Sources:* "About Us, Driving Toward Success," Sonic, https://corporate.sonicdrivein.com/about-us; O'Donnell, Rita, "Ready, Set, Skate: Sonic Adds a Dash of Competition to Employee Training," HR Dive, August 7, 2018, https://www.hrdive.com/news/ready-set-skate-sonic-adds-a-dash-of-competition-to-employee-training/529377/; "2018 Dr. Pepper Sonic Games, Sonic National Treasure, Unlocking Your Potential, http://www.drpeppersonicgames.com/index/gallery.

## NOTES

[1] Monika Hamori, Jie Cao, and Burak Koyuncu, "Why Top Young Managers Are in a Nonstop Job Hunt," *Harvard Business Review*, http://hbr.org/2012/07/why-top-young-managers-are-in-a-nonstop-job-hunt/.

[2] Carmen Nobel, "First Minutes Are Critical in New-Employee Orientation," Harvard Business School Working Knowledge Research & Ideas, last modified April 1, 2013, http://hbswk.hbs.edu/item/7193.html; and Daniel Cable, Francesca Gino, and Bradley Staats, "Breaking Them in or Eliciting Their Best? Reframing Socialization Around Newcomers' Authentic Self-Expression," *Administrative Science Quarterly* 58 (2013): 1–36.

[3] Peter Vanden Bos, "How to Build an Onboarding Plan for a New Hire," Inc., last modified April 2010, http://www.inc.com/guides/2010/04/building-an-onboarding-plan.html.

[4] "Industry Insight: Strategic Onboarding—Help New Hires Belong and Deliver Results," *Training*, https://trainingmag.com/trgmag-article/industry-insight-strategic-onboarding-help-new-hires-belong-and-deliver-results; Arlene S. Hirsch, "Don't Underestimate the Importance of Good Onboarding," *SHRM.org*, August 10, 2017, https://www.shrm.org/resourcesandtools/hr-topics/talent-acquisition/pages/dont-underestimate-the-importance-of-effective-onboarding.aspx

[5] Tayla Bauer, *Onboarding New Employees: Maximizing Success*, SHRM Foundation's Effective Practice Guidelines Series (Alexandria, VA: SHRM, 2010).

[6] Raymond Noe, *Learning System Design*, SHRM Foundation's Effective Practice Guideline Series (Alexandria, VA: SHRM, 2009).

[7] Lorri Friefeld, "Training Magazine Ranks 2018 Training Top 125 Organizations," *Training*, https://trainingmag.com/training-magazine-ranks-2018-training-top-125-organizations.

[8] Joe Flynn, "Linking Human Capital Management and Learning to Business Outcomes," *Learning & Training Innovations* 4 (2003): 12–13.

[9] "2018 Training Industry Report," *Training*, https://trainingmag.com/trgmag-article/2018-training-industry-report/.

[10] Hodell, Chuck, "All About ADDIE," Association for Talent Development (ATD), https://www.td.org/newsletters/atd-links/all-about-addie.

[11] Hodell, Chuck, "All About ADDIE," Association for Talent Development (ATD), https://www.td.org/newsletters/atd-links/all-about-addie.

[12] Edward Salas and Janis Cannon-Bowers, "The Science of Training: A Decade of Progress," *Annual Review of Psychology* 52 (2001): 471–499.

[13] Cliff Purington and Chris Butler, *Built to Learn: The Inside Story of How Rockwell Collins Became a True Learning Organization* (New York: AMACOM, 2003); and "Tailored Services: Training & Simulation," Rockwell Collins, http://www.rockwellcollins.com/Services_and_Support/Tailored_Services/Training_and_Simulation.aspx.

[14] Ronald Sims and Serbrenia Sims, *The Importance of Learning Styles: Understanding the Implications for Learning, Course Design, and Education* (Westport, CT: Greenwood Press, 1995).

[15] Alice Starcke, "Building a Better Orientation Program," *HR Magazine* 41 (1996): 107–112.

[16] Robert Eichinger and Michael Lombardo, "Learning Agility as a Prime Indicator of Potential," *Human Resource Planning* 27 (2004): 12–15.

[17] Salas and Cannon-Bowers, "The Science of Training."

[18] Kenneth Brown, "Using Computers to Deliver Training: Which Employees Learn and Why?" *Personnel Psychology* 54 (2001): 271–296.

[19] Salas and Cannon-Bowers, "The Science of Training."

[20] "Career Progression," Booz Allen Hamilton, http://www.boozallen.com/careers/life-at-booz-allen/career-progression.

[21] Dan Wentland, "The Strategic Training of Employees Model: Balancing Organizational Constraints and Training Content," *SAM Advanced Management Journal* 68 (2003): 56–63.

[22] "Strengthening Our Nation's Workforce with Demand-Driven Solutions: Registered Apprenticeship Trends in Information Technology," U.S. Department of Labor, Office of Apprenticeship Training Employer and Labor Services, Employment and Training Administration, doleta.gov/oa/brochure/Information%20Technology_new.pdf.

[23] Irwin Speizer, "State of the Sector: Training," *Workforce Management*, July 2005, 55–58.

[24] Salas and Cannon-Bowers, "The Science of Training."

[25] "Caterpillar Customer Training," Caterpillar, https://caterpillaruniversity.com/.

[26] Jonathan Pont, "Employee Training on iPod Playlist," *Workforce Management*, August 2005, 18; and "Home," 1st Class Solutions, http://www.1stclass.com/podcasts-provide-another-tool-for-employee-training/.

[27] Speizer, "State of the Sector."

[28] Brown, "Using Computers to Deliver Training."

[29] Irwin Speizer, "Simulation Games Score with Trainees," *Workforce Management*, July 2005, 60; and "'Simulation Training' Prepares Medical Staff for Real Thing," U.S. Department of Veterans Affairs, http://www.va.gov/health/NewsFeatures/20111117a.asp.

[30] Rick Newman, "How Sullenberger Really Saved US Airways Flight 1549," *U.S. News*, last modified February 3, 2009, http://money.usnews.com/money/blogs/flowchart/2009/02/03/how-sullenberger-really-saved-us-airways-flight-1549; and "'Simulation Training' Prepares Medical Staff for Real Thing," U.S. Department of Veterans Affairs, http://www.va.gov/health/NewsFeatures/20111117a.asp.

[31] David Zinger, "Game On: A Primer on Gamification for Managers," *T+D*, last modified May 8, 2014, http://www.astd.org/Publications/Magazines/TD/TD-Archive/2014/05/Game-on-a-Primer-on-Gamification-for-Managers.

[32] Bill Roberts, "Gamification: Win, Lose, or Draw?" *HR Magazine* 59 (2014): 29–35; Garry Kranz, "Learning Gets a Higher Degree of Attention at Workplaces," *Workforce*, January 8, 2014, https://www.workforce.com/2014/01/08/learning-gets-a-higher-degree-of-attention-at-workplaces/; and Joyce Gioia, "What Will Human Resources Look Like in the Near Future?" *Workforce*, last modified April 3, 2013, http://www.workforce.com/articles/what-will-human-resources-look-like-in-the-near-future.

[33] Roberts, "Gamification."

[34] Zinger, "Game On."

[35] Ibid.

[36] Sally Hovis, "Developing Capable Leaders Through Blended Learning," *T+D*, last modified May 7, 2012, http://www.astd.org/Publications/Magazines/TD/TD-Archive/2012/05/Developing-

Capable-Leaders-Through-Blended-Learning; and "GC Services Creates a Cost-Effective Blended Learning Program for Leadership Development," Skillsoft Learning Re-imagined, last modified December 2, 2011, http://blogs.skillsoft.com/-learning-re-imagined/2011/12/gc-services-creates-a-cost-effected-blended-learning-program-for-leadership-development.html.

[37] George Stevens and Gary Frazer, "Coaching: The Missing Ingredient in Blended Learning Strategy," *Performance Improvement* 44 (2005): 8–13.

[38] Barbara Means, Yukie Toyanna, Robert Murphy, Marianne Bakia, and Karla Jones, *Evaluation of Evidence-Based Practices in Online Learning: A Meta-Analysis and Review of Online Learning Studies* (Washington, DC: U. S. Department of Education, 2010).

[39] Richard Pérez-Peña, "Starbucks to Provide Free College Education to Thousands of Workers," *The New York Times*, last modified June 15, 2014, http://www.nytimes.com/2014/06/16/us/starbucks-to-provide-free-college-education-to-thousands-of-workers.html?_r=0; Stephen Miller, "Starbucks and McDonald's Expand Educational Opportunities," April 10, 2015, *SHRM.org,* https://www.shrm.org/resourcesandtools/hr-topics/benefits/pages/starbucks-mcdonalds-education.aspx.

[40] Katie Lobosco, "Walmart's Perk for Workers: Go to College for $1 a Day," CNN, money.cnn.com, http://money.cnn.com/2018/05/30/pf/college/walmart-tuition-benefit/index.html.

[41] "Employee Scholar Program," UTC, http://www.utc.com/Careers/Work-With-Us/Pages/Employee-Scholar-Program.aspx.

[42] Douglas Shuit, "Huddling with the Coach," *Workforce Management*, February 2005, 53–57.

[43] James Darby, "L&D Best Practices: July/August 2014," *Training*, 2014, http://www.training-mag.com/trgmag-article/ld-best-practices-julyaugust-2014.

[44] "ESL in the News," ESL, https://www.esl.org/about-us/esl-in-the-news.

[45] S. Sparrow, "A Defining Time for Coaching," *Personnel Today* 20 (2005): 23.

[46] Ibid.

[47] Michael Johnson, "January–February 2005: California Requires Sexual Harassment Training," *SHRM Legal Report*, last modified January 5, 2005, http://www.shrm.org/-legalissues/legalreport/pages/cms_010852.aspx.

[48] Ibid.

[49] Joann Lublin, "Bringing Hidden Biases into the Light," *Wall Street Journal*, last modified January 9, 2014, http://online.wsj.com/news/articles/SB10001424052702303754404579308562690896896.

[50] Ben Chu, "Starbucks Is Daring to Invest in Its Employees with Today's Diversity Training, A Rare Choice That Could Be Money Well Spent," *Independent,* May 29, 2018, https://www.independent.co.uk/voices/starbucks-diversity-training-unconscious-bias-race-economics-a8374001.htm.

[51] Marc Bendick, Mary Lou Egan, and Suzanne M. Lofhjelm, "Workforce Diversity Training: From Anti-Discrimination Compliance to Organizational Development," *Human Resource Planning* 24 (2001): 10–25.

[52] "Welcome to the NIH Training Center," National Institutes of Health, https://hr.nih.gov/training-center.

[53] Ibid.

[54] David Harold, Walter Davis, Donald Fedora, and Charles Parsons, "Dispositional Influences on Transfer of Learning in Multistage Training Programs," *Personnel Psychology* 55 (2002): 851–869.

[55] Brian Blame, J. Kevin Ford, Timothy Baldwin, and Jason Huang, "Transfer of Training: A Meta-Analytic Review," *Journal of Management* 36 (2010): 1065–1105.

[56] Rebecca Grossman and Eduardo Salas, "The Transfer of Training: What Really Matters," *International Journal of Training and Development* 15 (2011): 103–120.

[57] Vinita Parker-Wilkins, "Business Impact of Executive Coaching: Demonstrating Monetary Value," *Industrial and Commercial Training* 38 (2006): 122–127.

[58] "Best ROI in Online Training Case? Return Business," *SHRM.org,* http://www.shrm.org/hrdisciplines/technology/articles/pages/roiinonlinetraining.aspx. (.

[59] Jack Phillips, "Calculating the ROI of E-Learning," ASTD, last modified December 27, 2010, http://www.astd.org/Publications/Newsletters/ASTD-Links/ASTD-Links-Articles/2010/12/Calculating-the-ROI-of-E-Learning.

[60] "NIH Senior Leadership Program," Office of Human Resources at the National Institutes of Health, http://www.trainingcenter.nih.gov/senior_leadership_program.html .

[61] Gregory Hurts and Kevin Williams, "Attitudinal and Motivation Antecedents of Participation in Voluntary Employee Development Activities," *Journal of Applied Psychology* 94 (2009): 635–653.

[62] "Financial Leadership Development Program," BAE Systems, 2012 FLDP Final Approved Brochure.pdf .

[63] Dimple Agarwal, Josh Bersin, Gaurav Lahiri, Jeff Schwartz, and Erica Volini, "From Careers to Experiences: New Pathways," 2018 Global Human Capital Trends, Deloitte Insights, March 28, 2018, https://www2.deloitte.com/insights/us/en/focus/human-capital-trends/2018/building-21st-century-careers.html; Forbes Coaches Council, "13 Reasons to Offer Leadership Training and Development to Millennials," Forbes Community Voice, forbes.com, December 22, 2017, https://www.forbes.com/sites/forbesco achescouncil/2017/12/22/13-reasons-to-offer-leadership-training-and-development-to-millennials/#30c9c837a14d.

[64] "Fred's Super Dollar," http://www.fredsinc.com.

[65] "About Us," Nordstrom, http://shop.nordstrom.com/c/about-us?origin=footer.

[66] Neal E. Baudette, "Tesla's Mass-Market Gamble," Sunday Business, *The New York Times,* July 1, 2018.

[67] Shawn Adams, "Costs Drive Safety Training Needs," *HR Magazine* 48 (2003): 63–66.

[68] Geri Tucker, "HR at the Corner of People and Strategy," *HR Magazine* 59 (2014): 42–44.

[69] Frank Joss, "Lesson Plans," *HR Magazine* 48 (2003): 72–76.

[70] John Contemn, "Journey to a Culture of Learning," *Training,* http://www.trainingmag .com/trgmag-article/journey-culture-learning.

[71] Kenneth Wesley and Gary Latham, *Developing and Training Human Resources in Organizations* (Englewood Cliffs, NJ: Prentice Hall, 2002).

[72] "Performance Expectations = Results + Actions & Behaviors," Berkeley Human Resources, University of California, Berkeley, berkeley.edu, https://hr.berkeley.edu/ hr-network/central-guide-managing-hr/managing-hr/managing-successfully/performance-management/planning/expectations, 2018.

[73] Sandra Robinson and Elizabeth Morrison, "Psychological Contracts and Organizational Citizenship Behavior: The Effect of Unfulfilled Obligations Civic Virtue Behavior," *Journal of Organizational Behavior* 16 (1995): 289–298.

[74] Brie Wailer Reynolds, "100 Top Companies with Remote Jobs in 2018," *FlexJobs.com,* https://www.flexjobs.com/blog/post/100-top-companies-with-remote-jobs-in-2018/.

[75] "Demographic Shifts Transform the Global Workforce," *EY.com,* http://www.ey.com/GL/ en/Issues/Business-environment/Six-global-trends-shaping-the-business-world---Demographic-shifts-transform-the-global-workforce.

[76] Maryann Hammers, "Wyndham Looks to Leap Language Gap," *Workforce Magazine,* July 2005, p. 17.

[77] Catherine Dunn, "Language Options for Career Training," *Fortune* 169 (2014): 36; Samuel Grignard, "Technology Is Changing Expatriate Training," *Workforce* 78 (1999): 106–108; "TDIndustries Named on the 2016 Fortune '100 Best Companies to Work For List'," http:// www.tdindustries.com/news/tdindustries-named-2016-fortune-%E2%80%9C100-best-companies-work-list%C2%AE%E2%80%9D; "Introducing Fortune's 2018 100 Best Companies to Work For List," http://fortune.com/best-companies/.

[78] Samuel Grignard, "Technology Is Changing Expatriate Training," *Workforce* 78 (1999): 106–108; "TDIndustries Named on the 2016 Fortune '100 Best Companies to Work For List'"; "Introducing Fortune's 2018 100 Best Companies to Work For List."

[79] Dennis Briscoe and Randall Schuler, *International Human Resource Management* (London: Rutledge, 2004), 271.

[80] Patricia Dig, "One Style Doesn't Fit All," *HR Magazine* 47 (2002): 79–31.

[81] "Fostering an Environment Conducive for Global Career Development," CSR Reporting Sony, August 23, 2017, https://sony.net/SonyInfo/csr_report/employes/diversity/index5 .html.

[82] Patricia Dig, "One Style Doesn't Fit All," *HR Magazine* 47 (2002): 79–31.

[83] *City of Canton v. Harris,* 489 US. 378 (1989).

[84] J. Garden, "B-schools: Only a C+ in Ethics," *Business Week,* September 5, 2005, 110.

[85] Randy Myers, "Ensuring Ethical Effectiveness: New Rules Mean Virtually Every Company Will Need a Code of Ethics," *Journal of Accountancy* 195 (2003): 28–33.

[86] Speizer, "State of the Sector."

[87] "Governance at IBM," 2017 *Corporate Responsibility Report,* IBM, https://www.ibm.com/ ibm/responsibility/2017/assets/downloads/IBM-2017-CRR-Governance.pdf.

[88] Gregory J. Milkman and Samuel Rubenfeld, "Compliance Officer: Dream Career?" January 15, 2014, *Wall Street Journal,* http://www.wsj.com/articles/SB10001424052702303 3302045792507221145387 50.

# Part 4

# Managing Employee Attitudes and Behaviors

# Chapter 9

# Performance Management

## Learning Objectives

**AFTER READING THIS CHAPTER, YOU SHOULD BE ABLE TO:**

1 Describe the purposes of performance management.

2 Describe the components of an effective performance management system.

3 Discuss how to develop useful performance measures.

4 Review the approaches used to evaluate employee performance.

5 Compare and contrast the usefulness of sources for employee performance data.

6 Develop an effective approach for providing employees with performance feedback.

7 Describe the merits of alternative approaches to disciplining employees.

8 Explain how an organization's demands affect its performance management system.

9 Discuss how a firm's environment affects its performance management system.

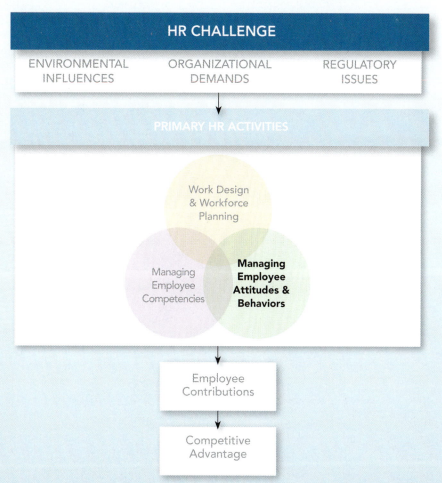

**HR CHALLENGE**

| ENVIRONMENTAL INFLUENCES | ORGANIZATIONAL DEMANDS | REGULATORY ISSUES |

**PRIMARY HR ACTIVITIES**

Work Design & Workforce Planning

Managing Employee Competencies

**Managing Employee Attitudes & Behaviors**

Employee Contributions

Competitive Advantage

# Why Performance Management Is So Important

As a manager, you are dependent on your employees. When your employees achieve their objectives, you receive accolades. When they perform poorly, your performance review as a manager and related incentives, including bonuses, may be affected. Put simply, your job performance is tied directly to your employees' performance. How well your employees perform is, to a large extent, a function of the effort they expend, but it is also a function of their level of motivation and the extent to which they have been trained and provided with the resources they need to succeed. Your goal as a manager, therefore, is to motivate the employees who report to you to work hard and continually improve what they do, making sure they have the necessary resources to succeed. As shown in Exhibit 9.1, one of the *primary HR activities* is to manage employee attitudes and behaviors. One way that managers do this is by having in place the right performance management programs. **Performance management** involves two related activities: (1) effectively evaluating the performance of your employees against the standards set for them, and (2) helping them develop action plans to improve their performance. Performance management, done well, aligns individual efforts with organizational goals.[1]

**performance management**

The process of managing two related activities: (1) effectively evaluating the performance of your employees against the standards set for them, and (2) helping them develop action plans to improve their performance

**EXHIBIT 9.1**

Strategic Management of Human Resources Framework

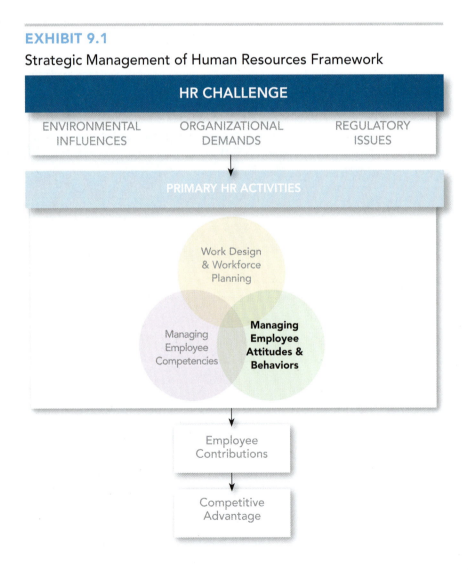

As a manager, you need to be able to answer questions such as these:

- How can I best measure the performance of my employees?
- What's the best way to give my employees developmental feedback to improve their performance?
- How should I communicate that information to employees?
- How should I manage poorly performing employees?

Perhaps no other human resource (HR) management activity is changing as rapidly as performance management. In this chapter, we will describe the traditional approaches to performance management that are still widely used across many industries. We will also highlight the newer trends that are becoming more prevalent, especially in knowledge-based industries and firms hiring large numbers of millennials, a group that expects more ongoing and frequent feedback than previous generations. After reading this chapter, you should be in a better position to design and implement a performance management system that motivates your employees to display the necessary attitudes and behaviors at work to help your company achieve a competitive advantage.

## Purposes of Performance Management

Traditionally, performance management activities have been used for administrative or developmental purposes, if not both.[2] Administratively, as we will discuss in Chapters 10 and 11, firms use performance evaluations to make decisions regarding their employees' salary adjustments, merit raises, and incentive rewards. For example, how do you know how much raise to give an employee? In many companies, this decision is based on the employee's performance evaluation.

As we discussed in Chapter 5, managers must make decisions regarding the promotions, demotions, transfers, terminations, and even layoffs of individuals. On what basis are these decisions made? Understanding your employees' current performance, as well as their potential to perform, will help you make decisions about the movement of employees within, or out of, your organization. Managers also use performance evaluation data for disciplinary purposes—that is, to reinforce the attitudes and behaviors employees should display on a daily basis.

The second purpose of performance management is *developmental* in nature—using performance evaluation information to help employees improve their performance in order to add more value to the company. This purpose is more likely to be the primary focus for firms that are moving away from traditional approaches to performance management.[3] Performance evaluations serve a vital role in terms of identifying the types of training needed by employees. Especially when employees are not performing at a satisfactory level, a developmental approach is important, as it focuses on finding out if there are areas in which the employee is able to improve performance and, if so, identifying a course of action to help the employee meet his potential. A developmental approach may also involve disciplinary actions to signal to employees that current actions or behaviors may not be acceptable, or on a more positive note, be part of employee career development and succession planning.

When you understand how to use performance evaluations for different administrative and/or developmental purposes, you can start to think about how to better manage the performance of your employees. Being clear about the purpose(s) of the performance management process and its relationship to achieving a

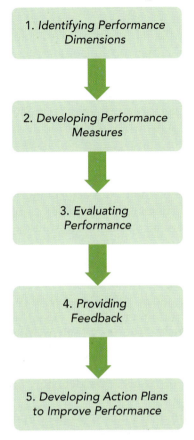

**EXHIBIT 9.2**

Steps in the Performance Management Process

1. *Identifying Performance Dimensions*

2. *Developing Performance Measures*

3. *Evaluating Performance*

4. *Providing Feedback*

5. *Developing Action Plans to Improve Performance*

competitive advantage before beginning its design is critical to the future success of the process.[4] As shown in Exhibit 9.2, there are five steps related to developing and implementing a good performance management process, which start with identifying performance dimensions.

## Step 1: Identifying Performance Dimensions

If you were asked to evaluate the instructor for one of your courses, what would you say? Would you say your instructor is "good," "average," or "poor"? Or would you think about it for a minute and break down different aspects of your instructor's performance and evaluate each one of them separately? You might rate your instructor as "good" in terms of being prepared for class, "average" for maintaining student interest during lectures, and "good" for grading fairly. If you focus on a single overall evaluation of your instructor, you are relying on a **global performance measure**—a single score to reflect overall performance. If you choose to consider separate parts of the instructor's performance, you are identifying **performance dimensions**.

Performance dimensions relate to the specific tasks and activities employees must perform to do their jobs, and the competencies employees need to successfully perform those tasks and activities. Now suppose that two employees exhibit similar performance levels overall (average), but they excel at different dimensions of their jobs. One employee might excel at helping his coworkers, whereas another might excel at working with her customers. By breaking their performance down into

**global performance measure**

the use of a single score to reflect an individual employee's overall performance.

**performance dimensions**

the specific tasks and activities employees must perform to do their jobs, and the competencies employees need to successfully perform those tasks and activities.

different dimensions, you are able to identify where each employee is making the biggest contribution and where each employee needs to improve. The first step in a successful performance management system, then, is to determine the performance dimensions you should evaluate. PwC, one of the largest audit, assurance, consulting, and tax companies in the world, has identified five competencies, a form of dimensions, that it uses to evaluate employees in its client-services practices.[5]

A job's performance dimensions should reflect the reasons it exists in the first place. For example, it wouldn't make much sense to evaluate a receptionist on the number of innovative products she develops for her company, because a receptionist is not likely to be directly involved in developing products. Rather, she's likely to be responsible for greeting customers, answering inquiries on the telephone, and the like. These tasks reflect the essential functions of the job that should be evaluated. A primary source of information for identifying performance dimensions is job analysis. As we discussed in Chapter 4, each job within a company exists to perform certain tasks, duties, and responsibilities. The performance dimensions should reflect these tasks, duties, responsibilities, and competencies required for their performance. Understanding the concept of performance dimensions serves as a starting point for developing an effective performance management system. As a manager, you need to understand what performance dimensions are important for a job; that is, what are the tasks, duties, responsibilities, and competencies that define the essence of the job and/or that are required for the organization to achieve its goals and objectives.

## Step 2: Developing Performance Measures

Knowing what performance dimensions should be evaluated does not necessarily translate into an effective performance management system. Rather, you have to be able to measure an employee's level of performance on the dimensions you have identified.[6] Effective performance evaluation systems use performance measures that are valid, have clear standards, and are specific. Let's look more closely at each of these criteria.

### Valid Measures

Performance measures must be reliable and valid. In our discussion of selection decisions in Chapter 7, we brought up the concepts of reliability and validity. *Reliability* refers to how well a measure yields consistent results over time and across raters. *Validity* is the extent to which you are measuring what you want to measure, and how well that is done.[7] Essentially, validity means that your performance measures reflect the actual performance of your employees.

Sometimes, however, performance evaluations go awry because the measures used are deficient or contaminated. A performance measure is said to be **deficient** when important aspects of an individual's performance are not measured. For example, measuring only the number of phone calls made by a sales representative to potential clients fails to recognize additional and important aspects of her job: actually making and closing sales. A performance measure is said to be **contaminated** when it captures information that is irrelevant to an individual's job performance.[8] Considering our sales representative example again, if the person's manager evaluates the rep's typing speed or the neatness of the employee's desk, the overall measure of her performance is likely to be contaminated by irrelevant information. In other words, you have to make sure the performance measures you use reflect all the essential performance dimensions required to achieve organizational goals, and only those dimensions.

**deficient performance measure**

an incomplete appraisal of an individual's performance, in which important aspects are not measured

**contaminated performance measure**

a performance measure that is irrelevant to an individual's actual job performance

## Performance Measurement Standards

**performance standards**

the level of expected performance

One key consideration in developing performance measures is clarifying the level of expected performance, the **performance standards**.[9] Consider an automobile salesperson. Is selling 10 cars in one month an indication of a "good," "average," or "poor" performance? Without a standard, or benchmark, just knowing the person's level of performance won't give you enough information to evaluate the employee's effectiveness.

Managers can use a number of standards for evaluating employee performance. For example, they might rely on some objective performance measure, such as number or dollar amount of sales, number of mistakes, and quantity of output. Performance standards can also be qualitative. Managers might use a simple "yes" or "no" format, or use a scale with anchors ranging from "unsatisfactory" to "excellent", to evaluate employees on whether they performed some task successfully." The Office of Personnel Management (OPM) provides detailed instructions to managers on how to develop performance standards. This agency is the chief HR agency for the U.S. government and sets personnel policy for federal workers. The OPM recognizes that the performance dimensions, which it refers to as "elements," tell employees what they have to do, and performance standards tell employees how well they have to do the elements of their jobs. These standards can be quantitative, qualitative, or some combination of the two.[10]

Standards must be clear and reflect the entire performance spectrum. An evaluation will not be of much use if the typical employee receives the highest possible rating because average performers and outstanding performers would receive the same ratings. At the same time, however, the standards cannot be so high that they are unattainable. If employees do not feel they can reasonably reach the standards set for them, their motivation to try to do so will likely diminish.

## Specificity

**specificity**

the clarity of performance standards

Performance evaluations are most effective when the standards are associated with high levels of specificity. Whereas validity focuses on the extent to which the performance standards reflect the actual tasks, duties, responsibilities, and competencies for which employees are responsible, **specificity** refers to the clarity of those performance standards. For example, when evaluating the dimension of customer service, a performance standard that simply focuses on evaluating whether employees provide "excellent" customer service is much less specific than a performance standard that is more narrowly construed—for example, one that evaluates whether employees help customers determine which products or services they most want or need.

Greater specificity affords two benefits.[11] First, it makes a standard clearer, and managers are likely to be more consistent when they evaluate employees on that standard. This specificity helps improve the reliability of the performance management process. Moreover, greater specificity means that a wider array of job tasks is likely to be evaluated, rather than focusing on some overall global assessment.[12] As a result, companies are likely to have a better idea about how different employees are performing different aspects of their jobs. Second, greater levels of specificity help employees understand how different aspects of their job should be performed.[13] Telling an employee he has poor customer service skills does not provide the same level of developmental potential as identifying specific aspects of customer service in which his performance is lacking.

The Office of Personnel Management (OPM), referenced earlier, provides a handbook for managers to teach them about the importance of, and process for, measuring employee performance. A critical focus of this handbook is explaining to managers the importance of setting specific performance measures and ensuring that they are tied to the desired results. The handbook notes the importance of measuring and recognizing accomplishments that help an agency achieve desired results, as opposed to measuring activities that may not lead to desired organizational outcomes. An activity might be answering customer questions, while an accomplishment would be providing accurate guidance to customers. Note the difference. Which is likely to help the agency achieve its goals? Simply answering a question, or providing accurate guidance?[14]

# Step 3: Evaluating Employee Performance

Managers can evaluate the performance of their employees in a number of ways. They can compare and rank order the employees, rate them against preset standards, or evaluate the results or outcomes of their performance. These methods vary in several important ways. First, some methods focus on measuring performance outcomes (e.g., quantity, speed, sales), whereas others focus on competencies, which include employee traits or behaviors.[15] *Traits* are the employees' attributes, such as their knowledge, courtesy, or some attitudinal measure. In contrast, methods that focus on behaviors strive to capture the extent to which employees display the desired behaviors related to doing their jobs. The various methods also differ in terms of their usefulness for meeting the administrative or developmental purposes of a firm's performance management system.

## Individual Comparisons

Perhaps the simplest form of performance evaluation is to compare employees to one another to discern their relative standing along some performance dimension. In a simple **ranking approach**, managers rank order employees from best to worst along some performance dimension or by virtue of their overall performance. For example, a manager might rank order employees based on their sales volume for a month. The person with the highest sales would be ranked number 1, the person with the second-highest sales would be ranked number 2, and so on. When managers have quantitative performance data, rankings are quite easy to do.

A variation of the ranking approach is the **paired comparison** method. In this approach, each employee in a business unit is compared to every other employee in the unit. The rater then assigns a point value to the better individual in the pair being compared. After all individuals are compared to one another and their points added up, they are ranked from the most points to the least. Exhibit 9.3 shows how

**ranking approach**

an evaluation approach in which employees are evaluated from best to worst along some performance dimension or by virtue of their overall performance

**paired comparison**

an evaluation approach in which each employee in a business unit is compared to every other employee in the unit

## EXHIBIT 9.3

Example of a Paired Comparison

| Employee for Paired Comparison | Employee Being Rated | | | | | |
|---|---|---|---|---|---|---|
| | **Bob** | **Sue** | **John** | **Anil** | **Magni** | **Karen** |
| Bob | — | | | | ✓ | ✓ |
| Sue | ✓ | — | | ✓ | ✓ | |
| John | ✓ | ✓ | — | ✓ | | ✓ |
| Anil | ✓ | | | — | | |
| Magni | | | ✓ | ✓ | — | |
| Karen | | ✓ | | ✓ | ✓ | — |
| **Point Total** | **3** | **2** | **1** | **4** | **3** | **2** |

a paired comparison works. For example, Bob is rated as having better performance than Sue, John, and Anil. As a result, Bob receives a total of three points. In contrast, Anil is rated as having better performance than Sue, John, Magni, and Karen, giving him a total of four points. After all employees are evaluated, Anil has the highest ranking, with four points. Bob and Magni have the second-highest ranking, with three points. Sue and Karen have the second-lowest ranking, with two points each, and John has the lowest ranking with just one point.

**forced distribution**

a form of individual comparisons whereby managers are forced to distribute employees into one of several predetermined categories

Another form of individual comparisons is the **forced distribution** approach. In this approach, managers are forced to fit (distribute) employees into one of several predetermined categories based on their performance. Exhibit 9.4 shows an example of what a forced distribution would look like on a bar chart. In this example, a manager would be required to rate 10% of her employees as "very good," 20% as "good," 40% as "average," 20% as "poor," and the remaining 10% as "very poor." Thus, if the manager had 100 employees, she could give only 10 of them a "very good" rating. Basically, the forced distribution in our example is the same approach used when a teacher grades on a bell curve. There will be more employees receiving an average evaluation (a C on the bell curve for a class of students), and fewer receiving a high or very low evaluation (As or Fs if being graded on a bell curve). Forced distribution systems prevent managers from rating all employees as "outstanding," "average," or "poor." They must use the entire range of the performance scores. This approach forces managers to be more critical in terms of which employees truly are "exceptional," "average," or "poor." As discussed in Company Spotlight 9.1, General Electric (GE) used the forced distribution method for many years but has now moved to a different approach.

Of course, all three of these individual comparisons have advantages and disadvantages. On the one hand, using individual comparisons is a relatively easy approach to design and implement. Managers simply need to determine a basis for the comparisons, or rely on an overall global assessment, and then they need to compare individuals to one another. In addition, the comparisons can be used for administrative purposes, such as determining who to promote and how to distribute incentives or allocate merit raises. If a company is forced to lay off employees, these methods may help managers decide who to let go. Over the years, many companies adopted the GE forced distribution approach. Microsoft used the forced distribution system but abandoned the approach in 2013. Yahoo introduced the forced distribution approach in 2013 and experienced legal challenges within a few years after doing so. Employees claimed that the forced distribution system discriminated against men when it was used to reduce head count.[16]

Obviously, as shown by the Yahoo example, there are some drawbacks to using comparison approaches. For instance, what do you do if two employees display

**EXHIBIT 9.4**

Example of a Forced Distribution Performance Evaluation

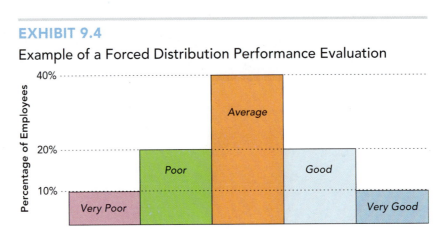

## COMPANY SPOTLIGHT  9.1

### Forced Distributions at General Electric (GE) Have Gone Away

While many companies use a forced distribution approach, perhaps the best known of these is the system that GE used for evaluating managerial and professional staff. Under the guidance of former CEO Jack Welch, GE focused on 4 *Es* when ranking managers and executives: high *energy* level, ability to *energize* others around common goals, the *edge* to make tough yes/no decisions, and the ability to consistently *execute* and deliver on promises. Once assessed, individuals were assigned to one of three groups—a top 15% (1s), a middle 75% (2s), and a bottom 10% (3s). If employees were placed in the bottom 10%, there was good chance they would be told to look elsewhere for employment. As Welch noted, "A company that bets its future on its people must remove that lower 10 percent, and keep removing it every year—always raising the bar of performance and increasing the quality of its leadership."

Now, however, this forced distribution system is gone at GE. In its place is a more robust and agile system that involves employees in performance development rather than performance appraisal, focuses on team inspiration and empowerment, and works with employees to use customer input to set real-time priorities. Speed and collaboration has increased and employees are more engaged. Time to market has improved dramatically, as has speed of innovation. GE also has developed an in-house app, called PD@GE, that enables the company to gain insights from employees and managers across the company. The idea is that more information provides better data and can lead to more continuous improvement.

*Sources:* Cohan, P., "Why Stack Rankings Worked Better at GE Than at Microsoft," *Forbes*, July 13, 2012, http://www.forbes.com/sites/petercohan/2012/07/13/why-stack-ranking-worked-better-at-ge-than-microsoft/; Marquez, J., "GE's People Power: Conaty Made Jack Welch a Believer," *Workforce Magazine*, August 2, 2007, 26–30, https://www.workforce.com/2007/08/02/ges-people-power-conaty-made-jack-welch-a-believer/; Grote, D., "Forced Ranking: Making Performance Management Work," *Harvard Business School Working Knowledge Archive*, November 14, 2005, https://hbswk.hbs.edu/archive/forced-ranking-making-performance-management-work; and Abelson, R., "Companies Turn to Grades, and Employees Go to Court," *The New York Times*, March 19, 2001, https://www.nytimes.com/2001/03/19/business/companies-turn-to-grades-and-employees-go-to-court.html; Sloan, Nathan, Agarwal, Dimple, Garr, Stacia, and Pastakia, Karen, "Performance Management: Playing a Winning Hand, 2017 Global Human Capital Trends," February 28, 2017, https://www2.deloitte.com/insights/us/en/focus/human-capital-trends/2017/redesigning-performance-management.html; Bodell, Lisa, "It's Time to Put Performance Reviews On Notice," April 27, 2018, https://www.forbes.com/sites/lisabodell/2018/04/27/why-performance-reviews-are-irrelevant-today/#7c0889604b63.

equal performance levels, but you must rank order them? Similarly, what if 20% of your employees deserve to be rated as "very good" or "outstanding," but you are forced to limit this rating to only 10% of employees? In such a case, you will have to make distinctions among your employees that are not actual reflections of their performance.[17] Ranking employees also gets considerably more difficult as business units grow in size. What if you have to compare 200 employees or 2,000 employees to one another? You could do so more easily with the forced distribution approach than you could with the ranking or paired comparison approach, but none of the three is ideal. Aside from the time constraints, managers might not have enough information to accurately rate or rank their employees with a high level of confidence in the results.

Finally, although comparative approaches are often helpful for administrative purposes, they are not as useful for developmental purposes. Rankings and distributions boil down to a single overarching rating for employees that often does not capture the specifics of why they are performing at a certain level. In other words, being ranked "5" as an employee simply reflects your current performance; it doesn't tell you much about what you can do to be ranked a "1," "2," "3," or "4."

## Absolute Approaches: Measuring Traits and Behaviors

**absolute approach**

the evaluation of employees' performance by comparing employees against certain "absolute" standards along a number of performance dimensions

Rather than comparing or ranking their employees against one another, many companies use **absolute approaches** to evaluate the performance of their employees. These approaches involve comparing employees against certain "absolute" standards (rather than against each other) along a number of performance dimensions (rather than simply making a global assessment about them). Each employee is assessed in terms of how well he or she performs on a set of performance dimensions based on some predetermined standards of performance. As a result, each employee's evaluation stands independent of other employees' evaluations. In theory, all employees could score "high," "average," or "low." Absolute approaches are also conducive to evaluating employees in terms of their traits, or attributes, as well as their behavior. Next, we discuss these two types of approaches.

### Attribute-Based Approaches

**graphic rating scale**

a method of evaluating employees based on various traits, or attributes, they possess that are relevant to their performance

The most common attribute-based approach is the graphic rating scale. Using **graphic rating scales**, raters evaluate employees based on various traits, or attributes, they possess that are relevant to their performance. Exhibit 9.5 shows an example of a graphic rating scale. As shown, a rater might be asked to evaluate the extent to which an individual is cooperative when performing his job—for example, to rate the person as "poor," "below average," "average," "above average," or "outstanding." The performance dimensions that can be used in a graphic rating scale are really only limited to the imagination of the manager using the scale.[18] For example, employees might be evaluated in terms of the extent to which they possess certain traits, such as product knowledge, creativity, and the like. Because the graphic rating approach provides a format for breaking down performance into a number of attributes, it is more suitable for developmental purposes than the comparative approaches noted earlier. Employees and their managers can see which attributes they scored high or low on and identify areas for improvement.

Graphic rating scales suffer from some limitations, however. Perhaps the most serious limitation is that when scales are poorly designed they can be ambiguous, and the performance standards can be interpreted differently by different raters. This problem is most likely to occur if the dimensions being rated are not described in some detail, and definitions of "outstanding," "average," "good," and "poor" ratings are not provided. For example, what does it really mean to be "above average" on a trait such as being cooperative? One manager might rate an employee as "above

### EXHIBIT 9.5

### Example of a Graphic Rating Scale

| Evaluate employee performance on the following performance dimensions. Circle the most appropriate rating to reflect the employee's performance on each performance dimension. | | | | | |
| --- | --- | --- | --- | --- | --- |
| **Performance Dimension** | **Rating** | | | | |
| | **Poor** | **Below average** | **Average** | **Above average** | **Outstanding** |
| Courteous | 1 | 2 | 3 | 4 | 5 |
| Cooperative | 1 | 2 | 3 | 4 | 5 |
| Knowledgeable | 1 | 2 | 3 | 4 | 5 |
| Quality of work | 1 | 2 | 3 | 4 | 5 |
| Quantity of work | 1 | 2 | 3 | 4 | 5 |
| Product knowledge | 1 | 2 | 3 | 4 | 5 |
| Creativity | 1 | 2 | 3 | 4 | 5 |

average" in terms of the person's cooperativeness, and another manager might rate the employee as just "average." This difference in rating results from each rater having a different belief about what constitutes "average" and/or different information about the employee being evaluated.

## Behavior-Based Approaches

Attribute-based approaches overcome some of the limitations of comparative approaches because they rely on a variety of performance dimensions and evaluate employees along a range of performance standards. However, focusing on workers' attributes alone can be somewhat misleading. Some attributes truly reflect an employee's job performance, but it is more likely that the attributes predict the person's *potential* to perform well rather than his or her actual performance. Put simply, possessing an attribute does not necessarily mean that an employee is using it to perform better and help the organization achieve its goals. To overcome this limitation, some companies rely on behavior-based approaches that emphasize examining the extent to which employees actually display certain behaviors on the job. The most common approaches are the critical incident approach, forced-choice approach, behaviorally anchored rating scales (BARSs), and behavioral observation scales.

In the **critical incident approach**, the evaluation criteria consist of statements or examples of "exceptionally good" or "poor" performance employees display over the course of the evaluation period. One of the primary advantages of focusing on critical incidents is that the emphasis is on actual behaviors rather than traits employees display on the job. Because of this emphasis, raters have clear examples to refer to when evaluating employees. However, to effectively use a critical incident approach, managers must keep track of their employees' behaviors. Although this might be easy to do when a manager is responsible for only a few employees, it grows exponentially more difficult as the number of employees being evaluated by a manager increases. In addition, raters might not be in a good position to monitor employee behavior throughout the day or over time. Sales managers provide a good example. Often, sales representatives work remotely. Because the sales reps are out of the office for an extended period of time, the manager is not in a position to regularly observe many of these employees' behaviors.

When managers use the **forced-choice** approach, they must choose among a set of alternative statements regarding the ratee. As Exhibit 9.6 shows, each statement is designed to be equally favorable or unfavorable. The rater is forced to pick the statement that is most reflective of the individual's job performance. In many cases, the statements viewed as "higher" from the company's point of view might not be known to the rater; the rater simply picks the most accurate statement. The idea here is to mitigate the chances of bias creeping into the evaluation—that is, the chances a manager will rate people either particularly high or low, or otherwise fall prey to other rating errors.[19] However, each statement actually has a predetermined value assigned to it reflecting its relative value to the organization and distinguishing exceptional employee behaviors from poor employee behaviors.[20] After a manager has chosen among the statements, each employee is scored to determine his or her overall evaluation of the individual's performance.

**critical incident approach**
a behavior-based evaluation approach where the evaluation criteria consist of statements or examples of exceptionally good or poor performance employees display over the course of the evaluation period

**forced-choice**
a behavior-based evaluation approach where managers must choose among a set of alternative statements regarding the person being rated

## EXHIBIT 9.6

### Example of the Forced-Choice Approach

| (1) _____ Is effective | (OR) | _____ Is efficient |
|---|---|---|
| (2) _____ Follows directions | (OR) | _____ Takes the initiative |
| (3) _____ Turns in work on time | (OR) | _____ Turns in high-quality work |

**EXHIBIT 9.7**

Example of a Behaviorally Anchored Rating Scale (BARS)

| Performance Dimensions | | *Prepared for Class:* **The extent to which the professor is well prepared to lead a class discussion on a particular topic and answer students' question.** |
|---|---|---|
| High | 5 | Professor has examples from recent news stories relevant to the topic. Professor is familiar with the assigned reading material. PowerPoint slides are well developed prior to class discussion. |
| | 4 | PowerPoint slides are well developed prior to class discussion, and professor is familiar with the assigned reading material. |
| Average | 3 | Professor is familiar with the assigned reading material and has some PowerPoint slides prepared for class. |
| | 2 | Professor is familiar with the assigned reading material but does not have PowerPoint slides prepared for class. |
| Low | 1 | Professor does not have any PowerPoint slides prepared for class discussion and is not familiar with the assigned reading material for the lecture. |

**behaviorally anchored rating scale (BARS)**

a behavior-based evaluation approach where raters must evaluate individuals along a number of performance dimensions with each performance rating standard anchored by a behavioral example.

One approach that integrates some of the advantages of the graphic rating scales and the critical incident approach is the **behaviorally anchored rating scale (BARS)**. Similar to graphic rating scales, BARS require raters to evaluate individuals along a number of performance dimensions. However, a BARS goes beyond a graphic rating scale by anchoring each of the rating standards with a particular type of behavior that warrants a specific rating. So, instead of simply choosing between "below average" and "above average" ratings, the rater associates each rating score with a specific example of an actual behavior that typifies "below average," "average," or "above average" performance.[21] Exhibit 9.7 shows an example of a BARS used to evaluate how prepared college professors are for their classes.

One of the major advantages of the BARS approach is that it gives all raters a frame of reference for evaluating each dimension of an employee's performance.[22] Thus, the consistency of performance ratings across different raters should improve. The main disadvantage of the approach is that it takes more time and effort to develop the behavioral anchors for a BARS. Although information for a BARS can be collected from many sources, including the ratee,[23] collecting all the information, as well as writing and scaling the critical incidents for each dimension of all of a firm's jobs can be time-consuming for managers and expensive for the company.[24] Moreover, BARS are job specific. As a result, a distinct BARS evaluation form needs to be created for each job.

**behavioral observation scale (BOS)**

a behavior-based evaluation approach that requires raters to evaluate how often an employee displays certain behaviors on the job

The BARS approach requires raters to evaluate whether an employee displays certain behaviors on the job. A **behavioral observation scale (BOS)** requires raters to evaluate how *often* an employee displays certain behaviors on the job. Similar to BARS, BOSs are based on critical incidents that differentiate high and low job performance. The primary difference between the two is that raters are able to assess the frequency by which a wide array of different behaviors, related to specific performance dimensions, are displayed on the job. Exhibit 9.8 shows an example of a BOS used to evaluate how prepared professors are for class.

## Results-Based Approaches

Rather than an attribute or a behavioral approach, some companies use results-based methods that rely on objective performance dimensions, such as production or quality measures. The measures are not necessarily tied to the job's specific tasks

## EXHIBIT 9.8

Example of a Behavioral Observation Scale (BOS)

| Prepared for Class: The extent to which the professor is well prepared to lead a class discussion on a particular topic and answer students' questions. | | | | | | | | |
|---|---|---|---|---|---|---|---|---|
| Performance Dimensions | Almost Never | | | Sometimes | | | Almost Always | |
| Professor has examples from recent news stories relevant to the topic. | 1 | | 2 | | 3 | | 4 | 5 |
| Professor is familiar with the assigned reading material. | 1 | | 2 | | 3 | | 4 | 5 |
| Professor's PowerPoint slides are well developed. | 1 | | 2 | | 3 | | 4 | 5 |
| Professor's PowerPoint slides are prepared in advance of the class. | 1 | | 2 | | 3 | | 4 | 5 |

and duties. They are tied to the outcomes employees achieve.[25] There are two primary results-based methods: the direct measures approach and management by objectives.

With a **direct measures approach**, managers measure the outcomes of their employees' work. The outcomes could be related to factors such as sales, productivity, or absenteeism. Because the approach focuses on quantifiable outcomes, the results are very clear and meaningful when the right measures are evaluated. For example, sales revenues generated are clearly an important indicator of an employee's sales performance in a retail establishment, so long as the focus is on making sales that help achieve organizational goals and not solely on making sales for the sake of achieving the goal. What we mean is the following: A sales associate with a set goal of sales revenues of $50,000 per month needs to understand that any product returns from customers will be deducted from his total sales. Otherwise, the sales rep, to meet his goal, could pressure customers into purchases they later regret and end up returning for a refund.

As with the other approaches discussed here, there are several limitations to the direct measures approach. First, not all jobs are associated with easily identifiable, objective outcome measures. What objective outcomes exist for a guidance counselor, a receptionist, or even a manager? Should receptionists be evaluated based on how many calls they answer? Or should they be evaluated on a more subjective behavioral dimension, such as how they handle the calls? Second, focusing solely on certain outcomes can lead to other outcomes being neglected. For example, overemphasizing sales in a retail outlet might create a disincentive for the store's employees to help one another. The associates might figure that if they take the time to help another colleague, their sales will suffer.

**Management by objectives (MBO)** is another results-based approach for performance management. Rather than focusing on direct measures of performance, managers using the MBO approach meet with their employees and jointly set goals for the employees to accomplish during a particular time period. Ideally, the goals that are specified are objective in nature and easy to measure. At the end of the evaluation period, the rater and the ratee meet again to discuss the ratee's performance during the review time period. If the ratee met or exceeded the goals, the evaluation is positive; if the ratee failed to meet the goals, the evaluation is less favorable. As you might imagine, some jobs are not very conducive to the MBO approach because they lack objective or quantifiable goals tied to employee performance. Another potential problem is that if the goals are set too narrowly, employees are likely to strive to meet

**direct measures approach**

a results-based evaluation approach in which managers measure the outcomes of employees' work such as their sales, productivity, or absenteeism

**management by objectives (MBO)**

a results-based evaluation approach where managers meet with their employees and jointly set goals for the employees to accomplish during a particular time period

only those targets and neglect other aspects of their jobs that are not directly evaluated. Despite the drawbacks, the MBO approach is a powerful method for helping raters and ratees agree on what goals are most important and the performance levels needed to meet them.

## Sources of Performance Data

There are many different sources of data to use for a firm's performance management system. Next, we discuss each one separately.

### Supervisors

Because supervisors are ultimately responsible for the performance of the employees who they oversee, it's logical that they would be a key source of performance data. Indeed, supervisors are often in a good position to provide such data. However, as we have explained, this ability depends on the opportunities that the supervisors have to actually observe their employees' performance. Put simply, managers might not have the time to constantly monitor what their employees do throughout the day, nor do they always work in close proximity to them. As a result, the data they provide generally include only what they were able to observe, and that data may not necessarily represent the full picture of an employee's performance.

### Coworkers

In a team work environment, or when employees perform interdependent tasks and have related responsibilities, their peers are often in a unique position to comment on certain aspects of their performance. For example, they may be more able to comment on how well employees cooperate and support others, as well as their actual task performance, better than their supervisors. An employee's coworkers are also likely to have a solid understanding of the particular challenges associated with their jobs. Managers face several potential downsides when they try to collect performance data generated by coworkers, however. First, if the coworkers are close friends, or if they do not like each other, their interpersonal relationships might influence their ratings of one another. Second, there are also concerns when peer evaluations are used in an administrative context. If employees have to rate each other and those ratings are used to make decisions about raises or promotions, coworkers will have an incentive to rate other employees lower to make themselves look better. That is the reason why many firms use coworkers' evaluations for developmental purposes rather than administrative purposes.

### Self-Appraisals

**self-appraisal**

the process of an employee evaluating his or her own performance

A **self-appraisal** occurs when an employee evaluates his or her own performance. People are generally very aware of how they are performing their jobs on a daily basis. As a result, self-appraisals can be a useful source of data. Of course, the obvious drawback of using self-appraisals is that employees will have an incentive to artificially inflate their own evaluations, particularly if the data are to be used for administrative purposes. At the same time, however, asking individuals to reflect on their own performance can be a very useful starting point and developmental tool to help employees improve their own performance.

### Subordinates

Many jobs in organizations require the supervision and oversight of others. In these positions, it is important to assess how well the supervisor is doing in terms of managing his or her employees. Therefore, another source of performance data is to ask subordinates to rate their supervisors. Understanding how the employees view their manager is useful information that might not otherwise be available to middle or upper management. This type of information is especially important. One of the most common reasons given for employees leaving an organization is their relationship with their immediate supervisor.

As you can imagine, however, there are challenges related to using these data. For example, subordinates may fear that their managers will retaliate if they say anything negative about them. The problem is likely to be magnified if the information subordinates provide isn't kept anonymous, or if employees think their managers might be able to tie comments directly back to them[26]—which can happen if a manager has only a few subordinates. Second, it is important to be sure to separate how well liked a supervisor is from how good he or she is at supervising. A supervisor might be very well liked by her subordinates, but not very good at getting them to work as hard and effectively as possible. Third, if the evaluations provided by a manager's subordinates are weighted too heavily, the manager will have an incentive to put the satisfaction of his employees first rather than put the firm's goals first.

## Customer Evaluations

Customers can also be a good source of performance data. Automobile manufacturers, hotels, restaurants, and many other service industries often try to gather customer information regarding the performance of their employees, supervisors, and business units. Because customer satisfaction is a critical determinant of a company's success, it makes sense to ask customers for input. However, you need to consider several challenges related to gathering customer-generated data. First, the data might not be equally relevant for all jobs. Consider a restaurant: Gathering data from customers related to the performance of servers is clearly appropriate— after all, servers directly affect the quality and enjoyment of customers' dining experiences. However, gathering data from customers related to the performance of the restaurant's dishwashers might not be as appropriate (unless there are problems with dirty dishes). Second, trying to reach out to busy customers and provide them an incentive to take the time to complete a survey or answer questions about the performance of employees can be time consuming and expensive. Moreover, if some customers don't respond to your questions or surveys, you're less likely to get a complete picture of your employees' performance. Customers with particularly bad or particularly good experiences with your firm are more likely than others to provide information. Despite these challenges, incorporating customer data into your performance management process is often an excellent idea. Just remember to ensure that a representative sample of customers participate in the process.

## 360-Degree Appraisals

As you have learned, there are many different sources for performance data, each with its own advantages and disadvantages. In an attempt to try to capture relevant data from different sources, some companies use **360-degree appraisals.** This approach involves gathering performance data from as many sources as possible—- supervisors, peers, subordinates, and customers. Because this approach tends to be very comprehensive, the performance of employees is more accurately depicted. As you can imagine, however, sorting through all the performance data can be cumbersome. Indeed, one of the primary disadvantages of the 360-degree appraisal approach is the time it takes for managers to make sense of the different, and sometimes conflicting, information. After all, different raters are likely to observe different dimensions of an individual's performance or have in mind different standards of effectiveness when rating the person.[27] For example, a person's peers might think an individual is performing well in terms of his or her cooperation. Meanwhile, the employee's subordinates and supervisors might be less enthusiastic about her productivity. Whose perspective is more accurate? Despite these problems, many companies such as Kellogg's utilize 360-degree appraisals.[28] In fact, more than 85% of Fortune 500 companies use 360-degree appraisals in their leadership development programs.[29]

**360-degree appraisal**

a comprehensive measurement approach that involves gathering performance data from as many sources as possible—supervisors, peers, subordinates, and customers

**EXHIBIT 9.9**

Example of the Impact of Different Weights in Evaluations

| Performance Dimension | Employee Ratings | Equal Weight | Scores | Example 1: Adjusted Weights | Scores | Example 2: Adjusted Weights | Scores |
|---|---|---|---|---|---|---|---|
| Clearly conveys course material | 1 | 20% | 0.20 | 30% | 0.30 | 50% | 0.50 |
| Is prepared for class | 3 | 20% | 0.60 | 30% | 0.90 | 20% | 0.60 |
| Maintains an entertaining class | 5 | 20% | 1 | 20% | 1 | 10% | 0.50 |
| Provides excellent feedback | 5 | 20% | 1 | 10% | 0.50 | 10% | 0.50 |
| Grades fairly | 3 | 20% | 0.60 | 10% | 0.30 | 10% | 0.30 |
| *Total Score* | | | *3.4* | | *3* | | *2.4* |

Evaluation Ratings:
1 = poor, 2 = slightly below average, 3 = average, 4 = slightly above average, 5 = outstanding

## Weighting Performance Criteria

One thing to consider when evaluating the performance of employees is the relative importance, or *weight*, of each performance dimension. In every organization, each job differs in terms of how it adds value to the company. In some jobs, the *quantity* of products produced is most important. In other jobs, the *quality* of the products produced is of utmost concern. Some jobs require high levels of employee cooperation and teamwork, while others require high levels of creativity and innovation. To complicate matters further, each job comprises multiple performance dimensions that vary in terms of their relative importance.

Recall our performance evaluation for a college professor. What are the key performance dimensions of a good professor? Being prepared for each class is certainly an important dimension of teaching, but is it enough? What about the quality of the lecture? You also have to consider how responsive the professor is to students' questions, as well as how fairly the professor grades exams. How much weight should each performance dimension carry?[30] Should being an entertaining teacher be as important as conveying knowledge in a way that enhances students' learning? Both are relevant, but are they equally relevant?

Exhibit 9.9 provides an example of how decisions you make regarding the relative weights of different performance dimensions affect an employee's evaluation. As you can see, the overall score for a single employee will vary, depending on how the performance dimensions are weighted. In this example, the college professor would receive the highest evaluation score when all the performance dimensions are weighted equally. When the weights are adjusted, as in Examples 1 and 2 in Exhibit 9.9, the professor's summary score changes. These adjustments obviously have important implications for administrative issues such as promotion decisions and merit raises for employees. As a result, employees are likely to be particularly sensitive to how the dimensions of their jobs are weighted. In fact, employees may have an incentive to focus their energies on some job dimensions at the expense of others. In Example 2 in Exhibit 9.9, if clearly conveying course material represents half the evaluation score, it is reasonable to expect that teachers may disproportionately focus their energies on that aspect of their job, perhaps at the expense of grading fairly or providing excellent feedback to students. Given that most jobs are multidimensional, managers need to take the time to think about which dimensions, if any, are more important than others, and adjust the relative weight placed on each accordingly.

## Performance Measurement Errors

As discussed in Chapter 7, when people make hiring decisions, certain biases can creep into the process.[31] The same is true when it comes to the performance management process. A manager commits the **halo error** when her overall positive view of an employee's performance biases the ratings that she gives the person on the individual criteria that make up his performance.[32] In contrast, a manager commits the **devil's horn error** when his overall negative view of an employee biases his ratings such that the individual receives lower ratings on specific performance dimensions than she really merits. The **contrast effect** occurs when a manager artificially inflates or deflates an employee's rating after comparing the person to another individual. For example, an employee with average performance might get a higher rating than he deserves if he is compared to an employee with poor performance; or an employee with average performance might get rated lower than she deserves if she is compared to an employee with outstanding performance.

There are several additional potential errors worth noting. The **primacy error** reflects situations in which a rater's earlier impressions of an individual bias her later evaluations of the person. For example, if a rater has an early positive impression of an employee, the rater might pay particular attention to later performance information that is consistent with that impression and discount information that is inconsistent with that impression. In contrast, a **recency error** reflects situations in which a rater narrowly focuses on an employee's performance that occurs near the time of the evaluation. **Similar-to-me errors** occur when managers rate employees who resemble them in some way more highly than they rate more dissimilar employees. For example, if the manager and ratee both went to a particular college, have similar opinions, or simply have similar personalities, the manager might artificially inflate her evaluation of the individual because of the similarity. Put simply, there is a tendency for individuals to be more favorable of others who are more like them than different from them, and this tendency can creep into their measurements.

Some raters may also commit restriction of range or distributional errors. As noted earlier in this chapter, raters often must evaluate individual performance along one scale or other. For example, raters may be asked to assess the extent to which individual employees are "poor," "average," or "outstanding." Sometimes raters have a tendency to commit leniency, strictness, or central tendency errors. Raters commit the **leniency error** when they consistently rate employees on the higher end of the scale—that is, rating everyone as a "4" or a "5" on a 5-point scale.[33] In contrast, they commit the **strictness error** when they consistently rate employees on the low end of the scale—such as rating everyone as a "1" or a "2" on a 5-point scale. When raters evaluate everyone as average, regardless of their actual performance level, they commit the **error of central tendency**, which reflects the unwillingness of raters to rate individuals as very high or very low. In these situations, for example, a manager may rate all her employees as a "3," or "average," out of 5 points. Some organizations encourage this rating by not requiring an explanation if an employee is rated as average.[34]

There are several steps companies can take to reduce the chances that these biases will occur. As noted earlier in this chapter, one approach is to incorporate more specificity into the rating formats. Defining more precisely what is being evaluated helps raters focus more on the relevant performance dimensions. A second approach

**halo error**
a bias that occurs when a positive characteristic of a person affects the evaluation of the person's other attributes

**devil's horn error**
a bias that occurs when a negative characteristic of a person affects the evaluation of the person's other attributes

**contrast effect**
a bias that results when an evaluation of one or more persons is artificially inflated or deflated when compared to the evaluation of another person

**primacy error**
a bias that occurs when a rater's earlier impressions of an individual bias his or her later evaluations of the person

**recency error**
a bias that occurs when a rater narrowly focuses on an employee's performance that occurs near the time of the evaluation

**similar-to-me errors**
a bias that occurs when evaluators rate employees who resemble them in some way more highly than they rate employees who are dissimilar

**leniency error**
a bias that occurs when a rater consistently rates employees on the higher end of an evaluation scale

**strictness error**
a bias that occurs when a rater consistently rates employees on the low end of an evaluation scale

**error of central tendency**
a bias that occurs when raters are unwilling to rate individuals as very high or very low on an evaluation scale

**frame-of-reference training**

training that aims to help raters understand performance standards and performance dimensions

is to train raters—to familiarize them with the errors that can occur and encourage them to avoid them.[35] A third approach, called **frame-of-reference training**, aims to help raters understand performance standards and performance dimensions.[36] This training helps raters understand and identify different standards or levels of performance. In essence, it is intended to calibrate, or align, different raters so that they will be able to reach a consensus on varying levels of performance.[37] This approach also helps raters develop common evaluation standards.[38] Finally, companies can use multiple raters. If one rater exhibits bias, having multiple raters helps smooth out the bias. Reducing bias is one of the reasons why firms use 360-degree appraisals.

# Step 4: Providing Feedback

The fourth step in an effective performance management system involves providing feedback to employees to help them improve their performance.[39] To be effective, the feedback must be provided in a timely manner and in a professional and positive way.

## When to Appraise Employees

Companies vary in terms of how often they provide performance feedback to their employees. Most supervisors are required to formally appraise their employees every six months or once a year. Providing feedback to your employees on an ongoing basis, however, is ideal. In fact, largely because millenials expect more frequent feedback, as already noted, more companies are moving to an approach for feedback that is more frequent than once or twice a year.[40] As a manager, if you don't provide ongoing feedback to your employees, the feedback you give them at the formal appraisal time may come as a surprise and be less well received and less effective. After all, how useful is it to tell your employees in a single meeting that they did something wrong six months ago, or that they have consistently been underperforming? Moreover, failing to let your employees know immediately that they did something wrong is implicitly telling them that their performance is satisfactory. In other words, they may not even realize that their performance is less than satisfactory. And, of course, the longer managers wait to discuss performance problems with their employees, the longer they and their firms will be forced to have to deal with the substandard behavior. Unfortunately, managers are typically very comfortable providing employees with positive feedback but are more reluctant to provide them with negative feedback. This reluctance exists even though the manager knows that the poorly performing employee will benefit the most from clear feedback and developing a plan for improving his performance.

## The Feedback Meeting

In addition to deciding when to formally appraise your employees, there are a number of factors managers need to consider when providing feedback. We discuss these factors next.

### Separating Evaluation from Development

Recall that from an administrative perspective, performance evaluations help managers make decisions regarding employees' salary adjustments, merit raises, and other incentive rewards. Managers also use performance evaluation information to help their employees develop and improve their performance. More than likely, your employees will not want to talk about how they can improve their performance while they are simultaneously lobbying you for a raise during a performance appraisal session. As a result, some companies schedule separate feedback meetings—one to help employees improve their performance and a second to make administrative decisions based on their performance.

### Targeting Behaviors or Outcomes Rather Than the Individual

A second major consideration for a feedback meeting is to separate the behaviors or outcomes of an employee's performance from the employee himself. For example, telling an employee that she didn't handle customer complaints well is more constructive than telling her she is a bad employee. By focusing on specific behaviors or outcomes, managers are more likely to be able to help employees identify specific areas to improve. Also, by not labeling employees as bad or good, employees are likely to be more open to their managers' suggestions as to how they might improve.

### Being Balanced in Your Appraisal

Recall that jobs generally consist of multiple performance dimensions. In most cases, employees' performance on their respective job dimensions will vary. It is quite likely that they will excel at some dimensions and have room for improvement on others. During an appraisal meeting, it is important to discuss the full spectrum of these dimensions. Even if an employee's overall performance rating is not satisfactory, you don't want to diminish the positive contributions the person has provided. In fact, you want to encourage the person to continue to excel in those areas, while improving their performance on the dimensions that are not at a satisfactory level.

### Encouraging Employee Participation

When employees are active, rather than passive, participants in the appraisal process, they are likely to view the process as more fair and useful. Asking employees to share their thoughts on how well they perform different aspects of their jobs, as well as asking about what factors may have helped or constrained their performance, are important ways to engage employees in the feedback conversation. By doing so, you are signaling to an employee that your agenda is not simply to judge him, but to help him improve. And by engaging him and considering his thoughts and concerns, you are taking positive steps toward creating an open dialogue regarding the person's development. This approach is a critical component for the last step of the performance management process—developing an action plan.

## Step 5: Developing Action Plans to Improve Employee Performance

Simply providing employees with feedback about their performance is not enough to improve it. Rather, effective managers take another step: They work with their employees to diagnose the source of any performance problems that they might have and help devise strategies to remedy them. Doing so, however, requires a clear understanding of the nature of the performance deficiency, the development of a plan to address the performance problems, and, when necessary, effective discipline of employees.

### Understanding the Causes of Poor Performance

As Exhibit 9.1 shows, the contributions employees make are a function of their competencies, attitudes, behaviors, and work environments. Performance deficiencies can therefore be related to any of these three factors. For example, a performance problem might not be due to the amount of effort an employee is exerting, but rather the fact that she lacks certain knowledge, skills, and abilities. Punishing employees for performing poorly when they want to perform well and are working as hard as they can is not likely to be an effective way to help improve their performance.

Performance problems can stem from factors related to an employee's work environment. For example, salespeople in rural areas often have to drive long distances to call on their customers. As a result, the number of sales calls they're able to make per day will be fewer than, say, the number that salespeople located in New York City are able to make. Obviously, this difference is a factor related to their work environment—not their performance—and is out of their control. There may also be something related to the design of employees' jobs, the technology they use, or the support or performance of their coworkers that prevents them from achieving excellent performance levels. Think about a situation in which finishing a project depends on receiving information from others. If those supplying the information are tardy in providing it or don't provide accurate information, the employee completing the project is not going to succeed through no fault of her own.

Sometimes, however, the root of the problem does indeed stem from the amount of effort an employee is exerting. Dealing with lack of effort or lack of motivation requires a different approach than dealing with skill deficiencies or the work environment as the source of poor performance. When lack of motivation or effort is the case, the person's manager can respond in a variety of ways. One way is to tie employees' annual raises to their performance reviews. Another is to provide employees with explicit goals and certain rewards if they reach those goals. As we will discuss in Chapter 11, this type of incentive model can be quite effective at maximizing employees' performance. Alternatively, as a manager, you may work jointly with each employee to develop a plan of action to help improve the employee's performance.

## Taking Action

With a clear understanding of where performance deficiencies exist and a discussion with your employee about the potential causes of those performance deficiencies, you are in a position to jointly develop an action plan to help improve that performance.

The first step in developing an action plan is to examine ways to remove barriers to employee success—obstacles that make it difficult for employees to be successful in their jobs. If the performance evaluation and appraisal meetings identify competencies as the leading cause of poor performance, for example, then training and development activities may be a viable solution. As discussed in Chapter 8, managers can use training and development programs to address skill deficiencies that may contribute to poor performance. Coaching and mentoring are two training tactics that are particularly useful in helping employees improve. Coaching typically focuses on an employee's performance improvement (usually in the short term, and usually relative to specific skills). Mentoring involves a longer-term relationship in which a more senior employee teaches a junior employee how the organization works and nurtures that person as she progresses in her career.

If the cause of poor performance is a result of the work environment, the solution may rest in aspects of the work design. As discussed in Chapter 4, some factors to consider are the design of the job, the competencies of coworkers, and technological considerations that constrain what employees are able to do in their jobs. It might be the case that an employee is being asked to perform more tasks than is possible to complete in a single workday. Alternatively, the technology in place may limit how well she can perform on the job.

If the cause of poor performance isn't a result of competencies or the work environment, but rests with the level or quality of an employee's performance, the following are some actions you may pursue:

- *Review the performance dimensions with your employee.* Are your employees clear about what they are expected to do to be successful? Sometimes employee performance is not a function of competencies, the work environment, or even motivation. The problem is lack of clarity about what is expected. Employees simply may not have a full understanding of all the aspects of their job. When this is the case, a review of the job description should provide clarity as to what employees are to do in the course of their workday. You might also clarify which performance dimensions you measure, in order to signal to an employee what aspects of their jobs are most important.
- *Review the standards of performance with your employee.* Sometimes employees understand what is expected of them, but they do not have a firm grasp on what it means to be successful at each task. Your employees should be clear on the types of performance that are considered "poor," "average," and "good" for each performance dimension. This clarity might be accomplished through discussion of the evaluation measures and the types of attitudes or behaviors that are indicative of each potential rating. This level of clarity is a major benefit of the BARS evaluation form. A BARS has clear behavioral anchors that identify the differences between the ratings for each of the performance dimensions.
- *Ensure that the performance measures are accurate.* The performance evaluation may be contaminated, deficient, or inaccurate. In such a case, you might discuss with an employee ways to more accurately evaluate his or her performance on the job. You may also consider adjusting what is evaluated to make sure your measures reflect the full array of behaviors important to your firm.
- *Evaluate potential role concerns.* In Chapter 4, we discussed role conflict, role overload, role underload, and role ambiguity. If any of these are present, they may lead to diminished performance. Employees may have conflicting pressures from their supervisor, customers, and colleagues that prevent them from performing all their tasks effectively. If this is the case, it might be useful to consider how to provide additional support to help balance these roles, or to consider how the job might be redesigned to allow employees to succeed in their job.

The second component of an action plan is to reach agreement on performance targets and timelines for achieving improved performance. For example, establishing clear targets of improvement, such as decreasing error rates by 10% or increasing sales by 10%, and setting a particular point in time for doing so provides clear goals for employees. This approach is much more constructive than simply telling employees to improve, and it provides employees with a benchmark to judge their improvements to see how they are progressing. In addition to using formal targets and timelines, effective managers engage in informal feedback and regular discussions with employees to see how they are doing in their jobs, and they work with them to continuously improve.

As a manager, you want to be supportive of the development of your employees, and if the steps you have taken are successful, the result will be a happier and more productive workforce. At the same time, however, it is important to recognize that employees must perform at an acceptable level, and failure to reach that level of performance over a reasonable period of time may indicate that an employee is not a good fit for the job. In situations in which the tactics we have discussed fail, managers may need to resort to discipline.

## Trends in Performance Management

Many organizations have realized that they have spent a lot of time and money on complex and rigid performance management systems that have not been effective in achieving company goals. As a result, a large number of organizations are revising their performance management systems. Increasingly, employers are seeking simplicity and focusing on making their processes more agile, more developmental, and more focused on providing feedback more frequently. A significant part of the changes occurring involve moving away from once or twice-a-year formal performance reviews to more frequent feedback check-ins in the form of conversational discussions that create a greater line of sight to company goals. Company Spotlight 9.2 describes how Deloitte used evidence-based management to create a new performance management system for its 65,000 plus employees that meets these criteria.

Regardless of the new approach selected, employees are continuing to receive feedback, just more frequently, and the basic tenets of performance management described already remain applicable. An effective system needs clarity of purpose, clear identification of what will be measured and how that will be done, observation

## COMPANY SPOTLIGHT **9.2**

### Using Evidence-Based Management to Change the Performance Management Process at Deloitte

An analysis of the performance management process at Deloitte yielded the following results: Each year, Deloitte was spending 2 million staff hours on setting performance goals, completing evaluation forms, and conducting formal reviews. Even with this investment of time, the process was not in sync with organizational objectives. As a result of the in-depth analysis, the company decided to take a simpler approach to its performance management process. Gone are once-a-year-reviews, 360-feedback tools, and objectives flowing downward from upper management. The focus now is on speed, agility, constant learning, and new ways of collecting data.

Before the changes, the company set objectives at the beginning of the year for each of its over 65,000 employees. Once a project was completed, each employee's manager would evaluate the employee's performance relative to her objectives. The manager would indicate if the employee excelled or did not excel. The end-of-project evaluations then factored into the year-end employee rating. The year-end rating came out of a complex consensus meeting process involving discussions of hundreds of employees relative to their peers. Each employee had an assigned counselor to represent him in these consensus meetings. While employees saw the process as fair, the company realized that this once-a-year process was less relevant in today's dynamic work environment. This awareness, along with an examination of the research on performance ratings and a study of high-performing teams at Deloitte, fueled the desire to find a better, more effective approach to performance management.

In designing its new process, Deloitte began by clarifying the purpose of performance management at the company. The outcome of this process was the identification of three objectives: to recognize (compensation and promotions), see (performance snapshots), and fuel (strengthen) performance. The new system is still a work in progress but is driven by clarity of purpose. Employees receive more ongoing, future-focused feedback, and they have greater opportunity to work to their strengths. Additionally, the process itself now can be more responsive to changing organizational objectives. After two years in place, the company already had data demonstrating the positive impact of the changes.

*Sources:* Buckingham, Marcus, and Goodall, Ashley, "Reinventing Performance Management," *Harvard Business Review*, April 2015, https://hbr.org/2015/04/reinventing-performance-management; Bank, Erica, "Reinventing Performance Management at Deloitte," https://www.td.org/insights/reinventing-performance-management-at-deloitte.

of employee performance, clear and accurate and ongoing feedback to the employee, and employee development plans designed for continuous improvement. An important component of any effective performance management system is ensuring it drives results and enables the company to have a competitive advantage. If that can be done with a more agile and simpler system, and often it can, then that should happen. The company will save time and money and have better results. Many companies are finding that to be the case.[41]

## Disciplining Employees

You probably think of discipline as negative actions taken by managers, with actions such as excessive tardiness, absenteeism, dishonesty, theft, and violence warranting serious and immediate discipline. However, discipline can also be positive in nature because it's designed to encourage employees to behave appropriately at work. A useful way to think about discipline is that it sends a strong signal to employees about how they should behave or otherwise perform at work. There are two prominent approaches to discipline: progressive discipline and positive discipline.

### Progressive Discipline

**Progressive discipline** refers to a process by which an employee with disciplinary problems progresses through a series of disciplinary stages until the problem is corrected.[42] As shown in Exhibit 9.10, there are typically four steps in this process. In the first step, the employee receives a verbal warning stating that his or her behavior or performance is not acceptable. The second stage involves writing up a reprimand, giving it to the employee, and documenting it in his or her personnel file. If the problem remains, the third stage of the progressive discipline is suspension. Finally, if the problem continues, the final stage is termination. Of course, companies bypass these stages if the problem is gross misconduct at work. Stealing, fighting, drug use, violence, and the like often result in immediate termination rather than progressive discipline being administered.

The primary advantages of progressive discipline are that it clearly informs employees that there is a problem and provides them with the opportunity to improve their performance. If a problem is corrected, there is no need to take further disciplinary steps. One criticism of progressive discipline, however, is that it puts a priority on punishment rather than corrective action. Therefore, some companies instead use positive discipline.

**progressive discipline**
a process by which an employee with disciplinary problems progresses through a series of disciplinary stages until the problem is corrected

### Positive Discipline

With **positive discipline**, the disciplinary process is not punitive; rather, it focuses on constructive feedback and encourages employees to take responsibility for trying to improve their behaviors or performance at work. The key to positive discipline

**positive discipline**
a disciplinary process that is not punitive but focuses on constructive feedback and encourages employees to take responsibility for trying to improve their behaviors or performance at work

## EXHIBIT 9.10

### Steps of Progressive and Positive Discipline

|        | Progressive Discipline | Positive Discipline |
|--------|------------------------|---------------------|
| Step 1 | Verbal warning | The employee and manager verbally agree as to how the employee must improve. |
| Step 2 | Written reprimand | The manager and employee hold a follow-up meeting and outline a new action plan; written documentation is kept. |
| Step 3 | Suspension | Employee is given a final warning of termination. |
| Step 4 | Termination | Termination occurs. |

is to help employees identify their problems early and address the causes of their problematic behavior. As Exhibit 9.10 shows, like progressive discipline, positive discipline also consists of four steps. The first step involves getting the employee and his or her manager to verbally agree about how to improve the problem. The second step involves having another meeting to explore why the problem was not corrected and to arrive at a new action plan. At this stage, there is written documentation of the meeting and a plan to address the problem. The third step involves a final termination warning. If the problem is not rectified, the final step, termination, occurs.

The steps in Exhibit 9.10 appear to be similar for both progressive and positive disciplinary procedures. However, positive discipline utilizes employee counseling. Essentially, it uses problem solving instead of punishment. The advantages of positive discipline are that the meetings are more constructive for employees, and employees feel that they are being treated with respect. The disadvantage, however, is that it requires more time and effort by managers to administer the process. Moreover, not every manager is adept at functioning in a counseling role. The results of using positive discipline, however, can be impressive. Verizon reduced all grievances by 63% and disciplinary grievances by 86% in the year after they installed the positive discipline approach, Tampa Electric Company (TECO) reduced sick-leave hours per employee from 66.7 in the year before implementation to 31.2 eight years later, and the Texas Department of Mental Health saw turnover drop from 48.5% to 31.3% to 18.5% in the two years following implementation.[43]

A few caveats are worth noting regarding discipline. First, employees must clearly understand the rules, regulations, and procedures in order for any discipline to be effective. In other words, they need to know they are doing something wrong. As discussed in the previous section, this information may be addressed simply by having a performance appraisal with an employee to discuss the situation. Doing so may avoid unnecessary discipline by helping to effectively manage performance expectations. Second, the discipline should happen swiftly. Why? When employees aren't disciplined immediately for a problem, they often don't know the problem exists, and it may be unreasonable to expect them to correct it.

Principles

Practice

# Performance Management in Practice: Organizational Demands

As shown in Exhibit 9.11, while the basic principles of performance management apply to all companies, how performance management systems are designed and implemented are likely to vary across contexts. Because each company is unique and operates in a distinct context, it is important to examine how firms use performance management systems in light of their strategies, company characteristics, cultures, and employee concerns. We'll start with organizational demands.

## Strategy and Performance Management

A firm's strategy affects the specific performance dimensions the company emphasizes and the methods it uses to evaluate its employees. Let's look at each of these factors more closely.

### Which Performance Dimensions Are Emphasized

Earlier in this chapter, we discussed the fact that each job within a company comprises multiple performance dimensions. However, the importance of each dimension is likely to vary based on the company's strategy. A key task for a manager is to consider

**EXHIBIT 9.11**

Performance Management in Practice

| Context | Practice Issues |
|---|---|
| **Organizational Demands** | |
| *Strategy* drives . . . | • Which performance dimensions are emphasized |
| | • The performance evaluation method used |
| *Company characteristics* determine . . . | • Which performance evaluation method is used |
| | • Who carries out the process |
| *Culture* establishes . . . | • The objective of the performance management system |
| | • Which evaluation approach is used |
| | • Effectiveness of performance management approaches |
| *Employee concerns* include . . . | • Perceptions of procedural and distributive justice |
| | • Employees' responsiveness to performance feedback |
| | • Achieving work/life balance |
| **Environmental Demands** | |
| *Labor force* influences . . . | • Accuracy of performance evaluations |
| | • The need to evaluate diversity efforts |
| *Technology* affects . . . | • The performance management process |
| | • How telecommuters are evaluated |
| *Globalization* impacts . . . | • What is evaluated |
| | • The acceptability of the performance management system |
| | • Who provides performance data |
| *Ethics/social responsibility* shapes . . . | • Employees' perceptions of the performance management system |
| | • How employees react to surveillance and monitoring |
| | • How ethically employees behave at work |
| **Regulations** | |
| *Regulations* guide . . . | • Efforts to reduce discrimination in the performance management process |
| | • The importance of documenting employee performance |

his or her company's strategy when deciding how much weight to place on the different performance dimensions to reflect how jobs add value to the company. Consider the job of a sales representative in a call center in a company with a strategy that emphasizes low costs and high volume of sales calls. Now, compare this job to one in a call center in a company whose strategy emphasizes customer service. In the cost-oriented company, call center representatives will add more value when they make more phone calls. In contrast, in the company with a customer service strategy, the quality of the interaction between a representative and a customer is likely to be of the utmost concern. As a result, managers in the two call centers are likely to weight each performance dimension related to a sales representative's performance differently.[44]

### The Performance Evaluation Method Used

In addition to which performance dimensions are emphasized, a company's strategy influences the performance evaluation method used. Recall that managers can use a comparative approach, an absolute approach, or a results-based approach. Each approach affects how employees do their jobs. Consider the job of a software engineer. How might the three performance evaluation approaches affect how a software engineer performs her job? A comparative approach is likely to foster a competitive climate, in which employees strive to achieve a high ranking by outperforming their coworkers at the expense of helping each other. With an absolute approach, each software engineer is evaluated based on his or her attributes (coding skills, knowledge of the products, etc.) and behaviors (engaging with customers, participation on project teams, etc.), so strife among employees will be less of a problem.

Which approach should be used? The strategy of a company might lead its managers to emphasize one approach over another. If individual output is the primary objective, the firm's managers might be inclined to use a comparative approach to signal to employees the importance of writing a lot of code. However, if innovation and quality project completion are important, a comparative approach might give employees a disincentive to help one another out. And if customer satisfaction is the strategy, a behavioral approach might allow managers to evaluate their employees based on how much code they write, as well as how they work with each other. We can imagine similar concerns in other jobs as well. In a production facility, for example, the extent to which employees focus on production volume, the quality of production, or teamwork will reflect the strategic priorities of the company and affect which evaluation approach is used.

## Company Characteristics and Performance Management

Which performance evaluation approach is used and who carries out the performance management activities are influenced by a company's size and stage of development.

### Which Performance Evaluation Approach Is Used

The size of a company directly influences the feasibility of using each performance evaluation approach. As discussed earlier, one of the major advantages of a comparative approach is that it allows managers to rank order employees. It's easier for managers in small companies to realistically know how well employees perform relative to one another. However, as companies grow and hire more employees, comparing each of them to one another becomes less feasible. Consider the challenges of using a comparative approach in a company with 10 employees as opposed to a company with 1,000 employees. With 10 employees, most managers could probably rank order the employees with a pretty high level of accuracy. But the addition of each employee exponentially increases the number of comparisons that have to be made. In addition, managers will be in less of a position to monitor their employees closely. As a result, the accuracy of the rankings is likely to diminish.

Larger companies are in a better position than small companies to use absolute performance evaluation approaches. Doing so also provides employees with more specific information about how well they are doing along a variety of performance dimensions. However, developing an absolute performance evaluation system is often time consuming and expensive. For example, it might not be the best investment for a small firm with only three employees to incur the expense associated with designing a BARS. However, a company with a larger number of employees may be able to realize a greater return on investment (ROI), especially if there are a lot of employees performing the same job. Spreading the costs of developing the system across 1,000 employee evaluations is much more feasible than across three employee evaluations. Moreover, larger companies and more mature companies are likely to have more financial resources at their disposal to allocate to develop absolute performance evaluation systems. Also, as we pointed out earlier, performance management processes are changing.

The companies leading the change are usually larger companies, including Cisco, IBM, and Patagonia, with more formalized systems already and more resources for experimentation.[45]

### Who Carries Out the Process

A company's size affects who carries out the performance evaluation process. Smaller and less-well-established companies are less likely to have support staff or HR departments to help design and implement their performance management systems. Rather, in these organizations, line managers are likely to be expected to perform these duties.[46] As companies grow and become more mature, they are likely to add HR staff or at least hire consultants to develop or revise the performance management process. This involvement of HR isn't to say that managers in larger organizations don't participate in the performance management process; rather, the amount of administrative support available to them is simply likely to be greater.

## Culture and Performance Management

A company's culture influences the purpose of the performance management process in several ways. First, it influences the choice of evaluation approach that managers will use. Second, how employees perceive the firm's cultural values will affect how they react to those approaches.

### The Objective of the Performance Management System

Suppose you work for a company that has a highly competitive culture, and managers emphasize that employees either succeed or look elsewhere for work. In an environment such as this, an administrative approach to performance management might be consistent with the firm's culture. In contrast, in cultures that prioritize the well-being of employees and their long-term employment, managers may be more likely to focus on developmental approaches.[47]

### Which Evaluation Approach Is Used

Given its culture, which performance evaluation approach should a firm use? Each of the primary performance evaluation approaches (comparative, attribute, behavioral, and results) has different attributes. In a highly competitive, cutthroat culture such as that of the National Football League, a comparative approach may be preferred—and expected. In contrast, in a culture characterized by a concern for employee welfare and employee loyalty, such as not-for-profit organizations like the Red Cross, absolute approaches may be preferred. Similarly, focusing solely on results rather than how employees perform their jobs may run counter to a culture that strives for continuous improvement in employee performance. 3M, a company that prides itself on innovation, is a good example. Some of 3M's best products were actually created by accident.[48] MRY, a branding and technology giant, encourages its employees to build new things and chase their dreams to foster an entrepreneurial culture; thus, its performance management process has to encourage such behavior.[49]

### Effectiveness of Performance Management Approaches

Any discrepancy between a firm's cultural values and how its performance management system is designed can result in negative reactions by employees, as well as lower morale and greater turnover on their part. However, when a firm's performance management systems are consistent with its cultural values, the result is more likely to be a reinforcement of those values and a renewed focus on what is necessary for the company to succeed.

## Employee Concerns and Performance Management

An important perspective to consider in the performance management process relates to employee concerns. As we have stated numerous times already, a major goal of performance management is to encourage employees to work to help the company achieve its goals. When employees perceive that their performance management system is effective, they will be motivated to perform at a high level. For this perception to exist, a number of concerns need to be addressed when the system is designed or revised. These concerns include perceptions of procedural and distributive justice, the existence of potentially conflicting interests, and the impact of the performance management system on the work/life balance of employees.

### Perceptions of Procedural and Distributive Justice

The performance management process is one particular management activity that is subject to many instances of employees' justice perceptions. From a distributive justice perspective, when employees perceive that performance evaluations reflect their true performance during the evaluation period, they are more likely to accept the evaluation and work toward the company's goals. And when employees understand the rationale regarding why they received the performance evaluations they did, as well as what it would take to improve their performance, they are more likely to accept the evaluations and take steps to sustain or improve their performance.

Even if they agree with their evaluations (distributive justice), employees might disagree with different aspects of the performance management process (procedural justice) if it's not designed appropriately. Employees' perceptions of procedural justice can be affected throughout the performance management process. For example, if employees feel that their performance evaluations were deficient and failed to reflect the true scope of performance dimensions they perform, or if they feel that their performance evaluations included performance dimensions that were beyond their control or irrelevant to their job (contamination), they may view their evaluations as unfair. It is also possible that employees may believe that the performance standards set for them were too hard or that the process was biased. They might also question whether different raters were truly in a good position to evaluate their performance.[50] Alternatively, employees might not feel that they were provided with sufficient guidance as to how they would be evaluated or how performance problems they experienced would be handled.[51] Finally, employees might not believe they were given enough feedback to understand how to improve their performance or know which performance dimensions they should have focused on.[52]

As this discussion suggests, managers have to be concerned with both distributive and procedural justice in the performance management process. When distributive and/or procedural justice concerns emerge, the impact on employees may be significant. Most directly, when employees disagree with the evaluation or have concerns about how different stages of the evaluation process are carried out, the performance evaluation process is less likely to motivate them. Over time, this situation can lead to feelings of mistrust and anger, and it can affect employees' loyalty to the company.[53]

### Employees' Responsiveness to Performance Feedback

In addition to perceptions of procedural and distributive justice, how employees respond to performance management feedback in general can vary especially if they and their managers have different objectives for the performance evaluation process. As noted earlier, performance management systems can be used for developmental or administrative purposes. Both purposes are valuable to a company's success. However, they can lead to conflicting responses, particularly during performance reviews. On the one hand, managers might be required to rely on performance management systems to make decisions about promotions, merit raises, layoffs, and the like. On the other hand, employees might want to focus on the feedback and developmental functions of the performance management system to help improve their performance and earn higher ratings in the future.[54] Although employees might be open to critical feedback used for developmental purposes, they are less likely to be as open to the same feedback being used for administrative purposes, particularly when the evaluation is tied to outcomes such as pay and job security.[55]

### Achieving Work/Life Balance

Throughout the previous chapters, we have explored how achieving work/life balance is an increasing concern for many employees. We have also talked about the steps that companies can take to help employees realize this balance through policies such as flexible work schedules. The performance management system a company uses can reinforce or conflict with the other activities it implements to support the work/life balance needs of its employees. This conflict can be especially problematic if the amount of time employees need to put into their jobs to meet their performance standards requires them to spend less time at home or enjoying other personal activities.

A somewhat related concern stems from how the performance management process works when employees telecommute or work flexible hours. Traditionally, supervisors and employees work similar hours in the same location, providing their supervisors with the opportunity to observe them regularly. But how do supervisors or other evaluators gather performance data about employees if they aren't at work all the time? Employees might be concerned that their raters don't understand or appreciate the work they do off site, or they might think that there is a bias against individuals who work remotely or on different schedules. Alternatively, employees might discover that even though they've been given the opportunity to telecommute or modify their work schedules to accommodate their personal activities, if they take advantage of these programs, they are less likely to be evaluated highly by their managers.

## Performance Management in Practice: Environmental Influences

Influences in the external environment play a role in performance management. In particular, labor force trends, technology, globalization, and ethical considerations strongly influence the decisions managers must make about how the performance management processes in their firms should be implemented. Next, we discuss these issues.

## Labor Force Trends and Performance Management

As the workforce becomes more diverse, the performance management system used within a company may need to be reevaluated in terms of both the accuracy of the performance evaluations being administered and what is being evaluated.

### Accuracy of Performance Evaluations

When a firm uses a more subjective appraisal process, minority group members may have greater concerns about the fairness of the process.[56] Research has explored some of the possible fairness issues related to performance appraisals. In one study, researchers found that male employees reacted more unfavorably to performance appraisal feedback from female supervisors than from male supervisors.[57] Another study found that as the proportion of a company's workforce became more racially diverse, the effects race had on the company's performance ratings decreased.[58] This finding suggests that as the workforce becomes more diverse, the influence of diversity on performance management may diminish. Nevertheless, the concern is that managers may intentionally or unintentionally allow biases, such as the similar-to-me bias, to affect the outcome of performance reviews. Fortunately, there are steps companies can take to improve the accuracy and fairness of their evaluations. As noted earlier in this chapter, companies can incorporate more specificity into their rating formats, train raters to help them avoid biases,[59] and help raters understand the specific performance evaluation dimensions that need to be emphasized.

### The Need to Evaluate Diversity Efforts

If firms are going to take steps to embrace diversity and increase it within their organizations, they also must hold managers accountable for their diversity efforts,[60] as do companies such as Procter & Gamble, Allstate, and Texaco. There are several ways to include diversity efforts in the performance management process. Companies can track the number of women and minorities they have in managerial positions or positions targeted for diversity initiatives. The ability to develop employees with diverse backgrounds for higher-level positions can also be included as part of managers' performance evaluations. Alternatively, a company using a behavioral approach for performance feedback could ask a person's coworkers, subordinates, and supervisors to relate incidents that show how well the person works with and/or manages women and minorities. Although doing so can take some time and effort, it can help employees identify areas for improvement and increase their ability to work in a diverse environment.

## Technology and Performance Management

Advances in technology affect performance management in several ways. Managers must rethink how they evaluate employees who telecommute, how employee performance data are collected, and how employees receive feedback. Next, we discuss each of these aspects.

### The Performance Management Process

Companies use a wide array of technologies to monitor aspects of the performance of their employees, such as counting the number of keystrokes employees type or the number of calls they make and receive. The trucking industry makes extensive use of technology to monitor the movement of their trucks, locate vehicles, control speed, and keep track of driver speed, braking, cornering techniques, and unauthorized stops. Technology is available that provides an in-cab display in red, yellow, or green to reflect driver habits. While some truckers view the technology as an invasion of privacy, the industry sees it as increasing safety.[61] Managers can also use the Internet or their companies' intranets to administer online surveys to gather additional performance data from an employee's coworkers, vendors, subordinates, and even customers. Once all the data are collected electronically, the manager then can tabulate the results for a wider array of feedback to improve the accuracy of the performance evaluation.

Technology can also be used to provide employees with instant feedback about how they're doing in their jobs, allowing them to see their performance evaluations and track how well they are progressing toward goals.[62] Considering the fact that many companies provide formal employee feedback only semiannually or annually, the ability to dramatically increase the frequency with which feedback is given is certainly a valued improvement in the performance management process, and companies that are moving to more real-time feedback processes are increasingly

## COMPANY SPOTLIGHT  **9.3**

### Technology as an Enabler of Performance at Patagonia

Using an easy-to-use interface in a mobile app called COMPASS, developed by HighGround, Patagonia has implemented a new performance management process that has paid off well for the company. Patagonia designs and manufactures outdoor apparel and accessories and has a goal of being transparent with customers about its products and with employees about their performance. Before COMPASS, Patagonia had used technology to digitize the formal annual review process documents. The system was difficult to learn and use, and consequently, it was not well used.

After years of considering the best way to reboot the performance management process, the company implemented its new process with a focus on team-centric performance. As part of the process, employees use COMPASS and objectives and key results methodology to set financial and stretch goals. They check in at least quarterly with their managers. Year-end performance ratings are a thing of the past. Goal attainment leads to bonuses.

Initially, employees were reluctant to give candid feedback during their check-ins, but that has since changed, and developmental conversations are much more useful. Most important, the company has seen a positive relationship between both individual and teams on financial and talent measures when they use the regular check-in and feedback processes available.

In working with HighGround to develop the app, the company created a new mission for its performance development process: "to improve employee performance through effective goal settings that leveraged the crowd." The results so far indicate they are achieving their mission.

*Sources:* Sloan, Nathan, Agarwal, Dimple, Garr, Stacia, and Pastakia, Karen, "Performance Management: Playing a Winning Hand, 2017 Global Human Capital Trends," February 28, 2017, https://www2.deloitte.com/insights/us/en/focus/human-capital-trends/2017/redesigning-performance-management.html; Fisher, Anne, "How Patagonia Keeps Employee Turnover 'Freakishly Low'," June 9, 2016, http://fortune.com/2016/06/09/patagonia-employee-turnover/; Weinfurt, Andrea, "The Employee Development Honor Roll: Patagonia," HighGround Blog, October 16, 2016, https://www.highground.com/resource/blog/the-employee-development-honor-roll-patagonia.

relying on the technology to make that process easier.[63] As shown in Company Spotlight 9.3, technology has played a vital role in increasing the communication and feedback for employees at Patagonia.

### How Telecommuters Are Evaluated

In earlier chapters, we have discussed how technological advances have made it possible for many employees to telecommute. Telecommuting can complicate performance management: If employees are not at the office, how are they evaluated? After all, managers have less direct communication and face-to-face interaction with telecommuters than they have with in-house employees. Consequently, managers have less opportunity to personally evaluate the performance of telecommuters, which has several implications.[64] First, managers can simply rely on traditional evaluation techniques and do their best to gauge the performance of telecommuters. Of course, with limited ability to observe the performance of their telecommuting employees, the quality of the data that managers gather and the feedback they provide is likely to be limited.[65] A second option is to modify how employees are evaluated. For example, managers might try to focus on the outcomes, or results, telecommuters achieve rather than their behavior.[66] A word of caution is in order here: Shifting to an outcome-oriented evaluation approach might work for some jobs that have clearly identifiable and objective outcomes; however, for many jobs, how employees do their work is just as important as (if not more important than) any outcome measure. Consider customer service representatives who work from home. Should they be evaluated based on how many customer calls they handle or based on the degree to which they satisfy customers? Sykes Home provides customer care services for its global clients using representatives who work from their own homes. The performance evaluations for these employees include quality assurance testing, formal performance evaluations, and feedback provided to the customer care professionals.[67]

## Globalization and Performance Management

When designing an international performance management system, a key issue is whether individuals on an international assignment should be evaluated based on dimensions and standards used in their home country or those adjusted to reflect the host country's culture. A second key issue is what is the best way to evaluate international assignees? The reality is that working internationally creates a number of challenges regarding both the content of the performance management system and the process by which it is carried out.

### What Is Evaluated

In the United States, many companies evaluate their managers and employees on quantifiable criteria such as efficiency, quantity of production, and sales. However, elsewhere in the world the ability of a firm's employees to maximize their performance on the same dimensions can be affected by local conditions related to the political environment, union relations, country, infrastructure, social norms, and cultural differences.[68] For example, an employee's ability to increase his firm's sales at an international facility might be limited by the local economic conditions, currency valuations, or level of poverty in the country. If the employee's company fails to consider such factors, it is relying on a performance evaluation system that doesn't reflect the challenges the employee faces. Thus, the different dimensions of the job need to be reviewed to ensure that they capture the relevant aspects of an individual's performance.

Companies must also clearly communicate the standards of performance for the performance dimensions for which employees are held accountable. What does it mean to succeed on each performance dimension? While improving the bottom line might be an important dimension in both the home and host countries for evaluating a manager, the level of improvement in an international culture that is possible can vary dramatically. In addition, how long does it take to reach the objectives? If an employee is assigned to a new facility, it may take considerably longer for the person to reach her performance expectations than if she is assigned to an established facility. What is achievable in six months in one location may take more or less time in another location. The performance standards need to reflect these potential differences.

### The Acceptability of the Performance Management System

Cultural differences can influence the acceptability of different performance management systems.[69] Some countries, for example, tend to be more individualistic, whereas others are more collectivistic. Holding employees accountable for how they individually perform is generally quite acceptable in individualistic countries, such as the United States. However, a research study that included five regions around the world found individual appraisal of managers to be widespread across U.S. multinational companies (MNCs) and other MNCs in the five regions studied. This same study also found convergence across performance management practices in these regions, with a few exceptions. For instance, MNCs in the Nordic region were more likely to adopt forced distribution evaluations than were MNCs in other regions. The researchers offer the following explanation for this result. In the Nordic region, the strong protections for employment and income security likely prevent a forced distribution process from being perceived as threatening to employees, unlike how it might seem in other countries with fewer worker protections. Overall, the research suggests that performance management practices may not be quite as different based on culture as one might expect. That does not mean that companies should not pay attention to local customs, especially when wanting to understand how to evaluate and develop employees at lower levels in the organization. In some countries, these employees may place a higher value on social relations, teamwork, and helping each other succeed, and may have different preferences about how the process is structured. The Adidas Group found that employees in Asia preferred a more traditional and structured approach to performance reviews, while U.S. workers wanted a more agile approach.[70]

In addition, the means by which performance standards are achieved can vary. In some cultures it might be more critical to a company's success for its employees to spend more time developing relationships with the unions, communities, and local leaders there than focusing solely on aspects within the company.[71] In other words, it's quite possible that for an international assignment to be a success, an employee stationed abroad might have to utilize different mechanisms than she would need to use in her home country.[72] Thus, managers evaluating employees in such situations must be certain to consider which performance dimensions are most relevant, what the appropriate standards of performance are, how the employees will interpret the performance dimensions based on their cultural experiences, and how they may need to work differently to reach their performance objectives.

### Who Provides Performance Data

Who should provide the data related to how well an expatriate is performing? Should the person's manager at the company headquarters compile the data? Or should the manager rely on raters in the foreign country to which the expatriate is assigned? There are two factors that influence who should provide performance data. First, raters from different cultures are likely to interpret an employee's behaviors differently. They will be inclined to rely on their own cultural values, which may or may not be consistent with the values of the employee or the home culture.[73] For example, aggressiveness might be a valued employee trait in the home country but disdained by people in the host country.

However, if employees adjust their behaviors to fit the cultures to which they are assigned, how will their performance look to raters in their home countries? Or should the employees be evaluated by raters in their host countries? Whose perspective is likely to be more accurate?[74] The second factor relates to the opportunity to observe employees when the home country managers of expatriates, for example, are located in a different country than the expatriates. Obviously, the ability of managers to observe employees in this situation will be severely compromised.[75] Thus, it is unwise to rely on one rater to evaluate an international assignee given the potential biases that can emerge, as well as the limited opportunity the person's supervisor will have to observe the employee's performance. A more appropriate approach is to rely on multiple raters from both countries.[76]

## Ethics and Performance Management

The performance management system a firm has in place affects the perceptions the company's employees have about whether they are being treated ethically, whether the evaluation process is ethical, and how ethically employees act on the job.

### Employees' Perceptions of the Performance Management System

Because performance evaluations can significantly affect a firm's employees, as a manager you need to ensure that your performance management system is ethical.

Not surprisingly, there is considerable overlap between employees' perceived fairness of the performance management system and their views on the ethicality of the system in place. Employees will view a system that has both procedural and distributive fairness as being more ethical.[77] Whether employees are allowed to participate in the performance management process can also affect their perceptions of how ethical it is. In particular, providing employees with a channel to voice their concerns about the process, the opportunity to challenge or disagree with the ratings they receive, and a chance to meet with their supervisors to discuss any discrepancies will improve the perceived fairness and ethicality of the system.

### How Employees React to Surveillance and Monitoring

Because technological advances have given companies new ways to monitor and control their employees, privacy issues have emerged—particularly when it comes to employees' use of the Internet and email. Using computer programs such as Time Doctor, WorkiQ, Todoist, Desk Time, and Asana, companies are able to monitor what websites their employees visit and monitor the completion of tasks and time spent on tasks.[78] TechWiss, RescueTime, and Xerox are among the companies that have used these types of technology to monitor how much time their employees spend surfing the Web.[79] Some companies also record their employees' conversations and track the number of keystrokes. Although these actions are legal,[80] how employees, managers, and society view them from an ethical point of view is open to debate. Moreover, it is possible that the use of these systems, even when done for legitimate reasons, can lead employees to believe that their managers don't trust them. If employees have ethical concerns about invasion of privacy or excessive surveillance, they may not respond in a positive way to these forms of monitoring. Clearly, this topic is controversial, and decisions to engage in employee monitoring need to be pursued with caution.

### How Ethically Employees Behave at Work

Well-publicized ethical issues at companies such as Worldcom, Hollinger International, Yahoo, Toyota, Volkswagen, Toshiba, Valeant, Turning Pharmaceuticals, Enron, Phillip Morris, Chevron, and Tyco have made people more aware of corporate ethics (or lack thereof). Indeed, a firm's performance system can affect whether its employees engage in behaviors that other stakeholders consider unethical. For example, a company that relies on a comparative evaluation approach for its employees might unintentionally be fostering a climate in which employees are willing to cheat or stab their coworkers in the back. Similarly, a performance management system that solely evaluates a corporation's financial performance might inadvertently encourage managers to engage in unethical (and perhaps illegal) accounting practices to improve the firm's bottom line. Managers might also fail to fill vacant positions or repair on-the-job safety problems because doing so might incur more costs and hurt their chances of reaching their financial targets and earning incentive pay. Furthermore, if administrative decisions made about promotions, layoffs, and the like are significant, the performance management system may help prompt employees to engage in unethical behaviors to maximize their potential income, protect their job security, or enhance their career progressions.

# Performance Management in Practice: Regulatory Issues

Of course, managers need to consider legal ramifications when they're designing and implementing their firms' performance management systems. Two issues that are directly related to regulatory issues are discrimination in the performance management process and the importance of documentation.

## Efforts to Reduce Discrimination in the Performance Management Process

In response to several lawsuits, Ford paid out $10.5 million over forced ranking-related discrimination claims on the basis of age, gender, and race.[81] Goodyear changed its forced distribution model, in part due to concerns about the influence of discrimination on the ranking of employees.[82] Other companies, such as Microsoft, Walmart, and Conoco, have faced legal action based on concerns of discrimination stemming from their employee performance management systems.[83]

These lawsuits serve as an important reminder that the performance management system you use must not be discriminatory. Some discriminatory actions in the performance evaluation or appraisal process may be intentional; however, managers may also unintentionally discriminate against employees. Sometimes these actions occur through biases such as the similar-to-me error that managers unknowingly commit as mentioned earlier with our reference to a diverse workforce. They may also stem from the evaluation approach used. Evaluating employees on outputs is much more objective than ranking them based on some general category such as "level of performance." Some of the evaluation approaches, such as BOS and BARS, which explicitly identify performance dimensions and levels of performance among those dimensions are conducive to helping raters focus on the performance of their employees without discriminatory considerations. As a manager, you need to remember the importance of job-relatedness, highlighted in Chapter 3. Striving to maximize validity, specificity, and clarity in performance standards are steps in the right direction to eliminating bias in the performance management process. The key to creating an effective and nondiscriminatory performance management process is to rely on evaluations that truly reflect employee attributes, behaviors, and/or outcomes that differentiate levels of actual job performance. Company Spotlight 9.4 demonstrates what can happen when a protected classification enters the performance review process.

## COMPANY SPOTLIGHT 9.4

### Age Not an Acceptable Performance Rating Criterion at MRA Systems

MRA Systems, Inc., is a Baltimore, Maryland, based subsidiary of General Electric that makes jet engines, components, and integrated systems for both commercial and military aircraft. The EEOC charged MRA with discrimination on the basis of age related to an employee's performance rating. The employee was 61 years old when he received a lower performance rating than his successful job performance warranted. He was also passed over for promotion to a higher paying position even though he was more qualified for the position than the younger person who got the job. The EEOC also charged that the employee was subjected to greater scrutiny on the job and was retaliated against when he filed a complaint at the company. MRA Systems was required to pay the employee $130,000 and provide substantial equitable relief for its discriminatory behavior. The consent decree that accompanied the settlement requires the company to provide at least two hours of required training on federal laws related to discrimination to anyone who participates in the performance evaluation process or assignment decisions.

*Sources:* "GE Subsidiary MRA Systems to Pay $130,000 To Settle EEOC Age Discrimination Suit," EEOC, June 3, 2010, www.eeoc.gov/eeoc/newsroom/release/6-3-10.cfm; Robert Rand, "Middle River Aircraft Must Pay Up for Age Discrimination," gazette.net, June 7, 2010, www.gazette.net/stories/06072010/businew175749_32567.php.

## The Importance of Documenting Employee Performance

Considering the potential consequences of performance evaluations, it should be obvious that you need to be sure to maintain documentation of decisions and actions throughout your performance management process. This involves documentation of the evidence—the factors—that led to your decision to assign a particular performance rating to an employee. Without documentation of an employee's performance, how do you know if they deserve a "3" or a "4" on your 5-point rating scale? Without proper documentation, how can you be certain you are not committing biases such as the recency bias because you can't remember the entire review period for an employee? Without documentation, how can you be sure you are not confusing events and perceptions of performance among 5 or 10 employees over the past six months?

Taking the time to document events and incidents isn't easy, but doing so will provide you with much more accuracy in your ratings, as well as assurance that you are providing the correct ratings for your employees. Given the implications these ratings may have for the careers and financial well-being of your employees, it is only fair to be as thorough and accurate as possible. In addition to documenting the incidents that led to your evaluation, it is equally important that you document all discussions and steps taken to help improve your employees' performance, as well as any disciplinary actions. If you encounter a situation in which you must suspend or terminate an employee, it is important that you be able to provide a timeline of the steps that you have taken to try to correct the person's performance.

## SUMMARY

Performance management is the process of evaluating the performance of your employees against the performance standards set for them and then helping them develop action plans to address any gaps identified. There are two primary purposes of performance management systems. First, they serve an administrative function by providing information managers use to make decisions about merit increases, layoffs, and the like. Second, they serve a developmental purpose by providing employees with information they can use to improve their performance in order to fuel the company's success further.

Managers must take five steps to design and implement an effective performance management system. First, they must identify a job's relevant performance dimensions. The performance dimensions of a job reflect the reason it exists. They help pinpoint the specific tasks and activities employees are responsible for in their jobs. Once the performance dimensions are identified, managers then turn to the second step: developing performance measures that serve as the basis for evaluating the performance of their employees. To be effective, performance measures must be valid, associated with clear performance standards, and specific.

The third step focuses on evaluating employees' performance. There are several different approaches managers can take: (1) individual comparisons, such as ranking, paired comparison, or forced distribution; (2) absolute approaches that are attribute- or behavior-based; and (3) results-based approaches, including direct measure and management by objectives.

The third step managers need to take to develop an effective evaluation system is to determine which sources of performance information to draw on. Managers can rely on information from the employees themselves, their coworkers, supervisors, and even customers. The choice of which sources of information to use should be based on the ability of the source to provide useful and valid information about the employee's performance.

The last two steps of an effective performance management system involve providing employees with feedback about their levels of performance and developing

action plans to improve their performance. When an employee performs poorly because of a lack of effort rather than ability, the manager may need to resort to discipline. Managers can use either progressive or positive discipline to help employees understand their performance deficiencies and improve. *Progressive discipline* is a process by which employees who have disciplinary problems progress through a series of disciplinary stages until the problem is corrected. *Positive discipline* is not punitive; rather, it focuses on constructive feedback and encourages employees to take responsibility for improving their behavior or work performance.

The choices managers make regarding the various options in the performance management system they use are influenced by organizational demands, environmental influences, and legal requirements. The organizational demands of a firm, such as its strategy, company characteristics, culture, and employee concerns, will affect the performance evaluation approaches managers use, the performance dimensions they emphasize, employees' responsiveness to the performance feedback they receive, and the like. Environmental factors require managers to look at how labor force trends, technology, globalization, and ethics affect the performance management system. Finally, because of legal considerations, managers need to try to reduce error and bias in the performance management process and to avoid wrongfully discharging employees.

## KEY TERMS

360-degree appraisal
absolute approach
behavioral observation scale (BOS)
behaviorally anchored rating scale
     (BARS)
contaminated performance measure
contrast effect
critical incident approach
deficient performance measure
devil's horn error
direct measures approach
error of central tendency
forced-choice approach
forced distribution
frame-of-reference training
global performance measure
graphic rating scale

halo error
leniency error
management by objectives (MBO)
paired comparisons
performance dimension
performance management
performance standards
positive discipline
primacy error
progressive discipline
ranking approach
recency error
self-appraisal
similar-to-me error
specificity
strictness error

## DISCUSSION QUESTIONS

1. Describe the two primary reasons organizations need a performance management process.
2. You have been tasked with developing a new performance management process for your company. What steps would you take to develop and set up the process?
3. What needs to happen to ensure a performance measure is effective? Why does that matter?
4. What are the advantages and disadvantages of the different sources of information used to evaluate the performance of employees?
5. What are the similarities and differences between progressive and positive discipline?

6. What are some of the main ways that organizational demands influence the performance management process?

7. Explain how environmental circumstances affect the design and implementation of a firm's performance management system.

8. What legal aspects must you consider when designing and implementing a performance management system? What are the possible consequences of not paying attention to these issues?

## LEARNING EXERCISE 1

Interview three people who are employed in different jobs and at different types of organization (for profit or not-for-profit, for example). Ask these individuals to share with you how the performance management process works at their companies and how the process is viewed by them and others in the companies.

1. Create a table comparing and contrasting what you have learned about the performance management process at these three companies. Identify the type of appraisal used by each organization.

2. Based on the information you learned in the interviews, discuss which, if any, of the companies, is most appealing to you and why, based on the performance management processes identified.

## LEARNING EXERCISE 2

Working in groups, obtain a job description for a job of interest to members of the group. After reviewing the job description, develop a performance management evaluation form that you might use to evaluate someone performing that job. In completing this exercise, it is important that you do the following:

1. Identify the performance dimensions to be evaluated.
2. Explain any weights you might assign to the performance dimensions.
3. Identify any standards you might create for the performance dimensions.
4. Create a form that might be used to assess the jobholder based on your responses to the first three questions.
5. Identify which sources of data would be best positioned to evaluate the jobholder.

## CASE STUDY 1: A NEW SYSTEM AT ADDILLADE AND PARTNERS

Addillade and Partners is a private medical practice with a full-time staff of about 15 nurses. Until now, the performance management system there has been based on a direct evaluation approach. The partners would simply rate how well each nurse they interacted with over the course of the year performed. However, some of the nurses have complained that the system isn't fair. One of the criticisms is that some managers are known to be good ones to work for—their nurses tend to receive high ratings and, as a result, high rewards. Other managers don't really provide any feedback; each nurse is simply given a score at the end of the review period without any insight into why he received that score or what he could do to improve.

Because Addillade relies so extensively on its nurses, the partners have decided to take steps to improve the perception of fairness of the system. In doing so, the partners are considering using the graphic rating scale in Exhibit 9.12 to evaluate the nurses:

**EXHIBIT 9.12**

## Proposed Graphic Rating Scale

Evaluate the employee's performance on the following performance dimensions. Circle the most appropriate rating for each.

| Performance Dimension | Rating | | | | |
|---|---|---|---|---|---|
| | Poor | Below Average | Average | Above Average | Outstanding |
| Courteous | 1 | 2 | 3 | 4 | 5 |
| Cooperative | 1 | 2 | 3 | 4 | 5 |
| Knowledgeable | 1 | 2 | 3 | 4 | 5 |
| Quantity of work | 1 | 2 | 3 | 4 | 5 |

### Discussion Questions

1. From an administrative perspective, what are some of the potential problems with this evaluation form? What are some of the potential problems from a developmental perspective?

2. What are the strengths and weaknesses of this evaluation form relative to a ranking form?

3. What recommendations would you make to improve the evaluation form?

4. Pick two other evaluation methods and describe how you would use them in this situation. What challenges does each present? Of the two, which approach is best? Why?

## CASE STUDY 2: SAP ELIMINATES ANNUAL PERFORMANCE REVIEWS

The annual performance review is a main feature of HR programs in most companies. A handful of companies, such as Accenture, Adobe, Medtronic, Gap, and Microsoft, are moving away from the traditional annual performance review and pursuing other methods. SAP is a very successful global company headquartered in Germany. The company provides support for cloud-based management software that enables thousands of clients to deliver performance feedback to millions of employees. While SAP will continue to provide support for performance feedback for other companies, it has decided to eliminate annual performance reviews for its own workers in the United States. SAP's chief HR officer for Germany, Wolfgang Fassnacht, told Reuters: "Grading workers did not work. People are open to feedback, also to harsh criticism, until the moment you start giving scores. Then the shutters go down." This change does not mean that SAP is abandoning all performance feedback, just that the annual reviews are slated to go away. The plan is to replace them with regular check-in discussions to provide feedback in real time and foster dialogue that can lead to better performance.

### Discussion Questions

1. Why do companies conduct annual performance reviews?

2. What are the challenges with conducting annual reviews?

3. What changes do you think would improve the annual review process?

4. What do you think of SAP's plans? Will they be successful? Why or why not?

*Sources:* Wright, Aliah, "Tech Company SAP Eliminates Annual Performance Review," *SHRM.org*, August 18, 2016, https://www.shrm.org/resourceandtools/hr-topics/technology/pages/sap-eliminates-annual-performance-reviews.aspx; Reuters, "SAP, Maker of Performance Review Software, Ditches Performance Reviews," August 12, 2016, http://fortune.com/2016/08/12/sap-ends-performance-reviews/.

## NOTES

1 Herman Aguinis, *Performance Management*, 4th ed., (Chicago Business Press, 2019).

2 M. Beer, "Performance Appraisal," in *Handbook of Organizational Behavior*, ed. J. W. Lorsch (Englewood Cliffs, NJ: Prentice Hall, 1987), 286–300.

3 David Dorsey and Rose Mueller-Hanson, "Performance Management That Makes A Difference: An Evidence-Based Approach," SHRM Science-to-Practice Series, SHRM, December 2017, https://www.shrm.org/hr-today/trends-and-forecasting/special-reports-and-expert-views/Documents/Performance%20Management.pdf).

4 Rose Mueller-Hanson and Elaine Pulakos, *Transforming Performance Management to Drive Performance: An Evidence-Based Roadmap*, 2018, New York: Routledge.

5 Sujan Patel, "The New Rules of Employee Performance Management," *Inc.*, inc.com, https://www.inc.com/sujan-patel/the-new-rules-of-employee-performance-management.html.

6 F. J. Landy and J. L. Farr, "Performance Rating," *Psychological Bulletin* 87(1) (1980): 72–107.

7 U.S. Department of Labor, *Testing and Assessment: An Employer's Guide to Good Practices* (Washington, DC: U.S. Department of Labor, Employment and Training Administration, 2000).

8 Cascio, *Applied Psychology in Personnel Management*.

9 H. J. Bernardin and R. W. Beatty, *Performance Appraisal: Assessing Human Behavior at Work* (Boston: Kent-Wadsworth, 1984).

10 "Performance Management Cycle: Developing Performance Standards," *Performance Management*, https://www.opm.gov/policy-data-oversight/performace-management/performance-management-cycle/planning/developing-performance-standards.

11 H. J. Bernardin, C. M. Hagan, J. S. Kane, and P. Villanova, "Effective Performance Management: A Focus on Precision, Customers, and Situational Constraints," in *Performance Appraisal: State of the Art in Practice*, ed. J. W. Smither (San Francisco: Jossey-Bass, 1998), 3–48.

12 Ibid.

13 P. Bobko and A. Colella, "Employee Reactions to Performance Standards: A Review and Research Propositions," *Personnel Psychology* 47(1994): 1–36.

14 "A Handbook for Measuring Employee Performance," U.S. Office of Personnel Management, March 2017, https://www.opm.gov/policy-data-oversight/performance-management/measuring/employee_performance_handbook.pdf.

15 Cascio, *Applied Psychology in Personnel Management*.

16 Allen Smith, "Yahoo's Forced Ranking Raises Legal Questions About Ratings," *SHRM.org*, February 4, 2016, https://www.shrm.org/resourcesandtools/legal-and-compliance/employment-law/pages/yahoo-forced-ranking.aspx.

17 B. M. Longnecker, "Rank & Yank: The Problems with Forced Rankings," *Workforce Management*, February 7, 2006, http://www.workforce.com/archive/feature/22/29/72/index.php.

18 Landy and Farr, "Performance Rating."

19 Cascio, *Applied Psychology in Personnel Management*.

20 Landy and Farr, "Performance Rating."

21 Ibid.

22 J. T. Austin and P. Villanova, "The Criterion Problem: 1917–1992," *Journal of Applied Psychology* 77(1992): 836–874; H. J. Bernardin and P. C. Smith, "A Clarification of Some Issues Regarding the Development and Use of Behaviorally Anchored Rating Scales (BARS)," *Journal of Applied Psychology* 66(1981): 458–463; and R. Jacobs, D. Kafry, and S. Zedeck, "Expectations of Behaviorally Anchored Rating Scales," *Personnel Psychology* 33 (1980): 595–640.

23 Austin and Villanova, "The Criterion Problem: 1917–1992"; and Bernardin and Smith, "A Clarification of Some Issues."

24 Bernardin and Smith, "A Clarification of Some Issues."

25 C. C. Hoffman, B. R. Nathan, and L. M. Holden, "A Comparison of Validation Criteria: Objective Versus Subjective Performance Measures and Self Versus Supervisor Ratings," *Personnel Psychology* 44(1991): 601–618.

26 D. Antonioni, "The Effects of Feedback Accountability on Upward Appraisal Ratings," *Personnel Psychology* 47(1994): 349–356.

27 W. C. Borman, "The Rating of Individuals in Organizations: An Alternate Approach," *Organizational Behavior and Human Performance* 12(1974): 105–124.

[28] Kellogg Company Qualtrics 360 Case Study, Qualtrics, https://www.qualtrics.com/wp-content/uploads/2014/04/Kellogg.360.pdf.

[29] Jack Zenger, "How Effective Are Your 360-Degree Feedback Assessments?" *Forbes,* March 10, 2016, https://www.forbes.com/sites/jackzenger/2016/03/10/how-effective-are-your-360-degree-feedback-assessments/#27c271e5a690.

[30] Ghiselli, "Dimensional Problems of Criteria."

[31] R. J. Wherry, Sr., and C. J. Bartlett, "The Control of Bias in Ratings," *Personnel Psychology* 35(3) (1982): 521–551.

[32] W. V. Bingham, "Halo, Invalid and Valid," *Journal of Applied Psychology* 23(1939): 221–228; E. L. Thorndike, "A Constant Error in Psychological Ratings," *Journal of Applied Psychology* 4(1920): 25–29; and Bernardin and Beatty, *Performance Appraisal.*

[33] J. S. Kane, H. J. Bernardin, P. Villanova, and J. Peyrefitte, "Stability of Rater Leniency: Three Studies," *Academy of Management Journal* 38(1995): 1036–1051; and J. P. Builford, *Psychometric Methods* (New York: McGraw-Hill, 1954).

[34] Rose Mueller-Hanson and Elaine Pulakos, *Transforming Performance Management to Drive Performance: An Evidence-Based Roadmap* (New York: Routledge, 2018).

[35] G. Latham, K. Wexley, and E. Pursell, "Training Managers to Minimize Rating Errors in the Observation of Behavior," *Journal of Applied Psychology* 60(1975): 550–555; and H. J. Bernardin and M. R. Buckley, "Strategies in Rater Error Training," *Academy of Management Review* 6(1981): 205–212.

[36] D. J. Woehr and A. I. Huffcutt, "Rater Training for Performance Appraisal: A Quantitative Review," *Journal of Occupational and Organizational Psychology* 67(1994): 189–205; and Bernardin and Buckley, "Strategies in Rater Error Training."

[37] S. G. Roch, D. J. Woehr, V. Mishra, and U. Kieszczynska, "Rater Training Revisited: An Updated Meta-analytic Review of Frame of Reference Training," *Journal of Occupational and Organizational Psychology* 85(2012): 370–395; and L. M. Sulsky and D. V. Day, "Frame-of-Reference Training and Cognitive Categorization: An Empirical Investigation of Rater Memory Loss," *Journal of Applied Psychology* 77(1992): 501–510.

[38] Woehr and Huffcutt, "Rater Training for Performance Appraisal: A Quantitative Review"; and Bernardin and Buckley, "Strategies in Rater Error Training."

[39] Beer, "Performance Appraisal."

[40] Sujan Patel, "The New Rules of Employee Performance Management," *Inc.*, inc.com, March 7, 2017, https://www.inc.com/sujan-patel/the-new-rules-of-employee-performance-management.html.

[41] Nathan Sloan, Dimple Agarwal, Stacia Garr, and Karen Pastakia, "Performance Management: Playing a Winning Hand, 2017 Global Human Capital Trends," deloitte.com, February 28, 2017, https://www2.deloitte.com/insights/ys/en/focus/human-capital-trends/2017/redesigning-performance-management.html; Rose Mueller-Hanson and Elaine Pulakos, Transforming Performance Management to Drive Performance: An Evidence-Based Roadmap, 2018, New York: Routledge; Dave Zielinski, "Performance Management Platforms Keeping Pace with Appraisal Trends," SHRM.org, March 20, 2018, https://www.shrm.org/rsourcesandtools/hr-topics/technology/pages/performance-management-platforms-trends-aspx.

[42] P. Falcone, "The Fundamentals of Progressive Discipline," *HR Magazine* 42(2) (February 1997): 90–93.

[43] T. Watson, "Discipline Without Punishment: A Best Practices Approach to Disciplining Employees," *Watson Training and Development*, April 15, 2014, http://www.watson-training.com/blog2/46-discipline-with-punishment-a-best-practices-approach-to-disciplining-employees.html.

[44] Ghiselli, "Dimensional Problems of Criteria."

[45] Nathan Sloan, Dimple Agarwal, Stacia Garr, and Karen Pastakia, "Performance Management: Playing a Winning Hand, 2017 Global Human Capital Trends," February 28, 2017, https://www2.deloitte.com/insights/ys/en/focus/human-capital-trends/2017/redesigning-performance-management.html.

[46] Anonymous, "Good Performance Management Needs Good Line Managers," *ACAS*, February 2012, http://www.acas.org.uk/index.aspx?articleid=3677.

[47] D. M. Rousseau, *Psychological Contracts in Organizations: Understanding Written and Unwritten Agreements* (Thousand Oaks, CA: SAGE Publications, 1995).

[48] Ibid.

[49] C. Clifford, "Keep Your Employees Loyal by Encouraging Them to Pursue Their Own Projects and Passion," *Entrepreneur*, October 17, 2013, http://www.entrepreneur.com/article/229416.

[50] I. Raemdonck and J. Strijbos, "Feedback Perceptions and Attribution by Secretarial Employees: Effects of Feedback Content and Sender Characteristics," *European Journal of Training and Development* 37 (2013): 24–48; and Rousseau, *Psychological Contracts in Organizations*.

[51] Falcone, "The Fundamentals of Progressive Discipline."

[52] C. Y. Westerman, K. B. Heuett, K. M. Reno, and R. Curry, "What Makes Performance Feedback Seem Just? Synchronicity, Channel, and Valence Effects on Perceptions of Organizational Justice in Feedback Delivery," *Management Communication Quarterly* 28 (2013): 244–263; and Rousseau, *Psychological Contracts in Organizations*.

[53] P. M. Hirsch, *Pack Your Own Parachute* (Reading, MA: Addison-Wesley, 1987); Rousseau, *Psychological Contracts in Organizations*; and S. L. Robinson and D. M. Rousseau, "Violating the Psychological Contract: Not the Exception But the Norm," *Journal of Organizational Behavior* 15(1994): 245–259.

[54] Austin and Villanova, "The Criterion Problem: 1917–1992."

[55] M. Beer, "Conducting a Performance Appraisal Interview," *Harvard Business School Cases*, January 1997, 1–16; and J. S. Black, H. B. Gregersen, M. E. Mendenhall, and L. K. Stroh, *Globalizing People Through International Assignments*.

[56] K. Kraiger and K. Ford, "A Meta-analysis of Rate Race Effects in Performance Rating," *Journal of Applied Psychology* 70(1985): 56–65; and Landy and Farr, "Performance Rating."

[57] D. Geddes and A. M. Konrad, "Demographic Differences and Reactions to Performance Feedback," *Human Relations* 56(12) (2003): 1485–1513.

[58] Kraiger and Ford, "A Meta-analysis of Rate Race Effects in Performance Rating," *Journal of Applied Psychology* 70(1985): 56–65.

[59] Latham, Wexley, and Pursell, "Training Managers to Minimize Rating Errors"; and Bernardin and Buckley, "Strategies in Rater Error Training."

[60] P. Babcock, "Diversity Accountability Requires More Than Numbers," Society for Human Resource Management, April 13, 2009, http://www.shrm.org/hrdisciplines/diversity/articles/pages/morethannumbers.aspx; and P. Digh, "The Next Challenge: Holding People Accountable," *HR Magazine* 43(11) (1998): 63–69.

[61] Robert Bowman, "Is New Truck-Monitoring Technology for Safety—or Spying on Drivers?" *Forbes*, https://www.forbes.com/sites/robertbowman/2014/02/11/is-new-truck-monitoring-technology-for-safety-or-spying-on-drivers/#1a6b9c7c4918.

[62] G. Dutton, "Round the Clock Performance Management," *Workforce*, April 2001, 76–78, http://www.workforce.com/articles/round-the-clock-performance-management; Sloan et al., "Performance Management: Playing a Winning Hand"; Dave Zielinski, "Performance Management Platforms Keeping Pace with Appraisal Trends," *SHRM.org*, March 20, 2018, https://www.shrm.org/rsourcesandtools/hr-topics/technology/pages/performance-management-platforms-trends-aspx.

[63] Zielinski, "Performance Management Platforms Keeping Pace with Appraisal Trends."; SHRM.org, March 20, 2018, https://www.shrm.org/rsourcesandtools/hr-topics/technology/pages/performance-management-platforms-trends-aspx.

[64] K. R. Murphy and J. N. Cleveland, *Understanding Performance Appraisal: Social, Organizational, and Goal-Based Perspectives* (Thousand Oaks, CA: SAGE Publications, 1995).

[65] Ibid.

[66] G. E. Gordon and M. M. Kelly, *Telecommuting: How to Make It Work for You and Your Company* (Englewood Cliffs, NJ: Prentice Hall, 1986).

[67] "Sykes: How It Works," https://www.sykes.com/jobs/work-at-home/u-s-faq/#how-it-works.

[68] H. Peretz and Y. Fried, "National Values, Performance Appraisal Practices and Organizational Performance: A Study Across 21 Countries," Society of Human Resource Management Foundation, November 2007, http://www.shrm.org/about/foundation/research/Documents/Fried%20Final%20Report%20508.pdf; and Black, Gregersen, Mendenhall, and Stroh, *Globalizing People through International Assignments*.

[69] H. B. Gregersen, J. M. Hite, and J. S. Black, "Expatriate Performance Appraisal in U.S. Multinational Firms," *Journal of International Business Studies* Fall 1996, 711–738.

[70] P. O'Clock, "The Role of Strategy and Culture in the Performance Evaluation of International Strategic Business Units," *Management Accounting Quarterly* 4(2) (2003): 18–29; Tony Edwards, Rocio Sanchez-mangas, Patrice Jalette, Jonathan Lavelle, and Dana Minbaeva, "Global Standardization or National Differentiation of HRM Practices in Multinational Companies? A Comparison of Multinationals in Five Countries," *Journal of International Business Studies*, 47(2016): 997–1021; Sloan et al., "Performance Management: Playing a Winning Hand."

71 Black et al., *Globalizing People through International Assignments*.

72 Ibid.

73 H. De Cieri and P. J. Dowling, "Cross-cultural Issues in Organizational Behavior," in *Trends in Organizational Behavior*, vol. 2, ed. C. L. Cooper and D. M. Rousseau (Chichester, UK: Wiley, 1995), 127–145; and Black et al., *Globalizing People through International Assignments*.

74 V. Suutari and M. Tahvanainen, "The Antecedents of Performance Management among Finnish Expatriates," *International Journal of Human Resource Management* 12(1) (2002): 55–75.

75 Ibid.

76 Black et al., *Globalizing People through International Assignments*; Suutari and Tahvanainen, "The Antecedents of Performance Management Among Finnish Expatriates"; and Gregersen et al., "Expatriate Performance Appraisal in U.S. Multinational Firms."

77 M. Schminke, M. L. Ambrose, and T. W. Noel, "The Effect of Ethical Frameworks on Perceptions of Organizational Justice," *Academy of Management Journal* 40(5) (1997): 1190–1207.

78 Kc Agu, "6 Software Tools for Monitoring Employee Performance," *The Blog, Huffpost*, huffingtonpost.com, updated December 6, 2017, https://www.huffingtonpost.com/kc-agu/post_11966_b_10099296.html.

79 T. Raphael, "Think Twice: Does HR Want to be a Digital Snoop" *Workforce Management*, http://www.workforce.com/articles/think-twice-does-hr-want-to-be-a-digital-snoop.

80 D. Griffin, "Employee Computer Usage Monitoring Law," *Houston Chronicle*, http://small-business.chron.com/employee-computer-usage-monitoring-law-1153.html; R. Richmond, "3 Tips for Legally and Ethically Monitoring Employees Online," *Entrepreneur*, May 31, 2012, http://www.entrepreneur.com/article/223686; and C. Muhl, "Workplace E-mail and Internet Use: Employees and Employers Beware," *Monthly Labor Review*, February 2003, 36–45.

81 A. Meisler, "Dead Man's Curve," *Workforce Management*, July 2003, http://www.workforce.com/section/09/feature/23/47/39/index.html; S. Armour, "Job Reviews Take on Added Significance in Down Times," *USA Today*, July 22, 2003, http://www.usatoday.com/money/workplace/2003-07-22-reviews_x.htm; B. Meier, "Ford Is Changing the Way It Rates Work of Managers," *The New York Times*, July 12, 2001, http://query.nytimes.com.

82 B. Dawson, "Failing Grade: Goodyear Faces Lawsuit over Evaluation System It Will Alter," *Rubber & Plastics News*, September 2002.

83 T. Osborne and L. A. McCann, "Forced Rankings and Age-Related Employment Discrimination," *Human Rights Magazine*, 31, 22, http://www.americanbar.org/publications/human_rights_magazine_home/human_rights_vol31_2004/spring2004/hr_spring04_forced.html.

# Chapter 10

# Compensating Employees

## Learning Objectives

**AFTER READING THIS CHAPTER, YOU SHOULD BE ABLE TO:**

1 Describe the purpose of compensation.

2 Discuss the importance of equity relative to a firm's compensation decisions.

3 Understand the process and rationale for establishing internal alignment of pay systems.

4 Explain how a firm ensures that it is externally competitive in what it pays.

5 Identify alternative compensation approaches that companies can use.

6 Describe the impact organizational demands have on how a company manages its compensation decisions.

7 Discuss environmental factors that affect the compensation that a firm offers.

8 Outline the regulations that affect how employees are compensated.

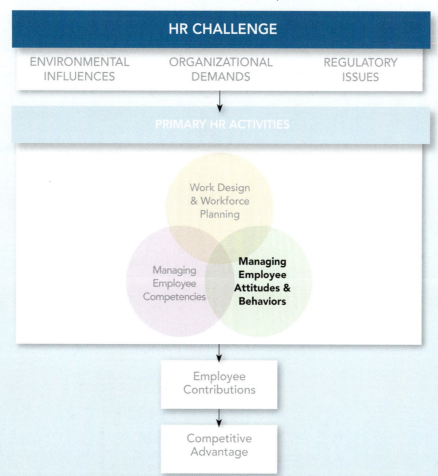

**HR CHALLENGE**

| ENVIRONMENTAL INFLUENCES | ORGANIZATIONAL DEMANDS | REGULATORY ISSUES |

**PRIMARY HR ACTIVITIES**

Work Design & Workforce Planning

Managing Employee Competencies

**Managing Employee Attitudes & Behaviors**

Employee Contributions

Competitive Advantage

# The Purpose of Compensation

If you come to work for us, we will pay you $30 per hour for the first 40 hours you work each week and $35 per hour thereafter. Will you work for us? What would you want to know before you make your decision? Would the type of work matter? Would you want to know how much other people who do the same kind of work (either at this company or in the industry in general) are making? Does what we are offering violate any pay laws?

In previous chapters, we discussed how companies design and plan for work and how they ensure that employees have the competencies they need to achieve organizational goals. Then, in Chapter 9, we began a discussion on how to manage employees' attitudes and behaviors by describing the performance management process. However, employees most likely will not be motivated to help you achieve company goals unless they feel that they are properly compensated for their performance. This chapter is about how pay decisions are made and what you, as a manager, need to know and do to ensure that the pay will attract, motivate, and retain employees. Thus, this chapter is also about the "Managing Employee Attitudes & Behaviors" circle in Exhibit 10.1. In this chapter, we discuss a number of questions that are important to consider when making compensation decisions, including the following:

- What factors should you consider when determining the salary range for a job?
- What is the best way to determine how much employees should be paid?
- How much of that pay should be guaranteed, and how much should be based on incentives?

## EXHIBIT 10.1

### Framework for the Strategic Management of Employees

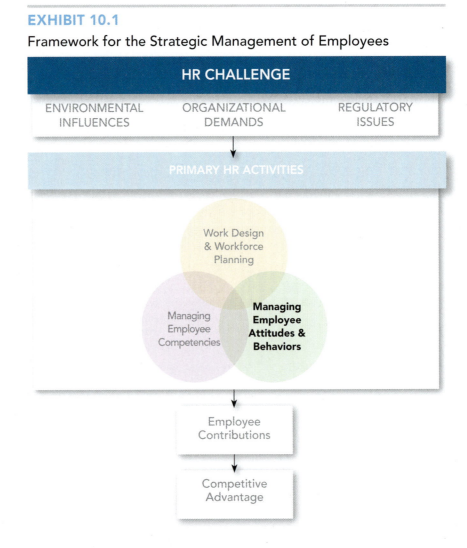

In this chapter, we will discuss pay equity and the decision-making processes used to establish pay rates and to assign pay to jobs and to individuals. As with the previous chapters, the second half of this chapter will help you understand some of the complex decisions that managers face because of organizational demands, environmental influences, and regulatory issues. As you study this chapter, keep in mind that the decisions you make about the pay for employees in your organization will affect how likely your company is to achieve and maintain a competitive advantage in the marketplace. As a manager, you will have input at various stages of the decision-making process. Thus, it is important for you to understand some of the theories related to compensation decisions, as well as the mechanics of how these decisions are made. And, it is equally important that you understand the legal implications of the decisions you make. Before we get into the specifics, though, we need to define what we mean by the word *compensation*.

## Total Compensation

**Compensation** refers to the monetary and nonmonetary rewards that employees receive in exchange for the work they do for an organization. In exchange for these rewards, employees are expected to be loyal and committed to their firms. Compensation can be either direct or indirect. Direct compensation includes the hourly wages or salaries paid to employees, as well as any incentives, including merit raises and bonuses or commissions they receive. Direct compensation can be fixed (wages), variable (commissions), or a combination. Indirect compensation includes the benefits and services employees receive, such as their health care insurance, paid vacations, lunches, company-paid training programs, and other "perks." This chapter focuses on direct compensation in terms of base pay and introduces the other components of a total compensation package. In later chapters, we discuss variable pay, such as incentives and bonuses, and benefits and other forms of indirect pay.

Over the past decade or so, most organizations have begun to refer to the total compensation package they provide as **total rewards**. The word *rewards* is believed to better reflect the many aspects of a compensation package (base pay, incentives, benefits, perks, and so forth) and to signal to employees that they are receiving more than just base pay. Some companies even include development and career opportunities in describing their total rewards. The goal behind this broad thinking is to motivate employees by helping them understand everything they are receiving from the organization in exchange for the work they do.

One company that understands the importance of this type of thinking is CH2M Hill, a global full-service engineering, construction, and operations firm that has been listed consistently among the world's most ethical companies from 2009 to 2017. In 2017, it was ranked number 22 on *Fortune*'s Top 50 Companies that Change the World list for its positive impact on society, and it also has received a long list of other awards and recognitions, including being recognized for its commitment to recruiting, developing, and advancing women in the workplace—the first firm in the engineering and construction industry to receive such recognition. CH2M includes employee ownership, professional development, tuition reimbursement, and work/life balance, among other benefits.[1]

The key to a successful compensation plan is a compensation philosophy that supports the goals of the organization. A **compensation philosophy** communicates information to employees about what is valued within an organization, enhances the likelihood of consistency in pay across the organizational units, and helps attract, motivate, and retain employees.[2] A survey by WorldatWork, the professional association for compensation professionals, reported that 9 out of 10 of the 600 companies responding had a compensation philosophy, and of those companies, 62% indicated they had a written compensation philosophy and another 31% had an unwritten compensation philosophy.[3]

---

**compensation**

the monetary and nonmonetary rewards employees receive in exchange for the work they do for an organization

**total rewards**

the sum of all the aspects of a compensation package (base pay, incentives, benefits, perks, and so forth) that signal to current and future employees that they are receiving more than just base pay in exchange for their work

**compensation philosophy**

communicates information to employees about what is valued within an organization, enhances the likelihood of consistency in pay across the organizational units, and helps attract, motivate, and retain employees

A clear idea of the compensation philosophy and its objectives enables a company to carefully construct a pay system that is aligned with the overall strategy of the organization and addresses internal alignment, external competitiveness, and employee contributions. When these factors are considered and the program is administered well, including being clearly communicated to employees, the compensation program assists the firm in achieving a competitive advantage. At SAS, a highly successful business analytics and business intelligence software company headquartered in Cary, North Carolina, the compensation philosophy takes into consideration the desire to pay employees competitively, while recognizing that the company's culture values egalitarianism.[4] Another company that understands the importance of a compensation philosophy tied to the desired corporate culture is Genentech, the company featured in Company Spotlight 10.1.

In the following sections, we discuss the concepts of internal alignment, external competitiveness, and employee contributions, as well as your role as a manager in making pay decisions. First, however, you need to have a solid understanding of equity theory. Consequently, we discuss it next.

## COMPANY SPOTLIGHT 10.1

### Why Everyone Wants to Work for Genentech

Total rewards is not the only reason 92% of employees indicate Genentech is a great place to work, but it certainly helps. Genentech, a subsidiary of Swiss drug giant Roche, is a leading biotechnology company focused on discovering, developing, and manufacturing medicines to treat serious diseases. The company is headquartered in San Francisco, California, and has 15,064 employees in the U.S. Genentech has a long list of awards including Fortune's 100 Best Companies to Work For for 2018, Best Workplace for Women in 2018, PEOPLE's 2018 Companies that Care, Best Workplaces for Giving Back 2018, and Best Workplaces for Millennials 2018. The company has made the Fortune 100 Best Companies to Work For list for 20 years.

In addition to a highly competitive salary (average base pay in 2018 was $135,913), the company provides cash bonuses, long-term incentives, and other rewards (average extra compensation in 2018 was $47,000). Employees receive 34 days of general paid time off and an unlimited number of sick days. Other benefits and perks include 401(k) contributions, subsidized childcare, fully paid sabbaticals, a generous transportation program, stock options, health insurance for part-timers, college tuition reimbursement (up to $10,000 per year), student loan debt repayment and much more. With this total rewards approach to compensation, it is no surprise that Genentech is consistently listed as a top company for employees.

*Sources:* "We Treat You Right," genentech.com, https://www.gene.com/careers/work-here/benefits; "Fortune 100 Best List," Fortune.com, http://fortune.com/best-companies/list; "Great Place to Work: Genentech," http://reviews.greatplacetowork.com/genentech.

## Equity Theory

Compensation is important to employees beyond the simple fact that most of us need money to buy the things we need and want and pay our bills. Employees also perceive that their compensation reflects how they are valued by their employer and people around them.[5] Compensation, therefore, is very important to employees and serves as a motivator at work. You probably have already studied a number of motivation theories in other classes, such as psychology. We introduced motivation theory in Chapter 4, when we described the job design process, and in Chapter 9, when we discussed performance management. We will talk more about motivation in Chapter 11, when we discuss incentive pay. In this chapter, we discuss one theory of motivation: equity theory.

Consider this scenario: You began working at a company eight years ago, and you gradually climbed the corporate ladder to arrive at your current midlevel management position. You think your salary is reasonable; you have gotten nice raises for your performance each year and for each promotion. You work hard because you have a strong work ethic and feel that your employer deserves a fair day's work for the salary you are receiving. In a casual conversation, a colleague in a similar job at the same level as you casually mentions his salary, which is considerably higher than yours. You know for a fact that this guy doesn't work nearly as hard as you do. After your initial shock, what is your response likely to be? Do you think you will continue working as hard as you have been, but ask for a raise? Do you think you will quit working as hard? What if you don't get a raise? Do you think you will stay with the company? Would your response be the same or different if the colleague worked for another company, but in a comparable job?

The situation just described involves a question of equity. According to **equity theory**, you and your employees will be motivated to work harder (provide inputs) when you believe that your compensation (outcome received) is at the right level for the work you are doing. As shown in Exhibit 10.2, people compare their input and outcome levels to those of other people in similar situations.

If employees know, or even just believe they are not receiving an appropriate level of compensation for their work (outcome), they will experience "disequilibrium." The disequilibrium, or inequity, can be either positive or negative. When the inequity is negative, employees believe they are not getting as much out of their jobs as they are putting into them relative to other people. Faced with this situation, employees are likely to try to resolve the inequity. They can do this in several ways. One way is by asking for a raise or a bonus. If that doesn't work, they can adjust their inputs to make their input/outcome ratio more equitable. In other words, they can stop working as hard as they once did, perhaps by putting

**equity theory**

the theory that employees compare their input (work effort) and outcome (wages) levels with those of other people in similar situations to determine if they are being treated the same in terms of pay and other outcomes

---

**EXHIBIT 10.2**

## Equity Theory

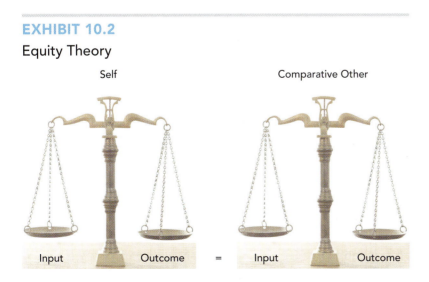

Self                    Comparative Other

Input     Outcome    =    Input     Outcome

in fewer hours, taking longer breaks, and so forth. Employees can also adjust their psychological perspective by rationalizing why there is inequity. They may try to explain the situation by seeking some other reasons for the difference, such as education, experience, or even political connections within the organization. If the reason they identify seems logical to them, they may reduce their feelings of inequity. A final option for employees is to quit their jobs if they believe that the inequity is too great and cannot be altered.

As a manager, you might not have much say about the actual pay structure within your firm. However, you are likely to have a great deal of input about how to reward your employees within that structure. Thus, it is important that you be aware of the importance of pay equity as you make recommendations for pay increases for your staff.[6]

To make matters more complicated, there are actually two labor markets in which inequities can exist: (1) the labor market within your firm and (2) and the labor market outside your firm. Companies try to develop compensation systems that are equitable both internally and externally. We discuss both the traditional job-based approaches, because many companies continue to use these methods to balance internal and external equity, and newer forms of pay. These newer forms of pay include skill-based pay, competency-based pay, and market pricing. Each of these are alternative approaches for designing compensation systems. We describe all these approaches within the context of how they are used to address a firm's internal alignment and external competitiveness.

## Internal Alignment

**internal alignment**

occurs when each job in a company is valued appropriately relative to every other job in terms of its ability to help the firm achieve its goals

**Internal alignment** occurs when each job in a company is valued appropriately relative to every other job in terms of its ability to help the firm achieve its goals. An example will help you understand this concept: Assume that you are a manager in a financial services firm with two employees reporting to you. One employee's job involves working with clients daily to help them with their financial needs. The other employee's job is an accounts payable position—making sure that the company's vendors get paid on time. Both jobs are important, but the first job is directly related to the purpose of the organization, which is selling financial services. The other job plays a supporting role. Which job do you think adds the most value to the company? If your answer is the sales job, you are correct. Therefore, in establishing a relative worth hierarchy for determining salaries, the sales job would be ranked higher than the accounts payable job and would receive a higher rate of pay.

Now, let's take a look at how companies establish internal alignment among their jobs. Keep in mind that as a manager, the more you understand the terminology we will be using, the better able you are to understand and explain to employees the internal pay structure within your organization. This information can also help you when you are negotiating your own pay.

Traditionally, companies have established pay rates for jobs, not for individuals performing the jobs. This point is important to remember as we examine the various types of job evaluation approaches used by companies. We tend to think that pay rates are established for employees rather than for tasks they perform, but it is the other way around. As you will learn in the following sections, a relative worth structure is developed for jobs, and then pay rates are assigned to those jobs.

Before a company can begin to establish the relative worth of its jobs and the pay for each job, it must have information available about the tasks, duties, and responsibilities required to perform each job. Recall that in Chapter 4, we described the job analysis process. The information derived from a job analysis is vital for establishing the relative worth of the jobs within the company through a systematic process called **job evaluation**. The four most common job evaluation approaches are job ranking, job classification, point factor, and factor comparison. The first two approaches, job ranking and job classification, are qualitative approaches. Point factor and factor comparison are quantitative approaches to job evaluation. Next, we give a brief overview of each approach. As you read about each one, consider the importance of having a well-defined job description resulting from a careful job analysis before you can effectively apply any of the approaches.

## Job Ranking

**Job ranking** involves reviewing job descriptions and listing the jobs in order, from highest to lowest worth to the company. This process is fairly easy to do when there are only a few jobs in the company. Accurately ranking jobs in a large company is much more difficult than ranking jobs in a small company. If you have only five jobs to evaluate, you probably know the jobs well even without looking at the job descriptions. But what if you had to rank 25 jobs? In this case, you would be less likely to know a great deal about all the jobs. Second, you would need some type of framework just to process all the information found in the 25 job descriptions. You would probably be able to decide which jobs were the most valuable and which were the least valuable without too much trouble. However, you would likely find it difficult to evaluate the jobs that fall somewhere in the middle. Such a system is also more difficult to justify to employees because ranking jobs is largely subjective. That is, the order is just a manager's opinion about which jobs are more valuable to the firm than others.

## Job Classification

**Job classification** involves developing broad descriptions for groups of jobs that are similar in terms of their tasks, duties, responsibilities, and qualifications. The job description for a particular job is then compared with the classification descriptions, and a decision is made about which description best fits the job. A wage range is attached to each classification, reflecting the relative worth of the jobs slotted into that classification.

The federal government has used a variation of the job classification system for many years. Visit http://www.opm.gov/policy-data-oversight/classification-qualifications/, and you will find a lot of information about how the federal job classification system works. Unlike some job classification systems that involve a solely subjective process of matching jobs to classifications, the government provides factor descriptions that can be used to develop scores for jobs to slot them into the appropriate classifications based on the score. The standards provided are meant to serve as a guide, not a replacement for the judgment of skilled compensation professionals or the knowledge of managers who make job classification decisions.[7]

In the federal government, the classification levels are referred to by the prefix *GS*, which stands for *General Schedule*, followed by a number. The higher the number, the greater the complexity and responsibility associated with the job, and the greater the qualifications required for performing the job. Naturally, the pay range is higher for jobs with higher GS numbers than for those with lower numbers; more senior jobs fit into an entirely separate pay schedule.

Sometimes managers want to reclassify jobs so that they can give a particular employee who merits it a large raise or because a job's duties have changed. The manager can then compare the revised job description to the classification guide to determine in which grade the job falls. The classification descriptions can also be used as input for preparing the new job description.

**job evaluation**
the systematic process of establishing the relative worth of the jobs within the company

**job ranking**
a type of job evaluation that involves reviewing job descriptions and listing the jobs in order, from highest to lowest worth to the company

**job classification**
a type of job evaluation that involves developing broad descriptions for groups of jobs that are similar in terms of their tasks, duties, responsibilities, and qualifications for the purpose of assigning wages

One criticism of the job classification system is that parts of the job being evaluated might fit into one job grade in the system, whereas other parts might fit into another grade. A decision then has to be made about which classification is the most appropriate. Because the pay range will differ depending on the decision, the outcome of the evaluation process is extremely important.

## Point Method

**point method (also known as point factor method)**

a quantitative method of job evaluation that involves assigning point values to jobs based on compensable factors to create a relative worth hierarchy for jobs in the company

**compensable factor**

an aspect of jobs, such as skill, effort, responsibility, and working conditions, that exist across jobs in a company, are needed by employees for the firm to achieve its objectives, and for which the company is willing to pay

**benchmark job**

a job that is used to represent the range of jobs in a company and that can be used for comparison with jobs in other companies for the purpose of establishing pay rates

The most commonly used type of job evaluation is the **point method**, sometimes referred to as **point factor method**. This quantitative approach uses a point value scheme that yields a score for each job. The scores for various jobs are then compared to determine their relative worth. The point method is developed by first identifying a set of factors for which the company is willing to pay. These **compensable factors** are chosen because they represent aspects of jobs that a company needs to achieve its goals. Typically, companies use compensable factors such as skill, effort, responsibility, and working conditions, but they can add other factors, such as innovativeness. Remember that we are focusing on evaluating a job, not a person performing a job, so compensable factors should be elements that appear in varying degrees across many jobs within the company.

With the point method, a point manual is used to determine the relative worth of jobs. The point manual contains a general description of each compensable factor, along with a description of each degree of the factor. Exhibit 10.3 defines one of the factors in a point method of job evaluation. An example of factor and point values is shown in Exhibit 10.4. The points assigned represent the relative weight of the factor in terms of its importance to the company. Any number of total points can be assigned, but 500 points is often used. And, although five is a typical number of degrees assigned, the number can be greater or smaller. The descriptions need to be carefully written to ensure that two different individuals evaluating the same job on the same compensable factors will arrive at the same results. In other words, clearly describing the compensable factors and defining what each degree represents will lead to a more reliable and valid process.

Once the point manual is ready, job descriptions for benchmark jobs can be compared with the factor descriptions, and the appropriate points can be assigned for these jobs. **Benchmark jobs** are used to represent the range of jobs in the company. These jobs need to be:

- Stable over time in terms of their responsibilities
- Well known and recognized

### EXHIBIT 10.3

#### Definition of Responsibility Factor

**Responsibility–This factor measures the type and level of responsibility associated with performing the duties of the job**

- 1st degree—Minimal responsibility expected, such as following directions as provided and reporting completion of duties

- 2nd degree—Limited responsibility, including ensuring that all policies and procedures are followed and that all tasks are completed in a timely manner

- 3rd degree—Responsibility for timely and accurate completion of assigned parts of projects

- 4th degree—Oversight responsibility for various aspects of the work, including some supervision of other workers and accountability for quality of outcomes

- 5th degree—Complete responsibility for ensuring that tasks are performed from start to finish, including providing supervision of other workers, managing budgets, and ensuring that finished projects are completed on time and with the highest quality

## EXHIBIT 10.4

### Point Values

| Factor | 1st Degree | 2nd Degree | 3rd Degree | 4th Degree | 5th Degree |
|---|---|---|---|---|---|
| **Skill** | | | | | |
| • Job knowledge | 20 | 40 | 60 | 80 | 100 |
| • Experience | 35 | 45 | 55 | 65 | 75 |
| **Effort** | | | | | |
| • Mental demand | 65 | 70 | 75 | 80 | 85 |
| • Physical demand | 20 | 25 | 30 | 35 | 40 |
| **Responsibility** | 70 | 85 | 100 | 115 | 130 |
| **Working conditions** | 30 | 40 | 50 | 60 | 70 |

- Clearly and concisely described
- Accepted in the external labor market for setting wage rates
- Compensated at an appropriate wage rate

The points assigned for each factor are added together to generate a score for the job. This score provides a way to compare jobs with each other to determine which jobs should be paid more and which less. Often, this process is conducted by a compensation committee to ensure that the results are reliable and valid.

As you can see, the point method brings more objectivity to the job evaluation process. The key to its success is threefold: (1) properly identifying the compensable factors and selecting the benchmark jobs, (2) assigning appropriate weights to each factor, and (3) accurately using the point manual.

Once the points are assigned, **job grades** are created to reflect the hierarchy of jobs within the company. Jobs with comparable points are grouped together to create the job grades. A company may have one job grade plan for all jobs. Typically, however, a company develops different structures for professional, technical, and other categories of jobs, such as clerical and skilled-trade jobs. Nonbenchmark jobs can then be evaluated and slotted into the hierarchy.

## Factor Comparison

**Factor comparison** is a quantitative type of job evaluation that involves ranking benchmark jobs in relation to each other on each of several factors, such as mental requirements, physical requirements, skill, responsibility, and working conditions. A determination is then made about how much of the hourly rate for a job is associated with each factor, as illustrated in Exhibit 10.5.

The factor comparison approach is actually a hybrid method for job evaluation that combines aspects of job ranking and the point method, but it also breaks the

**job grade**
a grouping of jobs with comparable points together to reflect the hierarchy of jobs within a company for the purpose of establishing wage rates

**factor comparison**
a quantitative type of job evaluation that involves ranking benchmark jobs in relation to each other on each of several factors, such as mental requirements, physical requirements, skill, responsibility, and working conditions, and then assigning a portion of the hourly rate for each job to each factor

## EXHIBIT 10.5

### The Factor Comparison Method of Job Evaluation

| Job | Hourly Rate | Skill | Responsibility | Working Conditions |
|---|---|---|---|---|
| Carpenter's assistant | $12 | $7 | $2 | $3 |
| Carpenter | $18 | $10 | $5 | $3 |
| Senior carpenter | $25 | $12 | $8 | $5 |
| Supervisor | $30 | $15 | $10 | $5 |

wage into smaller parts. Unfortunately, although this method can be quite accurate, it is also quite complex and would be challenging to explain to managers and employees.[8] Managers also need extensive training to properly use the method. And, because the monetary rates are included, as the market changes the rate, the plan has to be updated frequently.[9] As a result, the factor comparison approach is used less often than other approaches.

# External Competitiveness

**external competitiveness**

ensuring pay rates for jobs in a company are appropriately aligned relative to pay rates for similar jobs in the company's external labor market

**External competitiveness** ensures that jobs in a company are valued appropriately relative to similar jobs in the company's external labor market. Companies make decisions about what they want to pay relative to the external market, and these decisions affect how attractive the firm is to potential employees. They also affect the attitude and motivation of current employees.

To begin our discussion of how a company uses market data to set its pay rates, we first describe the process used to collect market data. We then discuss how to combine that information with the job evaluation process results to arrive at wage rates for jobs.

## Salary Surveys

**salary survey**

a systematic process for collecting information about wages in the external labor market

**Salary surveys** provide a systematic way to collect information about wages in the external labor market. However, salary surveys must be carefully constructed to ensure that the data gathered are reliable and valid. Managers can either conduct their own surveys or purchase survey data from a number of different sources, including professional organizations and human resources (HR) consulting firms. If you decide to purchase data, it is important to ask a lot of questions about the process used to collect the data, including the types of organizations included and the jobs analyzed. If your HR department provides the data for you, it is still important that you ask the same questions about the data provided.

Typically, salary survey data will come from companies in the same industry. For many jobs, it is also important to collect data from companies in other industries that might be competing with you for employees. A hospital and an airline operate in different industries, but both require accountants, marketing professionals, and other types of employees. The data should also come from the appropriate geographic labor market, which can be local, regional, national, or global, depending on the type of job.

Salary surveys should collect data for an organization's benchmark jobs because it would be too expensive and time consuming to try to collect data about every job in the company. Plus, there will be jobs in your company for which there are no comparable jobs in other organizations. Exhibit 10.6 contains a list of questions to consider when preparing to either conduct a salary survey or purchase one. Keep in

### EXHIBIT 10.6

#### Questions to Consider When Conducting a Salary Survey

- What is the goal for the survey? To cover base pay, variable pay, or benefits?
- What is the appropriate comparison group? Industry or individual professions? Local area or national?
- What questions will give me the data needed?
- What are the benchmark jobs to survey?
- Have I operationalized the job descriptions and the comparison data terms appropriately?
- How will I maintain the integrity of the data?
- Have I made sure that salary data from multiple salary surveys share a common date?

mind that if you are using salary from multiple surveys, you need to make sure the data share a common date—otherwise, they won't be comparable. Additionally, a new salary survey should be conducted at least every two or three years to ensure the company is staying competitive with pay.[10]

## Job Pricing

When the data collection for a salary survey is complete, the pricing of jobs begins. **Job pricing** is the systematic process of assigning monetary rates to jobs so that a firm's internal wages are aligned with the external wages in the marketplace. It is during this process that the organization's pay policy relative to the market is developed.

Job pricing is a multiple-step process. It begins with managers plotting the results of a salary survey for the benchmark jobs within their firm. To illustrate how the external data translate into internal compensation decisions, we will assume that the managers are using the point method to evaluate jobs. (Later in the chapter, we discuss alternative approaches to making pay decisions.)

As you can see in Exhibit 10.7, the *x*-axis represents the evaluation points associated with different jobs that are used to map their importance to the firm. The *y*-axis represents the salaries the external labor market is paying for those jobs. The result of combining the data for the jobs is a scatterplot. Notice that you can almost draw a straight line from the bottom-left corner to the top-right corner of the graph. In fact, that is what actually happens. The market line, also known as the **wage curve** or **pay policy line** (which may be a straight line, but is more likely to be curved), is drawn to represent the relationship between the job evaluation points and the salaries paid for the jobs. The wage curve can be drawn by hand through the points so that about as many points are above the line as are below the line, or a statistical regression process can be used to draw the line. (The regression approach is, of course, the most accurate.)

The next step is to plot the actual salaries paid for the benchmark jobs in the company and compare that result with the results from the market. Once again,

**job pricing**

the systematic process of assigning monetary rates to jobs so that a firm's internal wages are aligned with the external wages in the marketplace

**wage curve (or pay policy line)**

the market line that represents the relationship between the job evaluation points and the salaries paid for the various jobs in the labor market

---

### EXHIBIT 10.7

Wage Curve Developed from the Point Method of Job Evaluation

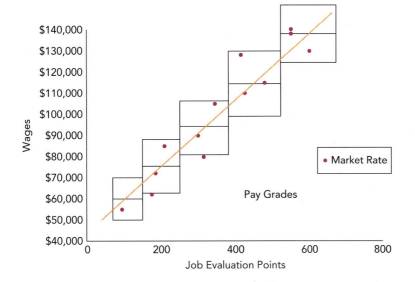

the job evaluation points are used. Any difference between the wages the company is paying and the wages being paid in the marketplace is noted. In short, the wage curve shows how similar the pay within a firm's job structure is to how the jobs are being paid in the labor market.

## Company Pay Policy

If a company's wage curve is below (or above) the market's wage curve, then decisions have to be made about whether to move the wages for those jobs up to the line, leave them as they are, or move them above the line. The company's pay policy will determine what is done and is driven by the strategic objectives of the firm's compensation philosophy and policies.

Companies can choose to pay *at the market* (follow), *above the market* (lead), or *below the market* (lag). Google and Costco are two companies that have decided to pay above the market for jobs in their industries.[11] They do so because they want to get the best talent and because they know that talented human capital is ultimately the key to success. Most firms, however, decide to pay at the market. Think for a minute about why that is the case. Many executives believe that if their company pays above the market, it might be incurring unnecessarily high labor expenses if there is a sufficient supply of workers willing to work at market wages. In contrast, if a company pays below market, it will have a harder time attracting employees.

Some firms choose to pay at the market but offer benefits that exceed what is typically offered for comparable work at other companies. An additional approach is to match as many jobs as possible to the market. This approach is used when a company's main focus is on external competitiveness rather than internal alignment.

## Pay Grades and Pay Ranges

Determining the actual pay rates for individual employees is governed by the pay range within which their jobs fall. Employees in a particular job should not be paid less than the minimum amount of the pay range, nor more than the maximum amount of the range. To establish pay ranges, managers decide which jobs are similar according to the job evaluation results and group those jobs into job grades. Often, there will be natural breaks in the point spread for the benchmark jobs that make it easy to decide which jobs logically should be grouped together into pay grades. The jobs in each pay grade will have the same pay range. Each pay grade will have a minimum and maximum number of job evaluation points (which appear on the horizontal axis), as well as minimum and maximum wage rates (which appear on the vertical axis).

If you once again refer to Exhibit 10.7, you will see that each range has a midpoint, as well as a minimum and a maximum. The midpoint of the range typically represents what an employee who is fully qualified and functioning at an acceptable level of performance should make and is drawn relative to the pay line the company intends to pursue. In the case of our example, the company is using the market line as its new pay line. The minimum represents what an entry-level employee would make, and the maximum represents what a highly qualified, longer-term employee would make. Wage ranges for high-level jobs can be 30%–60% above or below the midpoint, whereas entry-level wage ranges might be within 5%–15% of the midpoint.[12]

When establishing wage ranges, an important consideration is the degree of overlap. A small amount of overlap between two grades means that there is a great deal of difference between the salaries paid for the two jobs. In other words, less overlap means that there is more difference between jobs in each grade. The overlap decision is affected by the nature of the job (clerical versus professional) and other factors, such as what the firm wants to signal to employees in terms of upward mobility. When there is a lot of overlap, employees in a lower grade might actually have the same salary as employees in a higher grade. Thus, internal equity as well as external equity is a concern in determining the overlap of pay ranges.

Grades and ranges give managers some degree of flexibility when it comes to compensating employees who have different amounts of seniority, skills, and productivity levels. For example, an employee with one year of experience, who is still learning the job, would be paid lower in the pay range than would someone with five years of experience and a high level of performance.

Once the pay grades are determined, nonbenchmark jobs can be evaluated and slotted into the appropriate pay grades. Exhibit 10.8 summarizes the job pricing process. It is unlikely that you, as a manager, will have to actually collect the data, develop the wage curves, and determine job grades and ranges unless you choose a career in HR. (And, by the way, jobs in compensation typically are readily available and pay very well!) However, as a manager, you do need to understand the process and its implications. In the event that you are called on to actually use a job evaluation manual to make decisions about the point values for new jobs or restructured jobs within your firm, having this understanding will be invaluable. Most likely, unless you are in a small business, you will be given guidance from the HR department regarding how to set the salary for your employees within their appropriate pay grade range.

## Broadbanding

Over time, companies have worked to identify ways to reduce some of the complexity involved in the job pricing process. An approach that has worked well for some organizations is **broadbanding**, also known as **career banding.** Broadbanding consolidates a large number of pay grades into a few broad bands—usually 3 to 10 bands, or grades, as opposed to the larger number of grades traditionally used.

The maximum pay for a particular band can be as high as 100%–400% above the band's minimum pay.[13] For example, at your company, one person in the middle band might earn $10,000 per month, while another person in the same band might earn $18,000 per month—a 180% difference. The jobs in this band are all professional jobs at the company, ranging from comptroller to marketing manager. The jobs in the band are similar to one another in that they require approximately the same level of education and experience, as well as having similar levels of responsibility.

**broadbanding (also known as career banding)**

an approach used to reduce the complexity of a compensation system by consolidating a large number of pay grades into a fewer number of broad grades (or bands)

### EXHIBIT 10.8

#### Job Pricing Process

1. Conduct a salary survey.
2. Plot the salaries for benchmark jobs using job evaluation points for each job.
3. Draw the market line.
4. Decide on your company's line based on its pay policy.
5. Create wage ranges for your firm's job grades.
6. Adjust the wages for jobs within each grade, as needed, to match your company's pay policy.

Reducing the number of grades by using bands makes managing the system much easier, too, because the bands are typically wide enough that changes in the market don't require managers to adjust the bands as frequently. Another plus for broadbanding is that the pay range for a band gives you, as a manager, more flexibility to set the starting pay for one of your employees, and more room for you to give raises to your existing employees without going outside a band. Both IBM and Marriott adopted broadband pay systems which gave greater salary management responsibility to their line managers.[14]

When bands are used, it is important to ensure that there is some logical reason why jobs are in the same band. Managers also need to understand how the bands work and how to properly assign salaries within the bands. If this training does not happen, employees might believe that the company's salary decisions aren't based on objective criteria. Also, the flexibility in pay ranges afforded by bands can lead to higher wages overall for the company if processes are not in place to manage how increases are instituted.

Some companies actually use a combination of broadbands and job grades. For instance, a company that wants to make sure that functional expertise and people management are equally valued at bonus time might slot employees into bands based on such factors as level of decision-making, authority, and expertise, regardless of the functional area in which the employees work. For external benchmarking and establishing the range for base salary, the same firm might use job grades. At bonus time, the band in which a particular job is located would determine the percent of bonus paid. Other organizations are actually moving away from broadbanding and back to job grades. Company Spotlight 10.2 describes why the city government of

## COMPANY SPOTLIGHT **10.2**

### Broadbanding Versus Pay Grades for Fairfield City Employees

One might not think of a city government as a business, but local governments face many of the same decisions as any other type of business. Determining the compensation structure for employees is one of those decisions. Nearly 20 years ago, the city of Fairfield, Ohio, completed a salary study that resulted in the development of a broadband compensation structure with wide pay bands. The Clerical/Technical band ranged from $24,960–$74,774, for example. In 2017, the city commissioned a new study that led to the decision to move away from the broadband plan, which had three bands, to a point factor system, with 10 compensable factors and 14 pay grades. The change resulted in updating the pay structure for 50 nonunion employees. The study included surveying nearby and similar local governments. The results indicated that some positions were being overpaid relative to the market as a result of broadbanding, and some were being underpaid. Additionally, one of the city jobs fit into three bands, making it difficult to decide on the appropriate salary. Under the new system, no employee will be paid above the maximum of their range. The city plans to find other ways to keep the employees who will be affected by the new maximum motivated. For instance, the city may provide achievement bonuses if the employees meet their goals. Employees understand that the study was done by a third party and that it focused on positions, not the individual employee in the position.

*Sources:* Pitman, Michael D., "Fairfield to Adjust Employee Pay Structure," *Journal-News*, journal-news.com, December 6, 2017, https://www.journal-news.com/news/fairfield-adjust-employee-pay-structure/vMnpeK3v221rNbgspOcIMM/; "Fairfield City Council, Regular Meeting," December 11, 2017, https://d3n9y02raazwpg.cloudfront.net/fairfield-city/d8cf5f89-7799-11e7-b9a7-00219ba2f017-e25a7bab-4a4a-4d3b-98d9-7468461842bc-1512573422.pdf.

Fairfield, Ohio, a broadbanding plan that included three bands to a point factor approach that included 14 job grades.

## Pay for Individual Employees

Remember that up to this point, we have been talking about how to determine pay for jobs, not pay rates for individual employees. Once you have decided on the pay ranges for jobs, it is time to decide what to pay the actual employees performing the jobs.

The initial pay for a new employee will be based on a number of factors, including the person's previous work experience, education, training, and negotiating skills. Better negotiators often start at higher salaries. For current employees, salary increases can be tied to meeting quotas, completing projects, providing high levels of customer service, or the results of their performance appraisal.

Chapter 11 describes incentive pay in greater detail, including merit raises and sales commissions. This topic of incentive pay is important because the decisions managers make about performance-based pay affect employees' perceptions about how fairly they are being treated, their motivation level, and the company's bottom line. Companies are giving greater emphasis to performance-based pay in response to stakeholder concerns about overall firm performance and in acknowledgment of the substantial contributions employees make to achieving company goals. Even the U.S. government has adopted a pay-for-performance plan for many of its agencies.[15] This plan is in part the result of employee frustrations with a system that rewarded seniority more than contributions, as well as growing concerns about attracting top talent to government jobs.

Other issues have to be addressed in determining compensation for current employees as well. You may have an employee whose job is *red circled* or *green circled*. Red-circled jobs are those for which the person in the job is being paid above the maximum wage for that pay grade. In such an event, the manager can freeze the person's pay until the range catches up, reduce the person's salary (usually not a smart move unless you really want to get rid of the employee), reevaluate the job to make sure the job evaluation was done properly the first time, or upgrade the person's job description so that his or her job is evaluated at a higher grade. A green-circled job means, the person's salary is below the minimum of the range. The manager can leave the salary where it is (again, not a good move unless you want to get rid of the employee), reevaluate the job, reclassify the job into a lower grade, or give the person a raise. If there is a big difference between the person's current pay and his or her new pay range, the raise may be awarded in increments over time.

## Alternative Compensation Approaches

The job-based compensation approach is the predominant model used in most companies. However, more and more companies are experimenting with and adopting alternative approaches for compensation plans. These companies recognize that the human capital the employee brings to the job is critical for their organization's success. Think about the most creative person at an advertising firm or the most innovative software designer at a software company. Paying a person makes more sense than paying for a particular job in such contexts.

In contrast, paying for the job performed rather than what a person brings to the job makes more sense when job duties and responsibilities are relatively unchanging. However, job-based pay, especially when seniority is a big factor, is less likely to motivate employees to develop the knowledge, skills, and abilities (KSAs) that the firm needs for the future, and it doesn't recognize that the high level of knowledge and performance provided by employees makes a value-added difference. Of course, one central problem in moving to more employee-based pay systems is the need for good metrics to use as the basis of pay decisions.[16] Addressing the metrics issue is critical to reducing perceptions of inequity if a manager has control over setting the pay rates.

Some of the alternatives to the traditional job-based structures are skill- or knowledge-based pay, competency-based pay, direct market pricing, and broadbanding (which we have already described).

## Skill-Based Pay and Knowledge-Based Pay

**skill-based pay**

systems that require employees to acquire certain skills in order to receive a pay increase

**knowledge-based pay**

systems that require employees to acquire certain knowledge in order to receive a pay increase

**Skill-based pay** and **knowledge-based pay** systems require employees to acquire certain skills or knowledge to receive a pay increase. The skills or areas of knowledge are arranged in a hierarchy. An employee demonstrates mastery of each level of skill or area of knowledge by passing a test, passing a class, or serving in an apprentice role. Once the level has been passed, the employee receives a pay raise. These plans can be classified as depth oriented or breadth oriented. Depth-oriented plans focus on the employee gaining greater expertise (or depth) on existing skills. Breadth-oriented plans focus on employees gaining flexibility to perform a variety of jobs in the company while developing skill depth and self-management skills.[17] The goal of both of these pay plans is to ensure that a sufficient number of employees have the skills and knowledge an organization needs to succeed. The process also makes it clear to employees what they have to do to increase their pay.

These pay systems are not without problems, however. Some companies have found that they end up with more employees at higher levels of mastery than they need.[18] This outcome is expensive. Passing the test at each level automatically leads to a raise, so employees are getting paid at higher salaries than are really appropriate for their current jobs. Even though they have received a raise, employees may become frustrated because they can't use the skills they have acquired.

However, survey and academic research suggests that the benefits of skill-based plans outweigh the costs in the right settings, primarily in manufacturing and service jobs. Such plans have been associated with ensuring firms have the benefit of critically needed skills that may be used infrequently[19] and with increased productivity, lower labor costs, and fewer employees.[20] In a comparison that looked at job-based and market-based pay plans, researchers found that skill-based plans were superior because of these and other employee and organizational outcomes.[21]

In certain professions, such as consulting, medicine, and law, employees have specific credentials or levels of knowledge (MBAs, JDs, or certain computer certifications, for example) that allow firms to charge customers higher rates. As a result, companies are willing and able to tie pay to these higher-level credentials. In fact, they must do so in order to hire the professionals they need to achieve organizational goals.

## Competency-Based Pay

**competency-based pay**

a highly structured pay system that identifies the competencies employees need to master to be eligible for pay raises

Similar to skill- or knowledge-based pay, **competency-based pay** plans identify the competencies (e.g., attitudes, behaviors, abilities) employees need to master to be eligible for pay raises. The competencies are identified for the firm as a whole or for a particular work unit, and they are the competencies that are believed to be the most critical if the firm is to achieve its goals. Competencies might focus on customer service, teamwork, ability to motivate others, problem-solving, and creativity and innovation.[22] Employees receive higher compensation when they demonstrate that they have a higher amount of the competencies valued by the company.

For a competency-based system to succeed, managers need to clearly define the competencies employees need to have and outline a valid process for determining whether they have them. One plus of this system is that it keeps employees focused on continuous learning. The disadvantages are similar to the ones discussed for skills-based pay: Employees can obtain more competencies than their current jobs require, leading to higher labor costs for a firm, and employees can become frustrated if there isn't a clear path to use their additional training to advance within the organization.

## Market Pricing

Employers also can use **market pricing** to make employee-compensation decisions. Market pricing involves collecting salary information from the external labor market first rather than starting with the development of an internal structure based on the value of the jobs within the company. Data are collected on as many jobs as possible, with the remaining jobs included in the final pay structure. This approach came into vogue in the 1980s in part because jobs were changing rapidly as the use of technology became more prevalent.[23] Market pricing was the dominant approach used for job evaluation by companies participating in a WorldatWork survey in 2016.[24] In fact, 91% of 590 companies indicated they use market pricing as the basis for determining the relative value of jobs in their organization. The approach works well, as long as the data are accurate. Ignoring small sample sizes and other measurement problems can lead to incorrect inferences about the actual market pay rates for a particular job.[25]

Additionally, as noted earlier when we discussed salary surveys, it is important to make sure the data collected and used are all for the same time period; otherwise, it will not be an accurate reflection of the market. For instance, one company responding to a salary survey might provide data as of January 1 and report an annual salary of $50,000, while two other companies might provide data as of July 1 and report annual salaries of $50,500 and $51,900. If that happens, the company using the survey needs to age the January 1 data to the July 1 date to ensure the data accurately reflect the market. Aging the data involves determining a percent of increase in wages during the time period for which the data needs to be aged and then adjusting the data accordingly. Exhibit 10.9 shows why this matters. In our example, the mean salary increases by $333 annually and the median salary becomes $51,000 instead of $50,500. Thus, aging the data makes a difference in the market price for this job.[26]

Company Spotlight 10.3 describes Siemens' approach to market pricing.

**market pricing**
a method for determining pay for jobs by collecting salary information from the external labor market first, rather than starting with the development of an internal structure based on the value of the jobs within the company

### EXHIBIT 10.9

Aging Salary Survey Data

| Company | Date of Data | Hourly Wage | Adjusted Hourly Wage (Assumes 2% inflation from January–June) |
|---|---|---|---|
| 1 | January 1 | $50,000 | $50,000 × 1.02 = $51,000 |
| 2 | July 1 | $50,500 | $50,500 |
| 3 | July 1 | $51,900 | $51,900 |
| Mean Wage | | $50,800 | $51,133 |
| Median Wage | | $50,500 | $51,000 |

## Administering Compensation

Regardless of which compensation plan you use, it has to be carefully administered. A handbook for the job evaluation process, skill- or competency-based plan, market pricing, or broadbanding is only one part of effective administration

## COMPANY SPOTLIGHT  **10.3**

### Market Pricing at Siemens AG

Siemens AG, a 170-year-old German firm, has over 350,000 employees worldwide and is one of the world's largest industrial enterprises. Its revenues are near $90 billion. So how does a company of this magnitude decide how to pay employees? Siemens has found that market pricing is an effective way to have a competitive pay strategy. This data-driven approach helps managers ensure that pay at Siemens is in line with pay at other companies. More important, it helps the company attract the right talent, which is particularly important as the company continues to transition to the digital age and work to maintain its focus on businesses serving society's needs.

In the United States, market pricing is easier to do because there is better data available than in many other parts of the world where the company does business. Siemens uses both general and industry-specific salary surveys, making sure there is appropriate and sufficient salary data to represent the market accurately. The company also focuses on its internal market to find the right balance between the external and the internal markets.

*Sources:* Moore, Greg, "The Ups and Downs of Market Pricing at Siemens," Compensation Focus, WorldatWork, June 2017, https://www.worldatwork.org/docs/compensation-focus/2017/06-12-2017/the-ups-and-downs-of-market-pricing-at-siemens.html; Gharib, Susie, "How to Run a 170 Year Old Company Like a Startup," *Fortune*, October 4, 2017, http://fortune.com/2017/10/04/joe-koeser-siemens-ag-secret-to-success.

of a compensation program. Three other key elements are needed: training for managers, communication, and evaluation. We discuss each of these elements next.

Anyone involved in making employee pay decisions needs to receive training on how the process works. Topics to cover would include how pay rates are set at the company and how frequently they are reviewed, how pay raises are determined, and what can and cannot be communicated to employees about the firm's pay system. When a point method is used, managers need training on how to use the job evaluation handbook to score jobs, slot them into grades, and decide how much to pay for them.

Companies also have to decide how much information they should share with their employees about the compensation system. Most companies have closed pay systems. With a *closed* system, the details about individual pay rates are not made public except as required by law for high-ranking executives of publicly traded companies. The law requires publicly traded companies to include in their annual reports a breakdown of the components of the total compensation package. Public organizations in many states are required to disclose what they pay their employees. These organizations have *open* pay systems.

Companies that voluntarily make their pay information public believe that transparency is important and that the more information employees have, the more equitable the system will be perceived to be. Companies that use a closed system believe that there are many reasons why pay differences exist, and that some of those reasons are difficult to explain to employees. These firms believe, therefore, that it is better not to make too much information available. A company's compensation philosophy will guide these decisions.

With both open and closed systems, however, all companies and managers need to carefully consider what employees are told about their pay and how they are given that information. They should operate under the assumption that pay comparisons will occur, whether sanctioned or not.[27] Information that is carelessly conveyed can have a long-term negative effect on employee morale and productivity, while carefully crafted, honest, and thoughtful communication will enhance employees' perceptions of equity and justice. Social media also must be considered when planning how to communicate about pay, and how pay information is being communicated. Social media allows employees more access to more information about coworkers, thus increasing social comparison costs that affect compensation perceptions.[28]

The company also has to regularly review its compensation system. Without such a review, you might not know when external market salaries might rise, and your company would be at a competitive disadvantage. Keeping salary information current is only one reason for a regular review of the company's compensation system, however. The system also needs to be evaluated to ensure that employees in protected classes are being equitably paid, to ensure that managers are being trained as to how the compensation system works and properly rewarding employees, and to ensure that any changes in the company's values or strategic objectives are reflected in the firm's compensation system.

When changes are needed in the compensation system, the process for communicating those changes to employees must be carefully orchestrated. One study found that implementing a new pay system led to a long-lasting emotional response, which affected employee attitudes and behaviors. In this particular case, employees who responded positively to the changes were less likely to leave the organization. Giving employees ample opportunity to talk with managers and to respond anonymously to the new system can help employees have a voice and be more accepting of the new pay system.[29]

**Principles**

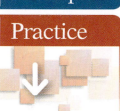

**Practice**

# Compensation in Practice: Organizational Demands

As with all other employee-management decisions, compensation decisions must be made within the appropriate context of a firm's organizational demands and environmental influencers. Exhibit 10.10 lists some of these elements. In this section, we examine how a company can manage employee compensation within these contexts so that it achieves the objectives of attracting, maintaining, and retaining the employees needed for the firm to have and maintain a sustained competitive advantage. We also will emphasize your role as a manager in making decisions about compensation. As with the first half of this chapter, we focus more on the broader topic of compensation in general, with an emphasis on base pay. Chapter 11 addresses organizational demands and environmental influencers relative to incentive pay, and Chapter 12 addresses benefits as well as safety, to round out our discussion of total compensation. As a manager, you are in a critical position to understand how the organizational demands and environmental influencers affect both how the company pays employees and their perceptions about that pay.

## Strategy and Compensation

A firm's strategy directly affects the internal value of its jobs, the wages it pays, and the pay mix it uses.[30] Firms that align pay with strategy, understanding that compensation is inextricably linked with technology, financial decisions, marketing, and operations, gain a competitive advantage over firms that do not ensure such alignment.[31]

### Internal Value of Jobs

A company's strategy will determine the tasks, duties, and responsibilities it considers most valuable for achieving its goals. Jobs that involve those tasks, duties, and responsibilities will receive the highest rewards. However, because the strategies of

**EXHIBIT 10.10**

## Compensation in Practice

| Context | Practice Issues |
|---|---|
| **Organizational Demands** | |
| *Strategy* drives . . . | • Internal value of jobs<br>• Compensation mix |
| *Company characteristics* determine . . . | • Ability to provide compensation<br>• Types of compensation |
| *Culture* establishes . . . | • Priorities of the firm's compensation policies<br>• Employees' expectations and attitudes toward compensation |
| *Employee concerns* include . . . | • Equity versus equality<br>• Fairness of rewards |
| **Environmental Demands** | |
| *Labor force* influences . . . | • Level of compensation<br>• Form of compensation employee desires |
| *Technology* affects . . . | • Ease of collecting compensation data<br>• How compensation is tracked and delivered<br>• What is considered compensable work |
| *Globalization* impacts . . . | • Where compensation decisions are made<br>• Acceptableness of compensation<br>• Pay rates |
| *Ethics/social* responsibility shapes . . . | • What compensation signals to employees<br>• Attitudes about the living wage and comparable worth |
| **Regulations** | |
| *Regulations* guide . . . | • What laws employers must follow in making compensation decisions<br>• What rights employees have regarding what they are paid |

firms differ, as explained earlier in the chapter, the same job can be valued differently from one company to another. Keep in mind, too, that if a company's strategy changes, the compensation system will need to change as well to ensure that it continues to help the firm achieve its overall goals. Now, let's look at some examples.

Consider KPMG, which provides audit, tax, advisory, and related services.[32] This company has a differentiation strategy and focuses on quality and innovative capabilities, as well as technologies that enhance quality. Core jobs for the company include accounting and information technology (IT) specialist jobs. Logically, the firm will pay more for those jobs than for support jobs, such as sales and HR management. The core jobs have a bigger impact on the company's bottom line. In fact, the company likely will pay wages higher than the market to attract the very best accounting and IT staff. The firm might even offer more variable pay as a way to further enhance employees' salaries and make the company an attractive employer.[33]

Now, consider a firm such as Airstream, which pursues a differentiation strategy by selling "adventure," marketed as "Live Riveted," and focusing on quality, community, and image.[34] While Airstream will hire accountants and IT specialists, the core jobs in this firm are design, engineering, and sales jobs, so employees in these jobs receive the highest pay. As you can see, the same jobs—the jobs of accountant and IT specialist in this case—can be valued differently, depending on the business of the company and its strategy.

Consider another example. In many fast-food restaurants, such as McDonald's, the focus is on maintaining low costs, standardization, and efficiency. Most of the core jobs will be very specialized and require low skills. As a result, the pay for these jobs will be low. A manager in an organization with a low-cost strategy would be tasked with ensuring that costs are kept down, that employees are efficient, and that employees follow the standards of the company. The manager would be paid to achieve these goals.

### Compensation Mix

A firm's strategy will affect the pay mix it offers employees. Many companies are reconsidering the amount of base pay versus variable pay that is included in employee compensation packages and considering more incentive pay plans.[35] A problem with base pay is that it ties the firm to a fixed dollar amount that becomes larger as cost-of-living adjustments and merit pay are added to the base.

As a result of inflation, many firms give their employees **cost-of-living adjustments (COLAs)** to offset the increases in the prices of goods and services they purchase and to keep salaries from lagging the external market. The consumer price index (CPI) is used as the basis for determining the amount of a COLA. The CPI consists of a market basket of food, energy, transportation, medical, and other goods and services that are regularly consumed by urban households, and it is calculated based on changes in the prices of these items. The data to calculate the CPI come from 75 urban areas in the United States and about 22,000 retail and service establishments and 5,000 housing units.[36]

Merit increases are not automatic. **Merit increases** are awarded based on how well an individual has performed. Like a COLA, however, a merit increase permanently raises a person's wages. Even if the worker's performance declines, the previous merit increase still remains part of his or her base pay. To offset the permanency of merit raises, quite a few firms are increasing the amount of variable pay they offer to employees. In fact, a lot of managers believe that offering employees more variable versus base pay can effectively shape their behavior.[37] Variable pay can include bonuses, commissions, stock options, and other forms of monetary rewards that do not become a permanent part of a person's base pay. Chapter 11 provides more discussion of these types of pay. For now, we will discuss the value of variable pay.

A pharmaceutical company, such as Pfizer, would have to consider whether more of the pay it offers its employees should be in the form of direct base pay, or whether a large percentage of it should be variable. The research staff might receive bonuses based on their individual performance and/or department's performance, or the company's performance as a whole. The sales reps are likely to receive commissions (variable pay) tied to their ability to convince physicians to write prescriptions for the company's drugs. They may or may not receive base pay as well. Research has shown that managers and employees who receive stock options behave in ways that are more beneficial to their firms because part of their pay (the stock options) is linked to the performance of the firm.[38] You will learn more about how sales commissions and other performance-based incentives work in the next chapter.

Overall, a company's strategy will determine the mix of base pay and variable pay and the mix of monetary and nonmonetary rewards it offers. Managers need to understand how this works so they can make appropriate decisions about pay. A firm's strategy and compensation philosophy also determines the extent to which other types of rewards, such as benefits, are available. A Mercer Total Rewards Survey reported that less than 32% of the respondents felt that their total rewards and business strategies were aligned.[39]

## Company Characteristics and Compensation

Along with strategy, the characteristics of a company have a major impact on its compensation decisions in terms of what the firm is able to offer its employees and

**cost-of-living adjustment (COLA)**

an adjustment given to employees to offset the increases in the prices of goods and services they purchase and to keep salaries from lagging the external market

**merit increase**

a salary increase awarded based on how well an individual has performed his or her job

the type of compensation provided. The age and stage of development of the company, as well as other characteristics, such as its size, play key roles in these decisions.

### Ability to Pay

Why might a firm pay less-than-market wages? Start-up and small firms might not be in a position to do otherwise. This situation could create some problems relative to attracting employees, but this is not always the case. Microsoft paid lower wages when it first started but was still able to attract highly qualified employees because the work they would be doing was on the cutting edge, and Microsoft gave shares of the company to the employees as well. The employees were betting on eventually making a lot of money by forgoing higher wages in the beginning of their careers with the firm. We all know the rest of that story.

More established companies have more resources and can pay at or even above-market wages. If a company is profitable, it will more likely offer higher salaries relative to the market. Keep in mind, however, that the age and size of the company are subordinate to the company's pay philosophy and that the company strategy should drive the pay philosophy. A new, small start-up might actually pay above-market wages for its size, age, and industry to ensure that it starts off with top talent. As a manager, part of your job will be to help employees understand your company's pay philosophy and why it exists.

Larger companies and more-established companies generally have greater resources and can pay higher wages. For example, SAS, the statistical software company mentioned earlier in the chapter, is known for paying above-market wages. Keep in mind that even in companies like this, some jobs are paid at the market rate and some are paid above it, as discussed in the earlier section on strategy. Whether a job is a core job or a support position affects the decision about level of pay.[40]

### Types of Compensation

The size and age of a firm play a major role in determining the type of pay it offers. As mentioned earlier, start-up firms often give stock options to their employees to offset their inability to pay market wages. Older, more established firms focus on finding the best balance between base pay and variable pay. Larger firms generally have more complex pay systems, in part because of the many types of jobs they have and the differing degrees to which those jobs contribute to the profitability of the firms. Larger firms can also offer more benefits and services to employees because of economies of scale. Generally, the more employees at the firm, the better deals the firm is able to strike with third-party benefit and service providers. Also, larger firms pay more overall than smaller firms.[41]

## Culture and Compensation

The culture of an organization has a major impact on the compensation decisions its managers make. Specifically, the culture establishes the priorities for the pay policy of the firm. It also plays a large role in terms of employees' expectations and attitudes about the rewards offered to them. Let's take a look at each of these issues.

### Priorities of a Firm's Compensation Policy

An organization's culture affects the pay policy of the firm both directly and indirectly. Overall, the pay policy of a company should complement its culture. In thinking about culture and rewards, it is important to remember that even the best intentions can lead to unwanted outcomes. If the culture is one of competition with individual rewards given, employees will be less interested in collaboration and being part of a team, and more interested in maximizing their own rewards.[42] If the organization values teamwork, then the pay policy needs to make it clear that teamwork will be rewarded. If the culture values innovation, the pay policy should emphasize that the company will provide higher rewards for employees who exhibit this value.

### Employees' Expectations and Attitudes about Compensation

An organization's culture sends a message to the firm's employees about what rewards they can expect to receive. For example, in a culture that values learning, employees will expect to receive higher pay for engaging in learning activities. Employees in cultures in which they know they are valued tend to have a more positive attitude toward their compensation than those in harsh and competitive cultures. In the latter environment, employees tend to be suspicious and distrustful of the compensation decisions managers make.[43] In turn, a firm's compensation system sends a message to employees about the company's culture by rewarding the types of behaviors desired in the culture.[44]

As a manager, you might not be able to change the entire corporate culture of your firm. However, you can do a lot to inform your employees about how pay decisions are made within it and what employees need to do to achieve higher pay levels. You are also in the best position to know what types of rewards are valued by your employees.[45] For example, if employees greatly value higher base pay, trying to offset a lower-pay plan with perks such as employee recognition programs isn't likely to motivate workers.

## Employee Concerns and Compensation

How your employees perceive the psychological contract they have with your firm will be due, in large part, to the company's pay decisions. These decisions include what the compensation signals to the employees about how they are valued and how the firm implements the process. Thus, significant employee concerns relative to compensation center on equity and fairness issues. You should be familiar with both of these issues by now. Let's take a look at how they play out relative to compensation.

### Equity Versus Equality

Earlier in the chapter, we discussed equity theory: Employees compare their inputs to their outputs and contrast them against those of people who are similarly situated to them, either within the company or outside it. If there is a perception that the rewards are inequitable, then the person will seek a way (or ways) to rectify the situation.

Consider what happens in an egalitarian organization where the goal is to compensate all employees at the same level. The idea is that doing this eliminates status differences and will foster a more cooperative work environment. The reality, however, is that not all jobs require equal KSAs or have equal levels of responsibility or accountability, and not all employees have the same motivation to perform their jobs. Thus, while having an egalitarian pay structure appears to be more objective than some other types of pay structures and appears to reduce equity concerns, such a system fails to address differences that are legitimate reasons for pay variability among employees.

In setting a pay structure, managers must carefully consider their decisions and acknowledge the consequences of the choices that they make. As a manager, you need to understand these and other employee concerns about compensation so that you can address them appropriately.

### Fairness of Rewards

When it comes to compensation decisions, employees are particularly sensitive to justice issues. If employees believe there is distributive justice, they might be less concerned about procedural justice. Typically, however, employees want to understand that both the process and the outcomes are fair. Employees know that even if they get a good outcome (such as a significant raise) this time, that might not happen the next time around if the process is poorly designed.

In addition, interactional justice is important. If an employee feels that he doesn't have a good relationship with you as his manager, he will be concerned about the fairness of your decisions, including those that relate to his compensation. Therefore, as a manager, it is your responsibility to make sure that your employees understand the pay process and how their pay was determined, and they know that you are treating them fairly.

**Salary compression** (also referred to as **pay** or **wage compression**) and **salary inversion** are additional fairness issues. Salary compression occurs when the pay for jobs in the external marketplace rises faster than the pay for jobs inside the organization, so that new employees are making the same wages as current employees. Salary inversion happens when the new employees negotiate for even higher wages than the current employees are making.[46]

Let's look at the job of college professor as an example. In the late 1980s, the numbers of students enrolling in business schools increased exponentially. As a result, universities needed to hire qualified faculty to teach these students. In order to attract and hire faculty in what had become an increasingly tight labor market, pay rates began to increase faster than the pay rates for faculty already employed, and that continues to be the case. Faculty fresh out of PhD programs start their academic careers making much higher salaries than faculty who have been at their schools for a long time.

We have used an academic example, but the same situation occurs in many other occupations across all types of organizations, especially those organizations that hire individuals with advanced degrees or highly specialized credentials. Any time there is a shortage of workers in the labor market, organizations end up paying higher salaries to attract needed employees, and it is often not economically feasible for the company to increase the salaries of existing employees to the same levels. Thus, salary compression happens, and with it come concerns about internal equity. When firms decide to make salary adjustments for a job to address equity issues, they have to decide whether all the longer-term employees in that particular job should be raised to the market level or not. Doing so implies that these employees would be able to obtain new jobs in the marketplace at market wages.

**salary compression (also referred to as pay or wage compression)**

a situation that occurs when the pay for jobs in the external marketplace rises faster than the pay for jobs inside the organization, resulting in new employees receiving equal salaries to current employees

**salary inversion**

a situation where new employees have negotiated for higher wages than the current employees are making

# Compensation in Practice: Environmental Influences

Along with organizational demands, environmental influences are a determining factor in how organizations set up their compensation systems. Labor surpluses and shortages affect pay levels. Technology has made administering systems easier and has made access to compensation data more available. Globalization has increased the complexity of pay decisions. In this section, we take a closer look at these and related environmental influencers.

## Labor Force and Compensation

Recall what you learned in your economics courses about supply and demand. As the supply of a good or service increases and demand decreases, what happens to its price? What about the reverse—when the supply declines and demand increases? Wages for jobs work the same way as prices for products. From a company perspective, then, the ideal world is one in which the labor supply far exceeds the demand for labor. In that environment, companies can keep wages down and still attract, maintain, and retain highly qualified workers. The opposite is also true: When the labor market is tight, companies have to use more of their profits to attract, maintain, and retain employees. Overall, the labor market influences the level of compensation firms offer, the form of that compensation, and market wages.

Remember that the labor market can be loose overall, but tight for particular jobs. Right now, for instance, the labor market is tight for many science, technology, engineering, and math (STEM) jobs. Companies with IT employees as part of their core workforce may need to pay above-market wages, but they also need to emphasize other total rewards, such as career opportunities and work/life balance.[47]

## The Level of a Firm's Compensation

What would you do if you had seven McDonald's restaurants in Billings, Montana, and were finding it difficult to attract quality applicants? When actually faced with this problem, the owner of these restaurants had to begin offering higher-than-minimum wages to attract workers. With lots of service jobs available, and few applicants to fill them, wages in Billings had continued to go up. The McDonald's franchiser was paying upward of $7 per hour (the minimum wage at the time was below $7), but other employers in the area were advertising as much as $15 per hour, plus benefits, for service jobs. Thus, trying to maintain the lower wages that are part of McDonald's low-cost strategy was hard in Billings.[48] This example shows how labor market supply and demand have a huge impact on market wages. By now, you are very familiar with how important it is that a firm decides whether to follow, lead, or lag the market and some of the organizational demands that influence that decision.

Obviously, we do not know everything about the impact of the various pay-level decisions. We do know, however, that leading the market helps a firm attract better-qualified workers (and more of them), helps retain workers, and reduces pay dissatisfaction. That is why Target announced in 2017 that it would raise its minimum wage to $10 an hour in October of that year and increase the hourly wage to $15 an hour by 2020. In its press release making this announcement, Target noted that it had a long history of investing in its team members and had always offered market-competitive wages. By putting the proposed increases in place, the company noted it would be "providing even more meaningful pay" for its employees. At the time of the announcement, $11 an hour was higher than the minimum wage in 48 states and matched the minimum wage in Massachusetts and Washington.[49]

Paying at the market rate results in attracting and retaining employees, containing labor costs, and reducing pay dissatisfaction. And, while lagging the market also helps contain labor costs, it makes an organization less attractive to prospective employees and leads to greater pay dissatisfaction. Thus, the decisions you make about your firm's pay relative to the external labor market are indeed important. Often, a hybrid policy may be the best approach. Jobs that are more critical to the firm can receive above-market wages, whereas less-critical jobs receive market or below-market wages. Jobs in high demand in the labor market may require higher compensation as well.

In reality, a firm may actually use a combination of pay strategies for a single job structure, depending on the availability of workers. If there is an abundance of workers for the entry-level jobs in the structure, their pay could be below or just at market. At the same time, a smaller supply of workers for higher-level jobs in the structure might necessitate paying above-market wages for those jobs.[50]

## Forms of Compensation That Employees Desire

Researchers have found that people have specific pay preferences and that individuals in the labor market will be more attracted to organizations with pay practices that match their pay preferences.[51] Millennials seem to seek out organizations that are providing clearly defined career opportunities and greater work/life balance.[52] When the labor market is loose, preferences such as these are less of a concern to firms because people looking for work will be less demanding. In contrast, people become more demanding in terms of the pay and other rewards that they expect when the labor market is tight.

## Technology and Compensation

Technology has vastly reduced the challenges of managing complex compensation systems, but it has created new challenges as well. It has made it easier to collect salary data and deliver pay. It has also affected what is considered compensable work. Let's take a look at each of these issues.

### Ease of Collecting Salary Data

Before the Internet, employers had to collect salary survey data with paper-and-pencil methods and then compile it—a slow process at best. Now, employers can access online salary surveys and conduct salary surveys online. These activities—accessing salary surveys and conducting surveys—have increased the speed with which employers and workers can access the most current salary information.

In addition to salary surveys provided by professional organizations and job sites such as Monster.com, sites such as Salary.com and PayScale.com have grown in terms of the accuracy and comprehensiveness of information they provide. Before you make any decisions based on salary data from sites such as these, however, make sure you research how and when the data were collected to ensure that they accurately represent the jobs of interest to you. Think about the consequences of using incorrect data if you are using these data to negotiate your own salary or if you are negotiating salary with an employee you are hiring.

### How Compensation Is Tracked and Delivered

With the advent of sophisticated database programs and expert systems, employers have been able to develop and implement computer programs to simplify the job evaluation process and to maintain all their compensation records. Employees have greater access to their pay information through their companies' employee portals as well.

Many companies are able to have employees input their work hours, with the data going directly into the company's accounting software. This ability saves the firms even more processing time. When the employees are consultants, lawyers, or other professionals who get paid based on the number of hours they bill clients, this ability to input data directly into the system has another advantage: It allows customers to more readily gain access to what their charges will be. For mobile professionals, the ability to input their time records directly online for compensation purposes helps ensure that they will be paid in a timely manner.[53] And, with online banking, companies can deposit employees' paychecks directly into their accounts so they don't have to worry about when and where to pick them up.

### What Is Considered Compensable Work

When employees telecommute, managers need to put in place clear policies that communicate what constitutes compensable work time. This way, employees understand what time they will be compensated for and what constitutes unauthorized off-the-clock work. To control off-the-clock work, managers should require employees to complete timesheets and certify that they are correct, in accordance with the company's telecommuting policy. Supervisors also need to verify the accuracy of the timesheets. The company's telecommuting policy should be consistently enforced, and any disciplinary measures should be outlined.[54]

## Globalization and Compensation

Global organizations have to decide whether they want to centralize or decentralize their compensation systems. That is, they have to decide where pay decisions will be made—either at headquarters or in the countries in which they are operating.[55]

In addition, the laws and norms of countries will affect the extent to which certain pay practices are accepted by employees. Let's now look at each of these two issues.[56]

## Where Pay Decisions Are Made

Global total rewards strategies are increasingly important. Global companies with centralized compensation systems are more satisfied with them and view them as more effective than companies with decentralized processes. Centralized systems provide a consistent link between results and rewards, and provide a greater likelihood of internal and external equity being achieved. However, the strategy does not mean that regional and country-specific differences in compensation are not considered. Quite the opposite, in fact. What it means is that they are integrated within a single compensation philosophy ensuring decisions reflect the goals and views of the company.[57]

In deciding where pay decisions are made, keep in mind that there are many cultural and local pay law differences around the world. Definitions of total reward package terms can vary significantly around the world. Earlier in this chapter, we used Siemens in a Company Spotlight. With business operations in more than 200 countries around the world, including Germany, Brazil, India, and several Middle Eastern countries, Siemens adopts its pay practices to address employment laws and practices relative to compensation in each place.[58] Also, whether the compensation is set by the headquarters or by the local office can affect interpretation of wage laws if not carefully designed, resulting in employees being able to claim they are working for two employers simultaneously—the headquarters and the local office.[59]

## Acceptableness of Compensation

Comparative studies of compensation in various countries have found some similarities and differences in the acceptability of various forms of compensation. For instance, in a study of compensation preferences in Hong Kong and China, several differences were identified. In Hong Kong, workers were interested in profit sharing and mortgage assistance. In China, workers were interested in individual bonuses and a housing provision.[60]

For expatriates, the picture is even more complicated. The complication occurs partly because companies have tightened their approach to global staffing and, in so doing, have made changes that affect how employees perceive the acceptability of their compensation. Globally, companies are just as concerned as U.S. companies with how well their compensation packages attract, maintain, and retain employees, whether those employees are host-country nationals (HCNs), third-country nationals (TCNs), or parent-country nationals (PCNs).

Paying PCNs is perhaps the most complicated aspect of global compensation. HCNs and TCNs will often be paid the host-country wage, while companies traditionally have tried to keep PCNs whole. That means that PCN salaries have been adjusted upward to account for the higher living costs in some countries versus the comparable costs in the home country. The converse is not true. Wages are not adjusted downward if living costs are actually less. Hence, when a PCN is from a country with considerably higher wages than the host-country wages, the PCN can be making a significantly higher wage than an HCN or a TCN in a comparable job, creating equity concerns.

One way to manage the compensation of PCNs is to use the balance-sheet approach, which involves looking at what a PCN was making prior to the international assignment and adding incentives for taking the foreign post and any pay adjustments needed to keep the employee at the same income level she was experiencing. The adjustments can include incentives for hardship assignments (assignments to countries with poor living conditions), dangerous assignments (say, to war-torn countries), or primitive assignments (assignments to countries or regions that are remote, such as the Australian outback). Therefore, the compensation for a global assignment typically involves adding current base pay and benefits to incentive and equalization adjustments.[61]

### Pay Rates

There are still significant pay-rate and pay-practice differences around the world—even within countries. Many U.S. companies doing business abroad have been criticized for paying low wages relative to American wages when they are following the laws in the country where they are doing business. Take China, for example. In March 2004, the Ministry of Labor and Social Security in China issued minimum-wage regulations for the first time.[62] In June 2007, the highest minimum wage in China was in Shenzhen, equal to $106 a month. In 2018, Shanghai's minimum wage was the highest, at 2,420 yuan a month, roughly double the minimum wage in smaller cities in China and equivalent to $357 USD a month.[63] Compare that to the United States, where the federal government requires a minimum wage of $7.25 per hour, and many people work 40 hours a week and receive a monthly wage of $1,257 as a result. This difference seems significant. However, the minimum wage in China might actually have equal or greater buying power compared to the minimum wage in the United States. Therefore, before generalizations are made, many factors, such as cost of living, have to be taken into consideration. That fact doesn't justify taking advantage of workers and paying them less than the minimum wage or just the minimum wage when a company can afford to pay more. Remember that the company's compensation philosophy should drive its practices around the world, not just in the United States.

Minimum wage differences are just one part of the total rewards that differ around the world. Other differences include required leave, health insurance, and other benefits. These differences make it imperative that a company carefully consider its total rewards philosophy when adopting a global mind-set. Doing so will help make sure that its goals are achievable. For instance, a company that wants to offer pay for performance as a central part of its total rewards package may find there are limitations in some countries on how that can be done.

## Ethics/Social Responsibility and Compensation

Perhaps as much as or more than any other HR activity, compensation is surrounded by ethical and social issues. What compensation decisions signal to employees about their firms' values and what people's attitudes are about living-wage and comparable worth issues are just a few of the ethical and social responsibility challenges associated with compensation.

### What Compensation Decisions Signal to Employees

The old adage "What gets rewarded is what gets done" carries strong ethical implications. Enron and related scandals raised the consciousness of many people about how compensation practices can lead to unethical behavior. By setting up a system that rewarded employees for goals that were short term and easily manipulated, employees with less than strong moral grounding (and even some who had been more grounded) found themselves engaging in unethical behavior to achieve the rewards. Managers who tie compensation to performance need to think long and hard about the possible consequences of their decisions regarding what will be the basis for those performance-based incentives. Tying pay-for-performance rewards to production quantity might have an entirely different outcome than tying pay-for-performance rewards to production quality.

Further, when performance is difficult to isolate and measure because of interdependent work, there can be negative outcomes from pay-for-performance, but the opposite is also true. When the performance in an interdependent work setting can be isolated and appropriately measured, there can be benefits from a pay-for-performance approach. Context does matter.[64]

### Attitudes About the Living Wage and Comparable Worth

An ethical and social responsibility issue that has been oft debated in Congress and in state legislatures is a concept called the **living wage**. The concept is generally described as providing a fair wage to a person so that basic living needs can be met. Much controversy surrounds this concept, however, because of the differences in opinion that exist about what minimal amount of income would constitute a living wage, as well as about whether it is the employer's obligation to ensure that employees make a living wage. Employers must pay the legally mandated minimum wage, but many have difficulty with the idea that they have to pay more than that for low-skilled jobs.

A few local governments have been able to enact living-wage legislation. Nassau County, New York, has a living wage of $16.07 per hour or $13.73 with health benefits for county employees and businesses with contracts with the county over $25,000. They have had a living-wage law in effect since 2007.[65] Company Spotlight 10.4 describes how Costco has made a decision as a company to offer a living wage even though it isn't required by law to do so.

**Comparable worth** has been another hotly debated topic. Comparable worth focuses on eliminating the gender inequity in wages because jobs held by women traditionally have been underpaid relative to similar jobs held by men. With comparable worth, jobs in the organization would be valued relative to other jobs

> **living wage**
> the concept that employees should be paid a wage that ensures that their basic costs of living are met

> **comparable worth**
> focuses on eliminating inequity in wages by ensuring that jobs that require similar levels of education and experience, and have other characteristics in common, are paid at a similar wage, regardless of gender

## COMPANY SPOTLIGHT 10.4

### Making a Living Wage at Costco

A blog on the job website Indeed.com named Costco Wholesale number one on its 2018 list of the top-rated companies in terms of pay and benefits practices. The Indeed blog analyzed data from 18 million employer reviews of companies to create its list. Costco is a multinational, membership-only warehouse that sells items in bulk quantities at low prices. The company is also the world's largest retailer of organic foods, choice and prime beef, wine, and rotisserie chicken.

Costco has long believed in paying employees a living wage. Its wages, even for entry-level employees, is well above what other retailers pay. The starting wage is $11.50 an hour, and the average wage is $21 per hour. The company also offers a graduated wage program, in which the more hours employees work, the higher their wage becomes. The pay of Costco's CEO is still well into the millions, but it is much less than that of other retail CEOs. In addition, the company offers excellent insurance and other benefits. Around 88% of the employees receive company-sponsored health insurance. During the last economic recession, Costco gave many of its workers a $1.50 per hour wage increase, spread over three years. Unlike many other retailers, the store is closed on Thanksgiving Day. Turnover at the company is less than 6% for associates and less than 1% for executives. By paying a living wage and treating its employees well, Costco truly embodies its philosophy that employees are its most important assets.

*Sources:* Short, Kevin, "11 Reasons to Love Costco That Have Nothing to Do with Shopping," Business, *Huffington Post*, December 6, 2017, https://www.huffingtonpost.com/2013/11/19/reasons-love-costco_n_4275774.html; "Top-Rated Workplaces: Compensation and Benefits," Indeed.com, February 27, 2018, http://blog.indeed.com/2018/02/27/best-places-compensation-benefits/; Lucas, Suzanne, "The Top 15 Companies in Compensation and Benefits," *Inc.*, March 2, 2018, https://www.inc.com/suzanne-lucas/the-top-15-companies-in-compensation-benefits.html.

within the organization, regardless of whether they are traditionally "male" jobs or "female" jobs. This process ensures that the value to the company is the driver in establishing wages rather than the labor market being the determinant.

Minnesota, which has enacted comparable worth legislation for state and local government, does a regular analysis to determine what inequities still exist between male and female jobs. An inequity exists when females are being paid less than males, even though their job evaluation ratings indicate that they should be paid at least equally. Also, the differences cannot be explained by performance issues or length of service issues. A January 2014 analysis showed that 99% of local governments were in compliance. Previously, women were paid 81% of the wages paid to men in jobs with comparable job evaluation ratings. The inequities most often found were between city clerks and maintenance workers. In the schools, a number of "female" jobs—jobs for secretaries, food service workers, and teacher's aides—were paid less than "male" jobs for custodians. In the 2014 review, one of the largest remaining differences was for the job of deputy clerk. Females were paid on average $3.38 per hour less than males doing the same job.[66]

As you can imagine, the idea of comparable worth has had only limited success. Employers are concerned with the added direct labor costs associated with reclassifying jobs. The Equal Pay Act of 1963 (EPA) requires equal pay only for jobs that are substantially the same.

## Compensation in Practice: Regulatory Issues

A number of regulations exist that affect decisions that employers make about compensation. These laws also affect what rights employees have relative to what they are paid. Both of these topics are covered by reviewing three pieces of legislation that affect compensation.

In Chapter 3, we discussed one piece of legislation that is directly related to compensation, the EPA. Recall that the purpose of this Act is to ensure that males and females are paid equally when they perform jobs similar in terms of their skill requirements, responsibilities, working conditions, and so forth. In the following sections we cover additional significant legislation that affects compensation decisions. Specifically, we discuss the Davis–Bacon Act, the Walsh–Healey Public Contracts Act (PCA), and the Fair Labor Standards Act (FLSA).

### Davis–Bacon Act

**Davis–Bacon Act**

requires contractors and subcontractors with contracts in excess of $2,000 with the federal government to pay their workers a minimum wage that is at least equal to the local prevailing wages, and to provide them with the local prevailing benefits

In 1931, Congress passed the **Davis–Bacon Act**, which requires contractors and subcontractors with contracts in excess of $2,000 with the federal government to pay their workers a minimum wage that is at least equal to the local prevailing wages and to provide them with the local prevailing benefits. The Davis–Bacon Act is administered by the U.S. Department of Labor.[67] Even minimal presence of a union in the local area can result in a higher prevailing wage because union wages are typically higher than nonunion wages.[68]

### Walsh–Healey Public Contracts Act (PCA)

**Walsh–Healey Public Contracts Act (PCA)**

applies to contractors with contracts over $10,000 that are involved in either manufacturing or providing goods and services to the U.S. government, and requires these firms to pay their workers the federal minimum wage for the first 40 hours they work in a particular week, and 1.5 times the minimum wage for any additional hours they work during the week

The **Walsh–Healey Public Contracts Act (PCA)**, passed in 1936, applies to contractors with contracts over $10,000 that are involved in either manufacturing or providing goods and services to the U.S. government. The Wage and Hour Division of the Department of Labor enforces it. Under the Act, firms must pay their workers the federal minimum wage for the first 40 hours they work in a particular week, and 1.5 times the minimum wage for any additional hours they work during the week.[69]

# Fair Labor Standards Act (FLSA)

The **Fair Labor Standards Act (FLSA)** is the most significant piece of legislation governing what can and cannot be done with regard to compensation. Congress passed this Act in 1938 to improve labor conditions for workers by ensuring that they would earn enough to have a minimum standard of living. The minimum wage provision of the Act remains one of the most controversial parts of the legislation. Many employers argue that a higher minimum wage would have a negative effect on their ability to stay in business. At $7.25 an hour, working 40 hours a week for 52 weeks a year, an individual would earn only $15,080. This amount would make it hard for a single person to maintain a minimum standard of living, and impossible for an individual with a family to do so.

The FLSA regulates the use of child labor, specifies what types of workers must be paid the minimum wage, and stipulates the pay rate for overtime work.[70] The Department of Labor oversees company compliance with the FLSA. As a manager, you need to be sure that decisions you make comply with this law, so let's take a look at its most significant parts.

> **Fair Labor Standards Act (FLSA)**
>
> governs what employers can and cannot do with regard to compensation, including regulating the use of child labor, defining the difference between exempt and nonexempt employees, setting a minimum wage, and stipulating the pay rate for overtime work

## Minimum Wage

At the time of this writing, most employees in the United States were entitled to a **minimum wage** of $7.25 per hour. This rate became effective July 24, 2009. Congress has debated raising the minimum wage to $10.10 an hour, and there has been some push to raise it even further, to $15 an hour. Each state has the option of setting its own minimum wage, however. In July 2018, 29 states plus the District of Columbia already had higher minimum wages than the federal minimum wage. Georgia and Wyoming actually have a state minimum wage of $5.15 an hour; however, since federal law trumps state law, they have to pay workers at least the required $7.25 per hour. Washington, D.C., has the highest minimum wage at $13.25 an hour, with plans to increase that to $15 per hour effective July 1, 2020. Several other states have put in place legislation that will continue to increase their minimum wage over the next few years as well. Additionally, New York has set its minimum wage to vary by geographical location in the state and size of employer. In New York City, large employers currently are required to pay $15 per hour, while small employers (10 or fewer employees) pay $13.50, with an increase to $15 by the end of 2019. Downstate New York employers currently pay $11 per hour and will increase the rate to $15 an hour by the end of 2021.[71]

The cities of Portland, San Diego, New York, and a few others have worked to increase the minimum wage for the city. The state of Oklahoma, on the other hand, passed a law preventing cities and towns from raising the local minimum wage.[72] The Department of Labor website (https://www.dol.gov/whd/minwage/america.htm) contains a link to information about the minimum-wage laws of the various states and the District of Columbia.[73]

There are some exceptions to the minimum wage requirement. People under the age of 20 can be paid less than the minimum wage during their first 90 consecutive days of employment; employees who receive more than $30 in tips per month may be required by their employer to count their tips as wages under FLSA requirements (although the employer must still pay at least $2.13 per hour in wages to these employees), and in no case should the employee be paid less than the minimum wage; and full-time students employed in colleges and universities, retail or service stores, and agriculture can be paid from 85% to 100% of the minimum wage if their employer has obtained a special certification.[74]

> **minimum wage**
>
> the lowest hourly wage that an employer can pay to workers

## Exempt Versus Nonexempt Employees

Managers need to know if their employees are exempt or nonexempt. **Exempt employees** do not receive overtime pay for hours worked over 40 in a workweek,

> **exempt employee**
>
> an employee whose job classification does not require the payment of overtime pay for time worked in excess of 40 hours a week

**nonexempt employee**

an employee who receive overtime pay for hours worked in excess of 40 hours in a workweek

while **nonexempt employees** do receive overtime pay. Executive, administrative, professional, and outside sales employees who receive salaries are typically considered to be exempt employees. The distinction between what constitutes an exempt employee versus a nonexempt employee is actually quite complex, however. For example, Congress has specified that certain computer professionals are also exempt if they earn at least $27.63 per hour.[75]

The FairPay Overtime Initiative, which went into effect in 2006, attempted to clarify which employees were eligible to be classified as exempt and resulted in jobs at many companies being reclassified. This initiative strengthened overtime rights for approximately 6.7 million American workers, 1.3 million of whom were low-wage workers who did not get overtime under the old rules. Then, in 2014, concerned that basic overtime protections had been eroded such that some managers were not even making the equivalent of the minimum wage, and in part because of the FairPay Overtime Initiative, President Barack Obama signed a Presidential Memorandum directing that Department of Labor Secretary Tom Perez update the rules and work with businesses and workers to fix this issue. A major concern was that businesses that wanted to treat workers fairly in terms of wages were being undercut by competitors who followed the letter rather than the intent of the FairPay Overtime Initiative. One example given was that of two New Jersey gas station managers working 65 hours per week and making less than the equivalent of the minimum wage because they were classified as exempt employees.

In May 2016, the Department of Labor updated salary and compensation levels for determining whether an executive, administrative, or professional worker should be classified as exempt. This update extended protection to over 4 million workers. Specifically, workers making less than $47,476 annually, or $913 per week, would be considered nonexempt and entitled to overtime pay. Employers could use nondiscretionary bonuses and incentive payments (e.g., commissions) to cover up to 10% of the new standard salary level. Further, employees who made over $134,004 were to be considered highly compensated employees (HCEs) and under most circumstances labeled exempt even if they did not meet all the criteria for classification as an exempt employee. The effective date for the new provisions was December 1, 2016. Going forward, automatic updates to the thresholds would occur every three years, starting on January 1, 2020.[76] However, shortly before this new plan was to start, Donald Trump was elected president of the United States, and the implementation of this initiative was delayed. As of the writing of this chapter, the Department of Labor was involved in rulemaking to revise this regulation. Until that process is completed, the standard reverts to the FLSA overtime pay requirements from 2004, which set the threshold at $455 per week or $23,660 annual salary.[77]

### Overtime

**overtime**

work hours that exceed the number of hours established as the normal workweek

Nonexempt employees who work more than 40 hours in a week are considered to be working **overtime** and are entitled to receive pay at the rate of 1.5 times their regular pay for that additional time. Managers should use the Department of Labor's guidelines and its website to determine whether employees must be compensated for rest and meal breaks (rest breaks, yes; meal breaks, usually no), whether employees "on call" must be compensated, and whether employees attending training programs must be paid for that time.

### Child Labor

The last significant part of the FLSA to discuss here is the child-labor provision. Prior to the passage of the FLSA, it was not uncommon for young children to work long hours, often in dangerous conditions, such as in factories. Today, youths under the age of 16 can work on a restricted basis: Those who are ages 14 and 15 can work after school hours (defined as between 7 a.m. and 7 p.m.) during the school year, but no more than 3 hours on a school day and no more than 18 hours per week; they can work 8 hours during a nonschool day and 40 hours during a nonschool week. Between June 1 and Labor Day, they can work until 9 p.m. Youths 16 years and older have no work-hour restrictions, but they cannot work in hazardous jobs if they are under age 18. Examples of hazardous jobs include those involving driving a motor vehicle, doing wrecking and demolition work, operating saws, and being exposed to radioactive substances.[78]

### Recordkeeping

Employers must keep certain information for each nonexempt employee, including the person's:

- Full name and Social Security number
- Address
- Birth date, if the employee is younger than 19
- Gender
- Occupation
- Time and day when the person's workweek starts
- Daily hours worked
- Total weekly hours worked
- Basis and rate of pay
- Overtime earnings
- Additions and deductions from pay
- Total wages by pay period
- Date of pay and pay period[79]

Payroll records, sales and purchase records, and collective bargaining agreements need to be retained for at least three years. Records such as time cards and other sources of information for wage calculations should be retained for two years.[80]

## SUMMARY

*Compensation* refers to the monetary and nonmonetary consideration employees receive in exchange for the work they do. The compensation can be direct, such as hourly wages and salaries, or indirect, such as benefits. When designing compensation packages, often referred to as *total rewards,* companies try to balance internal and external equity issues.

Internal equity is addressed by designing a process of internal alignment to ensure that jobs are properly valued relative to their worth to each other and to the company. The job evaluation process is used to do this. Job ranking and job classification are two qualitative job evaluation processes used. They are based on global evaluations of jobs. The point method and factor comparison method are two quantitative job evaluation approaches. They involve identifying and defining compensable factors and using benchmark jobs to set up the relative worth hierarchy of the jobs. In the point method, points are assigned to each degree of each compensable factor. In the factor comparison method, dollar amounts are assigned to each degree of each factor. Both approaches result in a job hierarchy.

External equity is addressed by ensuring that a company's pay is competitive with pay for similar jobs outside the company. This goal is accomplished by collecting salary information for benchmark jobs and comparing it to what the firm is paying for those jobs. Adjustments are then made to the pay based on the organization's chosen compensation policy. Companies can decide to pay at, below, or above the market for some of or all their jobs.

The process for deciding how much to pay individuals under the traditional job-based structure requires first grouping jobs into grades based on job evaluation

results; establishing a minimum, midpoint, and maximum dollar amount for that grade, based on market data and the firm's pay policy; and, finally, slotting individuals into the appropriate grades. Companies use an approach called *broadbanding* to reduce some of the complexity of this process. Reducing the number of grades and increasing their size in terms of minimum and maximum dollars give managers more leeway when it comes to setting the pay for their employees.

A number of alternative compensation approaches have evolved to address some of the complexity and challenges of the traditional job classification approach. Skill- and knowledge-based pay systems require employees to acquire certain skills or knowledge to receive pay increases. Lower-level skills or knowledge must be mastered before higher-level ones. Competency-based pay works in a similar way. This type of pay is based on employees mastering competencies that have been identified as supporting the firm's success. Firms also use direct market pricing, which involves collecting salary information from the external labor market first, rather than starting with the development of an internal structure based on the value of the jobs within the company.

Successful compensation plans are well designed and carefully administered. A handbook describing the process and training for managers who will be using the process are critical. A decision also has to be made about whether the pay system will be open or closed. Finally, the compensation plan should be reviewed regularly to ensure that information, including market salary data, is current and relevant to the goals of the company.

Organizational demands, environmental influencers, and the legal environment affect how compensation systems are designed and administered, as well as how they are viewed by employees. The strategy of a firm drives the internal value of jobs and the compensation mix offered employees. Company characteristics determine the firm's ability to pay and the type of compensation offered. Organizational culture plays a key role in establishing priorities for compensation policies and influencing employees' expectations about their firm's compensation. Employee concerns include equity versus equality issues and the fairness of the rewards offered.

The labor force influences the level of compensation firms must pay employees, the form of compensation desired by prospective employees, and market wages. Technology affects the ease with which data are collected, how compensation information is tracked and pay is delivered, and even what is considered compensable work. Globalization affects where compensation decisions are made, the acceptableness of different compensation systems, and pay rates. What compensation decisions signal to employees about their firms' values and what people's attitudes are toward the living wage and comparable worth are just a few of the ethical and social responsibility challenges associated with compensation.

Finally, the regulatory forces affecting compensation decisions are driven in the United States by laws that include the Davis–Bacon Act, the PCA, and the FLSA.

## KEY TERMS

| | |
|---|---|
| benchmark jobs | exempt employee |
| broadbanding | external competitiveness |
| comparable worth | factor comparison |
| compensable factor | Fair Labor Standards Act (FLSA) |
| compensation | internal alignment |
| compensation philosophy | job classification |
| competency-based pay | job grade |
| cost-of-living adjustment (COLA) | job evaluation |
| Davis–Bacon Act | job pricing |
| equity theory | job ranking |

knowledge-based pay
living wage
market pricing
merit increase
minimum wage
nonexempt employee
overtime
point method

salary compression
salary inversion
salary survey
skill-based pay
total rewards
wage curve
Walsh–Healey Public Contracts Act
    (PCA)

## DISCUSSION QUESTIONS

1. Prepare a short presentation on the meaning of compensation to employees and to companies, noting why there can be a mismatch between the two perspectives.

2. Why is equity so important to employees? What happens when employees believe their pay is not equitable?

3. Why are some jobs paid more than others in companies? What determines those differences, and why do the differences matter?

4. An employee of yours makes an appointment to discuss his salary with you. He feels that he is not being paid "at market." What does the employee mean? How would you validate that he currently is or is not being paid at market rate? What alternatives do you have if the employee is correct?

5. Choose a country in which you would like to live and research the compensation laws in that country. How does what you learned affect your willingness to live and work in that country?

6. What is the relationship between compensation and organizational culture? Discuss whether compensation can be used to change a company culture.

7. Talk to two or three of your peers about what they are looking for in terms of compensation for their first (or next) jobs. What conclusions can you draw from what you learned?

8. Many states have raised the minimum wage above the federal requirement. Discuss why this is happening and how it affects employers.

## LEARNING EXERCISE 1

As a manager, you will have employees come to you and tell you that they think they are underpaid. Assume that this has just happened. The employee in this case is an events planner who works for you in a large hotel in Chicago. The employee's current base salary after three years with the company is $55,000. The company tries to pay at market rate. Develop a plan of action for how you would respond in this situation.

1. Identify the information you would need to have to determine whether the employee's concerns are valid.

2. How would you resolve the situation if you were in a large company with a compensation staff in the HR department? How would you resolve it if you were a small business owner?

3. Find salary data for the job for the relevant labor market. Discuss how you decided on the relevant labor market, where you obtained the data, and whether there is a significant difference between what the employee is making and the relevant labor market salary for that job.

4. Discuss how you would approach the situation if you find that the employee is overpaid relative to the market.

## LEARNING EXERCISE 2

You will graduate from college soon and have been offered two jobs. Both jobs involve working in auditing, and both are a good fit for you and in cities of interest to you as places to live. One job is with a major accounting firm located in Atlanta. The other job is for a major insurance company in Boston. The salary for the Atlanta job is $57,000, with a $5,000 starting bonus. The second job is at $60,000, with no starting bonus.

1. Research the cost-of-living differences between these two cities and discuss what you learn.
2. What factors are considered in determining cost-of-living differences?
3. Given that both jobs are a good fit for you, which job should you take? Describe your decision process.
4. As an employer, what should you do to address cost-of-living issues that limit the number of job candidates willing to sign on to work for you?

## CASE STUDY 1: AN ETHICAL DILEMMA?

Her Majesty is a five-year-old, up-and-coming designer clothing chain in the Midwest catering to professional women. Samantha Santorina owns the chain and has five stores in three major metropolitan areas. Samantha takes pride in treating her employees well. She provides salaries above minimum wage for all her nonexempt employees, health insurance at low cost, and tuition reimbursement for all her employees who pass classes they take toward a degree at their local community college.

Samantha has one manager and two associate managers in each store. She has paid her managers more than the market rate in the areas where her stores are located since opening. Assume that the FairPay Overtime Initiative higher threshold of $47,476 for classifying employees as nonexempt rather than exampt has finally gone into effect. Samantha's managers currently make between $40,000 and $45,000 per year, depending on time in the job and performance.

After meeting with her accountant, Samantha has to make a tough decision. She has to decide between two choices: (1) hire another associate manager for each store to avoid having to pay overtime to her current managers, which would also mean paying benefits for this position; or (2) pay overtime to her current managers, who each regularly work 50 hours a week.

### Discussion Questions

1. Review the background leading up to the passage of the FairPay Overtime Initiative, as well as the FLSA guidelines for exempt and nonexempt employees.
2. What criteria should Samantha use in making her decision?
3. Make a proposal to Samantha about how to handle this situation. Is there another alternative she has not considered?
4. Because the new rule requires that the threshold be increased every three years, what advice would you give Samantha to help her plan for these changes?
5. Do you agree or disagree with having a higher threshold for classifying employees as nonexempt? Justify your response.

## CASE STUDY 2: COMPENSATION AT W. L. GORE

W.L. Gore & Associates is a company well known for its GORE-TEX fabric for protective outerwear. The company was included on *Fortune*'s "100 Best Companies to Work For" list for 20 consecutive years. Gore has received numerous other recognitions as well, including being ranked number 15 on the 2017 World's Best Multinational Workplaces list by the Great Place to Work Institute, was named a best workplace in France, Germany, Italy, Korea, Sweden, the United Kingdom, and China, and frequently has been used as an example of a company that is innovative. Rather than job titles, bosses, and organization charts, Gore uses a team approach, with leaders, sponsors, and team members.

The main objective of Gore's compensation plan is to ensure that employees, referred to as *associates,* are paid for their contributions to the success of the company. Their compensation plan is focused on both internal fairness and external competitiveness. Gore uses two approaches to achieve these goals. The first is straightforward and typically used by companies: comparing pay at Gore with pay for comparable jobs at other companies. In other words, Gore does a lot of benchmarking to be sure their salaries are competitive with the relevant labor markets. That takes care of the external competitiveness part.

The internal competitiveness part is what is different at Gore. The process works like this: Associates on the same team rank each other based on contributions to the company for the year. Team members provide a numerical ranking and can provide comments to support their rankings and identify strengths or areas for improvement of the associates they rank. This information is then used for determining raises.

### Discussion Questions

1. What type of compensation approach is Gore using to be externally competitive? What are the pluses and minuses of this approach?
2. Discuss the pros and cons of the internal competitiveness strategy at Gore.
3. Do you think that Gore can achieve its goals of internal fairness and external competitiveness with the two approaches used?
4. Would you want to work for this company? Why or why not?

*Sources:* Based on "A Successful & Innovative Leader Worldwide," Gore, http://www.gore.com/en_xx/careers/whoweare/ourreputation/gore-reputation.htm; and "Our Goals: Internal Fairness & External Competitiveness," Gore, http://www.gore.com/en_xx/careers/whatweoffer/compensation/compensation.html; "Gore Marks 20th Year on 100 Best Companies to Work For List," Gore, https://www.gore.com/news-events/press-release/enterprise-press-release-fortune-100-list-2017-us: "2017 World's Best Multinational Workplaces," Great Places to Work, http://www.greatplacestowork.net/best-companies/worlds-best-multinationals/the-list.

## NOTES

[1] "Newsroom: Awards, Industry Rankings," Jacobs CH2M, http://www.ch2m.com/newsroom?field_newsroom_target_id=29; "CH2M and Jacobs: A Winning Combination," Filing Relative to Proposed Merger of CH2M and Jacobs, Securities and Exchange Commission File No. 000-27261, http://d18m0p25nwr6d.cloudfront.net/CIK-0000777491/32bee14c-e91d-4b57-9b5b-20e640037170.pdf.

[2] Todd Henneman, "Pay 'Philosophy' Could Prompt Workers to Stay," *Workforce Management* 90 (2011): 18.

[3] "Compensation Programs and Practices Survey, A Report by WorldatWork," WorldatWork .org, August 2016, https://www.worldatwork.org/docs/research-and-surveys/survey-brief-survey-on-compensation-programs-and-practices-2016.pdf.

[4] Charlotte Garvey, "Agenda: Compensation & Benefits—Philosophizing Compensation," *HR Magazine*, last modified January 1, 2005, http://www.shrm.org/publications/hrmagazine/editorialcontent/pages/0105garvey.aspx.

[5] Ian Larkin, Lamar Pierce, and Francesca Gino, "The Psychological Costs of Pay-for-Performance: Implications for the Strategic Compensation of Employees," *Strategic Management Journal* 33 (2012): 1194–1214.

[6] Miriam Dornstein, "The Fairness Judgments of Received Pay and Their Determinants," *Journal of Occupational Psychology* 62 (1989): 287–299.

[7] "Classification & Qualifications," Office of Personnel Management, http://www.opm.gov/policy-data-oversight/classification-qualifications/.

[8] Donald Caruth and Gail Handlogten, *Managing Compensation (and Understanding It Too): A Handbook for the Perplexed* (Westport, CT: Quorum Books, 2001).

[9] Ibid.

[10] Sharon McKnight, "Is Your Salary Data a Toddler, a Teenager, or Ready for Retirement?" compensation.BLR.com, August 14, 2015, https://compensation.blr.com/Compensation-news/Compensation/Compensation-Administration/Aging-Salary-Data/; "How to Establish Salary Ranges," *SHRM.org*, May 23, 2018, https://www.shrm.org/resourcesandtools/tools-and-samples/how-to-guides/pages/howtoestablishsalaryranges.aspx.

[11] Rolfe Winkler, "Google Rated Top Employer for Pay and Benefits by Glassdoor," last modified May 23, 2014, http://blogs.wsj.com/digits/2014/05/23/google-rated-top-employer-for-pay-and-benefits-by-glassdoor/.

[12] George Milkovich and Jerry Newman, *Compensation* (New York: McGraw-Hill/Irwin, 2005).

[13] Ibid.

[14] Howard Risher, "How Much Should Federal Employees Be Paid? The Problems with Using a Market Philosophy in a Broadband System," *Public Personnel Management* 34 (2005): 121–140.

[15] Howard Risher, "Planning for the Transition to Pay for Performance: What Are the Practical Consequences of the Federal Government's Increased Emphasis on Pay for Performance and What Can Agencies Do to Prepare for this Change in Policy Direction?" *The Public Manager* 33 (2004): 29–34.

[16] Ed Lawler, "Pay Strategy: New Thinking for the New Millennium," *Compensation & Benefits Review* 32 (2000): 7–12.

[17] Gerald Ledford, Jr., and Herbert Heneman III, "Skill-Based Pay," *SIOP Science Series*, June 2011.

[18] Ibid.

[19] Atul Mitra, Nina Gupta, and Jason Shaw, "A Comparative Examination of Traditional and Skill-Based Pay Plans," *Journal of Managerial Psychology* 26 (2011): 278–296.

[20] Ledford and Heneman, "Skill-Based Pay."

[21] Atul Mitra, Nina Gupta, and Jason Shaw, "A Comparative Examination of Traditional and Skill-Based Pay Plans," *Journal of Managerial Psychology* 26 (2011): 278–296.

[22] Leanne H. Markus, Helena D. Cooper-Thomas, and Keith N. Allpress, "Confounded by Competencies? An Evaluation of the Evolution and Use of Competency Models," *New Zealand Journal of Psychology* 34 (2005): 117+.

[23] Brian Hinchcliffe, "The Juggling Act: Internal Equity and Market Pricing," *Workspan* 46 (2003): 46–48.

[24] "Compensation Programs and Practices Survey," A report by WorldatWork underwritten by Aon Hewitt, August 2016, https://www.worldatwork.org/docs/research-and-surveys/survey-brief-survey-on-compensation-programs-and-practices-2016.pdf.

[25] Robert Heneman and Peter LeBlanc, "Work Valuation Addresses Shortcoming of Both Job Evaluation and Market Pricing/Response," *Compensation & Benefits Review* 35 (2003): 7–11.

[26] Sharon McKnight, "Aging Salary Data: Is Your Data Ready for Retirement?" August 14, 2015, https://compensation.blr.com/Compensation-news/Compensation/Compensation-Administration/Aging-Salary-Data/.

[27] Robert Till and Ronald Karren, "Organizational Justice Perceptions and Pay Level Satisfaction," *Journal of Managerial Psychology* 26 (2011): 42–57.

[28] Larkin et al., "The Psychological Costs of Pay-for-Performance."

[29] Aino Tenhiälää and Robert Lount, Jr., "Affective Reactions to a Pay System Reform and Their Impact on Employee Behaviour," *Journal of Occupational and Organizational Psychology* 86 (2013): 100–118.

[30] Yoshio Yanadori and Janet Marler, "Compensation Strategy: Does Business Strategy Influence Compensation in High Technology Firms?" *Strategic Management Journal* 27 (2006): 559–570.

[31] Larkin et al., "The Psychological Costs of Pay-for-Performance."

[32] KPMG Services, https://home.kpmg.com/us/en/home/about.html.

[33] "Total Rewards: Creating a Sustainable Employment Deal for Global Companies," *Viewpoints*, Towers Watson, TW-NA-2012-25563.

[34] "Bethany Shepard, "12 Companies That Brilliantly Differentiated Themselves from the Competition," Hubspot, updated November 29, 2017, https://blog.hubspot.com/insiders/

branding-differentiation; "Adventure, Inspired by Airstream," Airstream, https://www.airstream.com/.

[35] Larkin et al., "The Psychological Costs of Pay-for-Performance."

[36] "Consumer Price Index Summary," Bureau of Labor Statistics Economic News Release, July 12, 2018, https://www.bls.gov/news.release/cpi.nr0.htm.

[37] Milkovich and Newman, *Compensation*.

[38] Yanadori and Marler, "Compensation Strategy."

[39] "Few Organizations' Total Rewards and Business Strategies Fully Align, According to Mercer Survey," Mercer.com, last modified May 19, 2014, http://www.mercer.com/content/mercer/global/all/en/newsroom/few-reward-and-business-strategies-align-say-mercer-survey.html.

[40] Ibid.

[41] Walter Oi and Todd Idson, "Firm Size and Wages," in *Handbook of Labor Economics,* ed. O. Ashenfelter and D. Card (Amsterdam: North Holland, 1999), 2165–2214.

[42] Eduardo Salas, Mary Kosarzycki, Scott Tannenbaum, and David Carnegie, "Aligning Work Teams and HR Practices: Best Practices," in *Reinventing Human Resources Management: Challenges and New Directions,* ed. Ronald Burke and Cary Cooper (New York: Routledge, 2004), 133–150.

[43] Caruth and Handlogten, *Managing Compensation (and Understanding It Too).*

[44] Annelies Van Vianen, "Person–Organization Fit: The Match Between Newcomers' and Recruiters' Preferences for Organization Cultures," *Personnel Psychology* 53 (2000): 115–125.

[45] Ronald Sims, *Managing Organizational Behavior* (Westport, CT: Quorum Books, 2002).

[46] Karen Hutcheson, Yelena Stiles, and Carolyn Wong, "The Top Five Problems in Faculty Pay," Strategy, Horizons, *NACUBO.org,* http://hrhorizons.nacubo.org/newsletter/past-issues/volume-7-issue-1/the-top-five-problems-in-faculty-pay.html.

[47] "Few Organizations' Total Rewards and Business Strategies Fully Align, According to Mercer Survey," Mercer.com, last modified May 19, 2014, http://www.mercer.com/content/mercer/global/all/en/newsroom/few-reward-and-business-strategies-align-say-mercer-survey.html.

[48] Linda Halstead-Acharya, "Tight Labor Market Fuels Recruiting Rivalry," billingsgazette.com, last modified June 3, 2006, http://billingsgazette.com/news/local/tight-labor-market-fuels-a-recruiting-rivalry/article_f8bb3456-6af5-5d25-a80e-0b8234a8b0ea.html.

[49] "Target Raises Minimum Hourly Wage to $11, Commits to $15 Minimum Hourly Wage by End of 2020," Target, A Bullseye View," corporate.target.com, September 25, 2017, https://corporate.target.com/press/releases/2017/09/target-raises-minimum-hourly-wage-to-11-commits-to.

[50] Caruth and Handlogten, *Managing Compensation (and Understanding It Too).*

[51] Daniel Cable and Timothy Judge, "Pay Preferences and Job Search Decisions: A Person-Organization Fit Perspective, *Personnel Psychology* 47 (1994): 317–348.

[52] "Few Organizations' Total Rewards and Business Strategies Fully Align, According to Mercer Survey," Mercer.com, last modified May 19, 2014, http://www.mercer.com/content/mercer/global/all/en/newsroom/few-reward-and-business-strategies-align-say-mercer-survey.html.

[53] Kelly Shermach, "Tracking and Invoicing Billable Hours Without Wasting Time," *Workforce Management*, last modified September 12, 2006, http://www.workforce.com/articles/tracking-and-invoicing-billable-hours-without-wasting-time.

[54] "General: What Factors Should We Consider Prior to Instituting a Telecommuting Practice?" *SHRM.org,* last modified January 30, 2012, http://www.shrm.org/templatestools/hrqa/pages/whatshouldweconsiderpriortotelecommutingpractice.aspx.

[55] Jessica Marquez, "McDonald's Rewards Program Leaves Room for Some Local Flavor," *Workforce Management* 85 (2006): 26.

[56] "Total Rewards: Creating a Sustainable Employment Deal for Global Companies," *Viewpoints*, Towers Watson, TW-NA-2012-25563.

[57] Ibid.

[58] "More Than 200 Countries and Counting," Siemens Locations, https://www.siemens.com/us/en/hoe/company/jobs/life-at-siemens.html.

[59] Ibid; Donald Dowling, "Avoid These Global Compensation and Benefits Plan Obstacles," *SHRM.org,* last modified April 22, 2014, http://www.shrm.org/hrdisciplines/global/articles/pages/global-compensation-benefits-plans.aspx.

[60] Randy Chiu, Vivienne Wai-Mei Luk, and Thomas Tang, "Retaining and Motivating Employees: Compensation Preferences in Hong Kong and China," *Personnel Review* 31 (2002): 402–431.

61 Dennis Briscoe and Randall Schuler, *International Human Resource Management* (London: Routledge, 2004).

62 "China Sets Minimum Wage Rules," *People's Daily*, last modified February 6, 2004, http://english.people.com.cn/200402/06/eng20040206_134134.shtml.

63 "Shanghai Gets Token Increase in Minimum Wage," *China Labour Bulletin*, http://www.clb.org.hk/content/shanghai-gets-token-increase-minimum-wage; "Employment and Wages," China Labor Bulletin, June 2018, http://clb.org.hk/content/employment-and-wage.

64 Charlie Trevor, Greg Reilly, and Barry Gerhart, "Reconsidering Pay Dispersion's Effect on the Performance of Interdependent Work: Reconciling Sorting and Pay Inequality," *Academy of Management Journal* 55 (2012): 585–610.

65 "Living Wage Overview," Nassau County Long Island, New York, https://www.nassaucountryny.gov/1597/Living-Wage.

66 "Minnesota Local Government Pay Equity Compliance Report," submitted to the Minnesota Legislature by Minnesota Management and Budget, last modified January 2014, http://www.beta.mmb.state.mn.us/doc/comp/pay-equity/payequity.pdf.

67 "Davis–Bacon and Related Acts," Wage and Hour Division (WHD), U.S. Department of Labor, http://www.dol.gov/whd/govcontracts/dbra.htm.

68 A. J. Thieblot, "A New Evaluation of Impacts of Prevailing Wage Law Repeal," *Journal of Labor Research* 17 (1996): 297–322.

69 "The Walsh–Healey Public Contracts Act (PCA)," U.S. Department of Labor, http://www.dol.gov/compliance/laws/coomp-pca.htm.

70 "Compliance Assistance—Wages and the Fair Labor Standards Act (FLSA)," Wage and Hour Division (WHD), U.S. Department of Labor, http://www.dol.gov/whd/flsa/.

71 "Minimum Wage: Congress Stalls, States Act," *CNN Money*, last modified April 28, 2014, http://www.money.cnn.com/2014/04/28/news/economy/states-minimum-wage/index.html; "State Minimum Wages/2018 Minimum Wage by State," National Conference of State Legislatures, January 2, 2018, http://www.ncsl.org/research/labor-and-employment/state-minimum-wage-chart.aspx.

72 Ibid.

73 "Minimum Wage Laws in the States, January 1, 2014," Wage and Hour Division (WHD), U.S. Department of Labor, https://www.dol.gov/whd/minwage/america.htm.

74 "Wages and Hours Worked: Minimum Wage and Overtime Pay," elaws—Employment Law Guide, U.S. Department of Labor, http://www.dol.gov/compliance/guide/minwage.htm.

75 "Fact Sheet #17E: Exemption for Employees in Computer-Related Occupations Under the Fair Labor Standards Act (FLSA)," U.S. Department of Labor, Wage and Hour Division, http://www.dol.gov/whd/overtime/fs17e_computer.pdf.

76 "Final Rule: Overtime, Defining and Delimiting the Exemptions for Executive, Administrative, Professional, Outside Sales, and Computer Employees Under the Fair Labor Standards Act," U.S. Department of Labor, Wage and Hour Division, https://www.dol.gov/whd/overtime/final2016/index.htm.

77 "Final Rule: Overtime," Wage and Hour Division (WHD), U.S. Department of Labor, dol.gov, https://www.dol.gov/whd/overtime/final2016/.

78 "Child Labor," Wage and Hour Division (WHD), U.S. Department of Labor, http://www.dol.gov/whd/childlabor.htm.

79 "Fact Sheet #21: Recordkeeping Requirements Under the Fair Labor Standards Act (FLSA)," U.S. Department of Labor, Wage and Hour Division, http://www.dol.gov/whd/regs/compliance/whdfs21.pdf.

80 Ibid.

# Chapter 11

# Incentives and Rewards

## Learning Objectives

**AFTER READING THIS CHAPTER, YOU SHOULD BE ABLE TO:**

**1** Explain the theories behind how incentive plans motivate employees.

**2** Compare and contrast the types of individual incentives.

**3** Discuss the major team- and group-based incentive plans.

**4** Compare and contrast the relative merits of the types of group-level incentive plans.

**5** Explain how to design an effective incentive plan.

**6** Describe how organizational demands affect a firm's incentive plans.

**7** Explain how environmental factors affect a firm's incentive plans.

## Why Are Incentive Plans Important?

Why do some employees work harder than others? This question is admittedly simple, but important. Most of us, at some time, have worked with people who did not work as hard as their abilities would indicate they could. Managers face this problem very often. What should they do? After all, as a manager, much of your personal success or failure, not to mention that of your company, rests on the performance of your employees.

As Exhibit 11.1 shows, employee competencies—knowledge, skills, and abilities (KSAs) and other characteristics—affect performance. Employees who have the competencies needed to excel at their jobs will be able to perform at a much higher level than employees without those competencies. Beyond competencies, the structure of the work environment—how jobs are designed and the effectiveness of a firm's workforce planning efforts—also affects the quality, type, and amount of effort individuals put into their work.

Other than knowing what to do, the ultimate purpose of incentives is to motivate—to motivate employees to work as hard as possible to reach certain goals by rewarding them when they do what is desired. Managers face a host of decisions that affect their incentive plans. For example, as a manager, you have to answer questions such as:

- What actions or outcomes should we base our incentives on?
- What types of incentives should we use?
- Should we focus on individual performance, team performance, company performance, or some combination of the three?

**EXHIBIT 11.1**

Framework for the Strategic Management of Employees

In this chapter, we look at how companies use the rewards associated with incentive plans to motivate their employees. We then discuss a variety of incentive plans that you, as a manager, can use to encourage your employees to engage in different types of behaviors.

# How Incentives Work

Let's look for a moment at how various incentive plans work in light of different motivational theories of behavior. As we do, think about the "incentives" that have motivated you to do well in school, do expected chores, or perform as expected on the job. Reinforcement theory, goal-setting theory, expectancy theory, and agency theory will help you understand how different incentive plans affect employees' attitudes and behaviors.

## Theories of Motivation

According to **reinforcement theory**, when people experience positive consequences, such as a reward, after they do something, they are likely to repeat that action, expecting the same outcome. Reinforcement theory, also known as **operant conditioning,** resulted from work by B. F. Skinner and others. These researchers believed that individuals learn about the relationship between actions and consequences and, as a result, modify their behavior accordingly.[1] For example, according to reinforcement theory, when employees are rewarded under a company's incentive plan for what they do, they are likely to repeat the same actions expecting to be rewarded again for doing so. As you will read about in this chapter, firms provide incentives in many different forms that have the potential to reinforce desired behaviors. A study by Bersin and Associates found that companies providing a lot of employee recognition, one type of employee incentive, have 31% lower turnover.[2]

The next theory of motivation is goal setting. Edwin Locke proposed this theory of motivation in the 1960s. Locke and Gary Latham have further refined the theory over the years. According to **goal-setting theory,** goals serve as a motivator to focus the efforts of employees when the goals are specific, challenging, attainable, and meaningful. Receiving feedback about progress toward goal attainment is also critically important.[3] In the employment context, when employees are committed to specific, challenging, yet attainable, goals, the goals serve as an anchor which focuses employee effort toward desired company outcomes.[4] By setting challenging goals rather than simple ones, employees are encouraged to push themselves to achieve them. Further, when individuals have specific goals rather than vague goals, they have a clear sense of the objective they are trying to realize and are more likely to focus their efforts toward that goal than other irrelevant or less relevant activities.[5] Setting a target for employees to decrease error rates by 10%, for example, provides more guidance than telling them to work harder to help improve company performance. Goals must be attainable to exert any influence on employee effort.[6] If employees perceive that there is no possibility of achieving a goal, they are not likely to work toward attaining it. Finally, employees must have confidence in their ability to achieve the goal (e.g., have the required KSAs) and receive adequate and timely feedback on their progress for goal setting to succeed.[7]

According to our third theory, **expectancy theory**, employees make decisions regarding how to act at work based on which behaviors they believe will lead to their most valued work-related rewards and outcomes. This theory of motivation is derived from work by Kurt Lewin in the 1930s and Edward Tolman in the 1950s.[8] As shown in Exhibit 11.2, three factors influence how incentives influence employee motivation on the job: expectancy, instrumentality, and valence. **Expectancy** refers to the degree to which employees believe that if they work toward a certain performance objective they will be able to achieve that objective. If employees don't believe they are capable of achieving the objective, their motivation to work toward

**reinforcement theory (also known as operant conditioning)**

positive outcomes occur when individuals learn the relationship between actions and consequences and, as a result, modify their behavior accordingly

**goal-setting theory**

goals serve as a motivator to focus the efforts of employees toward desired outcomes when the goals are specific, challenging, attainable, and when feedback on progress is provided

**expectancy theory**

employees make decisions regarding how to act at work based on which behaviors they believe will lead to their most valued work-related rewards and outcomes

**expectancy**

the degree to which employees believe that, if they work toward a certain performance objective, they will be able to achieve that objective

## EXHIBIT 11.2

Example of Expectancy Theory

*Performance Incentive:* **Employee's who exceed their annual sales target by 20% will receive a 10% bonus**

| *Expectancy* | *Instrumentality* | *Valence* |
|---|---|---|
| Do employees believe that the performance goal can be achieved? | Do employees believe they will actually be rewarded if they meet the goal? | Do employees value the 10% bonus? |

**instrumentality**

the perceived link between one's performance and receiving the reward or incentive payment promised; reflects whether employees believe that achieving an objective will be rewarded

**valence**

the degree of value employees place on different rewards

**agency theory**

managers can motivate their employees to act in certain ways by aligning employee interests with the interests of the firm's other stakeholders

it will diminish. **Instrumentality** reflects whether employees believe that achieving an objective will be rewarded. Employees will be less motivated to achieve an objective when there is not a direct or consistent link between the achievement and being rewarded for it. **Valence** is the degree of value employees place on different rewards. Employees will be more motivated to achieve incentives they value than ones they don't. For example, some employees might be more motivated by the potential to earn a weeklong vacation to Hawaii than an equivalent cash bonus. For other employees, the reverse will be true.

The final theory of motivation we include, **agency theory**, proposes that managers can motivate their employees to act in certain ways by aligning the employee's interests with the interests of the firm's other stakeholders—typically the company's owners. When one person (the principal, or owner) hires another person (an agent, or employee) to make decisions and work on his or her behalf, conflicts can occur. Agency problems may emerge if the two parties have different interests and goals. For example, a company's owner (principal) has an interest in maximizing the firm's profitability. In contrast, an employee (agent) has an interest in maximizing his or her own well-being, perhaps with "perks" such as higher pay and generous benefits. Providing the perks will reduce the firm's profitability, so the company has to believe that its desired outcomes will be achieved to be willing to make the investment required. Creating incentives to align the interests of principals and agents can help firms overcome agency problems such as this. For example, if employees are rewarded with a significant share of a company's profits, they will be more likely to take steps to improve the firm's performance. In other words, according to agency theory, when properly designed and implemented, incentive systems reward employees and managers for acting in the best interests of a company's owners.

# Types of Incentive Plans

Drawing from theories of motivation, companies have devised a wide variety of plans to encourage employees to work toward certain goals. One of the major distinctions among the different types of incentive plans is the level of their focus. Some incentive plans encourage superior individual performance. Other plans encourage entire groups to achieve some goal, or the plan may even focus on the performance of an entire company. A second distinction is whether incentives are used as an add-on to employees' base pay, or if they are used in place of some, or all, of an employee's base pay. We start our discussion of incentive plans with a focus on individual incentive plans.

## Individual Incentive Plans

Some of the individual incentive plans most commonly used by companies are: merit pay programs, lump-sum bonuses, piecework plans, standard hour plans, spot awards, and sales incentive plans. We review each of these in the following sections.

## Merit Pay Programs

Recall that we first mentioned merit pay programs in Chapter 10. Merit pay programs reward employees for achieving certain levels of performance over a predetermined time in the past. The logic for this approach is straightforward: Employees who perform at higher levels should receive greater rewards.[9] With a typical **merit pay increase**, employees receive a compensation adjustment based on the results of their performance evaluations. The performance ratings they receive are then used to allocate merit pay increases to them. For example, employees with a low rating of 1 (on a 5-point rating scale) might receive a merit increase of 0% or 1%. As performance ratings increase, so too does the amount of merit increase allocated to the employees. The highest performers receive the greater percentage increases to their base pay. Someone receiving a score of 3 might be rewarded with a 3% to 4% increase while someone with a score of 5 might be rewarded with a 5% increase, or even more.

**merit pay increase**
a compensation adjustment based on the results of an employee's performance evaluations

Some companies use a merit pay grid to determine the percentage of raises in a merit pay plan. This grid involves a graduated scale for merit raises that is tied to the job grade system and, thus, takes into account where the employee falls on the salary range attached to that job grade. Employees in higher grades who score high on their performance reviews actually could receive a lower percentage for high performance than someone who is in a lower grade receives. The rationale behind the merit grid is that the person in the higher job grade is already receiving a higher base salary so the dollar amount increase will still be larger even with a lower percentage than for the person in the lower job grade with a lower base salary who gets a higher percentage. Plus, with a maximum salary for the grade, it is important not to move a person's salary higher too quickly and exceed the maximum salary for the job grade. Okay, that was confusing, right? Take a look at Exhibit 11.3 to see how this process works. As you will see, even though Jyri receives a smaller percentage raise for high performance than Dapyne does, Jyri still receives a larger salary increase.

While merit pay increase plans are commonplace, they are not without problems.[10] In fact, in a survey of 150 senior managers conducted by Willis Towers Watson, only one-third felt that their incentive plans effectively differentiated pay based on the individual performance of employees. Only one in five respondents felt that merit pay plans worked. Here are some of the concerns raised by these executives and researchers about merit pay plans.[11] First, the increases are tied directly to employees' performance ratings, and this can be a problem if the ratings are not always accurate or reliable. As we discussed in Chapter 9, biases can creep into the evaluation process and threaten the accuracy of the ratings. When this occurs, employees will doubt the equity and fairness in their incentive systems. Second, because merit pay increases permanently raise the base salaries of employees, a company's labor costs can quickly escalate. Third, merit pay increases are backward focused. They reward

## EXHIBIT 11.3

### Merit Pay Increase Percentage Example

| Employee | Job Grade | Location of Current Salary in Job Grade Salary Range | Maximum Percent Merit Increase for Job Grade for Highest Performance | Current Base Pay | Merit Increase |
|---|---|---|---|---|---|
| Jyri Tigleman | 10 | Above midpoint | 3.5% | $170,000 | $5,950 |
| Daphyne Kucherman | 5 | At midpoint | 5% | $70,000 | $3,500 |

## EXHIBIT 11.4

Merit Pay Increases Versus Lump-Sum Bonus Payments

| Year | Base Salary | Merit Pay Increase 5% Annually | Base Salary | Lump-Sum Increase 5% Annually |
|------|-------------|-------------------------------|-------------|-------------------------------|
| 1 | $40,000.00 | $2,000.00 | $40,000 | $2,000 |
| 2 | $42,000.00 | $2,100.00 | $40,000 | $2,000 |
| 3 | $44,100.00 | $2,205.00 | $40,000 | $2,000 |
| 4 | $46,305.00 | $2,315.25 | $40,000 | $2,000 |
| 5 | $48,620.25 | $2,431.01 | $40,000 | $2,000 |

employees for their past performance rather than provide them with an incentive to work toward future goals. Moreover, because the increases are rolled into their base pay, the actual impact on an employee's weekly paycheck might not seem significant to employees. For example, a $2,000 raise spread out over 52 paychecks amounts to just over $38 per week—before taxes are deducted. As a result, it may be difficult for employees to differentiate merit pay increases from cost-of-living adjustments (COLAs). Finally, when merit increases occur year after year, employees tend to view the pay as an entitlement rather than as a motivator.[12] As a result of these drawbacks, many companies use other types of incentive plans.

### Lump-Sum Merit Bonuses

**lump-sum merit bonus**

a one-time payment based on an employee's level of performance

A variation of the merit pay increase is the **lump-sum merit bonus**. Like traditional merit pay programs, lump-sum bonuses are often based on an employee's level of performance. The primary difference is that lump-sum bonuses are not rolled into the employee's base salary—they are a one-time payment. This difference is important. Compared to merit pay plans, bonuses generally cost companies less because the payouts don't increase labor costs permanently.

As Exhibit 11.4 shows, there are several important cost differences between merit pay increases and lump-sum bonuses that accumulate over time. The most notable difference is that merit pay is permanently rolled into the base pay, resulting in a higher level of base salary for an employee throughout his or her tenure with an organization—even if the employee earns the payment only once. Second, the amount of the employee's compensation increases each year, even if the person continues to perform at the same level. For example, suppose the employee receives a 5% merit raise in year 1, which amounts to $2,000. If this level of performance holds steady over time, in year 4, a 5% merit increase would translate into $2,315.25. In contrast, with a lump-sum bonus plan, the incentive payments are distributed separately from the base pay. Further, because the costs of the payments are not rolled into the base pay of employees, companies can keep their salary levels lower and, instead, allocate higher lump-sum payments only to employees who meet the goals that have been set for them.

Many firms in the tech and finance industries use lump-sum bonuses. Exhibit 11.5 provides information about how the bonuses might be determined based on the role the person plays in the organization. This particular plan ties bonuses to a broadband compensation scheme and is based on the plan at an actual company, a 20-year-old software development company in the financial technology sector.

The "eligible bonus" is the amount that a fully performing employee could receive if both company performance and individual performance goals were met.

### Piecework Incentive Plans

As we have described, merit pay increases and lump-sum bonuses reward employees based on their past performance. In contrast, piecework incentive plans are more

**EXHIBIT 11.5**

## Bonus Eligibility by Band

| Band | Band Title | Band Description | Eligible Bonus % by Band |
|---|---|---|---|
| 6 | Executive Management | Provides enterprisewide strategic direction | 50% |
| 5 | Senior Management | Nonexecutive senior leader | 25% |
| 4 | Functional Area Leader; Senior Relationship Leader | Individual who provides functional area direction for a department; individual who provides high-level relationship management for customers | 15% |
| 3 | People Manager OR Advanced Professional; Domain Expert; Portfolio | Individual with people management responsibilities OR individual contributor with advanced technical/functional area qualifications as defined by the company; individual contributor who manages a portfolio of projects or processes; individual contributor with coaching/mentoring responsibilities; individual contributor with deep business unit expertise; individual who leads a product or service segment | 10% |
| 2 | Professional | Individual contributor with no people management, project, or process ownership | 7.5% |
| 1 | Associate | Entry-level technical- or functional-area contributor; administrative support staff | 5% |

forward-looking because they reward employees for their future performance. Under a **straight piecework plan**, employees receive a certain rate of pay for each unit they produce. Calculating a straight piecework plan is very simple. For example, a salesperson might be compensated $10.00 for every call made to a potential customer. The more calls a salesperson makes, the more he or she earns. Under a **differential piecework plan**, the pay employees receive per unit produced or delivered changes at certain levels of output. Returning to the salesperson example, a company might implement a differential piecework plan in which employees who make more than 10 calls in one hour receive $10.50 for each of the calls, compared to $10.00 per call for those failing to meet or exceed 10 calls.

A key advantage of piecework plans is that they focus employees' efforts directly on tasks that are valuable for company success. Piecework plans also very clearly tell employees what types of behaviors they need to exhibit. Employees know that if they perform well, they will receive higher levels of compensation. The simplicity of these plans and the ease of computing the anticipated compensation for different levels of productivity make them easy to communicate to employees.[13]

There are some potential problems associated with piecework systems. To be most effective, piecework plans depend on firms having clear, objective job outcomes on which to base their incentives. Unfortunately, not all jobs are so clear-cut. Many jobs require employees to perform a wide array of tasks that are difficult to measure. If, as a manager, you implement a piecework plan for this type of job, employees may focus their efforts on the parts of the job that are rewarded by the plan and ignore other important aspects of their jobs. As a result, piecework systems are generally most effective for jobs that are narrow in scope and involve the frequent performance of certain objective tasks. Manufacturing jobs, like those highlighted in Company Spotlight 11.1, which focuses on Lincoln Electric, are a good example. Second, piecework plans place a premium on volume. Without adequate controls, a firm might experience a high volume of products of diminished quality being

**straight piecework plan**

an individual incentive plan in which employees receive a certain rate of pay for each unit they produce

**differential piecework plan**

an individual incentive plan in which the pay employees receive per unit produced or delivered changes at certain levels of output

## COMPANY SPOTLIGHT 11.1

### Lincoln Electric

Lincoln Electric, a maker of arc-welding equipment based in Cleveland, Ohio, is a model of efficiency and productivity within its industry. The company has over 40 manufacturing locations and operations in over 160 countries. What has been the key to the company's success? If you ask anyone at Lincoln, they will likely point to the company's piecework incentive system, which has been in place and uninterrupted since 1915. Employees are paid based on the number of products they produce and a rating of the quality of those products. These factors enter into the equation to determine the annual bonus, which can range from as low as 25% of annual salary to 120%. With this system, an employee earns tens of thousands in annual bonus pay. In 2017, Lincoln handed out $97 million to 2,800 employees—an average of $25,131 per worker. When coupled with the reality that the company has not had a layoff in 69 years, it is clear how Lincoln Electric has been able to build and retain such a talented workforce.

*Sources:* Koller, Frank, "2017 at Lincoln Electric–No Layoffs for 69 Years and 84 Years of Amazing Profit-Sharing Bonuses," Frank Koller Blog, April 30, 2018, http://www.frankkoller.com/2018/04/2017-at-lincoln-electric-no-layoffs-for-69-years-and-84-years-of-amazing-profit-sharing-bonuses/; "Old-Fashioned Business Model Drives Lincoln Electric to the Forefront," North American Oil & Gas Pipelines, February 9, 2017, https://napipelines.com/business-model-lincoln-electric/pretty/Photo/0/.

produced. A third challenge is determining the firm's productivity standards that trigger the higher levels of incentive pay. The standards should be challenging for employees, yet attainable. Fourth, if the amount of work an employee can produce depends on the work of other employees or on the amount and/or type of equipment a firm has, for example, the person's output is less likely to be under his or her direct control. If this is the case, a piecework plan will be less motivating to the employee. Finally, when designing a piecework system, the company must ensure that the Fair Labor Standards Act (FLSA) rules for paying minimum wage and for overtime are taken into account. The average hourly wage cannot be less than the required federal minimum wage (or state, if that is higher) and overtime pay must be compensated appropriately.

### Standard Hour Plan

**standard hour plan**

an individual incentive plan in which the employee's pay is based on how much time an employee is expected to need to complete some task

**Standard hour plans** focus employees' attention on how quickly they can perform their tasks. With standard hour plans, a pay rate is set based on how much time an employee is expected to need to complete some task. If employees are able to complete their tasks in less time than expected, they still receive the full rate of pay for the task performed.[14] For example, if the standard time to install a new computer and its associated software is two hours, and a computer technician performs the job in one and a half hours, he will receive his hourly rate for the full two hours. Likewise, if employees are able to complete more tasks than they're expected to in a given time period, they will receive a premium for their higher level of work. For example, suppose a salesperson is paid $10.00 per hour and is expected to make 10 calls per hour. As Exhibit 11.6 shows, this translates into 6 minutes per call. Over the course of an eight-hour workday, the salesperson would be expected to make 80 calls. If it takes her only 45 minutes to make 10 calls, she would receive her $10 pay for the 45 minutes. Over the course of a day, if the salesperson actually makes 100 calls, she would be compensated for 10 hours' worth of work during those 8 hours. According to the standard hour plan, she would receive the equivalent of $12.50 per hour for that day rather than the $10 per hour she would have received if she had simply met expectations. This increase translates into a 25% incentive premium for her performance.

## EXHIBIT 11.6

### Sample Standard Hour Plan for a Salesperson

| Criteria | Standard Performance for 8-Hour Day | High Performance for 8-Hour Day |
|---|---|---|
| Base pay per hour | $10.00 | $ 10.00 |
| Performance level | 80 calls | 100 calls |
| Incentive premium | 0% | 25% |
| Final pay per hour | $10.00 | $ 12.50 |
| Final pay | $80.00 | $100.00 |

The primary advantage of the standard hour plan is that it encourages employees to work as quickly as possible to complete their tasks. If they are very efficient, they are able to perform more tasks than expected in a typical day, thereby increasing their take-home pay. Another benefit of standard hour plans is that, compared to piecework systems, the plan can be used to motivate employees who are doing more complex jobs—that is, jobs that involve different tasks or projects that are not necessarily standardized or simplified.[15] Automobile mechanic and attorney are examples of two jobs for which the standard hour plan is appropriate. At the same time, however, employees need some sort of motivation to pay attention to the quality of their work, not just the speed. It doesn't do any good for a company, or the customer, to have employees working very quickly but making a lot of mistakes or not delivering a high-quality product or service. For instance, when you take your car in for repair, you expect the mechanic to perform quality work so you don't have to bring the car back in for the same problem. Thus, if the mechanic can repair the car appropriately in less time, that is fine; but if not, the mechanic needs to take the full time expected to do the repair. To encourage employees to focus on quality as well as quantity, some companies require employees to correct their work on their own time if the quality of their work is low.

### Awards

A **spot award** is an incentive that companies use to encourage their employees to work toward specific outcomes. Managers give the awards (often cash) to employees "on the spot" when they exhibit certain behaviors or achieve certain outcomes associated with excellent performance. Spot awards give managers flexibility because they can be linked to a variety of employee actions at any time. Unlike merit raises and lump-sum bonuses, they don't depend on performance evaluations over the course of the review period. For example, a manager might give a cash award to the employee with the most sales, the employee who makes the fewest mistakes, or the employee with the highest customer satisfaction ratings. The strength of spot awards is that they can be tied directly to specific performance dimensions of employees' jobs and are paid only when desired performance levels are met. Given the flexibility of spot awards, it shouldn't be a surprise that 80% of private companies said they use short-term incentives to reward high-performing employees.[16]

Companies can use noncash awards as incentives as well. Vacations, merchandise, gift certificates, and paid time off from work are examples of some of the types of awards employees might be offered for achieving certain levels of performance. Here are some specific examples. At Zappos, every quarter, every employee receives $50 to reward to another employee for doing a good job. Managers, team leads, and supervisors are not eligible for these awards. In this peer-to-peer recognition system, employees can also hand out "Zollars" (Zappos dollars) to other employees. These Zollars can be collected and used in the Zappos office "Zollar store" for movie tickets,

**spot award**
a short-term incentive that companies use to encourage their employees to work toward specific outcomes

branded swag, or even to make a donation to a charity. JetBlue's peer-to-peer program is called Lift. Employees can recognize their colleagues for everyday and extraordinary actions and the colleague receives points to cash in for her or his choice of reward from the available selection. At CadmiumCD, the highest performing 10% of the staff are recognized in a company gathering. Each recognition gift is tailored specifically for the individual employee. For instance, someone who just had a baby might receive a gift certificate to a baby supply store.[17] Recognition programs such as these aren't always associated with monetary rewards, but they can still be powerful motivators.[18]

### Sales Incentive Plans

Sales professionals have an obvious impact on the performance of their firms. The more sales that these employees generate, the more business their companies enjoy. As a result, companies benefit from providing extensive sales-based incentives to these employees. There are three primary types of sales-incentive plans. The first type is a commission-based sales plan. A **straight commission plan** pays employees a percentage of the total sales they generate. For example, an employee working on a 1% straight commission plan who generates $1 million in sales would receive $10,000. If the person generated $10,000,000 in sales, he would receive $100,000 in compensation.

The primary benefit of this type of system is that high-performing employees receive high payouts and companies pay employees only for what they sell. However, employees working under these plans face a considerable amount of financial risk in terms of what they potentially earn. If a person sells nothing or very little, he or she receives little or no compensation under these plans. Another problem is that employees operating under commission-based pay systems can become so obsessed about their sales levels that they are hesitant to help their coworkers unless they are able to get part of their commissions. This issue may be particularly problematic when sales environments depend on collaboration and teamwork among employees. Further, sales professionals feeling pressured to make their quotas and receive larger commissions may also pressure customers to make purchases that they neither need nor want. Given these concerns, companies may replace commission-based pay systems with systems that are more team oriented.

Some companies rely on **straight salary plans** for their sales professionals. Employees receive a set compensation, regardless of their level of sales. As you can imagine, employees working under these plans might not be as motivated to sell as much as they can. However, the systems do provide employees with much greater personal income security. Also, because these plans remove the strong incentive to focus only on sales, employees might be more willing to spend time providing quality service to customers or working with existing customers. For example, in the financial services industry, there have been concerns about the practice of *churning*—investment brokers inflating their own commissions by increasing the number of transactions they make on a client's account, even if the transactions are not in the client's best financial interests.[19] This practice is less likely to happen when sales personnel are on a straight salary plan, as opposed to a straight commission plan.

In an attempt to capitalize on the benefits of both commission and salary incentive plans, some companies use a **mixed salary/commission plan**. This plan is also referred to as a **base plus commission plan**. In these systems, employees receive a lower base salary—perhaps only 50% or 70% of what would be offered under a straight salary plan. The remaining percentage is commission based. Here's an example: If an employee would normally make $50,000 under a straight salary plan, under a 70/30 plan (70% salary, 30% commission), she would earn a base salary of $35,000, and the rest of her compensation would be based on 30% of her commission plan (i.e., 1% of sales). If she sells $5 million, she would earn $35,000 in salary, plus 30% of $50,000 (1% of $5 million), or $15,000, resulting in a total salary of $50,000. If she sold $10 million, she would earn $35,000 in salary, plus $30,000 in commission.

---

**straight commission plan**

a plan that pays employees a percentage of the total sales they generate

**straight salary plan**

a plan in which employees receive a set compensation, regardless of their level of sales

**mixed salary/commission plan (also known as base plus commission plan)**

employees receive a lower base salary, perhaps only 50% or 70% of what would be offered under a straight salary plan, with the remaining percentage being commission based

## Group/Organizational Incentives

Rather than focus solely on individual incentive plans, companies can also implement group or organizational incentive plans. Group incentive plans are intended to motivate employees to work as a collective unit. The group might consist of a couple of individuals, an entire department, a business unit, or an entire company.

### Team Incentive Plans

When a company relies on teams, it is important to foster a collective sense of identity and cooperation among the team members. One method of doing so is to provide team-based incentives. In fact, piecework plans, standard hour plans, bonuses, awards, and merit pay can all be applied to entire teams as well as individuals. If a team reaches or exceeds its target objective, all of its members are rewarded equally, and if the team fails to meet its goals, none of the members receive the incentive. Company Spotlight 11.2 describes how Nike has moved to a new bonus system focused on company performance.

## COMPANY SPOTLIGHT **11.2**

### Nike's New System for Awarding Bonuses to Increase Pay Equity

As part of a companywide effort to create fairer internal pay, Nike announced that it would be increasing salaries for 7,000 employees out of its 74,000-employee workforce worldwide. At the same time, the company announced that it would be changing its bonus system. This major overhaul of the company's compensation system is one way Nike is working to address pay equity concerns and change the company's culture. The changes followed the results of an informal survey of female employees that indicated many of the respondents felt they had experienced gender discrimination in terms of promotions and in other ways. Nike did note that the raises being made were not gender specific and that the results of tracking their global pay equity indicated women were paid 99.9 cents for every $1 that men at Nike were paid. Nike says there are two goals for the changes: (1) to ensure pay is more competitive and (2) to "support a culture in which employees feel included and empowered."

An important, and perhaps the most substantive part of the compensation system change, relates to bonuses. Going forward, annual bonuses will be tied to a companywide budgeted earnings target, before interest and tax for the year, as opposed to the mixture of individual and team performance metrics used in the past. Eligible employees in the company will still have individual bonus targets. These targets could be 10% or 20% of annual compensation; however, the payouts will be uniform across the company. Also, eligible employees will now be able to choose how they want to receive stock awarded to them. They can choose stock options, restricted stock units, or a 50/50 mix. Overall, the company is hoping to create a clearer line of sight between what employees are doing and the outcomes for the company. The ultimate goal is to provide a more competitive and equitable total rewards program with bonuses playing an important role in achieving that goal.

*Sources:* Germano, Sara, "Nike to Adjust Pay for Thousands of Staffers After Internal Review," *Wall Street Journal*, July 23, 2018, https://www.wsj.com/articles/nike-to-adjust-pay-for-thousands-of-staffers-after-internal-review-1532369993; Salpini, Cara, "Nike to Raise Salaries After Internal Review," *Retail Dive*, July 24, 2018, https://www.retaildive.com/news/nike-to-raise-salaries-after-internal-review/528478/; Gurchiek, Kathy, "Nike Shoots for Pay Equity with Changes to Reward Program," *SHRM.org*, July 27, 2018, https://www.shrm.org/resourcesandtools/hr-topics/behavioral-competencies/pages/nike-shoots-for-pay-equity-with-changes-to-reward-program.aspx.

Team incentives make the most sense when employees perform tasks that are highly interdependent and when cooperation and collaboration are required for the team to be successful. The primary downside of team incentives, as with other group incentive plans, is the potential for free riders. **Free riders** are individuals who do not work as hard as the others on their teams. This behavior may take the form of being late for deadlines or just not doing their assigned part. You may have personally experienced such a person on a team you have been on in a class or at work. When this occurs, the hardworking team members are likely to feel they are getting a bad deal, and the team will tend to become dysfunctional. One solution to this problem is to have team members evaluate the contributions of each other through a peer appraisal or a 360-degree performance evaluation process. Another option we will discuss later in this chapter is to rely on a mixed-level system that rewards individual effort as well as team effort.

**free rider**

an individual who does not work as hard as the others on a team

### Gain Sharing Plans

**Gain sharing plans** are designed to help increase an organization's efficiency by increasing the productivity of the company's employees and/or lowering the firm's labor costs. Under these plans, employees earn a share of the gains of their productivity with the company. The gains may be realized in one of two ways. First, if the firm's collective productivity improves and the employees exceed some predetermined productivity level, they receive part of the monetary value of the increased productivity. Second, if employees are able to maintain the same level of productivity but do so with fewer costs, they share the gains of their increased efficiency. Two common plans that are used to realize these gains are Scanlon plans and Improshare plans.

**gain sharing plan**

a plan designed to help increase an organization's efficiency by increasing the productivity of the company's employees and/or lowering the firm's labor costs

A **Scanlon plan** can help reduce a firm's labor costs without corresponding decreases in productivity levels. Under this plan, employees make suggestions on how to improve a firm's productivity and offer those suggestions to a review committee for its consideration for implementation. If the review committee accepts the plan and its implementation results in increased efficiency, the gains of that efficiency are shared with employees. The incentive is based on improving the relative level, or ratio, of the firm's labor costs to the sales value of the products it produces. For example, a firm might have a target ratio of 0.1 for the company's labor costs relative to the sales value of its products. In this case, if the company expected to do $1 million in sales, it would strive to keep its labor costs to $100,000. If employees are able to achieve the same sales value of production with a ratio that's lower than 0.1, they share the gains of that increased efficiency with their company. In our examples, if the firm's workforce is able to realize $1 million in sales with only $90,000 in labor costs, the $10,000 in savings would be split among the employees and the company. By providing employees with a portion of any savings they help realize through participation and suggestions, companies are directly rewarding employees for taking steps to increase their productivity levels and for working harder toward the company's goals.[20]

**Scanlon plan**

a group-based incentive plan based on employee suggestions for increased efficiencies and productivity

A somewhat different approach to gain sharing is the **improshare plan**. Improshare plans are based on the number of hours a firm expects to take to reach a certain level of output. In essence, the plan is based on time savings per unit of production rather than just cost savings. To implement this type of plan, companies must first establish the expected hours per unit of productivity for a group of employees. If the employees are able to achieve a set level of productivity in fewer hours than expected, they receive an equal share of the hours saved in the form of pay.[21] Similar to the standard hour plan at the individual level, the primary impact of an improshare plan is that it encourages employees as a group to produce a greater quantity of output.

**improshare plan**

a group-based incentive plan based on the number of hours a firm expects to take to reach a certain level of output

The primary advantages of gain sharing plans are that they help foster a participative environment in which employees are able to help improve productivity and are rewarded for making useful suggestions. Because these plans operate at a group or plant level, all employees within the unit are encouraged to help one another succeed.[22] An additional advantage of gain sharing plans is their instrumentality—that is, there is a clear link between the effort employees expend and the rewards they receive.[23] As with team incentive plans, however, one potential problem is the existence of free riders in a group. Other potential problems are that the plan may be too complex for employees to understand[24] or the rewards may be viewed as unattainable, particularly in situations in which employees already operate at very high levels of efficiency.

## Profit Sharing Plans

Under **profit sharing plans**, company profits are shared with employees. Procedurally, profit sharing can be distributed to employees as cash or can be deferred. Under a **deferred profit sharing plan**, the incentive money paid to an employee is put into a retirement account for that employee. This plan has a tax advantage because the income the employee earns is deferred until he or she retires. After people retire, their earnings are generally lower so the income withdrawn from the retirement account is taxed at a lower rate.

> **profit sharing plan**
> a group-level incentive plan in which company profits are shared with employees

There are several other advantages of profit sharing plans. First, profits are obviously an important component of a company's success. Thus, implementing these plans helps keep employees focused on activities that are truly important. Moreover, by focusing employees' efforts on the performance of the entire company rather than solely on their own performance, profit sharing encourages collaboration and teamwork among employees. A final benefit of profit sharing is that employees are paid only when a company is doing well, a mechanism that helps maintain control over labor costs.

> **deferred profit sharing plan**
> a group-based incentive plan in which the incentive money paid to an employee is put into a retirement account for that employee

There are some downsides to profit sharing plans. In some instances, employees may be doing exceptionally well in their jobs and helping their coworkers excel, but their company's overall performance goal may not be being realized. The point here is that the profitability of a company is influenced by a multitude of factors, many of which are outside the control of employees. Competition, changes in consumer preferences, industry trends, and the like affect a company's profitability. With profit sharing plans, it is conceivable that employees might not be rewarded by their incentive plans, even though they have done everything they can to help their company succeed. A second potential problem with profit sharing plans is that employees might not see the fruits of their labor for a long time. It may take a while for the efforts of employees to translate into company profits. If this occurs, the gap between when performance occurs and when the reward is realized might be significant, thereby diminishing the motivating impact of these plans.

## Ownership Plans

Whereas profit sharing plans tie employee incentives to the profitability of a firm, ownership plans tie employees' incentives to the performance of a company's stock in the marketplace. Companies use two primary types of ownership plans: stock option plans and employee stock ownership plans (ESOPs).

**Stock option plans** provide employees with the right to purchase shares of their company's stock at some established price, such as its market value, for a given period of time. During that period of time, employees can exercise this right, and they can subsequently sell their shares. For example, an employee might be provided with a stock option plan to buy shares at $10 per share for five years. If the stock price rises above this to $30 per share, and the employee exercises her rights to purchase and sell the shares during the five-year period, she would realize a gain of $20 per share. **Broad-based stock option** plans are plans that apply widely to a firm's employees. More than 50% of a firm's nonexecutive employees are included in broad-based plans.[25]

> **stock option plan**
> a group-based incentive plan that provides employees with the right to purchase shares of their company's stock at some established price (often its market value) for a given period of time

> **broad-based stock option plan**
> a stock purchase plan that applies widely to a firm's employees

**employee stock owner-
ship plan (ESOP)**

a group-based incentive
plan in which a company
contribute shares of its
stock to a trust set up for
its employees

Under an **employee stock ownership plan (ESOP)**, a company contributes shares of its stock to a trust set up for its employees. In June 2018, there were 7,000 ESOP plans in the United States involving approximately 28 million employees. Publix is the largest ESOP at this time.[26] In a **leveraged ESOP**, the trust borrows against the company's future earnings, and as the debt is repaid, employees receive in their individual accounts shares of the stock held by the ESOP.[27] During the course of their employment, workers are updated as to the value of their stock accounts. When they retire or leave the company, they can sell their stock to the company or sell them on the open market. One of the major benefits of ESOPs is that employees are not taxed on the accumulated stocks until they receive their distribution upon separation from the company. Similarly, the company receives a tax deduction of the value of the stock transferred to the trust.[28] Remember when we discussed agency theory earlier in the chapter? If employees continue to accumulate considerable shares of company stock, they may adopt more of the perspective of the firm's owners in terms of how they do their jobs. Ownership plans can, therefore, increase the commitment of employees to the success of their companies.[29] Indeed, research suggests that ESOPs are associated with higher productivity and higher survival rates in companies.[30] Company Spotlight 11.3 describes how the ESOP at WinCo Foods is building wealth for its employees.

**leveraged ESOP**

a group-based incentive
plan that allows a trust to
borrow funds against the
company's future earnings,
and as the debt is repaid,
employees receive shares
of the stock held by
the ESOP in employee
accounts

One of the primary benefits of ownership plans is that they may serve to align the long-term interests of employees with those of the company. Because they do this, employees may be more inclined to exert the necessary effort in their jobs to maximize their value-added contributions. In addition, ownership plans do not require employees to use their own savings to participate. At the same time, however, there is still risk for employees. If employees rely on ESOPs as the main source of income for their retirement, their investment portfolios won't be well diversified. So, for example, if the company's stock does not perform well, its employees might end up holding worthless pieces of paper. This situation is exactly what happened to Enron's employees. Employees who were once worth millions on paper by virtue of what was in their ESOPs were suddenly worth nothing after Enron's demise.[31] Also, as is the case with other group-oriented plans, the risk of free riders is a problem. An additional potential problem with ownership plans is that employees might not feel that they can really make a difference, or that the ultimate measure—the stock price of their firms—is within their control.

### Mixed-Level Plans

**mixed-level plan**

an incentive plan in which
employees are exposed to
multiple incentive plans

Under a **mixed-level plan**, employees are exposed to multiple incentives. For example, at the restaurant chain Bubba Gump, one-quarter of a manager's bonus is based on the person's individual goals and the remaining portion is based on his or her store's performance.[32] The logic of using multiple incentive plans at different levels is that doing so can maximize the benefits of each plan while discouraging the downsides of each. Rewarding employees for their individual performance, as well as the performance of their teams or companies, encourages them to maximize their own performance, but not in a competitive manner or to the detriment of their coworkers. Employees who don't work well with their coworkers diminish their chances of realizing one of their incentives.

## Executive Compensation: Pay and Incentives

No aspect of compensation has been as controversial or received as much attention in recent years as executive compensation. It is almost impossible to pick up a newspaper or business magazine without seeing an article about problems with executive compensation or about unethical practices executives have participated in to enhance their own personal wealth. The average pay CEOs has skyrocketed relative

## COMPANY SPOTLIGHT 11.3

### Building Wealth Working at WinCo Foods—An Employee Owned Company

You probably have never thought about the grocery clerks at your local food store being millionaires. If you shop at WinCo Foods, you might need to think differently. The company has 98 stores in eight states. WinCo, headquartered in Boise, Idaho, has been employee owned since 1985. An Employee Stock Ownership Plan (ESOP) is the primary vehicle for the employees' retirement plan. The company also has a 401(k), and about 70% of its workers participate in that as well. Since 1986, shares have risen at a compounded annual rate of 18%. The ESOP purchased the company for $10 million in 1985, and today, the value of the shares held by company employees is valued at nearly $3 billion. Across the company, more than 400 front-line employees are already millionaires, and hundreds of employees have already retired as millionaires. Employees become owners after working at least 500 hours in their first six months of employment, are at least 19 years of age, and accumulate 1,000 hours each fiscal year.

Among the job titles at WinCo are shelf stockers, grocery clerks, and bakery workers. There are 130 workers with titles such as these at the Corvallis, Oregon, location. They have a combined retirement savings of around $100 million, and that is still growing. (Nope, that's not a typo.) A number of the workers already have retirement savings of over $1 million, and other employees are very close to becoming millionaires. An employee who received a company contribution of stock worth $5,000 in 1986, given the compounded annual rate of return of 18%, would find just that year's stock is now worth $863,000.

WinCo is well managed and is a steadily growing company that provides a wide selection of products at low prices with efficient and friendly service. The company does not advertise, shoppers bag their own groceries, and its main competitors include Walmart. Because employees know that their actions directly affect their retirement accounts, they tend to work as a team and police each other to ensure efficiencies occur and the work gets done, and gets done well.

*Sources:* "WinCo Foods Is Proud to Be Employee-Owned. . .," WinCo Foods, https://www.wincofoods.com/about/an-employee-owned-company; Josephs, Mary, "Millionaire Grocery Clerks: The Amazing WinCo Foods Story," *Forbes*, November 5, 2014, https://www.forbes.com/sites/maryjosephs/2014/11/05/millionaire-grocery-clerks-the-amazing-winco--foods-story/#624ff5945700.

to that of average workers. In 1983, CEOs earned just under 50 times the average worker. In 1993, that figure was almost 200 times, and in 2015, it was 335 times—which means that for every $1 earned by an average worker, the CEO is paid $335.[33]

Starting in 2018, companies were required to comply with a pay-ratio-disclosure rule that is part of the Dodd-Frank legislation of 2010. This rule requires companies to determine the compensation of the median-paid employee at the firm and compare that with the CEO as a ratio, as opposed to the traditional reporting using an average worker salary. Then, that information has to be disclosed. Among the first firms reporting this data were Honeywell, with a ratio of 333 to 1; Teva Pharmaceuticals, at 302 to 1; and Umpqua Holdings, at 55 to 1.[34]

Greater attention from shareholders and new and proposed legislation have led companies to reconsider how they provide executive compensation. Generally, a larger proportion of the pay mix for executives has been tied to performance for some time now. In fact, a 2006 survey of 350 firms by the *Wall Street Journal* and Mercer Human Resource Consulting found that over 80% of CEOs' compensation was at risk or dependent upon their firms meeting either their short- or long-term goals.[35] In 2016, that figure was at 60%–80%.[36]

Whether or not this linkage between CEO pay and performance is paying off for firms has been called into question. A study of U.S. CEO pay and long-term investment returns revealed that CEO pay was not generally well aligned with long-term company stock performance. Comparing 10 years of CEO pay figures to firm performance for 423 companies revealed that there was not a high correlation (R-squared = 0.0093) between CEO-realized pay (e.g., take-home pay after exercising stock options or becoming eligible for stock grants) and long-term investment returns at the majority of large-cap U.S. companies. Three-fifths of the companies had poor alignment with 23 of these companies actually underpaying their CEO for long-time performance and 18 overpaying their CEOs.[37]

Executive compensation includes the same components as other compensation packages—base salary, short- and long-term incentives, and benefits and services. Short-term incentives often include rewards based on financial measures of company performance. Long-term incentives such as stock options are used to encourage executives to try to improve their company's performance for a long period of time. This is done by aligning their pay with the long-term success of the company.

Executive compensation differs in the magnitude and mix of components, as well as perks not offered to other employees. These perks can include the use of a company plane, a car and driver, country club memberships, and even a bodyguard. A CEO's pay is typically established by a compensation committee made up of members of the firm's board of directors. These directors are often high-ranking executives from other companies. A major concern about the use of compensation committees to establish executive pay is the extent to which they can be unbiased. The members of the committee understand very well how the labor market works in terms of wages. As CEOs or vice presidents themselves, they know that market pay rates can be influenced by one company paying higher wages. Thus, these people have an incentive to provide greater rewards to the CEO of the company on whose boards they sit. In other words, what goes around, comes around; they know that approving higher wages for the CEO on whose board they sit will eventually pay off when their board reviews the market salaries for comparable CEOs.

It is worth mentioning that a number of CEOs are very aware of the controversial nature of their pay relative to their workers and have made adjustments in their pay in response. In fact, a few years ago, a number of high-profile CEOs agreed to a base salary of $1, with the rest of their income paid as performance-based pay. These CEOs included Meg Whitman of Hewlett-Packard, John Mackey of Whole Foods, Sergey Brin and Larry Page of Google, and Mark Zuckerberg of Facebook.[38] This is not to suggest that these executives don't reap the benefits of their efforts. Rather, they are tying their own financial gains to those of their companies. If their companies make money, they make money.

## What Makes an Incentive Plan Effective?

As a manager, you have a wide array of incentive plans from which to choose. To be effective, however, the plans need to meet several criteria:

- *Link to your firm's strategic objectives*. First, you have to know what exactly you are trying to accomplish with your incentive plan. Piecework systems, for example, are quite effective in settings that place priority on volume and efficient employee productivity. Commission plans help encourage employees to maximize their sales. Gain sharing plans encourage groups of employees to think about ways to improve the efficiency of their firms.

- *Have clear standards*. Effective incentive plans have clear standards of performance that employees strive to reach. One of the reasons piecework systems, sales incentives, and standard hour plans are effective is that they offer a clear link between pay and achieving some predetermined level of performance.[39]

- *Sample the full performance domain.* Effective incentive plans must give employees an incentive to excel in all aspects of their jobs. Managers must be careful not to focus solely on one performance aspect while neglecting others.
- *Be attainable.* The standards by which incentives are triggered must not only be clear, they must also be attainable. Recall goal setting theory and expectancy theory. If employees work hard and consistently fail to attain the incentives they hope to receive, the power of the incentive plan designed to motivate them will diminish.
- *Be easy to understand.* Incentive plans must be easy to understand. If employees don't know how to realize the incentives offered under a plan, the plan's motivational power will be weak.
- *Provide meaningful incentives.* As expectancy theory notes, incentives must be meaningful to employees. The more employees desire an incentive, the harder they will work to attain it.
- *Evaluated regularly.* A final criterion for effective incentive plans is that they must be regularly evaluated to ensure that they are actually motivating people to work toward the appropriate individual, team, and company goals.

Principles

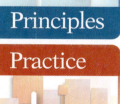

Practice

## Incentives and Rewards In Practice: Organizational Demands

As shown in Exhibit 11.6, the reward and incentive plans used by companies are likely to vary as they cope with different organizational demands, environmental influences, and regulatory issues. We start with how organizational demands—strategy, company characteristics, company culture, and employee concerns—affect the way incentive plans are designed and implemented, as well as how effective they are.

### Strategy and Incentives

Strategy influences incentives in several important ways. First, the strategic goals and direction of a company affect the types and levels of employee performance the company targets and the incentives it uses. Second, strategy influences which incentive plans are used for different groups of employees within companies.

#### What Is Rewarded

In our discussion of job design in Chapter 4 and performance management in Chapter 9, we noted that every job has multiple tasks and responsibilities. However, not all job duties are equally important for different strategic objectives. The strategic focus of a company should influence which tasks or behaviors are targeted with incentives.[40] A company with low cost as its strategic focus would likely reward different employee behaviors and outcomes than a company focusing on strategies such as customer service, innovation, or quality. In companies with a low cost focus, managers are more likely to target employee behaviors that directly contribute to the efficiency of the companies' operations. In contrast, a company pursuing a customer service strategy will be more concerned with encouraging attitudes and behaviors that lead to increased customer satisfaction, retention, and repeat business. A key task for managers is to consider their company's strategy when deciding which performance aspects to target. Ideally, they should be the ones that maximize the amount of value added to a company. And, as we have indicated, you need to consider the full array of tasks that your employees perform. If you

## EXHIBIT 11.6

Incentives and Rewards in Practice

| Context | Practice Issues |
|---|---|
| **Organizational Demands** | |
| *Strategy* drives . . . | • What is rewarded |
| | • Which incentive plans are used |
| *Company characteristics* determine . . . | • Feasibility of different incentive plans |
| | • Impact of incentives on employees |
| *Culture* establishes . . . | • Incentive plans managers choose |
| | • Employees' acceptance of incentive plans |
| *Employee concerns* include . . . | • Fairness of incentive plan standards |
| | • Likelihood of receiving incentives |
| | • Acceptability of incentive payouts |
| **Environmental Demands** | |
| *Labor force* influences . . . | • Using incentives to increase diversity |
| | • Desirability of different rewards |
| *Technology* affects . . . | • How incentives are managed |
| | • Incentive plans for a virtual workforce |
| *Globalization* impacts . . . | • What is rewarded |
| | • Acceptability of incentives |
| *Ethics/social responsibility* shapes . . . | • Ethical employee behavior |
| | • How employees and communities view executive incentive plans |
| **Regulations** | |
| *Regulations* guide . . . | • Bias and discrimination |
| | • Stock option backdating |

implement an incentive plan that is one dimensional and focuses on only a limited subset of tasks and behaviors, your employees may focus only on those tasks directly rewarded and neglect the performance of other important responsibilities.[41]

### Which Incentive Plans Are Used

The strategy of a company is related to the incentive plans used to motivate employees. If a company competes on a strategy that requires cooperation and teamwork among employees, groupwide or companywide plans might be more appropriate than individual incentive plans. Of course, individual incentive plans can be quite effective when other strategies are used. If customer service is the objective, a merit-based incentive may be more appropriate than, say, a standard hour plan or a piecework system that rewards employees for how fast they complete their tasks, rather than how satisfied they leave the firm's customers. Alternatively, in a company with a cost-focused strategy, incentive plans such as standard hour plans or gain sharing plans may encourage employees to reach and sustain certain productivity and efficiency levels.

To be effective, however, an incentive plan must be tailored in terms of how different employees add value to the organization. For example, production employees may add value through efficiency, sales employees may add value through generating sales, and research and development (R&D) employees may add value through the creation of new products. Each of these employees, therefore, needs to be provided with a distinct incentive plan that reflects how he or she contributes to the organization's strategic objectives. To accomplish this goal, managers might have to design multiple incentive plans to motivate different employees to maximize their efforts in specific ways. Trying to use a single incentive plan for all employees may not reflect differences in the nature of their contributions.

## Company Characteristics and Incentives

A company's stage of development and its size have a bearing on which incentive plans are feasible to use. A company's characteristics also affect the impact its incentive plans will have on its employees.

### Feasibility of Different Incentive Plans

In our previous discussion, we highlighted how the strategy of a company influences which incentive plans managers choose to use to motivate their employees. These choices are also influenced by a company's characteristics. Not all companies are in a position to every type of incentive plan. For example, a small, start-up company might not have enough financial slack to provide high levels of merit pay to its employees. Rather, the firm might be more inclined to use incentives that are paid only if the firm's employees improve the company's financial performance. In these cases, profit sharing plans, lump-sum bonuses, awards, or piecework plans—which are paid out only if the company benefits from the increased performance—may be more feasible than guaranteed salary increases.

### Impact of Incentives on Employees

The size of a company can affect how well its incentive plan motivates its employees. Consider the impact of a profit sharing plan in a company with 20 employees versus a company with 20,000 employees. In the smaller company, employees are more likely to have a clear line of sight regarding how their individual performance affects the performance of the entire company.[42] This perspective is likely to increase their instrumentality; they believe there is a stronger link between their efforts and the profitability of the company. When an employee is only one of thousands of employees, however, the direct link between his or her efforts and the company's overall profitability is likely to be—or at least is perceived to be—much weaker. Employees in this situation might believe that their performance simply does not make that much difference. As a result, the motivating impact of the incentive plan might be weaker than if the plan were used in a smaller company.

## Culture and Incentives

A company's culture affects the use of incentives in several ways. First, it influences the likelihood that managers will use the different incentive plans. Second, the shared perceptions among employees regarding the firm's cultural values influence their acceptance of incentive plans.

### Incentive Plans Managers Choose

A manager is likely to be most comfortable implementing an incentive plan that is consistent with the values of his or her company. In a company with a culture that encourages employees to work together to meet their departmental or unit goals, managers are likely to be more comfortable with a team-based incentive plan than with individual incentive plans. In contrast, in a high-performance culture that strongly values the accomplishments of individual employees, managers might be more comfortable with individual incentive plans. Different incentive plans send different signals to employees about what they should do at work, as well as how they should do it. The choice of which incentive plan you implement must reflect the

## COMPANY SPOTLIGHT 11.4

### When Everyone Quits

When Mark Moeller took over the family jewelry business, R. F. Moeller Jeweler in St. Paul, Minnesota, from his father in 1989, he decided to change the incentive system to encourage the salespeople to increase their productivity. Mark wanted to implement a mixed salary/commission plan to replace the straight salary plan under which the employees had been working. Shortly after he implemented the new system, however, all the nonfamily employees quit. The employees thought the personal risks with the pay-for-performance plan were too great (the plan reduced their base salary and provided them with 20% of the gross profit on the jewelry they sold). Over time, however, Moeller hired new employees who were not scared away by the sales-driven incentive plan. Once the right people were in place, sales took off. In fact, after a few years, the sales associates were put on straight commission to reward their outstanding efforts. The company has been family-owned since 1951 and now has three stores. Most recently, the company has continued to innovate, spinning off a new business, Atique, a virtual reality (VR) app that creates a virtual showroom for inspecting jewelry.

*Source:* Spector, B., "When Everyone Quits," *JCK Magazine* 172, no. 6 (June 2001): 258–264, http://www.jckonline.com/2001/06/01/family-business-crisis-when-everyone-quits; R. F. Moeller Jeweler, https://rfmoeller.com/; Ojeda-Zapata, Julio, "St. Paul Jeweler Offers Virtual-Reality App for Viewing Baubles in 360 Degrees," *Twin Cities Pioneer Press,* January 7, 2017, https://www.twincities.com/2017/01/07/st-paul-jeweler-creates-virtual-reality-app-for-viewing-baubles-in-360-degrees/.

cultural values of your company. Company Spotlight 11.4 highlights the impact of misalignment and alignment between incentives and culture at R. F. Moeller Jewelers.

### Employees' Acceptance of Incentive Plans

The culture of a company influences how employees perceive the appropriateness of the incentive plans it adopts. Any discrepancy between the design of a firm's incentive plan and a company's cultural values will result in a negative reaction from the employees. If inconsistencies exist between the plan and the culture, the result may be decreased, rather than increased, motivation to work toward your company's goals. Consider the options available for incentive plans for salespeople. As a manager, you can choose from a straight commission, a straight salary, or a mixed salary/commission plan. Which one should you choose?

One factor to consider is the underlying culture of your organization. If your company's culture is an individual performance–oriented culture, a straight commission system might be most appropriate. If your firm is more paternalistic and values taking care of employees, a salary or salary/commission mixed plan that provides employees with greater financial security is likely to be more consistent with your culture. Recall the reaction of the salesforce in Company Spotlight 11.4. The incentive plan was ineffective under the existing culture and worked only when all the nonfamily employees were replaced with employees open to a more performance-oriented culture.

A similar concern relates to how employees feel about the amount of compensation they have at risk—that is, the amount of their compensation based on incentive pay. With standard hour plans and piecework systems, for example, the financial security of employees is tied directly to their productivity. Employees do not earn incentives unless they hit certain performance targets. In contrast, plans such as merit-based pay and gain sharing do not carry this risk. The rewards are added to the employees' regular paychecks. The extent to which employees are willing to embrace these risks may be influenced by the cultural values of the company. For example, a company with a paternalistic history might face more resistance from its employees for shifting to an incentive-based pay plan than a company with a more performance-oriented culture.

## Employee Concerns and Incentives

In Chapter 10, we discussed the importance of employee concerns about fairness in a compensation system. Employees want to make sure that the level of their pay and the process for determining pay levels are fair. This concern about fairness includes their incentive pay, too. Specifically, employees can be concerned about the procedural justice related to their firms' incentive plans, the likelihood of their receiving the awards associated with the plans, and the actual incentive levels they receive.

### Fairness of Incentive Plan Standards

One design issue that influences employee perceptions of fairness relates to the standards that are set as part of their firms' incentive plans. Managers might develop very high standards for achieving particular incentives, bonuses, or awards such that very few people achieve them. Alternatively, performance standards may be set at a lower level that is easily attainable by many employees in a company. Consider a piecework system in which the average employee produces 20 units per hour. How would employees react if the standard for the higher incentive premium per unit were raised to 40 units per hour? If employees don't believe they can realistically produce 40 units per hour or more, they will view the plan as unfair.

A similar problem can exist with other incentive plans. The time standard in standard hour plans might be too short, for example, to allow employees to actually receive the incentive bonus. Likewise, individual or team incentives might be tied to goals that are unrealistic. Scott Testa, former CEO of Mindbridge Software, learned the importance of employee concerns and incentive system plans when he implemented a new incentive program for his salesforce. Employees were rewarded with long weekend trips to any destination, as long as the trips didn't cost more than $3,000. The problem was that the performance standard was unattainable. Salespeople who generated $200,000 per month in revenues had to bring in more than $500,000 per month in revenues for an entire year simply to qualify for the trips.[43] The idea for sales incentives and rewards has potential, but it must be attainable to have the desired impact on employees.

### Likelihood of Receiving Incentives

Employees are concerned about the instrumentality of a plan. As explained earlier, *instrumentality* refers to the perceived link between one's performance and receiving the reward or incentive payment promised. When this perception is compromised, employees will question the procedural justice of their incentive plans. For example, profit sharing plans and ownership plans are influenced by factors beyond the control of the employee. Employees operating under a profit sharing plan might be legitimately concerned that even if they work as hard as possible and meet or exceed their individual goals, they might not necessarily be rewarded.[44]

### Acceptability of Incentive Payouts

Beyond concerns about the process of how incentive plans operate, employees can also have concerns about the actual incentive payouts they receive. These distributive justice concerns can surface when either individual or team incentive plans are used.

When it comes to individual incentive plans, employees can be concerned about the amount of differentiation between high and low performers. Consider a merit pay program in which a high performer receives a 7% raise and an average performer in the same job receives a 3% or 4% raise. While this might sound like a big difference, when spread out over the course of a year, the actual dollar amount between these raises might not be that great. Thus, the high performers might not feel like their outstanding efforts are reflected in their incentive pay.[45]

A closely related concern has to do with incentive pay being rolled into employees' base pay over time. Low-performing employees who earn modest annual merit raises can earn more than high-performing employees who have less tenure. Of course, over time, the differences will lessen as the high performers acquire more tenure and merit pay. However, in the short term, the high performers might believe their base pay is insufficient in light of their outstanding performance.

Finally, distributive fairness concerns can also arise with regard to team- and group-level incentive plans. As noted earlier in this chapter, free riders are individuals in a work group who rely on their teammates to put in more effort for the team to achieve success. As a result, they achieve team success for free. In addition to free riders, social loafing can be a problem with group-based incentive plans.[46] **Social loafing** refers to a situation in which the motivation of individuals to exert effort diminishes when their outputs are combined with those of others.[47] One reason for this particular phenomenon is that their individual efforts are less likely to be noticed in a team setting compared to when they perform alone.[48] As a result, they don't feel their efforts will be rewarded, and this compromises their motivation to work hard. To overcome problems with social loafing, managers might turn to incentives that are able to reward both individual and team success. If controls are not in place to deal with nonproductive team members or free riders, high performers might ultimately look to move on to other teams or another company.

**social loafing**

a situation in which the motivation of individuals to exert effort diminishes when their outputs are combined with those of others

# Incentives and Rewards in Practice: Environmental Influences

The external environment ultimately affects incentive systems within companies. In particular, labor force trends, technology, globalization, and ethical considerations affect the decisions managers make when deciding which incentive plans to use.

## Labor Force Trends and Incentive Plans

Labor force trends in the environment affect the use of incentives in companies in several ways. First, managers need to think about how to reward employees in ways that support and embrace diverse workforces. Second, diversity can affect the types of incentive rewards different employee groups desire.

### Using Incentives to Increase Diversity

Throughout this book, we have discussed how different tools can be used to help employees and managers embrace diversity initiatives within companies. Recruitment and selection activities may help target underrepresented employee groups, and training programs may help employees appreciate and embrace coworkers with diverse backgrounds. Moreover, managers may be evaluated on how many women and minorities they have under their supervision.

If companies are truly serious about diversity, they need to reward their managers for embracing diversity efforts.[49] For example, companies can provide spot awards to managers who are able to recruit and retain employees from diverse backgrounds. Similarly, companies can include diversity measures as part of a manager's merit pay program and provide bonuses to managers who are outstanding mentors and coaches to diverse employees. A portion of a manager's incentive pay may be based on input from peers and subordinates regarding how well they work with and develop members of diverse backgrounds. At Georgia Power, for example, executives' incentives are linked to a diversity goal to increase the number of minorities and women in leadership positions.[50]

### Desirability of Different Rewards

As we have explained, the relative desirability of various incentive plans can vary. Moreover, the desirability of various plans is likely to change as the composition of the workforce changes. For example, rather than merit bonuses, some employees might prefer time off via additional vacation, shorter workdays, and so forth. The types of rewards offered may prove more or less valuable, depending on the age of the workforce. Younger employees may be more open to a greater emphasis on stock option programs that are associated with greater risk compared to older individuals who are closer to retirement.[51] Also, with a growing presence of women in the workforce, as well as a greater presence of dual-career families, some individuals may be more motivated by nonfinancial incentives, such as time off from work or flexible scheduling compared to straight cash-based rewards. Similarly, the values of Generations X and Y are different from those of older employees, and these differences influence what rewards and incentives they value. A study by Sloan Work and Family research network of Boston College indicated that Generation X workers place greater priority on personal and family goals than on career goals. For these employees, rewards that provide flexibility to address work/life balance may be more motivating than more traditional cash bonuses.[52] Jenny Floren, former CEO and founder of Experience, a leading provider of career services for college students and alumni, suggests that learning and growth are more important than money for Generation Y employees. As Floren noted, "The focus for these individuals is less about the compensation and more about the advancement, the improved capabilities and the recognition of achievement marked by a new position. Offering Generation Y employees a raise while keeping all other factors the same will not have the same impact as giving them new challenges."[53] In a separate study, Professor Julie Cogin found that younger workers expect more ability to balance work with their personal interests and family demands compared to baby boomers. Other scholars have described baby boomers as having a strong work ethic, being diligent on the job, and respecting authority relationship—characteristics that drive the incentives of interest to this group.[54]

## Technology and Incentives

In addition to labor force trends, technological advances affect incentives in organizations. One impact of technology is how incentives are managed. A second influence relates to incentives for virtual employees.

### How Incentives Are Managed

Technology influences the management of incentive systems. The most notable implication of technology on the incentive process is the use of online incentive plans. With online incentives, much of the administration of the plans is coordinated electronically. Online incentive plans are a great tool for managers because they serve a number of useful purposes. First, online incentive plans are ideal for standard recognition programs related to service awards or the completion of projects. When managers are in charge of a large number of employees, it might be difficult to remember each employee's anniversary or when each project is completed. Online programs can be designed to send managers email notices for service awards and track the progress of employees as they reach their incentive targets.

A second benefit of setting up online programs for incentives is the speed of recognition for employee accomplishments. Too often, incentive rewards are acknowledged at the end of the year or the end of the quarter. One of the major benefits of online incentive plans is that they help managers provide rewards when they are most powerful—right when they are earned. Companies such as L'Oreal and Southern Company have realized the benefits of using technology for providing faster recognition of achievements.[55] As noted earlier in our discussion of reinforcement theory, immediate recognition is one of the key principles of encouraging employees to repeat desired behaviors.

Technology can also reduce the cost of administering incentives. Fewer people have to be involved in the oversight of the program because the technology takes care of many of the details. With fewer staff needed to oversee the incentive plans, firms potentially have more money to put toward their incentive programs.[56]

Finally, online incentive plans allow companies to reward their employees with the types of rewards they want. Companies can choose the types of awards they offer their employees and allow employees to use online tools to select those they most value. For example, Hewlett-Packard (HP) uses its Recognition@hpe program to help reach employees around the globe. Using this system, supervisors around the globe can nominate and award employees for their outstanding work. The rewards can include cash, HP products, merchandise, and so forth.[57] By allowing employees input into the types of rewards they want, online incentive systems may help increase the valence of the rewards, thereby increasing the motivational power of the incentive plan. Of course, employees must have access to online incentive systems in order for them to be most useful. Although arranging computer access for all your employees might involve some initial start-up costs, the costs may be offset by the lower overall cost of administration and other benefits.

### Incentive Plans for a Virtual Workforce

Technology facilitates the use of virtual teams to achieve company goals. However, creating an incentive plan for a geographically dispersed team, or even individual workers, requires consideration of different factors than might be the case for workers in a shared location. Just as with face-to-face teams, completing projects on time, the quality of the work as measured by absence of errors, and meeting other goals are effective benchmarks to use as indicators of virtual team success and as a basis for awarding incentives. However, incentive plans that are tied more directly to observations of performance, such as merit based pay, can prove to be more difficult to administer in a virtual environment. As we discussed in Chapter 9, a concern with virtual employees is the challenge of observing their behavior. While technology allows tracking measures such as key strokes, searches completed, and other recordable tasks, those might not be the appropriate measures for many virtual workers. How do supervisors or other evaluators gather performance data if employees are not at work in the office all the time? Also, virtual employees might worry that their raters do not understand or appreciate the work they perform offsite, or that there is a bias against individuals who work remotely or who work varied schedules. Thus, designing an incentive plan for a virtual workforce requires careful planning, clear communication of expectations, and reasonable reliance on what technology can track.

## Globalization and Incentive Plans

Globalization affects the use of incentives in several ways. The decision to send employees to locations around the globe requires the use of different incentives for expatriate employees than might be used for domestic employees. At the same time, cross-cultural differences influence the acceptability and effectiveness of incentives as a motivational tool.

### What Is Rewarded

In a global company, different business units may have different objectives. A manager on assignment in Europe might be assigned to help penetrate an emerging market. A manager on assignment in Asia might be tasked with improving the efficiency of an establishment. These different objectives should be reflected in the incentive plans used for these managers.

Moreover, the ability of employees to meet incentive targets can depend on local conditions including union relations in a country, the country's infrastructure, or social norms.[58] As a result, it may not be realistic for companies to establish a global incentive plan for their employees. Rather, the plans might be more effective if they are customized to fit different regions or countries.

### Acceptability of Incentive Plans

When we discussed performance management, we looked at how cultural differences affect the acceptability of different evaluation approaches. A similar concern exists when we consider incentives from a global perspective. For example, as noted earlier in this chapter, incentives can be designed to reward individuals or larger groups of employees. In countries that are highly individualistic, employees might prefer incentives that reward their individual efforts. In contrast, in countries such as Japan that more highly value social relations, teamwork, and helping each other succeed,[59] employees might prefer incentive plans that do not force them to compete with one another. In addition to employee acceptance, managers in international locations might also be reluctant to implement certain incentive systems. In these situations, a company's plan might not be implemented at all or might be implemented in principle, but not fully embraced.

Firms also have to be sensitive to standards of living in different locations. For example, the cost of living (excluding rent) is twice as high in New York City as it is in China. By comparison, the cost of living (excluding rent) is 20% higher in Switzerland than in New York City.[60] Given these cost of living differences, a company with a global incentive program might have to make some adjustments to reflect such regional differences. The actions that trigger those rewards may have to be modified as well. Here's how one company differentiates based on location. Country managers at McDonald's located around the world are provided with a menu of business principles such as customer service, marketing, or restaurant reengineering to focus on as part of the company's "Plan to Win" program. Each country manager, in turn, identifies three to five areas he or she needs to focus on for the local market. At the end of the year, the country's incentive pool is based on how the region met its targets, as well as each unit's operating income. This plan allows for the impact of the local market to affect incentives rather than forcing a "one size fits all" approach, regardless of location.[61]

## Ethics, Social Responsibility, and Incentive Plans

The fourth environmental challenge, ethics and social responsibility, also comes into play when firms develop their incentive plans. First, the plans can directly affect how ethically employees and managers behave. Second, there is a growing concern regarding the ethics associated with the use of incentives for executives.

### Ethical Employee Behavior

By this point it should be clear that incentive systems can have a strong impact on how employees behave at work. It is important to keep in mind, however, that incentive systems must be designed such that they encourage ethical behavior. What is rewarded might not always lead to ethical behavior among employees.[62] Consider the use of piecework systems. Under these plans, employees have a strong incentive to increase the volume of their productivity. However, without appropriate quality controls, defective products of low quality or that are potentially hazardous to consumers might be produced. Likewise, a heavy emphasis on commissions could lead employees to steal customers away from one another to help grow their own sales figures. In other words, an incentive system that solely evaluates outcomes such as volume, sales, or financial metrics might not take into account how those results are achieved. As a manager, it is important for you to realize that your incentive plans can inadvertently encourage employees to engage in questionable or unethical behaviors to improve their chances of earning rewards.

Similar problems hold for incentive plans at the managerial level. Many managers are evaluated based on short-term financial performance measures such as a company's return on assets (ROA). ROA provides a snapshot of how efficiently a company is using its assets to generate its revenues. The logic for this incentive is that it motivates managers to try to earn more revenues per dollar the company has invested in assets. Unfortunately, managers could improve their ROA not by increasing revenue, but by lowering assets by firing employees, failing to fill vacant positions, or even neglecting to repair defective products because doing so might incur more costs that hurt their chances of earning their bonuses. If this approach were followed, a manager could earn a bonus based on improving her company's ROA, but at the expense of the company's long-term health.

### How Employees and Communities View Executive Incentive Plans

As we have indicated, how employees and communities view the incentives corporate executives receive has become a big issue. Consider the situation of former CEO Hank McKinnell of Pfizer. Between 2001 and 2006, Pfizer's shares lost more than 40% of their value while McKinnell received $79 million in pay.[63] When Marissa Mayer was named CEO of Yahoo, she was granted a compensation package that some experts estimate could have hit $250 million and that was tied almost exclusively to stock performance, not company performance.[64] As of 2016, she had already earned $100 million and that didn't include $55 million in guaranteed money if she stepped down. When Verizon purchased Yahoo in 2017, Mayer was expected to receive more than $23 million in compensation as the last CEO of Yahoo.[65] As you can imagine, employees, shareholders, and members of the community take exception to high payouts such as these being given to executives when the performance of their firms is lackluster. And these perceptions are even stronger when executive compensation grows while employees do not receive significant increases in their own pay, or when companies engage in downsizing activities or other workforce reduction tactics. Given these concerns, many companies have increased their use of long-term incentives that directly link executive pay with company performance, but, as noted earlier, there are many questions about how successful doing so actually is for a company.

## Incentives and Rewards in Practice: Regulatory Issues

Regulatory issues affect incentive plans. Two issues that are of particular importance are eliminating bias and discrimination related to incentive plans and how stock options are managed.

### Bias and Discrimination

Like a firm's other practices, its incentive plans must be neutral with regard to discrimination and bias. Members of protected classes need to have equal access to incentive plans and be assured that the design and implementation of those plans are based on performance rather than something illegal or discriminatory, whether explicit or implicit. This issue might sound simple to address, but it is not. One study, for example, found that more than one-third of the pay differences earned by men versus women were due to gender differences in the performance-based pay plans they participated in, rather than differences in their education, experience, occupations, or job levels.[66] In other words, men and women may not have equal access to pay-for-performance plans within companies. Clearly, the criteria used to allocate incentives must be free from bias. For example, because merit-based incentive plans are typically based on subjective performance evaluations, any biases that exist in the performance management process will carry over to a firm's incentive system.

Even when more objective measures are used for incentive plans, employees need to have an equal opportunity to excel at those aspects of their jobs that drive their incentive payouts. If there is unequal access based on biases or discrimination in the tasks employees perform, that unequal access may carry over into more results-based or objective indicators of performance. For instance, if women are denied opportunities to assume positions associated with commission-based pay or are excluded from jobs that are eligible for stock option plans, that might prove discriminatory. It is important that you, as a manager, take steps to ensure that all employees have the opportunity to excel in the incentive system, and that the system does not unfairly discriminate against particular groups of employees.

## Stock Option Backdating

One reason for increased skepticism regarding executive incentives relates to the use of stock option awards. A potential problem with stock option plans is the practice of **backdating**. Under this practice, companies pick a date when the company stock is low to be considered the date of the award. Under this practice, the recipient of the stock option immediately realizes a profit—simply by changing the date of the option. For example, a manager might be issued a stock option plan on June 1, when the stock price is $20. If the company backdates the stock option date to a time when the stock was priced lower (perhaps $15), the recipient automatically realizes a $5 profit per share when she sells her shares.

The motive of using stock options is to provide an incentive to managers and executives to help improve the value of the stock in the market. Backdating, however, adversely affects the motivation of executives to perform well because they are guaranteed a profit, even if their companies don't improve their performance. As noted by former Senate Finance Committee chair Charles E. Grassley (R–Iowa), "It's one thing for an executive to make big profits because he's improved his company, but it's a whole different thing to make big profits because he's playing fast and loose with the dating of stock options."[67] Securities and Exchange Commission (SEC) chair Christopher Cox echoed this sentiment when he noted, "What makes the option work as a powerful motivational tool is that, unlike a bonus, it isn't so much a reward for prior performance as it is an incentive for future performance. That's why the undisclosed backdating of options is such a serious potential problem."[68]

**backdating**
choosing the date for a stock award based on when the stock price was low, rather than using the exact date the stock award was issued, thereby creating an immediate profit for the individual

## SUMMARY

Incentive plans are important tools managers have at their disposal to motivate superior performance by employees. Drawing on goal setting theory, reinforcement theory, agency theory, and expectancy theory, incentives are powerful motivators in organizations because they explicitly reward employees when they do something desired by their firms.

Incentive plans can be categorized based on whether they emphasize the efforts of individual employees or collective efforts, such as those expended by teams, departments, or the company as a whole. Merit-based incentive plans are some of the most common plans in organizations. However, these plans reward employees based on their past performance. Other plans include individual incentive plans

such as lump-sum bonuses, piecework incentive plans, standard hour plans, awards, and sales/commission-based incentive plans.

Gain sharing plans reward employees for improving the efficiency of their organizations. Profit sharing plans reward employees for increasing their companies' profits. Ownership plans give employees partial ownership of their firms by awarding them company stock. If the company's market performance increases, employees benefit from the increases in the value of the stocks they hold.

The choices managers make regarding which incentive plans to use depends on the organizational demands their firms face, environmental factors, and legal requirements. A firm's strategy, company characteristics, culture, and employee concerns are organizational factors that affect the appropriateness of using different incentive plans, which criteria are emphasized to receive the incentives, and whether employees view their incentive plans as being fair. Environmental pressures force managers to consider how factors related to labor force trends, technology, globalization, and ethics affect the design and implementation of various incentive plans. Finally, legal considerations necessitate that managers take steps to ensure that their incentive plans are free from bias and discrimination and that they comply with legal requirements regarding the distribution of stock options.

## KEY TERMS

agency theory

backdating

broad-based stock option plan

deferred profit sharing plan

differential piecework plan

employee stock ownership plan (ESOP)

expectancy

expectancy theory

free rider

gain sharing plan

goal setting theory

improshare plan

instrumentality

leveraged ESOP

lump-sum merit bonus

merit pay increase

mixed-level plan

mixed salary/commission plan

profit sharing plan

reinforcement theory

Scanlon plan

social loafing

spot award

standard hour plan

stock option plan

straight commission plan

straight piecework plan

straight salary plan

valence

## DISCUSSION QUESTIONS

1. Discuss the relationship between motivation theory and incentive plans.

2. Some companies have moved away from individual commission-based incentive plans to team-oriented incentive plans. How do you think these changes will affect these companies? Which of these plans would be more likely to motivate you and why?

3. Choose two types of incentive plans and compare and contrast their advantages and disadvantages.

4. How might a small company with limited resources incentivize employees?

5. What type of incentive plan would you use in a company pursuing a cost strategy? What about in a company pursuing a quality or customer service strategy?

6. Choose a country and research the type of incentives used in the workplace in that country.

7. Explain how employees' perceptions of procedural fairness and distributional fairness are affected by the incentive plans under which they work.

8. What are other legal factors that should be considered when designing an incentive plan besides those addressed in this chapter?

## LEARNING EXERCISE 1

Interview five other students using the questions below. Be sure that they have each had a paid job. Prepare a summary of what you learned about their motivators. If you were their supervisor at work, which incentive plan do you think would be best? Would one plan work for all those you interviewed? Why or why not?

1. What motivates you to do well in your classes?

2. What types of paid jobs have you had?

3. What motivated you at each job?

4. Was there an incentive plan?

5. If there was an incentive plan, was it an effective motivator for you? Why or why not? If there was not an incentive plan, how would you like to have been incentivized?

## LEARNING EXERCISE 2

As noted in this chapter, a key component of effective incentive plans is that employees need to accept the plan. If they don't buy into the plan, employees are not likely to be motivated to work to their highest levels of performance. Put yourself in the position of the employees you might manage. Choose two different types of incentive plans. How would you feel if you were working as an employee in a company under each of the different plans you selected?

1. What would be your concerns? Why?

2. What aspects of each incentive plan would you find attractive? Why?

3. What recommendations would you make to a company to address your concerns to maximize your motivation for each plan?

## CASE STUDY 1: A NEW INCENTIVE SYSTEM AT LANE AUTOMOTIVE

You've been hired by Lane Automotive, a relatively large local automobile dealer, to design a new compensation and incentive system for several positions that make up the bulk of the firm's workforce. These positions are:

- **15 administrative positions:** These positions involve the day-to-day operational facets of running the dealership—answering phones, working at the customer service desk, filing paperwork, pulling records on vehicles, and so forth. These employees are currently paid on an hourly basis. The turnover rate is about 35% for these positions. There have been several complaints about the lack of courtesy and helpfulness of employees occupying these positions. Currently, these employees receive annual bonuses if the dealership exceeds its goals and merit pay increases once each year.

- **15 sales positions:** The employees occupying these positions are primarily focused on selling cars and are paid entirely on commission. The turnover among these employees is fairly high (about 80% leave each year), although a few of the salespeople have been with the dealership for a number of years.

- **17 service positions (mechanics):** The mechanics occupying these positions are paid on a standard hour plan (i.e., their pay is based on how much time it is should take to perform each repair). These employees regularly repair cars in less time than allowed under the standard hour plan. The turnover among these employees is very low. As in any other dealership, there have been some complaints about the quality of the service the firm's mechanics have delivered. A number of customers have had to bring their vehicles in several times before their auto problems were properly repaired.

The goals of the dealership are primarily to make money on the sale of new and used cars, but, in reality, most of the money is made through the service department. There are several challenges you must consider before you make your recommendations:

- The dealership's profitability is fundamentally influenced by the number of cars serviced and the quality of that service. In addition, the dealership's profitability is enhanced by (1) repeat business and (2) the company's reputation. Historically, repeat customers represent a sizable amount of business; the dealership gets to sell their used cars they traded in and also sells them new cars, as well as to continue providing service on their vehicles. Moreover, customer loyalty matters a lot because word-of-mouth advertising generates business.
- Service quality in terms of the sales process, as well as in the service department (mechanics), is a critical component of customer satisfaction and affects the amount of repeat business.
- The income salespeople earn is directly related to the profitability of each car they sell. The prices on the cars are somewhat negotiable. Under the current system, the sales staff and the dealership split the profits from every transaction 50-50.

### Discussion Questions

1. What are major problems that exist in this situation?
2. For each problem you have identified, explain how incentives may be a contributing factor to the problem or a solution to the problem.
3. What changes would you make to the incentive systems in place for these three groups of employees?

## CASE STUDY 2: EXECUTIVE COMPENSATION AT AB3D

AB3D Industries is a company with six manufacturing facilities that produce a variety of plastic-based children's toys. The company was founded in 1983 by Edward Pistrom, who served as the chief executive officer until 2005. Since then, several CEOs have filled the post quite successfully—continuing to meet the demand for safe and durable children's toys.

AB3D Industries has approximately 2,400 employees throughout the facilities. Each facility is run by a general manager and has staff who address the relevant employee and customer needs of those in key positions. The general managers of each facility report to the corporate staff, which consists of the CEO (chief executive officer), the COO (chief operating officer), and the directors of Human Resources, Legal, Sales, and Marketing. Since its founding, the company has maintained a healthy rate of growth in sales as well as in financial returns related to return on investments (ROI) and return on assets (ROA).

Despite the prosperous history of AB3D, over the past four years the company's performance has declined. Of the six manufacturing facilities, four have failed to

post any gains in productivity or revenue, while two have posted slight gains in productivity despite diminished levels of revenue at the facilities. Put simply, the performance of the facilities and the company as a whole has been poor. The CEO for the past three years was fired due to this poor performance.

Over the past three months, a consulting company has worked with AB3D top management to identify potential candidates for the CEO position. After a lengthy search and extensive interviews, AB3D is excited about the prospect of one candidate in particular—Andrew Reason. Andrew essentially grew up in this industry. Over the past 16 years, he has worked his way up from the manufacturing floor through operations and marketing positions to assume a director of operations position at a competing firm. Based on numerous discussions, it is clear that Andrew is interested in the prospect of helping turn around the performance of AB3D industries. His main concern is that AB3D must be able to provide a compensation package compelling enough for him to take on the CEO role. The consulting company has suggested that the market average for base compensation for CEOs in this industry should be approximately $1,500,000. In addition to base pay, CEOs in this industry expect lucrative short-term and long-term incentives to reward them for exceptional performance. What should you offer to this top candidate?

### Discussion Questions

1. Research CEO pay for the manufacturing industry and write a short summary of what you learn. Indicate how hard or easy it was to find the data, indicating the sources you used.

2. What factors are you considering in setting the executive compensation package for this potential hire?

3. What compensation/incentive package would you recommend for the new CEO? Be sure to identify the base pay, as well as the forms of short- and long-term incentives you would recommend. Why would you recommend this package?

4. What implications, if any, would this package have for the workers at AB3D Industries?

5. What would you do to address any concerns the workers have about your executive pay plan?

## NOTES

[1] Richard M. Steers, Richard T. Mowday, and Debra L. Shapiro, *Academy of Maagement Review*, 29 (2004): 379–387.

[2] "The Muse, The Secrets to Motivating Your Team," *Forbes*, March 19, 2013, http://www .forbes.com/sites/dailymuse/2013/03/19/the-secret-to-motivating-your-team/.

[3] Edwin A. Locke and Gary P. Latham, "New Directions in Goal-Setting Theory," *Current Directions in Psychological Science* 15 (2006): 265–268.

[4] J. Nahrgang, D. S. DeRue, J. R. Hollenbeck, M. Spitzmuller, D. K. Jundt, and D. R. Ilgen, "Goal Setting in Teams: The Impact of Learning and Performance Goals on Process and Performance," *Organizational Behavior and Human Decision Processes* 122 (2013): 12–21; G. H. Seijts and G. P. Latham, "Learning Versus Performance Goals: When Should Each Be Used?" *Academy of Management Executive* 19, no. 1 (2005): 124–131; and E. A. Locke and G. P. Latham, *A Theory of Goal Setting and Task Performance* (Englewood Cliffs, NJ: Prentice Hall, 1990).

[5] G. P. Latham, "The Motivational Benefits of Goal-Setting," *Academy of Management Executive* 18, no. 4 (2004): 126–129.

[6] E. A. Locke, "Linking Goals to Monetary Incentives," *Academy of Management Executive* 18 (2004): 130–133.

[7] Locke and Latham, "New Directions in Goal-Setting Theory."

[8] Steers, Mowday, and Shapiro, "The Future of Work Motivation Theory."

[9] W. F. Cascio, *Applied Psychology in Personnel Management* (Englewood Cliffs, NJ: Prentice Hall, 1991).

[10] D. E. Terpstra and A. L. Honoree, "Faculty Perceptions of Problems with Merit Pay Plans in Higher Education," *Journal of Business and Management* 14 (2008): 43–59; and S. Park and M. C. Sturman, "How and What You Pay Matters: The Relative Effectiveness of Merit Pay, Bonuses, and Long-Term Incentives on Future Job Performance," *Compensation and Benefits Review* 44 (2012): 80–85.

[11] Anne Fisher, "Why Performance Bonuses and Merit Raises Don't Work," *Fortune.com*, February 24, 2016, http://fortune.com/2016/02/24/salary-bonuses-merit-raises-effectiveness/.

[12] R. L. Heneman and M. T. Gresham, "Performance-based Pay Plans," in *Performance Appraisal: State of the Art in Practice*, ed. J. W. Smither (San Francisco: Jossey-Bass, 1998), 496–536.

[13] G. T. Milkovich and J. M. Newman, *Compensation* (Boston: Irwin/McGraw-Hill, 1999).

[14] Ibid.

[15] Ibid.

[16] "2018 Incentive Pay Practices: Privately Held Companies," WorldatWork, https://www.worldatwork.org/docs/surveys/Survey%20Brief%20-%202017%20Incentive%20Pay%20Practices-%20Privately%20Held%20Compaies.pdf?language_id=1; Stephen Miller, "Short-Term Pay Incentives Offered to More Workers at Private and Smaller Companies," May 25, 2018, SHRM Compensation Data Center, https://www.shrm.org/resourcesandtools/hr-topics/compensation/pages/short-term-pay-incentives-at-private-and-smaller-companies.aspx

[17] Annabel Acton, "Innovator's Challenge: Unleash Peer-to-Peer Recognition," *Forbes*, June 6, 2017, https://www.forbes.com/sites/annabelacton/2017/06/06/innovators-challenge-unleash-peer-to-peer-recognition/#3a11cbd2c0b3; Sheila Marikar, "How to Reward One Employee Without Alienating the Others," *Inc.*, https://www.inc.com/magazine/201711/sheila-marikar/rewarding-employee-performance.html?cid=hmhero.

[18] "Using Gift Cards to Drive Employee Engagement," *Ceridian*, http://www.ceridian.com/resources/newsletters/2010/Jul/using-gift-card-incentives-to-drive-employee-engagement.html (August 22, 2014); and S. F. Gale, "Small Rewards Can Push Productivity," *Workforce*, June 2002, 86–90.

[19] "Churning," U.S. Securities and Exchange Commission, August 22, 2014, http://www.sec.gov/answers/churning.htm.

[20] J. B. Arthur and L. Aiman-Smith, "Gainsharing and Organizational Learning: An Analysis of Employee Suggestions over Time," *Academy of Management Journal* 44 (2001): 737–754; and J. K. White, "The Scanlon Plan: Causes and Correlates of Success," *Academy of Management Journal* 22, no. 2 (1979): 292–312.

[21] R. T. Kaufman, "The Effects of Improshare on Productivity," *Industrial and Labor Relations Review* 45, no. 2 (January 1992): 311–322.

[22] Ibid.

[23] Arthur and Aiman-Smith, "Gainsharing and Organizational Learning."

[24] D. Kim, "The Choice of Gainsharing Plans in North America: A Congruence Perspective," *Journal of Labor Research* 26, no. 3 (Summer 2005): 465–483.

[25] E. H. Kim and P. Ouimet, "Broad-based Employee Stock Ownership: Motives and Outcomes," *Journal of Finance* 69, no. 3 (2014): 1273–1319; and J. Blasi, D. Kruse, J. Sesil, and M. Kroumova, "An Assessment of Employee Ownership in the United States with Implications for the EU," *International Journal of Human Resource Management* 14 (September 2003): 893–919.

[26] Mary Josephs, "Fast Facts on ESOPs," *Forbes*, June 19, 2018, https://www.forbes.com/sites/maryjosephs/2018/06/19/fast-facts-on-esops/#32f501242b1b; Mary Josephs, "Millionaire Grocery Clerks: The Amazing WinCo Foods Story," *Forbes*, November 5, 2014, https://www.forbes.com/sites/maryjosephs/2014/11/05/millionaire-grocery-clerks-the-amazing-winco--foods-story/#624ff5945700.

[27] R. A. Culpepper, J. E. Gamble, and M. G. Blubaugh, "Employee Stock Ownership Plans and Three-Component Commitment," *Journal of Occupational and Organizational Psychology* 77 (2004): 155–170; J. Case, "The Ultimate Employee Buy-in," *Inc.*, December 2005, 107–116; and C. C. Shulman, "Employee Stock Ownership Plans: Part I," *Journal of Pension Planning and Compliance* 28, no. 4 (Winter 2003): 60–98.

[28] Case, "The Ultimate Employee Buy-in"; and Blasi et al., "An Assessment of Employee Ownership in the United States with Implications for the EU."

[29] Culpepper et al., "Employee Stock Ownership Plans and Three-Component Commitment"; R. J. Long, "The Effects of Employee Ownership on Organizational Identification, Employee Job Attitudes and Organizational Performance: A Tentative Framework and Empirical Findings," *Human Relations* 31 (1978): 29–48; and A. S. Tannenbaum, "Employee-Owned Companies," in *Research in Organizational Behavior*, vol. 5, ed. L. L. Cummings and B. M. Staw (Greenwich, CT: JAI Press, 1983), 235–265.

[30] Case, "The Ultimate Employee Buy-in"; and J. R. Blasi, D. Kruse, and A. Berstein, *In the Company of Owners: The Truth About Stock Options (and Why Every Employee Should Have Them)* (New York: Basic Books, 2003).

[31] A. Barrionuevo and S. Romero, "Enron Prosecutor Attacks Theory of 2001 Collapse," *The New York Times*, April 28, 2006, http://www.nytimes.com/2006/04/28/business/businessspecial3/28enron.html?_r=1&; and MSNBC, "Ex-Enron CEO Indicted," February 19, 2004, http://www.msnbc.msn.com/id/4311642/%5Benter%20URL%5D.

[32] D. Berta, "Bubba Gump Nets Low Turnover with Incentives," *Nation's Restaurant News*, September 12, 2005, 58.

[33] "2013 CEO-to-Worker Pay Ratio," August 21, 2014, http://edit.aflcio.org/Corporate-Watch/Paywatch-2014; and K. Dill, "Report: CEOs Earn 331 Times as Much as Average Workers, 774 Times as Much as Minimum Wage Earners," *Forbes*, http://www.forbes.com/sites/kathryndill/2014/04/15/report-ceos-earn-331-times-as-much-as-average-workers-774-times-as-much-as-minimum-wage-earners/.

[34] "Employee Reaction Is U.S. Employer's Biggest Challenge to Pay Ratio Disclosure Rule," Willis Towers Watson, willistowerswatson.com, October 9, 2017, https://www.willistowerswatson.com/en/press/2017/10/employee-reaction-is-us-employers-biggest-challenge; Jena McGregor, "As Companies Reveal Gigantic CEO-to-Worker Pay Ratios, Some Worry How Low-Paid Workers Might Take the News," *Washington Post,* washingtonpost.com, February 21, 2018, https://www.washingtonpost.com/news/on-leadership/wp/2018/02/21/as-companies-reveal-gigantic-ceo-to-worker-pay-ratios-some-worry-how-low-paid-workers-might-take-the-news/?noredirect=on&utm_term=.196586b29.

[35] Mercer Human Resource Consulting, "2006 CEO Compensation Survey and Trends," *Wall Street Journal*, http://www.mercer.com/summary.jhtml/dynamic/idContent/1089750.

[36] D. Cable and F. Vermeulen, "Stop Paying Executives for Performance," *Harvard Business Review,* February 23, 2016, https://hbr.org/2016/02/stop-paying-executives-for-performance.

[37] Ric Marshall, "Out of Whack: U.S. CEO Pay and Long-Term Investment Returns," MSCI, https://www.msci.com/ceo-pay; Jena McGregor, "A New Report Suggests a Fundamental Idea Behind CEO Pay Could Be 'Broken'," *Washington Post*, washingtonpost.com, October 6, 2017, https://www.washingtonpost.com/news/on-leadership/wp/2017/10/06/a-new-report-suggests-a-fundamental-idea-behind-ceo-pay-could-be-broken/?utm_term=.a1609c559e09.

[38] Houston Chronicle Web Staff, "CEOs with $1 Salaries," http://www.chron.com/jobs/slideshow/CEOs-with-1-salaries-67762/photo-4901147.php; and S. Frier, "Facebook CEO Zuckerberg's Base Salary to $1," *Bloomberg*, April 1, 2014, http://www.bloomberg.com/news/2014-03-31/facebook-ceo-zuckerberg-s-base-salary-falls-to-1.html.

[39] G. T. Milkovich, J. M. Newman, and B. Gerhart, *Compensation*, 10th ed. (Boston: Irwin/McGraw-Hill, 2010).

[40] R. L. Heneman, G. E. Ledford, Jr., and M. T. Gresham, "The Changing Nature of Work and Its Effects on Compensation Design and Delivery," in *Compensation in Organizations: Current Research and Practice*, ed. S. L. Rynes and B. Gerhart (San Francisco: Jossey Bass, 2000), 195–240.

[41] E. E. Lawler III, *Motivation in Work Organizations* (San Francisco: Jossey-Bass, 1994).

[42] Heneman, Ledford and Gresham, "The Changing Nature of Work."

[43] E. Tahmincioglu, "Gifts That Gall," *Workforce Management*, April 2004, 43–46.

[44] K. M. Bartol and E. A. Locke, "Incentives and Motivation," in *Compensation in Organizations*, ed. S. L. Rynes and B. Gerhart (San Francisco: Jossey Bass, 2000), 104–147.

[45] Y. Yandori and V. Cui, "Creating Incentives for Innovation? The Relationship Between Pay Dispersion in R&D Groups and Firm Innovation Performance," *Strategic Management Journal* 34, no. 12 (2013): 1502–1511; D. Ittycheria, "Developing a High Performance Organization," *Siliconindia*, June 2005, 12–14.

[46] S. Karau and K. D. Williams, "Social Loafing: A Meta-analytic Review and Theoretical Integration," *Journal of Personality and Social Psychology* 65, no. 4 (1993): 681–706; and R. L. Heneman and C. Von Hippel, "Balancing Group and Individual Rewards: Rewarding

Individual Contributions to the Team," *Compensation & Benefits Review* 27, no. 4 (1995): 63–68.

47 P. Vermeulen and J. Benders, "A Reverse Side of the Team Medal," *Team Performance Management: An International Journal* 9, no. 5/6 (2003): 107–114; and B. Latane, K. D. Williams, and S. G. Harkins, "Many Hands Make Light the Work: The Causes and Consequences of Social Loafing," *Journal of Personality and Social Psychology* 37, no. 6 (1979): 822–832.

48 M. C. Schippers, "Social Loafing Tendencies and Team Performance: The Compensating Effect of Agreeableness and Conscientiousness," *Academy of Management Learning and Education* 13, no. 1, (2014): 62–81.

49 P. Digh, "The Next Challenge: Holding People Accountable," *HR Magazine* 43, no. 11 (October 1998): 63–69.

50 Georgia Power website, "Measuring Progress, Diversity and Inclusion," http://www .workforce.com/articles/gifts-that-gall; and F. McCloskey and J. Barber, "Georgia Power Turns a Crisis into a Diversity Journey," *Diversity Factor* 13, no. 4 (Fall 2005): 16–22.

51 A. Canik, C. Crawford, and B. Longnecker, "Combating the Future 'Retirement Gap' with Tailored Total Rewards," *IHRIM Journal*, September/October 2004, 32–37.

52 "Interview with Paulette Gerkovich, Catalyst," *Sloan Work and Family Research Network at Boston College*, February 2005.

53 W. G. Castellano, *Practices for Engaging the 21st Century Workforce: Challenges of Talent Management in a Changing Workplace* (Upper Saddle River, NJ: Pearson Education, 2014); "Managing Generation Y as They Change the Workforce," January 8, 2008, http://www .reuters.com/article/pressRelease/idUS129795+08-Jan-2008+BW20080108; and "Business Wire 2008," http://www.pr-inside.com/managing-generation-y-as-they-change-r376306. htm.

54 J. B. Becton, H. J. Walker, and A. Jones-Farmer, "Generational Differences in Workplace Behavior," *Journal of Applied Social Psychology* 44 (2014): 175–189; B. R. Kupperschmidt, "Multi-generation Employees: Strategies for Effective Management," *The Health Care Manager* 19 (2000): 65–76; and H. C. Yu and P. Miller, "The Generation Gap and Cultural Influence—A Taiwan Empirical Investigation," *Cross Cultural Management* 10 (2003): 23–41.

55 A. C. Poe, "Agenda/Awards & Incentives, Online Recognition," *HR Magazine*, June 2002, http://www.shrm.org/publications/hrmagazine/editorialcontent/pages/0602agn-awards .aspx.

56 Gilster, "Online Incentives Sizzle—And You Shine."

57 I. Speizer, "Good Intentions, Lost in Translation," *Workforce Management*, November 21, 2005, 46–49; "Recognition@hp," https://www.recognition.hp.com/hprecognition/login.do.

58 J. S. Black, H. B. Gregersen, M. E. Mendenhall, and L. K. Stroh, *Globalizing People Through International Assignments* (Reading, MA: Addison-Wesley, 1999).

59 J. Eisenberg, "How Individualism–Collectivism Moderates the Effects of Rewards on Creativity and Innovation: A Comparative Review of Practices in Japan and the U.S.," *Creativity and Innovation Management* 8, no. 4 (December 1999): 251–261.

60 "Quality of Life Index for Country 2018 Mid Year," *Numbeo.com*, http://www.numbeo .com/quality-of-life/rankings_by_country.jsp.

61 Zack's.com, "McDonald's Plan to Win Strategy on Track—Analyst Blog," *Nasdaq.com*, May 30, 2014, http://www.nasdaq.com/article/mcdonalds-plan-to-win-strategy-on-track-analyst-blog1-cm357521; B. Kowitt, "Why McDonald's Wins in Any Economy," *Fortune*, August 23, 2011, http://fortune.com/2011/08/23/why-mcdonalds-wins-in-any-economy/; and J. Marquez, "McDonald's Rewards Program Leaves Room for Some Local Flavor," *Workforce Management* 85 (2006): 26.

62 S. Kerr, "On the Folly of Rewarding A While Hoping for B," *Academy of Management Executive* 9, no. 1 (1995): 7–14; and Heneman et al., "The Changing Nature of Work."

63 C. Hymowitz, "Sky-High Payouts to Top Executives Prove Hard to Curb," *Wall Street Journal*, June 26, 2006, p. B1.

64 E. Jackson, "Marissa Mayer's Compensation and Stock-Selling not Linked to Performance," *Forbes*, http://www.forbes.com/sites/ericjackson/2014/08/17/ marissa-mayers-compensation-and-stock-selling-not-linked-to-performance/.

65 Alian Selyukh, "Verizon Closes the Yahoo Deal; Yahoo CEO Marissa Mayer Resigns," National Public Radio, June 13, 2017, https://www.npr.org/sections/thetwo-way/2017/06/ 13/5327772877/verizon-closes-the-yahoo-deal-ceo-marissa-mayer-resigns.

[66] J. Farrell and S. J. Glynn, "What Causes the Gender Wage Gap?" Center for American Progress, April 9, 2013, http://www.americanprogress.org/issues/labor/news/2013/04/09/59658/what-causes-the-gender-wage-gap/; K. W. Chauvin and R. A. Ash, "Gender Earning Differentials in Total Pay, Base Pay, and Contingent Pay," *Industrial and Labor Relations Review*, July 1994, 634–649; and Milkovich and Newman, *Compensation*.

[67] K. Day, "SEC to Clarify Rules on Backdating of Options," *Washington Post*, June 14, 2006, http://www.msnbc.msn.com/id/13306323/.

[68] J. Hanna, "The Costs and Benefits of Sarbanes–Oxley," *Forbes*, http://www.forbes.com/sites/hbsworkingknowledge/2014/03/10/the-costs-and-benefits-of-sarbanes-oxley/; J. L. Ossinger, "Buy a 'Backdating' Stock?" *Wall Street Journal*, February 2, 2007, http://online.wsj.com/news/articles/SB117038715807795878; and K. Day, "SEC to Clarify Rules on Backdating of Options," *Washington Post*, June 14, 2006, http://www.msnbc.msn.com/id/13306323/.

# Chapter 12

# Employee Benefits and Safety Programs

## Learning Objectives

**AFTER READING THIS CHAPTER, YOU SHOULD BE ABLE TO:**

1. Understand how a firm's benefits and safety programs shape employee attitudes and behaviors.

2. Describe the major characteristics of each of the mandatory employee benefits that firms must provide to employees.

3. Discuss the different types and major characteristics of voluntary benefits.

4. Outline the key components of effective benefits administration.

5. Explain the key components of an effective safety program.

6. Discuss how a firm's organizational demands affect its benefits and safety programs.

7. Identify the environmental factors that affect the benefits and safety programs firms implement.

8. Describe the regulatory issues related to benefits and safety.

**HR CHALLENGE**

| ENVIRONMENTAL INFLUENCES | ORGANIZATIONAL DEMANDS | REGULATORY ISSUES |

**PRIMARY HR ACTIVITIES**

- Work Design & Workforce Planning
- Managing Employee Competencies
- **Managing Employee Attitudes & Behaviors**

Employee Contributions

Competitive Advantage

# Employee Benefits and Safety Programs

In Chapter 1, we asked if you would be more willing to work for a company that had an attractive benefits program with coverage for dental care, vacation time, tuition assistance, and the like, or a company that did not offer these options. When we introduced the concept of Total Rewards in Chapter 10, we used Genentech as an example of a company that offers top pay and a wide range of benefits (see Company Spotlight 10.1). Many other companies have adopted a "more is better" philosophy in designing their benefits plans. However, probably just as many have cut back on benefits due to rising costs of health care. In 2018, the Bureau of Labor Statistics (BLS) reported that benefits represented 31.8% of employer costs of compensation.[1]

Benefits affect how employees feel about their company and their job. Many employers understand this fact and use benefits as one way to manage employee attitudes and behaviors. Managing employee attitudes and behaviors, as you know by now, is an important part of the framework for managing employees for competitive advantage as shown in Exhibit 12.1. Benefits offerings can take a variety of forms to address health and wellness issues, including providing health insurance, employee assistance programs, health promotion programs, health risk appraisals, and work and family balance programs.

## EXHIBIT 12.1
### Framework for the Strategic Management of Employees

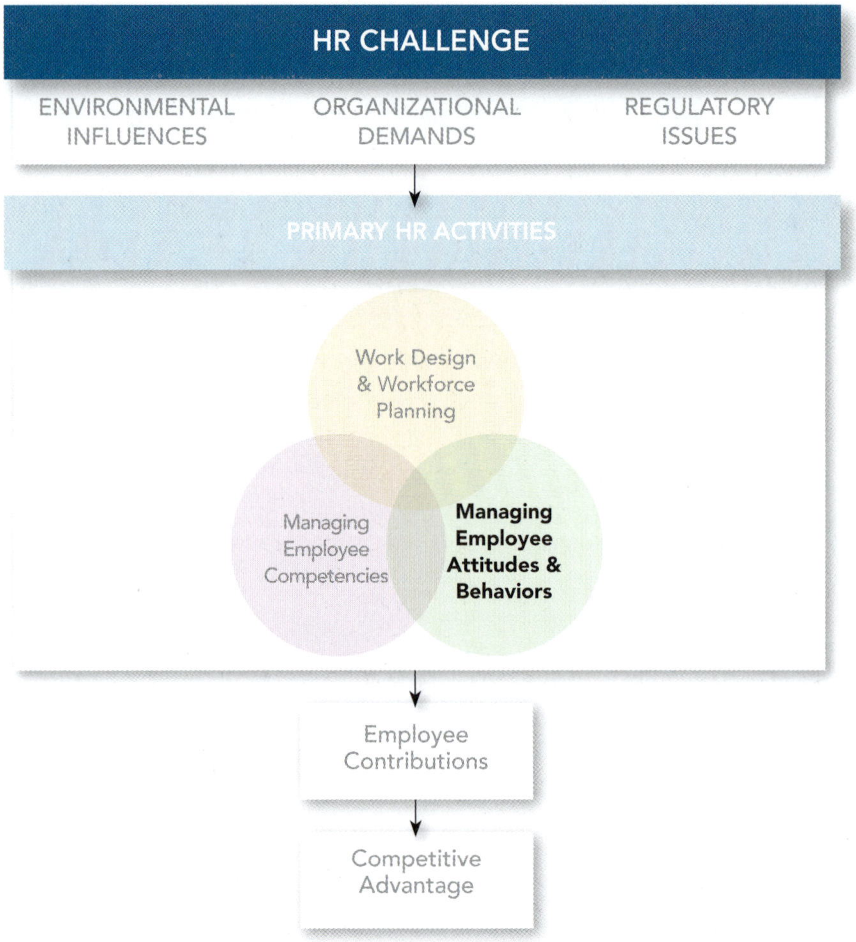

In this chapter, we discuss safety in the workplace, a topic intimately related to health and wellness. Overall, we will address questions such as the following that managers will need to be able to answer:

- Which benefits programs are most appropriate for your workforce?
- What are the regulatory requirements regarding benefits programs?
- How can you ensure the safety of your employees?

On a personal level, having an understanding of the different practices we discuss in this chapter will help you make informed decisions when choosing a new employer and choosing among the benefits offered to you.

As you read this chapter, keep in mind, too, that internal equity, external competitiveness, and proper administration of your firm's benefits and safety programs are just as important as they are for the monetary portion of employee compensation. So, even though your role as a manager may not require that you develop benefits and safety policies or make decisions about which benefits to offer to employees, you do need to know what is available and how and where more detailed information about these programs can be obtained in the company.

Take a minute to read Company Spotlight 12.1 to learn about the amazing employee benefits at Zappos, a company that clearly understands the short- and long-term value of an exceptional benefits program.

## Benefits and Safety Philosophy

A firm's benefits and safety philosophy drives the decisions it makes as to what it offers beyond what is mandatory. In developing such a philosophy, a firm needs to understand the needs and preferences of its workforce. For instance, you are probably familiar with Maslow's hierarchy of needs. According to this theory of motivation, individuals are motivated by five levels of needs. Starting with the lowest level and climbing to the highest, the needs are physiological, safety and security, belongingness, self-esteem, and self-actualization. Motivational theories such as this one help companies understand that all employees have some basic needs, but that their needs differ. These differences depend on each employee's current circumstances. An employee who worries about putting food on the table and paying for housing and transportation is going to be more concerned about fulfilling those needs than achieving a certain level of status within the firm. Employees who have their basic physiological needs met will be more interested in benefits such as life insurance and retirement accounts that provide a safety and security net for them. Thus, a firm's benefits and safety philosophy needs to account for differences such as these.

In addition to understanding that employees have different needs depending on their life circumstances, companies have to decide how much they are willing to invest in benefits and safety programs for their employees beyond what the law requires. The decisions a firm makes about these programs sends a signal to employees about what the company values, as do the decisions about pay in general. A firm's philosophy should support the mission, vision, and values of the firm. We now provide an overview of the mandatory benefits that firms are required by law to provide. Following that discussion, we will discuss voluntary benefits and safety programs.

## Mandatory Benefits

In the United States, mandatory employee benefits include Social Security, workers' compensation, unemployment compensation, and family and medical leave. Additionally, beginning in 2015, employers became responsible for

## COMPANY SPOTLIGHT 12.1

### Hot Benefits! That's Zappos

In 1999, Nick Swinmurn decided he could create a better shoe store—an online shoe store. And he did. The store started as a website offering the best selection in shoes anywhere. Today, that online shoe company consists of 10 separate companies under the Zappos Family umbrella, and they sell a lot more than shoes.

The Zappos Family has more than 1,500 staff members, most of whom work in the Zappos Fulfillment Centers. Exceptional customer service and an exceptional shopping experience are at the heart of the success of the company and the reason gross merchandise sales exceeded $1 billion by 2008 and continue to grow. Zappos was ranked number 20 on the Great Place to Work 2015 Best Retail Workplaces list and has been on the *Fortune* 100 Best Companies to Work For list many times over the years.

So, what kind of benefits does a company that is this successful provide to its employees? Take a look at this partial list:

- 100% of medical, dental, and vision premiums paid for employees
- Primary care visits, eye exams, generic prescriptions, and dental exams and cleanings are free
- Matching 401(k) plan
- Wellness coaches, a nap room, fitness center and classes, weight management program, and fitness challenges
- Housing benefits and free shuttle service
- Employee library
- Free food and coffee
- Free training classes
- On-site concierge services, dry cleaning, bank, car washes, alterations, and more
- Endurance event reimbursements
- $50 monthly coworker bonuses
- 40% discount at Zappos.com, with free next-day delivery to your desk
- Mandatory weekly team fun

   And much more!

*Sources:* Based on "The Happy Wackiness of Zappos.com," ABC News, last modified October 26, 2011, http://www.abcneews.go.com/blogs/business/2011/10/the-happy-wackiness-of-zappos-com/; and Zappos.com, http://www.about.zappos.com and https://jobs.zappos.com; and Chew, Jonathan, "The 20 Best Workplaces in Retail," November 24, 2015, http://fortune.com/2015/11/24/best-workplaces-retail/; Liggins, Terri, "Zappos' Top 10 Power Perks Ranked," Zappos.com, June 1, 2016, https://www.zappos.com/about/zappos-top-10-power-perks-ranked.

the Employer Shared Responsibility provision of the Patient Protection and Affordable Care Act (ACA). We discussed the Family and Medical Leave Act (FMLA) in Chapter 3; let's now take a look at the purpose and requirements of the other mandatory benefits.

## Social Security

The idea of social insurance began in Europe in the nineteenth century. At its core, social insurance protects people against job-related risks—disability, death, unemployment, and so forth. The goal of social insurance is to improve not just the lives of individual participants in social insurance plans, but society as a whole.

The **Social Security Act** was one of the first social insurance programs implemented in the United States. President Roosevelt signed it into law in the

**Social Security Act**
a social insurance program funded by payroll taxes to provide retired workers with a continuous stream of income after their retirement, benefits for dependents and survivors of covered workers, and benefits for disabled workers and their dependents, as well as insurance coverage for the elderly

United States in 1935, and it went into effect in 1937. The Act created the Old-Age and Survivors Insurance (OASI) program, which later became the Old-Age, Survivors, and Disabilities Insurance program (OASDI). Its purpose was to provide retired workers with a continuous stream of income after their retirement. Later, other provisions would be added to cover dependents and survivors of covered workers, as well as disabled workers and their dependents, and to provide health insurance coverage for the elderly.[2]

The Social Security Act was passed in the United States in part because workers were becoming less likely to have extended families to care for them in their later years as more people moved from the family farms to the cities to work in industry. At the time he signed the law, President Roosevelt stated, "We can never insure one hundred percent of the population against one hundred percent of the hazards and vicissitudes of life, but we have tried to frame a law which will give some measure of protection to the average citizen and to his family against the loss of a job and against poverty-ridden old age."[3]

Social Security is funded by payroll taxes. The 2019 Social Security tax rate is 12.40% of an employee's salary, shared equally between the employee and employer on earnings up to $132,900.[4] Employers withhold Social Security taxes from employee paychecks and submit the funds to the Internal Revenue Service (IRS). Self-employed workers must pay the full Social Security tax themselves each year. This tax is the OASDI portion of the Federal Insurance Contributions Act (FICA) tax that is withheld from employee paychecks. Most people have to work for at least 10 years to receive full credit, which accrues at the rate of about four credits per year, depending on a person's earnings. The amount of Social Security income retirees receive is a percentage of their average lifetime earnings. However, lower-income workers actually receive a higher percentage than upper-income workers.[5] Keep in mind that Social Security was meant to supplement an individual's retirement or disability income, not fully replace it.

**Medicare** is the health insurance portion of Social Security for retirees age 65 or older and disabled workers; it is the second part of the FICA tax and became law in 1965. Your Social Security credits count toward Medicare eligibility. Employers and employees contribute equally to the Medicare taxes.[6] The tax rate for Medicare for 2019 is 1.45% of a worker's total earnings. The total FICA tax rate for employees for Social Security (OASDI) and Medicare combined as of 2019 is 15.30%, paid equally by employee and employer, or fully paid individually if self-employed. Additionally, individuals with income of over $200,000 and married couples with income over $250,000 who file taxes jointly pay an additional 0.9 percent in Medicare taxes.[7]

## Unemployment Insurance (UI)

The **Federal–State Unemployment Insurance (UI) program**, created by the Social Security Act of 1935, provides temporary financial assistance to eligible workers who lose their jobs through no fault of their own. Almost all workers are covered by the program. The eligibility requirements are determined by state laws. Railroad workers, veterans who have recently served in the armed forces, and civilian federal employees are covered by other, similar programs.

Because UI is a partnership between the states and the federal government, states must meet the federal guidelines developed for the UI program. In all but three states, funding for this benefits program is based on an unemployment tax that employers are required to pay. Employers must pay a minimum amount of federal unemployment tax if they have one or more employees in each of at least 20 calendar weeks, or have one or more employees paid $1,500 or more in wages in any calendar quarter. The tax rate each employer pays is determined by the individual states and based on the number of unemployment claims filed against

---

**EXHIBIT 12.2**

Requirements for Collecting Unemployment Insurance (UI) Benefits

- Meet state eligibility requirements
- File a claim at the appropriate state unemployment insurance agency, or telephone if permitted in your state
- Make sure to provide accurate, current information
- Follow the guidelines for continued eligibility for benefits including reporting income and job offers on a regular basis
- Register with the state's employment service for reemployment assistance and/or training program information

*Source:* Based on "State Unemployment Insurance Benefits," Employment & Training Administration, U.S. Department of Labor, updated June 6, 2018, https://workforcesecurity.doleta.gov/unemploy/uifactsheet.asp.

the employer. Three states—Alaska, New Jersey, and Pennsylvania—actually collect taxes from employees to fund the program.[8]

Public employment offices or other approved agencies pay out the compensation to unemployed workers who are required to demonstrate that they are actively seeking reemployment. When unemployment in the United States is high, the federal government sometimes increases the number of weeks from the standard maximum of 26 weeks. After the last recession, Congress passed an emergency benefit program that extended unemployment benefits up to 73 weeks, with the actual length varying from state to state. That extension expired in December 2013. UI benefits range from 12 weeks in Florida and North Carolina to 30 weeks in Massachusetts, but most states still follow the 26-week standard.[9] Funding for an extended time period is shared between the states and the federal government. Exhibit 12.2 outlines what you would need to do to collect unemployment benefits if you were laid off from your job.

## Workers' Compensation Insurance

**workers' compensation**

a social insurance program that provides cash benefits and medical care to workers when they suffer injuries or illnesses related to their employment

**Workers' compensation** was actually the first type of social insurance developed widely in the United States. In 1911, the state of Wisconsin established the first workers' compensation program that was not declared unconstitutional. All 50 states, as well as the District of Columbia, Puerto Rico, and the U.S. Virgin Islands, have some type of workers' compensation programs, although Texas and Oklahoma permit employers to opt out of their workers' compensation insurance programs. Typically, workers' compensation provides cash benefits and medical care to employees when they suffer injuries or illnesses related to their employment. It also provides survivor benefits to dependents of workers who die due to work-related incidents. Workers who receive these benefits are not permitted to sue their employers for damages of any type.[10] The federal government has its own program and also administers the Longshore and Harbor Workers' Compensation Act, which covers all longshore and harbor workers in the United States. The Black Lung Benefits Act of 1972 covers coal miners who have black lung disease, and the Energy Employees Occupational Illness Compensation Act of 2000 covers employees, employees' survivors, contractors, and subcontractors of the Department of Energy (DOE) exposed to beryllium, as well as private companies that provided beryllium to the DOE.[11] In most states, employers are required to have a workers' compensation program regardless of the number of people they employ.[12]

The federal government has no involvement in the administration or financing of workers' compensation programs, nor does it have reporting requirements or standards for determining what constitutes a "tax-qualified" plan. Thus, information about the actual costs of workers' compensation and the number of workers covered under the various state and U.S. territory plans is not always readily available.[13]

Workers' compensation begins paying for an employee's medical care immediately after a workplace injury occurs. After a waiting period of three to seven days, it pays temporary disability benefits, and it also pays permanent partial and permanent total disability to workers with permanent disabilities caused by their work. Other costs covered include rehabilitation and training for employees who cannot return to their preinjury jobs, and benefits to survivors of employees whose work-related injuries lead to death.[14]

Employer costs for workers' compensation include insurance premiums and deductibles that have to be met. If an employer is self-insured, meaning the employer funds the workers' compensation plan rather than buying insurance from a provider, the costs of the plan equal the administrative costs related to it plus any benefits paid out to employees.[15] Employers can reduce their share of these costs by focusing on strategies such as educating employees about wellness and safety, ensuring that the workplace is free of hazards that could lead to injuries or illnesses, establishing "return-to-work programs" to get employees back on the job faster, and doing a better job of tracking claims to identify where health and safety problems in their companies might be present.[16] Later in the chapter, we talk more specifically about regulations for employee safety programs.

## The Patient Protection and Affordable Care Act (ACA) Employer Shared Responsibility Provisions

The Patient Protection and Affordable Care Act (ACA) was a long-awaited effort to extend health care to the many Americans not covered by an employer or other private plan. President Barack Obama signed the Act into law on March 23, 2010. The law had several goals: improving quality and lowering health care costs, providing greater access to health care, and providing new consumer protections. Some of the main features of the law included ending preexisting exclusions, requiring employer health plans to cover young adults up to age 26 on their parent's plan, ending lifetime limits on coverage for all new health insurance plans, limiting administrative costs by insurance companies, and providing certain types of preventive care at no cost. Different parts of the plan were scheduled to start at different times.[17]

Employers with 50 full-time employees, or a combination of full-time and part-time employees equal to 50 full-time employees, during the previous calendar year are required to be in compliance under the ACA's **Employer Shared Responsibility provisions** of Section 4980H of the Internal Revenue (IRS) Code. For purposes of the ACA, a full-time employee is someone who works on average 30 or more hours per week. Employers who meet the requirements to comply with the Act are known as *applicable large employers.*[18]

Under these provisions, employers are required to offer affordable health coverage to their full-time employees and their dependents or be subject to an Employer Shared Responsibility payment. The health coverage offered by the employer must provide a minimum level of coverage. The coverage must be offered to 95% of employees if the employer has 100 or more employees, and offered to 70% of employees if the employer has 50 to 99 employees. Small businesses with fewer than 50 employees are exempt from the ACA. The coverage is considered affordable as long as the employee's share of the cost of the coverage is less than 9.5% of the employee's annual household income. Employers may be subject to the payment if at least one full-time employee is receiving a premium tax credit because he is purchasing individual coverage in an Affordable Insurance Exchange, also known as a Health Insurance Marketplace. The provisions apply to for-profit, nonprofit, and government employers.[19] If an employer has fewer than 25 full-time employees, or full-time equivalent employees, the employer may be eligible for a Small Business

**Employer Shared Responsibility provisions**
a requirement under the Affordable Care Act (ACA) for employers with 50 full-time employees or the equivalent to offer affordable health coverage to their full-time employees and their dependents, or be subject to an Employer Shared Responsibility payment under certain conditions

Health Care Tax Credit. The purpose of the credit is to help cover the cost of providing health care coverage for employees.[20]

# Voluntary Benefits

**Voluntary benefits**, sometimes referred to as discretionary benefits, are those that an employer voluntarily chooses to offer its employees. Voluntary benefits primarily focus on health, wellness, and welfare; life management; and retirement. Many of these benefits would be extremely expensive for employees if they had to purchase them outside the group plans provided by their employers. Even if employees have to pay a portion of the cost, a group plan lowers that amount considerably.

The March 2018 Employee Benefits news release by the U.S. Bureau of Labor Statistics (BLS) reported that 69% of workers in the private sector were receiving employer-provided medical care benefits.[21]

In this section, we discuss health and wellness programs, life management, and retirement programs. These categories cover most of the types of voluntary benefits typically offered by firms.

## Health and Wellness Programs

Traditionally, companies have provided health insurance benefits to employees. Now, many companies have expanded their health-related benefit offerings to include benefits that focus on both health and wellness. These benefits often include health care plans, prescription drug plans, vision and dental care, and mental health and substance abuse benefits.

Companies have recognized the importance of integrating benefit offerings to contain rising costs. At J. B. Hunt Transport Services, for example, truck drivers have a job that lends itself to poor health habits. Eating unhealthy food at truck-stop diners and other eating establishments, sitting in the truck cab all day, and smoking can lead to increased incidences of high blood pressure and obesity. Add to that the time away from home and family for long periods of time and infrequent contact with others, and you have a recipe for serious health problems. After reviewing medical claims histories for drivers, J. B. Hunt came up with the Better Health for Life plan. This plan, which stresses exercise, weight management and proper diet, smoking cessation, disease management, and personal health coaching. After only two years, the company saw a measurable, positive impact due to better health of its drivers and the associated lower health care plan payouts. While the company doesn't use the Better Health for Life branding currently, it does still use many of the benefits that were part of that campaign and has now incorporated the use of telemedicine to make health care for nonemergency situations more accessible to its employees.[22] In the next sections, we describe various types of health and wellness programs provided by employers.

### Health Care Plans

Employer-sponsored health insurance premium costs rose 203% between 1999 and 2015. Clearly, that increase outpaced inflation and workers' earnings. Deductibles increased during this time as well. There was some good news, however. The cost of family premiums slowed from an average of 11% annual increase to an average of 5% in 2015.[23] In 2017, premium renewal rates rose again to 7%, after five years of hovering around 5%.[24]

Health care costs have increased for a variety of reasons. Individuals are living longer and working longer. Whether we like it or not, there is often a correlation between one's age and the need for health care. Additionally, newer medical technologies and newer drugs for treating everything from headaches to cancer are often costly. Companies employ a number of different approaches to maintain health

**EXHIBIT 12.3**

Helping Employees Make Good Consumer-Driven Health Plan (CDHP) Choices

- Provide information about all of the health care options available to employees in an easy to understand format

- Give employees examples of how costs differ for all available health care options, including the CDHP if offered

- Cover part of the costs related to health care plans

- Provide information sessions for employees so they can get answers to questions from benefits experts

- Once a health care option is selected, provide information and tools to help employees know how to select doctors, specialists, hospitals, tests, and prescriptions on a cost and quality basis within the selected plan

*Source:* Based on Aita, S. Joseph, "A Rational Approach to Consumer-Directed Health Care: Engaging Consumersand Providers in Controlling Costs," *Compensation & Benefits Review* 36 (2004): 40–47.

care costs. These approaches include traditional healthcare plans, managed care, high-deductible health care programs, generic and mail-order drugs, and wellness programs. Exhibit 12.3 shows what employers can do to help their workers choose wisely among the available health care plans.

**Traditional Health Care Plans**   *Traditional plans* include those available through insurance carriers, community-based plans such as Blue Cross/Blue Shield, and employer self-insurance. Under these traditional fee-for-service plans, an employee typically has to meet a deductible before the insurance plan pays for most medical services and even then the plans sometimes pay only 80% or less of the remaining costs. Employees can choose the doctors they want and usually don't have to live in a certain geographic location to participate in the plan. The plans generally do not pay for preventive care and may pay only part of the costs of diagnostic tests.

**Managed Health Care Plans**   *Managed health care plans* are approaches to health care cost containment and include health maintenance organizations (HMOs), preferred provider organizations (PPOs), point-of-service plans (POSs), and exclusive provider organizations (EPOs). Major differences in the four types of plans include how payments are made and the way medical costs are determined. These plans provide health care to members for a set monthly fee for a comprehensive set of services. Primary care physicians serve as gatekeepers.

    **Health maintenance organizations (HMOs)**, the first type of managed health care programs, originated in 1973 when the Health Maintenance Organization Act became law and allowed third-party payers to participate in health care payments. *Third-party payers* are companies, insurers, or other entities that negotiate health care options for employees rather than the employees doing so directly.[25] HMOs became very popular in the 1980s. They often require that the employees live within a designated service area and use doctors and facilities that are specified by the HMO. The plan pays for medical services if the health care providers are designated in the plan. Each employee identifies a primary care physician and goes to that person, who can then refer the employee to a specialist within the HMO if needed. Employers with 25 or more employees must give employees the opportunity to join a federally qualified HMO.

    A second approach to managed health care is the use of **preferred provider organizations (PPOs)**. In a PPO, an employer negotiates with health care providers, usually in a network, for discounts. The providers must follow strict standards about the number of diagnostic tests they order, and must adhere to other cost controls. The employer also gives its employees an incentive to use the preferred providers. When they do, the rates they pay are lower. Thus, employers save money on their health

**health maintenance organization (HMO)**

a type of managed care health insurance program that requires employees to designate a primary care physician and have any visits to a specialist referred by the primary care physician

**preferred provider organization (PPO)**

a type of managed care program in which the employer negotiates with health care providers, usually in a network, for discounts and services for health care coverage for employees

**copay**

the minimum amount employees must pay for health care, as determined by their health insurance plan

**point-of-service plan (POS)**

a hybrid of a health maintenance organization (HMO) and a preferred provider organization (PPO), in which individuals can also receive treatment outside the network, but must pay a higher deductible

**exclusive provider organization (EPO)**

requires the use of doctors, specialists, and hospitals in-network except in an emergency

**consumer-driven health plan (CDHP)**

alternative health care plan that lets employees choose a higher deductible or other more expensive alternatives, put money into a savings plan, and choose their health care providers

**health savings account (HSA)**

a special account established through employers, banks, credit unions, insurance companies, and other approved financial institutions into which an employee sets aside money pre-tax to help pay for his or her health care options

**high-deductible health plan (HDHP)**

a plan that requires the employee to pay first few thousand dollars of medical costs each year, with the plan paying only when employee has a major medical problem; results in monthly premium cost savings for employee and employer; also called *catastrophic health plans*

**account-based health plan (ABHP)**

a consumer-driven plan that pairs a group health plan with a tax-advantaged medical spending account

care costs, employees have a greater choice of doctors than they do with an HMO, and doctors are assured a flow of patients. If employees use a doctor not in the PPO network, they pay a higher **copay**. A copay is the minimum amount an employee must pay for health care, including a doctor's visit, a prescription, or diagnostic test.

The third type of plan is a **point-of-service plan (POS)**. This plan can be described as a hybrid of an HMO and a PPO. In a POS, the employee can decide which plan to use as needed. The employee might use the HMO component to see a primary care physician, but receive treatment following a referral through an in-network physician in the PPO. Individuals can also receive treatment outside the network but must pay a deductible of $500 or more.

The fourth type of managed health care plan is relatively new. An **exclusive provider organization (EPO)** requires the use of doctors, specialists, and hospitals in-network except in an emergency. The idea behind this plan is that limiting the number of providers enables the plan provider to better manage costs, leading to lower costs for the employee in terms of premiums and copays. Some organizations actually cover all the premium cost for participants in this type of plan. Also, by having a specified set of providers, the employee in the plan can see a specialist without getting a referral from a primary care physician. However, if the employee goes outside the network, the cost of care is not covered.

In a survey of over 11,000 employers and more than 20,000 health care plans in 2017, United Benefit Advisors found that, on average, POSs had the highest total annual health plan cost to the employee, followed by PPOs, EPOs, and then HMOs. Costs for employees annually ranged from $3,318 for HMOs to $4,347 for POSs. From an employer standpoint, EPOs were the most expensive, followed by PPOs, POSs, and HMOs. Costs for employers per employee on average ranged from $5,699 for HMOs to $6,945 for EPOs.[26]

Employers have adopted a variety of alternative approaches to address the concerns about health care plans. These alternatives come under the rubric of **consumer-driven health plans (CDHPs)**. CDHPs put more of the decision-making under the control of employees. The main idea behind CDHPs is that giving employees more responsibility for their health care costs will cause them to pay more attention to their health and their health care–related treatments and plans. These plans are popular with employers. In 2018, 40% of employers responding to a survey by SHRM reported offering CDHPs to their employees, a 17% increase from 2017.[27] Under a CDHP, employees have choices about whether to select a plan with a higher deductible or select other alternatives that are more expensive, how much to put into a savings plan for health care purposes, and which health care providers to use. Unfortunately, one research study has identified a negative outcome of the choice of a CDHP. In this study, enrollees in a high-deductible plan were much more likely than individuals in other plans to discontinue use of chronic-illness medications.[28]

In the past several years, more employers have turned to **high-deductible health plans (HDHPs)** as a way to manage the costs of employee health care plans. HDHPs are also referred to as *catastrophic health plans* because they don't pay for the first few thousand dollars of a person's medical costs each year. They pay only when the employee has a major medical problem. Because of their high deductibles, these plans are less costly for employers, and employees' monthly premiums are lower, too.

Employees in a HDHP can also participate in a health savings account. **Health savings accounts (HSAs)** were created as part of the Medicare Prescription Drug Improvement and Modernization Act of 2003. HSAs are an example of an **account-based health plan (ABHP)**, a consumer-driven plan that pairs a group health plan with a tax-advantaged medical spending account. HSAs provide a way for employees to pay for their immediate health care expenses not covered by an

## EXHIBIT 12.4

### Example of How an HSA Works

| Coverage for a 45-year-old male employee and his spouse | | | |
|---|---|---|---|
| | Deductible | Monthly Cost | Employee's |
| Annual Cost | | | |
|    Company health plan | $ 2,700 | $ 1,000 | $ 12,000 |
|    HDHP | $ 4,000 | $ 500 | $ 6,000 |
| Employee's savings | | | $ 6,000 |
| Minus HDHP | | | $ 4,000 |
| Difference | | | $ 2,000 |
| | | | |
| Contribution to HSA | | $ 7,000* | |
| Annual spending on health care | | $ 2,500 | |
| Annual savings | | $ 4,500 | |

*\*Maximum annual contribution in 2019 for family coverage*

**Rules:**
- Qualified health care expenses during the year would be paid from the employee's HSA
- Any amounts not spent roll over to the following year
- The savings are tax deferred and can be used for the employee's future qualified health care or retirement needs

HDHP and save money on a tax-free basis. Exhibit 12.4 shows how HSAs work. The employee in the example is 45 years old, married, and wants to include his spouse on his health care plan. He has two choices of plans provided by his employer. In the company health plan, a traditional plan, he has to pay $1,000 per month for his share of the plan versus only $500 a month for his share if he chooses the HDHP. However, his deductible for the traditional plan is $2,700 versus $4,000 for the HDHP. So, what is the best choice? The difference in the two annual premiums is $6,000, $2,000 more than the $4,000 deductible under the HDHP plan. And, because he can put the $4,000 for the deductible into an HSA pretax and let it accumulate if not spent, he has the potential to have a nice sum at retirement if the money is invested well.

As you can see from the example, the basic idea behind an HDHP is that you save money on the cost of the HDHP compared to having a health care plan with a lower deductible, and you can put aside the difference to cover medical costs you incur. In 2019, the maximum annual HSA contribution for a single person is $3,500, and $7,000 for a family. These amounts increase annually to account for inflation. In 2019, the minimum deductible for an HDHP by law has to be at least $1,350 for an employee and $2,700 for family coverage. The annual maximum out-of-pocket copay cannot exceed $6,750 for an employee or $13,500 for a family.[29] HSAs can be established through employers, banks, credit unions, insurance companies, and other approved financial institutions. HSAs provide a triple-tax advantage for users: (1) contributions reduce taxable income, (2) the earnings build up tax free, and (3) distributions for qualified expenses are not taxed.[30]

**Health Reimbursement Account**   A **health reimbursement account (HRA)** is another form of ABHP and is another mechanism for paying for the health care costs of employees. There are several differences between HSAs and HRAs, even though the purpose of each is to reimburse employees for qualified medical expenses. An employer, an employee, or an employee's family member can put money into an HSA. In contrast, only the employer can set aside money in an HRA. Employers can

**health reimbursement account (HRA)**

an account into which employers put money to reimburse employees for qualified medical expenses

deduct the costs of HRAs on their taxes in the same way they can deduct the costs of the health care insurance they provide their employees. When an employee leaves the company, whether for retirement or other reasons, funds left in the account are accessible to the employee. However, the accounts are not portable; they remain with the employer that provided them, and they cannot be used for retirement income. In an HSA, the funds belong to the employee and can be rolled over to the next plan year and withdrawn for retirement, subject to a penalty if the withdrawal occurs before age 65. With only a few exceptions, employees who have an HRA cannot have an HSA.[31]

In its sixth annual Aetna Healthfund Study, Aetna found that HSA and HRA users, when compared to PPO members, reported fewer emergency room visits, a higher rate of generic drug use, lowered medical costs overall, fewer nonroutine visits to the doctor, and other substantial differences. They were also more likely to engage in positive behaviors such as participating in health assessments, and they had taken a more engaged role in managing chronic conditions.[32] These differences result in health care cost savings. The greatest results were found for employees with HSAs.

**Self-Funded Plans**   Instead of contracting with an insurer such as Blue Cross/Blue Shield or Cigna to design and deliver all or part of their benefits programs, companies can decide to *self-fund* their programs (i.e., self-insure). Many large employers and a growing number of medium-sized and small employers make this decision each year. By self-funding, employers avoid having to pay premiums and taxes on those premiums, and they avoid some of the state requirements for benefits. When employers self-fund, they typically employ the services of a third-party administrator to oversee the plan. Because these plans are not subject to state mandates, they actually offer employers more flexibility, which is one of their attractive features. Self-funding can save money for the company, but it is not without risks. For example, if a number of the firm's employees suffer catastrophic illnesses, the fund may end up with greater costs than income for a year. By self-funding, a company is assuming that the money that it sets aside for employee medical costs, including what the employees pay into the fund, will be sufficient to cover all costs incurred.[33]

**Prescription Drug Benefits**   Prescriptions are a major expense for health care plans. In fact, many prescription costs have increased more than other health care costs. Companies reduce prescription costs by requiring employees to purchase *generic drugs* rather than brand-name drugs. Generic drugs have the same formulas as brand-name drugs, but many employees prefer the brand name. Caterpillar, Inc. has coined a term for this preference, "the purple pill syndrome," named after Nexium, which is widely advertised as "the purple pill" and because of the extensive advertising that leads patients to ask their doctor to prescribe it for them.

In one year, Caterpillar spent about $156 million on prescription drugs, an amount equal to 25% of its health care costs. To reduce these costs, Caterpillar first tried a two-tier and then a three-tier copay system. In a two-tier system, brand-name drugs cost more than generic drugs. In a three-tier system, insurance companies have different payment schedules for brand-name drugs, generic drugs, and drugs on a formulary list. A formulary list identifies drugs that the insurance company has decided are the most cost-effective for treating certain conditions. At the time, about 78% of companies were using a three-tier system. When the three-tier system didn't cut costs as much as Caterpillar wanted, it chose to go to a step therapy program whereby employees have to pay the full cost of brand-name drugs if a generic is available unless their doctors require the brand name. One concern with this approach, however, is that employees might end up not getting prescriptions they need and then experience health problems that affect their productivity and make the health care costs of their firms go even higher.[34]

In the 2017 benefits survey noted earlier, results indicated that, for the second year in a row, more health care plans were using drug plans with four or more tiers than one to three tiers. In fact, 72.6% of plans had four or more tiers and 32.6% of plans had as many as six tiers.[35] Another way to cut prescription costs is to require employees to obtain their prescriptions through a mail-order service. The prescribing physician writes the prescription so that the medicine can be dispensed for three months at a time. The firm and its employees receive volume discounts as a result, and administrative costs are reduced. Other cost-saving strategies include deciding whether lifestyle drugs, such as Viagra, will be covered by a company's insurance plan and/or if employees need to get prior authorization from their firms' insurers before certain drugs can be dispensed to them.[36]

**Vision and Dental Insurance**   Many employers include dental and/or vision coverage in their regular health plans or include them as separate options. These plans can be offered through HMO or PPO plans, and they can also be included as part of traditional fee-for-service plans.

Better dental hygiene products and better care starting at a younger age, fluoridation, and awareness programs have led to less tooth decay and gum disease and helped hold down costs. Dental coverage usually includes basic and major restorative care, and orthodontia, with a large percentage of the cost of preventive care being covered. In years past, many employers provided dental insurance with the cost fully covered by the employer. More recently, dental insurance is seen as a voluntary benefit and employers are paying from 0 to 50% of the premium cost.[37] What employers are starting to learn, however, is that encouraging employees to seek regular dental care can cut down on other health care costs. Dental decay and disease has been linked to cardiovascular risks and preterm, low-birth-weight babies, osteoporosis, and oral infections associated with diabetes. Many of these conditions could be caught earlier or prevented with regular dental care.[38] Sometimes the plans include certain restrictions, such as the minimum amount of time an employee has to have participated in the plan before certain procedures, such as root canals, are covered. When selecting a dental plan, employers typically look for carriers with broad networks of doctors in terms of their locations and the services they provide, generous discounts, and high service quality.

Vision insurance can also be included as part of a firm's health care options. Typically, the employer and employee both pay for the coverage. Managed care vision companies provide employees with a network of optometrists and ophthalmologists from which to choose. Usually, vision plans pay at least partially for eye exams, glasses or contact lenses, and, occasionally, LASIK surgery.

## Wellness Programs

Research suggests that the quickest way to lower health care costs is to lower the number of Americans who are overweight, drink too much, or smoke.[39] Workplace problems such as absenteeism and injuries on the job are often correlated with employee health and safety issues and lead to increased insurance costs. Because lifestyle choices such as smoking, excessive drinking, overeating, not wearing safety equipment, and not exercising are responsible for 50% to 80% of health care expenditures, it isn't surprising that companies have devised a number of programs to keep employees healthy.[40]

These programs, known as **wellness programs**, are typically categorized as lifestyle programs, such as memberships in fitness clubs, or disease management, including prevention and management of chronic illness. In 2018, 62% of employers were offering wellness programs, and 73% offered wellness resources and information.[41] This percentage represented an increase from the previous year. Overall, organizations

**wellness program**
an employer provided program designed to keep employees healthy; can include programs such as smoking cessation, weight loss management programs, and memberships in fitness centers

were more likely to have improved wellness benefits than any other benefit offerings. The disease management programs provide the most short-term return-on-investment (ROI), however, the lifestyle management programs affect employee overall well-being, and that is important in the long term.[42] The purpose of these programs is to reduce health insurance costs by encouraging employees to become educated about their own health and to participate in programs to improve their health in general as well as their health and safety on the job.

Wellness programs typically include the following:[43]

- A health-risk assessment to identify employees at risk for chronic diseases
- The identification of programs and incentives to motivate employees
- Education and awareness programs to promote the wellness effort
- Efforts that encourage employees to take responsibility for their own health
- An evaluation of the program's outcomes

Company Spotlight 12.2 describes the wellness program at Hasbro, a leading manufacturer of children's games and toys. In addition, Exhibit 12.5 lists some of the key ingredients for a successful wellness program.

Because wellness programs make employees more aware of health and safety risks and educate them about how to stay healthier, companies that use the programs

## COMPANY SPOTLIGHT 12.2

### Making Great Toys Goes Hand-in-Hand with Wellness at Hasbro

Ever played Monopoly, tossed a Nerf ball, or engaged with My Little Pony or Transformers? If so, you were using Hasbro products. This global play and entertainment company is committed to "Creating the World's Best Play Experiences." As part of its commitment to its employees and to being a socially responsible company, Hasbro, founded in 1923, includes a wellness program in its benefit offerings.

The Hasbro Wellness Program is led by an Employee Network Wellness Team. The program takes a comprehensive approach to prevention and starts by raising awareness of the importance of healthy lifestyles to achieve healthy outcomes. The program employs tools such as employee networks, human resources (HR) partners, surveys, external resources, and ongoing communication to engage employees. A few examples of activities provided to employees in the U.S. include:

- Mindfulness meditation classes
- Nutrition workshops
- Fitness challenges
- Biometrics screenings
- Quarterly wellness lunch and learns
- Healthy food in the on-site cafeteria

For its wellness efforts, Hasbro received recognition in 2016 by the American Diabetes Association as a "Health Champion." Hasbro has also been included on Snacknation's list of corporate wellness programs to copy. Overall, Hasbro is recognized as one of the World's Most Ethical Companies and ranked number one on the 2017 100 Best Corporate Citizens List.

*Sources:* "CSR at Hasbro, About Hasbro," Hasbro, https://csr.hasbro.com/en-us/csr/about-hasbro; "CSR Employees, Employee Safety, Health, and Wellbeing," Hasbro, https://csr.hasbro.com/employees/promoting-health-wellness; "Awards," News & Information, Hasbro, https://csr.hasbro.com/en-us/news/awards-2017; "45 Kick-Ass Corporate Wellness Programs to Copy," Snacknation, https://www.snacknation.com/blog/successful-corporate-wellness-programs/.

## EXHIBIT 12.5

### Keys to a Successful Wellness Program

- Be clear on the goals and objectives when designing the plan.
- Ensure that senior management is committed to the initiative and will provide financial resources.
- Involve employees at all levels and demographic groups in the design of the program.
- Define accountability for program management early in the process.
- Provide adequate resources to support intended goals and ensure sustainability.
- Provide clear and frequent communication throughout the design process and afterward.
- Include an incentive program to encourage employees to use the program.

expect to realize substantially lower health insurance costs. Unfortunately, the employees who usually participate are the ones who are already a firm's healthier employees. Thus, companies have found that just having a wellness program is not enough to change the behavior of employees. Instead, firms are using incentives to encourage their employees to participate in their wellness programs.[44] IBM provides its employees with the opportunity to earn a $100 credit toward a wellness device, such as a FitBit or sit-stand desk, if they complete the Wellness Checkpoint and select a Commit to Health program on the company's CaféWell. In addition, the company holds a quarterly wellness drawing, in which employees can win 12,000 BluePoints worth approximately $3,000. To participate, employees complete Commit to Health Incentives each quarter.[45]

A common criticism of wellness programs is they don't typically take into consideration the design and furnishing of an employer's workplace. Health hazards such as poorly ventilated heating and cooling systems and nonergonomically designed work setups can create health problems for employees.[46] However, safety programs, which we discuss later in this chapter, often do address these issues. Another criticism relates to concerns of discrimination and privacy when employees are required to participate in health assessments. Only legally permissible information should be shared with employers. An employer who uses information from a health screening in a way that labels a person as disabled and negatively affects his job opportunities may be violating the ADA.

### Employee Assistance Programs

Conditions such as anxiety, depressive disorders, and substance abuse affect a worker's ability to perform her job. According to the National Council on Alcoholism and Drug Dependence (NCADD), drug abuse alone costs employers around $81 billion annually.[47] The National Safety Council, an addiction resource center known as Shatterproof, and the non-partisan and objective research organization NORC at the University of Chicago have developed a calculator that enables a company to determine how much substance abuse might be costing the company. The calculator uses data from the government on industry- and state-specific employment costs and drug use, and can be found at www.nsc.org/drugsatowork. Based on results from the calculator, a Chicago health care company estimates that it could have as much as $227,000 or more in substance abuse costs from its 1,000 workers due to lost time, health care costs, and turnover. Overall, estimates are that an employee who recovers from substance abuse can save his company $3,200 a year.[48]

To help employees cope with mental health issues, substance abuse, and life challenges, companies offer **Employee Assistance Programs (EAPs)**. EAPs were started in the 1970s, primarily to provide a resource for managers dealing with employees who had or appeared to have substance abuse problems. When Ford

**employee assistance program (EAP)**

resources for employees dealing with personal problems, including attorney consultation, child-care and elder-care options, budget information, addiction recovery, and family counseling

## EXHIBIT 12.6

### What You Should Do If You Suspect an Employee Has a Substance Abuse Problem

*Watch for indicators. Note if the employee:*
- Frequently misses work because of an "illness," especially on Mondays or Fridays
- Is involved in frequent accidents at work
- Returns from lunch with glassy eyes or smelling of alcohol
- Changes his attitude toward his coworkers and you

*As a manager you should:*
- Confront the employee about his behavior, making sure to focus only on the problems at work
- Let the employee know that you are going to be closely monitoring his behavior
- Stress that your concern is that the employee's job is not getting done, or is not being done properly, and that this situation has negative consequences for the organization
- Make the employee aware that your organization has an EAP and that information shared through the EAP is confidential
- Set a time to follow up with the employee to see if his performance has improved

Motor Company launched its EAP in 1976, it had one purpose: to combat workplace alcohol abuse because about 40% of workplace injuries were related to substance abuse. Today, Ford's EAP addresses a broad array of issues, ranging from helping employees locate day care to financial planning.[49]

EAPs have indeed evolved from their early focus on substance abuse. Today, an employee can use an EAP to consult an attorney, find out about child-care and elder-care options, get information on budgeting, and seek family counseling. Managers who suspect that an employee has a substance abuse or other personal problem can refer that employee to the company's EAP. Exhibit 12.6 explains what a manager should do if he or she thinks an employee has a substance abuse problem.

### Short- and Long-Term Disability Insurance

Many companies offer their employees the opportunity to participate in short- and long-term disability insurance plans. These plans pay a percentage of the employee's salary during the time the employee is out of work due to a disability. Typically, a **short-term disability plan** will pay you a specified portion of your salary for 6 to 12 weeks' time, depending on the plan. (Usually there is a maximum benefit per month, called a *cap*, that high-income-earning employees can collect.) The benefits usually start after the employee has missed one to two weeks of work.[50]

**Long-term disability** typically starts after a specified period of time (typically 6 to 12 weeks) from the time of a disability and pays a portion of the employee's salary until retirement age.[51]

Many employers are instituting *return-to-work programs* to return employees back on the job as soon as possible. These programs typically specify when an employee is eligible to return to work and under what conditions. These programs are important to the employer for productivity reasons, and are important to employees as well: work provides a sense of order and purpose for most people. Before rolling out a return-to-work program, however, employers need to carefully think how legal requirements such as those of the ADA, FMLA, Pregnancy Discrimination Act, workers' compensation, and the FLSA will affect the program.[52]

Employers considering such programs need to have a good understanding of the costs of having employees out on leave, have an organizational philosophy and policies about how leave should be managed, and ensure that employees are not put in a position to have to return to work too early. Accidental Death and Dismemberment (AD&D)

**short-term disability plan**

an insurance plan that pays a specified portion of an employee's salary when the employee is out of work for a limited time due to a disability

**long-term disability**

an insurance plan that typically starts after a specified period of time (usually 6 to 12 weeks) from the time of a disability and pays a portion of the employee's salary until retirement age

**Accidental Death and Dismemberment Insurance (AD&D)** is designed to compensate employees for the loss of a body part or to compensate the employee's family if an employee suffers the loss of a limb or dies accidentally at work. The insurance usually specifies how much will be paid for the loss of each body part or for an accidental death, and it is likely to be more valued by workers in manufacturing and skilled-trade jobs than by white-collar workers.

**Accidental Death and Dismemberment Insurance (AD&D)**

insurance designed to compensate employees for the loss of a body part or to compensate the employee's family if an employee suffers the loss of a limb or dies accidentally at work

## Life Management Benefits

Many employers offer a wide variety of life management services to employees. These services are typically referred to as work/life benefits. However, we have labeled them as *life management benefits* to more accurately reflect the idea that work is part of life rather than separate from it. Designed to help employees achieve a balance between their home and work responsibilities, these benefits include paid time off, child-care and elder-care assistance, financial planning, and concierge services. Many of the life management benefits that companies offer today were instituted in an attempt to retain women in the workforce. But the programs can certainly help retain both male and female employees. When employees know that the company will be responsive to accommodating their personal needs, they will, in turn, be loyal, committed employees. IBM has had as many as 50 different life management programs; Bank of America has had 30.[53] In the following sections, we provide an overview of some of the life management programs most frequently offered. Keep in mind that there are many other types of benefits available, ranging from commuter benefits to on-site dry cleaning and hair-care services to personal shoppers and pet boarding.

### Paid Time Off

When employees are able to get away from the workplace for rest and renewal, they are more productive when they return. Also, employees need to know that when they are sick, they can (and should) stay home. To accommodate the needs of employees for time away from the job, employers provide paid time off in the form of vacation, sick leave, bereavement leave, personal leave, and holidays. According to one health and workplace benefits survey, in 2017, 84% of employers offered paid vacation time, 71% offered paid sick leave, 45% offered paid maternity leave, and 26% offered paid paternity leave.[54]

Instead of breaking down leave into all these categories, some employers give employees a certain number of days per year to take as *paid time off (PTO)*. PTO leave can be a specified number of days per year and/or accrued on a monthly basis, based on the length of time a person has been employed. Many employees observe different religious holidays. PTO gives them the flexibility to take off the religious holidays of their choice rather than holidays designated by the firm.

Even though employees know they have PTO, they do not always use it. One survey found that workers in the United States left 226 million days of vacation unused in a year, for a total of $34.3 billion worth of time. Another study found that 41% of workers do not use all of their paid vacation time. In this last study, only 32% of workers indicated that their employers encouraged taking time off. The extent to which organizational leadership encourages taking PTO may affect whether or not workers use their time.[55] Some employers allow their employees to contribute their unused time off pay to a pool from which employees who are out of work for medical reasons can draw after they have used up their own leave.

### Educational Assistance

We discussed employer-provided tuition assistance in Chapter 8, so we only mention it briefly here. A 2018 Society of Human Resource Management (SHRM) survey found that 51% of employers offered undergraduate tuition assistance, and 49% offered graduate education assistance. Interestingly, in 2013, 61% of employers were offering undergraduate tuition assistance.[56] Employer either pay directly for their employees to attend school or reimburse them for all or a portion of their educational costs.

Employers offering tuition assistance believe that when their employees acquire more education, they bring more human capital to the workplace and are, therefore, more valuable on the job. Some employers will reimburse their employees only if they make a certain grade in their courses. Some employers require their employees to agree that they will remain with the company for a set period of time after completing their education. As long as certain requirements outlined by the IRS are met, an employer does not have to report as wages the first $5,250 per year provided to an employee under an educational assistance plan. The IRS requires employers to document the details of their educational assistance plans and ensure that access is not limited to highly compensated employees.[57]

### Child Care and Elder Care

Baby boomers—people born between 1946 and 1964—are most likely to feel the effects of child-care and elder-care responsibilities; hence, this group is sometimes referred to as the "sandwich generation." A study by the National Alliance for Caregiving and AARP in 2015 found that 6 in 10 family member caregivers were employed at some point over the year prior to the study, with 56% of caregivers working full time. The majority of these caregivers had to make changes in their work schedules to accommodate caregiving responsibilities. An earlier study by Gallup found that these employees cost their employers up to $33.6 billion per year because of absenteeism and lost productivity. Of these caregivers, 46% are male. Employees who are caregivers cost their employers anywhere from $25 billion to over $28 billion per year because of absenteeism and lowered productivity.[58] Providing long-term care insurance options to employees is one way to keep caregivers in the workplace. We discuss this option next.

### Long-Term Care Benefits

**long-term care insurance (LTCI)**

an insurance plan that provides assistance to aging, disabled, and ill persons who need daily help with tasks such as dressing, eating, or bathing for an extended time period

**Long-term care insurance (LTCI)** provides assistance to aging, disabled, and ill persons who need daily help with tasks such as dressing, eating, or bathing for an extended time period. Often, employers offer LTCI to the extended family members of their employees, including parents and in-laws. Generally, employees pay for the premiums for this insurance themselves. Making this benefit available to your employees can give them peace of mind; when they are at work, they know that their loved ones are being cared for. If employers pay some or all of the cost of the LTCI, the cost is fully tax deductible. The LTCI benefits that employees receive are also tax free.[59]

### Life Insurance

Life insurance provides financial protection, or income, for an employee's family in the event of the employee's death. Thus, life insurance has been described as "a basic pillar for retirement saving because it provides psychological comfort."[60] Employer plans are often limited to $50,000 of coverage,[61] although some employers offer an amount equal to 1.5 times the employer's annual salary or more, and/or allow the employee to purchase greater coverage than the employer provides. A lot of plans allow employees to buy insurance to cover their spouse and children at a group-rate cost as well.

### Financial Planning

Financial planning services increase the financial literacy of employees and can help them achieve financial security. For example, employees with debt problems often experience stress and anxiety. They may also look for a higher-paying job and leave the company.[62] Employees who take advantage of the financial planning programs their employers offer have a better understanding of how to manage their finances, gain more confidence about their future financial situation, and tend to be more supportive of and satisfied with their companies.[63] Other outcomes of financial education programs are reduced absenteeism and increased productivity.[64]

Some employees provide access to professional certified financial planners directly, whereas others make the information available to their employees via online financial portals or websites. Using the portals, employees can calculate how much money they need for retirement, how much money they need to save to send their children to college, and how much mortgages and loans will cost. Employers need to make sure that any financial planning information they provide to employees, whether through a financial planner or through a financial portal, does not violate laws regarding financial advice.[65] For instance, employers can only make recommendations to the employees—not tell them what to do—and should make sure to provide employees with the pros and cons of various options.

Benchmark Senior Living decided to take financial assistance for employees one step further. They created a nonprofit organization, the One Company Fund, with the purpose of providing one-time grants up to $5,000 to handle financial hardships. The hardship could result from a death, natural disaster, or other emergency situation.[66]

### Legal Services

Darden Restaurants, owner of the Olive Garden, LongHorn Steakhouse, Bahama Breeze, and other restaurants, offers legal services as one of its voluntary benefits for employees. Other companies that provide legal services as a benefit through a service provider, such as Hyatt Legal Plans, are 7-Eleven, Yum!, Sprint, and Pfizer.[67] This benefit typically provides employees with access to attorneys for assistance with everything from estate planning and adoption to legal representation if they are sued, all at a reduced fee. Generally, employees pay the full cost of the benefit. The company contracts with a legal services provider and pays some nominal charges to offer this as a voluntary benefit to employees.

## Retirement Benefits

A goal for most of us is to one day be able to retire from our jobs and to have time for travel, hobbies, and whatever else we don't get to do today because we're busy earning a living. If we want to do these things, we have to carefully plan for our retirement. In this section, we describe the Employee Retirement Income and Security Act (ERISA) and then describe the most frequently offered types of retirement accounts.

The **Employee Retirement Income and Security Act of 1974 (ERISA)** is a federal law that protects retirees in the private sector. Just a few of the benefit plans covered under ERISA are pension, health, disability, life and accidental death and dismemberment, and cafeteria plans. Under ERISA, private employers must have written plans documenting the pension benefits they provide their employees. The plans must specify what the benefits are, who is eligible to receive them (as well as when and how), and how the plans can be terminated by employers. ERISA's major function is to ensure that firms treat their employees fairly with respect to their retirement accounts.[68] We now describe some of the major provisions of ERISA.

**Vesting** refers to the time required before you own part or all of your retirement funds. The money you pay into your retirement funds plus interest earned on that money is 100% vested immediately. This means that you have a nonforfeitable right to those funds, even if you leave your employer before you reach retirement age.

**Employee Retirement Income and Security Act of 1974 (ERISA)**

a federal law that protects benefits for retirees in the private sector

**vesting**

the time required before you own part or all of your retirement funds

Your employer can require you to fulfill certain service requirements before you are vested in the money it contributes to your retirement. ERISA provides minimum standards for vesting; your employer can use a different standard, as long as the ERISA minimum is met.[69]

There are two ways in which employees become vested: *cliff vesting* and *graded vesting*. Under cliff vesting, employees become fully vested when they have three years of service. This type of vesting means that employees own the employer's contributions to their retirement funds after three years of working for the employer. An employer has the right to allow the employee to be fully vested before three years of service, but cannot require a longer vesting time if it uses cliff vesting. The other option, graded vesting, is a phase-in plan. Under a plan such as this, an employee must be fully vested—that is, entitled to her firm's contributions—within six years: After the second year of service, the employee must be vested at 20% of the employer's contribution. The percentage increases by 20% each year thereafter until 100% vesting is reached at the end of six years of service.

### Contributory versus Noncontributory Retirement Plans

Some employers make retirement plans available to their employees, but require them to fund their own accounts. However, most employers that offer plans such as these either make the entire contribution, provide some type of matching funds, or provide some combination of the two. A **noncontributory retirement plan** is one in which the employer puts funds into an employee's account without requiring the employee to make contributions. A **contributory retirement plan** is one in which the employer and employee both put money into the retirement account.

An employer can have both types of plans—noncontributory and contributory. George Washington University (GW) offers such a plan. Here's how it works: GW puts 4% of an eligible employee's annual salary into a retirement fund, without requiring the employee to put anything into the account. GW also offers to match some or all of the money the employee puts into the account at 1.5 times the total, up to a maximum of 6%. If the employee puts in 4% of her annual earnings, GW puts in 6% (4% × 1.5 = 6%). With the noncontributory amount (4%) and the contributory amounts (4% contributed by the employee plus 6% contributed by GW), 14% of the person's total salary would be going into her retirement account annually.[70]

### Defined Benefit Pension Plans

A **defined benefit pension plan** provides an annuity to eligible employees upon their retirement. The annuity is either a specified dollar amount each month or is based on a formula that usually involves multiplying the number of years an employee worked at a company by a designated percentage by the employee's last or highest salary. The salary amount can also be an average of a number of years' salaries—for example, the average of the person's salary for the last three years he worked for the firm. Under this type of pension plan, the employee is promised an annuity that increases the longer the person has been with the company. Consider an employee who has worked for a company for 30 years and was making $70,000 at her retirement. If the company has designated the percentage for determining the retirement income of its employees to be 3% (a typical amount), then the employee's retirement income each year would be computed as follows: 30 years × $70,000 × 3% = $63,000. Thus, her retirement income would be 90% of her preretirement salary.

Companies such as GM and Ford used defined benefit plans for many years. The plans at these and other companies were designed to entice employees to stay with the employer for a longer period of time so they could increase the value of their retirement income. Unions are particularly fond of these plans because their members are assured of a good retirement income. The downside for companies, however, is that when a lot of employees retire at the same time, a lot of money has to be paid out. If the company funds have not been carefully managed and/or are underfunded because fewer employees subsequently paid into the plan (or for some other reason), the company has to make up the difference.

The economy can play a major role in the success of these plans. Low, long-term interest rates, a stock market that isn't climbing rapidly, extensive regulations, and global competition from firms that don't provide retirement programs such as these create a huge financial burden on firms that are trying to manage their defined benefit plans.[71] Even companies that are financially strong and have fully funded defined benefit plans, such as IBM, have frozen their defined benefit pension plans. Beginning January 1, 2008, no IBM employees could accumulate additional benefits in their defined benefit plans. This change was expected to result in a $3 billion savings over five years.[72]

A large number of companies have turned their pension programs over to the **Pension Benefit Guaranty Corporation (PBGC)**, a not-for-profit organization created by the federal government that insures defined benefit plans.[73] Employees who receive their pensions under the auspices of the PBGC (because the pensions of their firms are either underfunded or insolvent) are limited to a maximum amount per year. That amount in 2019 for a 65-year-old retiree was set at $67,295.[74]

### Defined Contribution Plans

**Defined contribution plans** have found favor with employers over the years as an alternative to defined benefit plans. Under a defined contribution plan, the amount of retirement income is a function of how well the money put into the plan was invested. The employer specifies where the money is to be deposited, sometimes providing several options of places, and often gives employees the power to decide how that money is invested within a place. Research of employee participation in 401(k) plans, a type of defined contribution plan described in the following section, has found that employees are most likely to participate in defined contribution plans when the company matches their contributions, when they can borrow from the plan, and when they have choices about how to invest in the plan.[75] Next, we describe two types of defined contribution plans in more detail: 401(k) plans and cash balance plans.

**401(k) Plans**   A **401(k) plan**, named after the section of the IRS code that permits these plans, allows employees to defer receiving some of their compensation until retirement. The money contributed by the employee is taken out of the person's paycheck pretax, and it accumulates tax free until the person retires. Only when a person begins withdrawing the funds upon retirement is he taxed. There is a dollar limit on how much can be deferred each year, however. For 2019, the IRS set the limit at $19,000 for traditional and 401(k) plans. The IRS has a provision that permits employers to include an elective deferral provision for individuals over the age of 50 to make catch-up contributions.[76]

**Cash Balance Plans**   A **cash balance plan** is a type of defined benefit plan that operates like a defined contribution plan because it defines the benefit a person receives upon retirement in terms of a cash payout. What does that mean? The employer credits the participants' accounts with a pay credit and an interest credit. The pay credit might be a percentage, such as 5%, of the employee's compensation, whereas the interest credit can be either a fixed or variable rate tied to an index. One index that might be used is the one-year U.S. Treasury bill rate. The employer bears the risk in this plan because the employee is entitled to receive the stated account balance. If an employee is vested in the plan, she can take the account balance in a lump-sum payment upon leaving the company or at the time of retirement. Or, if she is retiring, she can draw an annual payment, referred to as an *annuity*, from the account.[77]

**Pension Benefit Guaranty Corporation (PBGC)**
a not-for-profit organization created by the federal government that insures defined benefit plans

**defined contribution plan**
a pension plan in which the employer specifies where the money will be deposited and often gives the employee the power to decide how the money will be invested, with the retirement income being a function of how well money put into the plan was invested

**401(k) plan**
a retirement plan that allows employees to defer receiving some of their compensation until retirement, with contributions to the plan taken out of the employee's paycheck pretax and the funds accumulating tax free until retirement begins

**cash balance plan**
a type of retirement account in which the employer credits the participants' retirement account with a pay credit and an interest credit and the employer bears the risk; the employee, when fully vested, is entitled to receive the stated account balance upon leaving the company or at retirement

## Pension Protection Act of 2006 (PPA)

When it was passed in 2006, the **Pension Protection Act (PPA)** was referred to as historic and groundbreaking. The legislation resulted in large part from the increase in the number of firms that were turning their pension plans over to the U.S. Pension Benefits Guaranty Corporation (PBGC) because they could not afford to pay the pensions. The Act was designed to strengthen the U.S. pension system. In essence, the PPA tightened rules relative to employer responsibilities for funding pension accounts and for administering and terminating pension funds.[78] The Act requires employers to pay more attention to how they are managing these funds, particularly if they have underfunded their pension plan. It also raises caps so that employers can set aside more money when the economy is doing well to offset the fact that less money goes in at other times. For employees, the Act makes sure more information is provided to employees, especially regarding their choices for their pension funds.

## Retiree Health Plans

A study by the Employee Benefits Research Institute (EBRI) found that a couple who retires at age 65 and lives to an average life expectancy would need targeted savings of $392,000 for the cost of health insurance and nonreimbursed medical expenses.[79] This news comes at a time when more and more companies are finding it prohibitively expensive to provide health insurance for retirees. In 1988, about 66% of firms with 200-plus employees provided medical benefits to their retired employees. By 2018, the percentage was 19%. Companies are either eliminating these benefits altogether or capping them at a specified dollar amount. Some companies allow employees to purchase health care benefits at employee group rates, and others also allow employees to carry over medical spending account funds into their retirement, as noted earlier.[80]

# Benefits Administration

Adequately and effectively communicating benefits, wellness, and safety program information to employees is critical to the success of these programs. Studies have shown that when firms do a better job of this, their employees are more knowledgeable about their programs and participate in them more frequently, and the service quality of the programs improves.[81]

Workers often don't know how much money their employers are spending on their benefits. To address this issue, an employer often provides a detailed listing of how much each benefit or service is costing the company in addition to the employee's basic salary. This information helps the employee understand more about their total rewards from the company. When considering changing jobs, employees can use this information to compare the total rewards packages other employers are offering.

Employers have to make decisions about which employees will receive which benefits, how much the employer will pay versus how much the employee will contribute, and how much choice among available alternatives the employee should be given. Exhibit 12.7 contains a list of the types of issues managers need to address when they are putting together a firm's benefits package.

Age, marital status, number of children, and other demographics of an employee affect the person's preferences for different benefits. To assist their employees with different types of needs, employers have developed a number of flexible benefit plans. **Flexible benefit plans**, also known as *cafeteria plans*, allow employees to choose which benefits they want to purchase from a menu of benefits. Some companies require all their employees to have certain benefits, usually health insurance, but allow them to

---

**EXHIBIT 12.7**

## Issues to Consider When Designing a Benefits Package

- Identify the objectives for the benefits program.

- Decide on the amount of funds available for benefits.

- Conduct a needs analysis to determine what employees desire, how the current plan is working, if there is one, and how it lines up with benchmark programs.

- Design the benefits program keeping in mind that a one-size-fits-all plan will likely not be appropriate.

- Develop and implement a communications strategy.

- Conduct periodic reviews to ensure the program still meets organizational and employee needs.

*Sources:* "How to Design an Employee Benefits Program," *SHRM.org*, June 16, 2015, https://www.shrm.org/resourcesandtools/tools-and-samples/how-to-guides/pages/howtodesignanemployeebenefitsprogram.aspx; and Tillman, Audrey, "Design Benefits for a Diverse Workforce," *SHRM.org*, December 12, 2012, https://www.shrm.org/resourcesandtools/hr-topics/benefits/pages/design-benefits-diverse-workforce.aspx.

---

choose which other benefits they want to purchase. Some companies provide a set amount of money or credits for each employee for benefits. Massachusetts General Hospital Institute of Health Professions provides its employees with credits to use for benefits. Employees decide how to distribute the allotted money, or credits, among the benefits they choose, sometimes with certain restrictions.

Integrating benefit plans is often one of the greatest challenges for merged companies. When Sears and K-Mart merged, a major concern of retired employees was whether they would still have a health plan after the merger went into effect. They did get to keep their plan, but had to start paying the full price of the premium if they were under age 65.[82]

# Safety Programs

One way organizations address worker health and wellness is through safety programs. Safety is regulated in the workplace by the Occupational Safety and Health Act (OSH Act). Of course, many companies have developed their own safety practices that go beyond those of the OSH Act. For the moment, however, let's look at what the Act requires. Safety starts with hiring employees who are more likely to be safe on the job and rewarding employees for following safety standards.[83]

## Programs Related to the Occupational Safety and Health Act (OSH Act)

The mission of the **Occupational Safety and Health Act of 1971 (OSH Act)** is to "send every worker home whole and healthy every day."[84] The Act covers private-sector employers and employees in all 50 states and certain territories and jurisdictions of the United States through the federal Act or through state-approved programs.[85] Since the passage of the Act, worker deaths are down, on average, from 38 a day in 1970 to 14 a day in 2016. Worker injuries and illnesses have also declined dramatically, from 10.9 incidents per 100 workers in 1972 to 2.9 per 100 in 2016.[86] These results come from a combination of efforts by OSHA, state partners, employers, unions, advocates, and safety and health professionals.[87] The Occupational Safety and Health Administration (OSHA) enforces the OSH Act and other safety and health regulations in the workplace; provides outreach programs, education, and compliance assistance to employers; and develops partnerships with employers and other groups interested in safety issues.[88]

**Occupational Safety and Health Act of 1971 (OSH Act)**
an Act requiring employers to provide a safe workplace for all employees and providing a process for investigation of complaints of unfair practices and a process for workplace inspections

OSHA requires an employer to provide a workplace that is free of known hazards to health and safety and that complies with OSHA guidelines. Compliance officers have the right to inspect businesses and can issue citations when health and safety hazards are discovered. Citations list the OSH Act violation, the financial penalty for the violation, and the time period within which the violation must be corrected. Employers can contest these citations before a hearing board.

Employers are responsible for notifying employees about OSH Act standards, and employees are responsible for following the standards. Employees have the right to report their concerns to OSHA and can even request an inspection without their employer finding out they made the request. Employees have the right to know how their complaints are handled and to be advised of any actions taken. They can also request an informal review of a decision to not inspect an employer.

### Inspection Programs

Because of the sheer number of workplaces that OSHA has authority to inspect, it has developed a system for inspection priorities. The administration's top priority is to inspect reports of imminently dangerous situations. The second priority is to investigate fatalities and catastrophes that have resulted in three or more employees being hospitalized. The third priority is to respond to employees' complaints about unsafe or unhealthy working conditions. These complaints can be anonymous. The fourth priority involves following up on referrals. Following an inspection, OSHA conducts follow-up and monitoring inspections to make sure any hazards are eliminated and employees are safe. OSHA also conducts planned inspections of high-hazard industries or occupations.[89]

### Partnership Programs

OSHA has developed a number of programs to recognize employers who are committed to ensuring that their workplaces are safe and healthy. The Strategic Partnership Program enables OSHA and its partners—employers, employees (and their unions and associations), and other stakeholders—to develop a written, signed agreement to work together to address critical safety and health issues and to measure the results.[90] Another OSHA program is the Voluntary Protection Program (VPP). This program focuses on establishing a cooperative relationship between OSHA and companies that have comprehensive safety and health programs. The program recognizes the outstanding efforts of such companies.[91] Company Spotlight 12.3 describes how Milliken & Co. came to be recognized on the 2017 America's Safest Companies list, in part by aligning its safety program with OSHA's VPP.

OSHA is also available for consultation services to help employers establish workplace safety and health programs. When a firm requests a consultation, OSHA will appraise its mechanical systems, physical work practices, environmental hazards, and current safety and health programs.

### Reporting Requirements

Employers have eight hours following the work-related death of an employee or a work-related accident leading to the hospitalization of three or more employees to report the accident to OSHA.[92] Firms are required to use OSHA Form 300 to log their work-related injuries and illnesses, and OSHA Form 301 to provide specific details about incidents leading to injuries or illnesses.

## Workplace Violence Programs

Workplace violence might not be a topic you typically associate with workplace safety, but it is an important one. Did you know that homicide is the fourth-leading cause of fatal occupational injuries?[93] The National Institute for Occupational

## COMPANY SPOTLIGHT 12.3

### Milliken & Co. Make Safety Job 1

In 2017, Milliken became the first company commemorated in America's Safest Companies Hall of Fame. This 150 year old, Spartanburg, South Carolina, based company has 7,000 employees and operates at 52 different locations. They describe their business as performance products, textiles, and chemicals. The leadership of the company knows that when people have a safety-oriented environment in which to work, they can focus on what they are hired to do to help the company meet its goals and maintain a competitive advantage.

The manufacturing industry offers all kinds of safety hazards, especially when chemicals are involved. With that in mind, Milliken insures that employees understand the importance of safety and are motivated to follow safety procedures. Safety training is part of the onboarding for new hires and their engagement in the training is actually measured on a points system. The company understands that buy-in of top leadership and management down through the ranks establishes the culture for a focus on safety. Weekly audits are used to identify possible hazards, safety is engineered into the manufacturing process, and safety and health training is ongoing. Safety checklists serve as regular reminders of what needs attention. The company's safety program is closely aligned with the OSHA Voluntary Protection Plan. The 26 Milliken factories in the U.S. have VPP certification. With this attention to safety first, it is no surprise that EHS Today made Milliken the first company inducted into its America's Safest Companies Hall of Fame after being recognized on the annual list three times. The award is based on innovative solutions to safety challenges, significantly lower injury and illness rates than industry average, top notch communications, commitment to incident prevention, and comprehensive training.

*Sources:* Smith, Sandy, and Valentic, Stefanie, "2017 America's Safest Companies," EHS Today, ehstoday.com, November 7, 2017, https://www.ehstoday.com/americas-safest-companies-awards/2017-america-s-safest-companies; "Milliken In America's Safest Companies for 2017," Milliken, milliken.com, September 14, 2017, (http://www.milliken .com/en-us/ourcompany/newsandmedia/Pages/Miliken-in-Americas-Safest-Companies-for-2017.aspx.

Safety and Health (NIOSH) has identified a number of risk factors for violence in the workplace. These include having contact with the public; delivering passengers, services, or goods; working alone or in small numbers; exchanging money; and working with unstable or volatile persons, such as in health care, criminal justice, or social service settings.

Violence in the workplace can be prevented in a number of ways. The environmental design of the workplace can be changed to maximize its visibility and lighting, and companies can install security devices and erect barriers between employees and customers. Administrative controls can be implemented to reduce the chances of workplace violence occurring. Employers should review the firm's staffing plans to ensure that the company's employees are not working alone or required to transport or store money. Providing conflict-resolution training to employees can also help employers diffuse situations that could become violent. This type of training is an example of an employee behavioral change companies can pursue. Most important, a zero-tolerance policy toward workplace violence is a critical component in reducing the threat and presence of violence in the workplace.[94]

## Ergonomic Programs

Employers can increase safety in the workplace through ergonomics. (Recall that in Chapter 4, we discussed the concept of **ergonomics,** which is the science of

**ergonomics**

the science of understanding the capabilities of humans in terms of their work requirements

understanding the capabilities of humans in terms of their work requirements.) An ergonomically designed workplace is one that is designed for the safe and efficient completion of tasks. The height of employees' desks, their visual distance from their computer screens, and the way in which they should lift heavy objects are all examples of ergonomically related issues about which employers need to be concerned. In fact, in the 2018 SHRM survey of employer benefits, out of 300+ benefits covered in the survey, offering a standing desk to employees was one of the leading benefits added by employers. In 2013, 13% of employers offered this benefit. In 2018, 53% were offering it. The offering of this benefit addresses medical research that shows the negative health outcomes of sitting for long periods of time.[95] Improperly designed workspaces or work processes lead to injuries and other health problems, which in turn affect employee productivity.

In 2002, the U.S. Department of Labor initiated a four-pronged, comprehensive approach to workplace ergonomics. This approach focuses on developing industry- and task-specific guidelines, enforcing the guidelines, providing outreach and assistance for businesses, and chartering a national advisory committee to identify gaps in research related to ergonomics in the workplace. The overall goal of the program is to "quickly and effectively address musculoskeletal disorders (MSDs) in the workplace."[96] The program was first rolled out for the nursing home industry, and other industries have been added.

Managers concerned with identifying conditions that can contribute to musculoskeletal disorders can start by reviewing the injury and illness records they submit to OSHA, as well as their firm's workers' compensation claims, group health insurance records, first-aid logs, absentee and turnover records, and employee complaints and grievances. By using these information sources, you can identify incidents of MSDs, such as carpal tunnel syndrome, tendonitis, and bursitis, and categorize them by job, department, division, task, and so on in order to determine whether there are injury patterns or trends occurring within your company and, if so, where.[97]

**Principles**

**Practice**

# Employee Benefits and Safety Programs in Practice: Organizational Demands

We have provided a lot of information in this chapter already, and by now, it goes without saying that decisions about employee management practices must take into account the organizational demands, environmental factors, and legal issues affecting firms. We have outlined significant issues to address in Exhibit 12.8. We start this section by discussing organizational demands and how they affect the benefits and safety programs companies design for their employees.

## Strategy, Benefits, and Safety Programs

An organization's strategy has clear implications for the design and delivery of the company's benefits and safety programs. The strategy determines the role these programs play in terms of the total rewards the firm offers its employees, as well as the funds available for the programs.

### Role of Programs in Total Rewards Package

As noted in Chapters 10 and 11, when we discussed compensation and incentives, and again throughout this chapter, decisions have to be made about the composition of a total rewards package. These decisions include how much of the compensation will be in the form of fixed versus variable monetary compensation and nonmonetary compensation in the form of benefits and services. The decision

## EXHIBIT 12.8

### Employee Benefits and Safety Programs in Practice

| Context | Practice Issues |
|---|---|
| **Organizational Demands** | |
| *Strategy* drives . . . | • Role in compensation package |
| | • Funds available for programs |
| *Company characteristics* determine . . . | • Types of programs |
| | • Availability of programs |
| *Culture* establishes . . . | • Attitudes toward benefits and safety |
| | • Who gets nonmandatory benefits |
| *Employee concerns* include . . . | • Perceptions of the fairness of the firm's benefits |
| | • Safety in the workplace |
| **Environmental Demands** | |
| *Labor force* influences . . . | • What benefits need to be offered |
| | • What safety modifications and training should occur |
| *Technology* affects . . . | • How benefits information is delivered |
| | • Concerns about safety for telecommuters |
| *Globalization* impacts . . . | • Types of benefits offered |
| | • Policies about benefits equalization |
| | • Norms relative to safety |
| *Ethics/social responsibility* shapes . . . | • Management of benefits |
| | • Comprehensiveness of safety programs |
| **Regulations** | |
| *Regulations* guide . . . | • What happens when workers change jobs |
| | • Protection of employee medical information |

is driven, in large part, by the firm's strategy. Firms with a low-cost strategy will minimize the amount of funds they spend on nondirect compensation. Generally, they might offer full-time employees a few basic benefits, such as reduced premiums on their medical insurance. However, they will be less likely to offer more elaborate benefits, such as legal services. Nonetheless, the companies will still offer safety programs because they know these programs may be required, and because they recognize that providing safer workplaces for their employees saves money in the long run.

Firms with a low-cost strategy can still appreciate the broader cost savings that come from providing benefits to improve the health of their employees. When they have this longer-term view, they are more likely to offer wellness programs and life management benefits to employees. Walmart, a company we have mentioned several times because of its well-known low-cost strategy, actually offers a wide range of benefit options to employees.[98] Offering the benefit options does not mean that Walmart pays for all of them, or even that every employee has a chance to receive or purchase them. For example, many of the benefits are not available to Walmart's large group of part-time employees, and the company's full-time employees have to pay all or a portion of their insurance premiums. Walmart uses its buying power to bargain with benefits providers just as it bargains with its other suppliers. Many other low-cost employers do not have the same amount of bargaining power when it comes to their benefits providers as Walmart does.

Firms with a differentiation strategy recognize that they need to offer higher levels of benefits to attract the human capital needed to achieve a sustained competitive advantage. These companies emphasize the importance of employees in the development of their corporate values and design "state-of-the-art" benefits programs. They recognize that employees are as attracted to firms by the benefits they offer as they are by the monetary compensation, and sometimes even more so.

### Funds Available for Benefits

The overall strategy of an organization affects how much money the company is willing to spend on employee benefits and safety programs. Companies that adopt a low-cost strategy will, obviously, want to minimize these expenditures. Companies with a differentiation strategy will weigh the pros and cons of offering various benefits and wellness programs and decide which are most likely to attract, motivate, and retain the types of employees the firms need. Obviously, firms like Genentech and Zappos, two firms we have highlighted in this book, understand the importance of benefits to employees. Managers can—and should—play a critical role as providers of information to decision-makers about the programs that are most attractive to potential and current employees.

A firm's strategy also affects how much it will invest in safety programs, although that decision is often easier to make than deciding how much to invest in benefit options. Some firms that pursue a low-cost strategy pride themselves on having an excellent safety record and fund such programs generously. These companies want to avoid fines, reduce downtime, and reduce or eliminate the other negative effects workplace safety violations and incidents can have, plus they understand that people matter to the success of the company so choose to take care of them.

## Company Characteristics, Benefits, and Safety Programs

The stage of a company's development, size, and industry affect the types of benefits and safety programs it offers, too. We take a look at each of these issues next.

### Types of Benefit and Safety Programs

One survey of medical care benefits offerings found that smaller employers were less likely to offer medical care benefits (56% of employers with fewer than 200 employees) than were medium-sized and large employers with 200 or more employees (98% offered medical care benefits). Additionally, 63% of employees at small firms were more likely to have at least a $1,000 deductible, compared to only 39% of employees at larger firms with a deductible of at least $1,000.[99] These findings were not surprising, given the typical correlation between firm size and firm resources.

An exception to the typical relationship between firm size and benefit offerings is the case of start-up firms. Particularly in the 1990s, many start-up firms in the software industry offered a wide range of benefits to employees to attract and retain them, and that trend has continued. In fact, technology firms have had a lot to do with the increase in the types of life management programs available to employees today. The employees targeted most by these firms want to work hard and play hard, and they are often in short supply. Hence, firms get very creative when it comes to designing their benefits programs, offering employees everything from concierge services to meals at their workplaces. In order to compete for the best employees, many larger, older employers found that they needed to be more creative with the benefits they were offering to be competitive in attracting employees. Employees in medium to large companies tend to have greater access to health care benefits in particular. However, because small employers often choose to offer fewer benefits, or choose to participate in insurance pools with other small employers in their community, these employers might actually experience less of an impact of higher benefit costs due to an aging workforce than will large employers that have their own company-provided insurance plans.[100]

### Availability of Programs

The industry in which a company operates affects the benefits to which the company's employees have access. A study by Glassdoor in 2016 found that across all industries, finance had the highest-rated benefits packages, followed by information technology, and then manufacturing. Food service had the lowest rated benefits. The highest rated 401(k) retirement benefits were in finance, followed by education, and manufacturing. Food services, business services, and retail had the lowest rated. For employees wanting free food, IT, business services, and manufacturing are the place to be and they should stay away from education, retail, and finance.[101] When it comes to providing retirement benefit options, overall, smaller firms lag behind large corporations.[102]

All companies, regardless of their size, have to comply with OSHA safety guidelines. OSHA's *Field Inspection Reference Manual (FIRM)* does, however, allow its inspectors to adjust the penalties for violations imposed on firms based on their size: A 60% penalty reduction can be given to firms with fewer than 25 employees, a 40% reduction to firms with 26 to 100 employees, and a 20% reduction to firms with 101 to 250 employees. These reductions reflect the fact that larger employers typically have greater resources available to address safety issues and should, therefore, be penalized accordingly.[103]

## Company Culture, Benefits, and Safety Programs

A company's culture plays a key role in determining how the firm's employees will react to the benefits and safety programs the company implements and which employees will receive the nonmandatory benefits the firm provides.

### Employees' Attitudes Toward Their Firm's Benefits and Safety Programs

SAS, another company we have already highlighted in this book, provides a good example of how a company's culture can affect how employees feel about their benefits. SAS believes that "if you treat employees as if they make a difference to the company, they will make a difference to the company." SAS ensures employees know they make a difference through the extensive benefits and wellness programs it makes available. On-site child-care centers, elder-care information, an on-site employee health care center and fitness center, free snacks and beverages, and wellness programs are just some of the benefits the firm offers. Programs such as these have kept SAS in the top ranks of best places to work lists, including *Fortune's* Best 100 Companies to Work For and Great Places to Work for at least 15 years.[104]

Employees' attitudes toward safety are greatly affected by the safety culture in their companies. A United Kingdom construction company, Frank Haslam Milan Ltd. (FHm), had a goal of zero reportable accidents and achieved it. The company credits its success to its employees and even its customers who are involved in safety awareness and training programs. The firm's programs cover everything from first aid to driver awareness to control of substances that are hazardous to human health.[105] Company Spotlight 12.4 describes how UPS changed what its employees thought about safety in the workplace. UPS reduced injuries on the job and reduced turnover as a result of its safety awareness and training program led by employees.

Some of the methods used to educate employees about safety include safety posters, slogans, training sessions, incentives, and contests. These programs help remind employees of the responsibility they have to be safe on the job. By creating a culture of safety and ensuring that safety is a core value of a firm's senior managers, employers can reduce their workers' compensation claims, medical expenses, and liability for negligence.[106]

# COMPANY SPOTLIGHT 12.4

## UPS Turned Upside Down

United Parcel Service (UPS) has traditionally used a top-down management approach. But when the company found itself struggling with how to reduce its rising rate of on-the-job injuries, it decided to make a radical change. Instead of approaching its managers as it had traditionally done for 90-plus years, in 1995 UPS went to its employees—the drivers and parcel handlers—to seek their help in developing a new approach to safety.

The goal of UPS's safety program, called the Comprehensive Health and Safety Process (CHSP), is to ensure that every employee makes safety a personal value. CHSP has led to a 66% drop in lost time injuries since 2006. Another by-product of the program has been lower employee turnover. In 2005, UPS was honored with an Optimas Award for the innovation that went into improving its safety record.

UPS currently has over 450 management and administrative employees focused on protecting the health and safety of UPS workers. The 3,600 CHSP committees work directly on safety issues as well. They audit facilities and equipment, perform analyses of work practices and behaviors, lead training sessions, and make recommendations about equipment and process changes. Changes made as a result of the program include more ergonomically handheld computers for drivers and better facility layout.

Employees receive approximately 5.8 million hours of safety training each year. A core part of this training involves Safe Work Methods, a program focused on major risk areas for employees. These areas include job setup, slips and falls, pushing and pulling, lifting and lowering, powered equipment, and planning for the unexpected. In 2017, UPS incorporated virtual reality (VR) into nine of their Integrad training centers to enhance the training experience for their drivers. UPS is exploring how to apply VR training for other duties throughout their operations. Overall, the company invests $209 million each year in safety training.

*Sources:* Based on Shuit, D., "A Left Turn for Safety at UPS," *Workforce Management*, March 2005, 49–50; Jayaram, J., Smith, J., Park, S., and McMackin, D. "Framework for Safety Excellence: Lessons from UPS," Supply Chain 247, October 10, 2013, https://www.supplychain247.com/article/framework_for_safety_excellence_lessons_from_ups; "Safety Training Fact Sheet," UPS, http://www.pressroom.ups.com/Fact+Sheets/Safety+Training+Fact+Sheet; "Employee Safety," Empowered People UPS, http://www.sustainability.ups.com/committed-to-more/employee-safety/; and "UPS CHSP Committees Fact Sheet," UPS, https://www.pressroom.ups.com/pressroom/ContentDetailsViewer.page?ConceptType=FactSheets&id=1426321622969-973.

## Who Receives Nonmandatory Benefits

The degree of hierarchy in a firm's corporate culture influences decisions about who receives nonmandatory benefits and services. Consider a CEO who has access to a private jet, has a golf club membership, and has a personal assistant to run errands. These amenities are there to make the life of the executive less stressful. At the same time the CEO is enjoying these benefits, the lower-level employees in the company may be worrying about how they can afford the higher insurance premium the company is requiring them to pay.

## Employees' Concerns About Their Firm's Benefits and Safety Programs

Employers who understand their employees' concerns relative to the benefits and safety programs offered have an advantage in terms of both recruiting and retaining employees. Two of the major employee concerns are the perception of fairness when it comes to how the benefits are distributed and how safe employees feel in the workplace.

### Perceptions of the Fairness of the Firm's Benefits

Earlier in this chapter, we noted that diversity in the workplace has led to the need for a larger group of religious holiday options for employees. Diversity also plays a critical role in employee preferences for everything from type of health care options to educational benefits to retirement options and perceptions of fairness of benefit offerings. Consider the many demographic groups in the typical workplace: They represent differences in age, gender, marital status, ethnicity, and number of children (if any). In recent years, more companies have begun to offer domestic partner benefits, regardless of sexual orientation and marital status. Controversy still surrounds the practice, though. Other benefit issues frequently debated range from whether it is fair for employees with children to be given time off from work to care for them (when employees without children don't get equal time off) and whether employees with pets but no children, for example, should get benefits for pet care since employees with children get child-care options.[107]

One area in which the need for fairness clearly intersects with antidiscrimination law is age discrimination and benefits. As employees get older, the cost of providing benefits such as health care, disability, and pensions to them increases. These costs can ultimately affect the firm's ability to be competitive in the global marketplace.[108] However, older employees are also longer-tenured employees who provide much value to employers because of their knowledge, well-honed job skills, and conscientiousness. To retain these employees, treat all the employees fairly, and comply with the law, employers have found that they need to pay the extra costs associated with providing benefits to older workers. In fact, following the outcome of the U.S. Supreme Court case *Public Employees Retirement System of Ohio v. Betts*, 109 S.Ct. 256 (1989), Congress passed an amendment prohibiting discrimination against older workers "in all employee benefits except when age-based reductions in employee benefit plans are justified by significant cost considerations."[109] This amendment is known as the **Older Workers Retirement Protection Act**.

Finally, research has shown that procedural justice generally is a better predictor of satisfaction with benefits than distributive justice. However, in an open culture characterized by giving employees a lot of information about the company and their role in the company, distributive justice predicts satisfaction with the cost of benefits.[110]

**Older Workers Retirement Protection Act**

a law that prohibits discrimination against older workers in all employee benefits except when age-based reductions in employee benefit plans are justified by significant cost considerations

### Safety in the Workplace

News reports about safety in the workplace typically focus on sensational cases in which large numbers of employees are injured or killed. It goes without saying that employees expect a workplace in which they are not in imminent danger. But that is not their only concern about safety. Employees expect, at a minimum, to have equipment that is well maintained and functioning properly, ergonomically designed work areas, and protective gear for working in hazardous situations. An employer is responsible for providing these for employees and for training all employees about the proper operation of the equipment, use of protective gear, and their responsibility to keep the firm's workplace safe and free of hazards.

Falls because of slippery floors are a major cause of injuries in the restaurant industry. Researchers have found that factors related to the environment—for example, the friction of a restaurant's floors—affect whether employees report the floors as being slippery. And they also have found that factors related to employees themselves—for example, a person's age and recent experience with slipping—affect the likelihood of such reports being made.[111] This research provides a good example of the importance of training employees about safety in the workplace.

## Employee Benefits and Safety in Practice: Environmental Influences

The labor market, technology, globalization, and ethical and social responsibility issues all influence benefits and safety in the workplace. We explore each of these influencers in the following sections.

## The Labor Market and Benefits and Safety Programs

The labor market affects what benefits employers need to offer to attract workers, as well as the need for safety modifications and training. For example, in a tight labor market, offering more benefits to attract workers may be more cost-effective than trying to lure them with higher wages.

### What Benefits Need to Be Offered

We have already discussed how important it is for employers to be aware of the demographics of their employees to determine the benefits they should offer. The same is true for the labor market. Younger applicants will have different benefit expectations and needs than older applicants. Younger applicants are likely to be more interested in education, career pathways, and child-care benefits, whereas older workers are more likely to be focused on long-term care insurance and retirement benefits. Gender, marital status, and ethnicity affect applicant preferences for benefits. Also, in a tight labor market, employers have to be more creative in terms of the benefits they offer to attract workers. In contrast, in a loose labor market, they can offer fewer benefits and still attract qualified workers.

### Need for Safety Modifications and Training

An older workforce and having more individuals with disabilities in the workforce create challenges for workplace safety, but these challenges are not usually insurmountable. In fact, managers who recognize the contributions these groups can make are often willing to make modifications to ensure their safety. Let's once again use age as an example.

As we start to age, there are changes in our bodies that affect how we respond to situations that require strength and flexibility, postural steadiness, visual capacity, and mental processing. Employers who recognize the value of their older workers also recognize that many of the work modifications needed to reduce injuries in older workers are also important for preventing injuries in workers of other ages. That's why many firms encourage employees to participate in exercise programs that focus on strength and flexibility, as well as using techniques such as modifying one's work by using mechanical lifts to do the heavy lifting. Providing employees with education about changes in their visual capacity as they age so that they can receive the proper treatment, providing appropriate lighting for their tasks, and ensuring that materials to be read are easily viewable by older eyes are minor modifications that can help make the workplace safer and more "senior friendly."[112]

## Technology and Benefits and Safety Programs

Computers have greatly enhanced the ability of companies to manage their benefits programs themselves, as well as making it easier to outsource the task. In addition, technology plays a significant role when it comes to monitoring and managing workplace safety. The safety of telecommuters has also become a concern for employers.

### How Benefits Information Is Delivered

**employee self-service (ESS) application**

a Web-based program accessed via a company's intranet that employees can use to review their benefits information and make changes during open enrollment periods

**Employee self-service (ESS) applications** have redefined how employees access and manage their benefits. These applications are Web-based programs accessed via a company's intranet. Using ESS, employees can review their benefits information and make changes during *open enrollment periods*, the time during which company employees are authorized to make changes to their benefit preferences. Research shows that an ESS enhances the service delivery of a firm's benefits programs and improves employee communication, while significantly reducing operating costs for companies.[113]

In fact, employees have become so used to doing their banking and other business online that they expect to be able to access their benefits information online, too.

Companies with high numbers of blue-collar employees can provide computer kiosks if they are concerned about these workers not having access to computers to enroll in the benefits program. Online benefits management reduces the time a firm's HR personnel has to spend administering changes to the benefit status of employees—for example, if a worker marries or has a child. Web-based systems increase an employer's ability to manage the firm's liability by providing an easier way for the company to disseminate and track information related to programs such as the Consolidated Omnibus Budget Reconciliation Act (COBRA) and Health Insurance Portability and Accountability Act of 1996 (HIPAA), which we discuss later in this chapter. They also ensure that information such as this is consistently communicated to all of a firm's employees.

Companies can also use technology tools such as webinars, apps, podcasts, and Twitter chats to connect to employees, especially virtual employees, to communicate benefit offerings and related information. Technology can also be used to deliver benefit programs to employees. For example, we noted earlier in the chapter that J. B. Hunt provides a telemedicine option for employee healthcare. Caution should be exercised, however, to make sure the human touch in providing benefits and communicating with employees about benefits is not forgotten. Benefits are often quite complex and involve critical choices for employees. Benefits committees can be used effectively to ensure employees have a place to go with questions/concerns and that information is relied back to HR. The city of Plantation, Florida, has found such a committee to be very effective.[114]

### Telecommuting and Safety

While technology enables employees to work from home, it also raises concerns about workers' safety. In 2000, OSHA issued a policy specifically addressing home offices. OSHA indicated that it would not conduct inspections of employees' home offices, nor would it hold employers liable for home offices, and it does not expect employers to inspect these offices. It did, however, reaffirm that employers have a responsibility to report all work-related illnesses and injuries, regardless of where they occur.[115]

Workers' compensation laws typically do not distinguish between home offices and other work sites. Employers need to include information in their telecommuting policies, including the hours employees are required to work and identification of the areas of their homes that are their home offices. The policy should state that workers' compensation coverage applies only when employees are performing their jobs during their work times and in their home offices. An employer should also provide its telecommuters with guidelines explaining how to ensure that their home offices are safe. The guidelines should address issues ranging from proper ventilation and lighting to comfortable and safe office furniture.[116]

## Globalization and Employee Benefits and Safety Programs

Globalization has caused employers to look for ways to reduce labor costs to maintain their competitive advantage (or to gain such an advantage). Two main costs that employers are cutting are health care costs and retirement benefits. Health care costs in the United States are much higher than in other countries. For instance, according to the Organisation for Economic Co-operation and Development (OECD) Health Statistics, U.S. health spending in 2016 accounted for 17.2% of gross domestic product (GDP). The U.S. spending was 7.9 percentage points above the OECD average of 8.9%. These data suggest significant differences in the amount of spending. Globalization affects the types of benefits offered and policies about benefits equalization, as well as the norms for benefits and safety programs.[117]

## Types of Benefits Offered

Laws and norms differ among countries with regard to the types of benefits required or expected by employees. For instance, in Ireland and New Zealand, pensions are not tied to preretirement earnings, but rather are based on a flat rate. In the United States and Canada, pensions traditionally have been tied more directly to preretirement earnings.[118]

A study examining the relationship between national cultures and employee benefits reported that the cultural characteristic of uncertainty avoidance—that is, being uncomfortable in unknown, unstructured environments—was a major determinant of the managerial decision to offer welfare plans such as cafeteria plans, supplemental employment plans, and temporary disability plans. Those plans provide some degree of security to employees. The study further reported that there are benefits that are so commonly offered that no cultural differentiators were found, suggesting that managers have little discretion in deciding to offer them. These include death, dental, health, life, long-term disability, and severance benefits.[119]

However, the Social Security–type programs in many developed countries, including the United States, need to be reformed because many older workers are retiring, and fewer workers are paying into the programs to support them. Sweden, Germany, and Canada—three countries that have traditionally provided their citizens with strong social insurance programs—have adopted policies encouraging people to wait longer until they retire. Gradual retirement, partial retirement, and credit for caregiving activities are among the new practices in these countries. When older workers stay employed longer, the tax base for their contributions into Social Security–type programs remains stronger.[120] By 2050, most Organisation for Economic Co-operation and Development (OECD) countries are expected to have raised the retirement age to at least age 67.[121]

Major differences exist among countries in terms of the legally required amount of paid time off for employees. The United States has no legally required paid vacation or holiday. Every country in the European Union has at least four weeks of required paid vacation. Kuwait gets the prize for the most guaranteed time off with 30 paid vacation days and 13 paid holidays per year.[122] Another global concern is health care costs, which are rising around the world. Even in countries that have traditionally had government-financed health care programs, multinational companies are finding it necessary to offer supplemental health plans to employees to make up for the difference in what the governments provide and what the employees have to pay out of pocket.[123]

The Affordable Care Act Employer Shared Responsibility provisions only require employers to take into account the number of employees working in the United States when deciding if they must comply with the provisions. This information is true whether the company is U.S. based with a large number of employees abroad or a non-U.S. company doing business in the United States.[124]

One benefit not typically needed in the domestic workplace is kidnap and ransom (K&R) insurance. Typical K&R insurance covers a wide variety of benefits: security company fees, fees for professional negotiators and their travel costs, the bodily injury and lost salaries of abductees, psychological counseling for them and their families, and the cost of ransom money. The standard coverage amount is $1 million for a multinational employee, and it can be higher for executives.[125] Between $500 million and $1 billion may be paid out in ransom money each year. The good news is that through coordinated and successful efforts of the insurance companies that provide K&R insurance, the cost has fallen by about half over the past decade. The bad news is that the reduction in cost results from greater need for more employees to have coverage because data indicates having the insurance leads to a greater likelihood of being released by kidnappers through negotiation by the insurer.[126] The U.S. Department of State website (http://www.state.gov) maintains updated information on its Travel Advisories tab about countries where it is not safe to travel.

### Policies about Benefits Equalization

Benefits practices for expatriates vary around the globe and are more complex than even compensation for expatriates. Some companies take a benefits equalization approach to try to keep an expatriate "whole" relative to the benefits the person would have received if assigned to her or his home country. For instance, expatriates might not have a choice of whether to enroll in a country's social insurance program, and if they are required to enroll, the employer will pay the cost. Expatriates are also often provided with benefits beyond what they would receive at home. Annual leave time, educational expenses for their children, and family travel are just a few examples of these benefits.

Just as with compensation, decisions have to be made about using the going rate approach or using a balance sheet approach for providing benefits. The laws of a country can affect this decision. Antidiscrimination legislation passed in Hong Kong in 2006, for example, made it illegal for private companies to discriminate on the basis of ethnicity or race. Consequently, a company could not provide more benefits to an expatriate of Western descent than to other employees in the operation in Hong Kong who were not of Western descent unless the company could show that the Westerners possessed unique skills and abilities.[127]

Pensions are another benefit subject to differences around the world. For instance, in Denmark, most employees have to contribute to a defined contribution account, whereas in Singapore, there is a central fund that covers all residents, and in Mexico, there is a minimal government provided pension and some mandatory private pension plans.

Similarly, laws vary from country to country regarding health and safety, and so do countries' safety records. Thus, when doing business abroad, it is important to be cognizant of these differences.

### Norms Relative to Safety

Although you might expect safe working conditions to be the norm worldwide, that is not always the case, even in the United States. Most countries have safety standards, but they differ greatly in terms of how well the standards are enforced. What is considered acceptable in a manufacturing facility in Vietnam, for example, might not be considered acceptable in a manufacturing facility in the state of Washington. Country culture, past experience, and economic conditions affect norms about health and safety. Generally, however, more developed countries have better workplace safety practices.

## Ethics, Social Responsibility, and Benefits and Safety Programs

Ethics and social responsibility concerns relative to employee benefits have gained a lot of attention since Enron collapsed and so many of its workers were left without retirement income. This scandal and others have raised awareness about the need for ethical and socially responsible behavior regarding the benefits that firms promise employees.

### Management of Benefits

Downsizing, mergers and acquisitions, pension fund underfunding, and health screening programs may seem like a random list of corporate issues. What connects them is the impact they have on the benefits employees receive and the opportunities they present for companies to exercise ethical and responsible behavior in this regard.

When companies downsize, decisions have to be made about who stays and who goes, and also about what happens with the benefits for those who leave. Will health insurance continue to be available to individuals who take early retirement offers or whose jobs are eliminated? What happens to their retirement accounts? And what constitutes a "fair" early retirement offer?

What about when a merger or acquisition occurs? Which company's benefits plan will be continued, and how will any negative consequences of this decision for the employees involved be managed? Ethical issues relative to employee benefits also arise when employers require employees to participate in health screenings to receive certain benefits. Managers have to consider what is appropriate and what infringes on the rights of the employee.

### Comprehensiveness of Safety Programs

Hazards in the workplace can range from those created by a company's manufacturing processes to those created by such things as toxic fumes from new carpet. Managers have to make ethical and socially responsible decisions about how much information to share with employees about potential workplace hazards, as well as how to manage those hazards. Tyson Foods, a company that processes poultry, has had a number of workplace problems ranging from charges of discrimination to charges of dangerous work conditions. To address its need to exercise more social responsibility, Tyson developed the Team Member Bill of Rights. This Bill of Rights states that employees have rights to a safe workplace, adequate equipment and facilities, and continuing training.[128]

## Employee Benefits and Safety Programs in Practice: Regulatory Issues

We have already discussed many of the regulations that affect benefits and safety programs in the workplace. In this section, we discuss amendments to ERISA that affect what happens with some benefits when employees change jobs, as well as the protection of their medical information.

### What Happens When Workers Change Jobs

Two amendments to ERISA are particularly important for workers who leave an employer. They are the Consolidated Omnibus Budget Reconciliation Act (COBRA) and the Health Insurance Portability and Accountability Act (HIPAA).

The **Consolidated Omnibus Budget Reconciliation Act (COBRA)**, passed in 1986, provides for employees and their families who participate in a group health plan sponsored by an employer that has 20 or more employees to continue their coverage if the employee is no longer employed by the company providing the plan. COBRA gives the employee the option of continuing her group health insurance coverage, including dental and vision coverage, when she is terminated or leaves the job for a *qualifying reason*. For an employee, a qualifying reason is a layoff or a reduction in the number of hours the person works for a reason other than gross misconduct.[129] For up to 18 months after the employee leaves his job, he can pay the premiums to continue his health insurance coverage. Spouses and dependent children of an employee can qualify for coverage for up to 36 months if the spouse is eligible for Medicare, if the employee and spouse experienced a divorce or legal separation, or if the employee dies. When a child can no longer be classified as a

**Consolidated Omnibus Reconciliation Act (COBRA)**

an Act that provides for employees and their families to have the option to continue their group health, dental, and vision insurance coverage for up to 18 months when they are terminated for a qualifying reason as long as they pay the full cost of the premium

dependent because of age and/or no longer being enrolled in school full time, the child can obtain coverage for up to 36 months.[130]

President Bill Clinton signed the **Health Insurance Portability and Accountability Act (HIPAA)** into law in 1996. HIPAA makes it easier for workers to maintain their health care coverage when they change employers because it specifies that coverage under a previous employer's health plan counts for meeting a preexisting condition requirement under a new plan—as long as coverage is transferred within 63 days of the date that the person's coverage ended under his or her old plan.[131]

## Protection of Employee Information

In addition to HIPAA's portability protections, the Act also has provisions designed to ensure that only individuals who have a right to a person's medical information can access it. Employer group health plans come under the HIPAA guidelines. The plans cannot share information about you without your permission. In addition, under HIPAA, you have a right to see and to get a copy of any of your health records, and you can request that your communications with the record-keeper be kept confidential. This last provision means that you could specify that your doctor call you at your home rather than your office, if you wish, and the doctor would have to comply with any reasonable requests of this sort.[132]

## SUMMARY

Employee benefits and safety programs serve a critical role when it comes to firms attracting, motivating, and retaining workers. Managing the costs of these programs is a challenge for companies, especially in light of the escalating costs of health insurance, the most frequently offered employee benefit. However, firms that want to maintain a competitive advantage recognize that providing their employees with benefits and a safe workplace far outweigh the costs.

The law requires employers to provide employees with Social Security, unemployment compensation insurance, workers' compensation, family and medical leave, and affordable health coverage. Beyond these mandatory benefits, many employers provide benefits that address employees' health and wellness, retirement, and life management issues. Health insurance, a primary benefit that most employees want, can take the form of a traditional plan, an HMO, a PPO, a POS, or an EPO. Many employers have moved to consumer-driven health plans (CDHPs), often with a high-deductible health plan (HDHP) and health savings account (HSA).

Some of the most frequently offered types of retirement plans are defined benefit, defined contribution, and cash balance plans. Employers are moving away from defined benefit plans and relying more on defined contribution plans, such as 401(k) and cash benefit plans. Benefits designed for life management include employee assistance programs (EAPs), educational benefits, financial planning, and child-care and elder-care plans. ERISA provides guidelines for how many of the benefits, particularly retirement plans, are to be managed. In addition, HIPAA regulates employee benefits and ensures that employees' medical information is kept confidential.

The OSH Act requires employers to provide a safe workplace for all employees. OSHA oversees the OSH Act and partners with companies through various programs to ensure that workplaces are safe. OSHA also investigates complaints about workplace safety violations and fines employers who are out of compliance.

Organizational demands, such as a firm's strategy, company characteristics, and culture, as well as the concerns of its employees, affect how a company manages its

**Health Insurance Portability and Accountability Act (HIPAA)**

an Act that makes it easier for workers to maintain their health care coverage when they change employers because it specifies that coverage under a previous employer's health plan counts for meeting a preexisting condition required under a new plan

benefits and safety programs. Successful managers recognize that these factors dictate the benefits and safety programs their firms offer. For instance, a small start-up firm with a differentiation strategy and a culture that views employees as the firm's most critical resource will make different benefits choices than a larger, more established firm with a low-cost strategy and a hierarchical culture. Environmental factors, including regulations, influence decisions about benefits and safety programs as well. In order to compete for talent in a tight labor market, employers often have to offer workers more benefits than they do in a loose market. Technology has made it easier for companies to provide more and better information to employees about their benefits and safety. Globalization has forced employers to consider the types of benefits they offer to expatriates, host-country nationals (HCNs), and third-country nationals (TCNs), which are often affected by host country regulations, and whether they will equalize benefits for expatriates. Also, firms have to make decisions about how they will manage workplace safety because norms differ around the globe.

## KEY TERMS

401(k) plan

Accidental Death and Dismemberment Insurance (AD&D)

account-based health plan (ABHP)

cash balance plan

Consolidated Omnibus Budget Reconciliation Act (COBRA)

consumer-driven health plan (CDHP)

contributory retirement plan

copay

defined benefit pension plan

defined contribution plan

Employee Assistance Program (EAP)

Employee Retirement Income and Security Act (ERISA)

employee self-service (ESS) application

Employer Shared Responsibility provisions

ergonomics

exclusive provider organization (EPO)

flexible benefit plan

Health Insurance Portability and Accountability Act (HIPAA)

health maintenance organization (HMO)

health reimbursement account (HRA)

health savings account (HSA)

high-deductible health plan (HDHP)

long-term care insurance (LTCI)

long-term disability (LTD)

Medicare

noncontributory retirement plan

Occupational Safety and Health Act (OSH Act)

Older Workers Retirement Protection Act

Pension Benefit Guaranty Corporation (PBGC)

Pension Protection Act (PPA)

point-of-service plan (POS)

preferred provider organization (PPO)

short-term disability

Social Security Act

unemployment insurance (UI)

vesting

voluntary benefits

wellness program

workers' compensation

## DISCUSSION QUESTIONS

1. Why do companies offer benefits? How should a company decide which benefits to offer?

2. Research the misuse of workers' compensation benefits. Discuss why workers misuse this program, the enablers of the misuse, and identify strategies employers can use to stop the misuse.

3. Choose one type of voluntary benefit you are not very familiar with but think you would like to receive as an employee. Research that benefit and prepare a one-page summary of your research. Write the summary as if you were trying to convince management to offer that benefit to employees.

4. Your company is going to announce a new benefit for employees. Outline the points that need to be addressed before the announcement and as part of the announcement.

5. Research the history of the OSH Act. Why does the Act exist? Based on your research, discuss the effectiveness of the Act.

6. The culture in your company emphasizes making money more than ensuring safety. However, you know that a safe workplace will save the firm money in the short run and the long run. How would you make a case to senior management that developing a culture of safety would yield high returns for the company? Provide data to support your answer and indicate the source of the data.

7. Choose a country in which you would like to work. Research the types of benefits typically provided to employees in that country.

8. More and more employers are asking employees to participate in health screenings to receive a reduction in cost for health insurance. Discuss the ethical and legal issues that might result from such a requirement. Take a stand on the issue and justify your response. Be prepared to participate in a debate in class on this issue.

## LEARNING EXERCISE 1

Facebook has been banned by the city of Mountain View, California, from offering free lunch to its 2,000 employees who will be working at its new, soon-to-open location. The reason: When employees stay in and eat lunch, they don't go out and give business to local restaurants and other businesses and help the local economy. Google, located in Mountain View, hired its first chef over 20 years ago and set the bar for feeding employees. Other companies soon followed to be competitive. The city ordinance was passed in 2014 when Facebook announced its building project in Mountain View. The new rule was largely enacted in response to the city's largest employer, Google, providing those free meals. Under the rule, Facebook (and other companies moving to Mountain View) can subsidize up to 50% of the cost of employee meals at an in-house eatery and fully subsidize meals in restaurants open to the public.

1. Why do businesses offer free lunches as a corporate benefit?

2. What is a business's responsibility to its local community?

3. How do you think not being able to have a free gourmet cafeteria (such as the one at Google) will affect Facebook in hiring and retaining employees for this location?

4. What advice would you give Mark Zuckerberg about how to address this new rule?

*Sources:* Lee, Wendy, and Li, Ronald, "Mountain View's Unusual Rule for Facebook: No Free Food," *San Francisco Chronicle*, July 23, 2018, https://www.sfchronicle.com/business/article/Moutain-View-s-unusual-rule-for-Facebook-No-13096100.php; Malone Kircher, Madison, "Facebook Banned from Providing Free Lunch to Employees," *New York Magazine*, July 25, 2018, http://nymag.com/selectall/2018/07/facebook-banned-from-providing-free-food-to-employees.html.

## LEARNING EXERCISE 2

Your boss has asked you to develop a plan to reduce health care costs for the company. Currently, your company offers employees the choice of an HMO or a PPO. You are aware that one reason health care costs are on the rise in the company is the long-term costs of employee smoking, obesity, and an older workforce. At least 10% of the 350 employees in the company currently smoke (which they have to go outside the building to do). You believe that at least 20%

of the employees are obese, but that estimate is probably low. The average age of the employees is 52.

1. What can you legally do to address the effects of smoking and obesity on the costs of health care for the company? Are there any ethical concerns with what you have identified as being legal to do? Are there any ADA concerns?

2. How can age be taken into consideration in this situation without violating the ADEA?

3. What are some other ways in which health care costs could be reduced?

4. How would you communicate this information to your employees?

# CASE STUDY 1: KEEPING UP WITH ACUITY

As a manager at a mutually owned property and casualty insurer, you like to stay on top of what companies in your industry are doing. You have just read that Acuity Insurance, another mutually owned property and casualty insurer, has been ranked by the Great Place to Work Institute as a Top 10 Best Large Workplace in America for the past three years, ranking #9 in 2017. Before that, Acuity was on the top 5 Best Medium Workplace list for 10 consecutive years, ranking as the #1 company for five of those years. Also, in 2017, the company was named the Employer of the Year (Insurance) in the Stevie Awards for Great Employers contest, an international business awards competition.

The company has a voluntary turnover rate of less than 2% annually and offers amazing benefits for its 1,200 employees. Acuity is located in Sheboygan, Wisconsin. Your company, Traverse Property and Casualty Insurance, is located in Hartford, Connecticut, and has about the same number of employees as Acuity.

Acuity provides employees with a wide range of benefits and perks such as a free on-site fitness center with classes, on-site dry cleaning, subsidized cafeteria, and lunch with company officers on a regular basis. The company offers flextime and generous wellness benefits, including health and dental insurance, a vision plan, an EAP, and more. The CEO and president of Acuity, Ben Salzmann, believes that spending money on employee benefits and perks pays off in the long run.

The benefits offered are part of the overall culture at Acuity, ensuring employees know they matter to the company. That wasn't the case when Salzmann arrived at Acuity in 1999. Turnover was high and morale was low. That has now clearly changed.

Your company currently has a 25% annual turnover rate, and the last employee satisfaction survey suggested that employees are not satisfied with the company and not engaged in their work.

### Discussion Questions

1. Visit Acuity's website and read more about the company and the benefits offered to employees. What potential returns might Acuity yield by providing so many types of benefits and perks to its employees? (In responding, you may want to review motivation theory, including the discussion of motivation in Chapter 4.)

2. Currently, your company provides only basic benefits to its employees: a PPO health insurance plan (for which the company pays half the premium) and a 401(k) plan that is funded solely by the employees. What issues would you need to consider before deciding to increase the benefits offerings at your company?

3. Research the types of benefits that are typically offered in (1) the insurance industry, and (2) the region in which your company is located. Based on this information, prepare a recommendation to your CEO about whether or not a change should be made in the benefits program and what you anticipate the

outcome would be of making the change. Be sure to discuss what benefits you think should be added.

*Sources:* Based on "Acuity Toasts a Successful Culture," *HR Magazine,* 49 (2004): 48; Tyler, K., "Leveraging Long Tenure," *HR Magazine* 52 (2007): 54–60; "I Am Acuity," Acuity, https://www.acuity.com/public/i_am_acuity_brochure.pdf; and "Acuity Insurance Named a Best Company to Work For," Acuity Insurance, March 9, 2017, https://www.acuity.com/about/media-center/in-the-news/2017/acuity-insurance-named-a-best-company-to-work-for.

# CASE STUDY 2: CREATING A SAFETY CULTURE AT BORDER TRANSPORTATION

Border Transportation, located in Las Cruces, New Mexico, is a company that specializes in the delivery of medical equipment and supplies to hospitals, clinics, and medical supply companies in the Southwest and in Mexico. The majority of employees at Border Transportation are sales representatives, warehouse staff, and truck drivers. Currently, most of these workers are over age 45.

As a result of ongoing expansion, the company will grow from 225 employees to more than 500 employees in the next three years. Several government contracts have already been signed, and more are anticipated. The company has recently hired you as the warehouse manager. Part of your job is to oversee all safety programs for the company. These duties had been handled primarily informally by the dock supervisor prior to your coming onboard.

On your first day, the chief operating officer (COO) calls you in and gives you the following directives and information:

- Safety in the warehouse is becoming a real issue. The accident rate has tripled since last year. Something has to be done.
- Absenteeism has increased, especially on Fridays and Mondays.
- The company is spending 25% of its payroll costs on workers' compensation claims. Many of the claims are related to cumulative trauma disorders.
- You need to get rid of an employee in the warehouse who is reported to have AIDS.

## Discussion Questions

1. How would you respond to each of the directives from the COO? What steps would you take to instill a culture of safety in this warehouse?
2. Do you think a wellness program makes sense for this company? Provide support for your answer.
3. What do you think will be the biggest challenge in increasing safety and health at this facility?
4. How will you address the issue of the employee with AIDS?
5. Given the location in the Southwest and the company's work in Mexico, many of the employees have English as their second language. Do you anticipate that language will be an issue in creating and implementing a new safety program? If so, why and how will you address the issue? If not, why not?
6. How will you deal with employees who tell you that they have "always done it this way" when you try to improve safety procedures?

# NOTES

[1] "Employer Costs for Employee Compensation, March 2018," Bureau of Labor Statistics, U.S. Department of Labor, June 8, 2018, http://www.bls.gov/news.release/pdf/ecec.pdf.
[2] "The Basics of Social Security Updated with the 2006 Board of Trustees Report," FACTS from EBRI, Employee Benefits Research Institute (EBRI), last modified May 2006, http://www.ebri.org/pdf/publications/facts/FS-195_May06_SocSecBasics.pdf; and "Historical

Background and Development of Social Security," Social Security, http://www.ssa.gov/history/briefhistory3.html.

3 "Historical Background and Development of Social Security," Social Security Administration, http://www.ssa.gov/history/briefhistory3.html.

4 "Fact Sheet: Social Security, 2019 Social Security Changes," Social Security Administration, https://www.ssa.gov/news/press/factsheets/colafacts2019.pdf.

5 *How You Earn Credits 2018* (Washington, DC: Social Security Administration Publication No. 05-10072, 2018, https://www.ssa.gov/pubs/EN-05-10072.pdf.

6 Ibid.

7 "Fact Sheet: Social Security, 2019 Social Security Changes."

8 "Unemployment Insurance Tax Topic," U.S. Department of Labor, Employment and Training Administration, updated July 10, 2015, https://oui.doleta.gov/unemploy/uitaxtopic.asp.

9 "Policy Basics: How Many Weeks of Unemployment Compensation Are Available?" Center on Budget and Policy Priorities, Updated July 24, 2018, http://www.cbpp.org/sites/default/files/atoms/files/policybasics-uiweeks.pdf.

10 Ann Clayton, "Workers' Compensation: A Background for Social Security Professionals," *Social Security Bulletin* 65 (2003/2004): 7–15; and David F. Utterback, Alysha Meyers, and Steven Wurzelbacher, "Workers' Compensation Insurance: A Primer for Public Health," CDC Workplace Safety and Health, January 2014, http://www.cdc.gov/niosh/docs/2014-110/pdfs/2014-110.pdf.

11 Ibid.

12 John Kilgour, "A Primer on Workers' Compensation Laws and Programs," SHRM, last modified November 12, 2007, http://www.shrm.org/hrdisciplines/compensation/articles/pages/cms_000039.aspx.

13 Ishita Sengupta, Virginia Reno, and John Burton, Jr., *Workers' Compensation: Benefits, Coverage, and Costs, 2006* (Washington, DC: National Academy of Social Insurance, 2008).

14 Ibid.

15 Ibid.

16 A. Lipold, "Workers' Compensation Savings Strategies," *Workforce*, February 2003, 46–48.

17 "About the Law," HHS.gov/Healthcare, http://www.hhs.gov/healthcare/rights/; and "Key Features of the Affordable Care Act by Year," HHS.gov/HealthCare, http://www.hhs.gov/healthcare/facts/timeline/timeline-text.html#2014.

18 "Questions and Answers on Employer Share Responsibility Provisions Under the Affordable Care Act," Internal Revenue Service, http://www.irs.gov/uac/Newsroom/Questions-and-Answers-on-Employer-Shared-Responsibility-Provisions-Under-the-Affordable-Care-Act#Basics.

19 Ibid; also, "ACA Requirements for Medium and Large Employers to Offer Health Coverage," June 22, 2016, National Conference of State Legislatures, http://www.ncsl.org/documents/health/aca_requirements_for_employers.pdf .

20 "Affordable Care Act Tax Provisions for Employers," Internal Revenue Service, Employers, November 22, 2017, https://www.irs.gov/affordable-care-act/employers.

21 "Employee Benefits in the United States—March 2018," Bureau of Labor Statistics, U.S. Department of Labor, July 20, 2018, https://www.bls.gov/news.release/pdf/ebs2.pdf.

22 "J. B. Hunt Drives Its Team to Better Health: J. B. Hunt Customer Success Story," Aetna, last modified March 2007, http://www.aetna.com/employer/commMaterials/documents/Roadmap_to_Wellness/jb_hunt.pdf.; Jeff Della Rosa, "Then & Now: Rick George Promotes Telemedicine for J.B. Hunt," *Talk Business & Politics*, February 15, 2018, https://talkbusiness.net/2018/02/then-now-rick-george-promotes-telemedicine-for-j-b-hunt/.

23 "Visualizing Health Policy: Recent Trends in Employer-Sponsored Health Insurance Premiums," Henry J. Kaiser Family Foundation, January 5, 2016, http://kff.org/infographic/visualizing-health-policy-recent-trends-in-employer-sponsored-health-insurance-premiums/.

24 "2017 Executive Summary, Benefit Plan Design, and Cost Benchmarking Key Results," UBA Health Plan Survey, United Benefit Advisors, Indianapolis.

25 Katie Treadwell and Nicholas Cram, "Managed Health Care and Federal Health Programs," *Journal of Clinical Engineering* 29 (2004): 36–42.

26 "2017 Executive Summary, Benefit Plan Design, and Cost Benchmarking Key Results."

27 "2018 Employee Benefits: The Evolution of Benefits," shrm.org, June 2018, https://www.shrm.org/hr-today/trends-and-forecasting/research-and-surveys/Documents/2018%20Employee%20Benefits%20Report.pdf.

28 Jessica Greene, Judith Hibbard, James F. Murray, Steven M. Teutsch, and Marc L. Berger, "The Impact of Consumer-Directed Health Plans on Prescription Drug Use," *Health Affairs* 27 (2008): 1111–1119, doi: 10.1377/hlthaff.27.4.1111.

29 "IRS Announces 2019 HSA Contribution Limits, HDHP Minimum Deductibles, and HDHP Out-of-Pocket Maximums," *EBIA Weekly Newsletter,* Thomson Reuters, May 10, 2018, https://tax.thomsonreuters.com/blog/irs-announces-2019-hsa-contribution-limits-hdhp-minimum-deductibles-and-hdhp-out-of-pocket-maximums/.

30 26 CFR 601.603: Tax Forms and Instructions, Rev. Proc. 2018-30, IRS Document, https://www.irs.gov/pub/irs-drop/rp-18-30.pdf.

31 "Health Savings Accounts," IRS Publication 969-Main Content, http://www.irs.gov/publications/p969/ar02.html#en_US_2013_publink1000204039.

32 "Aetna HealthFund Consistently Delivering Meaningful Savings and Engaged Members," Aetna, http://www.aetna.com/news/AHF_study.pdf.

33 Rhonda Orin and Daniel Healy, "Ten Traps to Avoid When Negotiating Self-Funded Benefits Plans," *Compensation & Benefits Review* 38 (2006): 25–33; and Nancy Woodward, "Is Self-Funded Health a Path for Small Firms?" *HRMagazine* 51 (2006): 85–86.

34 Jeremy Smerd, "Firms Acting to Wean Employees off Brand Drugs," *Workforce Management* 85 (2006): 2.

35 "2017 Executive Summary, Benefit Plan Design, and Cost Benchmarking Key Results."

36 Gary Cain, "Benefit Plan Strategies to Reduce Health Care and Prescription Drug Cost Increases," *Compensation & Benefits Review* 35 (2003): 36–42.

37 Stephen Miller, "Dental Benefits Are Often Misunderstood, Underused," *SHRM.org,* July 18, 2017, https://www.shrm.org/resourcesandtools/hr-topics/benefits/pages/dental-benefits-underused.aspx.

38 Stephen Miller, "Preventive Dental Benefits Save Employers Money, Studies Find," *SHRM.org,* February 2, 2018, https://www.shrm.org/resourcesandtools/hr-topics/benefits/pages/dental-benefits-save-employers-money.aspx.

39 Hugh Waters and Marlon Graf, "Chronic Diseases Are Taxing Our Health Care System and Our Economy," STAT, May 31, 2018, https://www.statnews.com/2018/05/31/chronic-diseases-taxing-health-care-economy.

40 Kenneth Mitchell, "Managing the Corporate Work-Health Culture," *Compensation & Benefits Review* 36 (2004): 33–39; and Albert Crenshaw, "Debating the Impact of High-Deductible Health Plans," *Washington Post,* April 30, 2006, F08.

41 "2018 Employee Benefits: The Evolution of Benefits."

42 "Meet the Wellness Programs That Save Companies Money," *Harvard Business Review,* April 20, 2016, https://hbr.org/2016/04/meet-the-wellness-programs-that-save-companies-money.

43 "Risk-Assessment Strategies: Fairview's Wellness Program Cuts Cost, Number of High-Risk Employees," *IOMA's Report on Managing Benefits Plans* 6 (2006): 1–5.

44 "Incentives Key to Wellness Programs," *Occupational Hazards* 67 (2005): 16.

45 "2017 IBM Benefits and Programs Summary," IBM, http://www-01.ibm.com/employment/us/benefits/2017_IBM_Benefits_Summary_Regular_-_12.13.16_update.pdf.

46 M. Jamner and D. Stokols, *Promoting Human Wellness: New Frontiers for Research, Practice, and Policy* (Berkeley: University of California Press, 2000).

47 Sandy Smith, "Drug Abuse Costs Employers $81 Billion Per Year," March 11, 2014, *EHS Today,* http://ehstoday.com/health/drug-abuse-costs-employers-81-billion-year.

48 Alexia Elejalde-Ruiz, "Cost of Substance Abuse Hits Employers Hard, New Tool Shows," Chicago Tribune, April 6, 2017, http://www.chicagotribune.com/business/ct-workplace-substance-abuse-0407-biz-20170406-story.html#.

49 Gina Ruiz, "Expanded EAPs Lend a Hand to Employers' Bottom Lines," *Workforce Management* 20 (2006): 46–47.

50 Stephen Miller, "Disability Payments Up, But Fewer Workers Covered," *SHRM.org,* last modified July 2, 2014, http://www.shrm.org/hrdisciplines/benefits/articles/pages/disability-payments.aspx.

51 Ibid.

52 "Return-to-Work Toolkit for Employees & Employers," Office of Disability Employment Policy, U.S. Department of Labor, http://www.dol.gov/odep/return-to-work/.

53 "Life Beyond Pay—Work–Life Balance," *Economist* 379 (2006): 73–74.

54 Paul Fronstin and Lisa Greenwald & Associates, "The State of Employee Benefits: Findings from the 2017 Health and Workplace Benefits Survey," *Employee Benefit Research Institute Issue Brief,* April 10, 2018, https://www.ebri.org/pdf/briefspdf/EBRI_IB_448_WBS.10Apr18.pdf .

55 Jillian Berman, "Millions of Vacation Days Will Be Left Unused by American Workers," *HuffPost*, last modified December 1, 2011, http://www.huffingtonpost.com/2011/12/01/millions-of-vacation-days-unused-american-workers_n_1123780.html; and "Overwhelmed America: Why Don't We Use Our Paid Time Off?" U.S. Travel Association, August 2014, projectimeoff.com, http://www.projecttimeoff.com/sites/default/files/PTO_Overwhelmed America_Report.pdf .

56 Tom Cherry, "Rejuvenating Tuition Reimbursement Programs," *HR Magazine* 59 (2014): 79–85; "2018 Employee Benefits: The Evolution of Benefits."

57 "Publication 15-B (2017), Employer's Tax Guide to Fringe Benefits," Internal Revenue Service, https://www.irs.gov/publications/p15b#en_US_2017_publink1000193671.

58 "Caregiving in the U.S.," National Alliance for Caregiving and AARP Public Policy Institute, June 2015, http://www.caregiving.org/wp-content/uploads/2015/05/2015_CaregivingintheUS_Executive-Summary-June-4_WEB.pdf; and Lynn Feinberg and Rita Choula, "Understanding the Impact of Family Caregiving on Work," AARP Public Policy Institute, http://www.aarp.org/content/dam/aarp/research/public_policy_institute/ltc/2012/understanding-impact-family-caregiving-work-AARP-ppi-ltc.pdf.

59 M. Gordon, "Adding Long-Term Care Benefits," *Compensation & Benefits Review* 36 (2004): 47–52.

60 R. Storms, "Benefits That Save Retirement," *Compensation & Benefits Review* 34 (2002): 33.

61 Ibid.

62 E. Zimmerman, "Personal Debt Can Drive Employees to Distraction," *Workforce Management*, April 2006, http://www.workforce.com/archive/article/24/33/36.php.

63 T. Hira and C. Loibl, "Understanding the Impact of Employer-Provided Financial Education on Workplace Satisfaction," *Journal of Consumer Affairs* 39 (2005): 173–194.

64 J. Kim and E. Garman, "Financial Stress, Pay Satisfaction, and Workplace Performance," *Compensation & Benefits Review* 36 (2004): 69–76.

65 D. Robb, "Portals Offer Gateway to Financial Education," *HR Magazine* 50 (2005): 5–98.

66 Timothy Reilly, "One Company Fund," *Compensation & Benefits Review* 44 (2012): 176–179.

67 "Clients Benefiting from Hyatt's Group Legal Services," Hyatt Legal Plans, http://www.legalplans.com/about-hyatt-legal-plans/current-clients.aspx; "See What Employers Are Saying," Hyatt Legal Plans, legalplans.com, https://www.legalplans.com/employer/testimonials/.

68 "Employee Retirement Income Security Act—ERISA," Health Plans & Benefits, Employee Benefits Security Administration, U.S. Department of Labor, http://www.dol.gov/dol/topic/health-plans/erisa.htm; and "Compliance Assistance," Employee Benefits Security Administration, U.S. Department of Labor, http://www.dol.gov/ebsa/compliance_assistance.html.

69 "What You Should Know About Your Retirement Plan," Employee Benefits Security Administration, U.S. Department of Labor, http://www.dol.gov/ebsa/publications/wyskapr.html.

70 "Retirement," George Washington University, http://www.gwu.edu/retirement.

71 Geoffrey Colvin, "The End of a Dream," *Fortune* 153 (2006): 85–92.

72 Ibid.

73 "What You Should Know About Your Retirement Plan."

74 "PBGC Guarantee Limit for Single-Employer Plans Increases for 2019," Pension Benefit Guarantee Corporation, https://www.pbgc.gov/news/press/releases/pr18-06.

75 Leslie Papke, "Choice and Other Determinants of Employee Contributions to Defined Contribution Plans," *Social Security Bulletin* 65 (2003): 59–68.

76 "401(k) Contribution Limit Increases to $19,000 for 2019; IRA Limit Increases to $6,000," Internal Revenue Service, November 1, 2018, https://www.irs.gov/newsroom/401k-contribution-limit-increases-to-19000-for-2019-ira-limit-increases-to-6000.

77 "Frequently Asked Questions About Cash Balance Pension Plans," Employee Benefits Security Administration, U.S. Department of Labor, http://www.dol.gov/ebsa/FAQs/faq_consumer_cashbalanceplans.html.

78 "Fact Sheet: The Pension Protection Act of 2006: Ensuring Greater Retirement Security for American Workers," White House, last modified August 2006, http://georgewbush-whitehouse.archives.gov/news/releases/2006/08/20060817.html.

79 "Needed Health Savings in Retirement Going up Again," October 22, 2015, Employee Benefit Research Institute, https://www.ebri.org/pdf/PR1145.Hlth-Svgs.22Oct15.pdf.

80 Colvin, "The End of a Dream"; and Paul Fronstin and Nevin Adams, "Employment-Based Retiree Health Benefits: Trends in Access and Coverage, 1997–2010," *Issue Brief* No. 377, Employee Benefit Research Institute, last modified October 2012, https://www.ebri.org/pdf/briefspdf/EBRI_IB_10-2012_No377_RetHlth.pdf; Michael Hiltzik, "Your Vanishing Health Coverage: Employers Are Cutting Retiree Health Benefits at a Rapid Rate," *Los Angeles Times*, May 11, 2016, http://www.latimes.com/business/hiltzik/la-fi-hiltzik-retiree-health-insurance-20160511-snap-story.html; "2018 Employee Benefits: The Evolution of Benefits."

81 Robert Sinclair, Micheal Leo, and Chris Wright, "Benefit System Effects on Employees' Benefit Knowledge, Use, and Organizational Commitment," *Journal of Business and Psychology* 20 (2005): 3–29.

82 Charlotte Huff, "The Disappearing Benefit," *Workforce Management* 84 (2005): 34–38.

83 Pamela Babcock, "Safety Consciousness," *HR Magazine* 50 (2005): 66–70.

84 "OSHA 35-Year Milestones," Occupational Safety and Health Administration, U.S. Department of Labor, http://www.osha.gov/as/opa/osha35yearmilestones.html.

85 "All About OHSA," Occupational Safety and Health Administration, U.S. Department of Labor, https://www.osha.gov/Publications/3302-06N-2006-English.html.

86 "Commonly Used Statistics," Occupational Safety and Health Administration, U.S. Department of Labor, osha.gov, https://www.osha.gov/oshstats/commonstats.html.

87 "Commonly Used Statistics, Federal OSHA Coverage," Occupational Safety and Health Administration, U.S. Department of Labor, https://www.osha.gov/oshstats/commonstats.html.

88 "OSHA Enforcement," U.S. Department of Labor, OSHA, https://www.osha.gov/dep/index.html.

89 "OSHA Inspections," OSHA Fact Sheet, Occupational Safety and Health Administration, U.S. Department of Labor, https://www.osha.gov/OshDoc/data_General_Facts/factsheet-inspections.pdf.

90 "Partnership, An OSHA Cooperative Program," U.S. Department of Labor, OSHA, https://www.osha.gov/dcsp/partnerships/index.html.

91 "All About VPP," U.S. Department of Labor, Occupational Safety and Health Administration, https://www.osha.gov/dcsp/vpp/all_about_vpp.html.

92 "OSHA Inspections," OSHA Fact Sheet.

93 "Workplace Violence," Safety and Health Topics, Occupational Safety and Health Administration, U.S. Department of Labor, https://www.osha.gov/SLTC/workplaceviolence.

94 Ibid.; and "WPV Prevention Programs and Strategies," *Workplace Violence Prevention Strategies and Research Needs* (Cincinnati: CDC Workplace Safety and Health, NIOSH, 2006), 14–18.

95 "2018 Employee Benefits: The Evolution of Benefits."

96 "Safety and Health Topics: Ergonomics," Occupational Safety and Health Administration, U.S. Department of Labor, http://www.osha.gov/SLTC/ergonomics/index.html.

97 Ibid.

98 "Working at Walmart: Benefits," Walmart.com, http://walmartstores.com/Careers/7750.aspx.

99 Michelle Long, Matthew Rae, and Gary Claxton, "A Comparison of the Availability and Cost of Coverage for Workers in Small Firms and Large Firms: Update from the 2015 Employer Health Benefits Survey," February 5, 2016, Henry J. Kaiser Family Foundation, http://kff.org/private-insurance/issue-brief/a-comparison-of-the-availability-and-cost-of-coverage-for-workers-in-small-firms-and-large-firms-update-from-the-2015-employer-health-benefits-survey/.

100 Papke, "Choice and Other Determinants of Employee Contributions to Defined Contribution Plans."

101 Gloria Tian and Andrew Chamberlain, "The Best Industries for Benefits: An Analysis of Glassdoor Benefits Reviews," Research Studies, Glassdoor, May 12, 2016, https://www.glassdoor.com/research/studies/best-industries-for-benefits/.

102 "Employment Benefits in the United States, March 2018," News Release, Bureau of Labor Statistics, U.S. Department of Labor, July 20, 2018, https://www.bls.gov/news_release/pdf/ebs2.pdf.

103 "OSHA Field Inspection Reference Manual CPL 2.103," Occupational Safety and Health Administration, U.S. Department of Labor, https://www.osha.gov/Firm_osha_toc/Firm_toc_by_sect.html.

104 "About SAS: Awards," SAS, https://www.sas.com/en_us/news/awards.htm.

105 "Training Means Zero Accidents for FHm: Program Exceeds All Expectations," *Human Resource Management International Digest* 14 (2006): 23.

106 Babcock, "Safety Consciousness."

107 Nina Cole and Douglas Flint, "Opportunity Knocks: Perceptions of Fairness in Employee Benefits," *Compensation & Benefits Review* 37 (2005): 55–62.

108 Anna Rappaport, "Variation of Employee Benefit Costs by Age," *Social Security Bulletin* 63 (2000): 47–56.

109 "An Act," 35th Anniversary, Equal Employment Opportunity Commission, http://www.eeoc.gov/eeoc/history/35th/thelaw/owbpa.html.

110 Todd Arnold and Chester Spell, "The Relationship Between Justice and Benefits Satisfaction," *Journal of Business & Psychology* 20 (2006): 599–620.

111 Theodore Courtney, Yueng-Hsiang Huanga, Santosh K. Vermaa, Wen-Ruey Changa, Kai Way Lia, and Alfred J. Filia, "Factors Influencing Restaurant Worker Perception of Floor Slipperiness," *Journal of Occupational & Environmental Hygiene* 3 (2006): 593–599.

112 Cynthia Roth, "How to Protect the Aging Workforce," *EHS Today*, last modified January 20, 2005, http://www.occupationalhazards.com/Issue/Article/37390/How_to_Protect_the_Aging_Work_Force.aspx.

113 Jeff Koven, "Streamlining Benefit Process with Employee Self-Service Applications: A Case Study," *Compensation & Benefits Management* 18 (2002): 18–23; and Samuel Greengard, "Building a Self Service Culture that Works," *Workforce* 77 (1998): 60–64.

114 Kathryn Moody, "Why a Human Touch Matters Now More Than Ever for Benefits Technology," HRDive, hrdive.com, June 5, 2017, https://www.hrdive.com/news/why-a-human-touch-matters-now-more-than-ever-for-benefits-technology/444009/.

115 Edward Cherof, "August 2002: Legal Issues in Telecommuting," *SHRM.org*, last modified December 2006, http://www.shrm.org/legalissues/legalreport/pages/cms_000926.aspx.

116 Ibid.; and "Workers' Compensation: Telecommuting: Are Telecommuters Covered Under WC?" *SHRM.org*, last modified July 30, 2013, http://www.shrm.org/templatestools/hrqa/pages/wcandtelecommuting.aspx.

117 "Spending on Health: Latest Trends," Organisation for Economic Co-operation and Development, June 2018, http://www.oecd.org/health/health-systems/Health-Spending-Latest-Trends-Brief.pdf .

118 Edward Whitehouse, *Pensions Panorama: Retirement-Income Systems in 53 OECD Countries* (Washington, DC: World Bank, 2007), 43–45.

119 Elizabeth Oliver and Karen Cravens, "Cultural Influences on Managerial Choice: An Empirical Study of Employee Benefit Plans in the United States," *Journal of International Business Studies* 30 (1999): 745–762.

120 Angela Curl and M. C. "Terry" Hokenstad, "Reshaping Retirement Policies in Post-Industrial Nations: The Need for Flexibility," *Journal of Sociology & Social Welfare* 33 (2006): 85–106.

121 "Pensions at a Glance, OECD and G20 Indicators," Organisation for Economic Co-operation and Development, last modified November 26, 2013, http://www.oecd.org/pensions/pensionsataglance.htm.

122 "Countries with the Most Vacation Days," *WorldAtlas*, https://www.worldatlas.com/articles/countries-with-the-most-vacation-days.html.

123 "2014 Global Health Care Sector Outlook," Deloitte, http://www2.deloitte.com/global/en/pages/life-sciences-and-healthcare/articles/2014-global-health-care-outlook.html.

124 "Questions and Answers on Employer Share Responsibility Provisions Under the Affordable Care Act," Internal Revenue Service, http://www.irs.gov/uac/Newsroom/Questions-and-Answers-on-Employer-Shared-Responsibility-Provisions-Under-the-Affordable-Care-Act#Basics.

125 Sheri Merkling and Elaine Davis, "Kidnap & Ransom Insurance: A Rapidly Growing Benefit," *Compensation & Benefits Review* 33 (2001): 40–45.

126 "How Kidnapping Insurance Keeps a Lid on Ransom Inflation," *The Economist*, https://www.economist.com/finance-and-economics/2018/05/26/how-kidnapping-insurance-keeps-a-lid-on-ransom-inflation.

127 Pacific Bridge, Inc., "Hong Kong: New Anti-Racism Law Affects Expatriate Benefits Package," Global Focus Area, *SHRM.org*, http://www.shrm.org/hrdisciplines/global/articles/pages/cms_016121.aspx.

128 "Tyson and UFCW Mark Two Decades of Workplace Safety Progress," *UFCW.org*, last modified November 24, 2009, http://www.ufcw.org/tag/tyson/.

129 "Health Plans and Benefits: Continuation of Health Coverage—COBRA," U.S. Department of Labor, http://www.dol.gov/dol/topic/health-plans/cobra.htm; and "FAQs About COBRA Continuation Health Coverage," U.S. Department of Labor, http://www.dol.gov/ebsa/faqs/faq-consumer-cobra.html.

130 "FAQs About COBRA Continuation Health Coverage."

131 Eric Parmenter, "Employee Benefit Compliance Checklist," *Compensation & Benefits Review* 34 (2002): 29–39.

132 "Health Information Privacy," U.S. Department of Health and Human Services, http://www.hhs.gov/ocr/privacy/.

# Part 5

# Special Topics

# Chapter 13

# Labor Unions and Employee Management

## Learning Objectives

**AFTER READING THIS CHAPTER, YOU SHOULD BE ABLE TO:**

1 Explain why labor unions exist.

2 Describe the main purpose and key points of the laws regulating labor relations.

3 Discuss unfair labor practices.

4 Understand the different types of unions and union shops.

5 Explain the steps in the process of organizing a union.

6 Describe the collective bargaining process.

7 Explain the grievance process used in a union environment.

8 Discuss issues in managing labor relations in the future.

**HR CHALLENGE**

| ENVIRONMENTAL INFLUENCES | ORGANIZATIONAL DEMANDS | REGULATORY ISSUES |

**PRIMARY HR ACTIVITIES**

Work Design & Workforce Planning

Managing Employee Competencies

Managing Employee Attitudes & Behaviors

Employee Contributions

Competitive Advantage

## Labor Relations Overview

In the late 1700s, a group of businesses that made and sold boots decided to form a guild to protect against unfair competition. The bootmakers who worked for these employers decided that they needed to look out for themselves as well. They formed a society to bargain for wages and to restrict who could work for their employers. These actions ultimately led to the first labor case recorded in the United States. In this case, the Commonwealth of Pennsylvania brought charges against eight bootmakers for conspiring to coerce their employers to increase their wages.

Why did the case occur? In 1798, in Pennsylvania, employers had reduced the wages paid to bootmakers from $2.75 per pair for custom boots and $2.50 per pair for stock orders to $2.25 per pair for both types of boots. The bootmakers subsequently went on strike and successfully managed to restore their wages to their previous levels. The next year, employers reduced the bootmakers' wages again. When the bootmakers went on strike this time, their employers got together and decided to lock them out of their jobs. These events led to growing concern that workers were organizing. Employers responded by taking steps to suppress such activities. They charged the bootmakers with conspiracy against the employers. Ultimately, the eight bootmakers were found guilty of conspiracy and fined $8 each. The outcome in this case gave states the impetus to squelch union activity in the United States for the next 36 years or so.[1]

The labor movement eventually picked up momentum and has played a key role in securing better working conditions, wages, and benefits for workers, particularly in the manufacturing sector. Labor union membership in traditional industries, such as manufacturing, has been on the decline in the United States and in other developed countries in recent years. At the same time, efforts have increased to unionize groups of employees who have not typically been targeted by unions. These groups include adjunct faculty members and graduate students at universities, service workers in various industries, and information technology professionals and other knowledge workers. Further, as less developed countries bring in more industry, unions have turned their attention to improving working conditions for laborers there. Consequently, whether you are working domestically or globally as a manager, you need to be familiar with the laws that regulate labor union activity, the processes of unionization and collective bargaining, and the trends in labor relation activities. After a brief history of the union movement in the United States, we discuss each of these topics.

Labor relations affect all aspects of human capital management addressed in the framework shown in Exhibit 13.1. The presence of a union determines work design and workforce planning, how employee competencies are managed, and employee attitudes and behaviors. Thus, we include labor relations in this special topics section.

## Brief History of Labor Union Movement in the United States

Workers join unions for many reasons, including higher wages, better health and accident benefits, contractual provisions that ensure a safer workplace, greater job security, and having a voice in the workplace.[2] Skilled craftspeople were the first workers to unionize. Remember the bootmakers described at the beginning of the chapter? The society they formed was the first labor union in the United States. The first unions in Sweden were formed by printers. In Great Britain, the first unions were formed by building and printing trade workers. All of these unions were

**EXHIBIT 13.1**

Framework for the Strategic Management of Employees

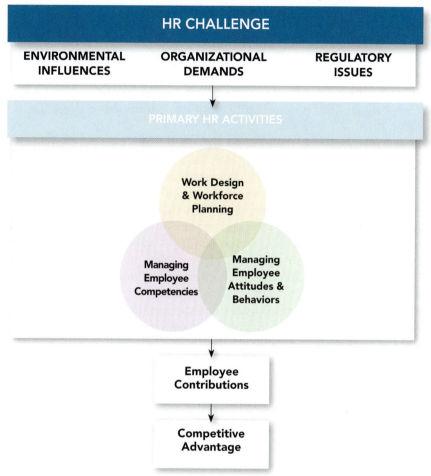

formed because the people in these trades were concerned about the competition they faced.[3] For example, as the transportation of products in the United States improved, bootmakers in Philadelphia found themselves competing for the first time with bootmakers in New York. This competition adversely affected their wages. Combine that situation with the advent of mass production, which reduced the need for skilled workers, and the foundation was laid for increased unionization.

In some trades, the ability of the skilled workers to move from one location to another affected wages within their industries and led to the formation of local unions. The local unions prevented tradespeople from other parts of the country from coming into a certain locale and bringing down wages.[4] (You will better understand the situation described here if you think about how many people today resent the fact that legal and illegal immigrants to the United States are often willing to work for lower wages than United States citizens will accept.)

Since the early days of labor unions, strikes have been used to achieve a union's objectives. Workers who continued to go to work during a strike became known as *scabs*, and their names were shared among local unions in an effort to ensure that they were not employable. Union members refused to work with nonunion members, and would even refuse to interact socially with them or live in the same boarding houses with them.[5]

By 1873, union membership had reached 300,000 in the United States. By 1878, however, membership was down to 50,000 due to a depression. Then, in 1886, the

American Federation of Labor (AFL) was formed, and unionism began to increase once again. Still, it wasn't until about 1933 that unions became firmly entrenched in the manufacturing sector. This change helped fuel an upturn in union membership. A pro-union U.S. president, Franklin Delano Roosevelt, and new legislation that made it easier for workers to unionize also played a part in the upsurge.[6]

In 2015, union membership in the United States reached a record low of 11.1%. This percentage was the lowest recorded by the Bureau of Labor Statistics since they began collecting this data in 1983. In 1983, the union membership rate was 20.1%.[7] Exhibit 13.2 describes the state of union membership in the United States in 2017 and shows that union membership has continued to drop since the low recorded in 2015.

Many reasons exist for the decline in union membership. Globalization has resulted in many traditional union jobs being moved to other countries, with manufacturing particularly hit hard. As manufacturing has moved abroad, U.S. job growth has occurred in the services sector and in small businesses, sectors of the economy that have historically been less likely than others to organize. Add to that the reluctance of local unions to spend money on organizing efforts—something that has traditionally been their responsibility—and you have a recipe for the decline of unions in the United States.[8] This decline in union membership is not just a U.S. phenomenon. Later in this chapter, we will look at unionization in other parts of the world.

Critics of unions say that employees don't support unions today because they are able to individually reap the benefits unions used to provide for them. Data from the Bureau of Labor Statistics suggests otherwise. For instance, in 2017, union workers had median weekly earnings of $1,041 per week, compared to $829 for nonunion workers. This spread of 27% has remained fairly constant since 2000, when the Bureau of Labor Statistics started tracking this wage data. Union members pay 1% to 2% of their salaries to their unions; that's a small price to pay relative to the benefits members reap.[9] Now, let's take a look at some of the regulations related to labor unions.

## EXHIBIT 13.2

### Union Membership in the United States 2017

| | |
|---|---|
| Overall union membership rate as percent of all wage and salary workers | 10.7% |
| Number of wage and salary workers who belong to a union | 14.8 million |
| Private sector workers rate of union membership | 6.5% |
| Public sector workers rate of union membership | 34.4 % |
| Occupational groups with highest union membership: | |
| • Education, training, and library | 33.5% |
| • Protective services | 34.7% |
| Occupational groups with lowest union membership: | |
| • Farming, fishing, and forestry | 3.4% |
| • Sales and related | 3.2% |
| • Food preparation and serving | 3.8% |
| • Computer and mathematical | 3.9% |
| Union membership, males | 11.4% |
| Union membership, females | 10.0% |
| State with highest union membership: New York | 23.8% |
| State with lowest union membership: North Carolina | 2.6% |

*Source:* Based on "Union Members—2017," Bureau of Labor Statistics, Economic News Release, January 19, 2018, http://www.bls.gov/news.release/union2.nr0.htm.

# Government Regulation of Labor Unions

Two of the earliest pieces of labor legislation were the Railway Labor Act of 1926 (RLA) and the Norris-LaGuardia Act of 1935. This legislation was followed by the passage of three Acts: the Wagner Act of 1935, also known as the National Labor Relations Act (NLRA), the Taft-Hartley Act of 1947, and the Landrum-Griffin Act of 1959. Jointly, the acts are referred to as the National Labor Code.

## Railway Labor Act of 1926

Prior to the nineteenth century, five laws had been enacted to handle rail labor disputes. Nonetheless, labor unrest in the railroad industry continued. Violent strikes and lockouts interrupted the rail transportation of people and goods in the United States, adversely affecting the economy. The **Railway Labor Act (RLA)** was passed in 1926 to try to provide a peaceful way for railroads and their employees to resolve their disputes. The RLA applies to common-carrier rail service and commercial airline employees (the latter of whom were included in the Act through provisions passed by Congress in 1936).

Besides providing a way for employees and railroads to peaceably resolve their differences, the RLA allows rail and airline employees to join labor unions. The Act also distinguishes between minor and major disputes. Boards such as the National Railroad Adjustment Board settle minor disputes. Employees can engage in strikes for major disputes, but not minor ones. Employers can use lockouts for major disagreements. The Act spells out provisions for handling major disputes, including collective bargaining guidelines, and it created the National Mediation Board (NMB) to handle these disputes and help parties resolve them.[10]

**Railway Labor Act (RLA)** provides a peaceful way for employees and railroads or commercial airlines to resolve differences, allows rail and airline employees to join labor unions, and distinguishes between major and minor disputes and what can happen relative to each; also created the National Mediation Board

## Norris-Laguardia Act of 1932

Congress passed the **Norris-LaGuardia Act** in 1932 to make it easier for employees to engage in union-organizing activities. Before the passage of the Act, employers had all of the power when it came to how workers were treated. Employers could have federal courts issue injunctions in cases involving or resulting from labor disputes if employees wanted to strike or otherwise interfere with the flow of work.[11] The Act also outlined the process to be followed for hearings, granted workers the right to collective bargaining, and stated that neither officers of a union nor the union itself would be held liable for unlawful activities of its members that could not be proven to have been instigated or approved by the union.[12]

**Norris-LaGuardia Act** made union-organizing activities easier for employees, outlined a process for hearings, and granted workers the right to collective bargaining

## Wagner Act (National Labor Relations Act of 1935)

Even after the passage of the Norris-LaGuardia Act, relations between labor and management continued to deteriorate because management in many companies refused to allow unions to represent labor. These poor labor–management relations cut across many industries, from automotive to textile, from steel to trucking. In 1934, the country was in the midst of the Great Depression, and 1.5 million workers went on strike. Many of these strikes became violent. A large number of the strikes were about wage increases, but one-third of them were over the right of unions to be recognized.[13]

Congress subsequently passed the **National Labor Relations Act (NLRA)**, known as the **Wagner Act**, in 1935. This Act is often regarded as the most important piece of labor relations legislation. The Act was passed for three main reasons: (1) to protect the rights of employees and employers, (2) to encourage these parties to engage in collective bargaining, and (3) to control their activities

**Wagner Act (National Labor Relations Act (NLRA))** protects the rights of employees and employers, encourages these parties to engage in collective bargaining, and controls their activities so the economy won't be adversely affected by their actions; also established the National Labor Relations Board (NLRB) so the economy wouldn't be adversely affected.[14] The Wagner Act established the National Labor Relations Board (NLRB) to oversee compliance with the Act. Let's take a look at some of the specific provisions of the Act relative to employee rights, unfair labor practices, workers not covered by the NLRA, and the establishment of the NLRB.

### Employee Rights

The NLRA protects private-sector employees from employer and union misconduct, such as attempts by employers to prevent unions from organizing and attempts by unions to coerce employees into joining them. The NLRA also ensures that employees have the right to organize a union where none currently exists. The specific rights provided under the NLRA to employees include the right to:

1. Form, or attempt to form, a union at their workplace.
2. Join a union, even if it's not recognized by their employer.
3. Assist in union-organizing efforts.
4. Engage in group activities (collective bargaining), such as attempting to modify their wages or working conditions.
5. Refuse to do any or all of the above unless a clause requiring employees to join the union exists.[15]

The NLRA also provides rights to employees who are not part of a union. These employees have the right to engage in **concerted activity**, which exists when two or more employees act together to try to improve working conditions, or when a single employee approaches management after conferring with other employees on their behalf or is acting on behalf of other employees. For example, if two or more employees talk with their employer about improving their pay, or if an employee does so on behalf of one or more of her coworkers, these employees have engaged in protected concerted activity.[16] Company Spotlight 13.1 provides an example of protected concerted activity involving the use of social media (a topic that will be specifically addressed later in this chapter).

### Unfair Labor Practices (ULPs)

**Unfair labor practices (ULPs)** are violations of the NLRA that deny rights and benefits to employees. These violations can be the result of employer or union activity. Such violations include threatening to take jobs or benefits from employees who attempt to form a union, reassigning workers to less attractive jobs than their current ones if they are involved in union activities, and telling employees they will receive greater benefits if they don't join a union. Labor unions violate the NLRA when they tell employees they will lose their jobs if they don't join the union or, when union employees are on strike, they bar nonstrikers from entering an employer's premises.[17]

Specifically, Section 8 of the Act defines the following ULPs:

1. Interfering with, restraining, or coercing employees in the exercise of their rights guaranteed in Section 7 of the Act.
2. Dominating or interfering with the formation or administration of any labor organization, or contributing financial or other support to it.
3. Discriminating against employees in terms of their hiring, tenure of employment, or any other term or condition of their employment, so as to encourage or discourage them from becoming members in a labor organization.
4. Discharging or otherwise discriminating against employees because they file charges or give testimony under the Act.
5. Refusing to bargain collectively with the duly chosen representatives of employees.[18]

**concerted activity**

when two or more nonunion employees act together to try to improve working conditions, or when a single employee approaches management after conferring with other employees on their behalf or is acting on behalf of other employees

**unfair labor practice (ULP)**

a violation of the NLRA that denies rights and benefits to employees; can be the result of employer or union activity

# COMPANY SPOTLIGHT **13.1**

## Is a YouTube Posting a Protected Concerted Activity?

Three construction workers at Rain City Contractors decided to publicly air concerns about unethical and illegal practices by their employer. They did so by posting a YouTube video about their concerns. These employees, all immigrants from El Salvador, were involved in building concrete foundations for a waterfront development known as Point Ruston, a mixed-use neighborhood that would include a four-star hotel. The development was taking place where for eight decades a company named Asarco had run a high-arsenic copper smelter.

The employees were concerned that the site was still contaminated with arsenic and other toxins. Their employer required them to wear badges that indicated they had been trained to handle hazardous materials, but they had never received any of this training. The badges actually belonged to other employees.

When the employees made the nine-minute YouTube video, they spoke in Spanish and hid their faces out of fear of retaliation by their employer. Ten days later, the three employees who did the video and two others who were their friends lost their jobs. The employees filed a complaint with the NLRB. While the investigation was ongoing, the employer threatened and interrogated other employees, making it clear that they were not to complain outside the company about working conditions. The employer alleged that the video was an attempt to bring a carpenters' union into the company.

The State of Washington fined the company $35,000 for not notifying workers about the potential exposure to arsenic. And, the NLRB determined that the video was protected concerted activity. The employees had the right to voice their concerns about their workplace safety. The video accurately described the working conditions.

On the second day of the scheduled hearing, the company agreed to a settlement that included back pay for all five workers from the date of their firing to the settlement date, and reinstatement to their former jobs. The workers chose not to return to work for Rain City Contractors.

*Sources:* Based on "Protected Concerted Activity, Lakewood, Washington, Construction Contractor, 19-CA-31580," National Labor Relations Board, http://www.nrlb.gov/rights-we-protect/protected-concerted-activity; and Lornet Turnbull, "Web Video of Workers Starts Department of Labor and Industries Probe," *Seattle Times*, last modified February 27, 2009, http://www.seattletimes.com/html/localnews/2008791757_youtube26m.html.

Although the Act identified these practices as "unfair," it did not make them crimes or impose any penalties or fines on people or organizations for their occurrence.[19]

### National Labor Relations Board (NLRB)

The **National Labor Relations Board (NLRB)** is an agency of the U.S. government that was created by Congress to administer the NLRA. This agency has two main functions. One function is to prevent and remedy unfair labor practices on the part of either labor organizations or employers. The second is to decide whether groups of employees want labor union representation so that they can engage in collective bargaining. This decision is based on the results of secret-ballot elections the NLRB conducts for employees.[20]

The two components of the agency are the board and the general counsel. The board is made up of five members, appointed to five-year terms by the president of the United States and approved by the United States Senate. Their role is quasi-judicial and involves making decisions in administrative proceedings. The president also appoints the general counsel (an attorney) to investigate and prosecute unfair labor practices and supervise the NLRB field offices as they process cases.[21] The general counsel is appointed for a four-year term and must be approved by the Senate.[22]

**National Labor Relations Board (NLRB)**

an agency of the U.S. government that was created by Congress to administer the National Labor Relations Act (NLRA)

# Taft-Hartley Act (Labor Management Relations Act of 1947)

For the 12 years after its passage, the NLRA was perceived by many as giving too much power to the unions. In response, the U.S. Congress passed the **Labor Management Relations Act of 1947,** commonly known as the **Taft-Hartley Act**. President Harry S Truman subsequently vetoed the Act, but Congress overrode his veto. The main purpose of the Act is to protect the rights of employees and make the NLRB a more impartial referee for industrial relations rather than having it serve as an advocate for organized labor.[23] Provisions of the Act are to:

1. Promote the full flow of commerce.
2. Prescribe the legitimate rights of employees and employers in their relations affecting commerce.
3. Provide orderly and peaceful procedures for preventing employees and employers from interfering with the legitimate rights of the other party.
4. Protect the rights of individual employees in their relations with labor organizations.
5. Protect the rights of the public in connection with labor disputes affecting commerce.[24]

This Act increased the reach of government regulation of collective bargaining (which is discussed in detail later in this chapter) and added new sanctions for violations in addition to those already existing under the Wagner Act. Specifically, these sanctions included criminal penalties in the form of fines and imprisonment, injunctions, and private suits for damages.[25] The Taft-Hartley Act also specified that the Bureau of Labor Statistics (BLS) would maintain a file of collective bargaining agreements. The BLS now collects agreements that cover 1,000 or more workers. These files are accessible through the BLS office in Washington, DC.

Next, we provide an overview of three outcomes of the Taft-Hartley Act: permissible types of union membership, national emergency strikes, and the Federal Mediation and Conciliation Service (FMCS).

## Union Membership

Among the most significant outcomes of the Taft-Hartley Act was the provision that employees cannot be forced to join a union. A total of 27 states, as shown in Exhibit 13.3, have passed **right-to-work laws** to prevent workers from having to join a union as a condition of employment, be forced to not join a union as an employment condition, or be forced to pay dues to a labor union or be fired for not paying such dues.[26] While there are 27 states shown as right-to-work states currently, the status of right-to-work laws in Missouri is in flux. In an interesting twist of events, the Missouri governor in 2017 signed right-to-work legislation into law. Then, in August 2018, voters in the state struck down this new legislation in a referendum known as Proposition A. The referendum was designed to hold up implementation of the right-to-work law, with the goal of having the law rolled back. This victory for the unions means that private-sector unions in Missouri can once again collect mandatory fees from workers who do not join the union that represents them in collective bargaining agreements.[27]

Organizations such as the National Right to Work Legal Defense Foundation and the National Right to Work Committee work to ensure that these rights of workers are not violated. The role of the foundation is to work through the courts to support individuals who have been victims of forced unionism. The committee lobbies state legislatures and Congress to eliminate forced unionism and works to educate people about right-to-work laws.[28]

Regardless of whether a state is a right-to-work state, the Taft-Hartley Act has led to safeguards for workers who do not wish to be forced to become union members

## EXHIBIT 13.3

### Right-to-Work States

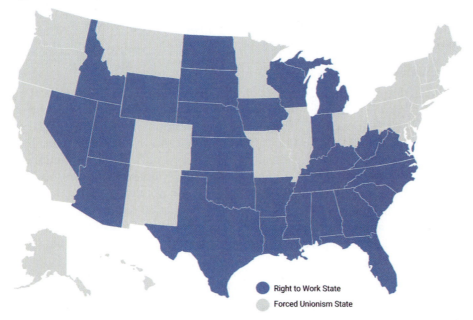

Right to Work State
Forced Unionism State

*Source:* "Right to Work States," Used with permission of the National Right to Work Committee (2018).

and redefined what types of union shops are legal under collective bargaining agreements. The most extreme form of union membership is a **closed shop**. A closed shop requires workers to join a union before they can be hired and requires employers to go to the union first to hire new employees. Only if union employees are not available can the employer recruit nonunion employees. The Taft-Hartley Act generally outlawed closed shops and ended the right of unions to decide who could be members of the union.[29]

In a **union shop**, all workers except managers in an organizational unit represented by a union must become members of that union within a certain period of time after being hired, or at least pay the equivalent of union dues. This type of agreement is referred to as a *union security clause*. Union shops are illegal in right-to-work states.[30]

In an **agency shop**, employees cannot be required to join a union but can be required to pay to a union an amount equivalent to initiation fees and dues that are considered to be a tax or service charged and are referred to as an *agency fee*. In exchange for these payments, the union acts as the bargaining agent for the employee. In reality, workers who are not union members can only be required to pay an amount equivalent to reduced union dues solely for the purpose of supporting the collective bargaining, contract administration, and grievance resolution services the union provides.[31]

The referendum vote in Missouri to roll back the state's right-to-work law was seen as a victory by unions, essentially reestablishing an important provision of agency shop agreements in Missouri. A recent Supreme Court decision, however, was seen as a major loss. In June 2018, the Supreme Court ruled that public sector employees could not be required to pay dues for nonpolitical work of unions. Look back at Exhibit 13.2 to see that 34.4% of public sector employees are unionized, a much higher percentage than the percentage of private sector employees who are unionized. This ruling effectively undid a practice that had stood since the 1970s. Under that practice, which is part of an agency shop agreement, nonunion members

**closed shop**

requires workers to join a union before they can be hired and requires employers to go to the union first to hire new employees

**union shop**

an arrangement under which all workers except managers in an organizational unit represented by a union have to become members of that union within a certain period of time after being hired, or at least pay the equivalent of union dues

**agency shop**

a labor union arrangement under which employees cannot be required to join a union but can be required to pay to a union an agency fee for purposes such as initiation

in the public sector were required to pay a fee even if they did not join the union. In exchange for the fee, the union acted as the bargaining agent for the employee. In its 5-4 vote overturning the practice, the Supreme Court cited concerns that requiring employees to pay a fee to be represented by the unions was, in effect, compelling workers to financially support public policy positions with which they disagreed because unions often take stands on policy issues.[32]

### National Emergency Strikes

The Taft-Hartley Act included a provision allowing the president of the United States to direct the appropriate state attorney general to issue an 80-day injunction against a strike or lockout. Before doing so, the following conditions must be met: (1) an entire industry or a substantial part of it is affected and (2) national health and safety are imperiled. When a strike is considered to constitute a **national emergency strike**, the president of the United States appoints an inquiry board to determine whether the two conditions are met. Specific steps exist for obtaining the injunction and following up after the injunction is ordered. After the 80-day injunction ends, the union can strike and management can lock out the union. Basically, the 80 days are to serve as a "cooling off period" for both parties with the hope that the strike or lockout will not happen.[33]

**national emergency strike**

a strike or lockout that affects an entire industry, or a substantial part of it, and national health and safety are imperiled

### Federal Mediation and Conciliation Service (FMCS)

The Taft-Hartley Act established the Federal Mediation and Conciliation Service (FMCS). The FMCS provides both unions and employers free mediation, conciliation, and voluntary arbitration for labor–management disputes. Its primary purpose is to prevent labor–management disputes from impeding the free flow of commerce. The agency also provides education and training programs designed to improve the working relationships between labor and management. For 2017, the FMCS reported that 87.1% of the cases in which it was involved in mediation with labor and management led to collective bargaining agreements.[34]

## Landrum-Griffin Act (Labor-Management Reporting and Disclosure Act of 1959)

The Labor-Management Reporting and Disclosure Act (LMRDA), known as the **Landrum-Griffin Act**, amended the Taft Hartley Act to protect union members from being abused by unions. It outlines the responsibilities of union officers, as well as the rights of union members, via a bill of rights that gives union members the right to free speech and due process, the opportunity to be involved in the nomination process for the election of union leaders, the right to receive copies of their collective bargaining agreements, and the right to sue their unions.[35] The Act also gives union members the right to vote on any increase in their union dues and requires unions to provide annual financial reports to the U.S. Secretary of Labor. Exhibit 13.4 provides an overview of union member rights.

**Landrum-Griffin Act (Labor-Management Reporting and Disclosure Act)**

protects union members from abuse by unions by outlining the responsibilities of union officers and providing a bill of rights for union members

## Types of Unions

We now provide an overview of the types of unions and discuss why they exist and how they are related. The types of unions have evolved over time and include local unions, city and statewide federations of local unions, and international unions. Local unions later joined together to form city and statewide federations. Statewide federations joined together to form national unions, and many of these have now become international unions.

## EXHIBIT 13.4

### Labor–Management Reporting and Disclosure Act (LMRDA) Overview of Union Member Rights

| Union Member Rights |
|---|
| **Bill of Rights** |
| Union members are guaranteed democratic rights that include: |
| • **Equal rights and privileges** for involvement in union elections and union business, subject to reasonable rules in the union constitution and/or bylaws |
| • **Freedom of speech and assembly** with regard to criticizing union officials, expressing different viewpoints, and holding meetings |
| • **Right to secret ballot vote** on rates of dues, initiation fees, and assessments |
| • **Protection of right to sue** the union, without reprisal |
| • **Protection from improper union discipline** and right to due process in disciplinary situations |
| Other rights: |
| • Receive a copy of the collective bargaining agreement |
| • Review union reports, constitutions, and bylaws |
| • Participate in union elections, including running for office |
| • Removal of elected union officers involved misconduct |
| • Protection from certain discipline in violation of law |
| • Protection from violence |

*Sources:* Based on "The LMRDA and the Union Members' Bill of Rights," The Association for Union Democracy (AUD), http://www.uniondemocracy.org/Legal/lmrda.htm; "Union Member Rights and Officer Responsibilities Under the LMRDA," Office of Labor-Management Standards, U.S. Department of Labor, http://www.dol.gov/olms/regs/compliance/members.htm.

## Local Unions

Local unions protect the interests of workers in a particular craft/trade or industry. For instance, Local No. 9 of the International Union of Operating Engineers is located in Denver, Colorado. Its members are in the stationary/skilled building maintenance trades. Members' dues are used to pay for worker representation and collective bargaining efforts and are set through a vote of the members.[36] Today, the lines between craft unions and industrial unions are blurring, but there are still some distinctions. **Craft unions** are organized to represent the interests of members with specialized craft skills. The United Association of Journeymen and Apprentices of the Plumbing and Pipe Fitting Industry of the United States and Canada Local 344 is an example of a local craft union in Lawton, Oklahoma. This union represents skilled plumbers and pipe fitters. **Industrial unions** have traditionally represented semiskilled and unskilled workers in a particular industry. For example, United Paperworkers International Union Local 1342 represents workers in the paperwork industry in Panama City, Florida.

Local unions are voluntary associations of workers who have banded together because of their shared economic interests. They might work for the same employer or for several employers. In any case, the members recognize that the union provides them with a greater voice with respect to their employers than they would have alone. Each member is entitled to one vote, and decisions are made by a majority vote. Elected officers and an executive board are empowered to act on behalf of the union. Members remain in good standing, as long as they pay their dues and other required fees and follow the guidelines for union membership. The goal of most local unions is to improve the wages, benefits, and working hours of members. A local union also provides a grievance mechanism for its members with the employer. We describe the grievance process later in this chapter.

After a local union is organized at a company, the union elects a **union steward** to serve as a liaison between the rest of the employees and the leadership of the union. The union steward is an employee of the company who serves in the role voluntarily. Typically, the formal agreement between the union and the employer

**craft union**

a union organized to represent the interests of members with specialized craft skills

**industrial union**

a union that has traditionally represented semiskilled and unskilled workers in a particular industry

**union steward**

a union member that serves as a liaison between the rest of the employees and the leadership of the union will specify the role of the union steward, including the amount of work time that the steward can spend on union activities.

## International Unions

**International unions** are federations of local unions. In essence, an international union is a "parent" for the local unions. Workers are members of the local union rather than the international union. However, the local union pays dues to the international union. International unions hold regularly scheduled conventions in which delegates from local unions participate. The international union elects officers and an executive board from among these delegates.

International unions provide services to local unions that would be more costly and/or difficult for them to provide individually. For instance, the federation is in a better position to lobby for legislation on behalf of the local unions than are the individual local unions. The Industrial Workers of the World (IWW) is an example of an international union. Its goal is to organize all industries into a single, worldwide union that cuts across industries and crafts.[37]

One of the fastest-growing and largest unions in North America is the Service Employees International Union (SEIU). In 2018, the SEIU had over 2 million members from the United States, Canada, and Puerto Rico. Members work in hospital systems, long-term care organizations, property services, and public services.[38]

Many U.S. and international unions have been part of a voluntary federation known as the AFL-CIO (formerly the American Federation of Labor–Congress of Industrial Organizations). The AFL-CIO consists of 55 unions representing 12.5 million workers.[39] The AFL-CIO has long been a force for change in the workplace in the United States, focusing on social and economic justice. However, that is changing. The AFL-CIO is made up of state federations and central labor councils that partner with state and community organizations to work to improve the lives of working families through local, state, and national campaigns.[40]

The SEIU and the International Brotherhood of Teamsters were the first groups to split from the AFL-CIO in 2005. The leaders of these two unions were concerned that the AFL-CIO was not doing enough to stop the decline in union memberships and was not making the labor movement a force to be reckoned with in the modern workplace.[41] These two unions joined with five others to form the Change to Win (CTW) coalition. CTW was created to become the leading voice for the labor movement in the United States. The organization believes a radical change is needed if U.S. unions are to survive.[42] Their primary goal is to bring together the 50 million American workers who are not working in jobs that can be outsourced to provide a voice for better wages and decent working conditions.[43]

## The Union Organizing Process

Company Spotlight 13.2 describes attempts to organize unions at Amazon. Conducting a union election costs about $1,000 per worker, whether the union wins or loses. In 2017, there were 1,366 NLRB-conducted certification elections, down from more than 7,000 per year in the 1960s. Unions won 940 of the 2017 elections.[44]

When a group of employees decide they would like to be represented by a union, their first step is to file a petition with the NLRB. Employees in the designated work unit, referred to as the **bargaining unit**, provide a dated signature on either a **union authorization card** or a signature card, indicating that they are interested in being represented by a particular union. At least 30% of the eligible employees must provide this card for the NLRB to consider the petition. The NLRB then assigns an agent from the appropriate regional field office to process the petition. The regional office of the NLRB holds a secret-ballot election, usually at the workplace. A majority vote in favor of the union is all that is required. The NLRB then certifies that the

# COMPANY SPOTLIGHT **13.2**

## No Unions Welcome at Amazon

Amazon was founded in 1994 and now has over 613,000 employees. The company has never had a successful unionizing effort. Not that there haven't been attempts to unionize. One attempt took place in January 2014 at the Amazon warehouse in Middletown, Delaware. A small group of maintenance and repair technicians voted 21–6 against joining the International Association of Machinists and Aerospace Workers. The workers had petitioned the NLRB to organize the union. The election itself was monitored on-site by the NLRB. The loss by the union followed intense efforts by Amazon to prevent the union vote from succeeding. Amazon had even brought in a law firm that specializes in preventing organized labor from getting a hold in a firm to help with its efforts. The company also held meetings to discourage employees from voting for the union. In an earlier unionizing attempt in 2000 by the Communication Workers of America, Amazon closed the call center where the workers were employed, reportedly as part of broader cost cuts. In other instances, employees who have raised the union issue have been terminated, although Amazon says the terminations had nothing to do with the unionization efforts.

Union representatives felt that the employees in Delaware had been pressured by management to not join the union. Amazon's take on the outcome was that the workers had made it clear they wanted to work directly with Amazon, and not through a union, to have their wants and needs met. The union spokesperson argued differently, saying that the unionizing effort was to give a voice to the workers to address issues ranging from safety to vacation time.

With Amazon's recent acquisition of Whole Foods Market, new allegations of the suppression of union organization surfaced when managers were instructed on how to head off union efforts. Amazon is often in the press because of its stressful, fast-paced work environment.

*Sources:* Based on Wingfield, Nick, "Amazon Proves Infertile Soil for Unions, So Far," *The New York Times*, May 16, 2016, https://www.nytimes.com/2016/05/17/technology/amazon-proves-infertile-soil-for-unions-so-far-html; Kopytoff, Verne, "How Amazon Crushed the Union Movement," *Time*, January 14, 2014, http://time.com.956/how-amazon-crushed-the-union-movement/; Sainato, Michael, "Amazon Training Videos Coach Whole Foods Staff on How to Discourage Unions," *The Guardian*, September 27, 2018, https://www.theguardian.com/business/2018/sep/27/amazon-whole-foods-training-video-union-busting-efforts-staff.

union represents the employees for collective bargaining purposes and requires their employer to bargain with the union.[45] Exhibit 13.5 provides an overview of the steps required in the union certification process.

One of the most challenging parts of the certification process is determining who is actually eligible to sign the union authorization card. The bargaining unit can consist of workers in a single location or from multiple locations. The bargaining

## EXHIBIT 13.5

### Labor Union Certification Process

Step 1: Workers decide they want to be represented by a specific union.

Step 2: 30% of eligible workers in the bargaining unit sign cards petitioning the NLRB for secret-ballot elections.

Step 3: A representation certification petition is filed with the NLRB.

Step 4: The regional office of the NLRB holds a secret-ballot election.

Step 5: The NLRB tallies the vote to determine if a majority of the workers voted for the union.

Step 6: The union is certified if the vote is positive.

Step 7: The employer is required to bargain with the union.

unit can also be limited to a specific group of craft workers or a single department. The NLRB determines who is eligible to be part of the bargaining unit, or the union and the employer jointly make this decision. Regardless of who makes the decision, the company is required to supply to the NLRB a list of names and addresses for employees who are eligible to vote in the representation election within seven days after the NLRB has indicated that an election will be held.[46]

**Excelsior list**

a list of names and addresses the company must supply of employees who are eligible to vote in the representation election for a union

This list is known as the **Excelsior list**. Here is an example of just how important this list is in a union election. The adjunct faculty at George Washington University (GW) successfully voted to be represented by SEIU, Local 500. The university challenged the outcome of the vote because it felt that some of the employees who had voted were not eligible to vote, and because they had been allowed to vote, other employees should have been allowed to vote as well. The NLRB said the appeal was without merit, and the federal appeals court agreed.[47]

## Role of Employees, Employers, and Union Organizers

Guidelines exist for what employees, employers, and union organizers can do during a unionization attempt. Employees can lobby coworkers to vote in favor of the union, but they can only do so during lunch and other break times. The employer gets to decide where the union literature can be distributed by employees. Employers can also require employees to attend company meetings so that management can present its view about the union being formed. These meetings can be held on company premises and during work hours. However, no meetings can be held in the 24 hours immediately preceding an election. Supervisors are permitted to have one-on-one meetings with employees about the union issue and can give employees written information as well.

Union organizers work for the unions and are not company employees. These organizers are not allowed to campaign for the establishment of a union on company property unless the workplace is remote, such as a logging camp. Organizers can distribute information in public areas at the work location or in public areas of the city. They can also call employees and visit them at their homes.[48]

## Card Checks and Neutrality Agreements

Federal law does provide an alternative route under which a union can be recognized by an employer outside the NLRB process. Employers can voluntarily recognize a union if employees show majority support, either through signed authorization cards or some other route. When the employer voluntarily recognizes a union as the bargaining representative for a group of employees, the status of the union cannot be challenged for a period of six months to one year after the first bargaining session occurs.[49]

**card check**

a process whereby a company recognizes a union once the union has produced evidence that the majority of workers have signed authorization cards indicating that they want the union to represent them

A **card check** is a process whereby a company recognizes a union once the union has produced evidence that the majority of workers have signed authorization cards indicating that they want the union to represent them. No election is held. Under a **neutrality agreement**, a company agrees that it will not express its views about unionization during the time when signatures are collected.

**neutrality agreement**

an arrangement in which a company agrees that it will not express its views about unionization during the time when signatures are collected

Unions prefer card checks and neutrality agreements because the NLRB does not become involved in the union certification process, and management loses its right to speak out about the possible effects of unionization. The AFL-CIO reports a more than 70% success rate when card checks and neutrality agreements are used.[50] Because the NLRA does not require secret-ballot elections, these activities are not illegal. However, under a card check, more than 30% of the eligible employees may have to sign the authorization cards or petition for the bargaining unit to be recognized.[51]

# Collective Bargaining

**Collective bargaining** is the process that labor unions and employers use to reach agreement about wages, benefits, hours worked, and other terms and conditions of employment. In this section we discuss this process.

## Good Faith Bargaining

The NLRB requires that employers and unions bargain in good faith. **Good faith bargaining** requires the parties to meet at a reasonable time and come to the bargaining table ready to reach a collective bargaining agreement. **Mandatory bargaining topics** must be negotiated and include compensation and benefits, hours of employment, and other conditions of employment. Pensions, insurance, grievance processes, safety, layoffs, discipline, and union security have also become mandatory bargaining topics. The law does not require an employer and a union to actually reach an agreement on the topics—only that they bargain in good faith.

The bargaining process can also address issues such as employee rights, managerial control, and benefits for retired union members. However, these topics are not mandatory and are referred to as **permissive topics**. With the fast-changing global economy, job security has become a critical component for collective bargaining.[52] No measures can be discussed that would be unlawful. For example, the two parties could not discuss a situation in which only union members could be hired, nor can the parties discuss discriminating against employees based on their membership in a protected class.

## Bad Faith Bargaining

Actions that constitute **bad faith bargaining** include bargaining with individual employees rather than union representatives, refusing to meet at reasonable times to engage in bargaining, and "going through the motions" of bargaining without the intent of reaching an agreement. Other activities that may or may not be considered bad faith bargaining include not being willing to schedule enough bargaining sessions and applying economic pressure to the other party.[53]

## Negotiating the Agreement

As a manager, you will find that there are many times when you are involved in negotiations. You will have to negotiate with customers, vendors, and/or employees. And, even if you do not actually represent your company in collective bargaining negotiations (assuming that you work in a union environment), you might be asked to provide those who do with certain information. Regardless of the type of negotiation, there are a few critical steps that should be followed to reach the best possible solution for all parties involved: (1) being prepared, (2) knowing the interests of the other party, and (3) understanding the consequences of not reaching an acceptable agreement. These steps apply to the collective bargaining negotiation process as well. We briefly discuss each of these components within the context of the collective bargaining negotiation process, and we discuss the major types of negotiation that are likely to occur.

### Preparing to Negotiate

Both parties involved in the negotiation—labor and management—spend considerable time preparing to negotiate. It is important that each side have current and accurate data to address the topics for negotiation. For instance, as noted previously, wages are a mandatory topic for negotiation in a collective bargaining agreement. Both

---

**collective bargaining**
the process that labor unions and employers use to reach agreement about wages, benefits, hours worked, and other terms and conditions of employment

**good faith bargaining**
the process that requires parties to meet at a reasonable time and come to the bargaining table ready to reach a collective bargaining agreement

**mandatory bargaining topics**
topics that must be negotiated, including compensation and benefits, hours of employment, and other conditions of employment

**permissive topics**
nonmandatory issues, such as employee rights, managerial control, and benefits for retired union members, that are often part of the collective bargaining negotiations and agreement

**bad faith bargaining**
entering into a collective bargaining situation with no intention of reaching an agreement, or in some other way violating the protocol for appropriate collective bargaining

parties will want to gather data about prevailing wage rates in the relevant labor market and be ready to make an offer during the negotiation that is reasonable based on that information. Of course, each side will seek to find wage information that is most advantageous for its part of the negotiation. The union will want data to support higher wages, while the company will want data to support lower wages.

If one party in the negotiation indicates that it is unable to make a concession, it is important that the party be able to substantiate its claims. For instance, if a representative of the company indicates that the cost of the benefits desired will adversely affect the operation of the company, the representative needs to be prepared with the appropriate financial data to support this argument. It is also imperative for the parties to know what their objectives are in order to make sure that they have the information they need to bargain well.

As you can see, preparing to negotiate requires paying careful attention to a lot of issues. In addition, preparation is an ongoing activity. As soon as a collective bargaining agreement is signed, it is time to start thinking about the one that will come next. During the preparation stage, the first-line supervisor can be a critical source of information about what employees are really expecting and desiring.[54]

### Knowing the Interests of the Other Party

Being prepared means entering into negotiation with some idea of what the other party will expect with regard to the final outcome. Understanding the interests of the other party—what the other party sees as critical relative to the outcome—puts the negotiator in a stronger position to bargain for concessions. Learning the interests of the other party takes a lot of time and effort, but the payoff is worth it.

Two commonly used types of negotiation strategies in labor negotiations are distributive and integrative bargaining. When a **distributive bargaining strategy** is used, there is a winner and a loser. The goals of one party are in direct conflict with the goals of the other party, and often each party wants to claim a fixed set of limited resources as its own, or at least maximize its share. Each party takes a defensive position during the bargaining sessions. In an **integrative bargaining strategy**, each party is more cooperative and works to make the outcome win–win. In this situation, one party can pursue its goals without precluding the other party from doing the same. Both sides cooperate to reconcile their differences and reach a mutually agreeable solution.[55]

**Interest-based bargaining** is basically an extension of integrative bargaining. In this situation, each party looks for common goals in order to meet the interests of the other party. Brainstorming, information sharing, and other techniques are used to ensure that the lines of communication between the two parties are kept open. The goal is to reach consensus so that both parties win.[56]

### Understanding the Consequences of Not Reaching an Acceptable Agreement

What happens if the parties to a union negotiation can't reach an agreement? Often, the result is either a strike by workers, a lockout of the workers by managers, or arbitration, with a third party making the decisions. The situation in which both parties have made their final offers and are not willing to make further concessions is referred to as an **impasse**.[57]

When an impasse occurs, the parties have several options. First, an impartial outside party such as the Federal Mediation and Conciliation Service, discussed earlier, can be called in to facilitate the negotiation. This facilitation can take the form of **conciliation**, which involves keeping the parties working on the agreement until they can resolve the issues at hand. The facilitation can also take the form of **mediation**, which involves the outside party working with each side to reach an acceptable agreement. Finally, **arbitration** can be used to resolve the issues. Unlike conciliation and mediation, in which a third party acts as an intermediary,

---

**distributive bargaining strategy**

a negotiation strategy in which each party takes a defensive position during the bargaining session resulting in a winner and a loser

**integrative bargaining strategy**

a negotiation strategy in which each party cooperates and works to reach a win–win outcome

**interest-based bargaining**

an extension of integrative bargaining in which each party looks for common goals in order to meet the interests of the other party

**impasse**

the situation in which both parties have made their final offers and are not willing to make further concessions

**arbitration**

a method of resolving disputes in which a third party acts as an intermediary and actually makes the decision about how the issue should be resolved

**mediation**

the arrangement whereby an outside party works with each side in a negotiation to reach an acceptable agreement

**conciliation**

a type of facilitation used when an impasse occurs in a collective bargaining session so that both parties keep working toward an agreement until they can resolve the issues at hand arbitration involves a third party actually making the decision about the issue. Recall that in Chapter 3, we introduced the concept of mediation and arbitration. More and more companies are using mediation and arbitration to resolve employee discrimination complaints and other grievances. Employees and unions also are using arbitration to resolve their disputes with individual employees. And labor arbitration or mediation is increasingly used by employers and unions to resolve collective bargaining labor–management disputes because this approach is more cost-effective and timely than taking the dispute to court.[58]

## The Grievance Process

Most collective bargaining agreements outline formal steps that must be followed to settle disputes between labor and management. These steps make up the **grievance process**. Officially, a **grievance** is a written charge by one or more employees that management has violated their contractual rights. Exhibit 13.6 lists the steps for employees to follow if they believe their rights have been violated.

The grievance process typically works as follows. First, the problem is reported to one's immediate supervisor who is obligated to investigate the matter and try to resolve the problem. The report can be written or oral, but it is usually written. The supervisor should then work with the union steward to resolve the problem. If the union steward does not believe that the problem is a legitimate grievance, no further action is taken. If these efforts do not result in a resolution, it goes to the next level of supervision. This time, the employee filing the grievance is represented by the union. Failure to resolve the grievance at this stage within the time allotted in the collective bargaining agreement (usually 5 to 15 days) results in the grievance being taken to a higher level of management, such as a plant manager or even the executives of the company. The highest level for the resolution of a grievance is spelled out in a union contract. If the grievance is still not resolved, the final step in the grievance process is to call in an arbitrator, who reviews the facts of the case and makes a determination about what action should occur. At this stage, the company and the union are both represented by high-level managers and union officials. If the union contract calls for binding arbitration (and most do), the arbitrator has the final say in the case.[59]

**grievance process**

formal steps that must be followed to settle disputes between labor and management

**grievance**

a charge by one or more employees that management has violated their contractual rights

### EXHIBIT 13.6

### Steps to Follow If Rights Have Been Violated

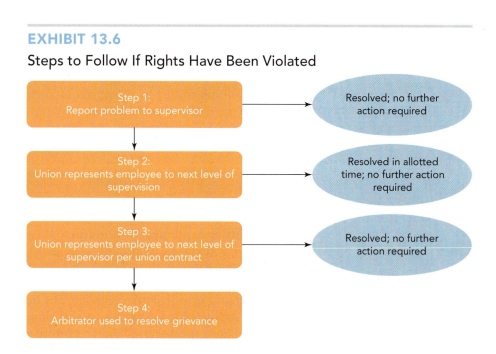

The employee's right to have a union representative involved in the process of disciplinary hearings resulted in large part from the 1975 landmark U.S. Supreme Court case *NLRB v. Weingarten, Inc.* In this case, the Supreme Court ruled that a union representative could be present when a supervisor conducted an investigatory interview to gather information that could result in the employee being questioned or disciplined, or when an employer asks an employee to defend his or her actions. As a result of this case, managers have to notify union representatives of the purpose of the interview. In addition, the employee has the right to select which union employee will be present.[60]

Managers need to be very familiar with the requirements of union contracts and understand the types of actions that lead to grievances. By doing so, they reduce the likelihood that they will have to participate in a grievance process. If a grievance is reported, the proper care and handling of it is critical. Conducting a fair and timely investigation, keeping your supervisor informed, and carefully documenting all activities related to the grievance are just a few ways to minimize the likelihood of the grievance going to an arbitration hearing.

# The NLRB's Role in Unfair Labor Practices

When an unfair labor practice (ULP) charge is filed with the appropriate NLRB field office, an investigation ensues to determine whether there is reasonable cause to believe that the National Labor Relations Act (NLRA) has been violated. If cause is found, the field office makes an attempt to help the parties involved reach a settlement agreement. If a settlement cannot be reached, a formal complaint is filed, and the case goes to the NLRB administrative law judge. The judge then issues a written decision, which can be appealed to the NLRB. If one of the parties believes the NLRB decision is not acceptable, it can file an appeal with the U.S. Court of Appeals. About 20,000–30,000 charges of ULPs are filed each year with the Court of Appeals.[61]

# Decertification

**decertification**

the process of terminating union representation, resulting in the union no longer representing the employees or engaging in collective bargaining on their behalf

If employees in a collective bargaining unit decide that they no longer want to be part of a union, they can petition the NLRB for decertification. **Decertification** means that the union will no longer represent the employees or engage in collective bargaining on their behalf. The decertification petition can be filed only within 90 days of the expiration of the collective bargaining agreement currently in force. As with certification, at least 30% of the employees in the bargaining unit must indicate that they no longer want to be represented by the union. A secret-ballot election is a requirement for decertification. In 2017, 168 decertification elections were held. Unions lost 118 of those and won 59.[62]

# Corporate Campaigns

**corporate campaign**

tactical strategies designed to identify and exploit opportunities to interfere with the normal operation of a business and affect its reputation

In the 1970s, unions began to use a strategy known as a corporate campaign to increase their presence and role in companies. A **corporate campaign** involves tactical strategies designed to identify and exploit opportunities to interfere with the normal operation of a business and affect its reputation. The goal is to create so much pressure on the company that it gives in to the union's demands. These campaigns begin with a power structure analysis aimed at identifying the vulnerabilities in stakeholder relationships that are critical to a company. The tactics used as part of the campaign range from sophisticated governance and financial initiatives to psychological warfare. Unions have used tactics such as introducing shareholder resolutions that restrict management and director authority, filing unfair labor practice claims that are not valid, and getting union-paid organizers hired to work for the company so that they can organize employees. This latter practice is known as *"salting."*[63] Corporate campaigns are an attempt to get around the NLRB's normal union certification procedures. Companies that have been targeted by campaigns such as these include Comcast, Borders, Sodexho, Taco Bell, and Nike.[64]

We don't want to give the impression that the unions are the only ones that don't play fair. Employers also engage in unfair and inappropriate activities to try to prevent unionization from occurring, as discussed earlier in this chapter. In a study in Canada, researchers found that the majority of the companies included had engaged in overt or covert tactics to keep the unions out. Among the reported activities were dismissing union activists and issuing threats or promises that were inappropriate. Interestingly, these actions had no effect on the certification process, but they did affect collective bargaining success and retention of the certification two years later.[65]

## Public-Sector Labor Relations

Prior to 1962, federal employees were not allowed to form unions. This prohibition was lifted by an executive order signed by President John F. Kennedy. It gave federal workers limited rights to unionize and bargain for nonwage items. The **Civil Service Reform Act** of 1978 set up the **Federal Labor Relations Authority (FLRA)** as the oversight agency for labor–management issues at the federal level. Other state and local laws protect government employees who want to participate in unions.

Unions such as the National Education Association (NEA) provide representation for specific groups of public employees. The NEA represents approximately 3 million members working in public kindergarten through university graduate programs across the United States.[66] Other unions, such as the Washington Federation of State Employees (WFSE), represent all employees in a particular state. These unions are also affiliated with the American Federation of State, County, and Municipal Employees (AFSCME), which is affiliated with the AFL-CIO.

**The Civil Service Reform Act**

granted permission to federal employees to form unions and established the Federal Labor Relations Authority (FLRA) as the oversight agency for labor–management issues at federal level

**Federal Labor Relations Authority (FLRA)**

oversight agency for labor-management issues at the federal level

## Trends in Labor Relations

We end this chapter by noting a number of trends in labor relations in the United States and elsewhere. Specifically, we address changes in union activities, new forms of employee organizations, and global unionization trends.

### Changes in Union Activities

Do labor unions have a place in the twenty-first century?[67] As we have indicated, in the United States, unions have been on the decline for some time, both in terms of the number of unions and the number of union members. The scope of unions is also changing. Employees are pulling away from the meganational unions they believe do not fully represent their cause.

The decline in membership has prompted unions to reach out to prospective members via innovations such as union credit cards, smaller unions that represent less than 50% of the workforce, and greater organizing efforts, consolidations, and mergers. Unions also have considered adopting new strategies, such as variable pay plans to protect employees' wages during difficult economic times. Recall from Chapters 10 and 11 that variable pay plans often include a portion of the salary that is fixed and a portion that is dependent on achievement of some goal, such as a production quota. With a variable pay plan, the percentage of the pay that is fixed is lower than in a traditional pay plan where all the salary is fixed; thus, there is more flexibility relative to what the company has to pay when the business is not doing well. Such plans also enable greater union/employee involvement in decision making relative to production issues, lead to improved communication between unions and management, and increase the input of unions into organizational strategy. Although seemingly anathema to the traditional philosophy of unions, which was to reduce the employment risks their members face, many U.S. collective bargaining agreements now include variable pay plans.[68]

## Social Media and Union Activity

Throughout this book, we have talked about how social media is affecting employee management activities. The NLRB has addressed social media and union activity as well. The NLRB began receiving complaints in 2010 regarding employer social media policies and practices and found reasonable cause that some of the policies and practices did indeed violate federal labor laws. Others did not. The NLRB responded by issuing three reports during 2011 and 2012 that described the results of its investigations into social media cases. The following is a summary of the findings and conclusions from these reports:

- Employees who discuss terms and conditions of employment with fellow employees via social media are engaging in "protected concerted activity."
- Employee complaints via social media about work that are not related to group activity among employees are not "protected concerted activity."
- Employer policies need to be carefully crafted so they do not prohibit activities, such as discussion of wages and working conditions, that are protected by federal labor laws.
- Unions can be found guilty of unlawful coercive conduct by how they use social media.[69]

The first decision issued by the NLRB regarding social media postings was made in September 2012 and involved the firing of a BMW salesman. This salesman had posted pictures on his Facebook page that showed what was described as an embarrassing accident at a Land Rover dealership near where he worked. The posting did not involve fellow employees. On the same day, he also posted pictures and mocking comments about serving hot dogs at a luxury BMW event. This posting did involve coworkers. A week after making these postings, he was fired from his job. The NLRB found that he was fired for the Land Rover posting and that he was not, therefore, fired for engaging in protected concerted activity.[70]

Several months later, the NLRB issued its second ruling regarding the use of social media, and inding in favor of five fired employees. These employees worked for a nonprofit organization and were fired because they participated in Facebook comments regarding a coworker who planned to complain to management about their work. The NLRB found that the Facebook conversation was protected concerted activity under federal labor law.[71]

## New Forms of Worker Organizations

As unions have continued to decline in membership, other groups have formed within organizations to represent workers. Some of these groups have affiliations with unions. They include affinity groups, such as those that focus on race, gender, or lifestyle and that lobby for the fair treatment of their members; worker centers that provide services, such as legal resources, to employees; and professional associations and guilds that provide services to their members. All of these groups attempt to ensure that members have a voice in the workplace.[72]

# COMPANY SPOTLIGHT **13.3**

## Communities Organized for Public Service (COPS) of San Antonio

Originally founded in Chicago, the IAF works to bring change to low- and moderate-income neighborhoods by revitalizing the local democracies within them. Its mission is to train people to take responsibility for their communities, thus getting citizens involved in public life by providing them with leadership and development training, for example. Often 10 to 20 people meet at a member's home to talk about issues and schedule conferences. Labor unions and community organizations, such as health centers, can also join the IAF. By focusing on institutional rather than individual members, the IAF ensures the continuity of the membership.

In 1974, another organization affiliated with the IAF, Communities Organized for Public Service (COPS), started in San Antonio, Texas. The group has been credited with leading to major transformations in the lives of citizens of San Antonio in the 44 years it has existed. Among the many accomplishments of this group is working with local cities, counties, school districts, and hospital districts to ensure employees receive a living wage. The organization has also collaborated with businesses and other organizations to provide scholarships to deserving public high school students so that they can attend college and have a better future than would otherwise have been likely.

*Sources:* Chambers, E. T., *Roots for Radicals* (New York: Continuum International Publishing Group, 2003); Osterman, P. "Community Organizing and Employee Representation," *British Journal of Industrial Relations* 44 (2006): 629–649; "Who We Are," Industrial Areas Foundation, www.industrialareasfoundation.org; "History," Industrial Areas Foundation, www.industrialareasfoundation.org/content/history; "Accomplishments," COPS/Metro, www.copsmetro. com/accomplishments; *Express-News* Editorial Board, "COPS Has Made City Better, Fairer," mySA, mysanantonio.com. March 23, 2016, https://mysanantonio.com/opinion/editorials/article/COPS-has-made-city-better-fairer-6974470.php.

Community-based organizations have also begun to provide a voice for workers. Some of these community networks are part of the Industrial Areas Foundation (IAF), a network of local faith- and community-based organizations throughout the country founded in 1940. The IAF organizing efforts are designed to effect change that often addresses conditions and outcomes for workers, including job training and minimum wages.[73] Company Spotlight 13.3 describes an IAF-affiliated network based in San Antonio, Texas.

A worker–management committee is another type of employee group. These groups originated in part out of the quality management and continuous improvement movement that occurred in the United States in the late 1980s. The movement's goal was mainly to increase the communication between workers and managers and aid in productivity improvements. These groups have been ruled illegal, however, when they engage in activities such as setting wages and establishing conditions of employment. When they do so, they are considered to have crossed the line and are viewed as attempting to become labor organizations which can only be certified by the NLRB. If you want to establish a worker–management committee, you need to make sure that its purpose is to share information and that all workers—not just union members—have the right to participate in the process.[74] Company Spotlight 13.4 discusses how the landscape for work–management cooperation is changing based on United Auto Workers (UAW) events at Volkswagen in Chattanooga.

## Global Trends

The United States is not the only country that has experienced a reduction in its union membership. In 2016, the labor union participation rate in Australia was

## COMPANY SPOTLIGHT 13.4

### Union Organizing Fails at Volkswagen, Chattanooga, Even with Management Support. . . But Did It Really?

In February 2014, employees at the Volkswagen (VW) manufacturing plant in Chattanooga, Tennessee, voted 712 to 626 against becoming members of the United Autoworkers (UAW). Because Volkswagen (VW) had not opposed the vote, union organizers believed they would win the election.

Volkswagen is a German company. In Germany, works councils are normal. The role of a works council is to bring management and workers together to make operations more efficient. United States labor laws, however, make it difficult to set up a works council without having a union to represent the workers.

The Chattanooga plant had opened in 2011 and is VW's only U.S. plant. The company planned to expand the size of the plant, resulting in the addition of 1,000 more jobs for area workers. Workers at VW in Chattanooga make about $19 an hour compared to $26 to $28 for veteran workers at automakers in Detroit. New hires in Detroit, however, are more likely to make $17 an hour.

The union initially challenged the outcome of the election but later withdrew the objection right before the NLRB was to hear the case. Soon after the UAW vote failed, numerous news articles reported information suggesting that Republican lawmakers in the state had interfered with the outcome of the election by threatening to withhold $300 million in tax breaks to VW if the union won. Without the incentives, VW would likely not expand its facility.

In an interesting turn of events, soon after withdrawing its objection to the election outcome, the UAW announced that it was forming UAW Local 42 to represent employees at the Chattanooga plant. The announcement stated that Local 42 would provide a voice for workers through the German works council approach for employee engagement. It further indicated that no employee would be required to join the union, and that the UAW was confident the management at VW would recognize the union if a meaningful number of workers signed to have Local 42 represent them in the workplace.

The UAW framed the announcement around becoming the works council partner with Volkswagen, and noted that it was a chance to do something that would be new and different. At that time, they further indicated that ongoing discussions with state officials included assurances that the incentives for VW's expansion would be forthcoming. Since then, however, the relationship between VW and UAW Local 42 has been rocky at best as VW has dealt with charges against the company for failure to follow emissions standards. There have been various attempts by small and larger groups to gain official union status, and even mention of the union situation in Chattanooga at VW strikes in Germany. The unionizing effort has made its way to the NLRB, then the D.C. Circuit Court, and back to the NLRB.

*Sources:* Based on Isidore, Chris, "Volkswagen Employees Say 'No' to United Auto Workers in Tennessee," *CNN,* last modified February 15, 2014, http://money.cnn.com/2014/04/21/news/companies/uaw-volkswagen/; Isidore, Chris, "UAW Drops NLRB Case to Organize Volkswagen," *CNNMoney,* last modified April 21, 2014, http://money .cnn.com/2014/04/21/news/companies/uaw-volkswagen/; Williams, G. Chambers III, "Is Volkswagen Preparing for a Union in Chattanooga?" *The Tennessean,* last modified July 15, 2014, http://www.tennessean.com/story/money/ cars/2014/07/15/volkswagen-ready-union-chattanooga/12670355/; and "UAW Charters Local 42 at Volkswagen in Chattanooga," UAW, last modified July 10, 2014, http://www.uaw.org/articles/uaw-charters-local-42-volkswagen- chattanooga; Brooks, Chris, "Trump's Labor Board Likely to Strip Auto Workers of Southern Victory," Labor Notes, January 10, 2018, http://www.labornotes.org/2018/01/trumps-labor-board-likely-strip-auto-workers-southern-victory.

14.5%, down from 25.4% in 1999. Sweden's labor union participation was 66.7%, down from 80.6% in 1999, and the United Kingdom was at 23.5%, down from 30.1% in 1999. Chile is one of the few countries in the Organisation for Economic Co-operation and Development (OECD) with a growth in labor union membership. In 1999, Chile's rate was 12.7% and in 2016, it was 17.7%.[75]

In Great Britain, the birthplace of the modern labor union, union membership has been declining since 1979. The changing structure of the British economy is believed to be the root cause. As manufacturing industries have declined in the country, so, too, has membership in the unions. More of the United Kingdom's public sector than private sector is unionized, and more women than men are union members.[76] Unions in Great Britain still have a voice in the workplace, but their economic impact has been significantly reduced.[77]

The impact of unions is still felt around the world, in developing countries, as well as in developed countries. In Mexico, unions have led to increased job training and greater productivity per worker, as well as improved the ratio of fringe benefits to total compensation and the value of benefits per worker. While these trends are positive, higher worker turnover has also been associated with union presence in Mexico.[78] Mexico actually has a complex system of unions that has existed for some time and is intricately connected to the government. Some people believe this relationship between the unions and the government is one reason wages have remained lower than they might otherwise be in a typical union environment.[79]

Globally, a number of laws and organizations affect workers' ability to join unions. The Universal Declaration of Human Rights by the United Nations (UN), and other conventions issued by the International Labour Organization (ILO), set forth the rights of workers to form and join trade unions. Some of the conventions specify that governments cannot interfere with this activity, whereas others protect workers from anti-union discrimination by employers.

Of course, just because such declarations exist does not mean that they are followed. For instance, there is a labor union in China, but it is the All China Federation of Trade Unions and is a product of the Chinese Communist Party. Thus, even though this union has 288 million members, it doesn't belong to the workers, like trade unions in other parts of the world. Collective bargaining does not occur because representing labor rights is secondary to serving the party. New labor legislation went into effect January 1, 2008, and appears to be making a difference. This legislation, known as the Law of the People's Republic of China on Employment Contracts, allows workers to have labor contracts and has led to an increase in wages. There was an unintended consequence, however. The higher wages have led to higher production costs, which have to be passed along to the consumer. These increases make the products less competitive in the marketplace. As a result of these wage increases and other issues, the economy has taken a downturn and China has begun outsourcing jobs overseas or eliminating jobs, which has led to worker unrest and protests. Leaders of these protests and worker strikes are often arrested or detained or experience state-sanctioned violence.[80]

Laws such as the Law of the People's Republic of China on Employment Contracts begin to address some of the issues surrounding fair trade practices. Specifically, Nike and other companies have been accused of exploiting workers by not paying them a fair wage and not providing better overall working conditions for them. Much of the debate concerns whether companies have an obligation to pay a "living wage." Recall that we discussed the concept of a living wage in Chapter 10 and noted that it is a complicated concept. However, the need for improved worker conditions and fair pay creates an opportunity for unions to provide a voice for workers in these developing countries.

Finally, large confederations of unions now exist that cut across country and continent borders. For instance, the European Trade Union Confederation (ETUC) includes unions from Eastern and Western Europe, and consists of 90 national trade union confederations in 38 countries and 10 European trade union confederations.[81] The International Trade Union Confederation (ITUC) includes the Asia-Pacific Regional Organisation, the African Regional Organisation, and the American Regional Organisation. The ITUC cooperates with the ETUC and has close relations with other union organizations around the globe.[82]

## SUMMARY

Labor unions exist to provide a collective voice for workers in bargaining with employers for higher wages, better benefits, safe and fair working conditions, and other conditions of employment. Labor union membership has been on the decline in the United States as a result of many traditional union jobs in manufacturing moving to other countries. Yet, research continues to show the benefits of union membership, including higher wages and better benefits for employees.

A number of regulations exist to govern labor–management relations. These include the Railway Labor Act of 1926, which provided a way for employees and railroads to handle differences, and the Norris-LaGuardia Act of 1932, which made it easier for employees to engage in union-organizing activities. The most significant legislation affecting labor and management relations was the Wagner Act, also known as the NLRA, which gave employees the freedom to join unions, defined unfair labor practices that were impermissible, and created the NLRB to administer the NLRA.

In 1947, Congress passed the Taft-Hartley Act to protect the rights of employees and employers because of a perception that the NLRA had given too much power to the unions. The Taft-Hartley Act protects employers from certain labor union practices that impede their business. The Landrum-Griffin Act was passed in 1959 to protect union members from abuse by unions. The Act outlines an employee bill of rights that gives union members, among other protections, the right to freedom of speech, the right to secret ballots, and the right to sue the union.

Unions exist in various forms. Local unions protect the interests of workers in a particular craft/trade or industry. A union steward serves as a liaison between the employees and the leadership of a union. International unions are federations of local unions and have stronger bargaining power and greater ability to lobby for legislation on behalf of union members.

The union-organizing process begins when workers decide to be represented by a specific union. If 30% of eligible employees indicate their desire to be represented by that union, a representation certification petition is filed with the NLRB, and a secret-ballot election is held. If the ballot passes, the union is certified, and the employer is required to engage in collective bargaining with that union.

Collective bargaining is the process of the employer and union reaching agreement about wages, benefits, and working conditions. Employers and unions are required to bargain in good faith on these mandatory bargaining topics. Collective bargaining agreements define the grievance process for resolving disputes between workers and management. These processes include involvement of a union steward or other union representative on behalf of or alongside the employee. Arbitration is the final step in resolving such disputes. If employees decide they do not want to be represented by the union any longer, they can initiate a decertification process. Federal employees can unionize and bargain for nonwage items. The Civil Service Reform Act of 1978 set up the Federal Labor Relations Authority as the oversight agency for the federal employee labor/management issues.

With the decline in union membership, unions have sought new ways to reach out to prospective members. These new approaches range from being open to variable-pay rather than fixed-pay plans; offering members more benefits, such as union

credit cards; developing stronger ties with public officials and political candidates who are pro-union; and consolidating and merging to pool union resources. New forms of employee organizations have developed as well. These can be in the form of affinity groups and community networks designed to provide support and resources for employees not protected by unions to ensure that they have a voice in the workplace.

Globally, union membership is declining. The UN's Universal Declaration of Human Rights and other conventions issued by the International Labour Organization define the rights of workers relative to forming and joining trade unions, but not all countries follow these conventions.

## KEY TERMS

agency shop

arbitration

bad faith bargaining

bargaining unit

card check

Civil Service Reform Act

closed shop

collective bargaining

conciliation

corporate campaign

craft union

decertification

distributive bargaining strategy

Excelsior list

Federal Labor Relations Authority (FLRA)

good faith bargaining

grievance

grievance process

impasse

industrial union

integrative bargaining strategy

interest-based bargaining

international union

Landrum-Griffin Act (Labor-Management Reporting and Disclosure Act)

mandatory bargaining topics

mediation

national emergency strike

National Labor Relations Board (NLRB)

neutrality agreement

Norris-LaGuardia Act

permissive topics

protected concerted activity

Railway Labor Act (RLA)

right-to-work laws

Taft-Hartley Act (Labor Management Relations Act)

unfair labor practices (ULPs)

union authorization card

union shop

union steward

Wagner Act (National Labor Relations Act)

## DISCUSSION QUESTIONS

1. Labor unions were much more powerful and larger during the Industrial Revolution than they are today. Why were unions so strong during the Industrial Revolution? What type of issues would they need to address to become more relevant today?

2. What are the major provisions of each of the three components of the National Labor Relations Act. Why are there three components? How relevant is this Act today? On what is your response based?

3. Prepare a short presentation for employers describing actions that constitute unfair labor practices during a unionization campaign.

4. Go to the website for the Change to Win labor federation (www.changetowin. org) and identify the affiliated unions. Choose one of the affiliates and research its purpose, history, and current membership. Identify how many local unions belong to the affiliated union you selected.

5. What can you, as a manager, legally do to prevent employees from unionizing?

6. If you were asked, as a manager, to provide input for the purposes of a collective bargaining process, what type of information would you provide?

7. One of your employees has come to you with a written statement indicating that her compensation is not fair. The employee is a member of the recognized union in your company. Describe how you would handle this complaint.

## LEARNING EXERCISE 1

Visit the website for two country-specific union federations. Prepare a table that compares and contrasts the foci of the two federations. Answer the following questions about each as you prepare your table.

1. What year was the federation started?
2. How many members does it represent?
3. Who is eligible to join the federation?
4. What is the focus of the federation?
5. What benefits are promised to members?
6. Do workers join local unions or just the national union?
7. Summarize what you learned. Include a reference list for sources of information.

## LEARNING EXERCISE 2

To learn more about the benefits of union membership, identify and interview someone who is a member of a union. In your interview, address at least the following questions.

1. How long have you been a member of the union?
2. Why did you join the union?
3. How has being a union member affected your job, including what you are required to do and your promotion opportunities?
4. What has been the biggest advantage to you as a union member?
5. Would you advise other workers to join the union? Why or why not?

## CASE STUDY 1: AVOIDING A UNION EFFORT AT TECHNOLOGIES ESSENTIAL

Jeannine Marquez has just become the CEO of Technologies Essential. The company is a 15-year-old, midsize computer software company headquartered in Columbia, Missouri. The company specializes in providing products that enable users to more fully implement SAP solutions. Most of the 569 employees are software developers. These employees are well paid and receive tuition reimbursement and excellent health and retirement benefits. The company rewards these employees well, as they are seen as the key to the company's success.

The software developers seem content with the company but the support staff are not. They believe that they are overworked and underpaid relative to the software developers. They receive less vacation and personal leave time, are required to take compensatory time off rather than receive overtime pay when they work more than 40 hours per week, and none of them make over $42,000 a year, even though many of them have worked for the company since it started and have supervisory responsibilities.

The CEO has just received a letter signed by 25 employees indicating they wish to join the Office and Professional Employees International Union (OPEIU). The letter

listed a number of grievances, including concerns about work schedules, concerns that other employees who had expressed an interest in joining a union were fired by the former CEO, and dissatisfaction with pay and benefits.

### Discussion Questions

1. Describe the steps that employees at Technologies Essential should take if they want to unionize.
2. Research the OPEIU. What would be the advantages to these employees if they did join this union? What would be the disadvantages?
3. If employees have been fired for unionizing, do they have any recourse?
4. What advice can you provide to Jeannine Marquez about how to address the concerns of these employees? Are there legal issues regarding unionization about which she needs to be aware as she begins to address the concerns? If so, what are they?
5. What is the best advice you can give managers to ensure they are not likely to face an effort by employees to unionize?

## CASE STUDY 2: NOT SO GRAND EMPLOYEE MORALE AT THE GRAND LIMITED HOTEL

For years, the Grand Limited has been known as the hotel to work for in the metropolitan area where it is located. The hotel has even received a number of awards for being a best place to work and for its family-friendly policies. It is not uncommon for workers to have been with the hotel for 25 years.

Now, the hotel is faced with new management and numerous retirements among its 500 employees. With a downturn in the economy, the new management of the hotel has decided to offer a lower wage structure and fewer benefits for new employees than it has offered in the past. The hotel is still paying the market rate for jobs similar to others in the area, and so far, it has been able to attract new employees. Unfortunately, the hotel managers have failed to take into consideration that many of the local hotels are unionized. There are rumblings that the newer employees are considering asking the local service industry union to represent them to bargain for better wages and benefits, as well as better working conditions. The newer employees are feeling disenfranchised and have little loyalty to the hotel. They believe they are not being treated equitably with the employees who have been around for a long time, As you can imagine, these issues are starting to spill over into the level of customer service provided to guests of the hotel.

You have been asked to serve as a consultant for the hotel to address these labor issues. A goal of management in bringing you in is to stop the employees from having a vote to be represented by a union.

### Discussion Questions

1. As the consultant, take a stand either for or against what management has done to date. Review the facts of the case and use those facts to support your argument. State any assumptions that you are using.
2. Describe what you would do to assist management in blocking the union. Be sure to address legal issues inherent in attempting to block a union effort.
3. Can you identify any value that could actually come from having the employees represented by a union?
4. Make a final recommendation to management about how to proceed in handling this situation.

## NOTES

1 Elias Lieberman, *Unions Before the Bar: Historic Trials Showing the Evolution of Labor Rights in the United States* (New York: Harper Press, 1950).

2 Joe Twarog, "The Benefits of Union Membership: Numerous and Measurable," *Massachusetts Nurse* 76 (2005): 9; and Dale Belman and Paula Voos, "Union Wages and Union Decline: Evidence from the Construction Industry," *Industrial & Labor Relations Review* 60 (2006): 67–87.

3 Lloyd Reynolds, *Labor Economics and Labor Relations* (Englewood Cliffs, NJ: Prentice Hall, 1978).

4 Ibid.

5 Ibid.

6 Ibid.

7 Dave Jamieson, "Union Membership Rate for U.S. Workers Tumbles to New Low," *Huff Post Politics*, last modified January 23, 2013, http://www.huffingtonpost.com/2013/01/23/union-membership-rate_n_2535063.html.

8 John Judis, "Labor's Love Lost," *New Republic* 224 (2001): 18–22.

9 Robert Grossman, "Unions Follow Suit," *HR Magazine* 50 (2005): 46–51; George Long, "Differences Between Union and Nonunion Compensation, 2001–2011," *Monthly Labor Review*, April 2013, 16–23; and Tami Luhby, "Want a Raise? Join a Union," *CNN Business*, February 24, 2015, http://money.cnn.com/2015/02/24/news/economy/union-wages/; "Union Members—2017," Union Members Summary, Economic News Release, Bureau of Labor Statistics, January 29, 2018, https://www.bls.gov/news.release/union2.nr0.htm.

10 Frank Dooley and William Thoms, *Airline Labor Law: The Railway Labor Act and Aviation After Deregulation* (Westport, CT: Quorum Books, 1990).

11 Reynolds, *Labor Economics and Labor Relations*.

12 Lieberman, *Unions Before the Bar*.

13 "The Wagner Act," Digital History ID 3445, http://www.digitalhistory.uh.edu/disp_textbook.cfm?smtID=2&psid=3445.

14 "National Labor Relations Act," National Labor Relations Board, http://www.nlrb.gov/about_us/overview/national_labor_relations_act.aspx.

15 "Employee Rights," National Labor Relations Board, http://www.nlrb.gov/rights-we-protect/employee-rights.

16 "Protected Concerted Activity," National Labor Relations Board, http://www.nlrb.gov/rights-we-protect/protected-concerted-activity; and "Employee Rights," National Labor Relations Board, http://www.nlrb.gov/rights-we-protect/employee-rights.

17 "Employer/Union Rights and Obligations," National Labor Relations Board, http://www.nlrb.gov/rights-we-protect/employerunion-rights-and-obligations.

18 "National Labor Relations Act," National Labor Relations Board, http://www.nlrb.gov/resources/national-labor-relations-act.

19 Edwin Beal, Edward Wickersham, and Philip Kienast, *The Practice of Collective Bargaining* (Homewood, IL: Richard D. Irwin, 1976).

20 "What We Do," National Labor Relations Board, http://www.nlrb.gov/what-we-do.

21 "The Board," National Labor Relations Board, http://www.nlrb.gov/who-we-are/board.

22 "The General Counsel," National Labor Relations Board, http://www.nlrb.gov/who-we-are/general-counsel.

23 Fred Hartley, Jr., *Our New National Labor Policy: The Taft-Hartley Act and the Next Steps* (New York: Funk & Wagnalls, 1948).

24 Ibid.

25 Beal et al., *The Practice of Collective Bargaining*.

26 "Right to Work States: Do You Work in a Right to Work State?" National Right to Work Legal Defense Foundation, Inc., http://www.nrtw.org/rtws.htm.

27 Eli Watkins, "Unions Notch Win in Deep-Red Missouri with Rejection of Right-To-Work Laws," *CNN Politics*, August 8, 2018, https://www.cnn.com/2018/08/07/politics/missouri-right-to-work-vote/index.html; Noam Scheiber, "Missouri Voters Reject Anti-Union Law in a Victory for Labor," *The New York Times*, August 7, 2018, https://www.nytimes.com/2018/08/07/business/economy/missouri-labor-right-to-work.html.

28 Ibid.

29 Beal et al., *The Practice of Collective Bargaining*.

30 Rossie Alston and Glenn Taubman, "Union Discipline and Employee Rights," National Right to Work Legal Defense Foundation, Inc., http://www.nrtw.org/RDA.htm; and "About

Your Legal Rights: Private Sector Employees," National Right to Work Legal Defense Foundation, Inc., http://www.nrtw.org/about-your-legal-rights-private-sector-employee.

[31] Beal et al., *The Practice of Collective Bargaining*.

[32] Jess Bravin, "Supreme Court Deals Blow to Public-Sector Unions," *Wall Street Journal*, updated June 27, 2018, https://www.wsj.com/articles/supreme-court-deals-blow-to-public-sector-unions-1530108179.

[33] Ibid.

[34] "Federal Mediation and Conciliation Service: Role and Function of the FMCS," January 2018, https://www.fmcs.gov/wp-content/uploads/ 2018/01/FMCS_role_and_function_2017-1.pdf.

[35] Beal et al., *The Practice of Collective Bargaining*; and "The LMRDA and the Union Members' Bill of Rights," Association for Union Democracy, http://www.uniondemocracy.com/pdfs/rights.PDF.

[36] "The IUOE," International Union of Operating Engineers, Local No. 9, last modified June 7, 2012, http://www.iuoelocal9.com/about_us.html.

[37] "Industrial Unions and Departments," Industrial Workers of the World, http://www.iww.org/en/unions.

[38] "Service Employees International Union," https://www.seiu.org/about.

[39] "About Us," AFL-CIO, http://www.aflcio.org/ about.

[40] "State Federations and Central Labor Councils," AFL-CIO, https://aflcio.org/about-us/our-unions-and-allies/state-federations-and-central-labor-councils.

[41] Thomas Edsall, "Two Top Unions Split from AFL-CIO," *Washington Post*, July 26, 2005, A01

[42] Marick Masters, Ray Gibney, and Thomas Zagenczyk, "The AFL-CIO v. CTW: The Competing Visions, Strategies, and Structures," *Journal of Labor Research* 27 (2006): 473–504.

[43] "Our Mission," Change to Win Strategic Organizing Center, http://www.changetowin.org/about.

[44] Jarol Manheim, *Trends in Union Corporate Campaigns: A Briefing Book* (Washington, DC: U.S. Chamber of Commerce, 2005); "Representation Petitions—RC," National Labor Relations Board, https://www.nlrb.gov/news-outreach/graphs-data/petitions-and-elections/representation-petitions-rc.

[45] "Conduct Elections," National Labor Relations Board, http://www.nlrb.gov/what-we-do/conduct-elections.

[46] Ibid.

[47] *The George Washington University and Service Employees International Union, Local 500*, Case 5-CA-32568.

[48] Gerald Mayer, "Labor Union Recognition Procedures: Use of Secret Ballots and Card Checks," Congressional Research Service Report for Congress, last modified April 2, 2007, assets.opencrs.com/rpts/RL32930_20070402.pdf.

[49] "Conduct Elections."

[50] Ibid.; Adrienne Eaton and Jill Kriesky, *Organizing Experiences Under Union-Management Neutrality and Card Check Agreements*, Report to the Institute for the Study of Labor Organizations, George Meany Center for Labor Studies, February 1999.

[51] Adrienne Eaton and Jill Kriesky, "Union Organizing Under Neutrality and Card Check Agreements," *Industrial and Labor Relations Review* 55 (2001): 42–59.

[52] Patrice Gelinas, "Flexibility Framework for Compensation and Job Security Negotiations," *Compensation & Benefits Review* 38 (2006): 24–29.

[53] Susan Woodhouse, ed., *The National Employer* (Atlanta: Littler Mendelson, 2006).

[54] Steven Thomas and Barry Wisdom, "Labor Negotiations in the Nineties: Five Steps Toward Total Preparation," *SAM Advanced Management Journal* 58 (1993): 32–37.

[55] Robert Walton and Richard McKersie, *A Behavioral Theory of Labor Negotiations* (New York: McGraw-Hill, 1965); "Module 5: Employee and Labor Relations," in *The SHRM Learning System* (Alexandria, VA: SHRM, 2007).

[56] "Module 5: Employee and Labor Relations."

[57] Woodhouse, *The National Employer*.

[58] Ronald Seeber and David Lipsky, "The Ascendancy of Employment Arbitrators in US Employment Relations: A New Actor in the American System?" *British Journal of Industrial Relations* 44 (2006): 719–756.

[59] "Module 5: Employee and Labor Relations."

[60] Ibid.

[61] "Investigate Charges," National Labor Relations Board, http://www.nlrb.gov/what-we-do/investigate-charges.

62 "Decertification Petitions—RD," National Labor Relations Board, https://www.nlrb.gov/news-outreach/graphs-data/petitions-and-elections/decertification-petitions-rd.

63 Manheim, *Trends in Union Corporate Campaigns*.

64 Ibid.

65 Karen Bentham, "Employer Resistance to Union Certification: A Study of Eight Canadian Jurisdictions," *Industrial Relations* 57 (2002): 159–185.

66 "About NEA," National Education Association, http://www.nea.org/home/2580.htm .

67 Hoyt Wheeler, *The Future of the American Labor Movement* (Cambridge, UK: Cambridge University Press, 2002).

68 Sean Karimi and Gangaram Singh, "Strategic Compensation: An Opportunity for Union Activism," *Compensation & Benefits Review* 36 (2004): 62–67.

69 "The NLRB and Social Media," National Labor Relations Board, http://www.nlrb.gov/news-outreach/fact-sheets/nlrb-and-social-medi.

70 Ibid.

71 Ibid.

72 Paul Osterman, "Community Organizing and Employee Representation," *British Journal of Industrial Relations* 44 (2006): 629–649; and *Rethinking Union Structures, Rebuilding Union Capacity*," *Futurework: Trends and Challenges for Work in the 21st Century,* Office of the Secretary, U.S. Department of Labor, http://www.dol.gov/dol/aboutdol/history/herman/reports/futurework/conference/relations/structures.htm.

73 "Who We Are," Industrial Areas Foundation, industrialareasfoundation.org.

74 Woodhouse, *The National Employer*.

75 "Trade Unions: Trade Union Density," OECD Employment and Labour Market Statistics (database), 2016, https://doi.org/10.1787/fbf99961-en.

76 Steve Schifferes, "The Trade Unions' Long Decline," *BBC News*, last modified March 8, 2004, http://news.bbc.co.uk/2/hi/business/3526917.stm.

77 Paul Williams and Alex Bryson, "Union Organization in Great Britain," *Journal of Labor Research* 28 (2007): 93–115.

78 David Fairris, "Union Voice Effects in Mexico," *British Journal of Industrial Relations* 44 (2006): 781–800.

79 Justino De La Cruz, "Mexico's Labor Law and Labor Unions in the 1990s," *Memento Economico* 124 (2002): 26–39.

80 Han Dongfang, "Labor Law Strengthens Chinese Union," *Asia Times*, last modified January 18, 2008, http://www.atimes.com/atimes/China_Business/JA18Cb01.html; Rebecca McCray, "China's Growing Labor Movement Threatens Beijing," *takepart*, March 16, 2016, http://www.takepart.com/article/2016/03/16/chinese-workers-labor-unions; Cherie Chan, "Labor Rights Movements Gaining Momentum in China," *DW,* May 1, 2016, https://www.dw.com/en/labor-rights-movements-gaining-momentum-in-china/18959557.

81 "Organisation and People," European Trade Union Confederation, etuc.org, https://www.etuc.org/en/organisation-and-people.

82 "The International Trade Union Confederation (ITUC) Is the Global Voice of the World's Working People," International Trade Union Confederation, https://www.ituc-csi.org/about-us.

# Chapter 14

# Creating High-Performing HR Systems

## Learning Objectives

**AFTER READING THIS CHAPTER, YOU SHOULD BE ABLE TO:**

1 Explain the principle of external fit.

2 Explain the principle of internal fit.

3 Explain how HR systems can be aligned with the contributions employees make.

4 Discuss how to manage an employment portfolio.

5 Explain what strategic performance drivers and HR deliverables are.

6 Evaluate the external alignment of your HR system.

7 Evaluate the internal alignment of your HR system.

8 Create a plan to change your HR system to make it more effective.

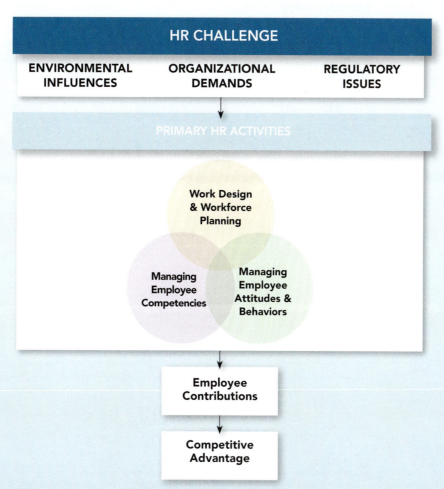

**HR CHALLENGE**

| ENVIRONMENTAL INFLUENCES | ORGANIZATIONAL DEMANDS | REGULATORY ISSUES |

**PRIMARY HR ACTIVITIES**

Work Design & Workforce Planning

Managing Employee Competencies

Managing Employee Attitudes & Behaviors

Employee Contributions

Competitive Advantage

In the beginning of Chapter 2, we introduced three axioms for effectively managing employees:

1. No two companies are the same.
2. There is no one best way to manage employees.
3. Using the wrong practice, or using the right practice poorly, can cause more harm than good.

After reading the previous chapters, you should have a pretty good idea about why these axioms are so important. As Axiom 1 states, each company is unique. Companies may compete for similar customers, offer similar products, and even have similar technologies. However, their cultures, sizes, stages of development, workforce compositions, and the like are unique. In addition, companies often face similar environmental challenges and regulatory issues. The relative impact they have on each company is different. By now, you are well familiar with Exhibit 14.1 which shows how these HR challenges influence the management of employees.

Axiom 2 highlights the fact that when managing employees, you can select from a wide array of HR activities. Consider how you select an employee. You may use interviews, personality tests, physical ability tests, or a number of other options. The best choice, however, depends on a number of factors—first, how the company is set up and how it competes in its market (see Axiom 1), and second, how the firm internally aligns itself. These factors, in turn, are directly affected by the HR challenges that you, as a manager, face. In other words, as a manager, you need to understand how and when to use the different HR practices.

**EXHIBIT 14.1**

Framework for the Strategic Management of Employees

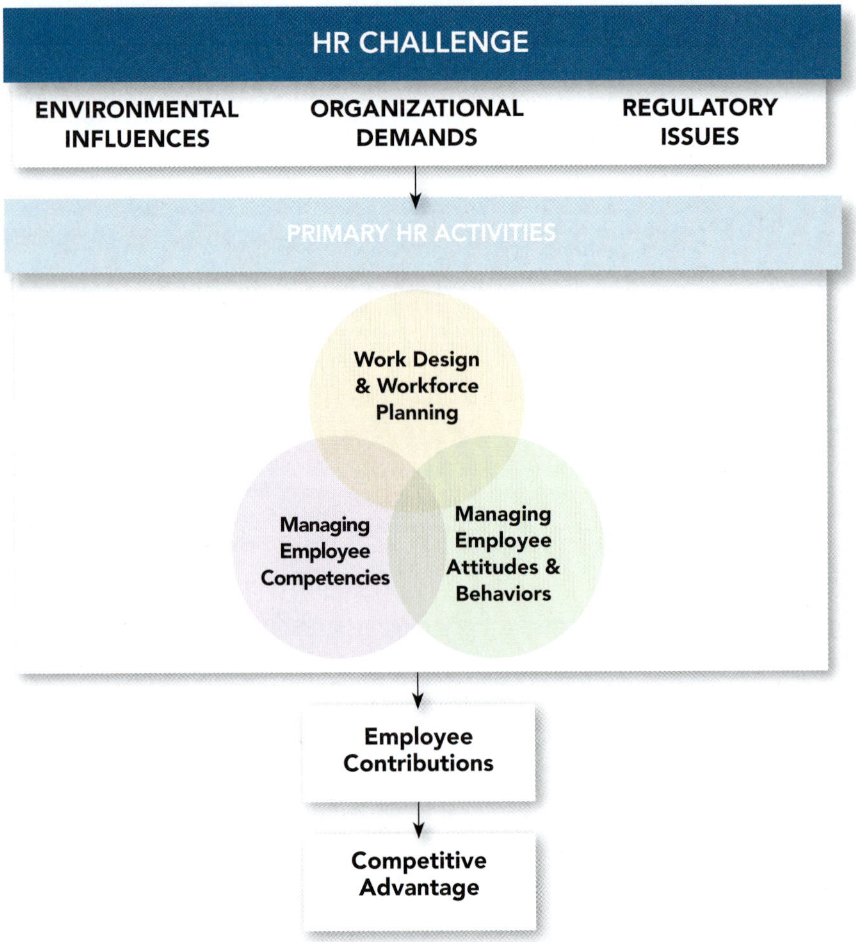

Axiom 3 shifts our focus to issues of design and implementation: A firm will experience problems if it designs and uses the wrong HR practices to manage its employees. Sometimes managers choose the wrong practices because they don't know enough about the tools they have at their disposal. Even if a firm chooses the right practices, how those practices are implemented can be problematic. For example, a team-based incentive-pay plan might work well with project teams, but it is not likely to be as effective in a company in which employees work independently.

Although there is no single best system with which to manage your employees, several fundamental principles can help guide your decisions and, in turn, determine whether your firm will have a high-performing HR system or a less effective system. In the next section, we focus on the key principles of high-performing HR systems.

# Principles of High-Performing HR Systems

In Chapter 1, we defined HR system alignment as a situation in which a firm's primary HR activities reinforce one another and support organizational goals. When they do, a firm's employees have the skills they need and exhibit the right attitudes and behaviors. The firm is also able to manage and allocate its work to make sure the right people are doing the right things when they need to be done.[1] As we discussed, there are really two forms of alignment to consider. External alignment refers to ensuring that the design of the three primary HR activities takes into account the HR challenges that companies face. In other words, managers must select HR activities that help their companies meet their organizational demands, cope with environmental factors, and comply with regulatory issues. The second form of alignment, internal alignment, focuses on ensuring that specific practices within each HR activity are consistent with one another and aligned across the primary HR activities. Next, we discuss both of these aspects in more detail.

## External Fit: Aligning HR Activities with HR Challenges

Throughout this book, we have emphasized the importance of choosing employee management practices in light of a number of challenges that managers face. We have focused on three sets of challenges: organizational demands, environmental influences, and regulatory issues. The key point of these influences is the importance of external fit. *External fit* refers to the alignment between the three primary HR activities and the HR challenges.

Each of the challenges affects which practices are used within companies, as well as the effectiveness of those practices. For example, a company's strategy influences how its jobs are designed, which workforce planning tactics are most appropriate for it to use, the recruitment and selection practices it chooses, the types of training and development it needs, and the performance evaluation methods it uses. Also affected by the firm's strategy are how the company compensates employees in different jobs, the incentive plans it chooses, and the decisions it makes about the benefits and safety and wellness plans it designs and offers. Companies that emphasize customer service, such as Nordstrom and Macy's, rely on different practices to manage their employees than companies that place greater emphasis on competing on the basis of costs, such as Dollar Tree, and Family Dollar.

At the same time, the other HR challenges, such as company characteristics, labor force trends, ethics, and regulatory issues, influence these same practices, albeit in potentially different ways. Some challenges affect which HR practices a firm needs in order to cope with changes in the environment. For example, the increasing diversity of the labor force affects how employees react to the use of different employee management practices. Similarly, the growing need for ethical and social responsibility on the part of firms affects which practices people and communities view as socially acceptable. Other challenges affect how employee management practices are carried out. Laws and regulations affect the wages employees must be paid, the types of interview questions prospective candidates can be asked, what companies must do to ensure that their workplaces and employees are safe, and the like.

Some of these challenges present opportunities for how to manage employees; others constrain which options a company is able to choose; still other challenges affect how a firm's HR practices will affect the company's ability to meet its goals. Adopting practices that facilitate the management of employees in light of these challenges is the first step toward designing an effective system for managing employees.

## Internal Fit: Aligning HR Activities with One Another

Throughout this text we have covered a lot of material regarding HR activities and the practices that comprise those activities. And, although we have focused on the primary practices individually in each chapter, the reality is that HR practices are rarely, if ever, used in isolation from one another. Rather, employees are exposed to multiple practices simultaneously, and the impact of one depends on the impact of the others.[2] For every job that exists within an organization, decisions are made regarding how the job should be designed or whether the job should be staffed by a full-time employee or through the use of contingent labor. Who occupies the job, as well as the person's knowledge, skills, and abilities, is a result of decisions managers made regarding the recruitment and selection process, as well as training and development activities. Decisions about the performance management process, how much to compensate employees, what types of incentive plans to implement, and which benefit programs to offer also have to be made to encourage the right attitudes and behaviors.

Although these might seem to be independent decisions, each decision influences other choices companies make about managing employees, as well as the effectiveness of those choices. To achieve internal alignment, you must first make sure that the specific practices used *within* each HR activity are consistent with one another. To be able to effectively manage employee competencies, it is important to ensure that the recruitment, selection, and training practices you use are reinforcing rather than conflicting with one another. For example, a state-of-the-art selection test will be useless if the firm's recruitment process fails to generate qualified candidates for a job. In turn, the quality of a firm's recruitment and selection procedures will affect the types of training programs employees need.

Beyond alignment among the practices within each primary HR activity, there must also be alignment *across* the primary HR activities. Each of the three activities described is critical; however, none is effective in isolation. As Exhibit 14.2 shows, work design and workforce planning; identifying, acquiring, building, and retaining employee competencies; and encouraging the right employee attitudes and behaviors must align with each other if they are to be effective.[3] A very low selection standard limits the job design options and affects how employees should be evaluated and rewarded. Similarly, if a company hires truly outstanding employees but then uses a forced-ranking performance evaluation method, the firm's managers might be forced to make arbitrary distinctions among employees that don't accurately reflect their performance. As a result, lower employee satisfaction and increased turnover could occur.

The degree of internal alignment determines whether companies realize synergies among their HR practices. Synergies occur when the combined use of specific HR practices is more powerful than the sum of their individual effects.[4] When we talk about synergies among HR practices, however, it is important to recognize that

**EXHIBIT 14.2**

Aligning a Firm's Internal HR Practices

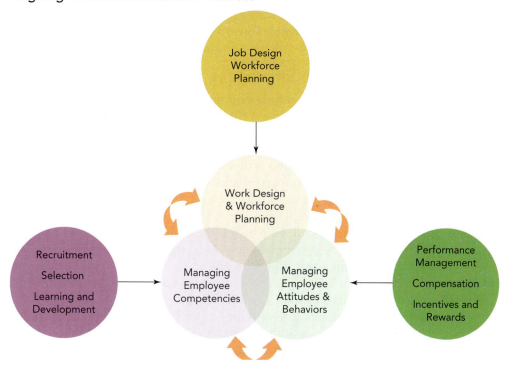

there can be positive synergies as well as negative synergies.[5] Deadly combinations and powerful connections are two ways to categorize what can happen with various configurations of employee management practices.

## Deadly Combinations

**Deadly combinations** occur when managers rely on HR practices that seem appropriate, but present problems when combined with other HR practices to manage employees.[6] There is a long list of deadly combinations that may potentially exist among the HR practices used to manage employees. The following are some situations that may potentially elicit deadly combinations[7]:

- If employees are motivated to work toward important goals, but do not possess all the competencies to do so, the results will be diminished employee performance and reduced organizational productivity.
- If employees possess the skills they need but lack sufficient motivation, their contributions to the company's success will be limited.
- If employees are capable and motivated but are limited in what they can do or are shorthanded due to poor job design or poor workforce planning, their ability to contribute to the organization will be limited.

## Powerful Connections

**Powerful connections** occur when HR practices are used in combinations that support and reinforce other practices that are in place.[8] For example, the use of a commission-based incentive system will reinforce the use of a performance management system that evaluates employees based on their sales levels. Using either one of these practices alone—the commission-based incentive system or the performance management system that evaluates employee sales—might encourage employees to achieve high sales levels. However, using the two practices together reinforces the importance of this objective for employees and is likely to be more

**deadly combinations**

occur when managers rely on HR practices that seem appropriate, but present problems when combined with other HR practices to manage employees

**powerful connections**

occur when HR practices are used in combinations that support and reinforce other practices that are in place

effective than either practice alone. Facebook, for instance, engages in extensive recruitment and selection activities to ensure that it has great talent within the organization. Once on board, employees are exposed to a fun work environment that is conducive to creativity and they are rewarded with attractive compensation and rewards to work as hard as possible toward the company's goals.[9]

## Aligning HR Systems with Employees' Contributions

As noted in Chapter 2, a company has a competitive advantage when it is able to create more economic value than its competitors. This outcome is achieved by providing greater value to customers relative to the costs of making a product or providing a service.[10] A competitive advantage can stem from a variety of sources. For example, it can result from holding protected assets, having extensive financial resources, maintaining state-of-the-art manufacturing technologies, providing excellent customer service or great product quality, or some other feature that separates a company from its competitors.

An effective management system helps align the contributions employees make so as to give the firm a competitive advantage. To do so, however, you need to have a clear understanding of how your employees add value in your particular company. Employees add value to their firms in different ways. Consider a firm that pursues a cost leadership strategy, for example. Cost advantages relative to competitors may stem from efficiency manufacturing, low-skilled labor, or very efficient highly skilled labor. The implications for how to manage employees may vary, depending on the source of the competitive advantage to realize cost leadership. Suppose a firm has three groups of employees: production workers, customer service representatives, and research and development employees. The value that production workers add relates to their individual and collective contributions toward achieving manufacturing efficiency for their firm. The research and development employees contribute to their firm by improving the technological superiority of the company's production process and product designs. Finally, the customer service representatives add value by maximizing the satisfaction of the firm's customers.

Although a cost leadership strategy might be the overarching focus of the company, because the firm's different employees contribute to that advantage in various ways, managing them all effectively is critical to achieving the competitive advantage. An effectively managed research and development group alone cannot lead to the achievement of company goals any more than an effectively managed group of production employees alone can lead to success. This approach also has implications for the design of HR systems to maximize employee contributions. As Exhibit 14.3 shows, the HR system you use to manage different groups of employees must reflect how they add value to your company.

Notice in Exhibit 14.3 that we have three groups of employees in a company. Because each group adds value in different ways, the HR system that maximizes their contributions must vary as well. To be most effective, the HR system needs to have a target or an objective (employee contributions); otherwise, employees will be left with no direction for how to focus their efforts. This target should reflect employees' contributions to the source of competitive advantage.

Indeed, research has shown that HR systems targeted toward certain company objectives are more effective than others. One study, for example, focused on how to design HR systems to improve employee safety. The study found that a system that included selective hiring and extensive training (managing competencies), contingent compensation (managing behaviors), and employment security, information sharing, high-quality work, teams, and decentralized decision-making (work design and workforce planning) was associated with a positive safety climate, improved safety orientation, and lower injury incidences.[11] Likewise, research has shown that HR

**EXHIBIT 14.3**

Aligning HR Systems with Employees' Contributions

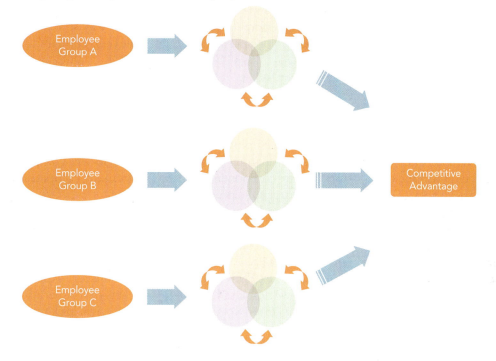

systems can be designed to encourage employees to provide high levels of customer service. In firms where customer service is paramount, the HR system should be designed both to provide employees with the skills and resources to be successful and to provide them with the discretion they need to meet their customers' demands immediately and reward workers for doing so.[12] One of the key strategic goals of Trader Joe's is to create an outstanding shopping experience for customers. One way the company accomplishes this is through its hiring and evaluation practices. Trader Joe's recruits, hires, and promotes people who love food and have fun, engaging personalities. Once on the job, employees are frequently evaluated based on customer-oriented metrics such as friendliness, helpfulness, and promotion of high team morale.[13]

As these sample HR systems point out, HR systems may be designed to target a variety of employee contributions, such as safety, customer service, productivity, creativity, quality, and the like. The key point is that to realize its intended impact, a system must align the three primary HR activities with employee contributions.

## Managing the Employment Portfolio

Up to this point, we have highlighted three key components of effective HR systems and how managers should go about aligning them. First, managers must take into account the HR challenges that exist within and outside companies. Second, effective managers strive for synergy among the three primary HR activities. Finally, effective managers target the employee management systems to maximize employee contributions to company success.

Beyond these three factors, however, managers have to consider the fact that different types of HR systems involve different types of costs and benefits. For example, training programs to develop employees' skills involve the costs related to the instruction, the lost labor productivity during the training, and the like. Although your firm might be able to make these investments, the question is whether it should. There are certainly financial considerations, but these decisions also reflect strategic considerations for the potential benefits that stem from those investments. From a strategic point of view, the key question is whether the investments in HR systems and the resulting employee competencies and motivation will actually help your company realize and sustain a competitive advantage. One way to make this determination is by taking a *portfolio perspective* of your employees' contributions. This perspective involves considering two factors: the strategic value and the uniqueness of the contributions they make.

## Strategic Value

**strategic value**

the extent to which the contributions of employees help their organization achieve a competitive advantage

**Strategic value** refers to the fact that employees contribute different things to their firms. The question is: How much do their contributions add to the company's success? Are the contributions a key component of how the company competes, or are they more peripheral to the company's competitiveness?[14]

As Exhibit 14.4 shows, the strategic value employees contribute to a firm affects a whole host of choices managers make, including whether to retain employees internally or turn to external sources, such as outsourced or contingent labor. In Chapter 5, we defined *outsourcing* as the practice of sending work to other companies. Increasingly, companies are realizing that it is prohibitively expensive, and not realistic, for a firm to be a world-class leader in all aspects of its operations. Because external service providers often focus on a single service and provide their services to many different companies, they are often able to attain greater efficiency in the performance of those tasks than a company could realize if it maintained the services in-house. By outsourcing tasks that are not strategically valuable, companies may be able to focus their efforts on activities that serve as a source for their competitive advantage.[15] For example, before its merger with Alaska Airlines in December 2016, Virgin America Inc. had the highest revenue per employee metric in the airline industry. This high efficiency outcome was the result of the company outsourcing jobs such as baggage delivery, reservations, catering, heavy maintenance, and more. Pfizer, a pharmaceutical company, provides another example of outsourcing. Pfizer outsources the majority of its clinical drug trials.[16] On the other hand, some companies have outsourced a large percentage of work and then realized that the company would be better served bringing the work back in-house. Target is one such company. About 70% of its information technology jobs were outsourced at one point, but by 2015, 70% of those jobs were being done by Target employees.[17]

Beyond outsourcing, companies may also turn to contingent labor—employees who are hired on a temporary or contractual basis, as opposed to being hired on a full-time or permanent basis—to perform certain tasks and responsibilities.[18] Trucking company Schneider National Inc.'s logistic operation subcontracts work to temporary staffing agencies and then those workers handle unloading shipping containers at Walmart warehouses.[19] Similar to outsourcing, relying on contingent labor and other forms of alternative labor is a way to achieve cost savings and strategic focus. According to a Bureau of Labor Statistics (BLS) survey, in May 2017,

**EXHIBIT 14.4**

### Strategic Value of Employee Contributions

| External Employment | → | Internal Employment |
|---|---|---|
| Low Strategic Value | | High Strategic Value |

## EXHIBIT 14.5

### Contingent and Alternative Employment Arrangements—May 2017

| Type of Employment Arrangement | Number of Workers | Percent of Total Employment |
|---|---|---|
| Contingent workers | 5.9 million | 3.8% |
| Alternative work arrangements | | |
| • Independent contractors | 10.6 million | 6.9% |
| • On-call workers | 2.6 million | 1.7% |
| • Temporary help agency workers | 1.4 million | 0.9% |
| • Contract firms | 933,000 | 0.6% |

*Source:* "Contingent and Alternative Employment Arrangements—May 2017," Economic News Release, Bureau of Labor Statistics, U.S. Department of Labor, bls.gov, June 7, 2018, https://www.bls.gov/news.release/conempl.nr0.htm.

contingent workers made up between 1.3% and 3.8% of total workers. The last time the same survey was conducted was in 2005. In February of that year, the percentages of contingent workers were actually higher, with a range of 1.8% to 4.1%. The range represents three different measures of contingent workers. All three measures include persons who do not expect that their jobs will last or who report that their jobs are temporary. Exhibit 14.5 provides additional data about contingent workers and alternative employment arrangements for May 2017.[20] A survey by the Aberdeen Group found that the top two benefits from using contract labor are the flexibility it gives a firm to quickly adjust its workforce (70% of respondents) and the ability it gives a firm to quickly hire workers with specialized skills (66% of respondents).[21]

When considering strategic value, the question is whether your company needs to have full-time employees perform certain tasks internally, or whether some external provider of these services could perform them more effectively or more efficiently. When employee contributions have a greater potential strategic impact, their companies are encouraged to make sure these positions are nurtured in-house so as to leverage their potential.[22] Given the importance of these positions, companies are often reluctant to outsource them or turn to contingent workers.[23] In contrast, as the strategic value of an employee's contributions decreases, the potential return from his or her contributions relative to the costs of maintaining the full-time employee internally diminishes. This is when it makes sense to turn to external sources.

Of course, the strategic value employees contribute to their firms varies across companies. Different strategies emphasize different internal business processes for competitive advantage. By extension, the strategic value of potential employee contributions oriented toward different business processes is likely to vary. For example, a company competing on costs might put a priority on operational efficiency. In a firm such as this, jobs in supply-chain management, logistics, and industrial engineering may be particularly valuable for facilitating efficiencies. IKEA, a global company that offers quality products at low prices, requires a very sophisticated engineering and logistics operation to do so. In contrast, in companies competing on innovation, jobs related to product development, research and development, and external collaboration might be most important. ServiceNow, a cloud-based subscription software-as-a-service (SaaS) provider that was named in 2018 as number one on the Forbes list of most innovative companies, requires a very entrepreneurial group of software engineers to achieve its goals.[24] In companies competing on customer service, jobs related to customer relations and sales and marketing may have priority. As a result, a highly valuable employee group in one company might be less valuable in another company, even when they are performing the same job.[25]

**EXHIBIT 14.6**

Uniqueness of Employee Contributions
and the Employment Relationship

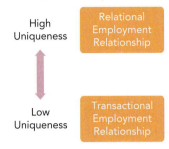

## Uniqueness

**uniqueness**

the extent to which the contributions employees make, and the necessary competencies to realize those contributions, are specialized to a company and not readily available in the open labor market

**Uniqueness** refers to the extent to which the contributions employees make, and the necessary competencies to realize those contributions, are specialized to a company and not readily available in the open labor market.[26] When employees make unique contributions to a company, they can set it apart from its competitors. In these cases, companies are more willing to invest in employees to realize those contributions.[27] In contrast, when the uniqueness of their contributions is based on competencies that are widely available in the labor market, there will be little incentive for a company to invest extensively to develop those skills.[28]

Of course, all employees require some degree of investment. The question that uniqueness raises is what type of investment to make. In general, the type of investment companies make depends on the nature of the relationship they have with their employees. This investment spans a continuum ranging from transactional to relational.

**transactional relationship**

a relationship that tends to focus narrowly on the performance of the necessary tasks, duties, and responsibilities that must be performed during a predetermined time period

**Transactional relationships** are best described as quid pro quo, or "a fair day's work for a fair day's pay."[29] Transactional relationships are economic in nature and focus on both parties meeting the basic terms of the contract they have with one another. These relationships tend to focus narrowly on the performance of the necessary tasks, duties, and responsibilities that must be performed during a predetermined time period. In contrast, **relational relationships** involve a much greater commitment to the individual by the company and vice versa. Relational relationships contain more of an emotional or social component that translates into a higher level of concern the parties have for one another. As Exhibit 14.6 shows, when employees make unique contributions, their companies tend to focus on building relational relationships with them. When they don't, companies tend to maintain transactional relationships with them.[30]

**relational relationship**

a relationship that involves a social or emotional commitment to the individual by the company and vice versa

## Mapping Your Employment Portfolio

It is possible to map the contributions employees make based on the strategic value and uniqueness of their contributions. As we have noted, the strategic value of certain positions influences whether a company will retain those positions internally or turn to external labor sources for them. Uniqueness influences the types of relationship that companies have with different groups of employees. In combination, the potential combinations of these two variables results in four types of employment groups: core employees, job-based employees, contract workers, and alliance/partners. In addition, four different approaches to HR investments emerge to manage each group: commitment-based, productivity-based, compliance-based, and collaborative-based HR systems. These are highlighted in Exhibit 14.7.

**EXHIBIT 14.7**

Diagram of an Employment Portfolio

|  | External Employment | Internal Employment |  |
|---|---|---|---|
| **High** | **Alliance/Partners** HR System: Collaboration | **Core Employees** HR System: Commitment | **Relational Relationship** |
| **Low** | **Contract Workers** HR System: Compliance | **Job-Based Employees** HR System: Productivity | **Transactional Relationship** |

*Uniqueness* (vertical axis)

Low — High (horizontal axis: **Strategic Value**)

### Core Employees

Based on their highly unique and valuable contributions, **core employees** are most likely to contribute directly to a firm's core competencies on the basis of what they know and how they use their knowledge.[31] As a result, these employees tend to be employed internally and treated as core workers in whom companies invest for their long-term success. The HR system used to manage these employees involves practices that support a **commitment-based HR system**. For example, a company may invest extensively in the development of core employees' competencies, empower them to use their competencies in the performance of their jobs, and encourage their full participation in decision-making and discretion on the job. Likewise, a firm might offer long-term incentives (stock ownership, extensive benefits, and so forth) to ensure that its core employees receive continued and useful feedback and adopt a long-term orientation to help the company achieve success.[32]

### Job-Based Employees

In addition to core employees, **job-based employees** also create value for firms. However, because these employees do not contribute in a unique manner, there is likely to be a fairly large number of them in the external labor market. As a result, companies do not have the same level of incentive to extensively invest in job-based employees' long-term development, well-being, and retention as they do for core employees.[33] Rather, managers are more likely to rely on a **productivity-based HR system**—a system that involves standardized jobs and selecting people from the external labor market who can contribute immediately in these jobs.[34] The types of rewards and incentives that are used for employees in positions such as these tend to focus on efficiency and productivity improvements. And, of course, companies are less likely to expend a great deal of money to develop people in these positions. Instead, they are more likely to emphasize a short-term, results-oriented performance management system.[35] Examples of job-based employees would include most retail associates and other service industry workers.

### Contract Workers

When the tasks a firm needs to be done are neither strategically valuable nor unique, the company may turn to **contract workers** to do these tasks.[36] Because of the limited uniqueness in these employees' contributions, external workers are often used to perform these tasks. And with limited strategic value, these

**core employee**
an employee who is most likely to contribute directly to a firm's core competencies

**commitment-based HR system**
an HR system of investing extensively in the development of core employees' competencies, empowering them to use their competencies in the performance of their jobs, and encouraging their full participation in decision making and discretion on the job

**job-based employee**
an employee who creates value for a firm but does not contribute in unique ways, and can be found in large numbers in the external labor market

**productivity-based HR system**
a system that involves standardized jobs and selecting people from the external labor market who can contribute immediately in these jobs, rewards based on efficiency and productivity improvements, and short-term results-oriented performance management systems

**contract worker**
an external employee whose contributions are neither unique nor of high strategic value to the organization

**compliance-based HR system**

a system that focuses on meeting preset rules, regulations, and/or procedures, with an emphasis on short-term productivity and the efficient performance of tasks that are limited in scope, purpose, or duration

employees do not contribute as much as core and job-based employees, and there is usually a good supply of them in the labor market. When managing contract workers, firms tend to emphasize **compliance-based HR systems**—systems that focus on meeting preset rules, regulations, and/or procedures. For example, these systems focus on short-term productivity and the efficient performance of tasks that are limited in scope, purpose, or duration. The job descriptions for positions such as these are likely to be standardized, and the training and performance management for these positions, if conducted, is likely to be limited to ensuring that the company's policies, systems, and procedures are met.[37] In addition, the compensation for employees in these positions is likely to be based on hourly wages and the accomplishment of specific tasks or goals.[38] Recall the example mentioned earlier in this chapter of the trucking company providing contract workers for Walmart warehouses.

### Alliance Partners

**collaborative-based HR system**

an HR system of managing external labor on a long-term basis through alliances or partnerships with a reliance on group incentives, cross-functional teams, and the like

**alliance partner**

an external employee who makes unique contributions but whose contributions are limited in terms of strategic value

The fourth group of employees are those who make unique contributions but whose contributions are limited in terms of strategic value. Because the contributions of these employees are not directly central to a firm's strategy, companies often look externally for these individuals. However, the contributions of these individuals are also unique to a company. To manage this group of employees, companies focus on establishing a **collaborative-based HR system** and turn to external labor on a long-term basis through alliances or partnerships.[39] While companies may be reluctant to invest in these **alliance partners** directly, there is investment in the relationship with these individuals. For example, many companies hire consultants to serve as an external source of knowledge for a particular project. Although some consulting relationships last only a short while, many constitute a partnership such that the external consultant works with internal employees on an ongoing basis. While both alliance partners and contract workers are external to a company, they contribute in different ways, with alliance partners applying their competencies in some unique capacity over a longer time frame. The longer-term relationships help preserve continuity and ensure trust among partners, and they engender reciprocity and collaboration between external individuals and internal employees.[40] Given the need for ongoing exchange, alliance partners are more likely to be managed with group incentives, cross-functional teams, and the like.

Many companies are under pressure to keep their HR costs down. From a strategic perspective, not all forms of employee contributions are equally critical to a company's success. While there are certainly many ways a firm can structure and manage its employment portfolio, adopting an architectural perspective helps managers make decisions regarding the level of investment in various employee groups to align their potential contributions with the long-term success of the company.

The first step is to evaluate the contributions of different employees of your firm, based on their levels of strategic value and uniqueness. This evaluation involves rating each group individually to arrive at a relative scoring for all employee contributions within your company. The second step involves mapping out your employees' contributions. Once you have done this, you will see how different employee groups contribute to your company's success. Exhibits 14.8 and 14.9 provide a hypothetical evaluation of the strategic value and uniqueness of a company's employee contributions. Exhibit 14.8 shows that in this case, customer service and sales add the most value, given this particular firm's strategic priority of providing good customer service. In contrast, the contributions of employees working in the firm's IT, logistics, and finance departments are not key factors for this company.

**EXHIBIT 14.8**

## Constructing an Employment Portfolio: Evaluating the Contributions of Your Employees

Business Strategy: Customer Service_____

Evaluate the extent to which each employee group provides strategic value and is unique.

| | |
|---|---|
| 1 | No value added |
| 5 | Modest level of strategic value |
| 10 | High level of strategic value |
| NA | Not applicable to our firm |

| Employee Group | How Much Value Added? | How Much Uniqueness? |
|---|---|---|
| Manufacturing | NA | NA |
| Research and development (R&D) | NA | NA |
| IT | 2 | 2 |
| Distribution | 8 | 2 |
| Legal | 2 | 7 |
| Marketing | 8 | 5 |
| HR | 5 | 7 |
| Customer service | 10 | 9 |
| Sales | 7 | 7 |
| Finance | 2 | 4 |
| Logistics | 3 | 3 |
| Other: _____ | NA | NA |

**EXHIBIT 14.9**

## Constructing an Employment Portfolio: Ranking Your Employees' Contributions

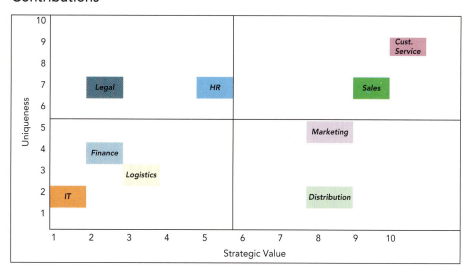

# Evaluating Your HR System: The HR Scorecard

Effectively creating a high-performing HR system involves evaluating the system. Is the HR system in place helping the company achieve its strategic objectives? Although there are a variety of ways to evaluate HR systems, one approach that has gained tremendous popularity is to build an HR scorecard. Pioneered by

Professors Brian Becker, Mark Huselid, and Dave Ulrich, an HR scorecard[41] helps assess the degree to which the links within HR systems and the contributions employees make to their firms actually help them realize a competitive advantage. To create an HR scorecard, you need to take the following steps:

1. Identify your firm's strategic performance drivers.
2. Evaluate your firm's external alignment.
3. Evaluate your firm's internal alignment.

## Step 1: Identify Your Firm's Strategic Performance Drivers

**strategic performance driver**

an activity that enables a company to realize the potential of its source of competitive advantage

Earlier in this chapter, we discussed the fact that a company's competitive advantage can stem from a variety of sources, such as low costs, product quality, customer service, and the like. **Strategic performance drivers** are the activities that enable a company to realize the potential of its source of competitive advantage. Companies pursuing a low-cost leadership strategy, for example, rely on operational excellence and cost controls to attain or maintain their position of cost leadership. Some key strategic performance drivers might be improved operational efficiency, reduced overhead, and increased productivity. Similarly, in a company with an innovation-based differentiation strategy, the key strategic performance drivers might be an increase in patent applications or a greater percentage of sales from new products. A company with a quality-based differentiation strategy might emphasize strategic performance drivers such as reduced scrap rates or fewer customer returns.

To translate a firm's strategic objectives into actionable activities, the source of a company's competitive advantage must be translated into strategic performance drivers. Senior managers within companies are often responsible for identifying their companies' strategic performance drivers.

## Step 2: Evaluate Your Firm's External Alignment

The second step in creating an HR scorecard is to evaluate your employee management system to assess the alignment of your primary HR activities with the source of your competitive advantage. Doing so involves two activities: translating your firm's strategic performance drivers into *HR deliverables* and evaluating the effectiveness of those deliverables.

### Translate the Strategic Performance Drivers into HR Deliverables

**HR deliverable**

what is needed from a firm's HR activities, or a mechanism by which an HR system creates value for a company

**HR deliverables** are what is needed from a firm's HR activities, or the mechanism by which an HR system creates value for a company.[42] Consider the strategic performance driver high-quality customer service. To realize high levels of customer service, companies need to attract and retain talented employees who are able to build and sustain long-term relationships with customers. As a result, the HR deliverables for the strategic driver high-quality customer service might be employment stability and high-quality employees. Consider an industry such as insurance that depends on long-term relationships with customers. Companies in that industry want professional sales staff and experienced customer service representatives who stay with the company to maintain strong relationships with customers while building relationships with new customers based on their experience. Similarly, consider another strategic performance driver: increasing new product offerings. What types of HR deliverables would be needed for this driver? Employee collaboration and creativity could be the HR deliverables that would enable companies to realize a strategic performance driver of new products. Many start-up tech companies rely heavily on employee collaboration and creativity to move the business forward.

Most strategic performance drivers incorporate elements of employee contributions, either directly or indirectly. A key strategic performance driver in a manufacturing plant, for example, might be the quality of the technology used in a production process and the efficiency of the employees. Employee productivity is an HR deliverable that is directly linked to achieving low costs, and the ability of employees to work with technological advancements may be an indirect contributor that enables the realization of technologies in place.[43] In other words, some HR deliverables are directly related to strategic performance drivers, and others serve as "enablers" to the drivers. Increasingly companies are realizing that AI alone won't get the job done in many instances. It is the combination of the right employees and AI that create the competitive advantage for the firm.

Exhibit 14.10 shows a hypothetical example of a company's assessment of the effectiveness of its strategic performance drivers. The company illustrated in this exhibit has identified three strategic performance drivers that are believed to help the company improve its competitiveness: improved customer service, improved product quality, and more new product offerings. To achieve these three strategic performance drivers, the firm has determined that employment stability, employee creativity, high-quality employees, and employee collaboration are the HR deliverables that, if fully realized, would maximize the strategic performance drivers.

### Evaluating the Alignment of HR Deliverables with the Strategic Performance Drivers

The second part of the second step in creating an HR scorecard is to evaluate the effectiveness of the HR deliverables. This evaluation is done by rating the extent to which the HR deliverables actually contributed to the strategic performance drivers. In Exhibit 14.10, for example, we can see some positives and some negatives for the company whose HR system we're evaluating. On the positive side, the company's ability to attract high-quality employees is a positive contributor to all three strategic performance drivers. However, the firm's employment stability is troubling because its turnover is a negative contributor to sustaining all three performance drivers. In addition, employee collaboration is positively related to the creation of new product offerings, as is employee creativity. At the same time, however, employee collaboration is not contributing to the realization of improving

---

**EXHIBIT 14.10**

Evaluating the Alignment of a Firm's HR Deliverables*

Please indicate the degree to which each HR deliverable in the chart below would currently enable each strategic driver, on a scale of −100 to +100. Empty cells indicate this is not a "key" deliverable for a particular driver. Examples of the extremes and midpoints on that continuum are as follows:

| | |
|---|---|
| **−100:** | This deliverable is **counterproductive** for enabling this driver. |
| **0:** | This deliverable **has little or no effect** on this driver. |
| **+100:** | This deliverable **significantly enables** this driver. |
| **DNK:** | Don't know or have no opinion. |

| Strategic Performance Driver | HR Deliverable | | | |
|---|---|---|---|---|
| | **Employment Stability** | **Employee Creativity** | **High-Quality Employees** | **Employee Collaboration** |
| *1. Improve customer service* | −80 | | +30 | |
| *2. Improve product quality* | −20 | | +20 | −20 |
| *3. Increase new product offerings* | −10 | +30 | +30 | +10 |

*Source:* Adapted from Brian Becker, Mark Huselid, and Dave Ulrich, *The HR Scorecard* (Cambridge, MA: Harvard Business School Press, 2001).

product quality. Clearly, some adjustments are needed to improve this company's odds of competing based on its strategic performance drivers.

Conducting an evaluation such as this will help you determine whether your HR deliverables are successful, as well as identify areas of your company that are underperforming. You can then target the deliverables that are unsatisfactory. To do so, however, you will have to further explore the HR practices that are used to manage employees. Step 3 of evaluating the HR system builds on the information from step 2 and focuses on examining how well or how poorly the practices used within the three primary HR activities are in alignment with the needed HR deliverables.

## Step 3: Evaluate Your Firm's Internal Alignment

The third step in creating an HR scorecard is to evaluate the degree of alignment between the firm's HR practices and its HR deliverables and evaluate the degree of alignment among the various HR practices themselves.

### Evaluating the Alignment of the HR Practices with the HR Deliverables

One of the key objectives of the third step of the HR system evaluation process is to determine whether the practices you are using for your primary HR activities (work design and workforce planning, managing employee competencies, and managing employee attitudes and behaviors) are helping or hurting the achievement of your firm's HR deliverables. This type of evaluation is easy to conduct. Exhibit 14.11 shows an example of such an assessment. Completing this assessment involves evaluating each practice on a scale of –100 to +100 in terms of whether the practice enables the HR deliverables.

In Exhibit 14.11, we can see that some of the practices are contributing in a positive way to the HR deliverables. For example, the activities associated with training and development and with compensation are helping to foster employment stability among the workforce. At the same time, the activities associated with selection, performance management, incentives, and benefits are negatively related to employment stability. With regard to selection, it may be the case that the company is failing to hire workers who are a good fit for the jobs for which they are being hired and/or the firm's culture. As discussed in Chapter 9, it is possible that the performance management process is contributing to employee turnover because employees perceive that there is a lack of distributive or procedural fairness

### EXHIBIT 14.11

Evaluating the Alignment of a Firm's HR System with Its HR Deliverables*

Please indicate the degree to which the following elements of the HR system facilitate the HR deliverables shown, on a scale of –100 to +100. Examples of the extremes and midpoints on that continuum are as follows:

| | |
|---|---|
| **–100:** | This dimension is **counterproductive** for enabling this driver. |
| **0:** | This dimension **has little or no effect** on this driver. |
| **+100:** | This dimension **significantly enables** this driver. |
| **DNK:** | Don't know or have no opinion. |

| HR Deliverable | Job Design | Workforce Planning | Recruitment | Selection | Training and Development | Performance Management | Compensation | Incentives | Benefits |
|---|---|---|---|---|---|---|---|---|---|
| *Employment stability* | 0 | 0 | 0 | –20 | +10 | –30 | +30 | –30 | –40 |
| *Employee creativity* | +40 | 0 | 0 | 0 | +20 | –30 | 0 | –40 | 0 |
| *High-quality employees* | 0 | –20 | +20 | +30 | –20 | –20 | +20 | –20 | 0 |
| *Employee collaboration* | +20 | 0 | +20 | +30 | –20 | –40 | 0 | –60 | 0 |

*Source: Adapted from Brian Becker, Mark Huselid, and Dave Ulrich, *The HR Scorecard* (Cambridge, MA: Harvard Business School Press, 2001).

with regard to their performance evaluations. Similarly, the firm's incentive systems might be misaligned, such that what is rewarded is not what employees value. Finally, the benefits package provided to employees might not meet the company's needs or be attractive compared to what other companies are offering.

Of course, these are simply speculations. But they do provide valuable information by showing areas of alignment and misalignment. When misalignments are identified, managers can look for ways to adjust the firm's HR activities to improve the realization of the company's HR deliverables and, ultimately, the firm's strategic performance drivers.

### Evaluating the Alignment Among the Firm's HR Practices

It is important to evaluate the alignment among a firm's HR practices themselves. As we have discussed, it is possible that the failure to achieve a firm's HR deliverables is due to negative synergies, or "deadly combinations," among the company's HR practices. As Exhibit 14.12 shows, evaluating the alignment among a firm's HR practices is done by assessing the degree to which each HR practice is consistent with each of the other practices.

In Exhibit 14.12, for example, we can see examples of positive connections and deadly combinations. On the positive side, the firm's training and development activities are consistent with how its jobs are designed and with the company's recruitment and selection activities. However, although the firm's performance management system and the incentive system are aligned with one another, they are inconsistent with how the company's jobs are designed and how employees are recruited, selected, and trained. Comparisons like these illustrate that managers can face numerous alignment issues among their firms' HR practices, which, in turn, can affect their firms' HR deliverables. When areas of misalignment are identified, this comparison provides a focus for discussion among managers to identify the sources of the problem. This diagnostic also pinpoints specific practices that are inconsistent with practices that are effective in achieving the desired HR deliverables.

### EXHIBIT 14.12

#### Evaluating the Internal Fit Among a Firm's HR Activities*

In the chart below, please estimate the degree to which the various HR management subsystems work together harmoniously, or "fit" together. Think of the degree of fit and internal consistency as a continuum from −100 to +100, and assign a value in that range to each relationship. Examples of the extremes and midpoints on that continuum are as follows:

| | |
|---|---|
| **−100:** | The two subsystems work at **cross-purposes.** |
| **0:** | The two subsystems have **little or no effect on one another.** |
| **+100:** | Each subsystem is **mutually reinforcing and internally consistent.** |
| **DNK:** | Don't know or have no opinion |

| | Job Design | Workforce Planning | Recruitment | Selection | Training and Development | Performance Management | Compensation | Incentives | Benefits |
|---|---|---|---|---|---|---|---|---|---|
| *Job design* | — | −30 | 0 | −20 | +10 | −20 | +20 | −50 | 0 |
| *Workforce planning* | | — | 0 | −10 | −20 | 0 | 0 | 0 | 0 |
| *Recruitment* | | | — | +20 | +20 | −40 | −10 | −40 | −10 |
| *Selection* | | | | — | 0 | −20 | 0 | −10 | −20 |
| *Training and development* | | | | | — | −10 | +10 | −10 | −10 |
| *Performance management* | | | | | | — | 0 | +20 | 0 |
| *Compensation* | | | | | | | — | +50 | 0 |
| *Incentives* | | | | | | | | — | |
| *Benefits* | | | | | | | | | — |

*__Source:__ Adapted from Brian Becker, Mark Huselid, and Dave Ulrich, *The HR Scorecard* (Cambridge, MA: Harvard Business School Press, 2001).

# Building Your Own High-Performing Organization

As you can probably tell, evaluating your HR system is a critical component of effectively managing your workforce. After all, if you don't conduct an evaluation, how do you really know if you are managing your employees as effectively as possible? In addition, organizations and environmental conditions continually evolve. As a result, it is important to continually assess the ability of your HR system to meet your company's changing needs.

Conducting such an evaluation is not enough, however. You must also think about what to do with the information you acquire during the evaluation. Often, this activity involves reassessing and redesigning the practices you use to manage your employees so they contribute more to your organization's competitive advantage. An HR scorecard is also an excellent starting point for redesigning how you manage your employees. You can use an HR scorecard to effectively redesign your HR system by doing the following:

1. Customizing your HR scorecard
2. Being consistent
3. Being specific
4. Following up on the implementation of the redesign

Next, we discuss how you go about doing these things.

## Customizing Your HR Scorecard

The first step in using an HR scorecard to redesign your HR system is to customize your firm's HR scorecard by following the three steps outlined earlier. Take a moment to identify the source of your company's competitive advantage. Is it productivity, product quality, customer service, product innovation, or some other strategic performance driver? Once you have identified the firm's strategic performance drivers, you can determine which HR deliverables are necessary to help achieve those drivers. Then, you have important strategic anchors to evaluate the effectiveness of the practices you use to manage your company's employees. You are also in a position to identify any misalignments among the firm's HR practices.

Sysco Corporation, for example, found that paying its delivery employees based only on the hours they worked wasn't helping create value for the firm. As Ken Carrig, former Sysco's executive vice president of administration, said, "The model didn't necessarily provide better customer satisfaction or profitability."[44] To align Sysco's HR practices with the employee contributions it was seeking, the company shifted to a pay system that rewarded its delivery employees for making more deliveries, making fewer mistakes, and improving safety.[45] Related, Family Dollar moved away from stock options for their employees to performance-based restricted stock and options. In doing so, they helped their employees focus on being accountable for activities that they controlled and helped the company achieve higher performance.[46]

## Being Consistent

A key point to remember is that much of the success of HR systems comes down to consistency. The presence of powerful connections or deadly combinations rests directly on the degree of alignment among your HR practices. In other words, you need to be sure that all the practices used to manage your employees reinforce, rather than counteract, one another. If employees are assigned to teams, for example, your performance management and incentive systems should involve a team component.

Rewarding team members based solely on their individual accomplishments will undermine the power of the system. If your HR practices are not consistent, employees won't accurately interpret the messages the firm is sending them and thus may not behave in expected ways.[47] In contrast, when the practices are consistent with one another, they create an environment in which employees share a common interpretation of what behaviors are important, expected, and rewarded. This, in turn, will motivate them to work toward the business objectives the firm is trying to achieve.

## Being Specific

Employees need to have a clear understanding of what it is they need to do to help their company succeed. In many ways, the various practices we have talked about in this text may be viewed as communications between management and employees. Practices determine the competencies of the workforce—how employees are expected to interact, as well as how they are to act in the performance of their jobs. One prominent part of understanding HR system effectiveness is that companies use different practices in an attempt to elicit needed role behaviors from employees given different considerations regarding strategy, technology, and the like.[48] Telling employees to make fewer mistakes on the job is not likely to be as powerful as explaining to employees how the number of mistakes they make affects company performance. If employees don't have a clear objective, they are not likely to reach that objective. Thus, implementing an effective HR system requires managers to be specific about what they expect from their employees and what the company needs them to do.

In many ways, implementing an effective HR system comes down to good communication. One of the keys to the successful implementation of a new performance review process at Adobe was providing bonuses every quarter that were clearly linked to performance. Prior to implementation of this new system, the company had noted an increase in attrition every year following the annual review process and awarding of the annual bonuses. Now, there is a more direct line of sight between performance and bonuses because the conversations about how employees are performing are more frequent. The bonuses, then, are tied to the results of those conversations.[49] However, there is a cautionary note to be offered here. One research study reported that workers who received performance-based pay were likely to work harder, but also were likely to experience high stress and low job satisfaction levels.[50]

## Following Up on the Implementation of a Redesign

Just because a company designs a particular HR policy doesn't mean the policy will be carried out is as it should.[51] In other words, what should be done might not be what is actually done.[52] For example, a company might institute a merit-based pay program to reward employees for their outstanding efforts. However, if the firm's managers rate all employees equally high on their performance evaluations, the pay program will fail to differentiate high versus medium or low performers. One outcome from this disconnection between the design and implementation of the program might be a decrease in motivation among the high performers. Similar situations may exist for other practices as well. A company policy for increased empowerment may be interpreted differently by different managers, resulting in inconsistency in its implementation throughout an organization. Some managers may view this as soliciting input from employees, while others may actually push decision-making down to employees.

This discussion highlights an important component of implementation: A company must take the time to help its managers understand how to implement a practice. Failure to follow up on the actual implementation of the policies that are intended to be used to help realize employee contributions will dramatically decrease their effectiveness in improving company performance.

## SUMMARY

One of the key themes of this chapter, and of this entire book, is that there is no single best way to manage employees. Rather, how employees should be managed depends on several HR challenges related to organizational demands, environmental influences, and regulatory issues. In addition to these considerations, there are several principles of high-performing HR systems that separate successful companies from not-so-successful ones. First, high-performing companies look at how their HR activities fit with the three HR challenges—organizational, environmental, and regulatory—they face. Second, high--performing companies internally align their HR practices to realize synergies from them. Third, high-performing HR systems target specific employee contributions that are critical for helping companies achieve a competitive advantage in the marketplace.

In addition to these three key principles, companies must also consider the costs and benefits related to maximizing the contributions their employees make. Different types of HR systems and activities involve different types of investments and costs. The key question is whether a particular investment will help a company achieve and sustain a competitive advantage. One approach to making tough investment decisions such as these is to view your workforce as an employment portfolio. By assessing the strategic value and uniqueness of their firm's different employee groups, managers are in a better position to evaluate the potential benefits that could stem from making those investments in terms of employee contributions. From a strategic point of view, will the investments in HR systems, and the resulting employee competencies and motivation, help the company realize a sustainable source of competitive advantage?

Many companies are now using HR scorecards to help evaluate the effectiveness of their HR systems. By identifying a firm's strategic performance drivers and key HR deliverables, an HR scorecard helps managers focus their attention on value-added activities. In addition, the scorecard helps managers evaluate the alignment between their firms' HR practices and HR deliverables. An HR scorecard provides managers with a clear snapshot of how well or how poorly they are managing their employees. This helps managers pinpoint specific practices that are inconsistent with one another and practices that reinforce one another and lead to the HR deliverables their firms desire.

## KEY TERMS

alliance partner
collaborative-based HR system
commitment-based HR system
compliance-based HR system
contract worker
core employee
deadly combination
HR deliverable
job-based employee
powerful connection

productivity-based HR system
relational relationship
strategic performance driver
strategic value
transactional relationship
uniqueness

# DISCUSSION QUESTIONS

1. Why are both external fit and internal fit important in designing HR systems?
2. Compare and contrast the concepts of *deadly combinations* and *powerful connections*. What is the value to a manager of understanding these concepts?
3. How would you go about identifying the employment portfolio for your company? Why does going through this process matter?
4. What is meant by the term "strategic performance driver?" What is the relationship of HR activities to strategic performance drivers?
5. Identify a company you are familiar with. How would you describe that company's strategy? Given its strategy, what do you think are the firm's strategic performance drivers? What are the firm's HR deliverables?
6. What is an HR scorecard, and what value does it add for a firm? HR scorecards are usually used in for profit businesses. How might a HR scorecard be of value to a not-for-profit organization?

# LEARNING EXERCISE 1

As a manager, you have a number of choices to make regarding how you manage your employees. Throughout this book, we have focused on three primary HR activities: work design and workforce planning, management of employee competencies, and management of employee attitudes and behaviors. The question you need to answer is when to use the various practices that make up the three HR activities. Use the following table to compare and contrast how a complete HR system might differ across four companies, each pursuing a different strategy:

| Primary HR Activity | Specific HR Activity | Cost Leadership Strategy | Innovation Strategy | Quality Strategy | Customer Service Strategy |
|---|---|---|---|---|---|
| | Which group of employees is likely to be viewed as "core"? | | | | |
| Work Design and Workforce Planning | Job design | | | | |
| | Workforce planning | | | | |
| Managing Employee Competencies | Recruitment | | | | |
| | Selection | | | | |
| | Training | | | | |
| Managing Employee Attitudes and Behaviors | Performance management | | | | |
| | Compensation | | | | |
| | Incentives | | | | |
| | Benefits, health, and wellness | | | | |

## LEARNING EXERCISE 2

Companies are increasingly acknowledging that their employees are a potential source of competitive advantage. At the same time, however, companies are increasing their reliance on external employees, such as contract labor and temporary workers.

1. As a manager, how would you strike a balance between the number of employees you retain internally and the number of external workers you employ?
2. What implications do you think your decisions would have for the morale, commitment, and effort of your employees?

## CASE STUDY 1: THE PUZZLING CLIMATE AT DIGITAL GAMING

Sitting at his desk, Bob Menendez is distraught over his current situation. Bob is the founder of a relatively young, small company called Digital Gaming (DG), which designs computer games. He has personally earned a lot of money and has a strong reputation in the electronic gaming industry for his vision and creativity. His computer games are routinely best sellers and rated among the top products in the industry, particularly for being lifelike, creative, and challenging. Recently, however, several industry analysts have noted that DG's games are not as creative as they once were, and that occasionally the company's software contains glitches.

Bob knows there is something true about these reviews. As an avid gamer himself, he sees that his products, although still high quality, have slipped a notch. Bob is equally concerned about the climate at DG. In the early years of the company's history, employees were highly engaged, full of energy, and completely committed to the company's success. Recently, however, Bob has noticed that some of the 100 programmers he employs seem distant and disengaged. Moreover, the turnover rate of his top programmers has more than tripled from its seven-year average of 10% to a point where DG continually has to hire new programmers. Interestingly, absenteeism and employee complaints are not a problem, and employees put in long hours.

Bob is confused: People are leaving his firm, but he doesn't really know why. As he tries to figure out what is causing the diminished product quality and increased turnover in his company, he wonders if the way he is managing his employees is the problem. He goes out of his way to hire the best and brightest job candidates. He doesn't recruit at top-notch schools because, in his experience, many of the really gifted programmers do not bother with school. Instead, he focuses on referrals from current employees, word of mouth, and advertisements in the top trade outlets. Rather than give applicants a typical employment test or interview, he simply asks them to do some programming on a computer in order to showcase their creativity and skills. Bob usually hires people with potential right on the spot, and he provides them with very attractive signing bonuses. Given the tight labor market for programmers, he is afraid that if he waits to make the offer, the most qualified candidates will take another job.

Once hired, DG employees typically work long hours. However, they have a lot of control over how they work. DG has a very informal culture. Some people show up for work in shorts and T-shirts, and many people work odd hours. For example, some programmers work all night and take the afternoons off. Employees are also given liberal training budgets that they personally manage to help stay on the cutting edge of their business.

The pay package Bob offers is also fairly generous. Base pay for employees is roughly the market average, but they can earn considerably more based on the amount of programming code they complete each month. Employees' computers are monitored by electronic software, not necessarily to evaluate what they do while they work, but to track how much work they finish by the end of the week. Bob then divides a monthly bonus among the programmers based on the volume of code they have completed. Each employee can access the company's intranet to see the status of his or her volume relative to that of DG's other programmers. As shown in the following table, employees in the top 10% of volume of code receive 40% of the bonus pool—a disproportionate share of the rewards available to employees.

| Employee Ranking on Performance Curve | Percentage of Bonus Pool |
| --- | --- |
| 90th–100th percentile | 40% |
| 70th–90th percentile | 30% |
| 40th–70th percentile | 25% |
| 20th–40th percentile | 5% |
| 0–20th percentile | 0% |

Bob evaluates an employee based on several key criteria: volume of completed work, ability to meet deadlines, and sales of the products he or she personally coded. Bob also considers how well each programmer complies with the stylistic preferences and unique formula that he developed for creating code when he founded the company. Although forcing programmers to stick to this protocol limits their creativity, Bob insists that the protocol is instrumental in producing successful programming games.

As Bob is thinking about the current climate at DG, his assistant interrupts to let him know that two more of his top programmers just submitted their letters of resignation. They are leaving to join a new start-up firm that competes directly with DG.

### Discussion Questions

1. What are the major problems at DG?
2. Create a table identifying the primary HR activities noted for DG and indicating whether or not they are contributing toward success or contributing to the problems identified. Indicate a reason for each response.
3. What changes to DG's HR activities would you advise Bob Menendez to make? Why?
4. How well do your changes work together. Specifically, what is the internal alignment of your proposed HR system? What additional changes would you suggest to achieve internal alignment?

## CASE STUDY 2: HOMELIFE

HomeLife is a relatively young company that competes in the consumer electronics and appliances industry (televisions, computers, kitchen appliances, etc.). The company describes itself as "making your life more enjoyable by making your home more efficient at an affordable price, regardless of how you define efficient." The company sells a large selection of items, and the range of the products that it carries spans the price spectrum from very low cost to very high end. For example, some of the company's kitchen ovens cost just under $400, while others cost well over $4,000. HomeLife also has low-end, affordable televisions under $400, as well as very pricey, large plasma televisions that cost over $6,000. It strives to be a low-cost leader for the quality of the product. Compared to its competition, HomeLife offers a very competitive price,

if not the lowest. In addition to the cost focus, the company prides itself on providing exceptional one on one customer service. The name of the company, HomeLife, is intended to reflect both the strategy and the philosophy of the organization. With a focus on costs and customer service, the name reflects the company's concern with the financial burdens customers face, as well as the vast amounts of information that customers must process when making purchasing decisions.

The name HomeLife also refers to the company's philosophy for managing its customer service representatives: HomeLife cares about its employees' long-term well-being and success, and offers them a very attractive benefits package including generous leave time, which encourages employees to balance work and family. Customer service representatives who work at HomeLife typically are hired through personal referrals of current employees, or occasionally an advertisement will be placed on the company website or another online job posting site when more than one opening exists. Each month, customer service representatives receive product training to explore the new products they will be selling to ensure that they are knowledgeable and can respond to customer questions.

To motivate them to sell, customer service representatives are rewarded on a commission-based pay plan. What is interesting about this particular incentive plan is that the customer service representatives have some discretion regarding the final price of the company's products. Most products have a standard markup of 10% to 25%, and the employee gets a portion of this profit. While many of the products sell for the list price, sophisticated buyers and repeat customers are often able to negotiate lower prices for their products. The challenge with this plan is that the company has a reputation for low costs, and customer service representatives who are not willing to negotiate the sales price are viewed as going against this objective. By lowering the prices, however, they are cutting into their own take-home pay. Additionally, while other employees at HomeLife provide valuable support to the customer service representatives, there is no incentive plan in place for them. However, turnover for these other employees is much lower, at 25%.

The company has done fairly well and now has six stores on the West Coast between San Francisco and Los Angeles. With a focus on low costs and customer service, the company has been able to sustain reasonable growth—it just opened two new stores—and a modest level of customer satisfaction among its consumers. At the same time, however, while the customer service representatives seem to be fairly happy and work hard, their turnover is around 70% per year. This turnover obviously involves costs associated with constantly hiring new employees, and it also has a negative impact on customer loyalty and the level of experience of the customer service representatives.

As the company has grown, Maria Gonzalez, president of HomeLife, has realized that she doesn't have the time or expertise to attend to all the issues related to policies for managing people. Recognizing that it is time for the company to have a full-time director of HR, Maria has decided to hire Daniel Hillman. Daniel has 10 years of HR experience at one of HomeLife's competitors in the industry. Maria was encouraged by Daniel's enthusiasm for creating a fun and effective workplace. During the course of their discussions, Maria told Daniel that her main goal for him in his new job is to design an HR system that reduces the turnover among customer service representatives, encourages them to work hard toward the company's competitive advantage of low costs and high customer service, and adheres to HomeLife's principles of taking care of its employees.

### Discussion Questions

1. Provide advice to Daniel regarding the nature of the HR system he should recommend for the customer service representatives at the six HomeLife stores.
2. Identify a key strategic performance driver for this organization.

3. How do the customer service representatives contribute to the strategic performance driver you identified?

4. Design an HR system to realize the strategic performance driver you identified. Be certain to explain how you would (a) design the work environment, (b) manage employee competencies, and (c) manage employee attitudes and behaviors.

## NOTES

[1] L. Baird and I. Meshoulam, "Managing Two Fits of Strategic Human Resource Management," *Academy of Management Review* 13 (1988): 116–128; J. P. MacDuffie, "Human Resource Bundles and Manufacturing Performance: Organizational Logic and Flexible Production Systems in the World Auto Industry," *Industrial and Labor Relations Review* 48 (1995): 197–221; and M. A. Huselid, "The Impact of Human Resource Management Practices on Turnover, Productivity, and Corporate Financial Performance," *Academy of Management Journal* 38 (1995): 635–672.

[2] K. Jiang, D. P. Lepak, J. Jia, and J. C. Baer, "How Does Human Resource Management Influence Organizational Outcomes? A Meta-analytic Investigation of Mediating Mechanisms," *Academy of Management Journal* 55, no. 6 (2012): 1264–1294; J. E. Delery, "Issues of Fit in Strategic Human Resource Management: Implications for Research," *Human Resource Management Review* 8 (1998): 289–310; and Patrick M. Wright and Gary C. McMahan, "Theoretical Perspectives for Strategic Human Resource Management," *Journal of Management* 18 (1992): 295–320.

[3] M. Audenaert, A. Vanderstraeten, D. Buyens, and S. Desmidt, "Does Alignment Elicit Competency-Based HRM? A Systematic Review," *Management Revue* 25 (2014): 5–26; R. Miles and C. C. Snow, "Designing Strategic Human Resource Systems," *Organizational Dynamics* 13 (1984): 36–52; R. S. Schuler and S. E. Jackson, "Linking Competitive Strategies with Human Resource Management Practices," *Academy of Management Executive* 1 (1987): 207–219; B. E. Becker and M. A. Huselid, "High-Performance Work Systems and Firm Performance: A Synthesis of Research and Managerial Implications," in *Research in Personnel and Human Resources Management*, ed. G. R. Ferris (Greenwich, CT: JAI Press, 1998), 53–101; and MacDuffie, "Human Resource Bundles and Manufacturing Performance."

[4] Delery, "Issues of Fit in Strategic Human Resource Management"; and D. P. Lepak, H. Liao, Y. Chung, and E. Harden, "A Conceptual Review of HR Systems in Strategic HRM Research," in *Research in Personnel and Human Resource Management*, vol. 25, ed. J. Martocchio (Greenwich, CT: JAI Press, 2006), 217–272.

[5] Delery, "Issues of Fit in Strategic Human Resource Management"; and B. E. Becker, M. A. Huselid, P. S. Pickus, and M. F. Spratt, "HR as a Source of Shareholder Value: Research and Recommendations," *Human Resource Management* 36, no. 1 (Spring 1997): 39–47.

[6] Becker et al., "HR as a Source of Shareholder Value."

[7] Jiang et al., "How Does Human Resource Management Influence Organizational Outcomes?"

[8] Becker et al., "HR as a Source of Shareholder Value."

[9] "Best Companies 2014," *Fortune*, http://fortune.com/best-companies/; T. Raphael, "At Google, the Proof Is in the People," *Workforce*, March 2003, 50–51; P. Withers, "Retention Strategies That Respond to Worker Values," *Workforce*, July 2001, 37–41; and B. Elgin, "Google: Why the World's Hottest Tech Company Will Struggle to Keep Its Edge," *BusinessWeek*, May 3, 2004; Google, *Bloomberg Businessweek*, May 2, 2004, http://www.businessweek.com/stories/2004-05-02/google.

[10] J. B. Barney and W. S. Hesterly, *Strategic Management and Competitive Advantage* (Upper Saddle River, NJ: Prentice Hall, 2006).

[11] A. Zacharatos, J. Barling, and R. D. Iverson, "High-Performance Work Systems and Occupational Safety," *Journal of Applied Psychology* 90 (2005): 77–84.

[12] I. Pena, and M. Villasalero, "Business Strategy, Human Resource Systems, and Organizational Performance in the Spanish Banking Industry," *International Journal of Human Resource Management* 21 (2010): 2864–2888; and H. Liao and A. Chuang, "A Multilevel Investigation of Factors Influencing Employee Service Performance and Customer Outcomes," *Academy of Management Journal* 47 (2004): 41–58.

[13] "Careers," Trader Joe's, traderjoes.com, https://www.traderjoes.com/careers.

[14] J. Barney, "Firm Resources and Sustained Competitive Advantage," *Journal of Management* 17 (1991): 99–120; M. Porter, *Competitive Advantage: Creating and Sustaining*

*Superior Performance* (New York: Free Press, 1985); and Wright and McMahan, "Theoretical Perspectives for Strategic Human Resource Management."

[15] A. Altuzarra and F. Serrano, "Firms' Innovation Activity and Numerical Flexibility," *Industrial & Labor Relations Review* 63 (2010): 327–339; A. Lopez-Cabrales, R. Vale, and J. Herrero, "The Contribution of Core Employees to Organizational Capabilities and Efficiency," *Human Resource Management* 45, no. 1 (Spring 2006): 81–109.

[16] Lauren Weber, "The End of Employees," *Wall Street Journal*, wsj.com, https://www.wsj.com/articles/the-end-of-employees-1486050443, updated February 2, 2017.

[17] Ibid.

[18] S. N. Houseman, "Why Employers Use Flexible Staffing Arrangements: Evidence from an Establishment Survey," *Industrial and Labor Relations Review* 55 (2001): 149–170.

[19] Lauren Weber, "The End of Employees," WSJ, wsj.com, Updated February 2, 2017, https://www.wsj.com/articles/the-end-of-employees-1486050443.

[20] "Contingent and Alternative Employment Arrangements—May 2017," Economic News Release, Bureau of Labor Statistics, U.S. Department of Labor, June 7, 2018, https://www.bls.gov/news.release/conempl.nr0.htm.

[21] "How Organizations Are Managing Contract Workers Now," *HR Focus*, November 2006, 5.

[22] M. Bidwell and J. R. Keller, "Within or Without? How Firms Combine Internal and External Labor Markets to Fill Jobs," *Academy of Management Journal* 57 (2014): 1035–1055; S. A. Snell, D. P. Lepak, and M. A. Youndt, "Managing the Architecture of Intellectual Capital: Implications for Strategic Human Resource Management," in *Research in Personnel and Human Resource Management*, ed. P. M. Wright, L. D. Dyer, J. W. Boudreau, and G. T. Milkovich (Greenwich, CT: JAI Press, 1999), 61–90; J. Purcell, "High Commitment Management and the Link with Contingent Workers: Implications for Strategic Human Resource Management," in *Research in Personnel and Human Resource Management*, ed. P. M. Wright, L. D. Dyer, J. W. Boudreau, and G. T. Milkovich (Greenwich, CT: JAI Press, 1999), 239–257; and M. A. Huselid, B. E. Becker, and D. Beatty, *The Workforce Scorecard: Managing and Measuring Human Capital to Drive Strategy Execution* (Boston: Harvard Business School Press, 2005).

[23] D. P. Lepak and S. A. Snell, "Examining the Human Resource Architecture: The Relationships Among Human Capital, Employment, and Human Resource Configurations," *Journal of Management* 28 (2002): 517–543; and M. Bidwell, "Do Peripheral Workers Do Peripheral Work? Comparing the Use of Highly Skilled Contractors and Regular Employees," *Industrial & Labor Relations Review* 62, no. 2 (2009): 200–225.

[24] Kathleen Chaykowski and Mark Coatney, "From Broke to Billionaire: How Fred Luddy Built the World's Most Innovative Company," *Forbes*, May 29, 2018, https://www.forbes.com/feature/innovative-companies-service-now/#50e5ff7fc603.

[25] D. P. Lepak and S. A. Snell, "The Human Resource Architecture: Toward a Theory of Human Capital Allocation and Development," *Academy of Management Review* 24 (1999): 31–48; and D. P. Lepak and S. A. Snell, "Managing the Human Resource Architecture for Knowledge-Based Competition," in *Managing Knowledge for Sustained Competitive Advantage: Designing Strategies for Effective Human Resource Management*, ed. S. Jackson, M. Hitt, and A. DeNisi (San Francisco: Jossey-Bass, 2003), 127–154.

[26] C. B. Perrow, "A Framework for the Comparative Analysis of Organizations," *American Sociological Review* 32 (1967): 194–208; R. H. Coase, "The Nature of the Firm," *Economica* 4 (1937): 386–405; and O. E. Williamson, *Markets and Hierarchies: Analysis and Antitrust Implications* (New York: Free Press, 1975).

[27] Bidwell and Keller, "Within or Without? How Firms Combine Internal and External Labor Markets to Fill Jobs."

[28] P. Cappelli and J. R. Keller, "Classifying Workers in the New Economy," *Academy of Management Review* 38 (2013): 575–596; B. Campbell, R. Coff, and D. Kryscynski, "Rethinking Sustained Competitive Advantage from Human Capital," *Academy of Management Review* 37 (2012): 376–395; and G. S. Becker, *Human Capital* (New York: Columbia University Press, 1964).

[29] D. M. Rousseau, *Psychological Contracts in Organizations: Understanding Written and Unwritten Agreements* (Thousand Oaks, CA: SAGE Publications, 1995).

[30] J. Jensen, R. Opland, and A. Ryan, "Psychological Contracts and Counterproductive Work Behaviors: Employee Responses to Transactional and Relational Breech," *Journal of Business and Psychology* 25 (2010): 555–568; and Lepak and Snell, "The Human Resource Architecture."

[31] Snell et al., "Managing the Architecture of Intellectual Capital"; and Purcell, "High Commitment Management and the Link with Contingent Workers."

[32] S. A. Snell and J. Dean, Jr., "Integrated Manufacturing and Human Resource Management: A Human Capital Perspective," *Academy of Management Journal* 35 (1992): 467–504; and J. T. Delaney and M. A. Huselid, "The Impact of Human Resource Management Practices on Perceptions of Organizational Performance," *Academy of Management Journal* 39 (1996): 949–969.

[33] Becker, *Human Capital*; Lepak and Snell, "Managing the Human Resource Architecture for Knowledge-Based Competition."

[34] M. J. Koch and R. G. McGrath, "Improving Labor Productivity: Human Resource Management Policies Do Matter," *Strategic Management Journal* 17 (1996): 335–354; Snell and Dean, "Integrated Manufacturing and Human Resource Management: A Human Capital Perspective"; and A. S. Tsui, J. L. Pearce, L. W. Porter, and J. P. Hite, "Choice of Employee-Organization Relationship: Influence of External and Internal Organizational Factors," in *Research in Personnel and Human Resources Management*, vol. 13, ed. G. R. Ferris (Greenwich, CT: JAI Press, 1995), 117–151.

[35] S. A. Snell, "Control Theory in Strategic Human Resource Management: The Mediating Effects of Administrative Information," *Journal of Management* 35 (1992): 292–328; and S. A. Snell and M. A. Youndt, "Human Resource Management and Firm Performance: Testing a Contingency Model of Executive Controls," *Journal of Management* 21 (1995): 711–737.

[36] Lepak and Snell, "The Human Resource Architecture"; and Lepak and Snell, "Examining the Human Resource Architecture."

[37] D. M. Rousseau and J. McLean-Parks, "The Contracts of Individuals and Organizations," in *Research in Organizational Behavior*, vol. 15, ed. L. L. Cummings and B. M. Staw (Greenwich, CT: JAI Press, 1993), 1–43.

[38] Lepak and Snell, "Examining the Human Resource Architecture."

[39] J. E. Mathieu, S. I. Tannenbaum, and E. Salas, "Influences of Individual and Situational Characteristics on Measures of Training Effectiveness," *Academy of Management Journal* 35 (1992): 828–847.

[40] J. H. Dyer, "Does Governance Matter? Keiretsu Alliances and Asset Specificity as Sources of Japanese Competitive Advantage," *Organization Science* 7 (1996): 649–666.

[41] B. E. Becker, M. A. Huselid, and D. Ulrich, *The HR Scorecard: Linking People, Strategy, and Performance* (Boston: Harvard Business School Press, 2001).

[42] Ibid.

[43] Ibid.

[44] C. Schneider, "The New Human-Capital Metrics," *CFO*, February 15, 2006, 24–27, http://ww2.cfo.com/strategy/2006/02/the-new-human-capital-metrics/.

[45] Ibid.

[46] HayGroup, "Family Dollar: Aligning Pay with Strategy," http://www.haygroup.com/ww/downloads/details.aspx?id=1128.

[47] C. M. M. Pereira and J. F. S. Gomes, "The Strength of Human Resource Practices and Transformational Leadership: Impact on Organizational Performance," *International Journal of Human Resource Management* 23, no. 20 (2012): 4301–4318; and D. E. Bowen and C. Ostroff, "Understanding HRM–Firm Performance Linkages: The Role of the 'Strength' of the HRM System," *Academy of Management Review* 29 (2004): 203–221.

[48] S. E. Jackson, R. S. Schuler, and J. C. Rivero, "Organizational Characteristics as Predictors of Personnel Practices," *Personnel Psychology* 42 (1989): 727–786; and Schuler and Jackson, "Linking Competitive Strategies with Human Resource Management Practices."

[49] S. Miller, "Employers Try Better Ways to Measure and Reward Performance," SHRM, August 14, 2017, https://www.shrm.org/ResourcesAndTools/hr-topics/compensation/Pages/better-ways-measure-reward-performance.aspx.

[50] C. Ogbonnaya, K. Daniels, and K. Nielsen, "Does Contingent Pay Encourage Positive Employee Attitudes and Intensify Work?" *Human Resources Management Journal*, 27 (2017): 94-112.

[51] D. P. Lepak and W. R. Boswell, "Strategic HRM and Employee-Organizational Relationship," in *The Employee-Organization Relationship: Application for the 21st Century* (Applied Psychology Series), ed. L. Shore, J. Coyle-Shapiro, and L. Tetrick (New York: Routledge, Taylor & Francis Group, 2012), 455–483; and E. Applebaum, T. Bailey, and P. Berg, *Manufacturing Advantage: Why High-Performance Work Systems Pay Off* (Ithaca, NY: ILR Press, 2000).

[52] M. A. Huselid and B. E. Becker, "Comment on 'Measurement Error in Research on Human Resources and Firm Performance: How Much Error Is There and How Does It Influence Effect Size Estimates?' by Gerhart, Wright, McMahan, and Snell," *Personnel Psychology* 53 (2000): 835–854; P. M. Wright and S. A. Snell, "Toward an Integrative View of Strategic Human Resource Management," *Human Resource Management Review* 1 (1991): 203–225; and P. M. Wright and W. R. Boswell, "Desegregating HRM: A Review and Synthesis of Micro and Macro Human Resource Management," *Journal of Management* 28 (2002): 248–276.

# Glossary

**360-degree appraisal**  a comprehensive measurement approach that involves gathering performance data from as many sources as possible—supervisors, peers, subordinates, and customers

**401(k) plan**  a retirement plan that allows employees to defer receiving some of their compensation until retirement, with contributions to the plan taken out of the employee's paycheck pretax and the funds accumulating tax free until retirement begins

**absolute approach**  the evaluation of employees' performance by comparing employees against certain "absolute" standards along a number of performance dimensions

**Accidental Death and Dismemberment Insurance (AD&D)**  insurance designed to compensate employees for the loss of a body part or to compensate the employee's family if an employee suffers the loss of a limb or dies accidentally at work

**Account-Based Health Plan (ABHP)**  a consumer-driven plan that pairs a group health plan with a tax-advantaged medical spending account

**adverse action**  an action taken against an applicant, such as turning the applicant down for the job

**affirmative action**  the process of actively seeking to identify, hire, and promote qualified members of underrepresented groups

**affirmative defense**  factual information presented by the defendent that leads to a claim by a plaintiff being defeated even if her or his claim is true

**agency shop agreement**  a labor union arrangement under which employees cannot be required to join a union but can be required to pay to a union an agency fee for purposes such as initiation

**agency theory**  managers can motivate their employees to act in certain ways by aligning employee interests with the interests of the firm's other stakeholders

**alignment**  the extent to which HR activities are designed to achieve the goals of an organization

**alliance partner**  an external employee who makes unique contributions but whose contributions are limited in terms of strategic value

**alternative dispute resolution (ADR)**  a process for resolving disputes among employees and employers using a mediator or an arbitrator

**alternative employment arrangements**  independent contractors, temporary help agency workers, on-call workers, and workers provided by contract firms.

**application**  a standardized form used by employers to collect job-related information about applicants

**arbitration**  a method of resolving disputes in which a third party acts as an intermediary and actually makes the decision about how the issue should be resolved

**assessment center**  a process of engaging job candidates in a series of simulations designed to evaluate their ability to perform aspects of the jobs they are seeking

**attrition**  a decision not to fill vacant positions that emerge as a result of turnover or other employee movements in a company

**audiovisual training**  providing instruction on a topic to employees by having them watch or listen to a video or other visual or audio presentation

**automation**  using machines to perform tasks that otherwise could be performed by people

**backdating**  choosing the date for a stock award based on when the stock price was low, rather than using the exact date the stock award was issued, thereby creating an immediate profit for the individual

**bad faith bargaining**  entering into a collective bargaining situation with no intention of reaching an agreement, or in some other way violating the protocol for appropriate collective bargaining

**bargaining unit**  a group of employees designated by the National Labor Relations Board (NLRB) or identified by the union and employer together as eligible to participate in a union election

**behavioral interview**  a type of interview based on the premise that past behavior is the best predictor of future behavior; involves asking job candidates to respond to questions about how they have handled specific job-related types of situations in the past

**behavioral observation scale (BOS)**  a behavior-based evaluation approach that requires raters to evaluate how often an employee displays certain behaviors on the job

**behaviorally anchored rating scale (BARS)**  a behavior-based evaluation approach where raters must evaluate individuals along a number of performance dimensions with each performance rating standard anchored by a behavioral example.

**benchmark job**  a job that is used to represent the range of jobs in a company and that can be used for comparison with jobs in other companies for the purpose of establishing pay rates

**biodata**  a shortened name for *biographical data*; refers to a standardized questionnaire that asks applicants to provide personal and biographical information to be compared with the same information for successful employees

**blended learning**  the use of multiple modes of training to accomplish a training goal, often with one part being online

**bona fide occupational qualification (BFOQ)**  a BFOQ exists when a protected classification can legally be used to make an employment decision

**broad-based stock option plan**  a stock purchase plan that applies widely to a firm's employees

**broadbanding (also known as career banding)**  an approach used to reduce the complexity of a compensation system by consolidating a large number of pay grades into a fewer number of broad grades (or bands)

**business necessity**  an employment practice that has some relationship to legitimate business goals and is essential to the company's survival

**card check**  a process whereby a company recognizes a union once the union has produced evidence that the majority of workers have signed authorization cards indicating that they want the union to represent them

**career fair**   an opportunity for employers to interact with a large number of potential applicants at one time

**cash balance plan**   a type of retirement account in which the employer credits the participants' retirement account with a pay credit and an interest credit and the employer bears the risk; the employee, when fully vested, is entitled to receive the stated account balance upon leaving the company or at retirement

**classroom training**   traditional learning that includes lectures, role plays, discussions, and other experiential activities

**closed shop**   requires workers to join a union before they can be hired and requires employers to go to the union first to hire new employees

**coaching**   short-term training provided one on one and primarily focused on performance improvement relative to a specific skill or ability

**cognitive ability test**   a test that measures general intelligence or levels of specific aptitudes, such as numeric fluency, general reasoning, verbal comprehension, mechanical reasoning, logical evaluation, and memory span physical ability test   a test that focuses on physical attributes of job candidates, such as endurance, strength, and general fitness achievement test (or competency test)   a measure of an applicant's current knowledge or skill level in relation to the job requirements work sample   a test in which the person actually performs some or all aspects of a job knowledge test   measures the extent to which an applicant has mastered the subject matter required to do a job personality inventory   a selection measure that identifies the extent to which an applicant possesses certain characteristics, such as assertiveness, self-confidence, conscientiousness, motivation, and interpersonal attributes

**collaborative-based HR system**   an HR system of managing external labor on a long-term basis through alliances or partnerships with a reliance on group incentives, cross-functional teams, and the like

**collective bargaining**   the process that labor unions and employers use to reach agreement about wages, benefits, hours worked, and other terms and conditions of employment

**commitment-based HR system**   an HR system of investing extensively in the development of core employees' competencies, empowering them to use their competencies in the performance of their jobs, and encouraging their full participation in decision making and discretion on the job

**comparable worth**   focuses on eliminating inequity in wages by ensuring that jobs that require similar levels of education and experience, and have other characteristics in common, are paid at a similar wage, regardless of gender

**compensable factor**   an aspect of jobs, such as skill, effort, responsibility, and working conditions, that exist across jobs in a company, are needed by employees for the firm to achieve its objectives, and for which the company is willing to pay

**compensation**   the monetary and nonmonetary rewards employees receive in exchange for the work they do for an organization

**compensation philosophy**   communicates information to employees about what is valued within an organization, enhances the likelihood of consistency in pay across the organizational units, and helps attract, motivate, and retain employees

**compensatory approach**   a process for deriving a final score for each candidate in the selection process by weighting outcomes on multiple selection measures differentially so that some items are weighted more heavily than others and a high score on one part can offset a low score on another

**competencies**   the knowledge, skills, abilities, and other talents that employees possess

**competency-based pay**   a highly structured pay system that identifies the competencies employees need to master to be eligible for pay raises

**competitive advantage**   a company's ability to create more economic value than its competitors

**compliance-based HR system**   a system that focuses on meeting preset rules, regulations, and/or procedures, with an emphasis on short-term productivity and the efficient performance of tasks that are limited in scope, purpose, or duration

**compressed workweek**   an arrangement that provides employees with the option to adjust the number of hours and days that they work within a week

**concerted activity**   when two or more nonunion employees act together to try to improve working conditions, or when a single employee approaches management after conferring with other employees on their behalf or is acting on behalf of other employees

**conciliation**   a type of facilitation used when an impasse occurs in a collective bargaining session so that both parties keep working toward an agreement until they can resolve the issues at hand

**concurrent criterion-related validity**   a type of criterion-related validity that involves administering the selection test and collecting performance measure scores concurrently

**Consolidated Omnibus Reconciliation Act (COBRA)**   an Act that provides for employees and their families to have the option to continue their group health, dental, and vision insurance coverage for up to 18 months when they are terminated for a qualifying reason as long as they pay the full cost of the premium

**construct validity**   how well a selection tool, such as a test, measures the job-related characteristic that it claims to measure

**consumer-driven health plan (CDHP)**   alternative health care plan that lets employees choose a higher deductible or other more expensive alternatives, put money into a savings plan, and choose their health care providers

**contaminated performance measure**   a performance measure that is irrelevant to an individual's actual job performance

**content validity**   the extent to which the selection test focuses on job relevant information that mirrors aspects of the job

**contingency recruiting agency**   an employment agency used by employers with payment made as a flat fee or percentage of the new hire's first-year salary, and paid only if the search is successful

**contingent labor**   employees who have no implicit or explicit expectation for ongoing employment

**contract worker**   an external employee whose contributions are neither unique nor of high strategic value to the organization

**contrast effect (within a company, see Chapter 9)**   bias that results when an evaluation of one or more persons is artificially inflated or deflated when compared to the evaluation of another person

**contrast effect (when recruiting, see Chapter 7)**   bias that results when an evaluation of one or more job applicants is artificially inflated or deflated compared to another job applicant

**contributory retirement plan**   a pension plan in which the employer and employee both put money into the retirement account

**copay**   the minimum amount employees must pay for health care, as determined by their health insurance plan

**core employee**   an employee who is most likely to contribute directly to a firm's core competencies

**corporate campaign**   tactical strategies designed to identify and exploit opportunities to interfere with the normal operation of a business and affect its reputation

**cost leadership strategy**   focuses on outperforming competing firms within an industry by maintaining the ability to offer the lowest costs for products or services

**cost-of-living adjustment (COLA)**   an adjustment given to employees to offset the increases in the prices of goods and services they purchase and to keep salaries from lagging the external market

**cost-per-hire**   the costs related to the recruitment part of hiring a new employee

**craft union**   a union organized to represent the interests of members with specialized craft skills

**criterion-related validity (also referred to as empirical validity)**   provides additional evidence of the validity of a measure by establishing a statistical relationship between the selection test and some measure of job performance

**critical incident**   a statement or example of exceptionally good or exceptionally poor performance that employees display over in the performance of their job

**critical incident approach**   a behavior-based evaluation approach where the evaluation criteria consist of statements or examples of exceptionally good or poor performance employees display over the course of the evaluation period

**Davis–Bacon Act**   requires contractors and subcontractors with contracts in excess of $2,000 with the federal government to pay their workers a minimum wage that is at least equal to the local prevailing wages, and to provide them with the local prevailing benefits

**deadly combinations**   occur when managers rely on HR practices that seem appropriate, but present problems when combined with other HR practices to manage employees

**decertification**   the process of terminating union representation, resulting in the union no longer representing the employees or engaging in collective bargaining on their behalf

**defamation of character**   occurs when someone makes written or verbal comments about a person and those comments are not true and cause harm to the individual, such as causing the person to be rejected for the job

**deferred profit sharing plan**   a group-based incentive plan in which the incentive money paid to an employee is put into a retirement account for that employee

**deficient performance measure**   an incomplete appraisal of an individual's performance, in which important aspects are not measured

**defined benefit pension plan**   a pension plan that provides an annuity to eligible employees upon their retirement with the amount paid per year based on a formula

**defined contribution plan**   a pension plan in which the employer specifies where the money will be deposited and often gives the employee the power to decide how the money will be invested, with the retirement income being a function of how well money put into the plan was invested

**demotion**   moving employees to lower-level positions within the company

**desktop training**   a training approach in which employees access a software program housed on their computers or on a server or in the cloud

**development**   prepares employees to take on additional responsibilities in different jobs, usually at a higher level

**devil's horn error**   a bias that occurs when a negative characteristic of a person affects the evaluation of the person's other attributes

**diary**   a journal or log of the tasks and activities that an employee performs throughout the course of a day, week, or month

*Dictionary of Occupational Titles* **(DOT)**   a list of concise job definitions created by the Employment and Training Administration and published by the U.S. Department of Labor

**differential piecework plan**   an individual incentive plan in which the pay employees receive per unit produced or delivered changes at certain levels of output

**differentiation strategy**   emphasizes achieving competitive advantage over competing firms by providing something unique for which customers are willing to pay

**direct measures approach**   a results-based evaluation approach in which managers measure the outcomes of employees' work such as their sales, productivity, or absenteeism

**disability**   a physical or mental impairment that substantially limits one or more major life activities

**discrimination**   treating people differently in employment situations because of characteristics, such as race, color, and gender, that have nothing to do with their ability to perform a particular job

**disparate impact**   discrimination that occurs when an employment practice results in members of a protected class being treated less favorably than members of a nonprotected class, even though the discrimination was not intentional

**disparate treatment**   treating individuals differently in employment situations because of their membership in a protected class

**distributive bargaining strategy**   a negotiation strategy in which each party takes a defensive position during the bargaining session resulting in a winner and a loser

**distributive justice**   perceptions of the fairness of what individuals receive from companies in return for their efforts

**diversity and inclusion training**   helps reduce discrimination by making employees more aware of the value of differences in the workplace and the need to create an open and welcoming environment for all employees

**domestic strategy**   a strategy that focuses primarily on serving the market within a particular country

**e-learning**   using the Internet, computers, and other electronic tools to deliver training programs

**employee assistance program (EAP)**   resources for employees dealing with personal problems, including attorney consultation, child-care and elder-care options, budget information, addiction recovery, and family counseling

**employee inventory**   a searchable database that can be used to identify employees who meet certain job requirements

**employee orientation**   a process designed to ensure employees understand the policies and procedures of the company when they first begin work, as well as understand how their job fits with the goals of the company

**Employee Retirement Income and Security Act of 1974 (ERISA)**   a federal law that protects benefits for retirees in the private sector

**employee self-service (ESS) application**   a Web-based program accessed via a company's intranet that employees can use to review their benefits information and make changes during open enrollment periods

**employer branding**   developing a long-term strategy to manage how a firm's stakeholders, including its current and future employees, perceive the company

**employee stock ownership plan (ESOP)**   a group-based incentive plan in which a company contribute shares of its stock to a trust set up for its employees

**employees**   individuals who work for a company

**Employer Shared Responsibility provisions**   a requirement under the Affordable Care Act (ACA) for employers with 50 full-time employees or the equivalent to offer affordable health coverage to their full-time employees and their dependents, or be subject to an Employer Shared Responsibility payment under certain conditions

**employment-at-will**   hiring provisions based on state laws that allow employers to terminate (or hire or transfer) employees at any time and that allow employees to quit at any time

**empowerment**   providing employees with higher-level tasks, responsibility, and decision-making in the performance of their job

**environmental influences**   pressures that exist outside of companies that managers must consider to strategically manage their employees

**equal employment opportunity (EEO)**   the term used to describe laws, regulations, and processes related to fair treatment of employees

**Equal Employment Opportunity Commission (EEOC)**   the federal agency responsible for enforcing compliance with antidiscrimination laws such as the Civil Rights Act of 1964 (CRA 64), the Age Discrimination in Employment Act (ADEA), and the Americans with Disabilities Act (ADA)

**equity theory**   the theory that employees compare their input (work effort) and outcome (wages) levels with those of other people in similar situations to determine if they are being treated the same in terms of pay and other outcomes

**ergonomics**   the science of understanding the capabilities of human in terms of their work requirements

**ergonomics**   the science of understanding the capabilities of humans in terms of their work requirements

**error of central tendency**   a bias that occurs when raters are unwilling to rate individuals as very high or very low on an evaluation scale

**essential functions**   the job tasks, duties, and responsibilities that must be done by a person in a job

**Excelsior list**   a list of names and addresses the company must supply of employees who are eligible to vote in the representation election for a union

**exclusive provider organization (EPO)**   requires the use of doctors, specialists, and hospitals in-network except in an emergency

**executive search firm, or headhunter**   see retained search agency

**exempt employee**   an employee whose job classification does not require the payment of overtime pay for time worked in excess of 40 hours a week

**expectancy**   the degree to which employees believe that, if they work toward a certain performance objective, they will be able to achieve that objective

**expectancy theory**   employees make decisions regarding how to act at work based on which behaviors they believe will lead to their most valued work-related rewards and outcomes

**external alignment**   the outcome of ensuring that the design of the three primary HR activities takes into account the HR challenges that companies face

**external competitiveness**   ensuring pay rates for jobs in a company are appropriately aligned relative to pay rates for similar jobs in the company's external labor market

**external recruiting**   the process of recruiting employees from outside the organization

**externships and internships**   ways for employers to connect with students in the workplace who could become future employees

**factor comparison**   a quantitative type of job evaluation that involves ranking benchmark jobs in relation to each other on each of several factors, such as mental requirements, physical requirements, skill, responsibility, and working conditions, and then assigning a portion of the hourly rate for each job to each factor

**fair employment practice laws**   state and local governments' employee management regulations

**Fair Labor Standards Act (FLSA)**   governs what employers can and cannot do with regard to compensation, including regulating the use of child labor, defining the difference between exempt and nonexempt employees, setting a minimum wage, and stipulating the pay rate for overtime work

**Federal Labor Relations Authority (FLRA)**   oversight agency for labor-management issues at the federal level

**final screening**   taking a more in-depth look at the applicants who make it through the initial screening prior to hiring them, including reviewing references, conducting background checks, and conducting additional interviews

**flexible benefit plan**   also known as *cafeteria plans*; type of benefit plan that allows employees to choose which benefits they want to purchase from a menu of benefits

**flextime**   a work arrangement in which employees may choose the starting and ending time of their workday, as long as they work the appropriate number of hours per day or week

**forced-choice**   a behavior-based evaluation approach where managers must choose among a set of alternative statements regarding the person being rated

**forced distribution**   a form of individual comparisons whereby managers are forced to distribute employees into one of several predetermined categories

**four-fifths rule**   a guideline generally accepted by the courts and the EEOC for making a *prima facie* case of disparate impact by showing that an employment practice results in members of a protected class being treated less favorably by an employment practice than members of a nonprotected class

**frame-of-reference training**   training that aims to help raters understand performance standards and performance dimensions

**free rider**   an individual who does not work as hard as the others on a team

**functional flexibility**   the ability of the firm to adjust the types of skills available in its workforce

**gain sharing plan**   a plan designed to help increase an organization's efficiency by increasing the productivity of the company's employees and/or lowering the firm's labor costs

**gamification**   adding game elements, game mechanics, and game design to nongame systems, or turning the content into a game with business objectives

**genetic information**   information about an individual's genetic tests and genetic tests of family members and/or about an individual's or family member's diseases or disorders

**gig worker**   an independent contractor, also known as a *freelancer*, hired by an employer on a temporary basis to perform specialized work

**global performance measure**   the use of a single score to reflect an individual employee's overall performance.

**global strategy**   a strategy whereby a company strives to achieve global efficiency

**globalization**   the blurring of country boundaries in business activities

**goal-setting theory**   goals serve as a motivator to focus the efforts of employees toward desired outcomes when the goals are specific, challenging, attainable, and when feedback on progress is provided

**good faith bargaining**    the process that requires parties to meet at a reasonable time and come to the bargaining table ready to reach a collective bargaining agreement

**graphic rating scale**    a method of evaluating employees based on various traits, or attributes, they possess that are relevant to their performance

**grievance**    a charge by one or more employees that management has violated their contractual rights

**grievance process**    formal steps that must be followed to settle disputes between labor and management

**growth need strength**    the extent to which individuals feel a need to learn and be challenged, a need to develop their skills beyond where they currently are, and a strong need for accomplishment

**halo effect (or devil's horns effect)**    a positive or negative characteristic of a job candidate that has more influence on the outcome of the evaluation than do other attributes considered

**halo error**    a bias that occurs when a positive characteristic of a person affects the evaluation of the person's other attributes

**harassment**    occurs when employees are subjected to unwanted and unwelcome treatment because of their race, color, religion, sex, national origin, age, disability, or genetic information

**Health Insurance Portability and Accountability Act (HIPAA)**    an Act that makes it easier for workers to maintain their health care coverage when they change employers because it specifies that coverage under a previous employer's health plan counts for meeting a preexisting condition required under a new plan

**health maintenance organization (HMO)**    a type of managed care health insurance program that requires employees to designate a primary care physician and have any visits to a specialist referred by the primary care physician

**health reimbursement account (HRA)**    an account into which employers put money to reimburse employees for qualified medical expenses

**health savings account (HSA)**    a special account established through employers, banks, credit unions, insurance companies, and other approved financial institutions into which an employee sets aside money pre-tax to help pay for his or her health care options

**high-deductible health plan (HDHP)**    a plan that requires the employee to pay first few thousand dollars of medical costs each year, with the plan paying only when employee has a major medical problem; results in monthly premium cost savings for employee and employer; also called *catastrophic health plans*

**high-impact learning organization**    a company that place a high value on learning

**high-potential employee**    an employee with the greatest likelihood of being successful and making significant contributions to achieving organizational goals.

**hiring freezes**    a temporary ban on the hiring of new employees for a specified period of time

**host-country national (HCN)**    an employee who is a citizen of the country in which the company's branch or plant is located, but the company is headquartered in another country

**hostile work environment**    exists whenever an employee is the subject of unwelcome harassment because of his or her membership in a protected class and that harassment is severe and abusive

**HR challenges**    challenges that managers must consider in the management of employees that relate to organizational demands, environmental influences, and regulatory issues.

**HR deliverable**    what is needed from a firm's HR activities, or a mechanism by which an HR system creates value for a company

**human resources department (HR department)**    a support function within companies that serves a vital role in designing and implementing company policies for managing employees

**human resources practices (HR practices)**    the practices that a company has put in place to manage employees

**impasse**    the situation in which both parties have made their final offers and are not willing to make further concessions

**impression management**    occurs when job applicants engage in actions to present themselves in a positive light to the interviewer with the idea of biasing the outcome of the interview in their favor

**improshare plan**    a group-based incentive plan based on the number of hours a firm expects to take to reach a certain level of output

**independent contractor**    external worker who performs work for an organization but maintains substantial control over the means and methods of their services

**industrial union**    a union that has traditionally represented semi-skilled and unskilled workers in a particular industry

**initial screening**    preliminary review of the information provided by job applicants and the collection of additional information to decide which applicants are worthy of more serious consideration for the job

**instructional objective**    a statement that describes what is to be accomplished in a training program and, therefore, drives the design of the program

**integrative bargaining strategy**    a negotiation strategy in which each party cooperates and works to reach a win–win outcome

**interactional justice**    how employees feel they are treated by their managers and supervisors in everyday interactions

**interest-based bargaining**    an extension of integrative bargaining in which each party looks for common goals in order to meet the interests of the other party

**internal alignment (with HR activities, see Chapter 1 and Chapter 14)**    the outcome of ensuring that specific practices within each HR activity are consistent with one another and aligned across the primary HR activities

**internal alignment (regarding jobs within a company, see Chapter 10)**    occurs when each job in a company is valued appropriately relative to every other job in terms of its ability to help the firm achieve its goals

**internal recruiting**    the process of seeking job applicants from within the company

**international strategy**    a strategy used by companies to expand the markets in which they compete to include multiple countries

**international union**    a federation of local unions

**job analysis**    the process of systematically identifying the tasks, duties, and responsibilities expected to be performed in a single job, as well as the competencies—the knowledge, skills, and abilities (KSAs)—that employees must possess to be successful in the job

**Job Characteristics Model**    a motivational model of job design based on five job dimensions and three psychological states of employees that affect employees' internal motivation and satisfaction, as well as absenteeism, turnover, and productivity

**job classification**    a type of job evaluation that involves developing broad descriptions for groups of jobs that are similar in terms of their tasks, duties, responsibilities, and qualifications for the purpose of assigning wages

**job crafting**    ways in which employees redesign their jobs to increase job satisfaction

**job description**   a written summary of the specific tasks, responsibilities, and working conditions of a job

**job design**   determining the tasks and responsibilities that employees in a particular job are expected to perform, as well as how they need to interact with their coworkers to realize those contributions

**job enlargement**   the assignment of additional tasks of a similar level of difficulty to employees

**job enrichment**   increases the level of responsibility and/or control employees have in performing the tasks of a job

**job evaluation**   the systematic process of establishing the relative worth of the jobs within the company

**job grade**   a grouping of jobs with comparable points together to reflect the hierarchy of jobs within a company for the purpose of establishing wage rates

**job posting**   the most frequently used technique for notifying current employees about job openings within the company

**job pricing**   the systematic process of assigning monetary rates to jobs so that a firm's internal wages are aligned with the external wages in the marketplace

**job ranking**   a type of job evaluation that involves reviewing job descriptions and listing the jobs in order, from highest to lowest worth to the company

**job rotation**   moving workers from one job to another job within the organization to provide exposure to different aspects of a company's operations

**job simplification**   removing decision-making authority from the employee and placing it with a supervisor

**job specialization**   the process of identifying the core elements of a job

**job specifications**   a description of the competencies—the knowledge, skills, and abilities (KSAs) or other talents—that a jobholder must have to perform a job successfully

**job-based employee**   an employee who creates value for a firm but does not contribute in unique ways, and can be found in large numbers in the external labor market

**knowledge-based pay**   systems that require employees to acquire certain knowledge in order to receive a pay increase

**labor demand**   the number and types of employees the company needs to meet its current and future strategic objectives

**labor shortage**   exists when the demand for labor exceeds the available supply of it (demand > supply)

**labor supply**   the availability of current or potential employees to perform a company's jobs

**labor surplus**   exists when the supply of labor is greater than the demand for it (supply > demand)

**Landrum-Griffin Act (Labor-Management Reporting and Disclosure Act)**   protects union members from abuse by unions by outlining the responsibilities of union officers and providing a bill of rights for union members

**learning**   the process of acquiring both tacit and explicit knowledge

**learning agility**   willingness to seek new experiences and opportunities to learn new knowledge and skills

**learning styles**   ways that people prefer to absorb and process new information

**legal compliance training**   ensures that a firm's managers and employees know what they can and cannot do from a legal standpoint

**leniency error**   a bias that occurs when a rater consistently rates employees on the higher end of an evaluation scale

**lesson plan**   a map of what should be done during each training session to achieve the stated objectives

**leveraged ESOP**   a group-based incentive plan that allows a trust to borrow funds against the company's future earnings, and as the debt is repaid, employees receive shares of the stock held by the ESOP in employee accounts

**line manager (manager)**   an individual who is responsible for supervising and directing the efforts of a group of employees to perform tasks that are directly related to the creation and delivery of a company's products or services

**living wage**   the concept that employees should be paid a wage that ensures that their basic costs of living are met

**long-term care insurance (LTCI)**   an insurance plan that provides assistance to aging, disabled, and ill persons who need daily help with tasks such as dressing, eating, or bathing for an extended time period

**long-term disability**   an insurance plan that typically starts after a specified period of time (usually 6 to 12 weeks) from the time of a disability and pays a portion of the employee's salary until retirement age

**lump-sum merit bonus**   a one-time payment based on an employee's level of performance

**management by objectives (MBO)**   a results-based evaluation approach where managers meet with their employees and jointly set goals for the employees to accomplish during a particular time period

**mandatory bargaining topics**   topics that must be negotiated, including compensation and benefits, hours of employment, and other conditions of employment

**market pricing**   a method for determining pay for jobs by collecting salary information from the external labor market first, rather than starting with the development of an internal structure based on the value of the jobs within the company

**McDonnell Douglas test**   a four-step test used to make a case of disparate treatment

**mediation**   the arrangement whereby an outside party works with each side in a negotiation to reach an acceptable agreement

**mentoring**   a longer-term relationship that involves a more senior employee teaching a junior employee how the organization works and nurturing that person as she progresses in her career

**merit increase**   a salary increase awarded based on how well an individual has performed his or her job

**merit pay increase**   a compensation adjustment based on the results of an employee's performance evaluations

**minimum wage**   the lowest hourly wage that an employer can pay to workers

**mixed motive**   a legitimate reason for an employment decision exists, but the decision also was motivated by an illegitimate reason.

**mixed salary/commission plan (also known as base plus commission plan)**   employees receive a lower base salary, perhaps only 50% or 70% of what would be offered under a straight salary plan, with the remaining percentage being commission based

**mixed-level plan**   an incentive plan in which employees are exposed to multiple incentive plans

**multinational strategy**   a strategy where companies establish autonomous or independent business units in multiple countries

**multiple-cutoff approach**   an approach in which an applicant performs all the measures of the job assessment process and has to reach a minimum score on each one to remain in the running for a particular job

**multiple-hurdle approach**   an approach in which applicants have to pass each step (hurdle) successfully to continue in the selection process

**national emergency strike**   a strike or lockout that affects an entire industry, or a substantial part of it, and national health and safety are imperiled

**National Labor Relations Board (NLRB)**   an agency of the U.S. government that was created by Congress to administer the National Labor Relations Act (NLRA)

**needs assessment**   a means to identify where gaps exist between what employees should be doing and what they are actually doing

**negligent hiring**   a hiring process in which an employer does not conduct a background check on an employee and that person commits a crime at work similar to the crime he or she committed in the past

**neutrality agreement**   an arrangement in which a company agrees that it will not express its views about unionization during the time when signatures are collected

**noncontributory retirement plan**   a pension plan in which the employer puts funds into an employee's account without requiring the employee to make contributions

**nonexempt employee**   an employee who receive overtime pay for hours worked in excess of 40 hours in a workweek

**Norris-LaGuardia Act**   made union-organizing activities easier for employees, outlined a process for hearings, and granted workers the right to collective bargaining

**numerical flexibility**   a form of flexibility related to the ease of adjusting the number of individuals working for a company

**Occupational Information Network (O*NET)**   an online database created by the U.S. Department of Labor that serves as a comprehensive source of information for many occupations

**Occupational Safety and Health Act of 1971 (OSH Act)**   an Act requiring employers to provide a safe workplace for all employees and providing a process for investigation of complaints of unfair practices and a process for workplace inspections

**Office of Federal Contract Compliance Programs (OFCCP)**   the federal agency responsible for developing guidelines and overseeing compliance with antidiscrimination laws relative to executive orders

**offshoring**   the practice of sending work that was once performed domestically to companies in other countries or opening facilities in other countries to do the work, often at a substantially lower cost

**Older Workers Retirement Protection Act**   a law that prohibits discrimination against older workers in all employee benefits except when age-based reductions in employee benefit plans are justified by significant cost considerations

**on-demand recruiting service**   an agency that charges based on the time it spends recruiting rather than paying an amount per hire

**on-the-job training (OJT)**   training that occurs when a manager or coworker teaches an employee how to perform some aspect of a job in the actual job location rather than in a separate training location

**onboarding**   the process used to socialize new employees to their jobs and the company, including helping them acclimate to the culture and goals of the company

**organization analysis**   an assessment used to determine a firm's progress toward achieving its goals and objectives

**organizational culture**   the set of basic assumptions, values, and beliefs of a company's members

**organizational demands**   factors within a firm that affect decisions regarding how to manage employees

**Outplacement assistance programs**   help employees who are being laid off find new jobs

**outsourcing**   the practice of sending work to other companies

**overtime**   work hours that exceed the number of hours established as the normal workweek

**paired comparison**   an evaluation approach in which each employee in a business unit is compared to every other employee in the unit

**panel interview**   a type of interview process in which several people interview an applicant at the same time

**parent-country national (PCN)**   an employee who is a citizen of the country in which the company is headquartered but working for the company in another location

**participation**   the extent to which employees are permitted to contribute to decisions that may affect them in their jobs

**Pension Benefit Guaranty Corporation (PBGC)**   a not-for-profit organization created by the federal government that insures defined benefit plans

**Pension Protection Act (PPA)**   an Act passed in 2006 and designed to strengthen the U.S. pension system by tightening rules relative to employer responsibilities for funding pension accounts and for administering and terminating pension funds

**performance dimensions**   the specific tasks and activities employees must perform to do their jobs, and the competencies employees need to successfully perform those tasks and activities.

**performance management**   The process of managing two related activities: (1) effectively evaluating the performance of your employees against the standards set for them, and (2) helping them develop action plans to improve their performance

**performance standards**   the level of expected performance

**permissive topics**   nonmandatory issues, such as employee rights, managerial control, and benefits for retired union members, that are often part of the collective bargaining negotiations and agreement

**person analysis**   an assessment of the gap between an individual's performance and desired job outcomes

**person–job fit**   the extent to which there is a good match between the characteristics of a potential employee, such as knowledge, skills, values, and the requirements of the job

**person–organization fit**   how well a person fits within the broader organizational culture

**podcast**   a digital recording that can be downloaded and played back later

**point method (also known as point factor method)**   a quantitative method of job evaluation that involves assigning point values to jobs based on compensable factors to create a relative worth hierarchy for jobs in the company

**point-of-service plan (POS)**   a hybrid of a health maintenance organization (HMO) and a preferred provider organization (PPO), in which individuals can also receive treatment outside the network, but must pay a higher deductible

**positive discipline**   a disciplinary process that is not punitive but focuses on constructive feedback and encourages employees to take responsibility for trying to improve their behaviors or performance at work

**powerful connections**   occur when HR practices are used in combinations that support and reinforce other practices that are in place

**prediction**   making a determination about how likely it is that candidates selected will be successful in the job based on their current ability to do the job or the potential they have to be able to learn to do the job and do it well

**predictive criterion-related validity**   a type of criterion-related validity that involves examining the relationship between selection measure scores taken prehire and performance scores collected at a later date

**predictive scheduling**   a set of laws that place obligations on employers to provide employee schedules ahead of time

**preferred provider organization (PPO)**   a type of managed care program in which the employer negotiates with health care providers, usually in a network, for discounts and services for health care coverage for employees

*prima facie* **case**   establishing the basis for a case of discrimination

**primacy error**   a bias that occurs when a rater's earlier impressions of an individual bias his or her later evaluations of the person

**primary HR activities**   encompass work design and workforce planning, managing employee competencies, and managing employee attitudes and behaviors

**private employment agency**   an agency that provides job search assistance for a fee, and often to select professions only

**procedural justice**   perceptions of whether the processes that are used to make decisions, allocate rewards, or resolve disputes, or that otherwise affect employees, are viewed as fair

**productivity**   the level of a firm's output (i.e., products or services) relative to the inputs (i.e., employees, equipment, materials, and so forth) used to produce the output

**productivity-based HR system**   a system that involves standardized jobs and selecting people from the external labor market who can contribute immediately in these jobs, rewards based on efficiency and productivity improvements, and short-term results-oriented performance management systems

**productivity ratio**   the employees (i.e., labor demand) needed to achieve a certain output level (i.e., level of sales, production, and so forth)

**profit sharing plan**   a group-level incentive plan in which company profits are shared with employees

**progressive discipline**   a process by which an employee with disciplinary problems progresses through a series of disciplinary stages until the problem is corrected

**promotion**   moving employees to higher-level positions, which often are associated with increased levels of responsibility and authority

**protected classifications**   the demographic characteristics that cannot be used for employment decisions, also called *protected classes*

**psychological contract**   the perceived obligations that employees believe they owe their company and that their company owes them

**public employment agencies**   not-for-profit employment agencies affiliated with local, state, or federal governments

*quid pro quo* **harassment**   occurs when submission to sexual conduct is made explicitly or implicitly a condition of employment

**Railway Labor Act (RLA)**   provides a peaceful way for employees and railroads or commercial airlines to resolve differences, allows rail and airline employees to join labor unions, and distinguishes between major and minor disputes and what can happen relative to each; also created the National Mediation Board

**ranking approach**   an evaluation approach in which employees are evaluated from best to worst along some performance dimension or by virtue of their overall performance

**re-recruiting**   the process of enticing qualified former employees to return to the company to work

**realistic job preview (RJP)**   a message that provides positive information about the job and company, as well as information that is likely to be less favorable to some potential applicants

**reasonable accommodation**   making modifications in how the work is done or in the work environment so that someone who is qualified for the job and who has a disability can perform the job

**recency error**   a bias that occurs when a rater narrowly focuses on an employee's performance that occurs near the time of the evaluation

**recruiting process outsourcing (RPO)**   an agency that contracts with an employer to administer some or all of the employer's recruitment functions

**recruitment**   the process of identifying potential employees, communicating job and organizational attributes to them, and convincing them to apply for available jobs

**recruitment value proposition**   a marketing concept used to design the advertising message in such a way that potential applicants can differentiate what one company offers to its employees from what other companies offer

**reference check**   contacting individuals whose names are provided by job applicants for the purpose of verifying employment information and gathering other job-related data about an applicant to use in making the hiring decision

**reinforcement theory (also known as operant conditioning)**   positive outcomes occur when individuals learn the relationship between actions and consequences and, as a result, modify their behavior accordingly

**relational relationship**   a relationship that involves a social or emotional commitment to the individual by the company and vice versa

**relevant labor market**   the geographic location in which one can reasonably expect to find a sufficient supply of qualified applicants

**reliability**   the extent to which a selection measure yields consistent results over time or across raters

**replacement chart**   method of tracking information about potential replacement employees for positions that could open up within organizations

**reshoring**   returning jobs back to the country of origin

**résumé**   an overview of an applicant's qualifications including education, previous work experience, and special skills and interests

**retained search agency**   an agency used for recruiting high-level positions, such as CEOs and vice presidents, with the agency paid a retainer for the work it does

**retaliation**   occurs when an employer takes an adverse action against an employee who has filed a discrimination complaint

**reverse discrimination**   a type of discrimination in which members of a protected group are given preference in employment decisions, resulting in discrimination against nonprotected groups

**right-to-work laws**   laws that prevent workers from having to join a union as a condition of employment, be prevented from joining a union as a condition of employment, be forced to pay dues to a labor union, or be fired for not paying such dues

**role ambiguity**   the uncertainty that employees may experience about the daily tasks expected of them and how to perform them

**role conflict**   tension caused by incompatible or contradictory demands on a person

**role overload**   too many expectations or demands placed on employees in the course of performing their jobs

**role underload**   having too few expectations or demands placed on employees in the course of performing their jobs

**salary compression (also referred to as pay or wage compression)**   a situation that occurs when the pay for jobs in the external marketplace rises faster than the pay for jobs inside the organization, resulting in new employees receiving equal salaries to current employees

**salary inversion**   a situation where new employees have negotiated for higher wages than the current employees are making

**salary survey**   a systematic process for collecting information about wages in the external labor market

**Scanlon plan**   a group-based incentive plan based on employee suggestions for increased efficiencies and productivity

**selection**   the systematic process of deciding which applicants to hire

**selection bias**   when one's personal views are allowed to affect the outcome of the decision-making process, rather than basing the decision on the results of the selection measures

**self-appraisal**   the process of an employee evaluating his or her own performance

**self-efficacy**   having confidence that one can perform a particular task

**self-managed team**   a type of team in which team members, rather than a supervisor, work collaboratively to make team decisions, including hiring, planning, and scheduling

**short-term disability plan**   an insurance plan that pays a specified portion of an employee's salary when the employee is out of work for a limited time due to a disability

**similar-to-me errors**   a bias that occurs when evaluators rate employees who resemble them in some way more highly than they rate employees who are dissimilar

**simulation**   a training activity that replicates the work the employees will be doing, without the safety and cost concerns often associated with various jobs

**situational interview**   a type of interview in which an interviewer poses hypothetical situations to the interviewee and gauges the person's responses relative to how the individual would be expected to respond in a similar situation on the job

**skill-based pay**   systems that require employees to acquire certain skills in order to receive a pay increase

**social loafing**   a situation in which the motivation of individuals to exert effort diminishes when their outputs are combined with those of others

**Social Security Act**   a social insurance program funded by payroll taxes to provide retired workers with a continuous stream of income after their retirement, benefits for dependents and survivors of covered workers, and benefits for disabled workers and their dependents, as well as insurance coverage for the elderly

**sourcing**   the process of identifying, attracting, and screening potential applicants who are not actively in the market for a new job

**specificity**   the clarity of performance standards

**spot award**   a short-term incentive that companies use to encourage their employees to work toward specific outcomes

**standard hour plan**   an individual incentive plan in which the employee's pay is based on how much time an employee is expected to need to complete some task

**stock option plan**   a group-based incentive plan that provides employees with the right to purchase shares of their company's stock at some established price (often its market value) for a given period of time

**straight commission plan**   a plan that pays employees a percentage of the total sales they generate

**straight piecework plan**   an individual incentive plan in which employees receive a certain rate of pay for each unit they produce

**straight salary plan**   a plan in which employees receive a set compensation, regardless of their level of sales

**strategic performance driver**   an activity that enables a company to realize the potential of its source of competitive advantage

**strategic value**   the extent to which the contributions of employees help their organization achieve a competitive advantage

**strategy**   a company's plan for achieving a competitive advantage over its rivals

**strictness error**   a bias that occurs when a rater consistently rates employees on the low end of an evaluation scale

**structured interview**   a type of interview that uses a set of predetermined questions related to the job and usually includes a scoring system to track and compare applicant responses

**subject matter expert (SME)**   an individual with the skills, knowledge, and expertise related to a particular job

**succession planning**   a process of planning for the future leadership of the company by identifying and developing employees to fill higher-level jobs within the company as they become available

**Taft-Hartley Act (Labor Management Relations Act)**   protects the rights of employees and makes the NLRB a more impartial referee for industrial relations, rather than having it serve as an advocate for organized labor

**task analysis**   identification of the gap between (1) the KSAs employees need in order to achieve organizational objectives and (2) the KSAs the employees actually possess.

**telecommute**   working away from the traditional office setting

**telecommuting**   employees working away from the traditional office setting, often with the use of technology

**temp-to-hire**   a person hired to work for the company for a short period of time but who may become a permanent employee

**The Civil Service Reform Act**   granted permission to federal employees to form unions and established the Federal Labor Relations Authority (FLRA) as the oversight agency for labor–management issues at federal level

**third-country national (TCN)**   a foreign national who works in a country other than her or his home country or her or his company's home country

**time and motion study**   systematic evaluation of the most basic elements of the tasks that comprise a job

**time-to-fill rate**   a measure of the length of time it takes from the time when a job opening is announced until someone begins work in the job

**total rewards**   the sum of all the aspects of a compensation package (base pay, incentives, benefits, perks, and so forth) that signal to current and future employees that they are receiving more than just base pay in exchange for their work

**training**   the systematic process of providing employees with the competencies—knowledge, skills, and abilities (KSAs)—required in order to do their current jobs

**transactional relationship**   a relationship that tends to focus narrowly on the performance of the necessary tasks, duties, and responsibilities that must be performed during a predetermined time period

**transfer**   moving employees to other jobs with similar levels of responsibility

**transfer of training**   the degree to which the information covered in the program actually results in job performance changes

**transition matrix**   a method for tracking the internal movement of employees throughout an organization over a certain period of time

**transnational strategy**   a strategy that strives to achieve the benefits of both a global strategy and a multinational strategy

**turnover**   the voluntary and involuntary termination of employees within an organization

**undue hardship**   a situation that exists when accommodating an employee would put the employer at a disadvantage financially or otherwise would make it difficult for the employer to remain in business and competitive

**unfair labor practice (ULP)**   a violation of the NLRA that denies rights and benefits to employees; can be the result of employer or union activity

**union authorization card**   also known as signature card; document indicating that an employee is interested in being represented by a union

**union shop agreement**   an arrangement under which all workers except managers in an organizational unit represented by a union have to become members of that union within a certain period of time after being hired, or at least pay the equivalent of union dues

**union steward**   a union member that serves as a liaison between the rest of the employees and the leadership of the union

**uniqueness**   the extent to which the contributions employees make, and the necessary competencies to realize those contributions, are specialized to a company and not readily available in the open labor market

**unstructured interview**   a type of interview in which questions are asked without a defined format, and the same type of information is not collected from all interviewees

**valence**   the degree of value employees place on different rewards

**validity**   the extent to which a selection method measures what it is supposed to measure and how well it does so

**vesting**   the time required before you own part or all of your retirement funds

**voice**   a specific form of participation that gives employees access to channels within their company to complain or express concerns about their work situation

**voluntary benefits**   benefits that an employer chooses to offer its employees without being required to do so

**wage curve (or pay policy line)**   the market line that represents the relationship between the job evaluation points and the salaries paid for the various jobs in the labor market

**Wagner Act (National Labor Relations Act)**   protects the rights of employees and employers, encourages these parties to engage in collective bargaining, and controls their activities so the economy won't be adversely affected by their actions; also established the National Labor Relations Board (NLRB)

**Walsh–Healey Public Contracts Act (PCA)**   applies to contractors with contracts over $10,000 that are involved in either manufacturing or providing goods and services to the U.S. government, and requires these firms to pay their workers the federal minimum wage for the first 40 hours they work in a particular week, and 1.5 times the minimum wage for any additional hours they work during the week

**web-based training**   learning experiences that are accessed through a secure website, such as online courses and webcasts

**wellness program**   an employer provided program designed to keep employees healthy; can include programs such as smoking cessation, weight loss management programs, and memberships in fitness centers

**work/life balance**   the balance between the demands of work and the demands of employees' personal lives

**Worker Adjustment and Retraining Notification (WARN) Act**   passed in 1989, mandates the amount of notice that workers, their families, and their communities must receive prior to a mass layoff

**workers' compensation**   a social insurance program that provides cash benefits and medical care to workers when they suffer injuries or illnesses related to their employment

**workforce planning**   the process of making sure that individuals with the right skills are where they need to be, at the right time, to meet a firm's current and future needs

**yield ratio**   a tool that provides a metric of the effectiveness of recruitment sources

# Author Index

Note: The letter 'n' following locators refers to notes

# Company Index

# Subject Index

Note: The letter 'n' following locators refers to notes